INTERNATIONAL HANDBOOK ON
MANAGEMENT AT WORK

International Handbook on Diversity Management at Work

Country Perspectives on Diversity and Equal Treatment

Edited by

Alain Klarsfeld

Employment Research Group, Toulouse Business School, ESC Toulouse, France

Edward Elgar
Cheltenham, UK • Northampton, MA, USA

Published by
Edward Elgar Publishing Limited
The Lypiatts
15 Lansdown Road
Cheltenham
Glos GL50 2JA
UK

Edward Elgar Publishing, Inc.
William Pratt House
9 Dewey Court
Northampton
Massachusetts 01060
USA

A catalogue record for this book
is available from the British Library

Library of Congress Control Number: 2009940638

Mixed Sources
Product group from well-managed
forests and other controlled sources
www.fsc.org Cert no. SA-COC-1565
© 1996 Forest Stewardship Council

ISBN 978 1 84720 890 3 (cased)

Printed and bound by MPG Books Group, UK

Contents

Contributors

Anne-Françoise Bender is an Associate Professor at the CNAM (Conservatoire National des Arts et Métiers), Paris. She specializes in career management, gender issues and diversity management. She has authored or co-authored articles (published in *Revue Française de Gestion* and *Revue Française de Gestion des Ressources Humaines*) and book chapters on these topics. She is the co-founder of the diversity management special interest group within the French-speaking HR academic society (AGRH – Association francophone de Gestion des Ressources Humaines).

Regine Bendl has been Associate Professor at the Vienna University of Economics and Business, Department of Management, in the working unit Gender and Diversity Management since 2002. She has published in German and English on diversity management and gender and organization theory. She was awarded with several prizes (for example, 2007 Best Paper Award EURAM (SIG Gender and Diversity in Management), EMERALD Highly Recommended Paper Award 2009). Currently she is the organizer of the EGOS Standing Working Group on Gender and Diversity. She is Associate Editor of *Gender, Work and Organization* and editorial board member of the *Canadian Journal of Administrative Sciences*, *Gender in Management: An International Journal* and the *British Journal of Management*. Since 2009 she has been Editor-in-Chief of *Diversitas: Zeitschrift für Managing Diversity und Diversity Studies*.

Inge Bleijenbergh is Assistant Professor at Radboud University in Nijmegen, the Netherlands. Her research interests are gender in organizations, European social policy and research methodology. She is the author of *Citizens Who Care: European Social Citizenship in EU Debates on Childcare and Part-time Work* (Dutch University Press, 2004) and has co-authored a number of articles, including (with C. Roggeband) 'Equality machineries matter: the impact of women's political pressure on European social-care policies', *Social Politics*, 2007, **14**(4), 1–23.

Lize A.E. Booysen is a Full Professor of Leadership and Organizational Behaviour at Antioch University, USA. She does research in the field of diversity, race, gender, leadership and change management. She holds a doctorate in business leadership from the University of South Africa as well as master's degrees in clinical psychology, research psychology and criminology, all with distinction. Lize Booysen is also adjunct faculty at the Centre for Creative Leadership, Greensboro, North Carolina, USA and has been involved in the 12-nation Leadership Across Differences (LAD) research project, steered by the CCL, since 2003. She participated in the GLOBE 65-nations research project on leadership, national culture and organizational practices during 1994–2003, steered by Wharton Business School at the University of Pennsylvania. Prior to joining Antioch in 2009, Lize was Full Professor at the Graduate School of Business Leadership, University of South Africa since 1992. She was also the Editor of the *South African Journal of Labour Relations*.

Verena Bruchhagen has been Head of Women's Studies at the Department of Educational Science–Sociology at the Technische Universität Dortmund, Germany, since 1996. She has written numerous publications on the issue of adult education in women's studies, managing gender and diversity, learning and teaching diversity, and is co-founder of the programme DiVersion: Managing Gender and Diversity, teaching and training professionals and adults in managing diversity.

Audrey Chia is Associate Professor of Management and Organization at the NUS Business School, National University of Singapore. She received her PhD from the University of Texas at Austin, USA. Her work has been published in various journals such as *Science Communication, Jurimetrics: The Journal of Law, Science, and Technology, Academy of Management Executive* and *Journal of Business Ethics.* She has co-authored two books, *The Three Paradoxes: Working Women in Singapore* (Aware Singapore, 1999) and *Culture and Management: A Casebook* (McGraw-Hill, 1990). Her research has been presented at international conferences on management, applied psychology and socioeconomics. Her current interests are workplace diversity and the repair of reputation and relationships.

Gwendolyn M. Combs is an Associate Professor of Management at the University of Nebraska–Lincoln, USA. Her research interests include human resource management and organizational behaviour. Her research examines diversity and group identity, and their relationship and impact on inter-group behaviour and organizational performance; affirmative action policy; and the influence of positive organizational constructs on employee attitudes and performance. She is a consultant on human resource policy development, diversity programme implementation and diversity training. She has published in journals such as *Human Resource Management, Journal of Organizational Behavior, Journal of World Business* and *Human Resource Development Quarterly.*

Annie Cornet is Professor in HEC – Business Economics at Liège University, Belgium. In 2001, she created EGID, a research centre on diversity and gender in management. She is a leading expert about gender and diversity in Belgium and has produced a number of articles, reports, books and handbooks on diversity management. Her research interests encompass organizational change and human resource management. She is the co-founder of the diversity management study group within the French-speaking HR academic society (AGRH).

Beliz Dereli graduated from Istanbul University Business Administration and Istanbul University State Conservatory Singing Department. She completed an MBA in Management Organization from Istanbul University in 1995 and a PhD in Human Resources Management from Istanbul University in 2003. Between 1992 and 1997 she worked as a human resources specialist in different sectors such as banking, textiles and tourism. Then she worked in ADECCO as senior recruitment consultant until 2002. Since 2002 she has been working at Istanbul Commerce University as an instructor and career planning centre manager.

Jürgen Grieger has occupied a vacant chair for Human Resource Management at Freie Universität Berlin since 2006. Among other things, he is interested in management theory, interpretative approaches to social sciences and human resource development/ organizational learning. At present he is working on hierarchy, authority, power and control in/of organizations as well as on corruption in organizations.

Edeltraud Hanappi-Egger has been Full Professor for Gender and Diversity in Organizations at the Vienna University of Economics and Business (WU Wien) and head of the Gender and Diversity Management Group since 2002. She holds a PhD in Computer Science and teaches in the area of diversity management from a multidisciplinary perspective. She has published more than two hundred articles on gender and technology, diversity management and organization studies. She was head of the Senate at WU, is a member of the University Board of the Graz University of Technology (TU Graz) and member of the 'Young Faculty' of the Austrian Academy of Sciences.

Rana Haq is an Assistant Professor at Laurentian University in Sudbury, Ontario, Canada. Her research interests are in employment equity and managing diversity in the workplace, international comparative strategic human resources management, cross-cultural communications, and organizational behaviour, as well as gender and diversity in entrepreneurship. She is a member of the Administrative Sciences Association of Canada (ASAC), the Academy of Management (AOM) and the Association of International Business (AIB).

Roswitha Hofmann was a researcher and lecturer at the Vienna University of Economics and Business Administration, Department of Management, in the working unit: Gender and Diversity in Organizations from 2002 to 2005. Since March 2005 she has held the position of an Assistant Professor. Her lectures include 'Introduction to organizational theories under gender and diversity perspectives'. She has published numerous articles in the field of diversity management. Her research interests are on sexual orientation and on diversity knowledge and competence in organizations.

Viktorija Kalonaityte is an Assistant Professor in the Department of Leadership, Entrepreneurship and Organization at the Linnaeus University in Sweden. Her research interests include gender and diversity in organizations and identity construction, viewed from feminist and postcolonial perspectives. Her most recent publications include an article on diversity as border control, published in *Organization*.

Alain Klarsfeld is Professor at Toulouse Business School, where he is also a research fellow at the Employment Research Group (ERG) and heads a specialized Master's programme in Human Resources Management (Mastère Spécialisé Responsable Ressources Humaines). He specializes in comparative human resource management, focusing on the management of competences, diversity management and corporate social responsibility. He has published in international scholarly journals, co-edited research monographs and is the co-founder of both the diversity management and the competence management special interest group within the French-speaking HR academic society (AGRH – Association francophone de Gestion des Ressources Humaines).

Iris Koall holds a PhD in Business Administration and has also been working for DiVersion, within women's studies, at the Technische Universität Dortmund, Germany, since 2000. She has written numerous publications about managing diversity as change process, and on cultural frameworks and equal opportunities. She connects the theory of social systems with questions of heterogeneity and paradox system construction, towards a theory of complex diversity management. At present she hold a position as Research

Director for ForTe – Research for Participation at the Faculty of Rehabilitational Sciences at the Technological University of Dortmund.

Jacqueline Laufer is a Professor at HEC Paris. Her research and teaching interests are in the field of human resource management, gender and organization, equal opportunities and diversity policies. She has worked as an expert for the European Union in the field of equal opportunities. She has published articles in the following journals: *Droit Social, Revue Française de Gestion, Feminist Economics, Travail et Emploi, L'Année sociologique* and *Travail, Genre et Société*. She is presently Deputy Manager of the CNRS (Centre National de la Recherche Scientifique) Network 'Mage', a European network of researchers dealing with the issue of gender and the labour market. She is member of the editorial board of the review *Travail, Genre et Sociétés*. She is member of the Conseil Supérieur de l'Egalité Professionnelle as qualified expert; she is scientific adviser for Comité consultatif de la HALDE (Haute Autorité de Lutte contre les Discriminations et pour l'Egalité, the French High Authority against Discrimination and for Equality).

Brigitte Liebig is Professor of Organizational Psychology at the University of Applied Science, Northwestern Switzerland (UAS NWCH), Department of Applied Psychology and directs the National Research Programme 'Gender Equality' (NRP 60) of the Swiss National Science Foundation. Her publications focus on gender and diversity issues in organizations, science and education, economy and politics. Current research projects include issues about social entrepreneurship, intercultural cooperation, entrepreneurial universities and women in freelancing.

Waheeda Lillevik is an Assistant Professor of Management and Human Resources at The College of New Jersey in Ewing, NJ, USA. Her research interests lie mainly in human resources management, management and organizational behaviour, particularly diversity management (with emphasis on acculturation), cross-cultural management and international HRM. Within these topics, she is also interested in how they intersect with corporate policy and governance, organizational citizenship, gender, ethics and flexible work arrangements.

Angeline Lim is a PhD student at the NUS Business School, National University of Singapore. Her research interests are workplace diversity, negative relationships and affect. She has presented her research at international conferences on management and industrial/organizational psychology.

Michael Meuser is a sociologist and Professor of Gender Studies in the Department of Sociology at the University of Dortmund, Germany. His research and teaching interests are in the fields of gender studies (with a special focus on masculinity and on gender politics), sociology of the body, sociology of knowledge and qualititative research methods. He is the author of numerous publications in the fields of masculinity studies, equal opportunity politics and qualitative methods. Topics of current research projects are the changing culture of fatherhood and the intersection of gender, class and ethnicity in schools.

Annalisa Murgia holds a PhD in Sociology and Social Research, at the Department of Sociology and Social Research, University of Trento, Italy. She is a member of the

Research Unit on Communication, Organizational Learning and Aesthetics, and of the Centre of Interdisciplinary Gender Studies of the University of Trento, where she is lecturer on the Master's in Gender Policies in the Labour World. Her researches focuses on work trajectories, with special regard to workers with atypical and precarious jobs, and on the social construction of gender in professional careers.

Julia Nentwich is Senior Lecturer of Organizational Psychology and Gender Studies at the University of St Gallen, Switzerland, where she is responsible for the teaching programme 'Gender and Diversity'. She holds a PhD from the University of Tübingen, Germany. Her major research interests at the Research Institute for Organizational Psychology are the social and discursive practices of gender and diversity. Current research projects tackle issues of change and change agency, female masculinities and the social construction of gender, technology and sustainability. She has published in international journals on these topics, in both English and German.

Eddy S.W. Ng is an Associate Professor at Dalhousie University, Canada. His research is in the areas of employment equity/affirmative action, workforce diversity, work values, career issues and the millennial generation. He has presented his research at the Academy of Management, the Administrative Sciences Association of Canada, the Canadian Psychological Association and the Canadian Industrial Relations Association. His work has also appeared in the *Canadian Journal of Administrative Sciences, Human Resource Management Review*, the *International Journal of Human Resource Management* and the *Journal of Business Ethics*.

Stella M. Nkomo is a Professor in the Department of Human Resources at the University of Pretoria, Pretoria, South Africa. Her particular fields of interest include diversity management, race and gender in organizations, change leadership and critical management studies. Professor Nkomo's internationally recognized work on race and gender in organizations and managing diversity appears in top management journals and edited book chapters. Professor Nkomo is the co-author of two books, *Applications in Human Resource Management* (Thomson-Southwestern Publishing, 2008) and *Our Separate Ways: Black and White Women and the Struggle for Professional Identity* (Harvard Business School Press, 2001).

Abhoy K. Ojha is a Professor in Organisational Behaviour and Human Resource Management with the IIMB, Indian Institute of Management, Bangalore, India. His research focuses on the social construction of performance in organizations, in particular in the innovation and healthcare sectors.

Renate Ortlieb is a Professor of Human Resource Management at the University of Graz, Austria. She has written numerous articles on the employment of migrants and workplace diversity, employee absenteeism, gender and power relations in organizations and company pension plans.

Mustafa Özbilgin is a Professor of Human Resource Management at Norwich Business School, UK. He researches and writes on equality, diversity and fairness at work from relational and comparative perspectives. He is the Editor-in-Chief of the *British Journal of Management* (Blackwell-Wiley) and *Equality, Diversity and Inclusion* (Emerald Press). His recent books include *International Human Resource Management* (Palgrave, 2004), *Global*

Diversity Management (Palgrave, 2007) and *Equality, Diversity and Inclusion* (Edward Elgar, 2009).

Barbara Poggio is an Assistant Professor of Sociology of Work at the University of Trento, Italy, where she coordinates the Centre of Interdisciplinary Gender Studies. Her research interests and publications focus in particular on the social construction of gender in organizations and on narrative analysis. She co-authored *Gender and Entrepreneurship: An Ethnographic Approach* (Routledge, 2005) and *Gendertelling in Organizations: Narratives from Male-dominated Environments* (Liber, 2007).

Pushkala Prasad is a leading scholar in the area of workplace diversity and she has researched workplace diversity in Scandinavian organizations as well as the diversity industry in Sweden. She is one of the co-editors of the *Handbook of Workplace Diversity* (Sage, 2006).

Barbara Sieben has been an Assistant Professor of Human Resource Management focused on Diversity at Freie Universität Berlin since 2007. Her research is based on multiparadigmatic approaches, informed by critical management perspectives. Next to workplace diversity, her research interests include emotions in organizations and the management of service work. She has published papers in journals such as *Managementforschung* and *Human Relations* and is co-editor of a volume on *Diversity Studies* (Campus, 2007).

Chris Steyaert has been Professor of Organizational Psychology at the University of St Gallen, Switzerland, since 2002; after obtaining a doctoral degree in Psychology from the Katholieke Universiteit Leuven (Belgium), he was connected to the Copenhagen Business School, Denmark and to the Entrepreneurship and Small Business Research Institute (ESBRI), Stockholm, Sweden. He has published in international journals and books in the area of diversity and difference, multilingualism and translation, forms of performing/writing research and the politics of entrepreneurship and creativity.

Jawad Syed's research interests include diversity and gender in organizations, cross-cultural HRM and organizational knowledge. In particular, Jawad has researched on diversity management in Australian and Pakistani contexts. Jawad has written widely on diversity and gender, including his articles in *International Journal of Human Resource Management*, *Asia Pacific Journal of Management*, *Asia Pacific Journal of Human Resources* and *Gender, Work and Organization*.

Ahu Tatlı is a Lecturer in International Human Resource Management in the School of Business and Management at Queen Mary, University of London, UK, where she has completed her PhD. Her research interests are in the field of equality and diversity in organizations with a particular focus on multi-level exploration of agentic power and strategies of the key actors in the field. Ahu has published widely in academic journals and books, as well as in practitioner journals in the areas of diversity management in public and private sector organizations in different industries, agency and change in organizations, and inequality and discrimination in recruitment and employment.

Adiam Tedros holds a PhD in Public Administration and has worked for the Swedish International Centre for Local Democracy since 2008. Her research focuses on state policies concerning urban planning and diversity. She has also taken part in a research project on individuals' experiences of equal treatment and/or discrimination across a range of Swedish institutions.

Ashley Terlouw is Professor of Sociology of Law at Radboud University Nijmegen, the Netherlands. She was a member of the Dutch Equal Treatment Committee between 2004 and 2008 and head of the refugee department of Amnesty International for the Netherlands. She worked at the District Court of The Hague from 1994 to 2001 as Senior Policy Advisor of the Staff Office on Refugee Law. She received her PhD in 2003 on cooperation between immigration judges. Her research interests are equal treatment, ethnicity and migration. Her additional functions are: Member of the Advisory Committee for Aliens (ACVZ) and board member and member of the appeal committee of the Dutch University Asylum Fund (UAF).

Marloes van Engen is Assistant Professor at Tilburg University, Nijmegen, the Netherlands. Her research interests are in the area of gender and diversity in organizations, work–family issues in organizations and the (human resource) management of diversity in organizations. She is taking part in the EU SUS.DIV Project – Sustainable Development in a Diverse World (Network of Excellence coordinated by the Fondazione ENI Enrico Mattei, Milan, Italy). She has published in *Psychological Bulletin*, *Journal of Organizational and Occupational Psychology* and *International Journal of Human Research Management*.

Cheryl Wyrick, PhD, SPHR (Senior Professional in Human Resources) is Professor and Chairperson of the Management and Human Resources Department at California State Polytechnic University Pomona, USA, where she has taught HR information systems, benefits, and training and development and other HR courses. An active volunteer, Cheryl has held various leadership positions in HR professional associations, including SHRM and the HR Certification Institute.

Patrizia Zanoni is an Associate Professor in the Faculty of Business Economics at Hasselt University, Belgium. Since 2009 she has led SEIN, the Research Institute for Identity, Diversity and Inequality Research. Drawing on various theoretical traditions including discourse analysis, labour process theory and institutional theory, her research investigates how 'different' identities are constructed and managed in organizations in function of productive goals and the generation of economic value. Her work has appeared in *Organization Studies*, *Human Relations*, the *Journal of Management Studies*, *Organization* and the *Journal of World Business*.

Acknowledgements

I would particularly like to thank the following direct or indirect contributors to the existence of this book project.

First, the contributors to the chapters themselves, for their chapters, the flesh and bones of the present book, and for the trust that they showed throughout this project, as well as those among the contributors who acted as voluntary reviewers during the first reviewing round: Anne-Françoise Bender, Annie Cornet, Iris Koall, Jacqueline Laufer and Waheeda Lillevik. Thanks to their participation, each first draft has benefited from three different reviewers.

The Academy of Management Gender and Diversity in Organizations (GDO) division comes into play. I would like here to give special thanks to Myrtle Bell, then President of the GDO, for opening so widely and welcomingly the door of GDO division to the newcomer to the Academy I then – August 2007 – was. I thus felt truly 'included' and encouraged to engage in collaboration with existing GDO members. The Academy of Management meetings in 2007 and 2008 provided ideal forums where the first contacts were made and where later discussions, at more advanced stages of the project, also furthered the advancement of this project, in the form of an international symposium.

Francine O'Sullivan, senior commissioning editor, Edward Elgar Publishing, beyond formally accepting this project, has been a firm supporter of this book throughout its period by her many suggestions and timely sending of advice or instructions, answering my many queries and those of the authors involved in the book project.

I also want to mention in particular the contributors to this book who supported the idea from its inception. I especially want to thank Rana Haq, Iris Koall, Mustafa Özbilgin and Jawad Syed, who reacted to this project by showing both enthusiasm and support at our first meeting in August 2007 in Philadelphia, and gave me the initial confidence that the whole project was worth delivering.

I am grateful to the Academy of Management International Theme Committee for their support, too. The Best International Symposium Award has been awarded to the symposium based on the present book's work-in-progress in August 2008 at the Annual Conference of the Academy of Management in Anaheim, California. This clearly signalled a strong interest from the academic community and motivated both the publisher and all participants to carry through the work towards the achievement of this book.

Perspectives from 16 countries on diversity and equal treatment at work: an overview and transverse questions
Alain Klarsfeld

Managing and developing diversity is on the political and business agenda in many countries. Diversity management has become an area of knowledge and practice in its own right in a number of countries. Yet all too often, it is referred to as a unifying concept, as if it were to be interpreted uniformly across cultures and countries. Much of the diversity literature is written by US or Anglo-Saxon scholars and suggests that diversity management represents a break from equality and equal opportunities at work. The purpose of this book is to restore diversity to its national contexts, and in particular to assess its relationship with equal employment legislation when such legislation exists. Countries covered by this volume are Austria, Belgium, Canada, France, Germany, India, Italy, the Netherlands, Pakistan, Singapore, South Africa, Sweden, Switzerland, Turkey, the UK and the USA.

Although it must be acknowledged that diversity may be a topic in the absence of such legislation, one particular question of interest to the authors of this book is to examine whether an equal employment legislation and 'diversity management' labelled as such existed at all in the different participating countries, and whether this 'diversity management' represented a break from equality concepts such as equal opportunity and affirmative action, as has been argued for about twenty years (Thomas, 1990; Thomas and Ely, 1996; Jain et al., 2003). The following chapters suggest that diversity management has not emerged as a concept in all participating countries, and where it has, a distinction between 'equality at work' and 'diversity management' is far from obvious. In many countries under review, diversity management appears strongly linked to equality and non-discrimination legislation, albeit in very country-specific ways. For some of the contributing teams to this volume, this link between diversity and compliance to equality legislations is sometimes termed a 'confusion', as they assume that diversity management should go beyond equality discourse and legislation (in other words, go beyond compliance with equality laws and moral imperatives) and should focus on the business benefits inherent in the diversity management concept (see the chapters on South Africa or the USA, for instance – Chapters 11 and 15). For other authors, no such remarks are formulated; on the contrary, as diversity management appears to be a vehicle towards institutionalizing equality at work, an ongoing process as seen from their own country's perspective (see the chapters on Sweden, Germany or France, for instance – Chapters 12, 6 and 5). But, with or without perceptions of limitations, and notwithstanding important differences in the various contexts of their adoption, diversity management and equality at work appear to be much more similar in content than the earliest advocates of diversity management had suggested, at least in the majority of countries covered by this book. However, this should not be interpreted as another normative assumption about diversity management, as a few countries, such as Canada and Belgium (at least as far as Flanders is concerned), seem to have developed an approach to diversity management in line with the vision of 'founding fathers' of this notion, i.e. the search for competitive advantage or other business-driven motives rather than compliance with anti-discrimination laws. Again, this underscores the need for contextualizing diversity management.

Beyond giving input on the relationship between diversity management and equal treatment legislations, this book's goal is to help scholars better contextualize the research they undertake in a given country and enhance their awareness of potential pitfalls in addressing 'diversity', equal treatment or affirmative action as 'natural' concepts. A better understanding of diversity will for instance help researchers appreciate the extent to which current research may or may not be generalized across countries, and whether and how 'diversity' has been constructed in various national contexts. For instance, in India, a country with a very diverse population, and strong equality legislation, diversity initiatives are very scarce in the private sector, whilst the public sector is subjected to 'reservation' quotas rather than 'diversity' labelled policies. In Singapore, 'harmony' and 'fairness' prevail over the term 'diversity' at the practitioner and policy-maker levels.

Although this book is not originally targeted to a non-academic audience, I make the assumption that, for the business community, and in particular for international businesses, it will help decision-makers appreciate the specifics of the countries they operate in as regards legal versus non-legal dimensions of diversity.

Finally, this book should also provide policy-makers and corporate leaders with benchmark data as regards how the concepts of diversity and equal treatment are understood in countries different from theirs, and the difficulties inherent in each country's 'path'.

Content specifications for the chapters

Although context is acknowledged as key to the development of this book project, a set of guidelines was provided to the teams of authors, if only to avoid the risk of a 'beauty contest' inherent in such an exercise. I also tried to take steps in order to avoid the context being conceptualized as static or deterministic (Özbilgin, 2009). Indeed, the country contexts presented in this book should be taken as possibilities, rather than as rigid constraints.

I informed authors that each chapter should use primary or secondary data, and be empirical, rather than theoretical, although theoretical frameworks could, of course, be used in order to help describe and/or understand the country's context.

The chapters were required to adopt a dynamic perspective, with retrospective data about dates when the first texts in the general and academic press in respective countries were issued, data about the legislation (dates, criteria covered), and if such data were available, case studies as well as macro data concerning the diversity of the workforce itself. Critical approaches were welcome, as authors were invited to distance themselves from developments taking place in their own countries. However, such approaches were not compulsory, as I assumed that a critical stance was not systematically the only relevant one for the interpretation of practices, be they in respect of laws or corporate management. Finally, each team was asked to provide a summary table based on a common template at the end of each chapter. This must be seen as a start of a reflection on comparability, rather than the outcome of it.

It was specified at the inception of the book project that each chapter should provide answers to the following questions, even if these were not to be considered limitative.

1. Is there equal treatment legislation in this country and what is its content? Since when? In particular, what dimensions of diversity does it address (gender, race, age, etc.)? To what degree is it enforced?
2. Even in the absence of such legislation, is there a public debate about diversity in this particular country, and if so, what is this debate, and concerning what type of diversity? How and when was it started if it was started at all? When do the first contributions appear in academia and in the press? Who are the actors involved in this debate, such as businesses, trade unions, political organizations, NGOs and other lobbies?
3. Is there empirical research about diversity in this country and what are the main contributions? What are the research questions being addressed by scholars about this country?
4. What is the relationship between diversity management and equal treatment/equal opportunity/affirmative action legislation if such legislation exists in this particular country?

Although the homogeneity of chapters is clearly a matter for improvement in subsequent editions of this book, I believe and hope that the above guidelines have helped each team of authors focus on a minimal set of requirements that could feed later discussions. In the next section, a brief summary is given for each chapter. Summaries reflect my decision to announce the structure of each chapter, and highlight some key findings as perceived from my own editorial perspective. Chapters cover Pakistan and Turkey, Austria, Belgium, Canada, France, Germany, India, Italy, the Netherlands, Singapore, South Africa, Sweden, Switzerland, the UK and the USA.

Summary of chapters

Chapter 1   *Pakistan and Turkey*

As an 'opener' to contextualizing diversity research from a country perspective, the first chapter, by Özbilgin, Syed and Dereli, shows how different historical paths influence the construction of gender diversity at the workplace in two large Muslim majority countries (MMCs). This chapter presents key historical underpinnings of gender equality at work in Turkey and Pakistan, assesses the interface between the state, religion and gender diversity from a historical perspective, and presents the current pictures of gender diversity especially in the workforce and political life in both countries. Gender diversity in Turkey has to be seen in relation to secularism, a strong component of Turkish history, whereas conversely in Pakistan, Islam was key in the foundation of the state and in the conceptualization of the role of women in society and the workplace. However, despite these historical differences, class differences of feminist thought and the associated polarization of achievements and failures in gender equality at work are strikingly similar in both countries. This sheds new light on how gender is constructed in MMCs, and beyond, points to the relevance of a country-based approach for the study of diversity management. What this chapter also tells us is that further research is needed along other dimensions of diversity than gender in both these countries.

Chapter 2   Austria

Bendl, Hanappi-Egger and Hofmann explain that Austria has a long history of being encompassed by a larger political regime, first as part of the Roman Empire, then under Habsburg rule as a member of the Austrian–Hungarian Empire. Throughout these periods Austria was embedded in highly culturally diverse environments. In order to provide a complex and accurate picture of contemporary Austria, the chapter first offers an historical framing, which has shaped the scientific and political debates during recent decades. In addition to providing structural data, the authors present an overview of the current political debates and the legal situation for diversity management and equal treatment. Next, they focus on the university and practice-based diversity management discourse and research findings about the implementation of Austrian diversity management in for-profit and non-profit organizations. Their contribution shows that although diversity and diversity management are now established concepts in Austria, the implementation of diversity management is still patchy, as only subsidiaries of foreign-owned multinationals, and a small minority of the largest companies listed on the Stock Exchange, have engaged in diversity initiatives, with SMEs that form the bulk of the Austrian economy lagging behind. Gender- and age-related measures dominate the scene in the diversity initiatives that were identified.

Chapter 3   Belgium

In their chapter, Cornet and Zanoni provide an overview of the specificity of diversity at the both the country level and the regional level, as Belgium comprises three regions with distinct policies. The text is structured in five sections. In the first, the authors sketch the position of women, the elderly, ethnic minorities, the disabled, and homo- and bisexuals on the Belgian labour market. The second section presents the Belgian anti-discrimination legislation and the third the public and private diversity initiatives. The authors then elaborate on the empirical research conducted on diversity in Belgium, and conclude with a reflection on the main distinctive issues concerning diversity within the Belgian context. In the Walloon context, characterized by heavy industry (metallurgy and mining) with only a few highly technological development poles, and higher unemployment rates, the notion of diversity remains relatively little used. In the more technology- and service-oriented Flanders, on the contrary, the shortage of labour in the recent years, together with the problem of the ageing of the working population, has favoured the diffusion of diversity management as one of the strategies to attract employees with non-traditional profiles into paid work.

Chapter 4   Canada

In their chapter, Haq and Ng start by describing and assessing the major piece of workplace equality legislation in Canada, the employment equity legislation. It can be concluded from their contribution that progress has been substantial for the various protected groups since the enactment of various pieces of Canadian equality legislation.

In its final section, the chapter provides input on diversity management understood as a business-case-driven practice. While employment equity seeks to redress past discrimination, managing diversity seeks to maximize the potential of all employees, including white males. The authors suggest that managing diversity is seen as less controversial when compared with employment equity given that it is more inclusive of everyone in the workplace rather than only those belonging to the four designated groups under the Equal Employment Act. As far as Canada is concerned, the focus on diversity signals a distinctive approach, more business-driven, more consensual, and more transversal, than the previous equal opportunities approach. Canada seems to have succeeded in developing diversity management practices that extend beyond compliance with equality laws.

Chapter 5   France
In the chapter on France, Bender, Klarsfeld and Laufer argue that the debate on diversity is not the result of a criticism or reframing of 'affirmative action', which does not exist as such in France for ethnic and racial minorities, and is actually illegal given the present legal framework. Rather, the rise of the diversity notion stems from a critique of the 'formal equality of rights model', which ignores the inequalities and the discriminations that it produces, and leads to the question of whether France should adopt affirmative action types of policies in the area of ethnic diversity. However, affirmative action, or 'positive action', as it is often termed in France, is considered by many as a risky strategy, one that privileges 'identities' and the self-seclusion of minorities rather than 'equality'. In the first section of their chapter, the authors bring a 'historical' perspective to their view of the implementation of equal opportunities for women, and the situation concerning the integration of immigrants and ethnic minorities. They present the French general legal anti-discrimination framework, and public policies in specific areas other than gender: disability, union affiliation, social deprivation, age, sexual orientation, religion. In the second section, they describe the advent of diversity as a response to the shortcomings of social policies and the integration of immigrants and their descendants. They conclude with the existing state of diversity research and pending issues in relation to the implementation of diversity policies, in particular that of ethnic statistics, subject of a heated debate in France at the time this chapter was finalized.

Chapter 6   Germany
In their chapter on Germany, Bruchhagen, Grieger, Koall, Meuser, Ortlieb and Sieben link gender, diversity and equal opportunities: they point out that, for the topic of equal treatment at work in Germany, gender and diversity are the most relevant anchors for research as well as for political and management practice. Diversity is seen here as a tool for society's achievement of providing equal opportunities. The authors make the assumption that diversity management will spread in Germany in both research and practice. The authors outline some of the barriers that will be hard to overcome, and also adverse effects of concepts such as diversity management when it serves only as a façade of legitimacy. However, according to them, there are strong drivers for an effective promotion of equal opportunities: legal forces, and demographical change – bred by increasing proportions of migrants, women and the elderly in the labour force – accompanied

by a shortage of highly qualified employees. They argue that political action on both the national and the local levels as well as the 'usual' processes of institutionalization will contribute to the wide distribution of the philosophy of diversity management and, more importantly, to the appreciation of diversity.

Chapter 7   India

The chapter by Haq and Ojha, is mainly dedicated to a depiction of India's affirmative action policies in the public sector, public education and political institutions, a critique of their outcomes, and proposals for reforms. India is unique in its outcome-based focus on numerical reservations, or quotas, for three designated groups: the Scheduled Castes (SC), the Scheduled Tribes (ST) and the Other Backward Classes (OBC) as part of its affirmative action policies. These policies have provided opportunities for advancement for members of the protected groups, but also an inflation in the number of protected groups, the definition of which is partly left to the initiative of each individual state included in the Indian federation. However, this type of legislation applies only to the public sector. Private sector organizations are not governed by affirmative action policies, and most have not shown any interest in implementing voluntary diversity programmes. The projected changes under discussion in India involve departing from a purely caste- or tribe-based system in order to include socioeconomic variables into a more complex model than the reservation, quota-based model.

Chapter 8   Italy

In this chapter, Murgia and Poggio defend the argument that, in comparison with other Western countries, in Italy the concrete implementation of diversity management practices in firms and organizations is still rather limited. It tends to focus on gender differences and often consists in circumscribed actions with scant efficacy with regard to the cultural change that should instead be at the basis of such an approach. Murgia's and Poggio's aim here is to conduct a reasoned analysis of diversity management in Italy, considering the situation of the Italian labour market, the legislative context, and the main schemes of organizational development undertaken in Italy by enterprises and consulting firms to enhance diversity. The authors attempt to show the strengths and weaknesses that characterize such developments. They focus in particular on gender diversity, as the dimension most widely considered in Italy.

Chapter 9   The Netherlands

In their chapter on the Netherlands, Bleijenbergh, van Engen and Terlouw provide input on the development of an anti-discrimination legal framework in their country and the debates that have surrounded it. Their chapter analyses a situation where an affirmative action legal framework – including self-report of ethnic origin – was put in place and later abandoned or mitigated because of employer claims and backlash from public opinion. This is an original feature when compared to the other countries featured in the book. The authors also insist on how different equality and diversity claims can compete and clash with one another. More precisely, the heated debate reported in their chapter bears on the tension between constitutional rights regarding religion (equal treatment with regard to religion, freedom of religion and freedom of education) and the right to equal treatment on the basis of gender and sexual orientation.

Chapter 10   Singapore

In the first section of their chapter, Chia and Lim present an original approach taken by the Republic of Singapore to bring forward the agenda of workplace equality: the tripartite model, a model whereby government, employers' organizations and trade unions promote best practice rather than the state issuing binding legislation. The section that follows discusses the treatment of four types of diversity in Singapore – ethnicity, gender, sexual orientation and age – from a legislative and sociopolitical perspective. They highlight that male–male sexual orientation is still illegal in Singaporean law, and homosexual behaviour is considered 'unacceptable' by an overwhelming majority of the population. The chapter also addresses the academic discourse surrounding the various types of diversity. Another original feature of Singapore, though not strictly employment-related, is presented: the Ethnic Integration Policy (EIP), a housing policy introduced to promote racial integration and harmony, and prevent the formation of racial enclaves by ensuring that every public housing estate had a balanced ethnic mix. Finally, a summary of the relevant issues and the implications they have for both research and practice are presented. As a concluding remark, the authors note that it remains to be seen if the tripartite model will be a suitable one for managing diversity, as this model is very recent, and evidence it still needed in order to properly assess its effectiveness.

Chapter 11   South Africa

In their chapter, Booysen and Nkomo begin with a brief overview of South African early history and cultures, the colonization and the forming of a republic, the apartheid regime and lastly the birth of its democracy and its cultural diversity. This is followed by a review of the legislation geared towards workplace equality and transformation in South Africa, which stretches beyond employment to include the promotion of blacks in the areas of corporate ownership and top management. Although progress has been achieved since 1994 as regards their employment status, blacks still are largely underrepresented at the managerial and professional levels. The outcome of workplace equality legislative measures and the difference between employment equity and diversity in the South African context are then discussed, followed by the current debates and issues surrounding cultural diversity. This is followed by an overview of diversity and employment equity research and practices in South African organizations. The authors point out that in South Africa, most organizations are still 'trapped' in the discrimination-and-fairness perspective, or what can be termed as 'righting the wrong' and complying with the law, and still have a long way to go towards promoting the other paradigms of diversity, which centre on the 'business case' argument, and value diversity as a potential source of learning.

Chapter 12   Sweden

Kalonaityte, Prasad and Tedros, in their chapter, argue that the Swedish appropriation of diversity management needs to be seen as a development of the ongoing national policy-making and institutionalized efforts to further equal treatment, migration management and gender equality. The purpose of the first section is to provide the reader with the Sweden-specific diversity terminology and the broader conceptual framework within which diversity needs to be viewed. In the second section the authors move on to review the current research debates on the status and the challenges associated with workplace diversity and equality. The second section is therefore an overview of the existing research orientations concerning workplace diversity and equality in Sweden. The chapter contrasts gender, as one policy area where Sweden is considered to be relatively successful, with ethnic integration, where many shortcomings are indicated.

Chapter 13   Switzerland
Switzerland has four official languages, two major religions and 26 cantons as sovereign legal and administrative entities. Another specificity of Switzerland is its strong 'breadwinner' culture, which expects women to be at home for childcare purposes. A federalist and democratic nation based on strong liberal values, Switzerland cherishes its myths about its rural origin, as Nentwich, Steyaert and Liebig explain in their chapter. Despite Switzerland's long tradition of dealing with its own internal diversity, the public debate on diversity in the work context began only recently. This paradox in the conception of diversity in Switzerland guides the authors as they discuss the entry and establishment of diversity practices in Swiss corporate and organizational life. First, they sketch the recent entry of diversity management into Switzerland, and show how the historical and local context of a specific 'diverse' Switzerland is aligned with the global idea of diversity management as it travelled from the USA. In the second section, they outline the diversity of the Swiss labour market and work life in general with regard to those dimensions that are considered the most significant: gender and culture. In the third section, they sketch the legal dimensions of diversity management, again moving between the specifically Swiss legal context and the broader (mostly European) legislative changes. And finally, they review some recent research projects in order to shed some light on the extent to which Switzerland forms a special case.

Chapter 14   The UK
Writing about diversity in the UK, Tatlı revisits the mainstream US-originated assumption that diversity management represents a break with equal opportunities. The first section of the chapter provides a background to the development of the diversity management discourse and structures in the UK. The now more than 30-year-old legislative and regulatory framework in the UK in relation to equality and diversity is introduced. Then diverse scholarly perspectives that are developed in the UK context are reviewed in order to account for the equal opportunities versus diversity management debate, mainly the theorization of the rationales for adopting diversity management. In the second section, Tatlı explores the discourses and practices prevailing in the field of diversity management in the UK context. She uncovers the complex and contested nature of diversity management processes by presenting empirical evidence against simplistic, a-historical, a-contextual and a-political notions of diversity management. The data display strong differences between the private sector on the one hand, and the public sector on the other, where legislation is traditionally binding. Diversity and equality policies tend to be more widespread in the latter. As far as the UK is concerned, and in spite of a dominant 'business case' discourse, in practice, the main driver for the adoption of diversity management policies appears to be, not the business case, but the search for legal compliance.

Chapter 15   The USA

In their chapter, Lillevik, Combs and Wyrick, after giving input on the early debates on gender and race equality in the first section, discuss the relevant legislation and policies dealing with the treatment of minority groups in the workforce. Enforcement issues, Supreme Court case law, and critiques formulated against affirmative action are dealt with in the third section. Next, research and public discourse about diversity management as a 'new' paradigm are addressed in a fourth section. This includes the definition of diversity, the rationales for the emergence of the concept of diversity, and a brief summary of US research and current debates about diversity, in particular as regards the relationship between equal opportunities, affirmative action and diversity management. Although it is a US-originated concept, stressing the benefits of a diverse workforce rather than compliance with legal requirements, diversity management appears to hold strong historical links with equal opportunities and affirmative action, and all three concepts are often perceived as one and the same by the general public. The authors insist on the strong backlash that exists among the US population against both diversity management and equal employment opportunities policies.

A typology of public policies regarding positive action

Each chapter includes a section on anti-discrimination legislation. In most – but not all – countries under study, states have introduced 'equality' legislations, in other words the removal of negative discrimination, and later on 'positive action' legislation, which seek to introduce temporary differential treatment for the attention of traditionally underprivileged population groups. Working on a variety of countries, themselves using a variety of criteria when it comes to operationalizing diversity (such as gender, national origin, disability), and a variety of positive action regulations, provides an overview of how constraining laws may be in relation to positive action. In the light of the material accumulated in this book, I offer Table 0.1 as an attempt to summarize the wide range of possibilities that the countries under study present to the reader. I hope that this will help policy-makers at the government and corporate level to remove some of the 'fog' that has surrounded the adoption of positive action measures, a fog that maintains a confusion between outcome-based quotas, and the collection of statistics for monitoring purposes. Table 0.1 suggests that such confusion does not hold, and aims to foster a discussion of the typologies of positive action legislations in the wake of Jain et al. (2003).

Research perspectives

In the future, more research should be devoted to assessing the relevance of this typology and its possible applications and limitations. Beyond state legislations, research efforts should try to extend beyond strictly focusing on the laws and adapt this typology to other levels of policy formulation such as the industry level and the corporate level: similar to states, industries (through collective bargaining) and corporations (through collective bargaining and internal, voluntary rules) as well as international institutions (such as the European Union) can put in place policies whose aim is to eliminate discrimination and develop and manage diversity. Once a clear typology is established, it becomes possible to conduct comparative research at these various levels on antecedents and consequences of such policies, in particular their efficacy in achieving organizational performance together with distributive and procedural justice.

Table 0.1   A typology of positive action legislations

Degree of constraint of positive action legislation	Definition	Examples of criteria/country as of July 2009
Equality of rights only. No reporting allowed	It is forbidden for employers to directly collect data and report figures on the criterion; action plans cannot target these criteria directly	Race and ethnic origin/ France and Sweden
Allowed reporting	Collecting data and reporting on the criterion is possible. This remains at the discretion of employers, and is highly controversial	National origin/France
Positive action encouraged	Collecting data and reporting on the criterion is compulsory, but not the setting of outcome targets, which remain at the discretion of employers. Employers have a broad duty to act, such as to engage in collective bargaining	Race and origin/UK (public authorities) Gender/France (until 2006)
Positive action compulsory – constrained process	Collecting data, setting targets, acting and reporting progress on the criterion is compulsory. Covered employers must demonstrate good faith action and progress. The target is remote and not binding in the short term. Sanctions may apply if there is a lack of 'good faith' and progress	Race and origin/Canada, USA, South Africa Ageing workers/France
Positive action compulsory – constrained outcome	Strict targets (quotas) have to be met for the criterion. Sanctions are imposed systematically when targets are not met	Caste and tribe/India Disability/France

References

Jain, H.C., Sloane, P.J. and Horwitz, F. (eds) (2003), *Employment Equity and Affirmative Action: An International Comparison*, New York: M.E. Sharpe.

Özbilgin, M. (2009), 'Equality, diversity and inclusion at work: yesterday, today and tomorrow', in M. Özbilgin (ed.), *Equality, Diversity, and Inclusion at Work: Theory and Scholarship*, Cheltenham, UK, and Northampton, MA, USA: Edward Elgar, pp. 1–14.

Thomas, D. and Ely, R. (1996), 'Making differences matter', *Harvard Business Review*, **74** (5), 79–90.

Thomas, R.R. (1990), 'From affirmative action to affirming diversity', *Harvard Business Review*, **68**, 107–17.

1 Managing gender diversity in Pakistan and Turkey: a historical review

Mustafa Özbilgin, Jawad Syed and Beliz Dereli

Introduction

Studies of gender in Muslim majority countries (MMCs) have traditionally focused on gender issues in the Middle East and the Arab world (e.g. Afkhami, 1995; Mernissi, 1987; Moghadam, 1997). This chapter is a departure from that tradition, and is focused on two non-Arab countries, Pakistan and Turkey. In this sense, the chapter accounts for the diversity of Islam and various gender norms and practices within MMCs. Previous research suggests that the compatibility of organizational values with the wider societal values is essential to the long-term success of organizations (Harzing and Sorge, 2003; Hofstede, 1984; Schuler and Rogovsky, 1998).

The focus of this chapter is upon managing gender diversity in Pakistan and Turkey. While other dimensions of diversity (e.g. cultural diversity, disability) are important, most of the literature in the two countries focuses on gender. Other areas are less developed and theoretically silent. They deserve in-depth future attention in their own right. We, however, argue that gender can serve as a cross-cutting lens through which other dimensions can be included in the diversity debate, as the managerial tools for leveraging gender diversity are more developed than tools for other strands of difference. Indeed, gender diversity is not a settled and resolved issue. Therefore the chapter does not choose to ignore other strands but focuses on one in order to highlight the ongoing relevance of gender issues in the context of employment in both countries.

Organizational–societal cultural congruence is not only important to productivity and worker satisfaction (Newman and Nollen, 1996), but also in terms of perceived organizational legitimacy that affects the long-term survival of the business (Giacobbe-Miller et al., 2003; Kostova and Zaheer, 1999). From an institutional perspective, coercive pressure is often brought about by the actions of governmental and other regulatory bodies that have control over an organization or its critical resources (DiMaggio and Powell, 1983; James and Wooten, 2006; Kostova and Roth, 2002; Oliver, 1991).

Cross-national differences in institutional structures are known to result in management practices that vary from country to country (Gooderham et al., 1999). Moreover, with a few exceptions (e.g. Ghorbani and Tung, 2007; Jain et al., 2003; Özbilgin, 2000; Syed et al., 2005; Syed, 2008), international comparative studies of gender equality in employment are almost negligible within an Islamic context, held back by barriers such as the lack of contextual understanding and a general dearth of gender-segregated data in MMCs. In this chapter, while we bring cross-national insights, drawing on a historical review of gender diversity in Pakistan and Turkey, we also present the information about the place of women in political life, decision-making process and working life in these two countries.

Historical contexts of gender equality in Pakistan and Turkey
Previous research has highlighted the importance of societal and historical contexts to fully understand the dynamics of diversity and equal opportunity in the workplace (e.g. Cox, 1995; Syed and Özbilgin, 2009; Triandis, 1995). History of intergroup relations presents the sociocultural background against which the social discourse and practices of equal opportunity are constructed (Alderfer and Smith, 1982). Accordingly, occupational roles tend to be segregated by gender or by ethnicity on the basis of assumptions about these and other forms of identity, having their roots in the history of the labour market and in differences in educational opportunities. In this section we explore the historical interplay between the state, religion and gender diversity in Pakistan and Turkey.

Islam, state and gender diversity in Pakistan
Whilst Islam was the *raison d'être* for Pakistan (the two-nation theory was based on the idea of separate homelands for Hindus and Muslims in the Subcontinent), the Turkish Republic was founded on the principles of secularism by clearly evacuating Islam from public life. This historical difference has resulted in different political orientations of each society, amply reflected in the distinct roles played by the military in the political evolution of both countries as the guarantor of national security: the guardian of secularism in Turkey, and the guardian of Islamic identity in Pakistan. These ideological differences were to have far-reaching implications for the future of social policies, including gender policies, in both societies.

To comprehend the true nature of gender discourse and female position in today's Pakistani society and organizations, it is imperative to investigate the historical evolution of Muslim feminist thought in pre-1947 colonial India. From the perspective of today's feminism, Minault (1998, p. 11) argues, it is important to recognize that in nineteenth-century India, men were the pioneers in the movements for women's education, rights and status. Men's participation in gender reforms was out of their genuine concern and idealism, and also out of their desire to harmonize their private lives and public roles and professions. Given the intense nature of seclusion faced by Muslim women, who had little access to education and other intellectual resources, it is not a surprise that men led the way to gender reforms in colonial India.

Minault treats the women's question as the story of three generations (p. 11): the first, men born before 1857, trained in traditional Islamic knowledge and literature, who first reflected upon Muslim family life, rituals and customs and proposed education programmes for women within private domains of religion and the four walls of the house; the second, the post-1857 generation with a blend of Islamic and Western education, who became skilled religious and social controversialists, and who first founded books, journals and schools for women's education and debated *purdah* (the veil); and the third, the first generation of women trained in schools, who contributed in public life through teaching in schools and writing on women's issues. By the end of the nineteenth century, there were clear signs of a social movement for gender reforms, furnishing its ideological rationale within the Islamic setting. The supporters of the reforms argued for more rights for women while challenging gender discriminatory cultural customs as well as the patriarchal interpretations of the religion that had kept Muslim women disadvantaged over many centuries. For instance, Sayyid Mumtaz Ali (1860–1935) was one of the main proponents of this ideology, chiefly known for his pioneering role in Urdu journalism for women. Mumtaz Ali founded the women's weekly journal *Tahzib un-Niswan* in Lahore in 1898 with the purpose of 'liberating women from outmoded customs and evil practices' (Minault, 1998, p. 73).

As a result of the diverse movements for gender reforms, there was a growing trend among upper- and middle-class urban Muslim women to attend modern schools and colleges (Jalal, 1991, p. 82). There were also signs of political activities of Muslim women, which were a breath of fresh air in the otherwise non-public and non-social roles assigned to them. The Anjuman-e-Khawatin-e-Islam (or the All India Muslim Ladies' Conference) was one such organization that claimed to represent the interests of all Muslim women. Founded in Aligarh in March 1914, the Anjuman's main objectives included the social and the educational uplift of Muslim women (Minault, 1981).

The revival of the Muslim League in the 1930s under the leadership of Muhammad Ali Jinnah (later to become the founder of Pakistan) opened a fresh chapter for Muslim women in the Subcontinent. Women were encouraged to take part in public life, though not as claimants of their rights so much as symbols of Muslims' cultural identity (Jalal, 1991, p. 84). Following the creation of Pakistan, women attained voting rights and the right to elect. The first legislature of Pakistan in 1947 had two women representatives, Begum Jahan Ara Shah Nawaz and Begum Shaista Ikramullah. Both of these women, along with other elite Muslim women in Pakistan, actively advocated women's political empowerment through legal reforms. They mobilized support that led to the passage of the Muslim Personal Law of Shariah in 1948, which recognized a woman's right to inherit all forms of property in the newly created state of Pakistan. They were also behind the futile attempt to have the government include a Charter of Women's Rights in the 1956 constitution. The 1961 Muslim Family Laws Ordinance covering marriage and divorce can be identified as the most important socio-legal reform supported by these women (FRD, 1994).

Under the Family Laws Ordinance, women were officially able to inherit agricultural property in consonance with Islamic law; second marriages were made contingent upon agreement by the first wife; divorce was made more difficult for men; women attained the right to initiate divorce for the first time; and a system of registration of marriages was also introduced. In practice, these laws generally protected the rights of educated and politically aware women. Women in rural areas and working-class women in urban areas were only marginally able to benefit from the new laws. A few women's organizations existed at that time, including the charitable All Pakistan Women's Association (APWA) and the progressive Anjuman-e-Jamhooriat Pasand Khawateen (Rouse, 1988, p. 6).

The class origins of those who were the vanguard of the feminist movement in Pakistan have played a major role in the articulation of women's issues at the policy level. Educated urban upper- and middle-class women have carefully demanded women's emancipation without creating a major upset by challenging their prescribed roles within society. This course has been described as an outcome of a deeper and largely subjective consideration: the stability of the family unit and by implication of the social order itself (Jalal, 1991, p. 79). Jalal suggests that, in today's Pakistan, Islamic identity of the state cannot be dissociated from the women's question in colonial India, when, threatened with the loss of their cultural identity in a sea of infidels, Muslims endeavoured to reinforce Islamic social life by protecting the stability of the family unit.

Women in Pakistan today

Women in power and decision-making   Four important challenges confronted women in Pakistan in the early 1990s: increasing practical literacy, gaining access to employment opportunities at all levels in the economy, promoting change in the perception of women's roles and status, and gaining a public voice both within and outside of the political process. There have been various attempts at social and legal reform aimed at improving Muslim women's lives in the Subcontinent during the twentieth century. These attempts have generally been related to two broader, intertwined movements: the social reform movement in British India and the growing Muslim nationalist movement. Since partition, the changing status of women in Pakistan has largely been linked with discourse about the role of Islam in a modern state. This debate concerns the extent to which civil rights common in most Western democracies are appropriate in an Islamic society and the way these rights should be reconciled with Islamic family law (Lewis, 2001).

Enhancement of women's political representation at national and local levels facilitated women's presence and voice in law-making and governance. Providing placement of women in positions of decision-making, and their participation in electoral positions at federal, provincial, and local levels under the Devolution Plan through the Local Government Ordinance 2001, is considered as the watershed for political empowerment of the women of Pakistan. It provides 33 per cent representation of women at all tiers of local elected bodies (with 39 964 women working as councillors) and 231 women representing in Federal and Provincial Assemblies as Members of the Senate and the National Provincial Assemblies on special women's seats out of 1170 seats. In addition, women can also contest elections on general seats. This has revolutionized political participation of women in Pakistan (Mahmood, 2007, p. 13).

On the other hand, establishment of 'Women's Political Schools' with assistance from donor agencies and 'District Resource Centres' for women are innovative projects infusing political vision and awareness among the women of Pakistan (CEDAW, 2007).

A melding of the traditional social welfare activities of the women's movement and its newly revised political activism appears to have occurred. Diverse groups, including the Women's Action Forum, the All Pakistan Women's Association, the Pakistan Women Lawyers' Association, and the Business and Professional Women's Association, are supporting small-scale projects throughout the country that focus on empowering women. The Pakistan Women Lawyers' Association has released a series of films educating women about their legal rights. The women's movement has shifted from reacting to government legislation to focusing on three primary goals: securing women's political representation in the National Assembly; working to raise women's consciousness, particularly about family planning; and countering suppression of women's rights by defining and articulating positions on events as they occur in order to raise public awareness (Islam for Today, 1994).

Women and economy in Pakistan   Although the proportion of population living below the poverty line in Pakistan fell sharply between 2001 and 2005, women have not benefited from economic growth to the same extent as men. Low social indicators coupled with limited access to income-generating opportunities have left women considerably more vulnerable to poverty than men. Women, as paid or unpaid labourers, are usually relegated tasks with low productivity and little investment in technology or extension efforts by government. In the urban context, an increasing proportion of women are working in the informal sector, in manufacturing and service-based activities. In the formal sector, some well-educated women are gradually moving into responsible positions in banks and other private sector offices (ADB, 2008, p. 1).

While not a panacea, women's access to finance is an important tool for poverty reduction. Microfinance programmes in Pakistan have increasingly focused on women and have been an important aspect of the country's poverty alleviation strategy. The Ten-Year Perspective Development Plan (2001–11) and the Three-Year Development Programmes (2001–04) of the government of Pakistan emphasize microcredit as the main approach to improving the conditions of poor Pakistani women (Niethammer et al., 2007, p. 3).

The small-to-medium enterprise (SME) sector can make a significant contribution to women's employment, which is particularly important in a country like Pakistan where the female labour force participation rate is 15.9 per cent, among the lowest in the region. This gap is even visibly larger in urban areas, where the female participation rate is as low as 9.44 per cent (Pakistan Federal Bureau of Statistics, 2006).

Even though 'hard data' are difficult to obtain, as research on female entrepreneurs in the SME sector is scarce, a survey undertaken by the International Labour Organization (ILO) of 150 women entrepreneurs in Lahore and the twin cities of Rawalpindi and Islamabad found 39 per cent of women from the sample engaged in small enterprises and 9 per cent in medium enterprises. Furthermore, the sample revealed that women entrepreneurs in the SME sector provide greater employment to women. On average, women entrepreneurs were found to hire more females than their male counterparts (Niethammer et al., 2007, p. 4).

Opportunities for rural women in Pakistan, especially in the North, where a majority of projects funded by IFAD (International Fund for Agricultural Development) are located, are limited. Nevertheless, women play a major role in the household economy that is invisible and unrecognized. Besides the household chores, women actively contribute to farm activities, collect firewood, fetch water and work in the fields. However, they are not allowed to go to market to sell their produce – they must depend on men. Since 1978, IFAD has supported 21 projects in Pakistan with loans for a total of US$387.5 million. The total estimated cost of the projects is US$2036.4 million. The projects have directly benefited approximately 1.6 million households in rural Pakistan, working to improve the livelihoods and productivity of rural poor people (ENRAP, 2007). Labour force participation rates show small increases despite economic growth, as presented in Table 1.1.

Many women withdraw from the labour force upon marriage, influenced by family attitudes, and because of unsafe travel conditions, discriminatory workplace conditions, and time pressures from domestic responsibilities. Unemployment rates in 2005–06 were higher for women, at 9 per cent compared to men at 5 per cent, but this gap has narrowed since 2003–04 when the unemployment rate of women was 13 per cent and of men 7 per cent (Table 1.2).

The proportion of women working in the non-agriculture formal sector of the economy is 26 per cent of total female non-agriculture workers. Women tend to be found

Table 1.1   Labour force participation rates (%)

	2003–04			2005–06		
	Total	Male	Female	Total	Male	Female
Pakistan	43.7	70.6	15.9	46.0	72.0	18.9
Rural	46.3	72.6	19.5	48.9	73.8	23.4
Urban	39.2	67.1	9.4	40.7	68.7	10.6

Source: GoP (2006).

Table 1.2   Unemployment rates (%)

	2003–04			2005–06		
	Total	Male	Female	Total	Male	Female
Pakistan	7.7	6.6	12.8	6.2	5.4	9.3
Rural	6.7	5.7	10.9	5.4	4.6	7.7
Urban	9.7	8.4	19.8	8.0	6.9	15.8

Source: GoP (2006).

in less-skilled areas (only 11 per cent are in senior managerial, professional, technician or clerical categories, see Table 1.3), and are forced into more part-time and piecework than men, despite lower earnings in this sector, so that they can remain at home. Changes in sociocultural norms and gender stereotypes are taking place, especially in urban societies where girls are increasingly encouraged to take up advanced education and to apply these skills in suitable professions. While some employment opportunities are increasingly available to women because of improved education, only certain sectors are considered suitable (ADB, 2008).

Women are blocked from reaching their full earning potential; investments in education are not maximized; and many women remain vulnerable to poverty, under- and unemployment, and dependence on others. If the demographic dividend of the youthful workforce – at least 45 per cent of which is female – is to be maximized in Pakistan, the exclusion of women from employment and productive opportunities needs to be more systematically addressed (ADB, 2008).

Secularism, state and gender diversity in Turkey
In Turkish society, relaxation of the religious strictures on gender segregation of public and private spheres of life during the declining years of the Ottoman Empire in the late nineteenth century enabled women's political activism to gain visibility. Following the national wars, the early years of the modern-day Turkish Republic in the 1920s witnessed significant legal and social changes in women's rights. Turkish women gained their political right to vote and to be elected to the Grand National Assembly in 1934 (Tekeli, 1993). In 1937, Turkey became a secular state by law, culminating in further relaxation of laws and social norms that previously constrained women's full participation in public life in

Table 1.3   Formal sector: distribution by major occupation groups (%)

Item	2003–04			2005–06		
	Total	Male	Female	Total	Male	Female
Legislators, senior officials and managers	24.9	26.7	5.9	25.6	27.9	7.1
Professionals	1.6	1.5	2.5	1.7	1.8	1.5
Technicians and associate professionals	3.8	3.2	9.8	4.5	3.4	13.2
Clerks	0.4	0.5	–	0.3	0.3	0.1
Service workers and shop and market sales workers	9.5	10.1	3.1	9.6	10.4	3.2
Skilled agriculture and fishery workers	–	–	–	0.2	0.2	0.3
Craft and related trade workers	31.1	28.4	58.6	30.9	27.4	59.1
Plant and machine operators and assemblers	6.1	6.7	0.2	6.7	7.4	0.5
Elementary (unskilled) occupations	22.6	22.9	19.9	20.5	21.2	15.0
Total	100.0	100.0	100.0	100.0	100.0	100.0

Source: GoP (2006).

Turkey (Bilge, 1995). Turkish women entered education, employment and other public domains of life in increasing numbers between the 1930s and the 1970s. This is, however, only one part of the picture.

Some argue that women were essential 'actors or pawns' in the republican project of modernity (Kandiyoti, 1988). The doors of gender equality were open to only those women who conformed to the Kemalist project of modernity. Yet women's activism was circumscribed by the dictates of an autocratic Westernizing state. Toprak (1988) reports the restraining impact of Kemalism on women's activism when it was considered inharmonious with the interests of the state. Tekeli (1991, pp.93–107) contends that the Kemalist revolution was not undertaken for women's own rights. It was rather used for the transformation that Kemalism aimed to accomplish at the level of the state. Tekeli argues that Atatürk evaluated the issue of women's rights in the context of the transformation of the state, and in this pursuit 'made use' of women's rights as much as he could.

Kemalist Turkey was to be a nationalist melting pot. Accordingly, there was an element of the 'otherness' of women who did not have the 'appropriate' ethnic and socioeconomic backgrounds. The banning of certain language groups was the source of many of Turkey's modern problems, including the Armenian problem. Although the Armenian problem dated from before the formation of the nation-state, it did not escape the Kemalist nationalization drive. Similar issues were faced in the Kurdish- and the Arabic-speaking areas of Turkey. Thus, whereas Kemalism brought 'emancipation' for upper-class women in urban areas, *the other* women's perspectives and issues remained marginalized within the 'mainstream' feminist discourse (Arat, 1997). These differences were later reflected in the emergence of Marxist feminism in Turkey.

The emergent Turkish feminist movement in the 1970s allied itself with Marxism, and the military *coup* in 1980 hit both the Marxists and the Marxist-feminists severely (Tekeli, 1993). However, Turkish democracy was restored in 1982. The first government after the *coup d'état* implemented liberal and *laissez-faire* policies that brought unforeseen changes to Turkish society. Both privately owned and state-owned television, radio and other mass media channels replaced the state monopoly in the 1980s, and public debates resumed about feminist concerns, ranging from women's employment and domestic violence to the rights of sex workers (Ecevit, 1993). However, in the late 1980s, the feminist groups in Turkey fragmented, reflecting widening disparities in the fortunes of their supporters from different classes and ethnic groups, from rural and urban areas, from secular and Islamic perspectives, and from different educational backgrounds. Within this social framework, the hard-core feminist movement in Turkey, which was still dominated by an elite group of academics or well-educated women from the urban centres of Turkey, enjoyed little success in reaching the lower socioeconomic segments of Turkish society.

Women in Turkey today

Women in power and decision-making   In Turkey, there are varied and multifaceted reasons for women's low levels of political participation, as in many other fields. One of the main reasons for the inadequate representation of women in politics and decision-making mechanisms in Turkey is the adverse nature of the structural and cultural organization of the political system and parties. This situation is exposed by certain non-governmental organizations (NGOs): the women's branches of political parties, which are viewed as a channel to enhance women's participation in political life, are not integral to decision-making processes, and they suffer from low political yield (KSGM, 2008).

Today Turkish women seem to participate in politics more actively than before. This may be attributed to rapid modernization and eradication of the patriarchal, traditional social structure. However, women are more active in local than in national politics. In the public sector, occupation and career opportunities for women are better than opportunities in the private sector. However, inequality still persists. In political parties, women remain as 'vote-gatherers' rather than as 'decision-makers.' Still, many – if not all – women are entering the political as well as the socioeconomic realm (Keskin, 1997).

According to the results of the General Elections of 2007, 50 out of 550 representatives in the Grand National Assembly of Turkey (TBMM) are female, which corresponds to 9.1 per cent. The proportions of female Members of Parliament (MP) in Parliament for the different election years are shown in Table 1.4 (KSGM, 2008).

Women and economy in Turkey   In Turkey, women's labour force participation and employment rates are far below those of other modern democracies. While in 1990 one woman out of three was employed, in 2004 this figure fell to one woman out of four. In the EU, one woman in two is in employment. Rural areas and the informal sector con-

Table 1.4   Proportions of female MPs in Parliament

Election year	Number of MPs in Parliament	Number of female MPs	Share in total (%)
1935	395	18	4.6
1943	435	16	3.7
1950	487	3	0.6
1957	610	7	1.1
1965	450	8	1.8
1973	450	6	1.3
1991	450	8	1.8
1999	550	22	4.0
2002	550	24	4.4
2007	550	50	9.1

Source: KSGM (2008).

Table 1.5   Labour force participation rate by urban–rural settlement and sex (15+) (%)

	2003	2004	2005	2006
Total for Turkey	48.3	48.7	48.3	48.0
Men	70.4	72.3	72.2	71.5
Women	26.6	25.4	24.8	24.9
Urban	43.8	44.5	45.5	45.5
Men	68.9	70.8	71.5	70.8
Women	18.5	18.3	19.3	19.9
Rural	55.5	55.4	53.1	52.2
Men	72.9	74.7	73.5	72.7
Women	39.0	36.7	33.7	33.0

Source: KSGM (2008).

tinue to provide the main employment opportunities for them. Unplanned urbanization, migration to urban areas and rapid feminization of the informal sector are among the important factors that impede women's participation in employment by creating social exclusion (Tisk, 2006, p. 3).

In Turkey, the labour force participation rate has fallen to very low rates in recent years and follows a decreasing trend over the year (see Table 1.5). The low labour force participation rate results from reasons such as (KSGM, 2008):

- Low educational level of the labour force;
- An annual rate of increase of the working-age population that is higher than the annual rate of increase of newly created jobs for that year;
- An increased migration to urban areas as a consequence of a decreasing trend of agricultural employment, which leads to a withdrawal of, in particular, women from the labour force;

Table 1.6   Unemployment rate by rural–urban settlement and sex (%)

	2003	2004	2005	2006
Total for Turkey	10.5	10.3	10.3	9.9
Men	10.7	10.5	10.3	9.7
Women	10.1	9.7	10.3	10.3
Urban	13.8	13.6	12.7	12.1
Men	12.6	12.5	11.6	10.9
Women	18.3	7.9	17.0	16.4
Rural	6.5	5.9	6.8	6.5
Men	7.9	7.3	8.1	7.6
Women	4.2	3.2	4.1	4.3

Source: KSGM (2008).

- Economic crises in 1994, 1999 and 2001;
- In an environment of high unemployment, people, particularly women, lose hope of finding a job and thus no longer seek one;
- Early retirement.

The unemployment rate is higher in urban areas than in rural areas. Unpaid family labour in agricultural activities in the rural areas is not registered as unemployment. Most of these unpaid family workers are women. The highest unemployment rate is found among women living in urban areas, which can be partially explained by the lower educational level of women than men and, thus, the inadequacy of their qualifications (Table 1.6) (KSGM, 2008).

In efforts to overcome the problems of low female labour force participation and high rates of female unemployment, support to and promotion of female entrepreneurship has recently become the most widely emphasized solution. While agencies in charge of promoting employment are working for alignment with the European Employment Strategy, the 'female entrepreneurship' component of this strategy is fully adopted in Turkey and, consequently, efforts to promote female employment are taken as tantamount to supporting female entrepreneurship (Toksöz, 2007, p. 62).

As is the case in many countries of the world, female entrepreneurship is seen as one of the main tools for solving the problem of employment of women in Turkey and, to this end, various projects, programmes and activities are carried out by public institutions, professional organizations and NGOs. However, gender-based discrimination obstructing entry into the labour market prevails in the female entrepreneurship field too (KSGM, 2008).

Since the beginning of the 1990s, there has been an increase in female entrepreneurship development activities by public institutions and civil-society organizations as well as international organizations in Turkey. This unforeseeable increase is the result of a growing interest in female entrepreneurship in relation to women's economic participation in Turkey. Promoting entrepreneurship among women has been seen increasingly as a solution to women's unemployment, as well as a means through which women can have a certain degree of economic independence (Ecevit, 2007, p. 7).

Table 1.7   Distribution of the employed by occupational group, 2006 (000s)

	Women	%	Men	%
Legislators, top-level directors and managers	157	2.7	1869	11.3
Professional occupational groups	511	8.8	959	5.8
Assistant professional occupational groups	409	7.0	915	5.5
People employed in bureaus and customer services	500	8.6	823	5.0
People employed in services and sales	483	8.3	2055	12.4
Qualified people employed in agriculture, animal husbandry, hunting, forestry and water products	2258	38.9	2854	17.3
People employed in works related to craftsmen	334	5.7	2845	17.2
Facility and machine operators, fitters	224	3.9	2112	12.8
People employed in jobs not requiring qualification	935	16.1	2088	12.6
Total	5811	100.0	16 520	100.0

Source: KSGM (2008).

In Turkey, the percentage of women in professional and semi-professional occupations is higher than the percentage of men in these occupations. However, the percentage of women in top-level management positions is low, which is a clear indication that not only the recruitment but also the promotion processes involve discrimination against women. According to the data given in Table 1.7, the rate of women among top-level managers is merely 7.7 per cent, which means that not even one out of every ten managers is a woman. There are serious barriers to the advancement of women to top positions. The phenomenon known as the glass ceiling in the literature indicates the existence of promotion criteria in favour of men, regardless of qualifications such as education, skills, and experience among women. If a decision for a promotion is taken, prejudices of male managers against women have an impact and in general women cannot go beyond mid-level managerial positions. This is applicable not only to the public or private sector workplaces, but also to professional organizations and trade unions where the workers are organized (KSGM, 2008).

As gender discrimination in the Turkish market arises from many different sources, it is necessary to address a variety of policies to remove it, such as anti-discrimination legislation and affirmative action or equal employment opportunity strategies. Also, educational policies could have pervasive effects greater than any other policies. The impact of education is quite substantial in improving women's situation in both market and non-market areas. It will not only increase women's labour force participation rates and their more equal access to male-dominated occupations, but also help to reduce discrimination against women by changing the discriminatory social norms in society (Palaz, 2002, pp. 10–11).

Table 1.8   Historical context of feminist thought in Turkey and Pakistan

	Turkey	Pakistan
Origin	Origins of feminist activism in the 19th century	Origins of the feminist movement in the late 19th century; All Pakistani Women's Association (APWA) est. 1949
Orientation	Three types of feminist movements: secular nationalist, Western individualist and modern Islamic	Two types of feminist movements: conservative Islamic and modern Islamic

Discussion

The historical positioning of women as symbols of Turkish nationalism by Atatürk facilitated women's visible participation in the public sphere of life, although those adhering to the customary Islamic traditions, such as women wearing headscarves, appear to be disadvantaged. In contrast, the historical situation of women as symbols of Islamic culture and Muslim identity in Pakistan practically prescribed traditional family roles as ideal for Muslim women, thus disadvantaging those women who aspired to have more participation in public life. However, despite these historical differences, class differences of feminist thought and the associated polarization of achievements and failures in gender equality at work are strikingly similar in both countries.

Table 1.8 offers an overview of the historical context and development of feminist thought within the two countries. The historical evaluation of gender discourse in Pakistan and Turkey indicates that women's political activism was a common push for improvement in women's rights in both countries. However, in contrast to Turkey, where women were treated as objects of national identity in visible defiance of the Ottoman Islamic traditions, women in Pakistani society were treated as objects of Islamic identity to defy the British colonial traditions. Thus, fundamentally opposite to the Kemalist encouragement of women in Turkey to participate in the public sphere of life, women's roles within the *chador* (a kind of veil) and *chardiwari* (four walls of the house) were prescribed as most suitable for them in order to protect their honour and Islamic traditions in Pakistan.

The pursuit of gender equality in Turkey owes much to Kemalism and the country's national project of Westernization, portrayed as equivalent to modernization, which sought to promote gender equality as a key national ideology from the late nineteenth century, and particularly following the reformations in the 1920s. These historical influences were to have far-reaching implications for the national agendas of gender equality, legal frameworks, and organizational policies and practices in both countries.

Conclusion

Our historical review of state, religion and gender diversity in Pakistan and Turkey suggests that different trajectories of interface between the state and religion lead to different approaches to gender diversity and its regulation in the context of work. The chapter has demonstrated that the interface of Islam and the state across the spectrum of Shariah-style theocracy to secularism fosters different cultures of gender diversity. Pakistan and Turkey provide useful examples of this historical difference.

Summary table for Pakistan and Turkey

	Turkey	Pakistan
Existence of anti-discrimination legislation	Turkey's candidacy of the EU means that the *acquis communautaire* of the EU will be adopted. This includes six aspects of diversity. Equality and freedom from discrimination are enshrined in Turkish Constitution. Turkey is also a signatory of CEDAW	Gender equality enshrined in the 1973 Constitution as an overarching principle; workplace harassment bill passed in 2009
Criteria covered by anti-discrimination legislation	Turkish Constitution stipulates and guarantees that everyone is equal	Gender, disability, harassment
Criteria for which the reporting of quantitative data and their communication to a public administration are compulsory	Census data contains information on gender, religion, age and other demographic data	Limited coverage in the public sector, federal and provincial departments. Little or no evidence in the private sector (except some MNCs)
Criteria covered by 'affirmative' or 'positive' action legislation other than unemployment- or income-based	Disability	Disability, gender
Existence of a discourse or debate on 'non-discrimination' or 'equality'	Equality by gender, ethnicity, religion and belief, sexual orientation are discussed in popular media	Gender equality discourse
Existence of a discourse or debate on 'diversity'	Diversity debate exists in a very weak form	Non-existent
Year or period when the 'discrimination' concept started to disseminate in management literature in the country	1995–96	2004
Year or period when the diversity concept started to disseminate in management literature in the country	2000–01	2004
Who pushed the 'diversity' agenda?	The subsidiaries of US corporations, the European Commission, the UN, voluntary organizations, academic environment, Union of Turkish Bar Associations	MNCs, NGOs, federal government

Table (continued)

	Turkey	Pakistan
Existence of a professional association representing diversity professionals and year of creation	Per-Yon members assume such a role	Women activists and NGOs
Existence of a professional association representing diversity scholars and year of creation	Women's Studies Congress	None

While economic, legal and socio-demographic structures in Turkey and Pakistan suggest that equal opportunity structures and practices in Turkey may provide useful examples from which Pakistani organizations may draw their inspirations, and vice versa, further investigation of the historical trajectories that the two countries have taken in terms of their configurations of state, religion and gender equality regimes suggest that Turkish practices could not be transposed with such ease. Indeed, the gender equality regimes in both countries are highly entrenched and embedded in their respective histories and unique trajectories of nation-building. While we demonstrated the primacy of the historical context over the essence of equality regimes in both countries, we also need to attend to variations between organizational perspectives in Pakistan and Turkey in order to question whether transfer of equality regimes may work at an inter-organizational level.

For many years, in both countries, women lived in worse conditions than men. Over time, the improving conditions in political approaches and educational background for women meant that they began to contribute to the household. In Pakistan, although women become more educated, unfortunately a majority of them cannot find jobs that are suitable for their skills and qualities. Between 2003 and 2006 the percentage of women working in craft and related trade increased most, compared to the other sectors. However, in the same period in Turkey, working women in urban areas increased while working men in urban areas decreased. This can be explained by the higher percentage of women working in professional and semi-professional occupations than men.

When we compare these two countries in terms of the percentage of the female workforce in top-level management positions, Turkish women's percentage is more than Pakistani women's. This situation may be explained by the more equal opportunities that are offered to highly educated and talented Turkish women. On the other hand, today, in both Pakistan and Turkey, women are beginning to participate actively in political activities and decision-making.

References

ADB (Asian Development Bank) (September 2008), 'Releasing women's potential contribution to inclusive economic growth – country gender assessment Pakistan', available at: http://www.adb.org/Documents/Fact_Sheets/PAK.pdf, 1 March 2009.

Afkhami, M. (ed.) (1995), *Faith and Freedom: Women's Human Rights in the Muslim World*, London: I.B. Tauris.

Alderfer, C.P. and Smith, K.K. (1982), 'Studying intergroup relations embedded in organizations', *Administrative Science Quarterly*, **27**(3), 5–65.

Arat, Y. (1997), 'The project of modernity and women in Turkey', in S. Bozdogan and R. Kasaba (eds), *Rethinking Modernity and National Identity in Turkey*, Seattle, WA: University of Washington Press, pp. 95–112.

Bilge, N. (1995), 'Laiklik ve Islam'da Ortunme Sorunu', *Cumhuriyet*, Turkey, 31 January.

CEDAW (Convention on the Elimination of All Forms of Discrimination against Women) (July 2007), Thirty-eighth session, 'Combined initial, second and third periodic report of Pakistan', available at: http://daccessdds.un.org/doc/UNDOC/GEN/N07/352/60/PDF/N0735260.pdf, accessed 25 February 2009.

Cox, T. (1995), 'The complexity of diversity: challenges and directions for future research', in S.E. Jackson and M.N. Ruderman (eds), *Diversity in Work Teams*, Washington, DC: American Psychological Association, pp. 235–45.

DiMaggio, P. and Powell, W. (1983), 'The iron cage revisited: institutional isomorphism and collective rationality in organization fields', *American Sociological Review*, **48**, 147–60.

Ecevit, Y. (1993), *Kadin Bakis Acisindan Kadinlar: Kentsel Uretim Surecinde Kadin Emeginin Konumu ve Degisen Bicimleri*, Istanbul: Iletisim Yayinlari.

Ecevit, Y. (2007), 'A critical approach to women's entrepreneurship in Turkey', available at: http://www.ilo.org/public/english/region/eurpro/ankara/publ/womenentr.pdf, accessed 1 March 2009.

ENRAP (Electronic Networking for Rural Asia/Pacific) (2007), 'Women in Pakistan: inching towards their economic and social empowerment', available at: http://www.enrap.org, accessed 26 February 2009.

FRD (Federal Research Division) (1994) 'Pakistan: a country study – the status of women and the women's movement', Library of Congress [www document], http://lcweb2.loc.gov/frd/cs/pktoc.html, accessed 22 March 2005.

Ghorbani, M. and Tung, R.L. (2007), 'Behind the veil: an exploratory study of the myths and realities of women in the Iranian workforce', *Human Resource Management Journal*, **17**(4), 376–92.

Giacobbe-Miller, J.K., Miller, D.J., Zhang, W. and Victorov, V.I. (2003), 'Country and organizational-level adaptation to foreign workplace ideologies: a comparative study of distributive justice values in China, Russia and the United States', *Journal of International Business Studies*, **34**(4), 389–406.

Gooderham, P., Nordhaug, O. and Ringdal, K. (1999), 'Institutional and rational determinants of organizational practices: human resource management in European firms', *Administrative Science Quarterly*, **44**, 507–31.

GoP (Government of Pakistan) (2006), Federal Bureau of Statistics, 'Labour Force Survey 2005–2006', available at: http://www.statpak.gov.pk./depts/fbs/statistics/lfs/lfs.html, accessed 28 February 2009.

Harzing, A. and Sorge, A. (2003) 'The relative impact of country-of-origin and universal contingencies on internationalization strategies and corporate control in multinational enterprises: world-wide and European perspectives', *Organization Studies*, **24**(2), 187–214.

Hofstede, G. (1984), *Culture's Consequences*, London: Sage Publications.

Islam for Today (1994), 'The situation of women in Pakistan', available at: http://www.islamfortoday.com/pakistanwomen.htm, accessed 26 February 2009.

Jain, H., Sloane, P. and Horwitz, F. (eds) (2003), *Employment Equity and Affirmative Action: An International Comparison*, Armonk, NY: M.E. Sharpe.

Jalal, A. (1991), 'The convenience of subservience: women and the state of Pakistan', in D. Kandiyoti (ed.), *Women, Islam and the State*, London: Macmillan, pp. 77–114.

James, E.H. and Wooten, L.P. (2006), 'Diversity crises: how firms manage discrimination lawsuits', *Academy of Management Journal*, **49**(6), 1103–18.

Kandiyoti, D. (1988), 'Women and the Turkish state: political actors or symbolic pawns?', in N. Yuval-Davis and F. Anthias (eds), *Woman–Nation–State*, London: Macmillan, pp. 126–49.

Keskin, B. (1997) 'Political participation patterns of Turkish women', available at: http://www.library.cornell.edu/colldev/mideast/womtur~1.htm, accessed 1 March 2009.

Kostova, T. and Roth, K. (2002), 'Adoption of an organizational practice by subsidiaries of multinational corporations: institutional and relational effects', *Academy of Management Journal*, **45**(1), 215–33.

Kostova, T. and Zaheer, S. (1999), 'Organizational legitimacy under conditions of complexity: the case of the multinational enterprise', *Academy of Management Review*, **24**, 64–81.

KSGM (Turkish Prime Ministry, General Directorate on the Status of Women) (2007), Turkish Statistical Institute (TÜİK), Household Labour Force Survey Results, available at: http://www.ksgm.gov.tr/Pdf/ekonomi_ing.pdf, accessed 10 December 2008.

KSGM (Turkish Prime Ministry, General Directorate on the Status of Women) (2008), 'Policy Document/Women in Power and Decision-Making', available at: http://www.ksgm.gov.tr/Pdf/kararalma_ing.pdf, accessed 1 March 2009.

Lewis, J.J. (2001), 'Pakistan: status of women and the women's movement', available at: http://womenshistory.about.com/library/ency/blwh_pakistan_women.htm, accessed 4 March 2009.

Mahmood, S. (2007), 'Presentation of Pakistan's combined Initial, Second and Third Periodic Report – introductory statement', available at: www.un.org/womenwatch/daw/cedaw/cedaw38/statements/delegations/Pakistan_intro_statement.pdf, accessed 28 February 2009.

Mernissi, F. (1987), *Beyond the Veil: Male–Female Dynamics in Modern Muslim Society*, Indianapolis, IN: Indiana University Press.

Minault, G. (1998), *Secluded Scholars: Women's Education and Muslim Social Reform in Colonial India*, Delhi: Oxford University Press.

Moghadam, V. (1997), *Women, Work and Economic Reform in the Middle East and North Africa*, Boulder, CO: Lynne Rienner Publishers.

Newman, K.L. and Nollen, S.D. (1996), 'Culture and congruence: the fit between management practices and national culture', *Journal of International Business Studies*, **27**, 753–79.

Niethammer, C., Saeed, T., Mohamed, S. and Charafi, Y. (2007), 'Women entrepreneurs and access to finance in Pakistan', *Women's Policy Journal*, **4**, 1–12.

Oliver, C. (1991), 'Strategic responses to institutional processes', *Academy of Management Review*, **16**(1), 145–79.

Özbilgin, M. (2000), 'Is the practice of equal opportunities management keeping pace with theory? Management of sex equality in the financial services sector in Britain and Turkey', *Human Resource Development International*, **3**(1), 43–67.

Pakistan Federal Bureau of Statistics (2006), *Labour Force Survey 2005–2006*, http://www.statpak.gov.pk./depts/fbs/statistics/lfs/lfs.html, accessed 1 March 2009.

Palaz, S. (2002), 'Discrimination against women in Turkey: a review of the theoretical and empirical literature', available at: http://eab.ege.edu.tr/pdf/2_1/C2-S1-M9.pdf, accessed 1 March 2009.

Rouse, S. (1988), 'Women's movement in Pakistan: state, class, gender', *Women Living Under Muslim Laws*, Dossier 3, June–July.

Schuler, R.S. and Rogovsky, N. (1998), 'Understanding compensation practice variations across firms: the impact of national culture', *Journal of International Business Studies*, **29**, 159–77.

Syed, J. (2008), 'Pakistani model of diversity management: rediscovering Jinnah's vision', *International Journal of Sociology and Social Policy*, **28**(3/4), 100–113.

Syed, J. and Özbilgin, M. (2009), 'A relational framework for international transfer of diversity management practices', *International Journal of Human Resource Management*, **20**(12), 2435–53.

Syed, J., Ali, F. and Winstanley, D. (2005), 'In pursuit of modesty: contextual emotional labour and the dilemma for working women in Islamic societies', *International Journal of Work, Organisation and Emotion*, **1**(2), 150–67.

Tekeli, S. (1991), 'Tek Parti Döneminde Kadin Hareketi de Bastirildi', in L. Cinemre and R. Çakir (eds), *Sol Kemalizme Bakiyor*, Istanbul: Metis Yayinlari, pp. 93–108.

Tekeli, S. (1993), *Kadin Bakis Acisindan Kadinlar 1980'ler Turkiye'sinde Kadinlar*, Istanbul: Detisim Yayinlari, pp. 15–50.

Tisk (2006), Tisk's Women Employment Summit, available at: http://www.umce-med.org/documents/17-07-2006-12-45-28TISK.pdf, accessed 28 February 2009.

Toksöz, G. (2007) 'Women's employment situation, Turkey', available at: http://www.ilo.org/public/english/region/eurpro/ankara/publ/womenemp.pdf, accessed 26 February 2009.

Toprak, Z. (1988), 'Cumhuriyet Halk Firkasindan Önce Kurulan Parti: Kadinlar Halk Firkasi', *Tarih ve Toplum*, March, 30–31.

Triandis, H. (1995), 'The importance of contexts in studies of diversity', in S.E. Jackson and M.N. Ruderman (eds), *Diversity in Work Teams*, Washington, DC: American Psychological Association, pp. 225–33.

2 Austrian perspectives on diversity management and equal treatment: regulations, debates, practices and trends

Regine Bendl, Edeltraud Hanappi-Egger and Roswitha Hofmann

Introduction

Austria has a long history of being encompassed by a larger political regime, first as part of the Roman Empire, then under Habsburg rule as member of the Austrian–Hungarian Empire. This was followed by a brief period as a republic, then as part of the German Nazi regime. Throughout these periods Austria was embedded in highly culturally diverse environments. Since gaining its independence as a neutral state in 1955, Austria's reputation has oscillated between a rather socio-romantic transfigured state defined by the waltz and Mozart, and a right-wing, conservative heartland, which disregards liberal and open-minded thinking. In order to provide a more complex and accurate picture of contemporary Austria, our text first offers a historical framing, which has shaped scientific and political debates during recent decades. In addition to providing structural data, we present an overview of the current political debates and the legal situation for diversity management and equal treatment. Next we focus on the university and practice-based diversity management discourse and research findings on the implementation of Austrian diversity management in for-profit and non-profit organizations. Specifically, this chapter will indicate the extent to which diversity management has been established in terms of knowledge, competences and practices in different Austrian contexts. Finally, we conclude our contribution with an outlook on future trends and driving forces in Austria.

Historical contexts and current political discussions on equal rights and diversity in Austria

Since the current Anti-discrimination Acts of the European Union[1] consider gender, ethnicity, religion/beliefs, sexual orientation, age and disability the most important diversity dimensions,[2] we attend to them in our historical framing, beginning with their development since the end of the nineteenth and the beginning of the twentieth centuries.

Gender

The First Women's Movement in Austria emerged in 1848. It was a struggle for civil rights, better working conditions and equal pay in the context of the 'March Revolution' against the Austrian monarchy. It was not until 1919, after the First World War, and the end of the Austro-Hungarian monarchy, that women's right to vote was incorporated into the Constitution of the First Republic of Austria. Soon afterwards, in 1929, the elimination of the discrimination of women was added to Austrian Constitution Law

(Article 7). The takeover of the Austro-Fascists in 1933 and of the National Socialists (Nazis) in 1938 brought a backlash against women's rights and reduced the role of women mainly to mothers and housewives. Due to the absence of men in all aspects of social and economic life, however, the regime was forced to modify its gender ideology during the last years of the Second World War in order to keep up war production and civil life. Thus more and more women entered previously male-dominated areas. But the situation changed radically when the men returned home from the battlefields and prisons. Again a backlash against women's rights occurred, and it was another 30 years until the second women's movement (see Geiger and Hacker, 1989) and the introduction of measures for more equality in the legislation and, thus, in everyday life.

In the early 1970s, as a consequence of social movements (e.g. the second women's movement, the students' movement, the peace movement) and the change of government from the conservative Austrian People's Party (1945–70) to the Social Democrats (1970–83), fundamental social and legislative reforms were accomplished with the help of the Austrian 'social partnership'.[3] New abortion rights were implemented (1974 – Federal Law 60[4]) and the Marriage Law was changed from a patriarchal model to one based on partnership (1975 – Federal Law 412[5]). The following years brought more changes in the legal situation, e.g. in 1989 parental leave became possible for men too, and in 1993 a law for equal treatment in federal services was implemented (1993 – Federal Law 100[6]), followed by an anti-discrimination law regarding working conditions (1992 – Federal Law 837[7]). In 1995 Austria joined the European Union and committed itself to the European laws concerning equal treatment and anti-discrimination (see Chapter 3).

Despite these legal developments, the situation of women and minorities is still shaped by patterns of inequality, such as job segregation and fewer chances for women in the job market, fewer promotion prospects, a shortage of childcare facilities, and an unequal division of reproductive labour (household, care). Furthermore, women still face discrimination when they retire due to their increasing participation in part-time work, inadequate and precarious work integration, and fragmented work biographies. Although women now earn 51 per cent of the university degrees, they hold only about 20 per cent of the top management positions and only 10 per cent of university professors are female. In 2005 the income gap between male and female workers was 31 per cent, between male and female employees 37 per cent.[8] In top positions the income gap was even greater at 41 per cent (Statistik Austria, 2008). These figures show that there is still a disparity between women's level of formal qualifications and their income, and their places in the hierarchies of organizations.

Ethnicity
Ethnicity is an important diversity factor in Austrian society, historically, as a consequence of the present territory of Austria being part of the Austro-Hungarian monarchy with Romanians, Bulgarians, Italians, Croats and Serbo-Croats, Hungarians, Germans, Czechs, Austrians, etc. Today, 13 officially acknowledged ethnic minorities live in Austria. About 1 per cent of the total population comprises Croats, Roma, Sinti and Lowara, Hungarians and Slovene people, as well as Czechs, who mirror the imperialistic history of Austria. Laws protect their rights (e.g. Federal Law 101[9] from 1959). These minorities, however, still suffer from discrimination, prejudice and exclu-

sion from resources and political power. Many other immigrants and refugees came to Austria joining these 'old' minorities as a result of political uprisings in Hungary (1956), Czechoslovakia (1968), Poland (1981) and Yugoslavia (1991), as well as due to the fall of the Iron Curtain (1989). Furthermore, in the 1960s and 1970, 'guest workers' from former Yugoslavia and Turkey were 'called' into the country in order to meet the labour market demands of postwar Austria's economic growth. Austria has also been for a long time the preferred destination for migrants and refugees from Asia and Africa, but this has been neglected or downplayed in public discourse. In 2006, 13 349 refugees came to Austria, mainly from India, Nigeria, Russia, Serbia/Montenegro and Turkey (Statistik Austria, 2007). From this perspective the dynamics of immigration have always played a crucial role in Austria. The increasing heterogeneity of the Austrian workforce, however, led to an ongoing discussion of equal opportunity programmes (see also Linehan and Hanappi-Egger, 2006).

Religion/beliefs
Ethnic diversity also raises questions of religious diversity. In Austria 14 different religious communities are officially recognized: the Austro-Hungarian monarchs were always allies of the Catholic popes and the dominant religious group continues to be Roman Catholic (representing 74 per cent of the population).[10] This is followed by the evangelical churches (4.6 per cent) and the Islamic community (4.3 per cent). One million of the approximately 8 million Austrians do not identify a religious affiliation. Thus Catholic values continue to have a strong influence in the political and cultural discourse, particularly in the public discussion on women's rights (e.g. abortion rights) and on sexual orientation.

Sexual orientation
As a consequence of the dominant role of the Catholic Church in Austria, hetero-normative patterns persist in Austria's culture, especially in comparison with other European countries such as the Netherlands, Denmark, Spain or Hungary. Although homosexuality has not been a basis for prosecution since 1971 and parliament passed laws for equal rights in 1979, discrimination of non-heterosexuals is omnipresent. Austrian gay, lesbian, bisexual and transgender (GLBT) organizations report that, although a law for same-sex couples has been in place since January 2010 (EPG)[11] gays and lesbians still do not have equal rights like married heterosexuals and there is still no legal protection against discrimination outside the workplace.[12]

Age
As in other north-western European countries, the Austrian population is ageing. Table 2.1 shows how the age structure is changing in Austria.

The population between 15 and 60 years is declining and the population over 60 years is rising. In 2005 the rate of employment of older people (55–64 years) was only 31.8 per cent. In the 1960s, due to attractive early-retirement opportunities, the number e.g. of male employees of age 60–65 shrank from 66 per cent to 44.9 per cent (see Butschek, 1992). In contrast to this, as a consequence of financial problems of the social security system, and the latest EU-driven pension reforms, people are being forced to remain longer in the workforce. Moreover, in order to meet the demands of the Lisbon strategy

Table 2.1   Age structure in Austria, 1951–2030 (% of total population)

Age	1951	1961	1971	1981	1991	2001	2006	2015	2030
Under 15 years									
Female	21.0	20.5	22.5	18.5	16.3	15.9	14.9	13.7	13.5
Male	25.1	24.6	26.4	21.6	18.6	17.8	16.6	15.2	15.0
15–60 years									
Female	62.1	58.9	54.3	58.4	59.6	59.9	60.4	60.0	53.7
Male	60.7	59.6	56.9	63.4	65.7	64.5	64.4	63.3	56.8
61–75 years									
Female	16.9	20.6	23.2	23.1	24.1	24.2	24.7	26.3	32.9
Male	14.1	15.8	16.7	15.0	15.7	17.7	19.0	21.5	28.2
Over 75									
Female	3.5	4.9	6.0	7.8	9.0	9.7	10.1	10.3	12.8
Male	2.8	3.3	3.3	4.1	4.3	4.6	5.5	6.6	9.1

Source: Statistik Austria (2008).

of 2000, a reduction of early pensions and an employment rate of 50 per cent of people between 55 and 64 is expected to be achieved by 2010.

Disability
Disability issues were widely discussed in Austria after the First and Second World War. Many people suffered from serious physical injuries during the two wars, since the Austrian territory was at the centre of the war zones. Therefore a law for hiring people with disabilities (Behinderteneinstellungsgesetz) was implemented in 1946 and the Austrian parliament passed a law for disabled ex-soldiers (Kriegsopferversorgungsgesetz) in 1950.[13] However, more than 60 years later, the discussion on anti-discrimination of different forms of disability is still unsatisfactory (see Chapter 3), as there exists no inclusive definition for all forms of disabilities. Also the status of data on disability is still insufficient. Following the results from a Eurostat survey (2002), 12.8 per cent of the employable people in Austria indicated that they are suffering from a chronic disease or disability. According to data from the Austrian Labour Market Service (AMS), in 2007 15 per cent of unemployed people (total 212 253) had disabilities. Legal safeguarding provisions (see Chapter 3) for disabled employees are often considered as an obstacle to recruiting people with disabilities.

To sum up, public discourses in Austria on equal treatment and diversity are still strongly driven by historical and economic circumstances as well as by social movements like the women's movement and the GLBT movement. It is also evident that EU membership in 1995 is influencing how gender, age, ethnicity/race, religion/belief, sexual orientation and disability are discussed in Austria today. In the last few years the public discourse on equal treatment in the workplace has been strongly informed by the EU Directive on Gender Mainstreaming and the EU discourse on diversity and diversity management.

   In the following section we outline the current legal situation in Austria and offer further insights about approaches to diversity there.

The current Austrian legal framework for equal treatment and diversity management
Today equal treatment is part of the Austrian Constitution Law (Bundesverfassungsgesetz, Version 10, April 1995). Article 7 (1) declares that all citizens are equal before the law, regardless of birthright, sex, societal status, class or belief. According to Article 14 of the Constitution, each Austrian citizen has the right to become a member of a religious community or a church. Only members of accredited churches (10)[14] and religious groups (4) have the right of public free practice of their religion. Other religious groups have only the right to practise their religion privately.

In 1997 a general anti-discrimination regulation for people with disabilities was added to the Constitution (Article 7 (1)), but Austria's current Constitution does not protect against discrimination based on ethnicity, age or sexual orientation.

Besides the previously mentioned legal changes in the 1970s, Austrian equal treatment policies were heavily affected by debates triggered by EU anti-discrimination policies and the signing of the Amsterdam Treaty in 1997. Article 13 contains a directive for all member states regarding the legal regulation of anti-discrimination and equal treatment:

> Without prejudice to the other provisions of this Treaty and within the limits of the powers conferred by it upon the Community, the Council, acting unanimously on a proposal from the Commission and after consulting the European Parliament, may take appropriate action to combat discrimination based on sex, racial or ethnic origin, religion or belief, disability, age or sexual orientation.

Consequently gender mainstreaming policy became more important in Austria, and public debates on anti-discrimination were fostered. In 2000 EU bodies passed two directives: the Equality in Employment Directive 2000/43/EC and the Racial Equality Directive 2000/78/EC. However, it was not until 2004 that the Austrian government implemented a corresponding law to the Treaty of Amsterdam and the two EC directives. In 2004, parliament passed the Act on the Equal Treatment Commission, the Ombudsman for Equal Opportunities (BGBl. No. 65/2004) and the Federal Equal Treatment Act (ETA) (BGBl. No. 66/2004) covering public employment. Since then there have been some revisions to these laws.[15] The recent revision of the Equal Treatment Act (BGBl. I No. 98/2008) regulates equal treatment regardless of gender (Part I), ethnic origin, religion or belief, age or sexual orientation (Part II) in work life. Part III includes regulations against racism with respect to all societal spheres. The revision also considers EC Directive 2004/113/EC for the Equal Treatment of Men and Women concerning access to the supply of goods and services.

The Treaty of Amsterdam (1999, Article 13) also strengthened the anti-discrimination policy concerning 'disability' in Austria, but this category is not part of the Equal Treatment Act (ETA). In this case the legislation refers to previously existing regulations concerning disabilities in work life. This is one reason why the Austrian ETA has been heavily criticized during recent years as weak and fragmented. Another reason is that the sanctions for discrimination are nominal.

As the ETA regulates only work life (with the exception of racism), protection against discrimination in everyday life is limited; especially, discrimination based on sexual orientation is not legally protected in Austria. Although the law for same-sex couples has, after years of discussion, been in place since 1st January 2010, it makes some clear distinctions between same-sex partnerships and marriages of heterosexual couples (see Benke, 2010). For example, in order to foster the (symbolic) inequality between marriage and same-sex partnership, a ceremony in the marriage licence bureau is not provided for the latter. Same-sex couples do not have the rights to adopt a child (not even the child of his or her partner) or to establish a 'family'. The legal and social situation of transgender and intersexual people is also still behind European standards (see Fels, 2006).

Along with the equal treatment discussions in the 1980s and 1990s and the public sector's incorporation of diversity measures within their organizations and services, demographic changes and population forecasts have generally led to a growing interest in diversity and diversity management in Austrian private sector organizations. While multinational corporations operating in Austria had to adapt their established global diversity management strategies to local societal and legal circumstances, Austrian companies have been confronted with managing diversity for the first time and have begun to implement diversity management. People in charge often refer to existing programmes for equal opportunity measures, gender equality and gender mainstreaming. They also adopt and adapt measures from the US diversity management discourse, as diversity dimensions associated with ageing and ethnicity have become salient as a result of local demographic changes (such as an ageing society and migration from Eastern Europe). These socioeconomic developments have led to a growing interest in diversity issues in research and practice. The following section gives an overview of important developments in diversity management in Austria.

Research and practices in diversity management in Austria
With respect to a management perspective, this section maps university- and practice-based diversity management discourse and presents results from diversity management implementation in Austrian for-profit and non-profit organizations.

University- and practice-based diversity management discourse
As Wise and Tschirhart (2000) show, academic interest in diversity management has substantially grown in the last few years based upon the number of diversity management articles published in top (ISI-ranked) academic journals. Influenced by US diversity management books (Cox 1993; Gardenswartz and Rowe, 1994b; Loden, 1996; Prasad et al., 1997; Thomas and Woodruff, 1999), and the first German diversity management texts (Krell, 1997; Koall, 2001), the term diversity management entered Austrian academic discourse in the mid-1990s (Mattl, n.d., 2001). However, an important boost to the field was the establishment of a Chair of Gender and Diversity in Organizations at the Vienna University of Economics and Business (Wirtschaftsuniversität Wien – WU Vienna) in 2002. The appointment meant that diversity management was officially included as field of research and teaching in academe, and the systematic production of academic diversity management texts began. The Group on Gender and Diversity Management at WU Vienna was also selected as a good-practice example in the EU survey on Diversity Management in Business Schools (see Pedersen et al., 2008).

The academic staff comprising this group (and the authors of this chapter are part of it) were and continue to be key players in the Austrian diversity research scene. As a first initiative, an edited book *Interdisziplinäres Gender- und Diversitätsmanagement: Einführung in Theorie und Praxis* was published mapping the terrain of diversity management for

Austrian contexts (see Bendl et al., 2004). The book was conceptualized as an interdisciplinary collection to show the complex and varied phenomena of diversity management. The book, therefore, encompasses organization theory through the lenses of diversity management, theoretical approaches and instruments, team development and human resources, labour economics, EU and Austrian legal bases as well as practice examples.

The introductory book was followed by another edited volume, *Agenda Diversität: Gender- und Diversitätsmanagement in Wissenschaft und Praxis* (Bendl et al., 2006). It contains research papers from German-speaking Europe, which were presented at the first academic Diversity Management Conference in Vienna in 2006. The intention of the conference was to stimulate an exchange between diversity management research and practice in an open process under structured conditions. In tandem sessions the practitioners presented their cases and the researchers commented on them in order to advance the theoretical development of the diversity management discourse. Institutions including Proctor and Gamble, Deutsche Bank and the City of Vienna served as practice examples for these discussions. These publications have contributed to a wide dissemination of a differentiated and contextually relevant diversity management literature that has reached other Austrian universities and colleges of higher education or of applied sciences (e.g. Häuslschmid, 2006).[16]

In the area of curriculum in Austrian universities, again WU Vienna serves as a good-practice example. The incorporation of the competence field of gender and diversity in organizations ('Kompetenzfeld Gender und Diversitätsmanagement') into the academic curriculum of business administration was also of high symbolic and practical value.[17]

Austrian researchers have also participated in many local, national and international organizations and conferences (e.g. AOM, EAEPE, EGOS, EOI Conference, EURAM, EURODIV, GWO Conference, ICRODSC, IFSAM, IHRM, IWOT, NWSA, WWW 08 Women's World Congress). Thus, in a short period of time, the work has been integrated into multiple national and international networks and communicated to various interest groups. It is also gaining recognition as Austrian researchers are assuming editorial roles within major journals and being awarded prizes for their contributions to the field.

A practice-based discourse on diversity has also emerged in Austria. Researchers entered this domain either by doing their own practice-based further education or by introducing further education in diversity management counselling (see, e.g., Austrian Society for Diversity – ASD). Practitioners raise diversity management issues by presenting case studies and describing their practices (e.g. Hartmann and Judy, 2005; Engel, 2007; Überacker, 2007; Pauser, 2007). A starting point for this kind of collaboration in Austria was the first practice-oriented conference on diversity management ('Wiener Fachtagung: Differenz als Ressource' – 'Managing Gender and Diversity') in 2003 and the first training course on diversity management ('Managing Gender and Diversity') (2003–04), both organized by VHS Ottakring. Since that time, practice- and counselling-oriented discourse has developed and diversified. One aspect has been the emergence of organizations and consulting groups specializing in diversity management training and/ or counselling (e.g. ImKontext, Prove (Diversityworks), Austrian Society for Diversity (ASD), Equalizent, VHS Ottakring). Many have identified a distinctive niche and are finding ways to compete in a small market. Increasingly, general organizational behaviour and human resource consultants are including diversity issues in their practices.

In 2008 the Austrian Standards Institute launched a diversity management directive

(ÖNORM S 2501). This directive was set up under the transdisciplinary consultancy of researchers, practitioners and the various stakeholders of the Austrian social partnership. The directive defines diversity and diversity management, and regulates the process of establishing and maintaining diversity management in for-profit and non-profit organizations. On the one hand, this directive can be considered as analogous to the diversity charters launched in other EU countries (see, e.g., http://www.charta-der-vielfalt.de/). On the other hand, it goes further: it sets standards that organizations wanting to be certified for their diversity management initiatives must meet. This directive and its accompanying mechanisms are prototypes that could prove useful if the European Standards Institute is to develop a directive for the EU countries.

In order to recognize good practice and progress towards diversity in Austria, different awards and prizes were set up. Beginning in the 1990s, corporations and organizations that had engaged successfully in equal treatment and equal opportunities for women were acknowledged ('Frauen- und familienfreundlichster Betrieb', 'Gläserner Schuh', 'E-Quality'). Meanwhile employers were also rewarded for best practice with diversity dimensions other than gender, such as age and sexual orientation (e.g. 'Bester Arbeitgeber', 'Meritus Award', TRIGOS Award, 'DiversCity Award').

All in all, these activities show that a professionalization of researchers and practitioners working in the field of diversity management has taken place. For the future we predict that this professionalization for both research and practice will continue – especially concerning the practices of SMEs, which are still underdeveloped. However, the time of diversity management pioneers in Austria is definitely over. Looking at Austria's changes regarding diversity management using Glasl and Lievegoed's (2004) model of organizational development, the next stage of differentiation will bring in even more expertise and specialization, which, for better or worse, is likely to trigger more standards and rules as well as competition within each community and more separation between research and practice. But, as always, we anticipate that there will be a handful of boundary spanners between research and practice.

Research on diversity management in Austrian for-profit and non-profit organizations
The implementation of diversity management has been very patchy. Subsidiaries of multinational enterprises (MNEs) such as BP, IBM, IKEA and Shell have implemented diversity management inclusively within the parameters of Austrian laws. However, as the majority of Austrian firms are small or medium-sized, their application of diversity management lags behind the implementation standards of large-sized firms and MNEs. The following three 2006 studies, described in Table 2.2, give detailed accounts of the status of diversity management in Austrian firms. Columns 3 and 4 show the foci and contexts of the studies.

In her quantitative study, Brunner (2006) examined the relevance of diversity management and the level of strategic implementation in Austrian companies of all sizes. Häuslschmid (2006) explored the *status quo* of diversity management for Austrian large-scale companies (Austrian top 500 corporations in 2004). Gitzi and Köllen (2006), in their study on participation in diversity management, identified the degree of workers' participation concerning diversity measures in Austrian corporations listed on the Austrian Stock Exchange. Although Brunner (2006) and Häuslschmid (2006) surveyed different types of Austrian corporations, their results are quite similar.

Table 2.2   Studies on diversity management in Austria

Author (year)	Aim	Research questions	Sectors	Form of survey
Brunner (2006)	To explore the relevance of diversity management in Austrian corporations	• To what extent is diversity management implemented? • Do these diversity management initiatives refer to strategic programmes or incremental measures?	Retailing Banking Electronic Further education Logistics Marketing Craft Energy Tourism Telecommunications Pharmaceutical industry	Mailed questionnaire 40 corporations Confirmative approach
Gitzi and Köllen (2006)	To evaluate the degree of participation with diversity management programmes in corporations listed on the Austrian Stock Exchange	• What significance does participation have in diversity management programmes?	Telecommunications Industry/production Banking	Analysis of websites 20 websites of corporations listed on the Austrian Stock Exchange Exploratory approach
Häuslschmid (2006)	To explore the *status quo* in Austrian large-scale enterprises in terms of degree of popularity, measures and multiplicity of diversity management programmes	• To what extent is diversity management popular and what are the reasons for personal diversity? • What are the main diversity dimensions used and which arguments of cost and benefit of diversity management are used? • Which measures are applied within diversity management initiatives?	Industry/production Retailing	Online questionnaire 56 corporations Confirmative approach

Popularity of and attitude towards diversity management   Both surveys show a positive attitude towards diversity management. Brunner (2006) found that the popularity of diversity management measures depends on which diversity dimensions (e.g. gender, disability, cultural diversity, sexual orientation) the diversity measures are targeted and the size and location of the corporation. Diversity management measures are more accepted in larger corporations than in smaller ones, especially when the aim is equal opportunity between women and men. Corporations located in eastern Austria are also more open to diversity dimensions of disability and sexual orientation than those in the western parts of the country. Also, large corporations considered diversity management as producing more benefits than medium and small firms. According to Häuslschmid (2006), diversity management will gain more importance in the future due to globalization, internationalization, changes in social values and attitudes, and greater individualization. With regard to the diversity paradigms (Aretz and Hansen 2002), in large companies diversity management is considered in the first instance as a learning and effectiveness approach.

Implementation   Brunner (2006) found that only 15 per cent of the 40 firms surveyed had a comprehensive diversity management programme, 15 per cent have almost reached the stage of having a comprehensive programme, and 15 per cent have recently started their diversity management initiatives. The greater the corporations' progress in implementation, the more managers perceive differences among their employees. Also, diversity management is discussed comprehensively in all departments in 33 per cent of the corporations. In 82 per cent of the corporations (33) diversity management is solely the task of human resources management, in 70 per cent of enterprises (28) it is the responsibility of the CEO, and in 32 per cent that of the public relations department (13). In 20 per cent of the cases, marketing (8), production (8) and administration (8) departments were responsible for setting up diversity management measures. Furthermore, according to Brunner (2006), 73 per cent of the companies employ a combination of a top-down and bottom-up diversity management strategy; 20 per cent manage diversity as a top-down strategy and only 3 per cent employ a pure bottom up strategy.

Altogether, Häuslschmid's (2006) results show that 19 per cent (8) corporations have a comprehensive diversity management strategy, 19 per cent (8) are in the preparation phase, and 53 per cent do not have a diversity management strategy.

Diversity dimensions   In terms of the different diversity dimensions of Austrian corporations, gender and age (Häuslschmid, 2006) or age and gender (Brunner 2006) get the most attention. Both those studies indicate ethnic background, disability and sexual orientation. As far as the other diversity dimensions, such as family status, language, education and experience etc. (Gardenswartz and Rowe 1994a) are concerned, according to Brunner (2006), education (36) and job experience (35) score highest and in Häuslschmid's survey (2006) professional competence (29) and personality (23) are mentioned most.

Measures   In Hauslschmid's (2006) study the measures that have been set up within diversity management refer to: flexible working hours (34), employee promotion (34), retirement transition programmes (29), equal opportunities (28), integration of disabled employees (27), language courses (26), work–life balance (24), religion (20), multilingual

Table 2.3   Diversity management measures in selected corporations

Corporation	Measures
Former Bank Austria Creditanstalt AG	• Flexible working hours • Support for childcare and kindergarten • Healthcare
Boehler-Uddeholm AG	• Corporate-wide guidelines
Telekom Austria AG	• Flexible working hours • Initiative for attracting young female employees • Public relations

Source: Gitzi and Köllen (2006).

material (20), integration of the older workforce (20), mentoring (15) and integration of homosexual employees (3). These measures correspond with those identified by Brunner (2006).

The third study on diversity management explored the degree of workers' participation within diversity management initiatives in corporations listed on the Austrian Stock Exchange. Although 20 corporations were listed in the ATX index in 2006, only three (former Bank Austria Creditanstalt AG, now Bank Austria, Boehler-Uddeholm AG and Telekom Austria AG) have diversity management measures. The following categories were applied in order to get a sense of how participation is enacted in the corporations – at least from a strategic perspective: measures of work–life balance, networking, corporate guidelines, awareness-raising measures, reintegration after absence, sponsoring or target group marketing. The three corporations showed that they had in place measures in different areas: work–life balance, networking, awareness-raising measures and corporate guidelines. More specifically, the three corporations employ the measures indicated in Table 2.3.

In a nutshell, according to Gitzi and Köllen (2006), the degree of participatory measures in diversity management is very restricted in the three corporations listed on the Austrian Stock Exchange. The degree of workers' participation does not seem to be a decisive criterion for the implementation of diversity management. Also, employee participation does not seem to be an objective of the companies. Collectively, these three studies (Brunner, 2006; Häuslschmid, 2006; Gitzi and Köllen, 2006) show that comprehensive programmes and practices of implementation are lacking but incremental engagement with diversity seems to be in place in Austrian corporations, even though it may not be carried out under the name of 'diversity management'. Also, the increase of participation of non-dominant group members due to diversity management in Austrian corporations is questionable, which shows that the bottom-up perspective of diversity management is not the driving force within and for diversity management in Austria.

Diversity management in Austrian universities
When we compare these results of studies on diversity management in for-profit organizations with those of public sector organizations, especially within universities, they are quite similar. Hanappi-Egger and Hofmann's (2006) survey on the implementation of gender and diversity management in 13 selected Austrian universities indicated that diversity

management endeavours are patchy. Even though Austrian universities already have a legal tradition of equal opportunities for women, beginning with the Working Group for Equal Opportunity in 1990 (Arbeitskreis für Gleichbehandlungsfragen), the Federal Government Equal Opportunities Act in 1993 (Bundes-Gleichbehandlungsgesetz), the implementation of coordination centres (Koordinationsstellen) and the promotion plan for women at all universities (Frauenförderplan), all interviewees reported a lack of resources in terms of both staff and infrastructure for gender and diversity management.

> The tasks related to gender and diversity management still remain largely the burden of committed individuals who initiate discourse and organize activities. . . . In addition, on average managerial and academic staff have no diversity management training resulting in a lack of adequate gender and diversity management strategies on the management level. . . . Furthermore, the promotion of women, gender mainstreaming and diversity management are considered to be concepts that compete with one another for resources. (Hanappi-Egger and Hofmann, 2006, pp. 121 and 123)

The recent annual university report of the Austrian Ministry of Science and Research (2008) points out that all 22 Austrian universities have met the legal obligation of producing a women's promotion plan. Equal treatment committees and arbitration commissions have been established at all universities. Coordination centres have also been set up at all universities, although their location and status differ (e.g. part of the Rector's Council Rectorate, independent service centre or in combination with an academic unit).

Universities continue to direct more attention to gender than to other diversity dimensions (with exceptional cases, e.g. University of Vienna), as they lag behind in official inclusion discourse. Yet student enrolments at Austrian universities portray another picture: in 2003, 15.9 per cent (29 577) out of 185 438 registered students in Austria were foreign students and their numbers are increasing rapidly so that, in 2008, 20.1 per cent of all students were foreigners (Universitätsbericht, 2008, p. 204). About 1 per cent of the Austrian students reported that they have physical disabilities affecting their mobility, and about 5 per cent report suffer from amblyopia; 3 per cent reported psychological problems (ibid., p. 239). Austrian universities have a variety of ways of working with students with specific needs. Generally there is a commitment to focus on barrier-free building access. Some institutions offer e-learning platforms, or employ an ombudsman.

Summing up the situation at Austrian universities, diversity management as an inclusive management concept is rarely put into practice. Only the University of Vienna has established a project group on diversity management, demonstrating at least some awareness of the topic. But the increasing internationalization, competitiveness and political pressure on university performance is expected to lead to a growing interest in constructively addressing diversity-related matters among staff and students.

Diversity management in the City of Vienna
The European Union's launch of gender mainstreaming in the 1990s prompted Austrian governmental and municipal organizations to set up further measures for gender and equality. However, the status of gender mainstreaming implementation varies depending on the objectives of the organization, the involved political parties, the relevant actors,

the local context, the degree of bottom-up movements and the level of organizational gender mainstreaming competence and, especially the amount of money spent on gender mainstreaming initiatives. But as gender mainstreaming focuses on only one dimension of diversity, governmental and communal initiatives have been taken to reduce discrimination linked to other diversity dimensions, e.g. ethnic background, beliefs, age, disability etc. For example, the City of Vienna has established a department for Promotion and Coordination of Women's Issues (MA 57 – Frauenförderung und Koordinierung von Frauenangelegenheiten) and two further divisions, Gender Mainstreaming (same term) and Anti-discrimination for Same-sex Lifestyles (Wiener Antidiskriminierungsstelle für gleichgeschlechtliche Lebensweisen). In 2004 the municipality also established a department for integration and diversity (MA 17 – Abteilung für Integrations- und Diversitätsangelegenheiten). Originally, the City of Vienna funded and administered only integration issues and support for citizens in settling in and making Vienna their home city. However, as today approximately 20 per cent of inhabitants of Vienna have other citizenships, the scope of the department has widened to better meet the needs of these groups by addressing diversity issues and engaging in political issues. This change in scope was accompanied by a change of institutional setting and name, from Wiener Integrationsfonds to Abteilung für Integrations- und Diversitätsangelegenheiten.

The department has about 45 staff members (about half are women; about half are men) from 14 countries and speak 23 languages (see Struppe, 2006). They work in four main areas: (1) living quarters and conflict, children; (2) youth and school; (3) housing, education and professions; and (4) society, health and social issues. Additionally, the staff members serve in regional branches in Viennese districts with large numbers of migrants and cooperate with other municipal departments. As far as the department's projects are concerned, they provide a wide range of services (see Struppe, 2006):

- further education in diversity issues for other municipal departments,
- an official glossary for the translation of forms etc. within the City of Vienna,
- dictionary for elections within Vienna in 13 languages (Wiener Wahlwörterbuch),
- cooperation with the police,
- voluntary assistance in conflicts,
- support media in order to give migrants information in their mother/father tongue,
- support for regional associations dealing with involving migrants in regional initiatives,
- other regional activities.

As this initiative of the City of Vienna shows, diversity is practised in Austrian and federal politics despite very restrictive Austrian immigration laws. Diversity is on the agenda of the City of Vienna and it can serve as a positive example for other municipalities in Austria. In fact, the City of Vienna's diversity management initiatives target both employees and clients.

However, compared to initiatives in some other European countries (e.g. the Netherlands, the UK), Austria cannot be considered a leader in diversity management. Its initiatives in the public and private sectors are often adaptations of strategies and processes from elsewhere to fit with the developments outlined earlier. This means that a stronger commitment to diversity management in business, education and politics is needed in Austria in order for it to become an inclusive country. Non-governmental organizations (NGOs) with expertise in diversity management (e.g. ZARA) exist to support such inclusive developments.

The future outlook – driving forces and trends from an Austrian perspective
Due to globalization, Austria will face future challenges like those of other EU member states (see also Münz, 2007). For example, Fotakis (2000) emphasizes the consequences of an ageing population and population decline in Europe. He states that Austria will face severe problems in the labour market and therefore force the government to promote immigration. Due to these driving forces, international companies are expected to move highly skilled people throughout Europe even for short periods of time. Thus, people with different cultural backgrounds will meet temporarily: 'labour tourism (short-term income seeking workers and contracted temporary employees) will increase. This will lead to new challenges in terms of ethnic diversity shifting the focus from the establishment of long-term diversity strategy to short-term measures' (Hanappi-Egger and Schnedlitz, 2009). Other trends they identify that have major consequences for managing diversity in Austria include evidence that younger Austrians (30–50 years) have a higher competence in dealing with diversity, a higher educational level, a higher employment rate among women and more diversified lifestyles than older Austrians (currently 50 plus).

The working programme (2009–14) of the current Austrian government, consisting of the Social Democrats (SPÖ) and the Conservative People's Party (ÖVP), also offers insights into gender and diversity issues that are considered important. The working programme identifies the following 'hot spots':

- *Labour market policies*   The aim is to increase the employment rate of women, the qualification level of people with migration backgrounds, and the employment rate of elderly people. These objectives should be realized by measures such as the promotion of women, and qualification initiatives for elderly people and people with migration backgrounds, by investing in the gender and intercultural competencies of labour market consultants and awareness-raising activities. In order to satisfy the labour demand, immigration of highly qualified people should be reorganized by establishing an immigration office and criteria to ensure a flexible and demand-oriented immigration model, clearly focusing on economic issues.
- *Research and science*   Generally the intention is to increase the number of women in top management positions, in particular in research institutions. Also it is recommended that further research be carried out on demographic changes as well as on migration.
- *Internal security*   As in the section on the labour market, increasing participation of women and the number of people with migration backgrounds is considered necessary to increase social cohesion.
- *Migration and integration*   It is explicitly stated that immigration must follow Austrian economic demands; therefore it should be organized by an immigration office consisting of representatives of the social partnership, and immigration of family members should be restricted. The improvement of the integration of

migrants in terms of better social, political and economic participation is stated as an aim, although specific measures are not mentioned.

- *Society, women, family and equal opportunity policies*   An explicit commitment to families highlights the importance of work–family balance and support for families. Women's promotion and their higher participation in employment as well as in top management are declared to be important objectives, along with closing the gender gap in earnings and achieving better integration of women with migration backgrounds and older women.
- *Generations*   There is a focus on anti-discrimination of older people.
- *Disability*   There is a focus on the importance of integrating people with specific needs, in particular women with low qualifications.

As topics of the Austrian government's working platform show, due to the political background of the involved parties, the different social categories are differently seen as relevant: while gender is considered important, sexual orientation is still ignored.

Also, modest attempts to consider intersectional aspects of diversity are proposed.

Summary table for Austria

Existence of anti-discrimination legislation	Yes
Criteria covered by anti-discrimination legislation	Gender, disability, sexual orientation, age, ethnicity, religion/belief
Criteria for which the reporting of quantitative data and their communication to a public administration are compulsory	Gender ('women's report'), ethnicity ('integration report'), annual data of Statistik Austria concerning the Austrian population (disabled employees, income, household and family structure)
Criteria covered by 'affirmative' or 'positive' action legislation other than unemployment- or income-based	Gender, age, disability
Existence of a discourse or debate about 'non-discrimination' or 'equality'	Yes
Existence of a discourse or debate about 'diversity'	Yes
Year or period when the 'anti-discrimination' concept started to disseminate in management literature in the country	1980s (women in management and equal opportunity programmes)
Year or period when the diversity concept started to disseminate in management literature in the country	2003
Who pushed the 'diversity' agenda	Academia, NGOs (trade unions, NPOs etc.), European Commission (legislation)
Existence of a professional association representing diversity professionals and year of creation	Austrian Society for Diversity (ASD) since 2004
Existence of a professional association representing diversity scholars and year of creation	Since 2006 (together with Germany and Switzerland), annual network meetings

Most important in the programme seems to be the promotion and participation of women in the working sphere. This group is further divided into targeted sub-groups, such as women with migration backgrounds (ethnicity), older women (age), and women with specific needs (disabilities), and specifically those sub-groups with respect to low education are seen as most relevant for specific actions and measures.

The fact that the government's working programme contains no precise measures regarding sexual orientation can be attributed to Catholicism's strong influence in Austria.

In conclusion, the 'Austrian' way of dealing with problems of diversity, namely 'waiting to see what will happen and hoping that solutions will emerge without strong efforts' is outdated. As a member of the European Union, Austria will face social, economic and demographic issues such as those of other EU countries. Based on the Lisbon Treaty, it is likely that driving economic forces will lead to a higher strategic and intersectional consideration of the different diversity dimensions. This gives hope that Austria's social reality, which is already in a state of flux, will keep on moving towards more inclusivity.

Notes

1. See European Union (2000a, 2000b).
2. In 2004 the Austrian parliament passed a national law on equal treatment (Gleichbehandlungsgesetz), which translated the EU directives into national law.
3. The 'social partnership' refers to a cooperative relationship between the employers' and employees' associations (social partners) in Austria. The aim of the social partnership is to solve conflicts of interest by consensual politics in order to avoid strikes and militant actions. The social partnership can be understood as an instrument of dialogue concerning social and economic politics. It consists of the Austrian Chamber of Commerce (Wirtschaftskammer Österreich), the Austrian Chamber of Agriculture (Österreichische Präsidentenkonferenz für Landwirtschaft), the Austrian Federation of Trade Unions (Österreichischer Gewerkschaftsbund) and the Austrian Chamber of Employees (Arbeiterkammer Österreich).
4. Federal Law 60, 29 January 1974 (Bundesgesetz 60, StGB).
5. Federal Law 412, 31 July 1975 (Bundesgesetz: Neuordnung der persönlichen Rechtswirkungen der Ehe).
6. Federal Law 100, 12 February 1993 (Bundesgleichbehandlungsgesetz – B-GBG).
7. Federal Law 837, 29 December 1992 (Bundesgesetz: Berichte der Bundesregierung betreffend den Abbau von Benachteiligungen von Frauen).
8. In Austria workers and employees are two different categories of employed people. They have different rights and duties and the social security as well as the retirement laws that apply to them are also different.
9. Federal Law 101, 14 April 1959 (Bundesgesetz: Minderheiten-Schulgesetz für Kärnten).
10. Source: Statistik Austria, population census 2001, in which there is a clear difference between urban and rural regions.
11. Bundesgesetz über die eingetragene Partnerschaft – EPG, BGBl. I, Nr 135/2009.
12. For more details, see http://www.rklambda.at.
13. Protection against discrimination because of ethnicity is also valid outside the work place.
14. See Bundespressedienst (2007), *Religionen in Österreich*, Bundeskanzleramt, Wien.
15. See http://www.ris.bka.gv.at.
16. In the context of the WU, several projects were undertaken and the authors specialized further in diversity management research by focusing either on different sectors or different diversity dimensions, e.g. age, gender, sexual orientation and the reproduction of heteronormativity. Subsequent publications consider diversity management in general, its connection with organizational change, knowledge and competence as well as with narratives. For a detailed list of publications, see www.wu-wien.ac.at/gender.
17. See, e.g., Hanappi-Egger and Hofmann (2007), Danowitz et al. (2009).

References

Aretz, Hans-Jürgen and Hansen, Katrin (2002), *Diversity und Diversity-Management im Unternehmen*, Hamburg and London: Lit Verlag.

Bendl, Regine, Hanappi-Egger, Edeltraud and Hofmann, Roswitha (eds) (2004), *Interdisziplinäres Gender- und Diversitätsmanagement: Einführung in Theorien und Praxis*, Wien: Linde-Verlag.

Bendl, Regine, Hanappi-Egger, Edeltraud and Hofmann, Roswitha (eds) (2006), *Agenda Diversität: Gender- und Diversitätsmanagement in Wissenschaft und Praxis*, München: Hampp.

Benke, Nikolaus (2010), 'Zum Bundesgesetz über die eingetragene Partnerschaft 2009: weder Ehe noch Familie', *Zeitschrift für Ehe- und Familienrecht*, July, 19–25.

Brunner, Iris (2006), 'Diversitätsmanagement in Österreich: eine kritische Bestandsaufnahme', unveröffentlichte Diplomarbeit,Wien, Wirtschaftsuniversität Wien.

Bundespressedienst (2007), *Religionen in Österreich*, Wien: Bundeskanzleramt.

Butschek, Felix (1992), Der österreichische Arbeitsmarkt. Von der Industrialisierung bis zur Gegenwart. Stuttgart.

Cox, Taylor (1993), *Cultural Diversity in Organizations*, San Francisco, CA: Berrett-Koehler.

Danowitz, Mary Ann, Hanappi-Egger, Edeltraud and Hofmann, Roswitha (2009), 'Exploration and exploitation in organizational change: developing and implementing a diversity management curriculum', *International Journal of Educational Management*, **23** (7), 590–603.

Engel, Roland (2007), 'Die Vielfalt der Diversity Management Ansätze – Geschichte, praktische Anwendungen in Organisationen und zukünftige Herausforderungen in Europa', in Iris Koall, Verena Bruchhagen and Friederike Höher (eds), *Diversity Outlooks. Managing Diversity zwischen Ethik, Profit und Antidiskriminierung*, Hamburg: LIT Verlag, pp. 97–110.

European Union (2000a), Council Directive 2000/43/EC, 29 June 2000.

European Union (2000b), Council Directive 2000/78/EC, 27 November 2000.

Fels, Eva (2006), 'Development of transgender politics in Europe', http://tgeu.net/PubAr/Documents/EU_ ILGApreGconf_evafels.pdf, last retrieval 22 June 2008.

Fotakis, Constantinos (2000), 'Demographic ageing, employment growth and pensions sustainability in the EU: the option of migration', Expert Group Meeting on Policy Responses to Population Ageing and Population Decline, UN Secretariat, New York, 16–18 October.

Gardenswartz, Lee and Rowe, Anita (1994a), *Diverse Teams at Work: Capitalizing on the Power of Diversity*, New York: McGraw-Hill.

Gardenswartz, Lee and Rowe, Anita (1994b), *The Managing Diversity Survival Guide. A Complete Collection of Checklists, Activities and Tips*, New York and Boston, MA: McGraw-Hill.

Geiger, Brigitte and Hacker, Hanna (1989), *Donauwalzer Damenwahl. Frauenbewegte Zusammenhänge in Österreich*, Wien: Promedia.

Gitzi, Andrea and Köllen, Thomas (2006), 'Die Rolle von Partizipation im Diversity Management: eine Praxisanalyse', in R. Bendl, E. Hanappi-Egger and R. Hofmann (eds), *Agenda Diversität: Gender- und Diversitätsmanagement in Wissenschaft und Praxis*, München–Mering: Rainer Hampp, pp. 25–43.

Glasl, Friedrich and Lievegoed, Bernard (eds) (2004), *Dynamische Unternehmensentwicklung, Grundlagen für nachhaltiges Change Management*, Bern, Stuttgart, Wien: Haupt Verlag.

Hanappi-Egger, Edeltraud and Hofmann, Roswitha (2006), 'Gender and diversity management at Austrian universities', in Günther Vedder (ed.), *Managing Equity and Diversity at Universities*, Hampp Verlag, pp. 111–26.

Hanappi-Egger, Edeltraud and Hofmann, Roswitha (2007), 'Gender- und Diversitätsmanagement: Qualifikationsbedürfnisse in der betriebswirtschaftlichen Universitätsausbildung', in Dieter Wagner and Bernd-Friedrich Voigt (eds), *Diversity-Management als Leitbild von Personalpolitik*, Wiesbaden: Deutscher Universitätsverl (DUV), pp. 153–71.

Hanappi-Egger, Edeltraud and Schnedlitz, Peter (eds) (2009), *Ageing Society. Altern in der Stadt, Aktuelle Trends und ihre Bedeutung für die strategische Stadtentwicklung*, Wien: Facultas.

Hartmann, Gabriella and Judy, Michaela (eds) (2005), *Unterschied machen. Managing Gender and Diversity in Organisationen und Gesellschaft*, Edition Volkshochschule, Wien: Verband Wiener Volksbildung.

Häuslschmid, Michael (2006), 'Diversity Management – eine Bestandsaufnahme in österreichischen Großbetrieben', unveröffentlichte Diplomarbeit, Salzburg, Fachhochschule Salzburg GmbH.

Koall, Iris (ed.) (2001), *Managing Gender and Diversity. Geschlecht, Kultur, Gesellschaft*, Hamburg: Lit Verlag.

Krell, Gertraude (1997), 'Mono- und Multikulturelle Organisationen? Managing Diversity auf dem Prüfstand', in Ulf Kadritzke (ed.), '*Unternehmenskulturen unter Druck' Neue Managementkonzepte zwischen Anspruch und Wirklichkeit*, Berlin: Edition Sigma, pp. 47–66.

Lineham, Margaret and Hanappi-Egger, Edeltraud (2006), 'Diversity and diversity management: a comparative advantage?', in Henrik Holt Larsen and Wolfgang Mayrhofer (eds), *Managing Human Resources in Europe. A Thematic Approach*, London: Routledge.

Loden, Marilyn (1996), *Implementing Diversity*, New York and San Francisco, CA: McGraw-Hill.

Mattl, Christiane (2001), 'Herausforderungen in Zeiten der Globalisierung', in Zebratl Special, Dokumentation der Tagung,Diversity Management. Kulturelle Vielfalt am Arbeitsplatz nutzen, herausgegeben von Zebra, VI.

Mattl, Christiane (n.d.), 'Diversity-Management. Die (kulturelle) Vielfalt am Arbeitsplatz nützen', http://www. work-life.at/pdf/div/DivManagementMattl.pdf, 23 March 2009.

Münz, Rainer (2007), 'Ageing and demographic change in European societies: main trends and alternative policy options, social protection', World Bank, Discussion Paper No. 0703, March.

Österreichisches Normungsinstitut (2008), ÖNORM S 2501 Diversity Management – Allgemeiner Leitfaden über Grundsätze, Systeme und Hilfsinstrument.

Pauser, Norbert (2007), 'Equalizent GmbH – Gleicher geht's nicht', in Iris Koall, Verena Bruchhagen and Friederike Höher (eds), *Diversity Outlooks. Managing Diversity zwischen Ethik, Profit und Antidiskriminierung*, Hamburg: LIT Verlag, pp. 386–97.

Pederson, Esben Rahbek, Tywuschik, Simon and Gardey, Sanchez Gonzalo (2008), 'Diversity management in business schools: emerging trends, new priorities and good practices', Symposium Report as part of the 'Activities promoting and developing the Business Case of Diversity' Project, http://ec.europa.eu/ employmentsocial/fundamental rights/pdf/pubst/stud/busicase en.pdf, accessed March 2009.

Prasad, Pushkala, Mills, Albert, Elmes, Michael and Prasad, Anshuman (eds) (1997), *Managing the Organizational Melting Pot. Dilemmas of Workplace Diversity*, Thousand Oaks, CA: Sage Publications.

Statistik Austria (2007 and 2008), http://www.statistik.at/web_de/statistiken/index.html, last retrieval 28 June 2008.

Struppe, Ursula (2006), 'Vielfalt fördern, Zusammenhalt stärken. Diversity Management am Beispiel der MA 17', in Regine Bendl, Edeltraud Hanappi-Egger and Roswitha Hofmann (eds), *Agenda Diversität: Gender- und Diversitätsmanagement in Wissenschaft und Praxis*, München-Mering: Rainer Hampp Verlag, pp. 83–94.

Thomas, R. Roosevelt, Jr. and Woodruff, Marjorie I. (1999), *Building a House for Diversity*, New York, Amacom.

Überacker, Jutta (2007), 'So divers ist Diversity Management', in Iris Koall, Verena Bruchhagen and Friederike Höher (eds), *Diversity Outlooks. Managing Diversity zwischen Ethik, Profit und Antidiskriminierung*, Hamburg: LIT Verlag, pp. 474–86.

Universitätsbericht (2008), *University Report*. Bundesministerium für Wissenschaft und Forschung, Minoritenplatz 5, 1014 Vienna.

Wise, L.R. and Tschirhart, M. (2000), 'Examining empirical evidence on diversity effects: how useful is diversity research for public-sector managers?', *Public Administration Review*, **60** (5), 386–95.

3 Diversity management in Belgium
Annie Cornet and Patrizia Zanoni

Introduction

This chapter presents the specificity of diversity and diversity management in Belgium. It addresses the need to further development of a more contextualized understanding of the diversity concept and approaches to its management. The diversity literature is today flourishing, yet the vast majority of studies remain based in the USA. Notwithstanding the important differences between the USA and other countries in the composition of the labour force, the nature of the applicable legislation, and the public debate around diversity, too often the US understanding of diversity is simply assumed to apply elsewhere (Konrad et al., 2006; Prasad et al., 2006).

Belgium is a small European country with a federal structure. Its main regions, Wallonia, Flanders and Brussels-Capital, are characterized by distinct socioeconomic and political profiles. As a result, diversity has partially distinct meanings and is managed in partially differing ways in the different regions. In this chapter, we shall provide an overview of the specificity of diversity at the country level and complement it with relevant information at the regional level.

As in many other European countries, diversity management became a hot topic in Belgium only around the turn of the century. Previously, diversity did not feature in the Belgian public debate on employment, which focused on the so-called 'groups at risk', such as the low educated and long-term unemployed (Lamberts et al., 2005). The concept of diversity emerged due to a combination of factors including changing labour market demographics, public diversity initiatives at the European, Belgian and regional levels, the publication of the first studies highlighting the position of specific groups in the labour market, and the emergence of diversity management in some private (multinational) companies. These factors have set certain sociodemographic groups in the spotlight, albeit to different degrees and in specific ways.

In the Belgian context, diversity refers today in the first place to ethnic minorities, above all 'historical' migrants including the Turkish and the Moroccan communities, migrants from Central Africa (above all the Democratic Republic of the Congo), less to migrant communities from Southern Europe (Italians, Greeks and Spanish) and increasingly to 'new' migrants from Eastern Europe and the rest of the world. For these groups, the focus is on access to employment. Women are also part of the diversity debate. However, differently from the above groups, the focus is for them as much on equal career opportunities as on employment. Only a few initiatives explicitly target men, mainly promoting better work–life balance. There is increasing attention by policymakers to employees above 45 years of age, low-educated young people, and, to a lesser extent, disabled people. Homosexuals and bisexuals remain to date at the margin of the debate, although there are a few awareness-raising initiatives against homophobia.

The text is structured in five parts. In the first section, we sketch the position of women, the elderly, ethnic minorities, the disabled, and homo- and bisexuals on the

Belgian labour market. The second section presents the Belgian anti-discrimination legislation and the third the public and private diversity initiatives. We then elaborate on the empirical research conducted on diversity in Belgium. We conclude with a reflection on the main distinctive issues concerning diversity within the Belgian context.

1.   The stratification of the Belgian labour market

In the last trimester of 2007,[1] Belgium counted 4450000 active and 338000 unemployed persons out of a total population of 10700000. The activity rate was 67.5 per cent, the employment rate was 62.6 per cent, and the unemployment rate was 7.1 per cent.

1.1   Stratification along nationality and ethnicity

In 2007, Belgium counted 932161 people with a foreign nationality, corresponding to 8.8 per cent of the total population. In contrast to North America and the UK, where minorities are measured by the census through self-identification in sub-ethnic groups, Belgium does not collect official data on the population of foreign origins. As the only official source of data is based on citizenship, and as second- and third-generation migrants can easily acquire Belgian nationality, official statistics tend to underestimate ethnic minorities. There is today still little consensus on how to define and identify this group (Centre for Equal Opportunities and Opposition to Racism, 2007). However, all existing figures show that, in Belgium, the 'allochtonous' population, that is, first-generation migrants and Belgians with origins in countries outside the EU, has much lower employment and activity rates than the average rates for native-born workers in both the public and private sector (Desmarez et al., 2004; Martens et al., 2005; Van den Cruyce, 2005).

As illustrated in Table 3.1, people with a foreign nationality are, in absolute numbers, quite evenly spread in the three Belgian regions: Flanders, Brussels and Wallonia. Flanders counts the most residents with foreign nationality, amounting to 331694. When measured as a percentage of the total population, however, the people with a foreign nationality represent 27.4 per cent of the population of the Brussels-Capital region, compared with 9.2 per cent of the population of the Walloon region and only 5.4 per cent of the residents in the Flemish region.

The barriers to foreigners' employment are numerous. Taking a 'deficit thesis' approach, several studies in the 1980s and the 1990s explained these differentials as a consequence of ethnic minorities' lack of education and training, qualifications, language skills in the host-country language, motivation, adaptation to host behavioural codes (in

Table 3.1   The population with foreign nationality in Belgium, by region in 2007

	Female	Male	Total	Proportion of foreigners (%)
Walloon Region	154667	162273	316940	9.2
Brussels-Capital region	142682	140845	283527	27.4
Flemish Region	160377	171317	331694	5.4
Total	457726	474435	932161	8.8

Source: FPS Economy – Directorate-general Statistics Belgium, Demographic Service.

terms of cultural distance with respect to the country of origin) and social capital (Neels and Stoop, 2000). In this literature, ethnic minorities are themselves seen as the cause of their unemployment (Adam, 2007).

At the end of the 1990s, however, studies began to investigate discriminatory mechanisms. In 1998, a study carried out for the International Labour Organization (ILO) highlighted discrimination based on cultural and national origin (Arrijn et al., 1998). Using a situation test methodology, the researchers found that during the recruitment process, candidates with Belgian or Moroccan backgrounds with similar qualifications – academic degree and professional experience – were treated differently. Ethnic minorities were invited less often to job interviews, selected less often after job interviews, and ultimately less often offered a job. For the first time, the discrimination of 'allochthonous' candidates was documented. These preliminary findings were later confirmed by a quantitative study undertaken by the Brussels Labour Market and Qualifications Observatory (De Villers, 2003), a mixed quantitative–qualitative study on discrimination against foreigners and persons of foreign origin on the labour market in Brussels (Martens et al., 2005), and a third study on the position of ethnic minorities on the labour market by Desmarez and colleagues (2004). Adam (2007) recently documented how employers justify the underrepresentation of foreign workers in their staff in terms of the latter's lack of confidence as well as colleagues', human resource managers' and clients' racism.

The effects of discrimination are also beginning to be studied more precisely in relation to the access of minorities to specific jobs and functions. There is evidence of horizontal segregation of minorities in sectors such as temporary work agencies, industrial cleaning, call centres, logistics and transport, characterized by badly paid and insecure jobs. This process has been labelled one of 'ethnicization' of jobs and/or 'ethnostratification' (Martens, 2005; Ouali and Rea, 1995). Moreover, Ouali (2007) showed empirically how women of foreign origin suffer double discrimination along both gender and ethnicity lines.

Next to direct discrimination due to stereotypes and prejudice, foreigners also face a number of structural administrative barriers, including the difficulty of obtaining a work permit, the eligibility criteria to apply for public jobs or subsidized work contracts, the recognition of foreign degrees and other qualifications and skills acquired through experience, and the eligibility criteria to obtain financial assistance and guidance in the process of looking for a job (Delhaye and Cornet, 2008).

1.2   Stratification along sex and age

Public statistics on the labour market are usually disaggregated along sex and age. Table 3.2 provides a picture of the position of different age groups and women and men on the labour market.

Comparing the position of men and women, we see that the latter have a lower employment rate,[2] 56.5 per cent versus 68.8 per cent for men, a higher unemployment rate, 8 per cent versus 6.4 per cent for men, and a lower activity rate,[3] 61.4 versus 73.5 per cent for men. The employment rate for women is lower than that for men in all age groups, but the gap is largest for the 55–64 age group of the population. For this last age group, the overall activity rate is one the lowest in Europe (36 per cent for Belgium, 49 per cent for Europe) (Romans and Preclin, 2008).

Table 3.2   Key Belgian labour market indicators by age and sex – fourth trimester 2007

		Aged 15–24	Aged 25–55	Aged 55–64
Activity rate (%)	Male	36.8	92.1	44.7
	Female	32.2	79.3	28.4
Belgium	Total	34.5	85.7	36.5
EU-15		49.9	85.1	49.6
EU-27		45.8	84.6	47.6
Employment rate (%)	Male	30.6	87.0	43.0
	Female	26.2	73.6	27.4
Belgium	Total	28.4	80.3	35.2
EU-15		41.1	80.1	46.9
EU-27		37.5	79.5	45.0

Sources: Institut National des Statistiques – http://www.statbel.fgov.be/; http://epp.eurostat.ec.europa.eu/cache/ITY_OFFPUB/KS-QA-08-027/EN/KS-QA-08-027-EN.PDF.

Further, concerning the specific position of women, as in other European countries, the labour market is characterized by occupational segregation by sex, with the concentration of women in service sectors and in a few female-dominated industries: the health sector, social services, education and distribution (Institut National des Statistiques – INS, 2002). The wage gap remains steady, with women earning almost 30 per cent less than men (Meulders and O'Dorchai, 2006; Sels and Theunissen, 2006a). There is also a strong vertical segregation, with the underrepresentation of women in managerial positions and women comprising less than 5 per cent of corporate board directors (Sels and Theunissen, 2006b).

The particularly low activity rate of individuals above 50 years of age has been explained as a consequence of a numbers of factors. Goyvaerts and Dessein (2004) mention the following factors. First, the Belgian population tends to enter the labour market late and retire early. During its short active life, a large part of the population works full time. Second, as women have entered the Belgian labour market relatively late in comparison with other European countries, older women are less present on it. Third, Belgium's highly industrial economy suffers more than others the effects of de-industrialization and the related lay-offs. Early retirement has long been used to reduce unemployment of older workers deriving from restructuring, and the trade unions strongly resist changing this policy. Fourth, state policies incentivizing early retirement in the 1980s and 1990s to increase the youth's employment rate have created widespread expectations of early retirement among employees that are difficult to reverse. Smets and De Mulder (2004) further mention the mismatch between elderly employees' lower productivity and higher salary costs, due to salary scales tied to number of worked years, representing a financial disincentive for employers.

The discrimination of elderly candidates in recruitment procedures has been illustrated by a recent study of the Centre for Equal Opportunities and Opposition to Racism. In 2008, the Centre analysed nearly 3000 employment offers. Among those, 11 per cent referred to age in a direct or indirect way, despite the fact that this is forbidden by law. In 2007, this rate was 7 per cent. In addition, in 2008, the Centre received 105 complaints

Table 3.3   Participation in professional life by degree of disability in 2002

	Belgium (%)	EU-14 (%)
Severe	18.3	24.3
Men	20.4	27.9
Women	15.9	20.5
Moderate	36.9	46.2
Men	54.2	57.6
Women	22.6	36.7
No disability	56.3	61.9
Men	69.2	75.1
Women	44.5	49.3

related to discrimination based on age. Among those, more than half (63) related to the work and 39 of them concerned the procedures used for the selection of workers.[4]

1.3   Segregation along (dis)ability

There are very few statistics on employment of disabled persons in Belgium. The most recent data that we found at the federal level are presented in a report of the National Institute of Statistics published in 2004 based on the Labour Force Survey 1996 results (Institut National des Statistiques – INS, 2004). These data reveal that disabled people still face huge barriers in accessing the Belgian labour market. Their employment rate is below the European average. Employment rates are lower for people with severe disabilities (18.3 per cent) than for people with moderate ones (36.9 per cent). Table 3.3 also shows the gap between men's and women's activity rates, with women's rates being lower than men's. Moreover, the gap between disabled people and non-disabled people increases with age, being particularly large for persons over 50.

Binamé and colleagues (Binamé and Mercier, 2004; Binamé et al., 2004) identified a range of reasons for the low employment of disabled people, including subjective and objective barriers, direct and indirect discrimination in employment, and 'employment traps' in the Belgian legislation. One of the barriers for many people who have been disabled from birth is their low education, derived from difficulties in school. Another barrier is the Belgian legislation, which discourages disabled people from working, as they lose part or all of their disability allocations. As the difference between starting salary and disability unemployment benefit is minimal, for this group working is not financially attractive.

1.4   Homosexuals and bisexuals

Little information is currently available on the position of homo- and bisexuals on the Belgian labour market. In 2008, 20 per cent (27 out of 135) of the grievances received by the Centre for Equal Opportunities and Opposition to Racism involved discrimination on the base of sexual orientation in the workplace (Centre for Equal Opportunities and Opposition to Racism, 2008). In most cases, harassment was reported, although there were also cases of discrimination in hiring and firing practices. As the Centre suspected that many instances of discrimination in the workplace are not reported, it commissioned a quantitative study on discrimination against gays, lesbians and bisexuals in the workplace (Vincke, 2008). The study reports the results of an online questionnaire completed by almost 2500 Belgian gays, lesbians and bisexuals. The analysis focuses on their experiences of homophobia in the workplace and on the consequences arising from them, checking systematically for potentially significant differences related to the regional language, sex, age, the level of training, and the size of the company. The study focused on homo- and bisexual employees' negative experiences in the workplace, both in general and in relation to sexual orientation. In general, negative experiences are mostly reported by older workers: firing, missed promotion, rejection for organizational reasons, lower pay for equal work, reclassification, job assignment or transfer, and forced resignation. Men stated more often that they were excluded during a selection process and that they missed an internal promotion. Sixty-five per cent of the sample report subtle homophobia in the form of gossip, allusions and mockery, while 12 per cent report more explicit homophobia in the form of insults and jokes. The Flemish more often report cases of firing and exclusion for organizational reasons than the Walloon, who more often report explicit homophobia. With regard to sexual orientation, 12 per cent of the respondents report that they were unable to benefit from promotion opportunities because of their homo- or bisexuality. This type of discrimination is more common in large and medium-sized enterprises.

2.   Equal treatment legislation

Belgium has an extensive legislation aimed at combating different forms of discrimination. National laws implement European directives, are implemented through regional decrees and complemented by collective labour agreements. The most recent national legislation consists of the laws of 10 May 2007[5] banning discrimination in all domains of federal competence. They implement three directives of the Council of the European Union (2004/113/EC, 2000/78/EC, 2000/43/EC) replacing the Anti-discrimination Law of 25 February 2003. One law concerns the equal treatment of men and women. Another, the Anti-discrimination Law, penalizes all forms of distinction, exclusion, restriction, or preference based on sex, age, sexual orientation, civil status, birth, property, religious or philosophical belief, political persuasion, language, current or future health status, disability, physical or genetic features, or social background in employment relations. A third law, the 'Anti-racism Law', forbids discrimination based on nationality, alleged race, skin colour, ancestry or national or ethnic origin.

The Law on Equal Treatment between Men and Women punishes any direct and indirect discrimination based on sex, pregnancy, childbirth or maternity, or on the basis of sex change. It regulates recruitment, selection and promotion (i.e. job offers and selection criteria), work conditions (i.e. contracts, work schedules, remuneration and holidays), dismissal, and additional social security regimes. Provisions contrary to the principle of equal treatment are null and void. Offenders can receive a prison term from eight days to one month and a fine. If harassment or violence is involved, the employer should take appropriate measures to stop it. Previous legislation complements this law. For instance, the Collective Labour Agreement 25 of 15 October 1975 of the National Labour Council regulates pay equality between male and female workers. It stipulates equal pay for same work or work of equal value, covering all elements and conditions of remuneration, including systems for evaluating duties. Pay refers not only to the basic salary, tips or services, and advantages, but also to holiday pay and additional non-legal social security schemes. A complaint may be filed by the employee either at the company or at the Labour Inspection. Further, the Law of 4 August 1996 on the well-being of workers regulates cases of sexual harassment.[6]

The second, general Anti-discrimination Law of 10 May 2007 applies to employment relations in both private and public organizations. It outlaws all forms of direct discrimination, indirect discrimination, injunction of discrimination or harassment, based on protected requirements, sexual harassment and refusal to set up reasonable facilities for a disabled person. Reasonable facilities include appropriate measures, taken according to the needs in a concrete situation, to allow a disabled person to access, participate and progress, unless these measures impose a disproportionate burden on the person who must adopt them. This load is not disproportionate when sufficient compensation is provided through existing policies in favour of people with disabilities. It applies to the conditions for access to employment (recruitment and selection), promotion, working and payment conditions (labour contracts, training and apprenticeship contracts, basic rules of work), termination of employment and affiliation to a workers' organization. Clauses contrary to the law or early renunciation to act are null and void. The victim may claim compensation amounting to the damages actually suffered or in the form of a fixed amount. The law also protects anyone who provides information on discrimination and any witness thereof from dismissal. In matters of racism, provision is also made for criminal penalties.

For regional competences, the European directives were implemented through decrees adopted by the Brussels-Capital Region on 4 September 2008, by the Ministry of the French Community on 12 December 2008, by the Walloon Region on 6 November 2008, and by the Flemish Community and Region on 10 July 2008.

The Law of 9 September 1996 further provides that employers, companies and organizations must produce data disaggregated by sex to be detailed in the social report[7] filed at the National Bank. The social report is mandatory for all companies with published annual accounts. It must be drafted following the model of the annual accounts at the end of the fiscal year. It should indicate the number of men and women employed on a full-time and a part-time basis, the total of full-time equivalents as well as the staff turnover during the fiscal year, by gender and level of education. It should further provide information disaggregated by sex on employees on subsidized employment schemes, full-time equivalents, and the amount of financial benefit, as well as on the number of employees attending training, number of hours of training attended, and the costs to the company. Concerning training, coaching or tutoring activities, the report should include disaggregated data on the participants and number of hours. For new employees, the type of contract and the level of education should also be indicated. For employees who are leaving the organization, next to this latter information the reason for terminating the contract should be mentioned. The social report should not only be published, but also communicated to the company's Work Council. If there is no Work Council, the report should be passed on to the union delegation. If there is no union delegation, the workers should be able to consult the report where the employment regulations are kept.

The Collective Labour Agreement of 9 March 1972[8] also obliges private companies with at least 100 employees to draft a human resource report disaggregated by sex, including:

- the employment structure and its development, presenting data broken down according to gender, age group, occupational category and division;
- the employment estimates, providing information broken down, as far as possible, according to occupational categories and including both quantitative and qualitative aspects;
- the decided or projected social measures in matters of employment, situated in the context of the two other points.

Moreover, companies that have filed a restructuring programme involving collective redundancies and those where the company's board makes a request for it are required to produce an annual report on equal opportunities for men and women (RD 27/08/93, BLD 25/09/93). The goal of such a report is to give an overview of the employment conditions, work regulations, functions and training for women and men in the company, but also an analysis and an evaluation for each occupational category of the specific situation of women concerning the conditions for employment and training, chances for promotion, qualifications as well as work conditions and pay. Disaggregated figures should be provided on all these aspects. These two last laws are however not enforced in practice.

The Royal Decree of 27 February 1990[9] aims at advancing measures to promote equal opportunities between men and women in public services. It envisages the designation of a person in charge of the initiatives to enforce equal opportunities in public organizations. It further proposes several actions such as the drafting of an equal opportunities plan and measures ensuring its follow-up.

Public service departments also have an obligation to employ disabled persons amounting to 3 per cent of their total staff (RD 5/3/2007, BLD 16/3/2007). Reasonable adjustments to the recruitment and selection procedure should be implemented.

Concerning age, the law of May 2007 sanctions any discrimination according to age in recruitment and employment. It further provides measures aimed at encouraging outplacement of older workers.[10] Any employer terminating employment of an employee above 45 years of age and who has at least one year of seniority must inform the beneficiary employee of his or her right to outplacement. The employee must formulate explicitly his or her request to benefit from this procedure. This includes the following services and consultancy: psychological support, setting up a personal assessment, assistance in working out and implementing a job search strategy, assistance in view of negotiating a new employment contract, assistance for integrating into the new work environment, and logistical and administrative assistance. To address the mounting financial problems deriving from a combination of a low activity grade of the elderly and an ageing population, a framework law called 'The Generations' Pact' was presented by the Belgian government to the parliament in October 2005.[11] The document proposes a new approach to the end of career, providing 66 concrete measures. They include bonuses and incentives for jobs for youth, a rise in the minimum retirement age, stricter conditions for pre-retirement (higher age, longer work career, with exceptions for certain heavy occupations), bonuses for unemployed individuals who accept a job, the possibility of lighter work for elderly employees (temporarily financed through public subsidies), the possibility to work a four-day week, and a bonus for those who keep working after 60 years of age.

The Belgian state established the Centre for Equal Opportunities and Opposition to Racism by the Royal Decree of 28 February 1993 and the Institute for the Equality of Women and Men through the Law of 16 December 2002. Both institutions are now competent for supporting victims of discrimination in court.[12]

The Institute limits its action to discrimination based on sex. It can suggest mediation or legal proceedings and launching of a civil action with the consent of the plaintiff, and can provide legal assistance to the person who files the complaint and who launches a civil action him or herself. The services rendered by the Institute are free of charge. The procedure for dealing with complaints was set up in 2005. In 2006, the Institute dealt with 156 requests, 58 per cent of which were filed by women, 36 per cent by men, 3.4 per cent by unknown (organizations) and 2.6 per cent by transsexuals. Of these requests, 28.8 per cent were related to employment. Of these, 44.4 per cent dealt with vacancies, selection and recruitment, 35.5 per cent with pregnancy and 21.1 per cent with working conditions.[13]

The Centre for Equal Opportunities and Opposition to Racism[14] plays a similar role for all other forms of discrimination. The Centre publishes a yearly report on complaints received. In 2006, the Centre received 2917 complaints.[15] Of these, 39 per cent concerned racial discrimination (nationality, so-called race, skin colour, national or ethnic origins), 11 per cent disability, 6 per cent religion or belief, 5 per cent sexual orientation, 4 per cent age, 3 per cent health condition, 2 per cent wealth, 1 per cent civil status, 1 per cent physical or genetic trait and less than 1 per cent political conviction. Compared to the previous year, the Centre received 77 per cent more grievances, probably due to an increased visibility of its activities thanks to the laws of May 2007 and the campaign around the European Year of Equal Opportunities for all. Only 2 per cent of the grievances filed in 2006 ended in a lawsuit. In the remaining cases, the Centre provided information and advice (70 per cent), forwarded the case to another competent body (15 per cent), or provided mediation to achieve conciliation (13 per cent).

The Belgian anti-discrimination legislation follows legal developments at the European level. Its implementation reflects the institutional complexity of the country, with competences on both the federal and regional levels.

3.   Overview of diversity initiatives

Next to the legal framework delineated above, a variety of public initiatives stimulate Belgian organizations to become more diversity-friendly. Most of these initiatives emanate from public agencies at the federal, regional and local levels, making use of awareness-raising campaigns, labels, financial incentives, and free consulting services to encourage organizations to achieve this (Cornet and Warland, 2008b; Union Européenne, 2006). In this section, we provide an overview of the most important initiatives.

3.1   Diversity initiatives at the federal level

In 2007, the Ministry for Employment and the Ministry for Public Services and Equal Opportunities, in agreement with Belgian trade unions, launched the federal label 'Equality and Diversity'.[16] The label rewards public and private employers who develop a diversity management plan covering at least two dimensions of diversity (age, sex, disability, or origin). In order to keep this label, an organization is re-evaluated every three years. Eleven companies received the label in 2007, and had it reconfirmed by the evaluation in 2008. That year, two additional companies were awarded the label.

The Centre for Equal Opportunities and Opposition to Racism organizes seminars with employers and union delegates aimed at raising awareness of discrimination at work and spreading information on diversity management. It also diffuses publicity material and organizes campaigns.[17] The Institute for the Equality of Women and Men has led some actions aimed at raising the awareness of companies about occupational equality between men and women. The main theme is pay equity. The Institute offers training and organizes awareness-raising initiatives targeting both employers and union delegates. Its EVA project[18] promotes the adoption of an analytical job classification to achieve pay equity. The Institute participates in assigning the 'Equality and Diversity' label, as companies are obliged to include gender equality in their business review and action plan.

To increase the employment of the population over 50 years of age, in 2001 the federal administration created the Professional Experience Fund.[19] The Fund subsidizes companies' actions to improve the well-being of employees above 45 years old by adapting the organization or the work conditions. Studies commissioned by the employer are also eligible for funding.

Furthermore, in its role as a public employer, the Belgian federal administration formulated a diversity action plan 2005–07[20] including 80 actions aimed at supporting the promotion of equality between men and women, the recruitment of disabled persons, and the integration of people of foreign origin in public functions. Examples are the screening of job offers and new networks for recruitment, help for preparation of the candidates to the selections, elimination of bias during the selection processes, more diverse commissions in charge of recruitment and promotion, accessibility of the services to the disabled, training, career support, work–life balance and targeted actions. Some administrations worked out a diversity management plan with the Diversity Unit of the Personnel and Organization Department of the federal administration, and each federal administration department appointed a civil servant to take part in the diversity network. A manual including over 80 examples of diversity management practices in the public administration was published (Cornet et al., 2007).

The Federation of Enterprises in Belgium has publicly taken a position on diversity in 2006. Its president launched an appeal under the title 'Diversity, a winning asset', which states the business case of diversity and invites companies to take action. The appeal was illustrated by five 'best cases' of diversity management. While the statement is a mere declaration of intent, not binding any organization, it does have some symbolic value and suggests that diversity is increasingly becoming an issue for employers. Some companies have profiled themselves as pioneers of diversity management: Randstad (temporary work agency), Colruyt (distribution), ISS (cleaning sector), IBM (IT consulting), Belgacom (telecommunications), Sodexo (catering), the Federal Police and the Belgian Army.

At the federal level, the trade unions have taken action on specific target groups rather than on diversity, for instance, on the theme of equality between men and women, the working conditions of migrant workers and, more recently, access to employment of people of foreign origin (second and third generation), the conditions of employment of youth and their difficulties in accessing the labour market, access to employment for persons older than 45, and, to a lesser extent, access to employment of disabled workers, and homophobia in the workplace. Despite their increasing participation in diversity initiatives, the Belgian unions have long had an ambivalent stance towards this concept. They have traditionally mistrusted diversity policies, which can easily be interpreted as a managerial strategy to prevent legislation protecting employees in the future. Unions fear in particular that these voluntary initiatives, focused on improving and using individual skills and abilities in a human resource management logic, downplay the problems related to discrimination and replace equal rights and treatment. From a union perspective, the best guarantee of objectivity and of limiting arbitrariness remains the adoption of clear and transparent procedures applicable to all workers (Burnotte, 2007; Cornet and Warland, 2008a; Peeters, 2004). Following this logic, unions are against measures that oblige companies to collect data on their staff disaggregated by origin. Although they adhere to the idea that discrimination should be made visible, unions are hesitant about any physical count based on patronymics, nationality of the parents or grandparents and, even more so, self-identification in ethnic groups, which could potentially be used by employers to pitch groups against each other (Buyssens, 2008).[21]

3.2 Diversity initiatives in the Brussels-Capital Region

With 40 per cent of its residents with a foreign nationality or origin, the Brussels-Capital Region has a particularly diverse population (Martens et al., 2005). Of the three Belgian regions, Brussels has the highest unemployment rate (17 per cent in 2008)[22] (Conter, 2000).

In 1996, in the Brussels-Capital Region and in the framework of the Territorial Pact for Employment,[23] the social partners decided to set up a project to fight against discrimination at the time of hiring. To fight against any form of discrimination in recruitment, ACTIRIS – the public agency for employment – opened, in collaboration with the Centre for Equal Opportunities, a dedicated service to receive complaints about employment. They organize seminars and training, and awareness-raising campaigns in companies, and finance the implementation of diversity plans and consulting services. The Brussels-Capital Region also drafted a diversity charter, which has been signed by several employers. Moreover, in 2004, it created a Unit on Equal Opportunities and Diversity[24] at the Directorate of Human Resources and Equal Opportunities of the Ministry of Brussels-Capital. The Unit deals with initiatives favouring equal opportunities for men and women.

3.3 Diversity initiatives in the Flemish Region[25]

The study on discrimination against candidates of foreign origins conducted for the ILO (Arrijn et al., 1998) stimulated the dialogue between the social partners and the Flemish authorities within the Flemish Economic Social Negotiation Committee (VESOC), resulting in 1998 in an agreement for the promotion of 'proportional employment' of ethnic minorities in both the public and the private sector.[26] The agreement aimed at implementing a long-term policy through yearly plans, including initiatives to ban discrimination by employers on the one side and to improve the qualifications and work experience of ethnic minorities on the other. The underlying principle is positive action, i.e. actions aimed at improving the access of the group to the labour market as well as its horizontal and vertical mobility, rather than on positive discrimination, whereby target groups are privileged over others. The main tool for the implementation of the VESOC agreement are so-called 'positive action plans'. Through these plans, Flanders supports organizations that want to attract more ethnic minority staff or improve the position of existing ethnic minority employees by providing funding and consulting services.

The yearly implementation plan of the VESOC agreement of 2000 extended the actions to the target group of the disabled, and the one of 2001 further included the elderly, explicitly mentioning the goal of equal opportunities for men and women. Since 2002, the positive action plans are called 'diversity plans' and have a broader scope, namely, the inclusion of women, the elderly, the disabled and ethnic minorities. The enlargement of the target group was stimulated by the positive economic conjuncture, which led to a shortage of labour.

Against this favourable economic background, the Trivisi think tank was launched in June 2000. Until the end of 2001, the project brought together business people, academics, representatives of the non-profit sector, employers and trade unions to identify critical success factors for diversity policies. In the same period, a series of collaboration protocols between the Flemish Ministry and ethnic minorities' associations, trade unions, employers' associations, representatives of temporary work agencies and entrepreneurs' associations were signed.

In November 2001, the Pact of Vilvoorde was signed by the Flemish Ministry and the social partners. The Pact translated the ambitions expressed by the Lisbon Summit to develop Europe into a dynamic, competitive knowledge economy in the Flemish context. It formulated 21 objectives pertaining to the competences of the Flemish Ministry (economy, employment, the natural environment, mobility, culture and welfare) to be met by 2010 to make Flanders a top economic region. Objectives 3 and 5 concern the position of specific sociodemographic groups on the labour market:

- *Objective 3*: In 2010 each individual of working age in Flanders has access to a decent job. The employment rate should be as close as possible to 70 per cent by 2010.
- *Objective 5*: In 2010, women and disadvantaged groups (including members of minority groups, the disabled and the low-skilled) are no longer underrepresented in the number of professionally active people. This is illustrated in particular by the fact that they are no longer overrepresented in the unemployment statistics.

In order to measure progress towards the achievement of the 21 objectives, indicators were developed by the Administration Planning and Statistics (today the Research Unit of the Flemish Government) and the Social-Economic Council of Flanders (SERV). The yearly evolution of the indicators is monitored to tune policy implementation. To reach the objectives formulated in the Pact of Vilvoorde within the legal framework defined by the Flemish Decree of 8 May 2002 (see above), two diversity platform texts were signed between the Flemish Ministry and the social partners on the one side and the representatives of ethnic minority associations (2002) and associations representing the disabled and the agencies for services to the disabled (2003) on the other. In the diversity platform text concerning ethnic minorities, the parties agreed on common actions to reduce the gap in qualifications, set up procedures for the recognition of competences gained elsewhere, organize language courses, career support, specific actions to facilitate recruitment, and the promotion of diversity management through the diversity plans (see above). They calculated that, depending on the economic growth, 2000 to 5000 jobs should be filled by ethnic minorities yearly. Agreed actions include softening of the criterion of nationality for certain permanent public jobs, hiring diversity consultants in the three main trade unions to raise awareness among militants and delegates, setting up a service on diversity for small and medium enterprises by the Entrepreneurs' Union (UNIZO), the creation of Jobkanaal, an intermediary between companies and ethnic minority candidates, to be organized by the main employers' association (VOKA) and two employees for the professionalization of the federations of ethnic minority associations concerning employment.

In the diversity platform text concerning the disabled, the parties agreed on a clear definition of the target group, stimulating diversity management through diversity plans, tailor-made coaching, training and intermediation, easier (administrative) access to subsidies for hiring disabled employees, reasonable adaptations by the employers, and access to career coaching and training.

In December 2003, the Diversity Commission of the Social-Economic Council of Flanders was created with the goal to follow up the initiatives implementing the proportional employment policy of the Flemish Ministry. This Commission is composed of the representatives of the organizations present in the Council and the representatives of the organizations representing the target groups.

Next to these multiple initiatives involving multiple actors – the Flemish Ministry, employers' associations, trade unions and ethnic minorities' associations – some companies have profiled themselves in the last years as pioneers of diversity management. Among the big companies, Ford Genk and Volvo Cars Gent in the automobile industry, Daikin in the cooling industry, Janssens Pharma in the pharmaceutical sector are all renowned for their developed policies in this area.

As a whole, it is clear that in the last decade, attention to the position of disadvantaged sociodemographic groups (so-called 'target groups' or 'groups at risk') and later to diversity by the main Flemish social actors has grown substantially. This is reflected both in the legislation and in the numerous agreements and initiatives that have emerged in this period. Although there is a will to pursue advances in this domain, as indicated by the identification of indicators and the creation of monitoring and evaluation procedures, Flanders has clearly chosen a policy focused on awareness-raising and incentives rather than legal obligations. This is shown by the virtual absence of support not only for setting up quotas for the employment of specific groups and positive discrimination, but even for testing discriminatory hiring policies by means of 'mystery candidates'.[27] We speculate that this consensus-based strategy results from a double specificity of the Flemish situation. First, the (projected) shortage of labour in the future is expected to create 'naturally' favourable market conditions for underrepresented groups on the labour market very soon. Second, all parties attempt to avoid a 'native backlash' at all costs, as this would play in favour of the extreme right party Vlaams Belang (Flemish Interest), which steadily gained votes in the period between 1991 and 2006.

3.4   Diversity initiatives in the Walloon Region[28]
The ministry of the Walloon Region launched in 2004 the Marshall Plan for economic development and the Strategic Plan for Social Inclusion, providing measures to combat discrimination in employment and increase the rate of employment of target groups like women, workers over 50 years of age, disabled persons, and men and women of foreign

origin. In 2006, the Walloon Minister of Economic Affairs launched a number of actions to raise the awareness of employers, including a 'Diversity and Human Resources in Wallonia' prize to reward best diversity management practices in companies, a diversity charter signed by 97 companies in 2008, and awareness-raising campaigns: seminars, a blog,[29] and a handbook (Cornet and Warland, 2008b). The Walloon Region further offers support to companies in the form of diversity consulting services.

The FOREM, the public agency for employment and training in the Walloon Region, collaborates at the local level with some centres for the integration of foreigners in the workplace.

Since 2005, the representatives of the employers and the trade unions have been involved in three committees set up within the Economic and Social Council of the Walloon Region (CESRW) dealing with discrimination in recruitment, childcare, and the integration of disabled persons in training and on the labour market. These committees can submit proposals of actions to the Walloon government. In 2000, they produced a document entitled *Multiculturalism, a company asset* (CESRW, 2000). However, as a whole, they have been relatively inactive. In 2006, a synthesis paper was drafted to report the perspectives of social partners on the existing tools regarding professional integration of disabled persons both in ordinary and adapted employment (ETA).

There are some non-profit organizations working for the integration of some target groups in employment, for example women with low qualifications or first-generation migrants. In general, there are few structured partnerships between them and companies.

As a whole, in Wallonia diversity management has to date been promoted above all by the public authorities with the aim of reducing unemployment rates of certain groups and fostering their social inclusion. Diversity is still perceived by most private companies as a low-priority topic. Larger and non-profit organizations are most likely to manage diversity. Among the former, public agencies and subsidiaries of multinationals are particularly active, public agencies because of their exemplary function and local branches of multinationals because of the requirement of their mother companies to develop and implement diversity management. Among the latter, diversity is often included in the organization's mission of supporting specific sociodemographic groups. In terms of sectors, the temporary work agency sector and the distribution sector, with relatively high concentrations of employees of foreign origin, appear to be the most active on diversity.

4. The empirical research on diversity

Despite the increasing attention to diversity, empirical research on this topic in Belgium remains limited. The vast majority of studies do not deal with diversity as such but rather investigate the disadvantaged position of specific sociodemographic groups on the Belgian labour market. Concerning sex differences, publications include studies on equal opportunities for men and women in public services (Hondeghem et al., 2004), gender analyses of official statistics (IWEPS and CWEFH, 2008; Kuppens et al., 2006). pay equity (Institut pour l'égalité des femmes et des hommes, 2000; Meulders and O'Dorchai, 2006), and the position of men and women on the labour market (Lamberts and Delmotte, 2004; Lamberts et al., 2005; Sels and Theunissen, 2006a, 2006b). Other publications deal with the position of disabled people in all sectors (Binamé and Mercier,

2004) or in public service (Binamé et al., 2004), with the position of the 'allochtonous' population in the Brussels-Capital region (Desmarez et al., 2004; Martens et al., 2005), in public service (Ceulemans et al., 2004) and on the labour market (Arrijn et al., 1998; Geets et al., 2006), and with homo- and bisexuals (Vincke, 2008).

Most studies show that these groups are underrepresented among the employees of both the private and the public sector due to discrimination, but also, for certain categories, to a lack of qualifications and access to networks. They further show the existence of both horizontal segregation (gender segregation but also ethnostratification of certain sectors) and vertical segregation (glass ceiling at different hierarchical levels) as well as a wage gap between men and women (Meulders and O'Dorchai, 2006), between native Belgians and people of foreign origin, and between hetero- and homosexuals (Meulders et al., 2004).

To date, only a few studies have taken into account the cumulative negative effects of different identity dimensions on the position of individuals on the labour market. For instance, Ouali (2007) has investigated the position of ethnic minority women at the intersection between gender and ethnicity and *Chronique Féministe*, the journal of the Women's University (Université-des-femmes, 2006), has dedicated a special issue on disabled women. More attention to these cumulative effects is, however, warranted (Cornet and Warland, 2008a). The position of an individual of foreign origin on the labour market will be strongly influenced, at the same time, by his or her education, sex, (dis)ability and family situation (e.g. whether or not he or she is a single parent).

Much less empirical research deals with diversity management practices in Belgian organizations. Bogaert and Vloeberghs (2005) investigated the approach to diversity management based on a sample of 64 Belgian organizations. They found that the most common practices were flexible working hours, work–family balance initiatives, and career path management initiatives. Language courses, adapted selection and recruitment procedures were also found, while training to eliminate cultural prejudice and in cross-cultural communication, often featuring among core diversity practices in the Anglo-Saxon practitioners' literature, were the least prevalent.

Cornet et al. (2007) compiled an inventory of more than 100 diversity management practices in the federal public sector in Belgium, the Netherlands, Sweden, France and the UK. These examples of practices covered the four dimensions of diversity, ethnicity, disability, gender and age, and all aspects of the HRM cycle, from recruitment to selection, evaluation and reward. Also, in the period 2006–07, a survey of practices in private and public firms in the Walloon region was financed by the Ministry of Economics. The results have recently been published in a manual for employers (Cornet and Warland, 2008b).

A team of researchers at the Higher Institute of Labour of the Catholic University of Leuven conducted an evaluation of the diversity plans subsidized by the Ministry of the Flemish Community (Lamberts et al., 2005) in the period 1999–2002. Of the evaluated organizations, 57 per cent had diversity plans dealing with specific groups (mostly ethnic minorities), 20 per cent dealing with all disadvantaged groups, and 20 per cent dealing with all employees. Most organizations implemented above all initiatives to do with recruitment and selection, newcomers' policy, and technical and language training. The researchers faced a general lack of figures concerning the evolution of the employment of ethnic minorities in the studied organizations and, where figures were available, found no clear positive effect of the plans on the employment of ethnic minorities in terms of recruitment, promotion and attrition. Most respondents declared, however, that the plans had improved the perception of management and employees on ethnic minorities, which seems to indicate that they mainly had an awareness-raising effect.

Finally, there are a number qualitative empirical studies based on data collected in Belgian organizations (Cornet et al., 2004; Cornet and Warland, 2008a; Zanoni and Janssens, 2007; Doyen et al., 2002; Janssens and Zanoni, 2005; Zanoni, 2008; Zanoni and Janssens, 2004), which develop the notion of diversity theoretically by analysing how specific organizational contexts affect both the understanding of diversity and its management. Although their findings are not statistically generalizable, these studies do provide an idea of how specific understandings of diversity are shaped by the context in which they are embedded. For instance, we note that many of the studied Flemish organizations start managing diversity for pragmatic reasons, especially to deal with an increasing presence of women, ethnic minorities and the elderly in organizations. Less attention is paid to the disabled and issues of sexual orientation are hardly addressed, as it is generally perceived as a topic pertaining to employees' private lives. These studies suggest that diversity management often emerges out of a need, leading to 'pragmatic' approaches.

Practices are first adopted to address specific problems encountered when certain sociodemographic groups enter the organization and only later bundled into a formal diversity management policy. They often become 'diversity management' when the organization communicates about them with other actors, for instance with public agencies in order to obtain subsidies or in exchanges of know-how with other organizations. *Ad hoc* practices are, for instance, flexible working arrangements to accommodate employees with caring responsibilities, reduced language requirements, or language courses and translations provided to help solve communication problems. Some of these initiatives are mainstreamed into general policies (i.e. working arrangements, recruitment processes, vacation policy, coaching and adaptation of work processes), while others target a specific group (language courses, job adaptation and places provided for praying). Diversity management policies tend to be more formalized from the beginning in local branches of multinationals, as these are more often required to report about them to headquarters, than in local (smaller) organizations. Yet some of these latter appear to have a quite successful 'pragmatic', partly informal, diversity management. In contrast to what the Anglo-Saxon literature on diversity suggests, only few companies employ certain groups because of their specific competences. For instance, migrants are in some companies hired for their linguistic and/or cultural knowledge (call centres, hospitals) or women for their relational skills or precision (industrial sector and food processing companies) (Janssens and Zanoni, 2005; Zanoni and Janssens, 2004).

5.   Reflections and conclusions

In this section, we offer some conclusive reflections on the specificities of diversity and its management in the Belgian context. One specificity concerns the emergence of the notion of diversity in the sphere of public policy at the turn of the century, as a more positive and encompassing term than the previously used concepts of 'groups at risk' and 'target groups'. The origins of diversity in Belgium are therefore quite different from the origins of this notion in the USA, where diversity emerged in the late 1980s as a business discourse alternative to equal opportunities and affirmative action discourses (Edelman et al., 2001; Kelly and Dobbin, 1998; McDougall, 1996). While diversity, as an 'umbrella' concept encompassing various types of differences, has today found its way into public Belgian discourse, the concept is still in an early phase of institutionalization (Zanoni and Janssens, 2008). Many public and private management initiatives still focus on one socio-demographic group, addressing the specific barriers it faces in participating in the labour market.

A second Belgian specificity is the uneven embeddedness of the notion of diversity in Wallonia, Flanders and Brussels. These differences derive from distinct socioeconomic situations in terms of predominant sectors and labour markets, and make it rather problematic to talk about one understanding of diversity at the national level. Rather, understandings of diversity have developed at different speeds and partly in different directions. In the Walloon context, characterized by declining heavy industry (metallurgy and mining) with only a few high-tech development poles, and higher unemployment rates, the notion of diversity remains relatively little used. Although unemployment rates might be higher for certain groups (the less educated, especially people with a foreign background, the elderly, women etc.), it is considered to be a general problem of the whole working population caused by the poor economic situation of the region, especially in the bigger cities and specific rural areas. The strong presence of both the Socialist Party and trade unions in Wallonia explains why, in the public discourse, the sociodemographic profile of the working class is de-emphasized, as these institutional actors have historically tended to look at diversity with suspicion, as a strategy to divide workers (Cornet and Warland, 2008a). However, the growing number of public-diversity-related initiatives in the last couple of years, involving employers, non-profit organizations, politicians and the trade unions themselves does suggest that diversity is becoming more accepted.

In Flanders, on the contrary, the shortage of labour in recent years, together with the problem of the ageing of the working population, has favoured the diffusion of diversity management as one of the strategies to attract employees with non-traditional profiles into paid work. Diversity management has been presented as a strategy to fill vacant jobs sustaining regional economic growth, diminish unemployment expenses, and generate state income to pay mounting retirement costs. Moreover, in a political context of rising xenophobia and success of Flemish nationalist extreme right parties, diversity management has offered a positive economic discourse around which the Socialist, Christian Democratic and Liberal Parties could reach consensus. Finally, the situation of the Brussels-Capital region is again specific. On the one hand, there is a large community of highly educated foreigners who are employed in the European institutions and the related service economy. On the other, the low-educated segments of labour, often ethnic minorities from non-EU countries, experience particularly great difficulties in accessing the labour market. Public diversity management initiatives generally aim at improving the position of this specific group.

A third Belgian specificity concerns how the institutional set-up of the country has affected the emergence of the notion of diversity and its specific understanding. The central role of employers–trade unions' negotiation in the economic sphere might explain why, up to now, it has been impossible to reach consensus about collecting data on ethnic background by residents in the country or even on the labour market. Employers fear that data collection might be the first step towards legally imposing quotas, limiting their discretion in matters of human resource management. Trade unions, as mentioned, fear that stressing the differential position of specific groups might lead to differential treatment of specific groups and fragment the labour class, ultimately damaging it. Without data on ethnic minorities' position on the labour market, however, developing, implementing and monitoring specific policies is highly problematic.

Fourth, it should be noted that diversity research in Belgium is still at its very beginning. This neglect is the joint consequence of the relatively recent emergence of the notion of diversity, the small size of the country and its internal institutional and socio-economic fragmentation, and the lack of official data on the labour market position of specific groups such as ethnic minorities, the disabled and homo-, bi- and transsexuals. While studies on specific groups exist, they are generally based on limited samples and

Summary table for Belgium

Existence of anti-discrimination legislation	Yes
Criteria covered by anti-discrimination legislation	Sex, age, sexual orientation, civil status, birth, property, religious or philosophical belief, political persuasion, language, current or future health status, disability, physical or genetic features, social background in employment relations
Criteria for which the reporting of quantitative data and their communication to a public administration are compulsory	Gender Disability for public service
Criteria covered by 'affirmative' or 'positive' action legislation other than unemployment- or income-based	Disability
Existence of a discourse or debate about 'non-discrimination' or 'equality'	Yes
Existence of a discourse or debate about 'diversity'	Yes
Year or period when the 'discrimination' concept started to disseminate in management literature in the country	1998 (ILO study)
Year or period when the 'diversity' concept started to disseminate in management literature in the country	2003–04
Who pushed the 'diversity' agenda?	University researchers, regional and federal government, Centre for Equal Opportunities and Opposition to Racism, trade unions, the European Commission, subsidiaries of US corporations, voluntary organizations
Existence of a professional association representing diversity professionals and year of creation	Network created by members of federal label diversity, 2008
Existence of a professional association representing diversity scholars and year of creation	No

deal with selected aspects of a group's disadvantage on the labour market. Studies of diversity are still rare (Bogaert and Vloeberghs, 2005; Cornet et al., 2007; Cornet and Warland, 2008b; Janssens and Zanoni, 2005; Zanoni, 2008; Zanoni and Janssens, 2007), as are studies that take an intersectional approach (Ouali, 2007).

Finally, the recent adoption of legislation implementing the European anti-discrimination directives of 2000 has certainly further contributed to the visibility of diversity in the country. As today the jurisprudence is still very limited, it is difficult to forecast the effects of these laws on employment relations. We deem it unlikely that the law will stimulate negative reactions comparable to the 'white male backlash' in the USA, as the 2007 laws do not enforce affirmative action through quotas and, moreover, Belgium lacks a lawsuit culture comparable to the one in the USA. In so far as employment relations remain collective and trade unions remain hesitant to use diversity as a means to enforce (specific) employees' rights out of fear of fragmentation of their constituency, diversity management is likely to remain a voluntary, consensual strategy between the state and the social partners.

Notes

1. http://www.statbel.fgov.be/.
2. The employment rate, or employment/population ratio, represents the share of persons in employment aged 15 to 64 out of the total population of the same age.
3. The activity rate, or labour force participation rate, represents the labour force (persons having or seeking work) as a percentage of the working-age population.
4. http://www.belgium.be/fr/actualites/2009/news_checklist_discrimations_age.jsp.
5. Published in the Belgian *Bulletin of Laws and Decrees* of 30 May 2007.
6. Published in the Belgian *Bulletin of Laws and Decrees* of 18 September 1996.
7. The required outline and forms that can be downloaded http://www.bnb.be - http://www.emploi.belgique. be.
8. Published in the Belgian *Bulletin of Laws and Decrees* of 25 November 1972.
9. Published in the Belgian *Bulletin of Laws and Decrees* of 8 March 1990.
10. Law of 5 September 2001 aimed at improving the employment rate, published in the Belgian *Bulletin of Laws and Decrees* of 15 September 2001, amended by the Law of 23 December 2005 on the solidarity pact between generations published in the Belgian *Bulletin of Laws and Decrees* of 30 December 2005.
11. Published in the Belgian *Bulletin of Laws and Decrees* of 30 December 2005.
12. http://www.iefh.fgov.be/, Information folder for the submission of grievances.
13. *Activities Report 2007*, see http://www.iefh.fgov.be.
14. www.diversite.be.
15. *Activities Report 2007*.
16. Federal Public Service Employment, Labour and Social Dialogue, Brussels www.emploi.belgique.be.
17. http://www.diversite.be.
18. http://www.iefh.be/eva.
19. http://www.emploi.belgique.be/fonds_de_lexpérience_professionnelle.
20. Federal Public Service, Personnel and Organisation, Unit, www.p-o.be.
21. A similar sort of distrust is found in the Belgian feminist movement. The fear is that diversity discourse will draw attention away from the cause of equality of men and women (Coene and Longman, 2008).
22. http://www.guidesocial.be/actualites/fortes-disparites-de-chomage.html.
23. http://www.eurofound.europa.eu/eiro/2000/05/feature/be0005313f.htm.
24. http://portail.irisnet.be/fr/region/region_de_bruxelles-capitale/ministere_de_la_region_de_bruxelles_ capitale/competences_et_organisation/secretariat_general/gestion_des_ressources_humaines/direction_ des_ressources_humaines/egalite_chances.shtml.
25. This section is based largely on Lamberts et al. (2005).
26. The VESOC agreement of 1998.
27. Some ethnic minorities organizations, such as Kif Kif and the Arabic European Liga, are however in favour.
28. http://emploi.wallonie.be/THEMES/EMPLOI/Diversité.html.
29. http://diversitegrh.canalblog.com/.

References

Adam, I. (2007), 'Immigrés et minorités ethniques sur le marché de l'emploi. Quelles politiques publiques en Belgique francophone?', in M. Martiniello and A. Rea (eds), *Immigration et Intégration en Belgique Francophone*. Etat des Savoirs, Louvain-la-Neuve: Acamedia–Bruylant, pp.179–92.

Arrijn, P., Feld, S. and Nayer, A. (1998), *Discrimination in Access to Employment on Grounds of Foreign Origin: The Case of Belgium*, Geneva: International Labour Office.

Binamé, J.P. and Mercier, M. (2004), *Responsabiliser les employeurs? Opportunité et faisabilité en Belgique d'un dispositif pour l'emploi des personnes handicapées*, Namur: Ministère des Affaires sociales et de la Santé de la Région wallonne. Accessible at: http://www.fundp.ac.be/medecine/psycho/docs/emploiph.pdf.

Binamé, J.P., Vos, S., Bollens, J., Depotter, V., De Muelenaere, A. and Grawez, M. (2004), 'L'emploi des personnes handicapées dans la fonction publique administrative fédérale', Faculté Notre-Dame de la Paix, Namur et Hoger Instituut voor Arbeid, KUL Leuven.

Bogaert, S. and Vloeberghs, D. (2005), 'Differentiated and individualized personnel management: diversity management in Belgium', *European Management Journal*, **23**(4), 483–93.

Burnotte, J. (2007), 'Les luttes contre les discriminations raciales: un enjeu fondamental de la lutte syndicale', www.dautresreperes.be © FAR 2007, 1–4.

Buyssens, E. (2008), 'La prophétie des grenouilles', *Politique: revue des débats*, octobre (56), 11–15. Accessible at: http://politique.eu.org/archives/2008/10/739.html.

Centre for Equal Opportunities and Opposition to Racism (2007), 'Monitoring socio-économique basé sur l'origine nationale pour mieux lutter contre les discriminations sur le marché du travail', paper presented at the Conférence interministérielle Emploi.

Centre for Equal Opportunities and Opposition to Racism (2008), *Rapport d'activités 2007 – activity report 2007*, Centre for Equal Opportunities and Opposition to Racism.

CESRW (2000), *La multiculturalité, un atout pour l'entreprise*, Liège, Belgique: Conseil économique et social de la région wallonne.

Ceulemans, E., Verhoeven, H., Ouali, N., Valkeneers, A. and Cambre, B. (2004), 'Diversiteit in de federale overheid. Studie naar de tewerkstelling van vreemdelingen en personen met een vreemde afkomst binnen het federaal administratief openbaar ambt', Bruxelles – Leuven: Afdeling Arbeid en Organisatie van de KULeuven, in samenwerking met het Instituut voor de overheid (KULeuven) en het Centre de sociologie du travail, de l'emploi et de la formation (TEF, ULB), Leuven.

Coene, G. and Longman, C. (2008), 'Gendering the diversification of diversity – the Belgian hijab (in) question', *Ethnicities*, **8**(3), 302–21.

Conter, B. (2000), 'Le chômage, révélateur de la dualité sociale à Bruxelles = Unemployment as revealing the social duality in Brussels', *Travail emploi formation*, **3**, 4–10.

Cornet, A., Delhaye, C. and Crunenberg, G. (2004), 'Gestion de la diversité: la recherche de la conciliation des logiques économiques et sociales', paper presented at the 16th congrès AGRH, Réconcilier l'économique et le social, Paris.

Cornet, A., Fonteyne, G., Verhaest, K. and Chakouh, N. (2007), 'Diversité et RH dans la fonction publique: bonnes pratiques en Belgique et à l'étranger. Bruxelles: Réalisé pour le SPF Personnel et Organisation.

Cornet, A. and Warland, P. (2008a), *GRH et gestion de la diversité*, Paris: Dunod.

Cornet, A. and Warland, P. (2008b), *La gestion de la diversité des ressources humaines dans les entreprises et les organisations: Guide à destination des employeurs*, Liège, Belgique: Editions de l'Université de Liège.

De Villers, M. (2003), 'Marché du travail bruxellois et discrimination ethnique: Approche des populations d'Afrique Sub-Saharienne (ou d'origine)', Observatoire bruxellois du marché du travail et des qualifications.

Delhaye, C. and Cornet, A. (2008), 'Rapport final d'évaluation et d'accompagnement du projet-pilote de job-coaching au sein du CRIPEL et du CRVI – Evaluation, Centre for Equal Opportunities and Opposition to Racism.

Desmarez, P., Van der Hallen, P., Ouali, N., Degraef, V., Tratsaert, K. (2004), *Minorités ethniques en Belgique: migration et marché du travail*, Gent: Academia Press.

Doyen, G., Lamberts, M. and Janssens, M. (2002), *Diversiteitsmanagment in de praktijk. [Diversity Management in Practice]*, Leuven: Hoger Instituut Voor de Arbeid.

Edelman, L.B., Fuller, S.R. and Mara-Drita, I. (2001), 'Diversity rhetoric and the managerialization of the law', *American Journal of Sociology*, **106**, 1589–641.

Geets, J., Pauwels, F., Wets, J., Lamberts, M. and Timmermans, C. (2006), *Nieuwe migranten op de arbeidsmarkt [New Migrants on the Labour Market]*, Leuven: Hoger Instituut voor de Arbeid.

Goyvaerts, K. and Dessein, B. (2004), 'Vlucht SN 50-plus naar Benidorm, klaar voor vertrek', *Over Werk*, **3**, 9–18.

Hondeghem, A., Scheepers, S., Decat, A. and Facon, P. (2004), *Studie naar de gelijkheid van mannen en vrouwen in het federaal openbaar administratieve*, Leuven: Instituut voor de overheid.

INS, I. N. d. S. (2002), 'Les matelots viennent de Mars, les femmes de ménage viennent de Vénus', Institut National des statistiques.

INS, I. N. d. S. (2004), 'Disabled people and employment', Info Flash (39 of 28).

Institut pour l'égalité des femmes et des hommes (2000), 'Evaluation et classification de fonctions – Des outils pour l'égalité salariale', Institut pour l'égalité des femmes et des hommes.

IWEPS and CWEFH (2008), 'Les facteurs de précarité. Photographie statistique de la situation des femmes et des hommes en Wallonie', IWEPS – Institut Wallon de statistiques.

Janssens, M. and Zanoni, P. (2005), 'Many diversities for many services: theorizing diversity (management) in service companies', *Human Relations*, **58** (3), 311–40.

Kelly, E. and Dobbin, F. (1998), 'How affirmative action became diversity management: employer response to antidiscrimination law, 1961 to 1996', *American Behavioral Scientist*, **47** (7), 960–84.

Konrad, A.M., Prasad, P. and Pringle, J.K. (2006), *Handbook of Workplace Diversity*, London: Sage Publications.

Kuppens, T., Steegmans, N., Van Aerschot, M., Poot, S. and Van Haegendoren, M. (2006), 'Femmes et hommes en Belgique: statistiques et indicateurs de genre', Institut pour l'égalité des femmes et des hommes.

Lamberts, M. and Delmotte, J. (2004), *Knelpunten op de arbeidsmarkt, kansen voor vrouwen?* [*Difficult-to-fill Vacancies on the Labour Market, Opportunities for Women?*], Leuven, Belgique: Hoger Instituut Voor de Arbeid.

Lamberts, M., Pauwels, F., Schryvers, E. and Van de Maele, M. (2005), *De weg naar evenredige arbeidsdeelname via diversiteitsplannen op organisatieniveau* [*The Route to Proportional Participation Through Diversity Plans in Organizations*], Leuven, Belgique: Hoger Instituut Voor de Arbeid.

Martens, A. (2005), 'Ethnostratification du marché de l'emploi', *Agenda interculturel*, octobre (236), 6–10.

Martens, A., Ouali, N., Van de Maele, M., Vertommen, S., Dryon, P. and Verhoeven, H. (2005), *Rapport de synthèse sur les discriminations des étrangers et des personnes d'origine étrangère sur le marché du travail de la Région de Bruxelles Capitale: Recherche dans le cadre du Pacte Social pour l'Emploi des bruxellois*, ORBEM, ULB, KUL.

McDougall, M. (1996), 'Equal opportunities versus managing diversity: another challenge for public sector management?', *International Journal of Public Sector Management*, **5**, 62–72.

Meulders, D. and O'Dorchai, S. (2006), 'The gender pay gap in Belgium', in *The Gender Pay Gap – Origins and Policy Responses: A Comparative Review of 30 European Countries*, European Commission Directorate-General for Employment, Social Affairs and Equal Opportunities, Unit G.1.

Meulders, D., Plasman, R. and Rycx, F. (2004), Special Issue: 'Gender, racial and sexual orientation earnings inequalities', *International Journal of Manpower*, **25** (3/4).

Neels, K. and Stoop, R. (2000), 'Reassessing the ethnic gap. Employment of younger Turks and Moroccans in Belgium', in R. Lesthaeghe (ed.), *Communities and Generations, Turkish and Moroccan populations in Belgium*, The Hague, the Netherlands: NIDI–CBGS Publications, pp. 279–320.

Ouali, N. (2007), 'Les femmes immigrées sur le marché du travail. Etat des savoirs', in M. Martiniello, F. Dassetto and A. Rea (eds), *Immigration et intégration en Belgique francophone*, Bruxelles: Academia Bruylant, pp. 269–85.

Ouali, N. and Rea, A. (1995), 'Insertion, discrimination et exclusion. Cursus scolaires et trajectoires d'insertion professionnelle de jeunes bruxellois', *Dossier TEF* (11), 158.

Peeters, A. (2004), 'La responsabilité sociale des entreprises', *Courrier hebdomadaire du CRISP*, 3 (1828), 1–47.

Prasad, P., Pringle, J. and Konrad, A.M. (2006), 'Examining the contours of workplace diversity: concepts, contexts and challenges', in A.M. Konrad, P. Prasad and J.K. Pringle (eds), *Handbook of Workplace Diversity*, London: Sage Publications, pp. 1–23.

Romans, F. and Preclin, V. (2008), *Population and social conditions Data in focus*, Eurostat.

Sels, L. and Theunissen, G. (2006a), 'Waarom vrouwen beter verdienen (maar mannen meer krijgen). Een kritisch essay over de sekseloonkloof', Leuven, Acco.

Sels, L. and Theunissen, G. (2006b), 'Genderjaarboek 2006 MVunited', Loopbaankloof: SF-Agentschap; Departement Werk en Sociale Economie.

Smets, J. and De Mulder, J. (2004), 'De eindeloopbaanproblematiek', *Over Werk*, **4**, 108–11.

Union Européenne (2006), 'Aperçu des initiatives pour la promotion de la diversité sur le marché belge de l'emploi', www.stop-discrimination.info.

Université-des-femmes (2006), 'Femmes et handicaps', *Chronique Féministe* (95–7).

Van den Cruyce, B. (2005), 'De ondergebruikte arbeidsreserve van vreemdelingen in België', Kwartallschrift Economie, www.statbel.fgov.be/studies/thesis_nl.asp?n=354 (2), 117–45.

Vincke, J. (2008), *Situation des lesbigays dans le monde du travail*, Bruxelles: Centre pour l'égalité des chances et la lutte contre le racisme.

Zanoni, P. (2008), 'Diversity in the lean automobile factory: exploring the relationship between difference, control and resistance', paper presented at the IERA Conference 'Diversity and New Employment Relations', Nijmegen School of Management, Radbond University Nijmegen, 30 June–2 July.

Zanoni, P. and Janssens, M. (2004), 'Deconstructing difference: the rhetoric of human resource managers' diversity discourses', *Organization Studies*, **25** (1), 55–74.

Zanoni, P. and Janssens, M. (2007), 'Minority employees engaging with (diversity) management: an analysis of control, agency, and micro-emancipation', *Journal of Management Studies*, **44** (8), 1371–97.

Zanoni, P. and Janssens, M. (2008), 'Contesting institutions across borders: the case of diversity management in a European branch of a U.S. multinational', paper presented at the EGOS, Colloquium 'Upsetting Organizations', 10–12 July.

Appendix

Table 3A.1   Official names of Belgian institutions

English	French	Dutch
Administration Planning and Statistics		Administratie Planning en Statistiek
Belgian Bulletin of Acts and Decrees	Moniteur Belge	Belgisch Staatsblad
Brussels Labour Market and Qualifications Observatory	Observatoire bruxellois du Marché du Travail et des Qualifications	Brussels Observatorium voor de Werkgelegenheid
Collective Labour Agreement		Collectief Arbeidsovereenkomst
Federation of Enterprises in Belgium	Fédération des Entreprises de Belgique	Verbond van Belgische Ondernemingen
Flemish Economic Social Concertation Committee		Vlaams Economisch Sociaal Overlegcomité (VESOC)
International Labour Office (ILO)	Bureau International du Travail	
National Institute for Statistics (NIS)	Institut National de Statistique	Nationaal Instituut voor de Statistiek
National Work Council	Conseil National du Travail	Nationaal Arbeidsraad
Professional Experience Fund	Fonds de l'Expérience Professionnelle	
Research Unit of the Flemish Government		Studiedienst van de Vlaamse Regering
Social-Economic Council of Flanders		Sociaal Economisch Raad van Vlaanderen (SERV)

4 Employment equity and workplace diversity in Canada[1]

Rana Haq and Eddy S.W. Ng

Introduction

> Canada is and has been a diverse nation composed of a wide variety of different peoples. Beginning with the 50 distinct aboriginal nations which were the original inhabitants of the country, and adding the French, the English, other European groups, Black Loyalists in 1776 and 1812, and the Chinese in 1858, Canada was a racially and ethnically diverse society even by Confederation in 1867.
>
> (McDonald, 1990, p. 2)

Immigration and multiculturalism have been the backbone of Canada's approach to nation-building, with the former being a source of Canada's ethnic, religious and racial diversity, and the latter representing the Canadian ideological construct for accommodating diversity (Breton, 1986). These realities have remained unchanged over time, but what is changing are the attitudes and policies governing how the diverse groups of individuals are treated within the social, economic and legal systems in Canada.

Socially, Canada has often been referred to as a 'mosaic', reflecting the reality that Canada is a nation of immigrants and encourages immigrants to maintain their distinctiveness as Canadians. The mosaic metaphor, first used in 1922 by an American writer, Victoria Hayward, continues to be very popular today for describing the multicultural nature of the Canadian society. The term 'mosaic' refers to the overall image formed when unique pieces of tile are aligned in a unified and coherent pattern, presenting an overall picture of unity and coherence (Fleras and Elliott, 1996).

The mosaic metaphor is in contrast to the 'melting pot' image that is attributed to the USA, where immigrants are encouraged to lose their ethnocultural distinctiveness in order to become 'American'. However, Fleras and Elliott (1996) state that both these metaphors are inaccurate and distorted oversimplifications of the two nations' strategy for managing diversity. In reality, Canada is not a pluralist haven where diversity is celebrated and minorities are integrated as full and equal participants, while the USA has not yet succeeded in 'melting' resistant differences, and segregations still exist on many levels.

In the USA, the landmark report by the Hudson Institute (Johnston and Packer, 1987) is cited as the impetus to managing diversity initiatives. In Canada, the 1984 Abella Report was instrumental in the birth of the federal Employment Equity Act (EEA) of 1986. Both documents confirm the changing nature and composition of the North American workforce and urge organizations to take appropriate measures to manage this increasing demographic diversity. The purpose of this chapter is to provide an overview of employment equity and workplace diversity in Canada. In particular, we shall discuss the Canadian employment equity legislation, with special attention to the advancement of women and visible minorities in the workplace, and recent developments in managing diversity initiatives specific to sexual minorities in Canada.

Changing demographics in Canada

Canada, like many industrialized countries, is experiencing low birth rates and an ageing workforce. Coupled with a sustained period of economic growth and low unemployment rates, Canada is facing a critical shortage of skilled workers (cf. Burke and Ng, 2005). The Canadian government has sought to address the skills gap by increasing worker immigration into the country. Between 2001 to 2006, more than 1.1 million people (an annual average of 242 000 immigrants) entered Canada under its aggressive immigration policy (Statistics Canada, 2007a). Immigrants represent almost 70 per cent of the growth in the Canadian labour force over the past decade, and it is estimated that they will make up 75 per cent of the workforce growth in 2016 and 100 per cent by 2025 (Burleton, 2002). Historically, immigrants to Canada have come from Europe, but Asia and the Pacific region have surpassed Europe as the principal source of immigrants over the past 30 years. Six in ten recent immigrants now come from Asia, including the Middle East (see Table 4.1). A majority of immigrants (70.2 per cent) also reported a mother tongue other than English or French, with Chinese, Italian, Punjabi, Spanish, German, Tagalog and Arabic making up the majority of languages spoken at home (Statistics Canada, 2007a).

This increasing ethnocultural diversity has created challenges for Canadian organizations. The Canadian multicultural policy was deliberately created to encourage immigrants to retain their cultural heritage rather than to assimilate. The Multiculturalism Act, passed in 1988, is aimed at helping people overcome barriers related to race, ethnicity, and cultural or religious background. It is a policy of inclusion and a means by which the federal government reaffirms multiculturalism as a fundamental value of Canadian society and of the Government of Canada. All federal institutions must take multiculturalism into account in all their activities, from hiring and promoting employees of all backgrounds to serving a diverse public. The Canadian government is therefore held accountable for ensuring that they 'carry on their activities in a manner that is sensitive and responsive to the multicultural reality of Canada' (Multiculturalism Canada, 2007).

Table 4.1   Immigrants by top 10 source countries, ten-year period (1997–2006)

Country	Continent	No. of immigrants	% of total
China	Asia	325 943	14.4
India	Asia	249 381	11.0
Pakistan	Asia	123 412	5.5
Philippines	Asia	122 853	5.4
USA	North America	66 097	2.9
Korea	Asia	65 139	2.9
Iran	Asia	63 711	2.8
UK	Europe	51 436	2.3
Sri Lanka	Asia	47 228	2.1
Hong Kong	Europe	46 671	2.1

Source: Citizenship and Immigration Canada (2006).

Legal framework for managing diversity
In Canada, employers are increasingly made accountable for their employment policies
and practices resulting from the growing diversity in the workplace. This is evidenced
by the legislation and policies that have been enacted and mandated by the federal
government. For example, the Canadian Charter of Rights and Freedom, as part of the
Constitution Act of 1982, guarantees certain rights and freedom of individuals without
precluding employment equity programmes (cf. Jain et al., 2003). Specifically, Section
15(1) states that everyone is equal before and under the law, and has the right to equal
protection and equal benefit of the law without discrimination, and in particular, without
discrimination based on race, national or ethnic origin, colour, religion, sex, or mental
and physical disability. In addition, the Canadian Human Rights Act (CHRA) prohibits
discrimination on the basis of eleven grounds:

> Discriminatory practices based on race, national or ethnic origin, colour, religion, age, sex,
> sexual orientation, marital status, family status, disability or conviction for which a pardon has
> been granted. (Canadian Human Rights Act, R. S. 1985, c H-6, s.2)

The federal Employment Equity Act itself was enacted in 1986 to remove barriers
in employment for historically disadvantaged groups. Its goal is to remedy past discrimination in employment opportunities and improve access and distribution of the
designated group members throughout all occupations. Under the EEA, a separate
administrative policy in the form of the Federal Contractors' Program (FCP) is used as
a tool to help achieve the goals of employment equity for companies wishing to supply
goods and services to the federal government. These are discussed in more detail later
in this chapter.

The Pay Equity Act[2] was also put in place in 1988 to mandate equal pay for work of
equal value (McDonald and Thornton, 1998). Fundamental to this policy is that female
jobs found to be of equal (or comparable) value to male jobs must be paid the same.
Such a policy is considered to be complementary to employment equity, since if equal
pay policy existed alone, then women would not be hired (Gunderson, 2002). Pay equity
ensures that women's job are paid fairly given their value (although occupation segregation continues), while employment equity attempts to reduce occupation segregation
among males' jobs by removing barriers that have kept women out (Weiner, 2002). In
order to facilitate a cross-national comparison with the other chapters in this volume,
this chapter will be devoted to employment equity in Canada, with particular emphasis
on women and minorities, given their historical discrimination and the progress that
has been made to date. A topical focus on minority experiences in the workplace is also
made, given the current challenges facing them in the Canadian labour market.

Employment equity in Canada
Employment equity officially came into effect with the passage of the Employment
Equity Act (EEA) in 1986. It follows the recommendations from the Royal Commission
of Inquiry on Equality of Employment, chaired by Judge Rosalie Abella. The 1984
report found that four designated groups, women, aboriginal peoples, visible minorities,[3]
and persons with disabilities, face insurmountable barriers leading to discrimination in
employment. Specifically, the Employment Equity Act states:

The purpose of this Act is to achieve equality in the workplace so that no person shall be denied employment opportunities or benefits for reasons unrelated to ability and, in the fulfilment of that goal, to correct the conditions of disadvantage in employment experienced by women, aboriginal peoples, persons with disabilities, and members of visible minorities by giving effect to the principle that employment equity means more than treating persons in the same way but also requires special measures and the accommodation of differences. (Employment Equity Act, 1995, c. 44, s.2)

Under the EEA, there are two mandatory programmes: the Legislated Employment Equity Program (LEEP) and the Federal Contractors Program (FCP). The former applies to federally regulated employers in four sectors (banking, transportation, communications and federal crown corporations) with more than 100 employees. Employers are required to develop an employment equity plan, set goals and time-tables for hiring and promoting representative numbers of designated groups, identify and eliminate discriminatory systems and practices in their organizations, replace them with non-discriminatory alternatives, implement special measures and make reasonable accommodation for differences. Employers are also required to collect data on their workforces, including the number of employees and representation of the designated groups by industrial sector, geographic location, employment status, occupational category, salary range, hirings, promotions and terminations (EEA, 2006; Labour Canada, 2006). The 1999 to 2008 Annual Reports are currently available on Labour Canada's website (http://www.rhdcc-hrsdc.gc.ca/eng/lp/lo/lswe/we/ee_tools/reports/annual/index-we.shtml).[4]

These data must be submitted annually, by 1 June, to the Ministry of Human Resources and Social Development Canada. The Employer Reports and Analysis Unit receives these reports and verifies them for compliance with the reporting requirements. Organizations that fail to report their results or annual plan are liable to face a financial penalty of up to $50 000 (EEA, 2007). The Minister of Labour prepares a consolidation of all the employer reports and an analysis of the results achieved, and tables a report in parliament.

As provided in the legislation, Human Resources and Social Development Canada issues guidelines and tools to employers on how to develop and implement employment equity programmes. In addition, it has regional employment equity consultants who assist employers in meeting their obligations under the EEA. For example, the assistance given to employers is usually through examining their employment systems, and refers to the policies, practices and conditions used by organizations to recruit, train, promote and compensate employees. The examination can determine if discriminatory practices are inherent in the way they recruit and select, train, develop, promote, evaluate, compensate, benefit, lay off, recall, discipline and terminate employees. They must also look closely at the conditions of employment. If necessary, they are advised to design and implement measures that will assist in eliminating discrimination. The LEEP presently covers 474 private sector employers and 29 crown corporations, with a combined workforce of 651 000 employees, plus another 358 160 employees in other federal agencies such as the Canadian Forces, Royal Canadian Mounted Police, and the Canadian Security and Intelligence Services (Labour Canada, 2006).

The EEA has had a significant impact on the employment practices of federally regulated organizations in Canada. While there has been recognition and support for the

EEA (Benimadhu and Wright, 1991; Cornish, 1996; Jain and Hackett, 1989; Kerthen, 1997; Kirby and Murrell, 1995; Kirchmeyer and McLellan, 1991), there have also been calls for more aggressive interventions (Blakely and Harvey, 1988; Henry and Jain, 1991). The original EEA of 1986 was often criticized for 'lacking teeth', as there was no sanction for failing to comply with the Act. For example, there were no standards, benchmarks or means to measure success if and when the goals are achieved (Henry et al., 1995), no effective penalties for non-compliance (Jain and Hackett, 1989), and employers took minimal action to improve the representation of the designated groups (Fleras and Elliott, 1996). The EEA was subsequently amended and strengthened in 1995 (and came into effect in 1996) to address these shortcomings. Some of these changes include: empowering the Canadian Human Rights Commission to conduct on-site compliance reviews (audits) and creating the Employment Equity Review Tribunal to issue 'court enforceable' orders (Agocs, 2002; Jain et al., 2003).

The EEA of 1995 is presently undergoing a second parliamentary review to ensure that it continues to meet the needs of designated groups and if it should be expanded to include other groups (Labour Canada, 2006). (Note: at the time of writing, the Parliament of Canada was prorogued and the motion of referral to the Parliamentary Committee conducting the review lapsed.)

Federal Contractors' Program
The Federal Contractors' Program (FCP) was established in 1986 under the EEA and applies to non-federally regulated organizations, with 100 or more employees, that supply goods and services to the federal government, and that have contracts of $200 000 or more. The FCP is a 'stand-alone' programme, rather than legislation, and it is authorized by the Treasury Board (Circular 1986-44). The intent of the FCP is for government programmes to be able to induce organizational change by controlling funding. The FCP is enforced by Human Resources and Social Development Canada, where positive action is an eligibility requirement for federal government funding. In the 1995 revision of the EEA, parliament required the FCP to become 'equivalent' to the LEEP (Section 42(2)).

Under the FCP, employers are required to complete a certificate of commitment indicating their readiness to participate in the programme. There is no required reporting for FCP employers and no systematic collection and inputting of data on employee representation. Under the LEEP, reporting data is highly structured and extensive. The FCP includes an 11-step criterion[5] that employers are expected to implement in order to reach the goal of fair representation for the four designated groups at each occupational level within the organization as available in the labour force.

In practice, the FCP is a voluntary programme in that no employer is required to do business with the federal government. If an employer believes that the cost of implementing the FCP is higher than the benefits of obtaining the government contract, it can choose to forgo the contract. It also excludes contractors in construction and legal services. Nearly half of all FCP employers are found in business services, machinery and equipment supplies, electrical, chemical, educational services, and transportation equipment (Labour Canada, 2006). Currently, the FCP covers 936 contractors employing over 1.1 million individuals, representing 6.9 per cent of the Canadian labour force.

Provincial employment equity policies
While this chapter is devoted to examining the federal EEA, the provinces and territories within Canada also enact legislation for employers that fall under their jurisdictions. The Province of British Columbia passed the Public Service Directive on Employment Equity legislation in 1994. Six other provinces also have some form of employment equity policy (Manitoba, 1983; Saskatchewan, Quebec, 1987; Nova Scotia, 1975; New Brunswick, 1984 and Prince Edward Island, enforced through human rights legislation), although only Quebec extends its mandate beyond the public service sector. The three remaining provinces, Ontario, Alberta and Newfoundland, have no employment equity policy or legislation. Six of the seven provinces with employment equity policies also have pay equity legislation, except for Saskatchewan. Alberta and Newfoundland have neither employment equity nor pay equity legislation, while Ontario has pay equity legislation but not employment equity (see Bakan and Kobayashi, 2000 for a comprehensive review).

Assessment of employment equity in Canada
One measure of the effectiveness of employment equity in Canada is the achievement of proportionate representation (numerical goals) among designated group members relative to their availability rates in the workforce. An analysis of the EEA *Annual Reports* (see Table 4.2) indicates that the progress in attaining proportionate representation has

Table 4.2   Representation of women and visible minorities under the Employment Equity Act (selected years)

Designated group	1987 (%)	1999 (%)	2001 (%)	2005 (%)	2006[a] (%)	Workforce availability (2001)
Women						
Private sector						
Banking	76.1	72.0	71.0	68.9	68.4	
Communications	39.6	41.5	41.3	40.8	40.6	
Transportation	16.9	25.2	24.7	25.3	25.3	
Other	21.3	26.3	28.0	30.7	30.7	
Total private sector	40.9	44.8	44.9	43.3	43.1	47.3
Federal public sector	42.0	51.4	52.1	53.5	52.2	47.3
Visible minorities						
Private sector						
Banking	9.5	15.8	17.1	22.9	23.5	
Communications	4.0	7.1	10.8	12.5	13.2	
Transportation	2.6	9.3	7.6	9.6	9.4	
Other	2.6	7.4	7.7	9.6	11.8	
Total private sector	5.0	10.5	11.7	14.8	14.9	12.6
Federal public sector	2.8	5.5	6.1	8.1	8.6	12.6

Note: [a] Most recent available data.

Sources: EEA, *Annual Reports 2000, 2002, 2006*; Labour Canada (2006).

been modest but steady since the implementation of employment equity in 1986. These improvements occurred in both the private (federally regulated industries) and public sectors, although both women and visible minorities remained poorly represented in senior management positions.

Women were either close to or had closed the representation gap in employment by 2001 (the most recent available census data). Female representation increased from 40.1 per cent to 44.9 per cent in the private sector, close to their external availability of 47.3 per cent, in 2001. Women met or exceeded their representation in the banking sector, but remained underrepresented in all other sectors, most notably in transportation. In the federal public sector, women's representation increased from 42 per cent to 52.1 per cent in 2001, far exceeding their availability rates, and their representation continued to climb to 53.5 per cent in 2005 (most recently reported data). Leck (2002) found that employment equity improved the human resource practices (e.g. employment policies that support employment equity), increased the presence and status of women, and narrowed wage gaps between men and women.

Women also made significant inroads into middle-level management and professional jobs (see Table 4.3). Leck and Saunders (1992) noted that women started to fill traditionally male-dominated positions such as supervisory roles as a result of employment equity. Furthermore, the percentage of women in senior management positions had climbed from 14.9 per cent in 1987 to 22.1 per cent in 2005, although it was still below their availability rate of 25.1 per cent in the 2001 census year. Leck (2002) attributed this to a change in attitudes towards women occupying staff roles (middle-management jobs)

Table 4.3   Representation of women and visible minorities in management and professional occupations (selected years)

Designated group	1987[a] (%)	1999 (%)	2001 (%)	2005 (%)	2006[b] (%)	Workforce availability (2001)
Women						
Senior managers	14.9	17.3	20.3	22.1	22.2	25.1
Middle managers	n/a	42.6	43.0	44.1	44.2	37.5
Professionals	n/a	42.3	45.2	46.0	46.3	52.8
Total	40.9	44.8	44.9	43.3	43.1	47.3
Visible minorities						
Senior managers	2.6	3.1	3.9	5.5	5.2	8.2
Middle managers	n/a	8.3	8.9	11.8	12.5	11.8
Professionals	n/a	14.6	16.7	20.4	21.3	13.8
Total	5.0	10.5	11.7	14.8	14.9	12.6

Notes:
[a] Data obtained from Agocs (2002).
[b] Most recent available data.

Sources: EEA, *Annual Reports 2000, 2002, 2006, 2007*; Labour Canada (2006).

since staff roles are considered to be 'less powerful' and therefore less dangerous or risky than line positions.

The representation of visible minorities has also climbed steadily, from 5 per cent in 1987 to 11.7 per cent in 2001 in the private sector, closing in on their availability rate of 12.6 per cent. Visible minorities met or exceeded their external availability only in the banking sector (see Table 4.2). Jain (1993) found that visible minorities were still underrepresented in some of the most prominent communication and transportation companies, such as Bell, the Canadian Broadcasting Corporation, CTV, Air Canada and Canadian National Rail. The rapid immigration of workers has contributed to the increase of visible minorities in the workforce, but employers have not been able to keep up with their employment (Bakan and Kobayashi, 2000). In the public sector, the representation of visible minorities had jumped from 2.8 per cent in 1987 to 8.1 per cent in 2001, but still fell short of their availability rate of 12.6 per cent. A 1997 study that examined the poor representation in the federal public service concluded that a lack of flexibility in the hiring process, lack of senior managers who are visible minorities, and the existence of strong 'old-boy' social networks presented barriers to the hiring and promotion of visible minorities (cf. Agocs, 2002).

Visible minorities also gained representation in middle-level management and professional jobs (see Table 4.3). In 2001, the representation of visible minorities in professional and technical jobs exceeded their external availability. However, their representation at senior management levels, at 3.9 per cent, was far below their external availability rate of 8.2 per cent. Jain and Lawler (2004) concluded that visible minorities, with the exception of professional and technical jobs, are ghettoized in lower-level positions. The Canadian Human Rights Commission Tribunal recently found that visible minorities at Health Canada were not promoted at a rate commensurate with their qualifications and experience (cf. Bakan and Kobayashi, 2000). Therefore, despite having exceeded their representation rates by 2005, visible minorities remain in support roles and at the bottom of the management scale. The overrepresentation of visible minorities at entry levels must not be viewed as having achieved equity in the workplace.

Federal Contractors' Program
Human Resources and Social Development Canada (HRSDC) commissioned a study to assess the relevance, effectiveness, and value of the Federal Contractors' Program (FCP) from 1995 to 2001. Data from employer self-reports indicate that representation for women and visible minorities showed improvements from 1995 to 1999 (Human Resources and Social Development Canada, 2002). However, these improvements largely disappeared in 1999, due in part to a reduction of resources in administering the FCP. The FCP also did not appear to have an impact on the contracting or purchasing position of the federal government. Less than 5 per cent of employers reported that they were discouraged from bidding on federal government contracts because of FCP requirements. However, Erridge and Fee (2001) interviewed purchasing managers in the public sector, and found that they were dismissive of the FCP. The lack of reporting requirement under the FCP has forced organizations to pay greater attention to other more pressing issues such as government audits. Erridge and Fee concluded that the FCP is a policy that is based on encouragement and no enforcement, and thereby cannot achieve its stated objectives. In 2005, Labour Canada estimated that federal contractors had

Table 4.4   Estimated representation of women and visible minorities under the Federal Contractors' Program (2001–04)

Designated group	Employees[a]	Representation (%)	Workforce availability[b] (%)	Representation Index[c] (%)
Women	108 656	39.1	47.3	82.7
Visible minorities	31 230	11.2	12.6	88.9

Notes:
[a] Based on surveys conducted on 224 contractors from 2001 to 2004.
[b] Based on 2001 Census data.
[c] Derived by dividing 'Representation' by 'Availability'.

Source: EEA, *Annual Report 2005.*

achieved over 88 per cent on the representation index for women and visible minorities (see Table 4.4).

Visible minority experiences in the workplace
Despite the progress that has been made since the implementation of employment equity in Canada, significant labour market inequity remains. For example, visible minorities continue to experience higher rates of unemployment compared to the average Canadian-born worker. Very recent immigrants,[6] a majority of whom are visible minorities, experienced an unemployment rate of 11.5 per cent, more than double the 4.9 per cent for the Canadian-born population despite being more qualified (Statistics Canada, 2007c). As a result, six in ten immigrants to Canada had to find work outside the occupational fields in which they were trained (Statistics Canada, 2003). Those who were fortunate enough to find employment, usually in sales and service or in processing and manufacturing jobs, earned considerably less compared to their Canadian counterparts with similar levels of education (National Anti-Racism Council of Canada, 2007). Even after 15 years in Canada, immigrants with a university degree are still more likely than Canadian born people to be in low-skilled jobs (Statistics Canada, 2008). This growing labour market segregation means that visible minorities are disproportionately employed in low-income and low-status jobs compared to Canadian averages.

In a survey conducted by the Conference Board of Canada (2004a), immigrants reported a lack of Canadian work experience, lack of recognition of foreign credentials, language barriers and unfamiliarity with the 'Canadian way' as impediments to labour market participation. Therefore it is not uncommon to hear reports of immigrants with university degrees and transferable job skills such as computer programming working as taxicab drivers in Toronto. Audrey Macklin, a Professor of Law at the University of Toronto, refers to this as a 'brain waste' when we end up with 'the most overqualified cab drivers, pizza-delivery men and caretakers in the world' (Marron, 2004). The failure to recognize the learning and credentials of immigrants alone cost them $3.4 to 5 billion annually in lost earnings due to unemployment or underemployment (Conference Board of Canada, 2004b). In light of this, employers, business leaders and professional bodies must work together to ensure that they recognize and utilize the skills and talents of immigrant labour to deal with a shortage of skilled workers and to gain a competitive advantage.

Building a business case for diversity

Canadian organizations are increasingly making diversity a priority (Canadian Business, 2004). In a recent national survey of managers and executives responsible for diversity in their organizations, there appears to be a gradual shift in Canadian organizations from a compliance-driven focus to a business-driven focus on workplace diversity (Conference Board of Canada, 2006). However, the survey also found that only half of the respondents had strategic plans for diversity, and made conscious efforts to create and sustain inclusive work environments. Therefore an opportunity exists for organizations to manage diversity to gain a strategic advantage in the competition for talent from an increasingly diverse labour market. The business case for diversity suggests that organizations that manage diversity well can attract, retain and motivate the best talents from all demographic groups (Ng and Burke, 2005). Culturally diverse employees who are career-satisfied are more likely to perform to their fullest potential (Cox and Blake, 1991; Catalyst and The Diversity Institute, 2007). Research studies have also shown that diverse groups can outperform homogeneous groups in problem-solving and creativity and contributing to the bottom line (Ng and Tung, 1998; Richard, 2000; Watson et al., 1993; Wright et al., 1995). Furthermore, employees from diverse backgrounds can provide organizations with knowledge about the diverse markets to reach a wider customer base (Cox and Blake, 1991; Robinson and Dechant, 1997).

The transformation from compliance with employment equity to managing diversity began in the late 1980s (Agocs and Burr, 1996). Managing diversity, which originated in the USA and is also being widely adopted in Canada, represents a voluntary corporate response to increasing diversity in the workplace. It gained popularity when human resource managers began promoting the business case associated with diversity by emphasizing the gains from a diverse workforce to serve a diverse customer base (Kelly and Dobbin, 1998). While employment equity seeks to redress past discrimination, managing diversity seeks to maximize the potential of all employees, including white males (Cox, 1991). As a result, managing diversity is seen as less controversial when compared with employment equity given that it is more inclusive of everyone in the workplace rather than only those belonging to the four designated groups under the EEA (Ng and Burke, 2005).

Evidence of the shift from compliance with employment equity to managing diversity is compelling. In a recent Conference Board of Canada study, a majority of Canadian employers indicated that they are managing diversity to acquire resources and to gain a competitive advantage in the marketplace. They include access to a broader talent pool, to be an employer of choice, to mirror an organization's customer base, and to improve customer–stakeholder relationships. Some employers also believe that managing diversity is a corporate social responsibility, that is, it is seen as the right thing to do. Few consider it to be a legal requirement, suggesting that they do not see it as compliance cost or an administrative burden, but rather a matter of strategic advantage. There is evidence that the shift from compliance with employment equity to the business case for managing diversity has resulted in more positive employment outcomes for minorities. As an example, in 2006, the private sector reported 14.9 per cent of visible minorities as compared to 8.6 per cent in the public sector, when the available rate for visible minorities in the workforce is at 12.6 per cent (see Table 4.2). See Table 4.5 for a development of employment equity legislation and workplace diversity management in Canada.

There has also been a noticeable shift from focusing only on the four designated groups specified under the EEA to a broader approach of managing diversity to include sexual minorities or gays, lesbians, bi-sexual and trans-gendered people (commonly referred to as sexual minorities in Canada). In 2005, Canada legalized same-sex marriage, and this recognition has led to changes in workplace attitudes and policies towards sexual minorities. Complementing this, the Supreme Court of Canada ruled in 2007 that a federal law denying benefits to same-sex spouses was unconstitutional. Today, as a result of protections under the Canadian Human Rights Code and the Charter of Rights and Freedoms, most employers in Canada provide the same benefits structure to all employees, regardless of sexual orientation, as part of their managing diversity policies.

As a result of these recent developments, sexual minorities are more open about their same-sex relationships and have gained access to important family benefits such as medical and dental benefits, parental leave, and other group benefits that were normally reserved for heterosexual couples. Organizations that were federally regulated since 1986 under the EEA, such as banks, and FCP employers, such as universities, were at the forefront of this broader inclusive managing diversity movement. For example, Beth Grudzinski, Vice-President, Corporate Diversity, at the Toronto-Dominion (TD) Bank says that they have been 'working hard to create an environment where every employee and customer feels comfortable, regardless of their sexual orientation' (Habib, 2009, p.E1). The TD Bank made same-sex benefits available to their 45000 Canadian-based employees in 2002 when it integrated with Canada Trust, which had already implemented these policies as early as 1995. They also have an Employee Pride Network of about 600 TD members to share their ideas, experiences and strategies that have helped boost the number of employees accessing same-sex benefits by 36 per cent over the past two years, between March 2006 and March 2008.

Summary and conclusion

The changing demographic profile of the Canadian population is having a considerable impact on the Canadian workplace and marketplace. It already has an English and French heritage; the influx of new immigrants, particularly from Asian and the Pacific region, is contributing to the diversity of the workplace and economy. This increasing ethnocultural diversity in the workforce has created challenges for Canadian organizations. The Canadian multicultural policy was deliberately created to encourage immigrants to retain their cultural heritage rather than to assimilate.

The Royal Commission on Equality in Employment, which resulted in the implementation of the 1986 Employment Equity Act in Canada, seeks to eliminate employment barriers facing historically disadvantaged groups, such as women, visible minorities, aboriginal peoples and people with disabilities. Although most Canadian organizations say that they value diversity, a majority have not yet achieved representation rates for women and visible minorities that match or exceed their availabilities in the workforce. An analysis of the data from the EEA *Annual Reports* also indicates that women and minorities are not at all well represented at senior management levels. Employers still have a long way to go to remove barriers that have prevented women and minorities from reaching senior management positions. Konrad (2007) suggested that one way to improve the representation of women and minorities is by providing training, mentoring and developmental opportunities to high-potential candidates. For example,

Vinnicombe and Singh (2003) found that women-only training can help women develop their leadership strengths in order to access leadership positions. Overall, employment equity has improved the human resource practices, such as employment policies that support employment equity, increased the representation of women and minorities in the workplace, and narrowed wage gaps in Canada. Employers see diversity as a strategic advantage rather than an administrative issue, which has contributed to the improved employment outcomes for women and minorities. In particular, visible minorities

Summary table for Canada

Existence of anti-discrimination legislation	Canadian Human Rights Act (1982)
Criteria covered by anti-discrimination legislation	Section (15) guarantees equality rights and equal protection under the law to individuals regardless of 'race, national or ethnic origin, colour, religion, sex, age, or mental or physical impairment'
Criteria for which the reporting of quantitative data and their communication to a public administration are compulsory	Employment Equity Act (1986) seeks to increase the participation of aboriginal peoples, people with disabilities, visible minorities and women in the workforce
Criteria covered by 'affirmative' or 'positive' action legislation other than unemployment- or income-based	Aboriginal peoples, people with disabilities, visible minorities and women
Existence of a discourse or debate about 'non-discrimination' or 'equality'	Yes
Existence of a discourse or debate about 'diversity'	Yes
Year or period when the 'discrimination' concept started to disseminate in management literature in the country	Blakely and Harvey (1988) first published the effectiveness of employment equity in the *Journal of Business Ethics*
Year or period when the diversity concept started to disseminate in management literature in the country	Christine Taylor from the Conference Board of Canada popularized 'Building a Business Case for Diversity' in 1995
Who pushed the 'diversity' agenda?	Canada was the first country in the world to enact legislation (the Multiculturalism Act) in 1985. Since then, private sector employers have begun to push the 'business case' for diversity agenda
Existence of a professional association representing diversity professionals and year of creation	The Human Resources Professional Association was first established in Ontario in 1990
Existence of a professional association representing diversity scholars and year of creation	The Women in Management Division of the Administrative Sciences Association of Canada (ASAC) was first established in 1989. The Division was renamed Gender and Diversity in Organizations Division in 2001. ASAC is the national association of management professors in Canada

exceeded their representation rate in the private sector, given the shift from compliance with employment equity to managing diversity because it is good for business.

Some gaps continue to exist, however. For example, visible minorities remain under-represented at senior management levels. To achieve true equality in the workplace, organizations will need to build a more inclusive workplace, by changing their employment practices such as policies on recognizing foreign credentials and work experiences, and by implementing organizational strategies to develop and promote a demographically diverse workforce. The current economic climate has already seen organizations laying off employees and reducing their training budgets. Forty-two per cent of organizations surveyed by the Society of Human Resources Management indicated that they will reduce expenses on programmes such as anti-harassment and diversity training (Zeidner, 2009). Organizations must exercise care in maintaining their programmes and diverse workforces so that the gains from diversity are not reversed.

Notes

1. The preparation of this chapter was supported in part by Laurentian University and Dalhousie University. The authors would like to thank Alain Klarsfeld for his leadership and guidance.
2. The Pay Equity Act, widely considered to be the most comprehensive in North America, was enacted in the Province of Ontario in 1988 (McDonald and Thornton, 1998). Since Canada is a federation, both the federal and provincial governments can enact legislation on labour standards. Separate legislation has since been enacted in other provincial jurisdictions (see Hart, 2002, for a review).
3. Visible minority, under criteria established by the Employment Equity Act (EEA), refers to a person who is non-Caucasian in race or non-white in colour. Under the EEA, an aboriginal person is not considered to be a visible minority.
4. The annual reports for a particular year appear the following year after approval from the Canadian Parliament.
5. For more details on the FCP, see http://www.hrsdc.gc.ca/en/lp/lo/lswe/we/programs/fcp/criteria/index-we. shtml.
6. Defined as those who have been in Canada for five years or fewer.

References

Abella, J.R.S. (1984), *Equality in Employment: A Royal Commission Report*, Toronto, ON: Minister of Supply and Services Canada.

Agocs, C. (2002), 'Canada's employment equity legislation and policy, 1987–2000', *International Journal of Manpower*, **22/23** (3), 256–76.

Agocs, C. and Burr, C. (1996), 'Employment equity, affirmative action and managing diversity: assessing the differences', *International Journal of Manpower*, **17** (4/5), 30–45.

Bakan, A.B. and Kobayashi, A. (2000), 'Employment equity policy in Canada: an interprovincial comparison', Cat. No. SW21-46/1999E.

Benimadhu, P.P. and Wright, R. (1991), 'Employment equity: impact of the legislation', *Canadian Business Review*, **18** (2), 22–5.

Blakely, J.H. and Harvey, E.B. (1988), 'Socioeconomic change and lack of change: employment equity policies in the Canadian context', *Journal of Business Ethics*, **7**, 133–50.

Breton, R. (1986), 'Multiculturalism and Canadian nation building', in A. Cairns and C. Williams (eds), *The Politics of Gender, Ethnicity and Language in Canada*, Toronto: University of Toronto Press, Chapter 2.

Burke, R.J. and Ng, E. (2005), 'The changing nature of work and organizations: implications for human resource management', *Human Resource Management Review*, **16** (2), 86–94.

Burleton, D. (2002), 'The demographic challenge: slowing population, aging workforce trends more severe in Canada than in the U.S.', *TD Forum on Living Standards*.

Canadian Business (2004), '*Diversity Pays*, 29 March.

Catalyst and The Diversity Institute (2007), 'Career advancement in corporate Canada: a focus on visible minorities – survey findings', retrieved 10 December 2007 from http://www.catalyst.org/files/full/Career%20 Advancement%20in%20Corporate%20Canada,%20A%20focus%20on%20visible%20minorities-%20 Survey%20Findings.pdf.

Citizenship and Immigration Canada (2006), 'Facts and figures 2006: immigration overview: permanent residents', retrieved 10 December 2007 from http://www.cic.gc.ca/english/resources/statistics/facts2006/permanent/12.asp.

Conference Board of Canada (2004a), *Performance and Potential 2004–05: How can Canada Prosper in Tomorrow's World?*, Ottawa: Conference Board of Canada.

Conference Board of Canada (2004b), *The Voices of Visible Minorities: Speaking Out on Breaking Down Barriers*, Ottawa: Conference Board of Canada.

Conference Board of Canada (2006), *Report on Diversity: Priorities, Practices, and Performance in Canadian Organizations*, Ottawa: Conference Board of Canada.

Cornish, M. (1996), 'Employment and pay equity in Canada: success brings both attacks and new initiatives', *Canada–US States Law Journal*, **22**, 265–78.

Cox, T.H. (1991), 'The multicultural organization', *Academy of Management Executive*, **5** (2), 45–56.

Cox, T.H. and Blake, S. (1991), 'Managing cultural diversity: implications for organizational competitiveness', *Academy of Management Executive*, **5** (3), 45–56.

Employment Equity Act: Annual Report 2000, Gatineau, QC: Human Resources and Social Development Canada.

Employment Equity Act: Annual Report 2002, Gatineau, QC: Human Resources and Social Development Canada.

Employment Equity Act: Annual Report 2005, Gatineau, QC: Human Resources and Social Development Canada.

Employment Equity Act: Annual Report 2006, Gatineau, QC: Human Resources and Social Development Canada.

Employment Equity Act: Annual Report 2007, Gatineau, QC: Human Resources and Social Development Canada.

Erridge, A. and Fee, R. (2001), 'The impact of contract compliance policies in Canada – perspectives from Ontario', *Journal of Public Procurement*, **1** (1), 51–70.

Fleras, A. and Elliot, J.L. (1996), *Unequal Relations: An Introduction to Race and Ethnic Dynamics in Canada*, Scarborough: Prentice Hall Canada.

Gunderson, M. (2002), 'The evolution and mechanics of pay equity in Ontario', *Canadian Public Policy*, **28** (1), 117–31.

Habib, Marlene (2009), 'Same-Sex at work. Report on diversity', *The Globe and Mail*, Section E, Monday, 26 January.

Hart, S.M. (2002), 'Unions and pay equity bargaining in Canada', *Relations Industrielle*, **57** (4), 609–29.

Henry, F. and Jain, H. (1991), 'When inequality is built right into the system', *The Globe and Mail*, 12 April.

Henry, F., Tator, C., Mattis, W. and Rees, T. (1995), *The Colour of Democracy: Racism in Canadian Society*, Toronto: Harcourt Brace and Company Canada.

Human Resources and Social Development Canada (2002), 'Evaluation of the Federal Contractors Program; Final Report. Evaluation and Data Development, Strategic Policy. Retrieved 21 December, 2009 from http://www.servicecanada.gc.ca/eng/cs/sp/hrcdc/edd/reports/2002-000615/spah183_e.pdf.

Jain, H.C. (1993), 'Employment equity and visible minorities: Have the federal policies worked?', *Canadian Labour Law Journal*, **1** (4), 389–408.

Jain, H.C. and Hackett, R.D. (1989), 'Measuring the effectiveness of employment equity programmes in Canada: public policy and a survey', *Canadian Public Policy*, **XV** (2), 189–204.

Jain, H.C. and Lawler, J.L. (2004), 'Visible minorities under the Canadian Employment Equity Act: 1987–1999', *Relations Industrielles*, **59** (3), 585–611.

Jain, H.C., Sloane, P.J. and Horwitz, F.M. (2003), *Employment Equity and Affirmative Action: An International Comparison*, Armonk, NY: M.E. Sharpe.

Johnston, W.B. and Packer, A.H. (1987), *Workforce 2000: Work and Workers in the 21st Century*, Indianapolis, IN: Hudson Institute.

Kelly, E. and Dobbin, F. (1998), 'How affirmative action became diversity management', *American Behavioral Scientist*, **41** (7), 960–84.

Kerthen, H. (1997), 'Equity in Employment as a Means of Minority Incorporation: Some results from a 1990 Toronto Survey', *Multiculturalism in North America and Europe*.

Kirby, D.C. and Murrell, A.J. (1995), 'Managing diversity within a global context: issues and directions for future research', Administrative Sciences Association of Canada, Windsor, Ontario, ASAC.

Kirchmeyer, C. and McLellan, J. (1991), 'Capitalizing on ethnic diversity: an approach to managing the diverse workgroups of the 1990s', *Canadian Journal of Administrative Sciences*, **8** (2), 72–9.

Konrad, A.M. (2007), 'The effectiveness of human resource management practices for promoting women's careers', in D. Bilimoria and S.K. Piderit (eds), *Handbook on Women in Business and Management*, Cheltenham, UK and Northampton, MA, USA: Edward Elgar, pp. 254–77.

Labour Canada (2006), 'Ten years experience: A background issues paper on the Employment Equity Act and

Federal Contractors Program in preparation for the parliamentary review 2006', Gatineau, Quebec: Human Resources and Social Development Canada.

Leck, J.D. and Saunders, D.M. (1992), 'Hiring women: the effects of Canada's Employment Equity Act', *Canadian Public Policy*, **18** (2), 203–20.

Leck, J.D. (2002), 'Making employment equity programmes work for women', *Canadian Public Policy*, **28** (S1), 85–100.

Marron, K. (2004), 'Equality struggle remains in law', *The Globe and Mail*, B-15, 19 April.

McDonald, N. (1990), '*The McDonald Guide to Managing Diversity*, Cross Cultural Communications International Inc. Winnipeg, Manitoba: Canada.

McDonald, J.A. and Thornton, R.J. (1998), 'Private sector experience with pay equity in Ontario', *Canadian Public Policy*, **24** (2), 185–208.

Multiculturalism Canada (2007), *Annual Report on the Operation of the Canadian Multiculturalism Act 2005–2006*, Gatineau, QC: Canadian Heritage.

National Anti-Racism Council of Canada (2007), *Racial Discrimination in Canada*, Toronto: NARCC.

Ng, E.S.W. and Burke, R.J. (2005), 'Person–organization fit and the war for talent: does diversity management make a difference?', *International Journal of Human Resource Management*, **16** (7), 1195–210.

Ng, E.S.W. and Tung, R.L. (1998), 'Ethno-cultural diversity and organizational effectiveness: a field study', *The International Journal of Human Resource Management*, **9** (6), 980–95.

Richard, O.C. (2000), 'Racial diversity, business strategy, and firm performance: a resource-based view', *Academy of Management Journal*, **43** (2), 164–77.

Robinson, G. and Dechant, K. (1997), 'Building a business case for diversity', *Academy of Management Executive*, **11** (3), 21–31.

Statistics Canada (2003), *The Changing Profile of Canada's Labour Force*, Ottawa: Minister of Industry.

Statistics Canada (2007a), 'Immigration in Canada: a portrait of the foreign-born population, 2006 census: immigrants came from many countries', retrieved 7 December 2007 from http://www12.statcan.ca/english/census06/analysis/immcit/asia.cfm.

Statistics Canada (2007b), 'Immigration in Canada: a portrait of the foreign-born population, 2006 census: findings', retrieved 10 December 2007 from http://www12.statcan.ca/english/census06/analysis/immcit/index.cfm.

Statistics Canada (2008), 'Immigrants' education and required job skills', retrieved 6 March 2009 from http://www.statcan.gc.ca/cgi-bin/af-fdr.cgi?l=eng&loc=2008112/pdf/10766-eng.pdf.

Vinnicombe, S. and Singh, V. (2003), 'Women-only management training: an essential part of women's leadership development', *Journal of Change Management*, **3**, 294–306.

Watson, W.E., Kumar, K. and Michaelsen, L.K. (1993), 'Cultural diversity's impact on interaction process and performance: comparing homogeneous and diverse task groups', *Academy of Management Journal*, **36** (3), 590–602.

Weiner, N. (2002), 'Effective redress of pay inequities', *Canadian Public Policy*, **28** (S1), 101–15.

Wright, P., Ferris, S.P., Hiller, J.S. and Kroll, M. (1995), 'Competitive through management of diversity: effects on stock price evaluation', *Academy of Management Journal*, **38** (1), 272–87.

Zeidner, R. (2009), 'Wielding the budget tax ax may be inevitable, but pink slips and benefits cuts don't have to follow', *HRMagazine*, February.

5 Equality and diversity in the French context

Anne-Françoise Bender, Alain Klarsfeld and Jacqueline Laufer

Introduction

For a few years now, a national debate has emerged in France around the notion of diversity and to some extent about the issue of diversity as a 'business case'. While the issue of equal opportunity between men and women had been on the agenda for many years, diversity, and specifically the dimension of ethnic diversity, has come forward in the public debate only in recent years, as a result of an increasing awareness of the difficulties and shortcomings linked to the French model of equality and integration of immigrants and their descendants.

Indeed, in France, contrary to the USA and the UK, the issues of equal opportunity and of diversity have developed recently as a result of a new awareness of the difficulties of the French model of equality based on equality of rights for all citizens. Formal equality of rights, according to the republican model, was originally based on a denial of any differences between citizens.

The central issue has been for a long time the implementation of equality between men and women, which has its roots in the French Revolution of 1789, and in the French Declaration of Human and Citizens' Rights (Déclaration des Droits de l'Homme et du Citoyen), which excluded women from the citizenship rights granted to men: liberty and equality (Fraisse, 1995).

While ethnic diversity was supposed to be dealt with by the model of integration of all individual citizens in the Republic, transcending all their individual characteristics – cultural, religious, social – it is the increasing awareness of the multiple inequalities and discriminations affecting ethnic minorities which has urged the need to tackle the issue of 'diversity' (Weil, 2005).

In France, the debate on diversity is not therefore the result of criticism of 'affirmative action', which does not exist as such in France for ethnic and racial minorities. Rather, it follows criticism of a model of formal equality of rights, which 'ignores' the inequalities and the discriminations that it produces, and leads to the question of whether France should adopt affirmative action types of policies in the area of ethnic diversity. However, affirmative action, or 'positive action', as it is sometimes termed in France, is considered by many as a risky strategy, one that would privilege 'identities' and the self-seclusion of minorities rather than 'equality' (Noiriel, 1998). Furthermore, while in the USA there is a long tradition of 'counting' ethnic and religious categories, in France, such a 'counting' appears illegal and illegitimate, in virtue of the principle that forbids any discrimination between categories and between individuals based on such criteria (Weil, 2005; Méron, 2009).

This emerging national debate on diversity will also be put in context with the development of a legal framework designed to tackle discrimination, especially in the field of employment. The new awareness of a variety of possible discriminations, together with the recent strengthening of anti-discrimination laws, developed simultaneously with the debate on diversity.

In the first section, we shall bring a historical perspective to the implementation of equal opportunities for women, and the situation concerning the integration of immigrants and ethnic minorities. We shall present the general legal anti-discrimination framework, and public policies in specific areas other than gender: disability, union affiliation, social deprivation, age, sexual orientation, religion.

In the second section, we shall describe the advent of diversity as a response to the shortcomings of social policies and the integration of immigrants and their descendants. We shall present the existing state of diversity-related research and pending issues in relation to the implementation of diversity policies.

We shall make frequent references to a distinction between two conceptions traditionally opposed to achieve equality: that of 'equality of rights', where everyone should be treated in the same manner; and that of 'positive action', where preferential treatment should be given to those who are subjected to inequalities (Kelly and Dobbin, 1998; Lyon-Caen, 1990). This distinction is widely acknowledged in the literature, although the terms vary considerably among authors to specify its underlying concepts.[1]

1.   The development of equality issues and of an equality legal framework

To understand the context in which the debate on diversity has relatively suddenly and rapidly emerged, it seems useful to give some perspectives on how the issues of gender equality and integration of immigrants in French society have been stated. Indeed, these two issues are the most salient in the diversity debate and emerging policies in France, as in other countries, although diversity does raise the issue of the many motives of discrimination in the employment sphere.

Concerning women's equality, the main problem has been the inefficiency of an equal-right principle to overcome the structural inequalities between men and women on the labour market and within firms. While women have had access to full-time employment, the ambiguities of public policies in the field of 'conciliation' between work and family have led us to consider that the implementation of professional equality could be considered as a secondary objective. As a consequence, in 2005, women's average wage was still 81 per cent of that of men. Even when partially controlling for occupational category (manual worker, clerical employee, management position etc.), women's average wage was only between 77 per cent and 94 per cent of that of men according to occupational category, management being the category where women's wages are smallest as a proportion of men's wages (77 per cent) (INSEE, 2005).

Concerning immigrants and ethnic minorities, the policies towards immigrants were aimed at 'assimilation' and there has been a paradoxical tension between a tendency to make immigrants 'invisible' and a tendency to assign them to a permanent status of 'marginality', through, for example, the use of the same word of *immigrés* (immigrants) to refer to people born abroad, but also to refer to people of foreign origin though born in France and holders of the French nationality (Fassin, 2002; Rea and Tripier, 2008).

1.1   Gender equality in France: from exclusion to positive action
Concerning women's equality and professional equality, France can be characterized by a relatively egalitarian culture, combined with a good legal basis for equality and with relatively women-friendly policies in the field of reconciliation between work and family. However, it can be said that equality between men and women is far from being achieved: employment segregation, glass ceiling phenomenon and unequal pay are still on the agenda (Laufer, 2003).

From inequality and protection to equality   During the nineteenth century, the unequal status of women in society led to a variety of legal and policy measures aimed at protecting the role of women workers as mothers. After affording special protection to children, the state extended it to women in 1892 through legislation restricting the length of the working day and prohibiting night work in manufacturing industry. The male-dominated unions supported this protective logic, given that it protected their male members' job status by excluding women from certain jobs (Lanquetin, 1998; *Travail, genre et sociétés*, 2001). A second aspect of this protective logic was the introduction in 1909 of eight-week maternity leave without interrupting the work contract. In the context of this protective logic, public policies have been aimed at protecting simultaneously women at work and the family, by considering women both as mothers and as workers.

The development of state feminism   Starting in the 1960s with the development of women's employment, a political, legal and institutional dynamic emerged, linked with increasing government intervention in the field of women's employment, described as 'state feminism' (Lévy, 1988). Central to this dynamic was the issue of moving from the principle of equality between men and women, which was written in the 1946 French constitution, to real equality.

The growing number of sociological studies on women's employment equality, the activities of women in trade unions and as representatives of women's associations, and the establishment of government bodies in charge of women's work issues have together contributed to a shift in how public policies have dealt with women's employment situation (Mazur, 1995).[2] However, for a long time, the reduction of discrimination against women, of sex-based segregation in the labour market, of salary inequalities between men and women and of sex-based differentials in access to vocational training and higher-level jobs have remained distant goals.

From the 1960s until today, French state feminism has had to confront the contradiction with policies that stressed the family role of women, an orientation described as 'familialism'. On the one hand, feminism and the various policy and administrative bodies linked with women's rights have worked towards the development of women's access to work and to employment equality; on the other hand, public policies have not, for example in the field of childcare, given enough recognition to the fact that both fathers *and* mothers were economically active (Commaille, 1993).

The legal framework of gender equality: from 'equal rights' to 'positive action'?   The principle by which the law guarantees women the same rights as men was established in the Preamble to the 1946 French Constitution. In accordance with this principle, equal rights were to be asserted gradually in political and economic contexts.

Following the constitutional statement, equal pay was the first issue addressed. In July 1946, a decree abolished lower pay rates for women. Collective agreements in 1950 extended the principle to equal pay. However, the principle of equal pay for the same work, or for work of equal value, was established only in 1972, in a law that omitted to specify what work of equal value meant and that left untouched many practices that gave rise to gendered pay differences as well as to the existing hierarchy of men's and women's jobs.

The principle that recruitment and dismissal should not be influenced by the possibility of pregnancy or by the sex and family status of the person was introduced with the law of July 1975, although exceptions were allowed if employers presented a 'legitimate motive' for treating women differently from men.

The 1983 law on professional equality improved equal rights for women in the world of work and defined 'equal value' to strengthen the application of equal pay legislation. Work of 'equal value' was defined as involving a comparable level of professional knowledge, or equivalent qualifications, experience and responsibilities. The onus of proof in the case of pay discrimination was reversed; it is now the employer who must produce the justification for unequal pay (Lanquetin, 2000). As for equal treatment in hiring and firing, the 1983 legislation abolished the notion of 'legitimate motive' from the 1975 law. Instead, a limited list of jobs was established where recruitment could favour one sex over the other.

A second objective of the 1983 law, referred to as the Roudy Law, after the Minister of Women's Rights who proposed it, was to inscribe in French employment law a coherent approach to employment equality. While monitoring sex equality at the company level was the essential objective, the new Roudy Law set out the social and economic information to be given annually by employers to the work council in the firm, made up of trade union and other representatives. The objective was to strengthen the process of collective bargaining between employers and trade unions, and to integrate a concern for professional equality into collective bargaining. A third objective of the 1983 law was to introduce the principle of positive action for women into the French legal code, in conformity with the EEC directive of 1976. Positive action was recognized as a necessary step beyond an equal rights approach to employment equality. The goal was to have an effective and tangible impact on the inequalities that characterize the situation of women in the labour market. The firm was the main unit targeted for action; management and unions were clearly designated as the key agents in the process of implementation of positive action, with collective bargaining expected to encompass equality at work (Laufer, 2003).

Two mechanisms were developed to further these goals. The first was a requirement for firms employing more than 50 employees to draw up an annual report on the comparative situation of women and men in the firm in terms of recruitment, promotion, pay, qualification, training and working conditions. Each work council at the firm level was to receive such a report. In this way, social partners were to be given a basis for debate and negotiation in the field of equal opportunity. A second mechanism concerned negotiated equality plans. These were to be instruments of positive action that set out temporary measures in favour of women in recruitment, promotion, training and working conditions at company level. However, they were not made compulsory but only encouraged through public subsidies.

A 9 May 2001 law on equal employment reinforced some of the provisions of the 1983 law, by making employment equality a major theme of collective bargaining. The law introduced more precise indicators in the annual report of the comparative situation of women and men. The negotiation on work equality was also made compulsory at the firm and at the sector level, either through specific negotiation on equality or by integrating equality objectives into the set of compulsory negotiations. Negotiations must take place every year or every three years, depending on whether the social partners have come to any agreement.

Positive action as understood in the 1983 law was still an option for French firms: equality plans were encouraged but not compulsory. In other words, tools were provided to employers, but no commitment was made to correct inequalities. This has changed since the 9 May 2001 law and the 2004 intersectoral agreement on gender equality. This agreement contains the first commitment, made by French employers collectively, to gradually reduce the residual 5 per cent pay differential measured by the French statistical institute INSEE. Finally, in March 2006, a law was passed that sets an explicit deadline for the fulfilment of the said objective: the end of 2010. This objective is to be implemented sector by sector. This law also grants women who take maternity leave the average individual pay rise granted to their colleagues. Whether the elimination of the gender pay gap will be effective by December 2010, and how strict the actual enforcement efforts by the government will be, remains to be seen.

1.2   Perspectives on the status of immigrants and their descendants

The emergence of the debate concerning diversity in France can be seen as being largely related to a growing and public awareness of the shortcomings of the French model of integration in respect of immigrants and their descendants, which is the subject of this section.

France has been a regular destination for migrant workers since the middle of the nineteenth century. The influx of immigrants has been moderate but steady ever since, in the region of 0.2 per cent of the French population annually. Migrants make up 5 million persons, or about 8 per cent of the French population, which was 64.3 million in January 2009. Out of these 5 million persons born abroad, 2 million have acquired French nationality (Héran, 2007; Pla, 2009). Roughly speaking, French migrants can be split into three equal components. In 2006, 1.7 million were born in another EU country, mainly Spain, Portugal and Italy, and 1.5 million were born in Maghreb (Algeria, Morocco, Tunisia). Finally, 1.4 million were born in another part of the world, mainly Sub-saharan African countries – Senegal and Mali being the principal countries concerned – and Asia – Turkey being the main provenance – followed by China (Borrel, 2006). Over the last 30 years, the proportion of immigrants in the French population has remained fairly stable, rising slightly from 7.4 per cent in 1974 to 8 per cent.

However, and in spite of the fact that immigration has for many years represented an important share of the French labour force, it can be said that 'France is a country of immigration which ignores itself' (author's translation from Schnapper, 1991; Rea and Tripier, 2008). This situation must be considered with regard to the French model of citizenship, which privileges an objective of 'assimilation' of immigrants, as opposed to the 'differentialist' vision, which characterizes other countries such as the USA but also the UK and Germany. While this differentialist vision can rely on various criteria, it leads to legitimizing the perception of a 'segmented humanity' (translation by author of Todd, 1994, p. 12, quoted in Rea and Tripier, 2008).

While the 'ordonnance de 1945' defined a legal basis favouring equal treatment of migrants (Weil, 2008, p. 86), French migration policy has ever since been characterized – like many other European countries – by recurrent debates and legal evolutions. For example, such issues as the limitation of the number of migrants because of the employment situation, the control of 'illegal' migration, the access to the status of foreign resident (especially through the 2003 and 2006 laws) and the issue of 'chosen migration' are all now seen in the context of the Schengen Treaty.[3]

Integration versus assimilation   The ambivalences of France's immigration policy can also be traced through the various notions and concepts that have emerged as to the status of immigrants and of their descendants.

Significantly, the notion of 'assimilation' has been progressively rejected because of its colonial and ethnocentric connotation, and replaced by the notion of 'integration' in numerous research papers and public debates (Dewitte, 1999). Significantly also, many other terms and notions have appeared in relation to the immigration issue: multiculturalism, exclusion, ethnicity, discrimination and, most recently, diversity. As noted by Dewitte (1999), this situation illustrates the unsettled debate as to what exactly is meant by the term 'integration', this debate being now increasingly influenced by the European context. If, theoretically, immigration is open to all national origins, European migrants are likely to be considered more favourably than those coming from African countries (Weil, 2005; Rea and Tripier, 2008).

Immigration: a legitimate research subject?   Another characteristic of the French situation concerning immigration is the fact that it has not, for a long time, been considered as a legitimate research topic for historians and for sociologists (Noiriel, 2001, p. 67). As noted by Noiriel (2001), this situation should be related to the 'epistemological obstacle', which represents the fact of understanding a phenomenon that 'radically questions the theme of national unity' (translation by the author from Noiriel, 2001, p. 68). This process has led to what Noiriel (2001) describes as 'an absence of social visibility of immigration in France' (translation by the author) and has been a powerful means to reduce, in the second generation, the cultural specificities of immigrant communities, without however suppressing them completely.

As far as sociological research is concerned, Rea and Tripier (2008) analyse this difficult emergence of research on immigration in a national context characterized by a 'denial of memory' (Rea and Tripier, 2008, p. 19) as to the status of immigration in French history and society.[4] In this context, research on immigration has first tended to deal nearly exclusively with the problems faced by immigration policies: health and accommodation of immigrants or work adaptation. Immigrants were considered only as an extra workforce. As Rea and Tripier emphasize, while immigration becomes a political issue, researchers tended to share the republican optimism as to the capacity of French society to fully integrate migrants. If they were of Marxist orientation, they would consider ethnic origin (like gender) as an obstacle to an analysis based on class. Again, it was as if a sociological study of racism and/or discrimination would risk confirming the existence of ethnic communities, a threat to the French model of integration, or would contribute to the fragmentation of working-class struggles, compromising the common objective of the anti-capitalist movement (Rea and Tripier, 2008). However, while French sociology has taken some time to study immigrants, major research was carried out in the 1970s on the situation of immigrants, on their relationships with other workers, on the absence of social and professional mobility, and on their relationships with unions (Tripier, 1990). Also, it should be noted that the sociology of immigration has progressively enlarged its scope in France as in other countries. It has extended to racism and to inter-ethnic relations, when it appeared that the presence of migrants had to be analysed on a long-term basis: 'Was the European situation getting closer to the American situation? What should national identity be in a diversified society?' (Rea and Tripier, 2003, p. 36).

Immigration and origin: a legitimate basis for positive action? Mirroring the difficult emergence of the study of immigration and integration in the French social sciences, French law does not deal with national, 'ethnic' or 'racial' origin as an area where specific positive action should be undertaken.[5] In this area, progress has been made towards more formal equality of rights, but there is a strong reluctance to adopt positive action legislation. Many commentators who agree that immigrants and their descendants suffer from discrimination on the labour market, and who are in favour of a stricter enforcement of the existing 'equality of rights' provisions now provided by the law (see section below), are opposed to any move towards positive action, and prefer the existing 'equality of rights' approach (Amadieu, 2004b).

1.3 General legal anti-discrimination framework in France

The general anti-discrimination legislation is an all-encompassing, equality-of-right framework, which forbids and penalizes discrimination based on an extensive list of criteria. It was developed gradually through the 1980s, 1990s and particularly in the 2000s following European legislation in 2000.

Equality of rights is at the very root of the 1789 Declaration of Human Rights. It was reaffirmed in the French 1946 Constitution's preamble and included in the 1958 Constitution. This was reinforced by Article 119 of the Rome Treaty and ILO Convention 111 of 1958, which was ratified by France in 1981. Under the influence of the Constitution, equality of treatment thus became a general principle of French labour law (Lattes, 1989).

Banning discrimination explicitly in employment matters came later. The French labour law anti-discrimination framework started in 1982 as a section devoted to the 'disciplinary' section (Sutter, 1983). It originally prohibited employers from adopting discriminatory decisions based on a limited list of criteria (gender, opinions, origin, union affiliation). Employment discrimination is an offence that is now punished by fines that can go up to €225 000 per discrimination for a company, €45 000 per discrimination for individuals, and up to three years' imprisonment for persons found guilty of discriminatory behaviour.

Discrimination criteria were recently expanded by EU directives adopted between 1997 and 2000, which triggered the adoption of the most serious advance in this area in France: a 2001 law that goes beyond the EU requirements. Since 2001, French law lists 16 prohibited discrimination criteria: origin, sex, family status, physical looks, family

name, disability, health condition, genetic characteristics, behaviour, sexual orientation, age, political opinion, union activity, religion, real or supposed nationality, ethnic
group or race. Beyond the prohibited criteria, French anti-discrimination law covers
most employment and human resource management decision areas (recruitment, training and development, compensation, promotion, discipline, among others) where initial
anti-discrimination laws focused on discipline. It also includes the European provisions regarding the reversal of the burden of proof prescribed by the European Union
after 1997:[6] as long as the employee can provide elements from which discrimination
may be presumed (but not firmly established), it is up to the employer to demonstrate
that he or she based his or her decision on objective, strictly job-related data. Before
this, the burden of the proof rested on the employee alone, although the French Cour
de Cassation (Supreme Court) had started to make use of this new proof mechanism
before it was introduced in French law, in particular in resolving union discrimination
lawsuits (Klarsfeld, 2005). In line with EU directives, French employment discrimination law also explicitly protects workers against indirect discriminations from 2001,
whereas previous texts did not refer to indirect discrimination. The French definition of
indirect discrimination is that of the EU and was adopted in the French legislation in
2008. Indirect discrimination exists 'where an apparently neutral provision, criterion or
practice would put persons having a [particular characteristic covered by the law] at a
particular disadvantage compared with other persons'.[7] Another feature is that it grants
a 'right to sue' to unions and non-governmental organizations in lieu of the victim of
discrimination, provided the victim agrees. No such right existed before 2001. All this
is a clear consequence of the influence of European directives (Lanquetin, 1995, 2000).
Moreover, claiming one's right under French legislation has been made considerably
more accessible since the creation of the HALDE (Haute Autorité de Lutte contre
les Discriminations et pour l'Egalité, High Authority against Discrimination and for
Equality) at the end of 2004. This Authority has the right to investigate management
practices following employee claims, seek settlements and inflict fines, albeit much lower
than those in standard courts. Quantitatively, the HALDE's activity in dealing with
complaints is rising sharply: 7788 complaints were lodged with the HALDE in 2008, up
from 6222 in 2007, 4058 in 2006 and 1410 in 2005, its first year of functioning (HALDE,
2006, 2007, 2008). Before the creation of HALDE, there were no statistics regarding discrimination lawsuits, but from interviewing labour lawyers, it can be assumed that such
litigations were very rare (Klarsfeld, 2005).

1.4   Specific equality provisions in areas other than gender
We shall see that, as far as union activity, disability, age and social deprivation are concerned, legislation goes beyond an 'equality of rights' approach and encompasses some
form of positive action. Such is not the case for religion and sexual orientation, which
tend to fall more under the 'equality of rights' approach. We shall not present gender
equality policies, which have been discussed above, in Section 1.1. The debate on the
introduction of ethnicity- and race-based policies and legislation will be dealt with in the
second section, devoted to the advent of the notion of diversity in France.

Union affiliation and activity   The first sources providing protection against discrimination for union activity derive from case law. Cour de Cassation (French Supreme Court)

decisions setting forth this principle can be tracked as early as the 1920s (Lyon-Caen et al., 1999). The first law providing explicit banning of union discrimination was issued in 1956. It is an 'equality of rights' legislation stating that union members and activists should not be discriminated against in terms of discipline. At present, union members are mainly covered by this legislation. Beyond strict equality of rights, union representatives benefit from special protection measures against dismissal: in order to dismiss a union representative – and a worker representative in general – employers are requested to solicit the approval of the labour administration, a protection from which no other category of worker benefits. This special protection is meant to compensate for the pressure and exposure to possible employer retaliation, to which union and worker representatives are subjected as part of their representation duties.

Disability   Disabled people are widely discriminated against on the French labour market and in society at large. At the end of 2006, they accounted for 8 per cent of the unemployed population, while they represented only 4.5 per cent of the workforce of French firms (Ministère du Travail, 2007). French law as regards disabled people started out as 'positive action' and still falls predominantly within this category. Indeed, the disabled form the first designated group for whom a strong affirmative framework has been designed in France, consisting in defining a recruitment quota of disabled workers to be hired by employers. Such legislation can be traced back to a 1924 law which imposed the recruitment of 'mutilated' World War One veterans. The term 'disabled worker' appeared in a law adopted in 1957 that defined the notion of 'employment priority' of disabled workers.[8] Ever since, the legislation adopted has tried to turn this 'priority' into actual employment, a challenge that still proves difficult to meet. A law passed in July 1987 obliges every French employer with more than 20 employees to employ a proportion of disabled workers of at least 6 per cent. This is typically a 'positive action' type of legislation, setting forth an explicit quota of disabled people to be hired by employers in order to remedy their unfavourable standing on the labour market. Employers not meeting this obligation have to pay a contribution to a body specializing in the integration of disabled people (the AGEFIPH, Association Nationale pour la Gestion du Fonds pour l'Insertion Professionnelle des Personnes Handicapées[9]). In 1990, another law was passed that prohibits discrimination based on disability and health status (unless justified by work requirements) as well as on private demeanors (Vie-Publique.fr). This latter piece of legislation is an 'equality of rights' legislation. Yet in 2005, 18 years after the enactment of the 1987 law, 27 per cent of all workplaces covered had not hired a single disabled worker, nor used a single subcontractor certified for employing disabled persons, and had opted for the payment of the full penalty instead (Amira, 2008).

The 2005 law sets much higher fines for companies that refuse to hire a 6 per cent target of disabled workers. The fine can go up to one year's pay of the national minimum salary[10] per missing disabled person for firms that have not initiated any action plan in favour of employing disabled people. It changes the mode of calculation of the percentage of disabled workers in favour of the latter, one of the main advances consisting in including subcontractors in the calculation perimeter of the total workforce upon which to base the 6 per cent share of disabled workers to hire. It includes more cases of disability in its perimeter. It sets up an obligation to bargain collectively every year in all covered firms and to bargain collectively every three years at the business-sector level.

It also introduces the European notion of 'reasonable accommodation' for disabled workers ('right to compensation' in the French legal terminology): employers have to make specific efforts to integrate disabled persons into the workplace. The burden of providing this reasonable accommodation rests both with the employer and with public authorities (Lattes, 2008).

Policy in favour of socially deprived urban areas   The 'politique de la ville' (literally, city policy) started out as a territory-based policy intended to improve accommodation of the poor in suburban areas (Weil, 2005). A certain percentage of publicly managed accommodation was allocated to the poor as part of a scheme to eliminate the slums around the major French cities in the 1960s and early 1970s. Although not explicitly targeting migrant workers or ethnic groups, the gradual elimination of slums concerned, *de facto*, migrant workers and their families, who composed the majority of the slum inhabitants. Throughout the 1970s, 1980s and 1990s and up to the present day, the 'politique de la ville' appears as a set of 'positive action' public policy responses to problems generated by the allocation of workers and their families to the worst part of the state-administered housing. Removing slums had removed neither poverty nor social segregation, due to the distance from the social housing to the more privileged city centres. Moreover, the architecture and urban planning of the publicly managed housing system, mainly anonymous, poorly maintained high-rise buildings, was also blamed for taking its toll on its inhabitants' quality of life, education, security and economic opportunities. The relocation of the poor into these buildings also coincided with the start of the recession after the first oil shock from 1973 onwards and the rise of unemployment. Against a background of riots and growing criminality, the 'politique de la ville' gradually came to include a range of initiatives from the early 1980s onwards, including priority education funding, youth training schemes, plans for fighting delinquency, drug addiction and dealing, plans for housing improvement, and, more recently (from the 1990s), tax incentives to attract employers into the deprived areas and foster economic development.

Age   Age turns out to be the main factor in employment discrimination in France (Guillemard, 2007), and has long been an official criterion of exclusion from the workplace, although it is undergoing dramatic legislative change at present. The very idea of 'early retirement' suggests that the exclusion of ageing workers has long been encouraged by social policies, rather than restricted by them. The same applies to age limits that, until recently, were used in most public sector and civil service jobs.[11] Such age limits are in the process of being removed at the time of writing (Agence France Presse, 2008; Collen, 2008). Awareness of the limitations in the funding of retirement, the low employment rate among older workers, evidence of discrimination affecting ageing workers (Amadieu, 2004a), but also the pressure resulting from European policies such as the European Employment Strategy and the 2000 European directive on equal treatment at work – all of these factors have prompted the idea that legislation should actively counter discrimination against ageing workers.

Beyond removing existing age discrimination and the inclusion of 'age' into the 'equality-of-right' legislation in 2001, French law now supports a positive action approach for ageing workers, in concordance with EU legislation. A national agreement between trade unions and employers' organizations on ageing workers was reached in March 2006, introducing an array of positive action measures: first, the agreement defines an employment target for the employment rate among workers aged between 55 and 65 to be raised from 36.8 per cent in 2006 to 50 per cent in 2010. Sector-level bargaining must define employment targets for ageing workers within their area of coverage; workers above 45 are entitled to a specific career interview every five years; employers have the possibility to hire ageing workers above 57 on fixed-term contracts for three years instead of 18 months, thus providing more flexibility of terms and conditions to ageing workers; the agreement prompts the removal of all limitations on the right of retired workers to continue working while receiving their retirement allowance. At the time of writing, a law was adopted whereby companies with 50 workers or more have to sign a collective agreement containing precise goals as to the proportion of ageing workforce to be achieved within a period of three years. Failing to sign such an agreement before 1 January 2010 will result in a penalty amounting to 1 per cent of the total wage bill.

Sexual orientation   There is a dearth of data on sexual orientation in France (Falcoz, 2008). Yet sexual orientation is one of the criteria covered by French law following the 2000 European directive regarding equal treatment at work. In spite of the difficulty inherent in measuring an invisible phenomenon, it was found, in recent research commissioned by the HALDE, that 4.1 per cent of men and 4 per cent of women in France admit to having had sexual relationships with someone of the same sex. Seventeen per cent of homosexuals have never revealed anything about their sexual orientation to their colleagues, while 66 per cent practise some form of dissimulation of their orientation. At least 40 per cent have experienced verbal discrimination in the form of derogatory comments on the way they dress, move, speak or on their hairstyle (Falcoz, 2008). Although they are covered by the umbrella legislation mentioned above, homosexuals still suffer from restriction of rights *vis-à-vis* heterosexuals, in the form of prohibition of homosexual marriages. Sexual orientations other than homosexuality (transsexuality, bisexuality) are rarely researched.

Religion   Religion parallels sexual orientation in that it is an 'invisible' form of diversity, one that will only surface if the employee reveals his or her religious beliefs. However, in the case of secularism (called '*laïcité*' in France), religion has been included in legislation for longer as a criterion on which no one can be discriminated against, and has given rise to an abundant case law. Numerous litigations have occurred whereby an employee has claimed the right to practise his or her religion at the workplace, or has sought to be exempted from certain tasks, or has been dismissed or disciplined for showing religious signs. However, beyond an equality-of-right framework, French law does not contain any 'positive action' provision in favour of any religion on the workplace, and court rulings in employment matters overall support the equality-of-rights conception. In the French conception of secularism, religion is a private matter. Everyone is free to practise his/her religion as long as it does not interfere with other people's freedom of beliefs and with the laws of the Republic. There has been a longstanding debate recently about the Islamic scarf in primary and secondary schools, the scarf conflicting with the banning of ostentatious religious affiliation signs in state schools and public services. The commission created to handle this question came to the conclusion that such banning was necessary in light of French secularism, but the decision was not taken light-heartedly and triggered much controversy in the Muslim community and elsewhere.

'Ethnicity', nationality and 'race'   These criteria are covered under the 'umbrella' equality-of-right legislation referred to above, but are not subjected to any positive action type of legislation. French law actually hinders anti-discrimination action in the area of ethnicity and race as it prohibits the collection of data about ethnic and racial origin,[12] let alone any positive action in favour of persons who would have been categorized through such data collection. Concerning nationality, the collection of data is legal and can provide a proxy, but positive action in favour of persons of a given nationality or their descendants would be considered discriminatory and is prohibited by the equality-of-right legislation described above. Such shortcomings in the French legislation partly explain the advent of the notion of diversity, as we shall see in the next section.

2.   The advent of diversity and diversity-related research

2.1   From the invisibility of migrants and their descendants to the notion of diversity
Although the 'social policies' described above probably improved the conditions, or at least limited the damage caused by years of poverty to specific ethnic groups as beneficiaries of such policies, they did not address ethnic or racial origin as such. That problems faced by many of the 'socially deprived' may be caused by ethnic prejudice and not just by lack of economic and social resources was never articulated, partly because such a frame of thought was a threat to the unity of France or of the working class, as shown in the preceding section. Yet research shows that groups of specific 'ethnic' origins, particularly people from North Africa and Africa, but also the 'black' and 'coloured' French from French overseas territories, clearly suffer a disadvantage on the labour market (CEREQ, 2004, 2006; Observatoire des Discriminations, 2004, 2005, 2006).

The debate on diversity and on the management of diversity has been developing in France for a decade, against a growing awareness that children of immigrants suffer a particular disadvantage that, according to many analysts, is not wholly explained by their social origin or by their place of residence. This evolution has led to an emphasis on the shortcomings of the French model of integration of immigrants and of immigrants' children. While unions had for a long time been the main channel of collective action and of access to citizenship rights for the immigrants, the development of a local community life, together with the development of the urban and housing problem, have moved the locus of integration to local life (Rea and Tripier, 2003).

The debate on the issue of diversity (and the development of the legal framework to fight discrimination) has shed light on relatively ignored phenomena: racism and discrimination in employment and career progression, which lead to the overlapping of a 'professional hierarchy' with an 'ethnic hierarchy' even if in principle the latter does not exist (Bataille, 1997); discrimination in access to employment (Rapport du Haut Conseil à l'Intégration, 1998; Rapport Fauroux, 2005; CEREQ, 2004, 2006, Observatoire des Discriminations, 2004, 2005, 2006); housing problems; and cities becoming the privileged setting of some of the key problems linked with integration, such as schooling and housing.

During that same period, the creation of the HALDE in 2004, the development of 'testing' studies as a procedure to evaluate the degree of discriminatory practices in firms, together with the development of a regulatory framework on discrimination, have contributed to make discriminatory practices increasingly visible and illegitimate in public opinion. A recent enquiry carried out by the HALDE indicated that among the personnel of private firms (employing more than 5000), 75 per cent think that it is very important to fight discriminatory practices; 31 per cent say that they have been victims of at least one discrimination and 27 per cent have witnessed such discrimination. A total of 74 per cent think that all the initiatives that prevent discriminatory practices are likely to improve the social climate (HALDE, 2007).

We would argue that, in France, the concept of diversity appeared in relation to the growing awareness, in the late 1990s, that problems faced by 'socially deprived' areas may be, if not caused, at least aggravated by employment discrimination towards specific ethnic origins (CEREQ, 2004, 2006). For instance, for youngsters of North African origin and holders of a low qualification obtained in 1998, the probability of being unemployed after five years on the labour market is 60 per cent higher than that of a young person whose parents were both born in France and with a similar qualification and presence on the labour market (CEREQ, 2006). Other researchers have shown that, for North Africans, the probability of exiting unemployment is about half that for French nationals, even after controlling for gender, age and education level (Gobillon et al., 2007). This awareness grew as a result of a strengthened EU employment strategy, legislation and programmes throughout the 1990s and 2000s, of non-governmental organizations active in the field of fighting ethnic discrimination, but also of specific business circles. It culminated after the November 2005 riots and the publication of the two CEREQ studies just mentioned and of the first widely publicized studies of employment discrimination around that year (Observatoire des Discriminations, 2004, 2005, 2006). This also coincided with the European Commission report on the 'business case' for diversity (European Commission, 2005).

We particularly argue that, in France, some specific business circles used the concept of 'diversity' as a vehicle to lobby for the adoption of proactive, positive-action types of legislation in favour of disadvantaged ethnic groups, as this legislation does not exist in the context of France. The role of the Montaigne Institute must here be underscored. This Institute, set up in 2000, is a voluntary think tank made up of corporate leaders, consultants and experts, under the leadership of Claude Bébéar, former CEO of the leading AXA insurance corporation. It has two main objectives. The first is to 'helpfully influence the public debate by putting forward pragmatic and original ideas'. The second is 'to contribute to the design of public policies in order to improve the French economic and social environment'.[13] The Montaigne Institute is one of the key players in promoting diversity, but at the same time positive action and its inscription in French law. The first item that appears on its agenda is 'diversity and equality of treatment'. In this realm, this think tank produced successive reports advocating the need for positive action in the area of employment and higher education (Sabegh and Méhaignerie, 2004; Blivet, 2004; Institut Montaigne, 2006). One of these reports is titled: 'Those forgotten by the equality of opportunities'.[14] The Montaigne Institute originated the 'Diversity Charter' (Charte de la Diversité, 2004), a voluntary commitment initially made by a small number of firms. The purpose of this charter is to respect and promote the application of the principle of non-discrimination in all its forms and at all stages of human resource management, in particular recruitment, training and development, and promotion, in order to reflect the diversity of the French society and in particular its cultural and ethnic diversity, at all qualification levels.[15]

Though not straightforwardly a positive action tool ('to respect and promote the application of the principle of non-discrimination' evokes equality of rights), the purpose of 'reflecting the diversity of the French society' opens the door to positive action, measurement and evaluation of progress, and is therefore consistent with the spirit of positive action, even though the 'remedial' element of positive action is not mentioned. The 'Diversity Charter' was signed by 40 large French companies in October 2004. In March 2008, it was signed by 1692 firms, according to its secretariat.[16] In June 2009, 2370 firms had signed it.[17]

Diversity recently became part of the legally binding vocabulary when French employers' organizations and trade unions also reached a collective agreement on 'diversity in the firm' in October 2006 (Accord National Interprofessionnel sur la Diversité dans l'Entreprise, 2006).[18] According to the agreement, an 'equality correspondent' is to be appointed in every French firm. Awareness training and communication programmes must be put in place in order to change management practices, the organization of which should be undertaken at both the company and the sector level. Firms must introduce recruitment processes based solely on skills and professional abilities, and exempt from discrimination, a demand coherent with already existing demands for equal treatment on the basis of skills. Careers should similarly be based on competence and performance, not on discrimination criteria. Sector-level bargaining should include diversity. Workers' representatives should be informed annually about diversity in the firm even in the absence of a collective agreement adopted at the sector or firm level. However, contrary to the Diversity Charter, no commitment is made by signatories to 'reflect' the French society in French firms. Nor does this agreement put in place any form of 'diversity goal' or of measurement of progress.

The last initiative to mention is a 'diversity label' (*label diversité*), a voluntary norm promoted, in September 2008, by the French Association for Quality Assurance (AFAQ, Association Française pour l'Assurance de la Qualité). In order to comply with this voluntary norm, employers first have to complete a diagnosis of their standing *vis-à-vis* the discrimination criteria set forth in French law, identify the 'risks' of discrimination of their operations and their existing management systems to promote diversity. Beyond this internal analysis, the top management of the firm must define 'diversity goals', design and implement an action plan towards the fulfilment of these, review progress annually, appoint a diversity correspondent and put in place a complaints management process. In March 2009, that is, seven months after its official launch, only seven firms had received this award (*Le Monde*, 2009).

Beyond these initiatives, a few firms have voluntarily adopted 'positive action' plans and, in some cases, collective agreements, in favour of recruiting and promoting workers of diverse origins (see below, the section devoted to corporate practice). However, these initiatives remain isolated.

In short, France does not have a positive action legislative framework in the area of ethnic and cultural diversity, as it does for gender – even though the latter remains quite theoretical and has not yet triggered a vast implementation of gender equalities policies, the public service lagging even behind – unions, disability, age and deprived urban areas. Most efforts benefiting groups of diverse ethnic origins come under the banner of social policy or measures in favour of the unemployed, the young and the inhabitants of deprived areas (of whom many are from underprivileged ethnic groups).

2.2   *Research on equal opportunities and diversity policies in France*

Given the relatively recent emergence of diversity policies in France, research has so far concentrated on gender equality policies, which have been initiated at a slow pace in the 1980s. But even that research was mostly carried out by sociologists and not by management scholars. It was only in 2006 that a special-interest group was constituted in the AGRH (French-speaking HRM research Association) on the subject of diversity and equal treatment practices. On 15 January 2009, it organized the first academic conference ever held by French management scholars on 'gender and diversity'. Gender inequality, along with other kinds of discrimination in organizations, with the possible exception of age, was simply not considered to be a human resource management issue. In this context, management research on equal employment and diversity is in its infancy in France. A few doctoral studies are starting, however, to be conducted on those issues.

2.3   *Research on gender equality policies in French organizations*

For many years, sociological – mostly – and management research has highlighted the unequal and sometimes segregationist use of the feminine workforce by French employers – showing results very similar across countries: women were employed for their so-called 'feminine' qualities and skills in low-paid, non-qualified factory jobs (Guilbert, 1966; Kergoat, 1982), feminine occupations were denied the prestige and qualification level that masculine jobs gained (Maruani, 1989), male-dominated organizational cultures and practices maintained stereotypes against women and prevented any significant career progress (Laufer, 1982; Aubert, 1982; Laufer and Fouquet, 2001).

Training and qualifications   In the 1980s, following the Roudy Law, a few gender equality initiatives have been taken by industrial companies, mainly to increase the qualifications and skills of their feminine workforce (Doniol-Shaw and Junter-Loiseau, 1989). Laufer (1992) conducted five field studies among the 25 or so equality programmes (Plans d'actions pour l'égalité professionnelle) initiated. She highlighted the selective and pragmatic emphasis put on women's professional training. Firms' initiatives were driven by opportunity rather than by willingness to achieve gender equality. Employers largely disregarded the question of gender discrimination and ignored, at that time, the question of work and non-work roles articulation.

Feminization of the workforce   More recently, initiatives have been taken by employers and employment services to attract and qualify women in industries such as the building sector, transport and industrial maintenance, which experienced a labour shortage. A longitudinal field study conducted in industrial companies in Alsace (Forté et al., 2005) highlights the various professional trajectories of women, very often non-promotional, which the authors explain by general resistance (by men and by women) to female management, and by the preponderance of technical qualification in those cultures – these women being mostly less qualified than their male co-workers. They conclude that acquiring formal qualifications may be the necessary, though not always sufficient, step for women's durable inclusion in those sectors.

Career management for women managers and professionals   Since the 1990s, a few French firms have started to address the 'glass ceiling' issue faced by women managers. Although these were initially subsidiaries of US firms (such as Hewlett-Packard studied by Belle, 1991), French multinationals started to address this issue mostly at the turn of the century (Bender and Pigeyre, 2004). In France, as in other countries, the 'glass ceiling' effect appears largely due to the hegemony of men in managerial hierarchies, very often with engineering academic training (Grandes Ecoles), accounting for masculine cultures and gendered representations of leadership attributes (Guillaume and Pochic, 2007).

In a special issue of the *Revue Française de Gestion* (Laufer, 2004), Belghiti-Mahut (2004) exposes the results of a survey in a large telecoms company. The predominant factor to which managers and professionals of both sexes attribute women's difficulties in reaching top management is societal stereotypes about women. Interestingly, the number of children is not a career handicap for the women surveyed, who apparently manage to reconcile private and professional demands. In the same issue, Pigeyre and Valette's article (2004) deals with women's careers in French universities. Their research highlights the different access of women to professorship positions, depending on the discipline (history, biology or management science) and on the conditions for promotion (based on research or competitive selection examination). Finally, Martin and Pignatel (2004) confirm the small number of women on French companies' boards. In 2003, they represented only 5.8 per cent of the mandates in the 500 largest French groups (and the 154 664 firms related to them). This rate has progressed by only 1.6 per cent since 1998. Women hold proportionately far fewer decision-making seats and powerful women remain a very small elitist club, present on many boards.

Management research has detailed the specificities of women managers' situations and their strategies to get to the top (Pigeyre, 2001; Laufer, 2005), as well as the variety of firms' practices regarding women's careers (Laufer, 2004). At the time of research, few specific measures – apart from the possibility not to work on Wednesdays[19] – were adopted for women managers. Employers generally perceive that the environment is already quite supportive: French law provides for paid maternity leave and fiscal measures help upper-middle-class couples to pay for nannies; companies' childcare provisions are also sometimes provided by their social committee (*comités d'entreprises*), run by workers' representatives. There remain many obstacles, however, for women who are in charge of families, such as an extended-hours work culture, mobility and travel demands from the employer, and prejudices against women's competences (Belghiti and Landrieux-Kartochian, 2008; Laufer, 2007).

Gender stereotypes   Chantal Morley, Marité Milon and Isabelle Collet (2009) recently carried out a content analysis of press articles written in French, including French and Swiss newspapers. They highlighted the constant reference, by journalists when writing about women, to private life and family matters, the fact that journalists allude much more to a supposedly 'feminine' management style than the women interviewed, who use more gender-neutral words, and the frequent allusion to the (seducing) physical appearance of the women. If journalists evoke men's private life (family responsibilities) in comparable proportion to women, men's extra-professional activities are much more alluded to, namely sport and music.

Negotiating gender equality at the company level The Génisson legislation (2001) gave a new impulse to collective agreements. Laufer and Silvera (2006) studied 40 company's agreements negotiated on this subject. They note that only large companies have signed such agreements, very often at the sole initiative of the employer given the lack of union mobilization of the subject. The agreements provide for flexible work-time arrangements, neutralization of maternity leave on a salary perspective, HRM practices designed to increase women's representation in certain masculine professions, and managerial ranks and effective pay equality. Fifteen out of 40 agreements refer to quantitative targets of recruitment or promotion of women. Gender-blind job evaluation systems also start to be studied in a gender-mainstreaming perspective (Lemière, 2006).

To our knowledge, however, there are no empirical studies on how these agreements have been implemented by the companies, with the exception of a government-sponsored study,[20] whose authors emphasize the difficulties they encountered in gaining access to the companies. The study reveals that the line management is very often unaware or little informed of the equality measures that have been negotiated between top management and unions. At best, HRM procedures such as recruitment and pay allocations are changing towards more equal treatment. However, certain issues are scarcely dealt with, such as working conditions and gendered representations of occupations. The access to the empirical field is therefore difficult for researchers. Only one doctoral dissertation has been produced on companies' practices and their perceptions by employees, men and women (Landrieux-Kartochian, 2005b), and it took place in a US-based consulting firm. Another doctoral research under way (Scotto and Boyer, 2009) studies two French companies having implemented gender equity and diversity policies. The first one, the utility company providing water to Paris ('Eau de Paris'), is well known in France for its commitment to anti-discrimination at work. Its management actively promoted the new 'diversity' label recently created to reward best practices. The second case is a medium-sized construction firm located in the South of France, Cari, whose top management decided to feminize its workforce for ethical and economic reasons, in a situation of workforce scarcity – at the time of the initiative. Another industrial company, which received the 'equality label', agreed to host a PhD student in economics in order to study the integration of women at the first line management level (Charbeau, 2006). As a sign of the changing times, French-speaking management scholars have recently published a handbook on gender and HRM (Cornet et al., 2008).

2.4 *Studies on other sources of discrimination*

Age discrimination French sociologists such as Volkoff (CREAPT) and Guillemard (CEE) have been working for many years on the difficulties faced by ageing workers. The first author, in collaboration with colleagues of his research laboratory, studies in particular how ageing workers face work organization constraints and can adapt to these evolutions (Volkoff and Pueyo, 2005; Molinié and Volkoff, 2006). His work mixes ergonomic and sociological perspectives.

Guillemard (2003) takes a more sociopolitical perspective on issues such as the inflexion of career patterns for ageing workers, the problem of early retirement and how to diminish it. She has also conducted many international comparisons on senior employment patterns and policies (Guillemard et al., 2004; Guillemard, 2007).

In management science, Marbot (2005) highlighted, in her doctoral dissertation, a psychological construct that she called the 'end of professional life' feeling. It is largely connected to perception of employer's practices towards ageing workers. It is worth mentioning that France has one of the lowest ageing workers' employment rates in Europe, with only about 38 per cent of people in employment when reaching the legal age of retirement (60) – the majority of new retirees being composed of people on early retirement financed by companies, unemployed people, inactive people and people unable to work for health reasons.

Bellini et al. (2006) conducted field work in 15 companies in the Poitou area in order to identify senior workers' management practices. They highlighted six patterns, among which were the following human resource strategies (the three other were more *ad hoc* practices):

- an opportunistic use of voluntary early retirement (through negotiated redundancies) to renew the workforce;
- an adaptation of workers' skills through transmission of know-how and encouragement of multi-skilling;
- a preventive adaptation of working conditions and jobs in order to capitalize on ageing workers' skills and enable their profitable retention in the company.

Only three companies adopted the last strategy.

In their doctoral research, Pijoan and Briole (2006) analysed the cognitive schemes of top managers in the geriatric sector regarding their ageing workers. The results show that positive representations of ageing workers do not necessarily lead to particularly inclusive human resource practices. In addition, inclusive strategies designed to specifically deal with ageing workers' needs (such as specific training and working conditions) may lead to their relative exclusion all the same, by combining such policies with recruitment targeted at young people.

Sexual orientation   Recent research has been conducted among homosexual persons to enquire about their experiences of discrimination and about related perceptions and personal strategies at work (Falcoz, 2008). It is the first of its kind in France, a country where gay and lesbian organizations have only recently really taken hold in very few and mostly state-owned companies. The survey reveals widespread perceived homophobia and the extent of strategies used by homosexual people in order to conceal their sexual orientation at work.

Disabled people   In management studies, very few articles or books have been dedicated to disabled employees. The subject was mostly dealt with by social scientists specialized in the field, who adopted legal, psychological and sociological points of view, but management as a whole neglected the issue, which was perceived as concerning only a very small minority of employees. The law passed in 2005 strengthened employers' obligations and the subject is now of growing interest – and financial consequences – for companies (Naschberger, 2007).

2.5 Research on diversity management

There has been little empirical research so far on organizational practices relating to 'diversity', in the anti-discrimination meaning of the word, before the year 2000. The concept of diversity was mainly used to refer to the international dimension of management and how to manage intercultural teams (Chevrier, 2003).

As diversity management practices – in the sense of anti-discrimination practices – seem to take hold in France, researchers have been starting to address the issue (Bender, 2004; Garner-Moyer, 2006). As mentioned above, in 2006, HRM academics working on these topics constituted a special interest group in the French academy of HRM (AGRH[21]), called 'diversity and equality', which comprises 25 members or so working on various types of discrimination and on diversity management.

Among them, Annick Bourguignon and Philippe Zarlowski (2009) conducted the first exploratory investigation of photographs in the French popular management press (mainly monthly magazines). They found that, unsurprisingly, men were much more often represented than women (79 per cent men/21 per cent women). Regarding ethnicity, visible minorities' representation in photographs was less than 10 per cent. Non-Caucasian people were mostly anonymous people at work and not the (named) persons highlighted in the adjacent article. The authors emphasize that the representation of the business world offered by this press is one 'where male, Caucasian and named persons (that is, 'real' persons) held dominant and enjoyable positions (they smile) over non-Caucasian, mostly female and anonymous workers'.

On diversity itself, we should mention a study of European companies' website communications on the theme (Singh and Point, 2004). The authors state that the continental conception of diversity remains anchored in 'assuring equality of treatment' and fighting discrimination, whereas UK companies presented a more strategic and business-anchored rhetoric about 'diversity as a strategic enhancer for the company'. A survey carried out a few years ago among HR professionals, lawyers and non-HR managers in the Toulouse area (Klarsfeld, 2005, 2007) shows paradoxical results: at the time of the study, there was a prevalence of perceptions of gender and age discrimination by HRM professionals, but also a near absence of litigation on the ground of such discrimination, while union discrimination formed the bulk of discrimination litigation. French scholars, however, have started to address and question the 'business case' for diversity, in particular in relation with gender equality (Landrieux-Kartochian, 2005a).

Other empirical materials produced up to now are mostly companies' presentations of their diversity management practices (Peretti, 2006; Barth and Falcoz, 2007). The latter presents various academic contributions that discuss with a critical perspective the concept and practices of diversity management as used in HRM and in marketing. Researchers have also started interviewing the newly appointed diversity managers and highlighting their diversity – sometimes integrated in HRM, sometimes directly reporting to the CEO, sometimes depending on broad corporate social responsibility managers (Broussillon et al., 2007). Finally, recently signed collective agreements on diversity attracted researchers' curiosity: Hélène Garner-Moyer (2009) analysed seven of them. Some agreements include well-structured tools for diagnosis, measurement – when allowed – and follow-up policies, especially when they focus on a few dimensions of diversity (i.e. age, gender, origins, disability). Other agreements, which probe 'diversity' at large and condemn all motives of illegal discrimination without emphasizing specific actions, tend not to set objectives or follow up actions and remain rather vague.

Up until recent years, there has been a relative absence of managerial research[22] related to racial discrimination – the field being mostly studied by sociologists – or to the integration and management of a workforce of diverse origins. As mentioned above, the legitimacy of such questions in human resource management is recent and still resisted by scholars who do not want to stigmatize supposedly 'different' workers. Some PhD students, however, are currently working on the subject.

At the end of the 1990s, a team of researchers, 'Observatoire des Discriminations', University of Paris I, conducted several studies on discrimination by examing CVs (Amadieu, 2004a). Through discrimination testing, they found that the principal factors of discrimination at the time of recruitment are, in order of significance, age, origin, handicap, gender and physical appearance. Consequently, another series of tests was realized on a larger scale (Cediey and Foroni, 2006). This stream of research has greatly contributed to raising the issue of employment discrimination in France.

With the purpose of identifying discrimination on profession trajectories, more research has been carried out by social scientists, who studied the relationships between employees' careers and their names in a French distribution company (Cediey and Foroni, 2005). The question of studying ethnic origin by statistical measures remains very controversial in France, as we shall see below.

Conclusion: some pending issues in the French debate on diversity

The issues related to diversity and to the management of diversity lead in France to numerous and intense debates. Without claiming to deal with all the topics included in this debate, we can identify some of the most salient issues. Two points can be emphasized.

The first has to do with the variety of the issues and policies that are now gathered under the umbrella of diversity, one of the main reasons being the 16 different points of illegal discrimination that are included in the 2001 French law. While it is essential to tackle all forms of discrimination, this situation does lead to some difficulties, in that the strategies that appear legitimate to erase discrimination vary according to the category under consideration. For example: compulsory gendered statistics to attest inequalities that affect women but illegal and illegitimate counting of 'ethnic diversity'; positive (or affirmative) actions that are legal and encouraged for the handicapped, legal but seldom implemented for women, and forbidden for other minorities etc. A main issue has to do with the risk that the emphasis put on diversity will overshadow the issue of equality between men and women. Indeed, one could emphasize the benefits of a transversal approach to discrimination that calls attention to the common discrimination processes towards many categories, such as indirect discrimination, stereotypes or 'glass ceiling' effects. However, women are not a minority, and gender discrimination is transversal to all other forms of discrimination, which raises the issue of the multiple discriminations faced by women (Lanquetin, 2009). Therefore the issue arises as to the capacity of an approach based on the sole (and often ill-defined) objective of diversity to integrate the full-fledged objective of true gender equality policies, which should mobilize the whole array of strategies provided by the gender equality laws in such a way as to develop a true 'equality culture' (Laufer, 2009).

A second question relates to the measurement of 'ethnic' or 'racial' discrimination and/ or diversity, an issue that leads to difficult debates since such a 'count' would challenge one of the main principles of the French Constitution, stating that any distinction on the basis of race is forbidden among French citizens (Weil, 2005). Such 'counting' also under- lies the issue of positive discrimination on the basis of those criteria, a strategy rejected by many political and social actors. In this context, it can be underlined that no consensus exists on the best practices to identify discriminatory behaviour – anonymous CV, testing, use of surnames – on the hypothesis that they constitute good indicators of ethnic origin.

While it is too early to say what will be the answer to this 'French Dilemma', it is obvious that this debate in itself led to major progress in awareness of discrimination processes and therefore to a more sound approach to diversity policies.

Summary table for France

Existence of anti-discrimination legislation	Yes
Criteria covered by anti-discrimination legislation	Origin, gender, family status, pregnancy, physical appearance, disability, health condition, genetic characteristics, demeanours, sexual orientation, age, political opinion, union activity, family name, nationality, ethnicity, race, religion
Criteria for which the reporting of quantitative data and their communication to a public administration are compulsory	Gender, age, disability
Criteria covered by 'affirmative' or 'positive' action legislation other than unemployment- or income-based	Disability, gender, age, area of residence, union activity
Existence of a discourse or debate about 'non-discrimination' or 'equality'	Yes
Existence of a discourse or debate about 'diversity'	Yes
Year or period when the 'discrimination' concept started to disseminate in management literature in the country	2003–04
Year or period when the diversity concept started to disseminate in management literature in the country	2003–04
Who pushed the 'diversity' agenda?	Influence of business circles in favour of positive action for persons of foreign origin, the European Commission, subsidiaries of US corporations, the French government, voluntary organizations
Existence of a professional association representing diversity professionals and year of creation	Yes, 2007
Existence of a professional association representing diversity scholars and year of creation	Yes, 2006

Notes

1. The choice of words proved to be a challenge in writing this chapter. Kelly and Dobbin (1998) use the term 'neutral' legislation instead of our 'equality of rights', and 'affirmative action' where we use 'positive action'. Lyon-Caen (1990) uses the term 'legal equality' (*égalité juridique*) for our 'equality of rights' and 'social equality' (*égalité sociale*) for our 'positive action'. Rather than the US 'affirmative action' expression, when referring to a remedial approach to equality, the French use the expression 'positive action' or 'positive discrimination', the latter being used to characterize the most extreme forms of remedial measures such as recruitment quotas. The term 'positive action' is the term used throughout the European Union Directives and European Court of Justice legal decisions on this issue.
2. Established in 1966, the Comité du Travail Féminin – CTF (The Committee on Women's Employment) was a major actor in promoting equality between men and women and an important locus of development for French state feminism (Lévy, 1988; Mazur, 1995; Lurol, 1999). The CTF also played a consultative role for all issues concerning women's economic activity and was responsible for examining all the points to be covered in Council Directive 76/207/EEC on equal treatment.
3. The evolution of French immigration policy must also be put in context with the provision of the Schengen Treaty, which from 1985 to 1996 defined a European intergovernmental, political asylum and frontier controls. These agreements specify who can enter the EU, who can freely circulate through the EU and who cannot, and legal measures to prevent illegal immigration.
4. Rea and Tripier emphasize that, in French sociology, the issues linked with the evolution of social classes and of class relations tended to underscore the status of immigration: immigrants were not considered as able to influence society at large (Rea and Tripier, 2008, p. 20).
5. The first article of the French Constitution says: 'the French republic . . . ensures equality before the law of all citizens without any distinction on the basis of origin, of race, of religion . . . ' (author's translation). Consequently the CNIL (National Commission for Data Protection and Freedom) forbids any collection of information on such 'sensitive issues' as 'race' or 'ethnic origin'. The statistical monitoring of 'ethnic' and 'racial' diversity is illegal in France. The legitimate information to be collected by census and researchers consists of name, nationality, nationality of origin, nationality and place of birth of parents, address. However, these data are not supposed to be included in firms or administrative personnel files (CNIL, 2005).
6. Directive 97/80, 15 December 1997.
7. Council Directive 2000/78/EC of 27 November 2000.
8. Law 57-1223, 23 November 1957.
9. National Association for the Management of the Fund in Favour of the Professional Integration of Disabled Workers.
10. €1321.02 per month in 2008.
11. For instance, until July 2008, EDF (French electricity utility)'s policies placed a ban on the recruitment of workers aged 40 and above for pensions reasons (minimum period of contribution to benefit from the company's pension scheme). The same reason applied in public sector jobs.
12. Loi no. 78-17 du 6 Janvier 1978 relative à l'informatique, aux fichiers et aux libertés, art.8.
13. 'Tout sur l'Institut Montaigne', 'Pourquoi l'Institut Montaigne', www.institutmontaigne.org, author's translation.
14. Sabegh and Méhaignerie (2004).
15. Diversity Charter, commitments 2 and 3, author's translation.
16. www.charte-diversite.com, accessed 15 March 2008.
17. www.charte-diversite.com, accessed 17 June 2009.
18. In France, collective agreements signed at the intersectoral level are binding for all private sector firms, although the penalty for not abiding by them is somewhat theoretical.
19. There is no school on Wednesdays in France.
20. *La mise en oeuvre des accords d'égalité professionnelle: Analyse de huit démarches d'entreprises.*
21. Association Francophone de Gestion des Ressources Humaines.
22. Some chapters in the previously cited books address this question, but without empirical material.

References

Accord National Interprofessionnel sur la Diversité dans l'Entreprise (2006) (National Collective Agreement on Diversity within Firms).
Agence France Presse (2008), 'Fin des limites d'âge à l'embauche chez EDF: la Halde satisfaite', 28 August.
Amadieu, J.-F. (2004a), *Enquête 'Testing' sur CV*, Adia/ Université Paris I – Observatoire des Discrimination.
Amadieu, J.-F. (2004b), 'Discrimination positive, mais injuste', *L'Express*, 1 November.
Amira, S. (2008), 'La loi d'obligation d'emploi des travailleurs handicapés du 10 juillet 1987: éléments de bilan', *Premières Synthèses*, no. 28.1, July, INSEE.

ANDCP (2005), *Le marché du travail est-il un marché du travail comme les autres ? Quel rôle pour les DRH?*, November.

Aubert, N. (1982), *Le Pouvoir usurpé? Femmes et hommes dans l'entreprise*, Paris: Éditions Robert Laffont.

Barth, I. and Falcoz, C. (eds) (2007), *Le management de la diversité, Enjeux, fondements et pratiques*, Paris: L'Harmattan.

Bataille, P. (1997), *Le racisme au travail*, Paris: La Découverte.

Belghiti-Mahut, S. (2004), 'Les déterminants de l'avancement hiérarchique des femmes cadres', *Revue Française de Gestion*, no. 151-4, pp. 145–60.

Belghiti-Mahut, S. and Landrieux-Kartochian, S. (2008), 'Le plafond de verre, encore et toujours', in A. Cornet, J. Laufer and S. Belghiti-Mahut (eds), *Genre et GRH, les défis de l'égalité hommes–femmes*, Paris: Vuibert, pp. 105–24.

Belle, F. (1991), *Etre femme et cadre*, Paris: L'Harmattan.

Bellini, S., J.-Y. Duyck, F. Laval, E. Renaud and S. Vauclin (2006), 'Une typologie des pratiques de gestion des seniors', *Revue Management and Avenir*, no. 7.

Bender, A.-F. (2004), 'Egalité professionnelle ou gestion de la diversité: quels enjeux pour l'égalité des chances?', *Revue Française de Gestion*, juin–août, 205–17.

Bender, A.-F. and F. Pigeyre (2004), 'De l'égalité professionnelle à la gestion de la diversité: quels enjeux pour la gestion des carrières des femmes?', in S. Guerrero, J.L. Cerdin and A. Roger (eds), *La Gestion des carrières, enjeux et perspectives*, Paris: Vuibert.

Blivet, L. (2004), *L'entreprise et l'égalité positive*, Paris: Institut Montaigne.

Borrel, C. (2006), *Enquêtes annuelles de recensement 2004 et 2005, près de 5 millions d'immigrés à la mi-2004*, no. 1098, August.

Bourguignon, A. and P. Zarlowski (2009), 'How French management magazines provide representations maintaining gender, ethnicity and double discrimination', paper presented at the AGRH Gender and Diversity International Conference, ESCP–EAP Paris, January.

Broussillon, George-Axelle, Evalde Mutabazi, Philippe Pierre and Aude Seurrat (2007), 'La figure du "Responsable Diversité" dans les entreprises en France. Tentative de typologie et dimensions identitaires', Actes de l'Université d'Automne de l'IAS, Colloque de Corte/3ème rencontres internationales de la diversité.

Cediey, E. and Foroni, F. (2005), 'Un diagnostic partagé sur les discriminations liées à l'origine et au sexe. Résultat d'une recherche-action au sein du Groupe CASINO', rapport ISM-Corum, http://www.ismcorum.org/stock_images/reference/rapport-casino-ism-corum.pdf, accessed 10 September, 2008.

Cediey, E. and Foroni, F. (2006), *Les Discriminations à raison de 'l'origine' dans les embauches en France. Une enquête nationale par tests de discrimination selon la méthode du BIT*, Genève : Bureau international du Travail (ILO).

CEREQ (2004), 'Les jeunes issus de l'immigration: de l'enseignement supérieur au marché du travail', *Cereq Bref* No. 205, février.

CEREQ (2006), 'Jeunes issus de l'immigration, une pénalité à l'embauche qui perdure', *Cereq Bref* No. 226, janvier.

Charbeau, L. (2006), 'Evaluation de la qualité du travail et inégalités de carrière entre hommes et femmes', XVIIe Congrès de l'AGRH – Le travail au coeur de la GRH, IAE de Lille et Reims Management School, Reims, 16 et 17 novembre.

Chevrier, S. (2003), 'Cross-cultural management in multinational project groups', *Journal of World Business*, **38**, 141–9.

CJD (2006), 'Faire de la diversité une ressource pour entreprendre', dossier de synthèse du travail de réflexion et d'expérimentation réalisé par le CJD sur le thème de la diversité dans les entreprises 2004–2006, Juin.

Collen, V. (2008), 'Un mouvement général de relèvement des limites d'âge', *Les Echos*, 14 November.

Commaille, J. (1993), *Les stratégies des femmes: travail, famille et politique*, Paris: La Découverte.

Cornet, A., J. Laufer and S. Belghiti-Mahut (2008), *GRH et genre: les défis de l'égalité Hommes–Femmes*, Paris: Vuibert.

CNIL (Commission Nationale de l'informatique et des libertés) (2005), Avis du 5 Juillet.

Délégation interministérielle à la Ville (2005), *Les politiques de la Ville depuis 1977*.

Dewitte, P. (1999), *Immigration et intégration: l'état des savoirs*, Paris, La Découverte.

Doniol-Shaw, G. and A. Junter-Loiseau (1989), *Les Plans d'égalité professionnelle: étude-bilan 1983–1988*, Paris: La Documentation Française.

European Commission (2005), *The Business Case for Diversity*, September.

Falcoz, C. (2008), *Homophobie dans l'entreprise*, Paris: La Documentation Française.

Fassin, D. (2002), 'L'invention française de la discrimination', *Revue Française des Sciences Politiques*, **52** (4), 403–23.

Forté, M., M. Niss, M.-C. Rebeuh and E. Triby (2005), 'La mixité professionnelle: les conditions d'un développement durable', *Document d'études*, No. 98, Dares.

Fraisse, G. (1995), 'Entre égalité et liberté', in *Ephesia, La place des femmes – Les enjeux de l'identité et de l'égalité au regard des sciences sociales*, Paris: La Découverte, pp. 387–93.

Garner-Moyer H. (2006), 'Gestion de la diversité et enjeux de GRH', *Revue Management et Avenir*, 7, 23–42.

Garner-Moyer, H. (2009), 'Quelle est la place du genre dans les accords sur la diversité?', paper presented at the AGRH Gender and Diversity International Conference, ESCP–EAP, Paris, January.

Gobillon, L., Magnac, T. and Selod, H. (2007), 'The effect of location on finding a job in the Paris region', CEPR 6199.

Guilbert, M. (1966), *Les fonctions des femmes dans l'industrie*, Paris: Mouton.

Guillaume, C. and Pochic, S. (2007), 'La fabrication organisationnelle des dirigeants. Un regard sur le plafond de verre', *Travail, Genre et Sociétés*, 1 (17), 79–103.

Guillemard, A.-M. (2003), *L'âge de l'emploi. Les sociétés face à l'épreuve du vieillissement*, Paris: Armand Colin.

Guillemard, A.-M. (2007), *Prolonger la vie active face au vieillissement. Quels leviers d'action? Les enseigne-ments de l'étranger*, Lyon: Editions Réseau ANACT (Agence Nationale pour l'Amélioration des Conditions de travail).

Guillemard, A.-M., P. Ansart, M. Legrand and M. Messu (eds) (2004), *Quand la vie s'allonge. France–Japon*, Paris: L'Harmattan.

Guyomar, M. (1999), 'La politique d'immigration française depuis 1945', in P. Dewitte (ed.), *Immigration et intégration: l'état des savoirs*, Paris: La Découverte.

HALDE (2006), *Annual report*.

HALDE (2007), *Annual report*.

HALDE (2008), *Annual report*.

Héran, F. (2007), *Le temps des immigrés*, Paris: Seuil.

INSEE (2005), 'Salaire net annuel moyen selon le sexe et la catégorie socioprofessionnelle dans le secteur privé et semi-public', http://www.insee.fr/fr/themes/tableau.asp?reg_id=0&id=38, accessed 26 September 2008.

Institut Montaigne (2006), *Ouvrir les Grandes Ecoles à la diversité*, Institut Montaigne.

Kelly, E. and Dobbin, F. (1998), 'How affirmative action became diversity management: employer response to anti-discrimination law, 1961–1996', *American Behavioral Scientist*, 41 (7), 960–84.

Kergoat, D. (1982), *Les ouvrières*, Paris: Le Sycomore.

Klarsfeld, A. (2005), *Lutter contre les discriminations et développer la diversité: les regards croisés de DRH, de consultants en recrutement et d'avocats en Midi-Pyrénées*, Rapport de Recherche EQUAL–ANDCP, Toulouse, octobre.

Klarsfeld, A. (2007), *Représentations et pratiques de lutte contre les discriminations et de développement de la diversité au Centre des Jeunes Dirigeants de Toulouse*, Rapport de recherche EQUAL–CJD, janvier.

La Croix (2008), 'Justice. Deux collégiennes exclues pour le port du foulard déboutées à Strasbourg', 5 December.

Landrieux-Kartochian, S. (2005a), 'Femmes et performance des entreprises, l'émergence d'une nouvelle prob-lématique', *Travail et Emploi*, 102, 11–20.

Landrieux-Kartochian, S. (2005b), 'L'intérêt managérial des démarches d'égalité professionnelle, un exemple de (ré)conciliation de l'économique et du social?', 16e Congrès de l'AGRH–Paris Dauphine, 15 et 16 sep-tembre.

Lanquetin, M.-T. (1995), 'La preuve de la discrimination: l'apport du droit communautaire', *Droit Social*, 5, 435–41.

Lanquetin, M.-T. (1998), 'L'égalité professionnelle à l'épreuve des faits', in M. Maruani (ed.), *Les nouvelles frontières de l'inégalité hommes femmes sur le marché du travail*, Paris: La Découverte, pp. 115–26.

Lanquetin, M.-T. (2000), 'Un tournant en matière de preuve des discriminations', *Droit Social*, 6, 589–93.

Lanquetin, M.-T. (2009), 'Egalité, diversité et discriminations multiples', *Travail, genre et sociétés*, 21, 91–106.

Lattes, J.M. (1989), *Le principe de non discrimination en Droit du Travail*, Thèse Université Toulouse I, sous la direction de Michel DESPAX, 2 tomes.

Lattes, J.M. (2008), 'Handicap, le droit à la compensation et le droit de la compensation', Proceedings of the Association Travail et Handicap dans la Recherche Publique (ATHAREP) Conference, Paris, 23 May.

Laufer, J. (1982), *La féminité neutralisée? Les femmes cadres dans l'entreprise*, Paris : Flammarion.

Laufer, J. (1992), *L'Entreprise et l'égalité des chances: enjeux et démarches*, Paris: La Documentation Française.

Laufer, J. (2003), 'Entre égalité et inégalités: les droits des femmes dans la sphère professionnelle', *L'Année sociologique*, 53 (1), 143–74.

Laufer, J. (2004), 'Femmes et carrières: la question du plafond de verre', *Revue Française de Gestion*, 4 (151), 117–27.

Laufer, J. (2005), 'La construction du plafond de verre: le cas des femmes cadres à potentiel', *Travail et Emploi*, **102**, 31.

Laufer, J. (2007), 'L'égalité professionnelle hommes-femmes', in I. Barth and C. Falcoz (eds), *Le management de la Diversité*, Paris, L'Harmattan.

Laufer J. (2009), 'L'égalité professionnelle entre les hommes et les femmes est-elle soluble dans la diversité?', in *Travail, genre et sociétés*, No. 21 (Special edition 'Egalité et Diversité', eds J. Laufer and R. Silvera).

Laufer, J. and Fouquet, A. (2001), 'A l'épreuve de la féminisation', in P. Bouffartigue (ed.), *Cadres: la grande rupture*, Paris: La Découverte, pp. 167–77.

Laufer, J. and R. Silvera (2006), 'Les accords d'entreprise sur l'égalité professionnelle', *Regards sur l'actualité*, Paris: La Documentation française, No. 317, janvier.

Le Monde (2009), 'Eric Besson demande aux préfets de promouvoir le "label diversité"', 4 March.

Lemière, S. (2006), 'Un salaire égal pour un emploi de valeur comparable', *Travail, genre et sociétés*, 1 (15), 83–100.

Lévy, M. (1988), *Le féminisme d'état en France:1965–1985*, Doctorat en Sciences politiques, Paris, IEP.

Ligue des Droits de l'Homme de Toulon (Human Rights League) (2002), http://www.ldh-toulon.net.

Lurol, M. (1999), 'Quand les institutions se chargent de la question du travail des femmes, 1970–1995?', *Travail, genre et sociétés*, **1**, 179–202.

Lyon-Caen, A. (1990), 'L'égalité et la loi en droit du travail', *Droit Social*, No. 1, janvier, 68–75.

Lyon-Caen, G., J. Pélissier and A. Supiot (1999), *Droit du travail*, Paris: Dalloz.

Marbot, E. (2005), *Les DRH face au choc démographique*, Paris: Editions d'Organisation.

Martin, V.K and I. Pignatel (2004), 'Les instances de pouvoir des 500 premiers groupes français', *Revue Française de Gestion*, **4** (151), 161–72.

Maruani, M.and C. Nicole (1989), *Au labeur des dames, métiers masculins, emplois féminins*, Paris: Syros.

Mazur, A. (1995), *Gender Bias and the State: Symbolic Reform at Work in Fifth Republic France*, Pittsburgh: University of Pittsburgh Press.

Méron, M. (2009), 'Statistiques ethniques: tabous et boutades', *Travail, genre et sociétés*, **21**, 55–68.

Ministère du Travail (2007), 'Le chômage des personnes handicapées en décembre 2006', http://www.travail-solidarite.gouv.fr/etudes-recherche-statistiques-dares/statistiques/travailleurs-handicapes/indicateurs-conjoncturels/chomage-personnes-handicapees-decembre-2006-.html, accessed 26 September 2008.

Molinié, A.-F. and S. Volkoff (2006), 'Fins de vie active et "pénibilités" du travail', in *La qualité de l'emploi*, Paris: La Découverte, Centre d'études de l'emploi, Collection Repères.

Morley, C., M. Milon and I. Collet (2009), 'Discours sur les dirigeant-e-s au regard du genre', paper presented at the AGRH Gender and Diversity International Conference, ESCP–EAP, Paris, January.

Naschberger, C. (2007), 'La mise en œuvre d'une démarche diversité en entreprise: Le cas de l'intégration des personnes en situation de handicap', Troisièmes rencontres internationales de la diversité/Third International Meeting of Diversity Management, 'Réussir la diversité/Successful Diversity Management', Corte, 4, 5 et 6 octobre.

Noiriel, G. (1998), *Le creuset français. Histoire de l'immigration. XIX ème–XX ème siècle*, Paris: Seuil.

Noiriel, G. (2001), *Etat, notion et immigration, vers une histoire du pouvoir*, Paris: Belin.

Observatoire des Discriminations (2004, 2005, 2006), *Baromètre ADIA*, CERGOR, Université Paris I.

Peretti, J.-M. (ed.) (2006), *Tous différents, gérer la diversité dans l'entreprise*, Paris: Editions d'Organisation.

Pigeyre, F. (2001), 'Femmes dirigeantes: les chemins du pouvoir', in P. Bouffartigue (ed.), *Cadres: la grande rupture*, Paris: La Découverte, pp. 269–80.

Pigeyre, F. and A. Valette (2004), 'Les carrières des femmes à l'université: "Les palmes de verre du cocotier"', *Revue Française de Gestion*, **4** (151), 173–89.

Pijoan, N. and Briole A. (2006), 'Expliciter les représentations des seniors chez des directeurs: une analyse à partir de cartes causales idiosyncrasiques', *Revue management et avenir*, **1** (7), 152–80.

Pla, A. (2009), 'Bilan démographique 2008', INSEE, January.

Rapport Fauroux (2005), *Les discriminations ethniques dans le domaine de l'emploi*, Rapport remis au gouvernement par Roger Fauroux le 8 Septembre.

Rea, A. and M. Tripier (2003, 2008 new edn), S*ociologie de l'immigration*, Paris: La Découverte.

Sabegh, Y. and L. Méhaignerie (2004), *Les oubliés de l'Egalité des Chances*, Institut Montaigne.

Schnapper, D. (1991), *La France de l'intégration*, Paris: Gallimard.

Schnapper, D. (1994), *La communauté des citoyens: sur l'idée moderne de notion*, Paris: Gallimard.

Scotto, M.-J. and A. Boyer (2009), 'Processus de féminisation et d'égalité professionnelle femmes/hommes dans les entreprises appartenant à des secteurs "masculins": l'exemple des secteurs de la production d'eau et du bâtiment', paper presented at the AGRH Gender and Diversity International Conference, ESCP–EAP Paris, January.

Singh, V. and S. Point (2004), 'Strategic responses by European companies to the diversity challenge: an online comparison', *Long Range Planning*, **37** (4), 295–318.

Sutter, C. (1983), 'L'égalité professionnelle dans les droits nouveaux', *Droit Social*, p. 684.
Todd, E. (1994), *Le destin des immigrés*, Paris: Seuil, Collection l'histoire immédiate.
Travail, genre et sociétés (2001), special edition, Le travail de nuit des femmes (eds Jacqueline Laufer and Rachel Silvera), No. 5, pp. 135–60.
Tripier, M. (1990), *L'immigration dans la classe ouvrière en France*, Paris: CIEMI/L'Harmattan.
Vie Publique.fr/Dossiers politiques publiques/La politique du handicap/Chronologie, accessed 5 May 2008.
Volkoff, S. and V. Pueyo (2005), 'How do elderly workers face tight time constraints?', in *Assessment and Promotion of Work Ability, Health and Well-being of Ageing Workers*, Elsevier ICS, Vol. 1280, pp. 17–22.
Weil, P. (2005), *La République et sa diversité: immigration, intégration, discriminations*, Paris: Le Seuil.

6   Social inequality, diversity and equal treatment at work: the German case

*Verena Bruchhagen, Jürgen Grieger, Iris Koall,
Michael Meuser, Renate Ortlieb and Barbara Sieben*

1.   Demographic development, equal treatment legislation, institutionalization and professionalization

1.1   Demographic and labour force structure

First, we give a short overview of the German population and labour force, in order to convey an impression of how population diversity is represented in German organizations. We concentrate on the diversity dimensions of gender, ethnicity/migration background, age and disability.

1.1.1   Gender   In 2006, around 82.3 million people – 42.0 million women and 40.3 million men – lived in Germany (Statistisches Bundesamt, 2008). Women are under-represented in the labour force: with a total labour force participation rate of people aged between 15 and 65 of 75 per cent, the participation rate of women is 68 per cent, compared with the men's rate of around 81 per cent (ibid.). Only 28 per cent of management positions are held by women (Holst, 2007). The comparatively low representation of women in the labour force, especially in management positions, can be traced back mainly to their roles as family and household caretakers and the very poor provision of governmental child care institutions in Germany. For many years, women's participation in the labour force has been increasing continuously, and women have become better educated. Nevertheless, the gender pay gap is tremendous: with women averaging only 82 per cent of men's pay, Germany is among those nations with the largest gender pay gap in Europe (Busch and Holst, 2008).

What is interesting to note is the setting in the former German Democratic Republic (GDR): until the breakdown of the communist government in the 1990s, Eastern Germany was characterized by full employment. This included women; the employment rate of women approached 100 per cent. Furthermore, women often worked in jobs that have been regarded by the Federal Republic of Germany's society as typically male, for example, crane operators or machinists. Since the reunification of the two parts of Germany, the labour force structure in Eastern Germany has adapted to that of Western Germany (Manske and Meißner, 1999).

1.1.2   Ethnicity/migration background   The employment of people with a migration background in Germany has a specific historical background: between 1955 and 1973, so-called 'guest workers' from foreign countries were recruited by the Federal Republic of Germany in order to respond to the extraordinarily high labour force demand. After having worked for some years, these migrant workers did not return to their countries of origin, as was expected. Instead, they and their families have remained in Germany. As mainly the second generation of these people have become better educated, they endeavour to achieve an adequate vocational career. Recognizing these historical roots, we speak about 'people with a migration background' here instead of using the terms 'race' or 'ethnicity'. Whereas 'race' is mainly associated with colour and 'ethnicity' with cultural commonalities, migration background refers to the fact of having immigrated into the focal country. The concept thereby broadens the traditional focus on citizenship, as it includes, in addition to 'foreigners', naturalized citizens, resettlers, and their direct descendants.

In 2006, 15.1 million people with a migration background lived in Germany. They represent 18.4 per cent of the total German population and 16.2 per cent of the German labour force (Statistisches Bundesamt, 2008). People with a migration background are strongly underrepresented in management positions and overrepresented in lower positions and jobs with undesirable working conditions. They are far from being included socially within organizations (Anders et al., 2008; Schmidt, 2007; Ortlieb and Sieben, 2010). However, there is a great heterogeneity in the migrant population. For instance, the study by Sinus Sociovison (2007) differentiates several milieus that are more or less linked to separation from or integration into the German society. These milieus are far less differentiated by ethnic, national or cultural background than by educational levels, values and lifestyles, which in turn are affected by the regional – urban or countryside – origin of their members. Accordingly societal inclusion rests mainly on the adaptation to middle-class educational and work habits (Beck and Perry, 2008).

1.1.3　Age　Similar to people with a migration background, older people face difficulties in getting a job. For instance, while the duration of a period of unemployment averages about 9 months, people older than 50 need on average 15 months to find a new job (Bundesagentur für Arbeit, 2007). In 2006, 16.3 million people aged 65 and above lived in Germany. Their percentage of the total population has been increasing for longer than 50 years (Statistisches Bundesamt, 2008). The labour participation rate declines dramatically with increasing age: while 85 per cent of the people aged between 50 and 54 participate in the labour force, this is the case for only 74 per cent of those between 55 and 59 and 33 per cent of those between 60 and 64. This decline can be partly attributed to extensive early retirement policies. Due to the compulsory retirement age of 65, only 3 per cent of the people aged 65 and above are part of the labour force. These facts represent a severe challenge in view of the demographic change: according to a forecast by the Commission of European Communities (2006), in 2050 nearly one-third of the German population will be 65 or older.

1.1.4　Disability status　Regarding the 8.6 million registered disabled people living in Germany in 2005, the labour force participation rate of people aged between 15 and 65 is about 50 per cent. The women's rate therein is 46 per cent and the men's rate 53 per cent (Statistisches Bundesamt, 2006). Difficulties in getting a job are similar to those of people with a migration background and people aged 50 and above. However, there are many non-profit organizations that employ disabled people for therapeutic and welfare reasons, some of which are sponsored by the German government.

1.2 Relevant laws

In Germany, several legal norms have addressed equal treatment and anti-discrimination at work for many decades:

- The most fundamental legal norm is Article 3 (3) of the Grundgesetz (GG, Federal Constitution Act) dating from 1949, which stipulates that no one should be discriminated against because of gender, race, language, homeland, origin, religious or political opinions, and no person should be disadvantaged because of disability.

- Likewise the Betriebsverfassungsgesetz (BetrVG, Works Constitution Act) – the law of industrial relations at the company level – embodies in § 75 principles for the equal treatment of employees. § 1 stipulates that the employer and the works council should ensure that all the people working in the company are treated according to principles of justice and equity. In particular, no discrimination because of race, ethnic background or origin, nationality, religion or faith, disability, age, political or trade union activity or attitude, gender or sexual identity should occur. Additionally, some of the works council's general tasks named in § 80 refer to equal treatment and diversity. For example, the works council must enforce real equality between women and men, enhance work–life balance, deal with the concerns of young employees, foster the employment of older people and the integration of disabled and other employees in special need of protection, promote employment of migrant employees as well as understanding between foreign and German workers and fight against racism and xenophobia. The BetrVG dates back to 1952. The most recent changes were passed in 2001, concerning among other things the representation of women employees in works councils and the obligation to fight against racism and xenophobia in organizations.

- To transpose the four well-known pertinent EU directives on anti-discrimination (2000/43/EG; 2000/78/EG; 2002/73/EG and 2004/113/EG) into national law, the Allgemeines Gleichbehandlungsgesetz (AGG, General Equal Treatment Act) was enacted in August 2006. Here, the legislators aimed at a comprehensive approach that unifies several dimensions of both diversity and life spheres into one single act. According to § 1, the employer is required to prevent or to eliminate discrimination because of race or ethnic background, gender, religion or faith, disability, age or sexual identity. Whereas the exact wording of the law is 'disadvantaging' (*Benachteiligung*), the prevalent concepts of direct and indirect discrimination are outlined in § 3. Regarding different life spheres and the respective legal spheres, the AGG refers to both civil law and employment law. The people to be protected thereby need not be regularly employed, as described in § 6 (1); people such as vocational trainees, job applicants and former employees are covered as well. § 7 forbids discrimination against these people for one of the above-mentioned reasons. This implies, for example, that job advertisements must be designed to be gender-neutral, or that jokes about disabled people are prohibited. The employer is obliged to implement preventive or reactive instruments (§ 12). Together with trade unions, staff and the works council, the employer must encourage compliance with the law (§ 17). Two further aspects are of special interest. These are, first, the right of action for individuals as well as for works councils or trade unions in the case of violations of this law stated in § 17 (2), and second, that injured people are entitled to compensation under § 15 while the burden of proof lies on the accused (§ 22).

Special minority groups are protected by further specific laws:

- Concerns of disabled employees are addressed by the formerly named Schwerbehindertengesetz (SchwbG, Disabled Persons Act; since 2001: Sozialgesetzbuch IX – SGB, Code of Social Law). For example, § 5 constitutes the employer's liability to employ disabled persons. If the company has more than 20 jobs, 5 per cent of the positions should be held by disabled people. Otherwise, following § 11, monetary compensation has to be made. In addition, disabled people receive an extra five paid absence days per year (§ 47), and they have the right to special dismissal protection (§§ 15–19). Furthermore, the law contains extensive norms about goals and instruments as to the vocational integration of disabled people. Its precursors date from the years 1961 and 1974.
- Pregnant women are protected by the Mutterschutzgesetz (MuschG, Law on the Protection of Expectant and Nursing Mothers), which, for example, prohibits the employment of pregnant women in jobs involving lifting (§ 4) or during the last six weeks of pregnancy (§ 3). Additionally, according to § 9 (1), the dismissal of women during pregnancy and for the first four months after childbirth is prohibited. This law was enacted in 1952, with its origins dating back to 1878.
- Young employees under the age of 18 are protected by the Jugendarbeitsschutzgesetz (JArbSchG, Young Persons' Protection of Employment Act), especially in relation to working and leisure times and physically demanding job tasks. This law also has a longstanding tradition: the current norms date from 1976, rooted in an initial version of 1839.
- Older employees – especially those with high tenure – have the right to special dismissal protection through the Kündigungsschutzgesetz (KSchG, Employment Protection Act), which was enacted in 1951.

It should be added that the 16 federal states of which Germany is composed have slightly different legislation on equal opportunities issues. The main focus of these laws is on equal opportunities for women and men as public service employees of educational and healthcare institutions and public administration in general. For instance, federal laws regulate the tasks and rights of equal opportunity officers and stipulate positive predisposition for women and people with disabilities within the course of personnel selection. That is, according to the law, women or disabled people are to be selected for a vacant position whenever their relevant job skills, knowledge and abilities are equivalent to those of male applicants or job applicants without disabilities.

1.3   Public discourse on the legislation

A debate lasted over many years before the adoption of the AGG. While the public service sector has already been covered by equal opportunities acts for many years, the private sector remained undisturbed. In the late 1990s, the German government planned to pass an equal opportunities act addressing the private sector (see the draft in Pfarr, 2001). Due to heavy criticism and reservations concerning such a law on the part of the employers, in 2001 the government stopped the draft bill. Instead, it signed an agreement with the employers' federations on the self-commitment of employers regarding equal opportunities on a voluntary basis. The government praised the ensuing improvements and exemplary company policies (BMFSFJ, 2003). However, it turned out that the agreement did not yield significant results (Krell and Ortlieb, 2004). Nevertheless, the discussion on an equal opportunities act addressing the private sector died down.

Later on, in 2006 the planned bill was replaced by the AGG. Again, after its enactment, mainly employers' federations complained about 'bureaucratic monsters', predicted high costs, and proclaimed the abolition of the freedom of contract. Others stated that, due to the burden created by these norms, employers might refuse to employ, for example, any women and migrants at all. Overall, in this debate, the AGG was assumed not only to damage employers but also those who were originally to have been protected. Conservative newspapers even presumed that the law and the corresponding debate might force Chancellor Angela Merkel to resign. At the time of writing, about three years after the enactment, the debate has cooled. As Bayreuther (2007) argued, respective legal imperatives already existed, and many of the fears accompanying the implementation of the AGG (e.g. of excessive claims for damages) have proved unfounded.

1.4   Equal opportunity concepts in German practice and debate: gender mainstreaming and diversity management

With regard to equal opportunities at work, two concepts have gained prominence and raised debate in Germany: gender mainstreaming and diversity management. These concepts cannot be described independently of each other (Meuser and Neusüß, 2004). In their application to the management of human resources, both aim at the implementation and fostering of equal opportunities in organizations. Gender mainstreaming is often related to public administration and diversity management to private enterprises, although this differentiation is not constitutive of their conceptual cores. However, it is rooted in their respective origins and regulatory character.

The approach of gender mainstreaming originates in the fourth world women's conference of the United Nations in Beijing in 1995. With the Amsterdam Treaty of 1997, gender mainstreaming became obligatory for the member states of the European Union. According to the European Council, gender mainstreaming means 'the (re)organization, improvement, development and evaluation of policy processes, so that a gender equality perspective is incorporated in all policies at all levels and at all stages, by the actors normally involved in policy-making' (Council of Europe, 1998, p. 15). According to this definition, gender mainstreaming is understood to be a cross-sectional task. It has (a) a personal dimension – all members of an organization are involved, (b) a thematic dimension – all programmes and decisions have to be checked with respect to gender equality, and (c) a formal dimension – all levels of an organization's hierarchy are involved.

In contrast, the concept of diversity management has its roots in the US human rights movement and the equal opportunities legislation it spurred. However, there is no corpus of legislation that would prescribe the implementation of diversity management. This concept encompasses strategies, programmes and instruments directed towards a constructive handling of the diversity of organizational members and other stakeholders, such as clients or investors, for example, regarding gender, age, ethnicity, sexual orientation and physical ability. The declared aim is to appreciate such diversity and to prevent any discrimination because of a certain group membership or of individual attributes since this, according to the proponents' arguments, may result in competitive advantage (Cox, 1993; Thomas, 2000). In the German discourse, diversity management emerged primarily as a human resource management concept in the late 1990s (Krell, 1996; Koall et al., 2002; Vedder, 2006; Krell, 2008a) and has been proliferating ever since, above all in private organizations (Süß and Kleiner, 2006a).

Returning first to gender mainstreaming, one of its main merits is that the concept implicitly challenges classical organization theory. According to the theory of (bureaucratic) organization from Weber to Luhmann, organizations are portrayed as gender-blind. This view is usually shared in organizational self-presentations. It is heavily questioned by the feminist theory of gendered organization (Acker, 1990, 1992). According to this theory, organizations have a gendered substructure that is not accidental, but an inherent feature. We need not decide on the correctness of either theory to notice that, with gender mainstreaming, gender becomes a parameter in an organization's self-observation that is potentially omnirelevant. When implementing gender mainstreaming, the organization becomes aware of its gendered substructure.

However, the politics of gender mainstreaming were not generally welcomed in Germany by feminists and protagonists of equal opportunity politics in favour of women. The reason is that the focus changes from women to gender. Thus, in principle, men are also included as beneficiaries of gender mainstreaming. It was suspected that gender mainstreaming could weaken women's politics. And indeed, quite a few public administrations cancelled the position of women's representative and installed the position of gender mainstreaming representative. Often the person remained the same, but the duties proliferated. A look at the implementation of gender mainstreaming reveals that this approach covers traditional women's politics as well as broader strategies that direct gender politics onto both genders. In recent years a central issue in debates on gender mainstreaming has been the question whether (and to what extent) programmes addressed to (specific groups of) men must be developed – for example, in favour of boys who are increasingly underachieving in school compared to girls. Therefore it builds on the acknowledgement that there is no gender-neutral reality, and it prescribes the consideration of the different living situations of women and men *ex ante* and continuously within all societal projects (Krell et al., 2008). Accompanying its implementation in organizational practice (for Germany, cf. www.gendermainstreaming.net), an academic discussion emerged around topics such as gender policy and organization, implementation and scope for design, instruments, and the relation between gender studies and gender politics (for an overview, cf. the contributions in Meuser and Neusüß, 2004). Nevertheless, looking back at ten years of implementing gender mainstreaming, we can observe that the conflict between women's politics and gender mainstreaming has cooled a great deal.

However, a new conflict has emerged: many protagonists of gender mainstreaming are very sceptical of diversity management. A main objection is that a focus on diversity reduces gender to one category among others (class, ethnicity, nationality etc.) in observing organizations. In this way, critics suspect that the social category of gender has decreased in significance and gender topics are marginalized in equal opportunity politics (e.g. Wetterer, 2002; Knapp, 2005; Stiegler, 2005). Furthermore, such critics accuse diversity management of being business-driven above all. The fear is that economic might outweigh (gender-) political goals. According to Bührmann (2005, p. 83), diversity management tends to become the dominating rationale even in public administration. This development must be seen as part of a restructuring of public administration according to the principle of 'New Public Management'. Following this principle, instruments that have been developed in private enterprises such as management by setting objectives or benchmarks are transferred to and adopted in public administration.

However, objections have not only been raised against diversity management. Regarding both concepts, gender mainstreaming as well as diversity management, critics argue that they tend to neglect the dimension of social inequality that characterizes gender relations and other social relations (e.g. with a view to class, ethnicity or sexual orientation). In particular, gender researchers argue that both approaches turn gender into a category that is stripped of its political implications (Bereswill, 2004; Wetterer, 2002). In both approaches, gender is acknowledged as a social or cultural construct. Yet, according to such criticism, the way gender is addressed invites the reinforcement of gender differences instead of their deconstruction. For example, both concepts imply the need to survey the gender ratio in organizations. Although the claims of these concepts include far more than this, some debates give the impression that using the terminology of gender implies nothing more than simple gender counting. And what is more, the procedure itself harbours the danger of affirming an understanding of male and female as discrete categories. Another contentious aspect is the call to acknowledge and value the specific competences and potentials of women and men, or of other social groups in the organization (e.g. differentiated by age, migration background etc.). With regard to gender mainstreaming, this call is described as an often unintentional reinforcement of gender stereotypes. Instead of being challenged, the gendered division of labour tends to be handled as a 'natural order' and as a resource that human resource management should rely on positively (Meuser, 2004, 2005). Analogous caveats have been raised against such approaches to diversity management that are based on an understanding of diversity as differences between social groups of employees (Krell, 2008a).

Looking more closely at the discourse of gender as a human resource or as human capital, it is important to note that mainly female resources are at stake. This discourse implicitly focuses on women, not on women and men. Gender is perceived as a human resource of women only. While aiming at strengthening the position of women in the labour force, an equation is reproduced that is well known from the history of the cultural construction of gender in Western society: to see only women as gendered beings.

In discussing the criticism raised against gender mainstreaming and diversity management by scholars of gender studies, it must be taken into account that the structures of relevance are different in scientific research, gender politics and organizational development. It is quite normal for scientific categories to change their meaning when expanding from science into praxis. This not only applies to gender. A certain degree of trivialization seems to be the price that scientific concepts generally have to pay when they become popular or 'successful' outside of academia (Meuser, 2004).

1.5   Institutionalization and professionalization of equal opportunities
As noted above, the AGG has a special relevance in equal opportunity legislation in Germany, given its comprehensive approach to diversity and different life spheres, including work in organizations. To support and accompany its implementation, the

Federal Anti-Discrimination Agency was established together with the enactment of the law in 2006 as an advisory institution for individuals as well as for companies. Several federal states subsequently founded or strengthened respective anti-discrimination agencies, for instance, Berlin and Brandenburg.

Equal opportunity legislation and diversity management are interrelated in several ways: first, diversity management concepts help employers to meet the legal standards set by the AGG (cf. Krell, 2008a; Merx and Vassilopoulou, 2007). As legislation is regarded as one of the main drivers for the institutionalization of practices, diversity management, which started to appear in German companies around the end of the 1990s, is expected to spread increasingly in the near future (cf. Stuber, 2006; Süß and Kleiner, 2006a). Second, in the academic realm, next to gender (which has a longer tradition), the topic of diversity is also increasingly becoming established. It is incorporated in university teaching (for an overview on diversity-related teaching activities in HRM, cf. Krell et al., 2006); comprehensive study and research programmes have been launched and diversity professorships have been established (e.g. at the Christian-Albrechts-University of Kiel for the discipline of sociology, for management at the Berlin Humboldt University, and for human resource management at the Freie Universität Berlin). Third, we observe attempts by political actors to use the terminology of diversity management. For example, the Ministry of Commerce and the Ministry of Family, Senior, Women and Youth Affairs have started to use diversity-related terms such as valuation of diversity in teams and in the population. In 2007, a campaign 'Diversity as an Opportunity' was launched, aiming especially at sensitizing employers to the benefits of ethnic and cultural diversity at work. This campaign includes the promotion of the 'charter of diversity', a letter of self-commitment to diversity principles that was composed in 2006 by the federal government together with large companies and has since been signed by many German employers.

2.   Research on diversity and equal treatment at work

2.1   *Historical background and related approaches*

2.1.1   Lines of development of the academic debate   In Germany, work-related research on single diversity dimensions has a long tradition, for example, with regard to gender (e.g. Krell and Osterloh, 1993), to age (Naegele, 2004, 2005), and to migration background (Bukow, 1996; Yildiz, 1997). It should be added that a problem focus on 'special' employee groups often prevailed, as for instance in the body of research on the 'guest workers' and related integration problems (e.g. Gaugler et al., 1985; Martin, 1991). This is one of the aspects that has changed with a focus on diversity and diversity management, for this focus is accompanied by a stress on potentials and opportunities. Another aspect is the focus on the mixture of social categories in the workforce and their handling.

However, explicit and systematic approaches to diversity and its management did not emerge until the 1990s. The first German publications included that by Kiechl (1993), who labelled diversity management as 'post-modern cultural activities in the enterprise', a German reader on 'creating diversity' by Jung et al. (1994), and a critical analysis by Krell (1996). She transferred the US diversity debate to the German context and scrutinized the notion of monocultural organizations. Since then, the body of literature on diversity and diversity management has been growing persistently. Contemporary diversity-related research considers, for instance, gerontological aspects like active ageing (Barkholdt and Naegele, 2007; Frerichs, 1998; Sporket, 2008), or diversity strategies related to the employment of people with migration backgrounds (Anders et al., 2008; Ortlieb and Sieben, 2008a).

Accompanied by corresponding developments in organizational practices and debates among practitioners, Süß and Kleiner (2006b) brought up the question ten years later of whether diversity is to be characterized as a management fashion. Gender mainstreaming (cf. Section 1.4), like the other relevant practice-oriented concepts nurturing research on equal opportunities, especially for the German public sector, has become powerful because of the political forces that promote gender politics, that is, equal treatment and opportunities (Tondorf, 2001).

Before going deeper into topics and theoretical approaches of current research on diversity, we briefly review some historical roots of the respective research on human resource management.

2.1.2   Research on human resource management   Inspired by the recognition of the changes in society's values (*gesellschaftlicher Wertewandel*), an early discussion of diversity-related topics emerged in the debate about German human resource management. Several concepts arose from this discussion. Their common denominator was a consideration of the individual orientation of employees, of differences within the workforce and a related concern for a differentiated treatment of employees. Building on considerations of work motivation, the idea was to enhance the organization's goal achievement by accounting for individual requirements of work quality. Conditions for higher employee performance were to be created through an individual structuring of work (e.g. flexible work time), compensation (in particular, flexible benefits systems), work–life balance as well as personnel development and career opportunities (cf. the contributions in Drumm, 1989a). These concepts were labelled 'Individualized Organization' (*Individualisierte Organization*; Schanz, 1977a, 1977b), 'Differential Job Design' (*Differenzielle Arbeitsgestaltung*; Ulich, 1978), and 'Individualization of Human Resource Management' (*Individualisierung der Personalwirtschaft*; Drumm, 1989b, 2000). Marr's (1989) 'Differentiating Human Resource Management' (*Differenzielle Personalwirtschaft*) is theoretically challenging; it is an HRM concept that builds on the ideas of individualization and the implementation of flexibility (for later developments see Fritsch, 1994; Wiegran, 1996; Morick, 2002). A theoretically based consideration of individual differences is to be achieved by criteria of differentiation on an individual level: (a) individual attributes, such as age, gender and occupation; (b) practical characteristics of the person, such as hierarchical, functional and institutional roles and positions; (c) characteristics of personality, such as motives, values and cognitive orientations; (d) abilities, such as expertise, social competence and ability to communicate; (e) personal living conditions, such as family status and duration of active work life. The main idea is that these attributes moderate the relationship between performance behaviour (as the dependent variable) and individual characteristics (as independent variables). Finally, the identification of homogeneous employee groups should be the practical basis for creating general rules for them (Morick, 2002).

Proponents of these concepts turn away from the assumption of what is called a standard employment relationship (*Normalarbeitsverhältnis*). They all stress the tension between the quest for equal treatment (prescribed by general rules and legal provisions) and the concern for individual circumstances and needs. However, despite their intention to deal with the employee's individuality, it is not their primary aim to account for the goals or interests of (groups of) employees. Rather, this concern is a means to enhance employee performance and thereby achieve the organization's goals. In his latest approach to a 'Differentiating Human Resource Management', Morick (2002) states that a discussion of this topic presumably will not be initiated until research on diversity is carried out on a broader basis.

The heterogeneity of the workforce is still acknowledged in other respects. In early attempts to analyse specific groups of employees, the following are distinguished (and nearly always treated as problematic groups): young people, elderly persons, women, foreigners and disabled persons (for an overview see Mag, 1989). It is the deviation from the 'standard employee' that makes members of these groups a specific clientele for HRM politics, a focus that at the same time paves the way for prejudice and stigmatization. Nevertheless, the analytic creation of different groups (or types or segments) of employees is a useful method of analysis. The criteria most frequently used are (for an overview see Schramm, 2004): (a) the offered labour (*Arbeitsangebot*) or sociodemographic characteristics (the traditional basis of diversity); (b) specific value orientations (*Werthaltungen*), for example, as to career, leisure or alternative engagement (Einsiedler, 1993; Inglehard, 1998); and (c) the modus of labour supply (*Erwerbsform*). The last is of particular importance because of its potential to describe and analyse existing forms of paid employment, that is, regular employment relationship, part-time employment, temporary (or irregular) employment and precarious employment (e.g. 'working poor'). The recent development of these employment forms is of special interest as well as the relevant outcomes and demands for an adequate creation of employment systems (Marsden, 1999; Schramm, 2007) and the alignment of HRM systems (Ridder et al., 2001).

2.2   Contemporary research: theories, methods, topics and epistemological underpinnings
A large part of diversity-focused research in Germany is practice-driven. Scientific approaches are dominated by researchers from the social and political sciences as well as by management researchers. In what follows, we try to achieve a systematic overview, which, due to the sheer variety, is a rather challenging venture (cf. Koall et al., 2007; Krell et al., 2007).

We begin with a recursive overview of theories and methods applied as well as predominant topics. Then we dig deeper into the scientific discourse on diversity and its management by discussing the epistemological underpinnings of respective studies. In a final step, we discuss the focus on single diversity dimensions versus a focus on intersectionality.

2.2.1   Theories and methods   A broad range of theories has been used in the German scientific discourse on gender and diversity. For instance, a systems theory perspective has been used to analyse diversity and diversity management by Aretz and Hansen (2002), Baecker (2005), Elmerich (2007), Knoth (2006), Koall (2001) as well as Labucay (2006). Lederle (2007) and Süß and Kleiner (2006a), who address the diffusion of diversity programmes and practices, ground their analyses on sociological neo-institutionalism. Additionally, Süß (2009) uses Giddens's theory of structuration. A. Becker (2006) refers to transaction cost theory in order to analyse the costs and benefits of diversity initiatives. Ortlieb and Sieben (2008a, b) resort to resource dependence theory in order to explain why people with a migration background are (not) employed in organizations. Poststructuralist approaches are applied by Koall (2001) and Krell (2003) in order to highlight and critically examine the (re)production of differences and power structures.

Methods applied in empirical studies on gender and diversity, or gender mainstreaming and diversity management, respectively, concentrate on surveys. To name some examples, Krell et al. (2006) conducted a questionnaire-based study among chair holders in Business Administration about their activities in diversity-related research and teaching. Stuber (2007) uses a survey to investigate the return on investment gained by the implementation of diversity management. Süß and Kleiner (2006a) rely on survey data in order to investigate the diffusion of diversity management in private organizations. Köppel et al. (2007) examine particularly the diffusion of cultural diversity management practices in Germany in this way. Other studies rely on expert interviews. For instance, Schmidt (2005) consulted gender mainstreaming representatives and other institutional actors who are responsible for implementing policy. Vedder (2006) relies on expert interviews and document analyses for his international comparison of diversity initiatives. Von Dippel (2007) conducted interviews with executives in public administration about their views on diversity management. Anders et al. (2008) integrate two approaches in their study on personnel structures and practices in Berlin companies. A quantitative approach based on telephone interviews with heads of personnel is combined with a qualitative approach based on case studies in selected companies. Even more sophisticated research designs are pursued in the discourse analysis by Lederle (2007), who analyses the implementation of diversity management in Germany and the ethnographic case study by Frohnen (2005), who in turn examines the social construction of diversity at work.

A currently unexplored area is the assessment of the construct of diversity itself. Most of the research concentrates on single diversity dimensions like age or migration background, partly combined with a second one, e.g. gender. Thus the intersections of multiple dimensions are seldom covered (cf. in more detail Section 2.3). Voigt and Wagner (2006) provide a methodological reflection in this regard by discussing the application of more extensive numeric diversity measures.

Furthermore, there are approaches that aim at clustering the field of diversity research. For example, M. Becker (2006) suggests a three-level model that allows the characterization of diversity studies by type of research, its subject, and by research paths in order to explore the state of the art systematically. Krell and Sieben (2007) propose a guide of diversity research that characterizes research questions by the method and the goal of the research. This guide allows us to highlight specific merits and blinders of respective approaches to diversity, and in particular it demonstrates the fruitfulness of multiparadigmatic research on connected topics. For a similar approach cf. Section 2.2.3, where we explore the epistemological underpinnings of diversity studies.

2.2.2 Business case and best practices The business case and economic efficiency of diversity and diversity management programmes are prevalent topics in the respective research. They have been analysed by Sepehri (2002) in international companies and by Gebert (2004) by means of a meta-analysis on the innovative capacity of teams. Weißbach et al. (2007) have analysed the commitment and success of intercultural teams, and Stuber (2007) has investigated the return on investment of diversity management.

Additionally, there is a broad range of publications addressing best practices. For instance, Jung and Küpper (2001) report on best-practice examples of gender mainstreaming. The volume on human resource management practices fostering equal opportunities, particularly between men and women, and edited by Krell (2008b), contains a series of best-practice examples building on gender mainstreaming as well as on diversity management. Best diversity practices are also covered by the volume edited by Koall et al. (2007). Another recent topic is age diversity (Bender, 2007). For instance, Frerichs and Sporket (2007, p. 1) point out that 'more than half of German companies do not hire employees above the age of 50'. By 'combating age barriers', organizations adapt to inclusion choices by moderating their already introduced HR instruments towards more flexibility of work, career development, lifelong learning and health promotion systems (Frerichs and Sporket, 2007; Sporket, 2008).

2.2.3   Epistemological underpinnings of research on diversity management   Let us now turn to another view of contemporary research on the topic of diversity management in Germany. By using case studies, we reveal the theoretical assumptions that underpin these respective studies. For this purpose, we draw on a differentiation of research approaches stemming from systems theory. We apply constructivist epistemology within social system theory as this perspective permits the highlighting of linkages between science and practice, and the respective logics of these systems. This approach is particularly fruitful since the research on diversity is, for the most part, practice- and problem-driven. Furthermore, it aims mainly at developing recommendations as to how the potentials of diversity may best be used, whether on behalf of individuals, of organizations or of society.

As Luhmann (1984) argues, theory is arranged according to constructed factuality, dedicated or reserved perspectives, building functions or relating to norms to describe the autopoietical demands of social systems. Regarding opposing sociological programmes of functional theory of social systems (Luhmann), on the one hand, and politically oriented critical theory (Habermas, 1981) on the other, we can analyse and criticize social systems either on the level of their autopoietical reproducing function and structures (functional) or on the level of possible political visioning (normative). Against this background (and following Witt, 1994), we distinguish research approaches by their functional or normative epistemological focus, that is, by the assumptions researchers hold about their objects and the aims they are directed at. Functional approaches try to achieve complexity reduction by referring to 'factual constraints', actions and communication of corporations. As Witt (1994, p. 344) points out, such approaches sometimes work subversively, since they may unmask the capitalist ideology. However, the affirmation of functional economic assumptions may tend to blend out social complexity (Grieger, 2004, p. 60). In contrast, normative diversity approaches are driven by ethical and political efforts. They support an understanding of discrimination, emancipation and justice, and try to balance discrepancies between economic and political systems. They correspond to critical perspectives that scrutinize and criticize the ideology

Table 6.1   Epistemological orientations of diversity research

Epistemological focus / Practice-oriented intention	*Functional*	*Normative*
Prescriptive	Functional-prescriptive orientation	Normative-prescriptive orientation
Descriptive	Functional-descriptive orientation	Normative-descriptive orientation

of inherent business necessity. As such, they often include implicit (idealistic) exceptional knowledge about reality. Furthermore, they are inherently reflective regarding their own schools of thought or standpoints (such as feminist, poststructuralist, critical).

Following Kappler (1976), Pfriem (1983) and Steinmann et al. (1976), we further distinguish prescriptive and descriptive intentions. This dimension describes the distinction between theoretical work and practical application. Scientists relate theory to practice basically in two ways (Ridder, 1990, pp. 217, 293; Witt, 1994, pp. 304f.): they aim either at explaining or at designing practice. In descriptive approaches, researchers observe practice in order to enhance the self-perception of practitioners in acting and reflecting. In contrast, in prescriptive approaches, good practice is invented; strategies or operationally usable instruments are developed.

The combination of these two dimensions results in four research orientations (see Table 6.1), which we use in the following to characterize the epistemological underpinnings of diversity research. However, it should be noted that considerable interference occurs. That is, some approaches may be characterized by more than one orientation or may appear at a transition zone between orientations.

FUNCTIONAL-PRESCRIPTIVE ORIENTATION   In such approaches, efficiency and functional relations of diversity management in business processes are observed. They are related to a presumably objective outer world, as being constructed or evolved by communication. Functionality acts as a norm (Kappler, 1976, p. 122) and is used as a discursive support for the relevance of factual diversity processes.

An initial example of such an approach is provided by Aretz and Hansen (2002; cf. also Aretz and Hansen, 2003). Following Parsons's structural-functional system approach, these authors develop a framework based on the AGIL scheme (i.e. adaptation, goal attainment, integration, latent pattern maintenance) which prescribes how corporations may fulfil the 'necessity' (Aretz and Hansen, 2002, p. 48) of dealing with diversity. Organizations are perceived to coordinate their four cultural subsystems in order to secure the function of latent pattern maintenance (via mission statements, values, visions), to integrate diversity into a team or group collective (by affiliation, tenure, unity in diversity), to adapt to the environment by mobilizing resources for diversity issues (by best practice, workflow, professionalization, rewards) and, finally, to secure the function of goal attainment by fostering leadership and responsibility (via hierarchy, career paths and job description). Aretz and Hansen (2002, p. 70) propose that diversity implementation should follow functional imperatives and be oriented towards business stages for diversity management. These comprise mobilizing resources, developing a vision, creating a shared need and making it last.

A further example is Sepehri's (2002) comparison of European, American and Asian diversity research. He claims that homogeneous business cultures have less visible internal discrimination and therefore pay less attention to diversity issues than heterogeneous cultures. These work with demographic differences to regulate their processes. Sepehri ascribes to diversity management the capacity to change homogeneous into heterogeneous cultures, to alter power relations, the exclusive formation of opinion and the oppression of social and human resources. However, he does not consider the requirements needed to get to the anticipated cultures and structures that enable the use of heterogeneous resources.

Against this background, it is useful to analyse to what extent diversity management may be functionally equivalent to an elitist regulation of complex systems (Koall, 2007). According to Luhmann (1970, p. 35), functions may not be viewed as objective standards but as discursively developed arrangements to fulfil autopoietical needs. Functions are changeable, by using a different frame of reference, by analysing expectations, and by defining a problem so that solutions are comparable rather than using fixed cause-and-effect relations for problem-solving. Functions of hegemony have to be considered if one wants them to be replaced. For this purpose, it is necessary to analyse how homogeneity is reproduced in an organization. To what needs does it respond in the social organizational setting and what alternatives may fulfil these needs in a different way?

FUNCTIONAL-DESCRIPTIVE ORIENTATION Here, factuality is mainly ordered by business objectives as well as by functional relations, which are defined as the implicit and explicit knowledge of managing an enterprise. These approaches work on the level of disenchantment (*Entzauberung*) and reconstruct principles of business reality. Using descriptive-functional approaches, researchers observe the performance and capacity of a system and scrutinize conditions to develop functional equivalents.

For example, M. Becker (2006, p. 5) observes a paradigm shift in the diversity discourse from affirmative action to the change of organizational culture. The management of a heterogeneous workforce relates to internal and external drivers as well as to agency and actor perspectives. Heterogeneity and homogeneity are more or less functionally applied in order to produce business outcomes. A functional orientation requires active, strategic and operative diversity management activities according to predefined business objectives. By optimizing diverse resources, a unique competitive positioning is fostered. Therefore, according to M. Becker (2006, p. 42), diversity management should be (labour)-market-driven and business-case-oriented.

Based on neo-institutional theory, Süß and Kleiner (2006b) observe processes of adoption and symbolic representation of diversity management, depending on expected rewards through legitimation. They show that diversity initiatives may be accompanied by isomorphic tendencies developed by several mechanisms: first, by economic or legal pressure; second, by the imitation of structures or behaviours judged useful for obtaining legitimacy and resources; and third, by normative pressure, stemming from professionalization (i.e. through trade unions, occupational networks, educational workers who develop an awareness about diversity issues). The functionality of diversity management is related to isomorphic processes rather than to economic justifications (Süß and Kleiner, 2006b, p. 536). Furthermore, the authors point out that diversity initiatives are still not structurally and strategically embedded. Thus, despite diversity initiatives, the homogeneity of personnel and organizational structures endures. The advantage of this functional reconstruction is that it highlights the gap between the ideology of economic advantage and the practical intentions or 'theory in use' (Argyris and Schön, 1974) of diversity management. Confronted with the complexity of social systems, it is interesting to observe which functions a so-called diversity management programme fulfils, if it tries to avoid complexity in that it is neither related to business objectives nor pursues processes of social innovation and development.

A. Becker (2006) provides a further example of a functional-descriptive orientation. He examines resource-oriented HRDM (human resource diversity management) on the basis of transaction costs theory. He connects the property rights' costs of non- or imperfectly imitable human resources to the competitive advantage of HRDM. This ensures an optimal internal and external creation and allocation of resources stemming from different stakeholders. Thus this perspective considers the diversity of stakeholders in connection with workplace diversity and resource mobility. According to the author, diversity is related to bounded rationality, individualism or opportunism. Such behaviour is moderated by the management's capacity to deal with heterogeneity. Hence HRDM depends first on the quality of the recruited personnel, second on appropriate communication systems and information technologies, and third on varying factor specificity and insecurity moderated by the firm's maturity stage (ranging from traditional, transitional, to transformed). Against this analysis, one may object that the binary distinction between functionally oriented rational firms and the irrational complexity of human beings is not adequate. Organizations may be described as complex social systems, which are also using subjective communicative capacities and legitimate functionality by relating to posterior constructed rational decisions (Luhmann, 2002).

Podsiadlowski (2002) relates to functional arguments by analysing the conditions of diversity-mature organizational settings. She shows that engagement with work, team and task matters more than demographic factors for the successful management of a diverse team (similar to the data reported by Williams and O'Reilly, 1998). Podsiadlowski's findings point to the importance of observing and changing the conditions in organizations as social systems. Only this enables a diverse workforce to act efficiently. In her study, input variables on the individual level were professional competences, motivation and commitment. Group input variables were time, benefits, task orientation and heterogeneity in status, education and profession. On the organizational level she considers variables such as leadership quality, culture and the structuring of processes. Trust, cohesion, time/space for communication and clear-cut responsibilities were relevant for positive group dynamics. Among positive factors for diversity management processes, she counts networking instead of hierarchical communication structures, team locality instead of demographic (nationality, gender, age) locality and a complex structure of task and performance. In her study, diversity management was disturbed by rivalry, which occurred in the form of marginalization of interactional needs, and of social pressure by an unclear division of resources, tasks and responsibilities. The lack of prescriptive expectations or organizational/team history and very distant cultures (e.g.

not as close as UK to USA) were most relevant for success. Open communication and moderated group dynamics were decisive for the success of diversity management.

Another approach to analysing functional relations in organizations is the theory of social systems. It allows the observation of how diversity – in terms of the complexity of social entities (interactions, organizations, societies) – is perceived and processed according to internally developed functions and structures of expectation (Baecker, 2001; Nassehi, 2005). Organizations reduce heterogeneity into homogeneity by their need to regulate communication, evaluate performance and control people. Diversity management tends to unfold heterogeneity; therefore it requires the development of functional equivalents to primary homogeneous functions in organizations. Unfolding complexity raises paradoxes to being able to practise diversity (Baecker, 2001; Lindsay, 1993; Özbilgin and Tatlı, 2008, p. 27; Lewis, 2000; Luhmann, 2005). Paradoxes (defined as logical contradictions within assumptions about normalcy, such as equality in difference) are covered by (business) rationales. Hence they reduce the necessity of reflection and of adjustment to environmental demands. Paradoxes have the power to challenge frameworks of reference, for example, the function–structure relationship in organizations (Koall and Bruchhagen, 2009). Unfolding paradoxes enhances the capacities of self-regulation by referring to communicative contexts and implicit rules of coded communication (Koall, 2001) to control complexity. Knoth (2006) focuses on communication in diversity processes from a radical constructivist point of view. He examines how information in diversity processes is generated by cognitive systems and reflected as meaning. Considering linguistic and cognitive prerequisites of diversity processing, he claims to rely rather on existentialistic problems of interaction (e.g. self-perception, isolation, contingence) than on demographic diversity. Barriers to interaction are used as communicative conflicts to stimulate change and enhance the perception of normalcy and otherness. Culture thereby emerges from complex interactions. This points to the difficulties in implementing a diversity culture. Furthermore, if the implementation remains on the level of buzz-words, diversity management turns out to be a façade of legitimacy (Knoth, 2006, pp. 200f.). According to Baecker (2007), mainstream diversity approaches resemble a unity management rather than a management of diversity, as they are directed towards a reduction of complexity rather than to its use and to the unfolding of paradoxes. By the recommendation of the strategic planning and controlling of diversity programmes and initiatives, complexity is strongly reduced.

A common denominator of German system theorists is that they seek to describe latent assumptions of research and practical applications as well as the conditions of systems' operations, such as organizational sense production and the construction of environmental relations (Baecker, 1994; Knoth, 2006; Koall, 2001; Labucay, 2006). Complex systems challenge mechanisms and conditions such as professionalization, modes of living, news and markets. Within this approach, communication might be perceived in its non-directed, latent, unintended, contingent (possible but not necessary) adjustment (Luhmann, 2002). Rather than being related to business rationales, traces of individual or collective micro diversity in interaction and self-organization are relevant for diversity processes (Baecker, 2005).

Whereas the former cited approaches rely on the social constructivist, communicative perspectives of social systems' analysis, Labucay (2006) deploys a more cybernetic one. She relates a system theory perspective to a cost–benefit analysis of diversity management. As she argues, organizations build their internal complexity self-referentially, but heterogeneity will produce coordination and steering problems. Operationally closed organizations possess the capacity to include diverse members (stakeholders) according to internally defined and shifting boundaries. This offers a development perspective towards more diversity in organizations. Diversity management may be interpreted as a functional device to control spaces and times of social system insecurity. Addressing diversity management within this perception of social systems theory, Labucay (2006, p. 77) combines the diversity issue with postmodern organizational analysis, which addresses the fragmentation and instability of organizational phenomena (cf. also Koall, 2001, pp. 23f.).

In her ethnographic sociological study, Frohnen (2005) describes how diversity is accomplished in the German subsidary of Ford. She explores how the employees find a way to cope with cultural heterogeneity, how the multicultural staff are 'doing diversity' in the workplace. In this case, diversity management is not analysed as a strategy of steering an organization; rather, it is seen as an everyday social practice. The doing and also the undoing of diversity is analysed as an individual as well as a collective functional device to deal with the social complexity of multinational corporations.

Relating to Gergen's (1999) discursive work on collective self-construction and dominance and hegemonic 'truth' production, Pless (1999) describes barriers and resistance to diversity management. Claims about functional business requirements are revealed to be social constructions. Barriers against diversity initiatives are described as a solely communicative construction of 'truth'. Suggesting a paradigm shift from dominance (with a modern and hierarchical ideology of 'different but equal') to partnership ('variety of perspectives is normal') puts relations in the centre of diversity processes. This effort focuses on interactional constructions of organizational factuality, the observation of symbolic networking and the perception of leadership as a cultivating function within relational work. The intention is to transform normative prescriptions into a strongly admired diverse reality. Therefore steering communication should be arranged by diversity norms, ethical principles and communication codes, and controlled by diversity councils and diversity managers. This visioning relies implicitly on prescriptive normativity, as it unmasks and reformulates functional relations.

NORMATIVE-PRESCRIPTIVE ORIENTATION   Following this orientation, researchers seek to work out recipes for best practice and develop instruments and models for a future, visionary enterprise. They might reflect their own political, normative standpoint; however, they only seldom reflect the inherent partiality that arises due to the interdependent levels of observer, actor and implementation (Grieger, 2004, p. 60). Labelling these political approaches as a 'theory of projection', Knoth (2006, p. 15) expounds the problem of using generally valid standards of social justice that lead to an ideological demarcation of demographic groups and vacuous, simplified regulated access according to demographic standards. However, these approaches add surplus to solely business ideology by relating political or collective demands to the diversity policy of organizations. Referring to analyses in which 'rational' business argumentation is confronted with political ambitions or ethical expectations, these normative ideas inspire the future (though uncertain) development of visions of diversity management capabilities and are more or less challenging functional business imperatives.

Domsch and Ladwig (2003) connect political diversity approaches to business structures by relating the hidden costs of discrimination to the benefits of diversity management. The focus of Domsch's (2006) analysis lies on the resistance to change towards equal opportunity practice and the lack of commitment to gender and diversity initiatives. He found that only a minority of contemporary organizations implement equal opportunities programmes strategically and systematically. Respective initiatives seldom find a reflection in the organizational culture, and commitment-enhancing practices such as gender- and diversity-related target agreements and incentives are lacking. Although these organizations have anticipated mega-trends such as demographic change and the search for high potentials, equal opportunity issues such as gendering in marketing (Domsch and Hadler, 1989), women in leadership (Domsch and Regnet, 1990), and double-career couples (Domsch et al., 1988; Domsch and Krüger-Basner, 1989; Domsch and Ladwig, 1998; Behnke and Meuser, 2003) have not been 'hot topics' with companies until non-discrimination legislation (AGG) was enacted in Germany in 2006 (cf. Section 1.5). As a quality tool in the sense of the EFQM (European Foundation for Quality Management), Domsch (2006) developed the genderdax model, by which companies are rated according to their gender and diversity efforts in leadership, policies and strategies and resulting levels of customer satisfaction, employee satisfaction and the impact on society. The idea is that a focus on equal opportunities in the management of partnerships, resources and processes may ultimately lead to excellence in business results. These considerations are political in the sense that they introduce social issues in a rather counterfactual way to mainstream practice. Business objectives are used as a framework to legitimate political approaches. Likewise, Harms and Müller (2004) focus on developing diversity leadership qualities. Based on findings stemming from intercultural research, they recommend relying on well-known leading attitudes and competences such as intensive communication, space for face-to-face interaction, management by walking around, being a champion of diversity and creative support of members of minority groups in leadership positions. But they remain sceptical about whether members of the dominant group can be trained to value 'otherness'. Reflective, sensitizing and awareness-raising programmes are a challenge for both leadership and executive development.

The analysis of Weißbach and Vorontsowa-Schnell (2003) may also be characterized as prescriptive as it offers practical solutions for diversity-related problems. The authors report on the handling of conflicts based on cultural differences in a Russian-German corporation. Conflicts occurred, for instance, due to workflow documenting procedures that were not accepted, to differing needs as to authoritarian versus self-organized relations between managers and subordinates and, above all, due to the stereotyping suffered by the group of East European immigrants. Moreover, the authors observed a remarkable gap between the high professional education of the Russian employees and their low organizational status. The authors conclude that, in order to solve diversity problems, participation is essential for members of dominant as well as of minority groups in training programmes (in communication procedures, technical terminology, leadership models, workstyles) and accompanying social events. This facilitates the development of hybrid cultural identities in the workforce. The authors also work on a counterfactual level, by mixing or combining observation, research and consulting. Their focus lies on how to enhance the capacity of organizations to deal with complicated diversity processes.

NORMATIVE-DESCRIPTIVE ORIENTATION   Such approaches also follow an emancipatory, ethical or political standard by reflecting the conditions and implications of reaching a particular vision. But they mostly resist developing standards for implementing successful diversity initiatives and stay on the level of analytic description, though taking a political standpoint.

The first politically oriented, here labelled normative-descriptive, analysis of diversity management stems from Krell (1996). She describes the functions and dysfunctions of homogeneous and heterogeneous organizations by reconstructing the characteristics of German fascistic '*Gemeinschaftskulturen*' and Japanese 'clan cultures' that may be regarded as prototypes for exclusive organizational cultures. Transferring diversity management to German conditions of society, it is apparent how differences in historical and cultural levels are created to distinguish 'ourselves' from 'others', for example, East from West Germans or 'deviant' from 'standard' employees (i.e. white, male, middle-class, native, not handicapped, without family responsibilities). Examining the appeal of diversity management, the author shows that the concept is ideologically charged with promises of harmony. Compared to affirmative action programmes, diversity management is expected to be less threatening to members of the majority group. That is also why there may be fewer chances to change standard employment conditions, for example to a stronger focus on work–family issues. The described dilemmas are stimulating discussion (Krell, 1996, pp. 346f.): who is participating in the definition of diversity? Who is regarded as an attractive human resource and who is excluded? Do we need a strong diversity culture to support heterogeneity? How much control or self-regulation does the implementation of diversity management need? Several visionary answers (Herrmann-Pillath, 2007; Domsch, 2006; Koall, 2007) respond to these dilemmas. As these examples show, political concepts of personnel management analysis deliver a framework for research on inclusive personnel management. They open up the view on relations of dominance that can reduce complexity, and point out ways to alter the existing order through negotiation processes.

Another topic subject to normative-descriptive-oriented analyses is diversity marketing. For instance, Schuchert-Güler and Eisend (2007) critically examine ethnomarketing instruments and show their stereotyping and normalizing effects. In her analysis, Seidel (2006, p. 252) suggests that diversity marketing bears more political and quality risks than profits for customers. She recommends connecting diversity marketing initiatives to internal organizational and cultural change. Sackmann et al. (2002) analyse the organizational change towards more diversity as a transfer from a homogeneous to a complex organizational culture and observe the impacts, prerequisites and transitions on the individual, team and organizational levels. On the organizational level, they identify time, resources and trust as key factors for changing dominant habits, privileges and perceptions. Change agents, who need knowledge, competences and motivation, are supported by the contemporary 'war for talents', which raises the significance of the 'soft factors' of diverse human capital. Hence normative visioning is here connected to the description of prerequisites for enabling cultural change. Hansen and Müller (2003, p. 34) also develop political diversity perspectives directed to change of organizational cultures. They relate the change of traditional gender biases to social drivers such as individualization and demographic development. With their analysis they describe the ambivalent constitutions of diversity management between market-based views and capacities to 'de-ice' gender cultures.

By his vision of 'open society/companies' to meet complexity demands, Herrmann-Pillath (2007) refers to evolutionary economics. Organizations as motors of social change still employ patterns of closed, homogeneous companies, but are confronted with contemporary environmental demands (e.g. interculturality, indigenous leadership, the decline of patriarchal organizational culture, individualization). Open companies are characterized by double inclusiveness, diffuse ambivalent membership rules, permanent stable networks instead of hierarchies, pluralism of business objectives, fragmentation of leading responsibilities and a stakeholder instead of mere shareholder orientation. By continuously supporting social change towards an open society or company, dominant standards are made dispensable. However, there is the paradox that diversity management is not power-neutral. Elites are needed to support diversity initiatives, but leading classes or elites reproduce anti-democratic structures on behalf of their privileges. Normative approaches suggest that elitarian cultural standards might be overcome in organizations by enhancing participative competences that can help to acquire orientation in complex societies and organizations (Koall, 2007).

Aretz (2006, p. 65) states that there is no empirically proven business relevance for the concept of diversity management, and he questions connected political-normative expectations as to the realization of emancipation and individualization in economic systems. He de-masks diversity management as a sublime disciplinary strategy that replaces hierarchical control by contextual supervision, transparency of decision processes, spontaneous self-exploitation and individual instead of collective bargaining. Subdued to the capitalistic logic, this raises economic efficiency – with consequences for privacy (*Lebenswelt*). The 'entreployee' (*Arbeitskraftunternehmer*, Pongratz and Voß, 2003) is a related paradoxical figure symbolizing the collapsed opposition of work and capital – a binary distinction formerly useful to legitimate exploitation and the distribution of resources. Through diversity management, this paradox might be resolved, proving the relatedness of constructing human and economic capital (Koall and Bruchhagen, 2009).

Therefore it is helpful to conquer binary distinctions by theoretical analyses such as the one we are pursuing here to describe the field of diversity research. There are further German studies (see also Regine Bendl in the Austrian contribution to this volume, Chapter 2) that question the naturalization of binary distinctions and deconstructing diversity from a poststructuralist perspective (Koall, 2001; Krell, 2003). As Baecker (2003) argues, diversity research is related to complex, paradoxical and network organizations. Against this background, the use of deconstructive methodology opens up ways to question normalcy, binary distinctions and dominance, and to reflect on visionary prescriptive recommendations for a sensible dealing with diversity.

2.2.4   Diversity dimensions versus intersectionality   Turning once again to predominant topics of diversity research, it has to be added that very many studies concentrate on specific social groups and thus on single diversity dimensions. A major part of the research in Germany focuses on gender, for example, Koall and Bruchhagen (2002), Bruchhagen and Koall (2007), or the comprehensive book on equal opportunities for women and men edited by Krell (2008b). The book by Hermes and Rohrmann (2006) on disability studies as well as the monograph by Ong (2005) on migrant employees (see also Friedrich-Ebert-Stiftung, 2006; Weißbach and Vorontsowa-Schnell, 2003) and by

Frerichs (1998) on older employees are further examples of research focusing on one single diversity dimension, considering also the heterogeneity within these groups.

Two perspectives dominate diversity research and practice (Krell, 2008a). In the first, the focus is directed on the differences between social groups. Such differentiating approaches have the merit of shedding light on the special situation of such groups, for example, of homosexual or elderly people in organizations. On the other hand, such a focus on differences is particularly susceptible to stereotypical ascriptions, and it runs the risk of overlooking the heterogeneity within groups – whose boundaries are anyway only barely definable. In contrast, in the second perspective on diversity, differences and similarities between group affiliations are accentuated. This focus, in turn, opens up a view on the intersections of social categories.

The concept of intersectionality enables the grasping of this complexity methodologically. The term 'intersectionality' refers to the fact that the position people hold in society and organizations is determined by belonging to different social categories. Moreover, a focus on intersectionality entails the combination of analytical and theoretical perspectives that especially allow the analysis of the hierarchies of different social categories or dimensions. Since the end of the 1970s, there has been ongoing work on epistemological, methodological and theoretical frameworks for research on gender and on other social categories, including associated inequalities and societal power relations. Critics have exposed missing links and blind spots in the dominant debates on differentness and sameness, otherness, as well as equity and inequality. However, the focus on the relation of different categories (such as gender, class and race) at the same time has raised the possibility that the analytical category of gender might run the risk of losing significance. In Germany this discussion is still continuing (e.g. Knapp, 2001, 2005), in particular with regard to gender versus diversity (cf. Section 1.4).

Increasingly globalized societies have also led to a stronger perception of heterogeneity and complexity and are challenging the way of studying and also practising difference. The scientific debate on this topic is intimately connected to debates on equal opportunities politics as well as to corresponding management concepts. In Germany, the issue of gender mainstreaming shaped the discussion of inequality until more politicization occurred due to the lack of quantitative and qualitative inclusion of people with migration backgrounds. We currently perceive respective efforts in response to the demographic change and the perceived social inequalities. However, in scientific as well as in political debates, there is still a kind of competition between different diversity dimensions and their 'relevance'.

Intersectionality offers a way to enrich respective research. Relevant concepts in this regard stem from US gender researchers. To begin with, Crenshaw (2000) offers metaphors on intersection to identify the various forms of subordination of race and gender. As to Crenshaw's metaphor of the 'cross-road', the following criticism has been raised: it certainly draws attention to the potential (simultaneous) discrimination of two dimensions, namely race and gender. However, it does not allow the analysis of the binary classification of gender as a basis for (sub)ordination in a heteronormative patriarchal culture. The main challenge is to combine connectional and methodological approaches in a way that allows the analysis and differentiation of categories of social differences without reproducing them. In this sense, McCall (2005) discusses prospects for a non-essentialist work with socially distinguished dimensions. McCall (2005) distinguishes three methodological approaches to intersectionality: anti-categorical, intra-categorical and inter-categorical. All three allow for describing structures and processes of inequity and inequality. All have their blinders, but respond to the challenge of working with 'the complexity that results from the burden of analysis expanding to include multiple dimensions of social life and categories of analysis' (McCall, 2005, p. 2).

In Germany, Knapp (2005) first discussed intersectionality as a new paradigm of feminist theory, followed by a wider argumentation of the (main) axes of inequality in interdisciplinary perspectives (Klinger et al., 2007). The increasing discussion of intersectionality marks out not only the changing forms of social inequality but also the structurally based continuity of inequality and discrimination (expressed in 'fitted' and actualized phenomena and forms).

The growing interest in intersectional analysis may be explained by the attempts of widening feminist approaches to become compatible with other heuristic and theoretical concepts as well as empirical realities. If we ask for the importance of an intersectional perspective and its compatibility in the field of diversity, we first have to contextualize the efforts to reflect and theorize conditions, experiences and practices of inequality. Early feminist discourses opened social categories of inequality as gender and class in relation to other categories. Moreover, the theoretical discourses have referred to social experiences (as stated above) of inequality and oppression and to the practice of 'doing difference'. An adequate theoretical approach must overcome earlier approaches that put the focus on one or a few leading dimensions of discrimination in order to be able to work on the multiplicity and complexity of oppression and discrimination. Furthermore, those categories that do not focus on the US mainstream triad of gender, race and class (such categories discussed include nationality, religion, citizenship) tend to be neglected. On the other hand, Münst (2008) points out that the empirical concept of a bi-national perspective in migration research would allow an adequate analysis that enables an integration of the specific social, cultural and economic status of migrants between two nationalities.

A more poststructuralist concept leads to an analysis of the constitution of social differences, referring to visible and invisible forms of discrimination in their multiple intersections. In this orientation, the theoretical and empirical framework of research challenges interdependent relations and different axes of inequalities and discrimination as well as the processes of hierarchy-building among the dimensions of diversity. To develop a theoretical framework for working on the phenomena of heterogeneity, diversity, difference and discrimination, the approach of intersectionality also seems to be attractive in the context of diversity discourses and research. For instance, Hardmeier and Vinz (2007) compare the epistemological underpinnings of diversity and intersectionality concepts, and discuss the respective contributions to gender research in the political sciences. Bruchhagen and Koall (2007) also address the potentials of combining intersectionality and diversity. They suspect that this combination may face the same dilemma that was pointed out, for example, with regard to the 'feminist degendering movement' (Lorber, 2000; Butler, 2004): how to overcome the powerful 'making of' decision and differentiation based on binary constructions? We are bound to use established terms, languages and the connected semantics. Instead of reproducing, reducing or avoiding the use of social and cultural differences, one possible resort is to reflect and critically examine the processes of constructing and deconstructing differences that occur in diversity research and practice.

In Germany, the combination of micro-meso-macro perspectives has been discussed in feminist theory (Knapp, 2001, p. 24) and for theories of social systems (Burzan et al., 2008). We expect that this need to combine and integrate different levels of analysis could also give new input to the German discussion of diversity concepts and could widen the understanding of complexity and interdependence. However, the application of intersectional concepts to diversity issues is still a 'work in progress' in Germany. Connecting the notion of intersectionality and the discourse on diversity raises the question whether the construct of diversity and the concept of diversity management are likely to capture the multiple relations of social inequality to which the term intersectionality refers. Having its origin in feminist theory, intersectionality was developed as a critical category with strong (gender-)political implications. It helps to overcome the rigidity of theoretically and methodologically binary-based research, and offers an alternative to pointing out the exclusivity or hierarchy of categories of discrimination (which runs the risk of losing others or of making them invisible). In distinguishing different strategies of diversity management, one can ask whether the focus on the interrelatedness of dimensions of inequality is preserved or whether these dimensions are perceived only as a source of multiple competences that should be exhausted for organizational development. In this case the focus changes from – negatively connoted – social inequality to – positively connoted – cultural differences.

3.   Outlook

As we have pointed out, for the topic of equal treatment at work in Germany, gender and diversity are the most relevant anchors for research as well as for political and management practice. Thus gender and diversity studies may resort to a broad spectrum of further research areas and concepts. Prominent management concepts that aim to foster equal opportunities are gender mainstreaming and diversity management. We assume that diversity management especially will spread continuously in Germany in both research and practice. It remains to be seen what levels of workplace equality will be achieved through these efforts and developments. We have outlined some of the barriers that will be hard to overcome, and also the adverse effects of concepts like diversity management, for instance, when it serves only as a façade of legitimacy. However, there are strong drivers for an effective promotion of equal opportunities: besides legal forces, above all the ongoing demographical change – which is especially caused by increasing proportions of migrants, women and the elderly in the labour force – accompanied by a shortage of highly qualified employees. Moreover, political action on both the national and the local levels as well as the 'usual' processes of institutionalization will contribute to the wide distribution of the philosophy of diversity management and, more importantly, to the appreciation of diversity.

We have argued that diverse theoretical positions are relevant to describe the field of diversity and its practical application as diversity management. This also applies to the doing of scientific diversity work, for instance, in the course of writing this chapter. The multidisciplinarity of our team has forced us to deal with our internal diversity regarding management approaches, disciplines and political heritages. We have argued that there is not and should not be one single valid meta-theoretical framing of business-related and science-related diversity work. Rising complexity leads to conflicts. However, the resulting struggles are useful and fruitful if they cause disturbance and involvement, and if they widen perspectives and open frameworks of scientific work.

Summary table for Germany

Existence of anti-discrimination legislation	Yes
Criteria covered by anti-discrimination legislation	Origin, gender, family status, pregnancy, disability, health condition, sexual orientation, age, political opinion, union activity and attitude, nationality, language, ethnicity, race, religion
Criteria for which the reporting of quantitative data and their communication to a public administration are compulsory	Disability, gender (only for public administrations)
Criteria covered by 'affirmative' or 'positive' action legislation other than unemployment- or income-based	Race or ethnic background, gender, religion or faith, disability, age or sexual identity
Existence of a discourse or debate about 'non-discrimination' or 'equality'	Yes
Existence of a discourse or debate about 'diversity'	Yes
Year or period when the 'discrimination' concept started to disseminate in management literature in the country	1980s
Year or period when the diversity concept started to disseminate in management literature in the country	1990s
Who pushed the 'diversity' agenda?	Diversity scholars, consulting firms, subsidiaries of US corporations, individual diversity managers, business circles, foundations, the European Commission, the German government
Existence of a professional association representing diversity professionals and year of creation	Yes, 2007
Existence of a professional association representing diversity scholars and year of creation	Yes, 2006 (together with Austria and Switzerland)

Additionally, diversity management concepts are at least partly politically inspired and connect hopes of emancipation with business objectives. In this sense, diversity management is shaped by a normative, political impetus that complements the business rationale. Diversity management entering the organization might work politically if it raises complexity and overcomes binary distinctions between 'right' and 'wrong' or 'social' and 'economic', and if we then reflect on the interdependence of powerful divides.

References

Acker, Joan (1990), 'Hierarchies, jobs, bodies. A theory of gendered organizations', *Gender and Society*, **4** (2), 139–58.
Acker, Joan (1992), 'Gendering organizational theory', in Albert J. Mills and Peta Tancred (eds), *Gendering Organizational Analysis*, Newbury Park et al.: Sage, pp. 248–60.
Anders, Violetta, Renate Ortlieb, Heike Pantelmann, Daphne Reim, Barbara Sieben and Stephanie Stein (2008),

Diversity und Diversity Management in Berliner Unternehmen. Im Fokus: Personen mit Migrationshintergrund. Ergebnisse einer quantitativen und qualitativen empirischen Studie, München and Mering: Hampp.

Aretz, Hans-Jürgen (2006), 'Strukturwandel der Weltgesellschaft und Diversity Management in Unternehmen', in Manfred Becker and Alina Seidel (eds), *Diversity Management. Unternehmens- und Personalpolitik der Vielfalt*, Stuttgart: Schaeffer-Poeschel, pp. 52–74.

Aretz, Hans-Jürgen and Katrin Hansen (2002), *Diversity und Diversity Management im Unternehmen. Eine Analyse aus systemtheoretischer Sicht*, Hamburg: LIT.

Aretz, Hans-Jürgen and Katrin Hansen (2003), 'Diversity Management. Ein Konzept für den Umgang mit Vielfalt und Komplexität', *Zeitschrift für Organisation*, **72** (4), 192–8.

Argyris, Chris and Donald Schön (1974), *Theory in Practice: Increasing Professional Effectiveness*, San Francisco, CA: Jossey-Bass.

Baecker, Dirk (1994), *Postheroisches Management*, Berlin: Merve.

Baecker, Dirk (2001), 'Why systems?', *Theory, Culture and Society*, **18** (2), 59–74.

Baecker, Dirk (2003), *Organisation und Management*, Frankfurt/M.: Suhrkamp.

Baecker, Dirk (2005), 'Effektives Durcheinander – der gesellschaftliche Umgang mit Vielfalt', *Vielfalt. Der Wert des Unterschiedes. Politische Ökologie*, **22** (91–2), 11–14.

Baecker, Dirk (2007), 'Why complex systems are also social and temporal', paper submitted to European Conference on Complex Systems, Dresden, 1–5 October (http://homepage.mac.com/baecker), Herdecke: University of Witten.

Barkholdt, Corinna and Gerd Naegele (2007), 'Konturen und Fragen einer sozial-gerontologischen Lebenslaufforschung – unter besonderer Berücksichtigung des Zusammenhangs von Arbeit und Alter', in Hans Werner Wahl and Heidrun Mollenkopf (eds), *Altersforschung am Beginn des 21. Jahrhunderts. Alterns- und Lebenslaufkonzeptionen im deutschsprachigen Raum*, Berlin: Springer, pp. 21–41.

Bayreuther, Frank (2007), 'Diskriminierungsschutz und Gleichbehandlung im Arbeitsleben – Eine rechtswissenschaftliche Analyse der Diskussion über das AGG', in Gertraude Krell, Barbara Riedmüller, Barbara Sieben and Dagmar Vinz (eds), *Diversity Studies. Grundlagen und disziplinäre Ansätze*, Frankfurt/M. and New York: Campus, pp. 179–200.

Beck, Sebastian and Thomas Perry (2008), 'Migranten – Milieus – Erste Erkenntnisse über Lebenswelten und wohnungsmarktspezifische Präferenzen von Personen mit Migrationshintergrund in Deutschland', *Forum Sozial*, **2** (5), 12–17.

Becker, Andreas (2006), 'Diversity Management aus der Perspektive der betriebswirtschaftlichen Theorie', in Manfred Becker and Alina Seidel (eds), *Diversity Management: Unternehmens- und Personalpolitik der Vielfalt*, Stuttgart: Schaeffer-Poeschel, pp. 205–38.

Becker, Manfred (2006), 'Wissenschaftstheoretische Grundlagen des Diversity Managements', in Manfred Becker and Alina Seidel (eds), *Diversity Management: Unternehmens- und Personalpolitik der Vielfalt*, Stuttgart: Schaeffer-Poeschel, pp. 3–48.

Behnke, Cornelia and Michael Meuser (2003), 'Doppelkarrieren in Wirtschaft und Wissenschaft', *Zeitschrift für Frauenforschung und Geschlechterstudien*, **4** (21), 62–74.

Bender, Saskia-Fee (2007), 'Age-Diversity: Ein Ansatz zur Verbesserung der Beschäftigungssituation älterer ArbeitnehmerInnen?', in Ursula Pasero, Gertrud M. Backes and Klaus R. Schroeter (eds), *Altern in Gesellschaft – Age, Diversity and Inclusion*, Wiesbaden: VS, pp. 185–210.

Bereswill, Mechthild (2004), '"Gender" als neue Humanressource? Gender Mainstreaming und Geschlechterdemokratie zwischen Ökonomisierung und Gesellschaftskritik', in Michael Meuser and Claudia Neusüß (eds), *Gender Mainstreaming. Konzepte – Handlungsfelder – Instrumente*, Bonn: Bundeszentrale für politische Bildung, pp. 52–70.

BMFSFJ – Bundesministerium für Familie, Senioren, Frauen und Jugend (2003), *Bilanz 2003 der Vereinbarung zwischen der Bundesregierung und den Spitzenverbänden der deutschen Wirtschaft zur Förderung der Chancengleichheit von Frauen und Männern in der Privatwirtschaft*, Berlin.

Bruchhagen, Verena and Iris Koall (2007), 'Losing Gender-Binary? Winning Gender-Complexity! Intersektionelle Ansätze und Managing Diversity', *Journal Netzwerk Frauenforschung NRW*, **22** (1), 32–42.

Bührmann, Andrea D. (2005), 'Plädoyer für eine "geregelte Deregulierung" zur Implementierung von Work–Life-Balance in Führungspositionen. Managing Diversity und Gender Mainstreaming im Spiegel aktueller empirischer Forschungsergebnisse', *Zeitschrift für Frauenforschung und Geschlechterstudien*, **23** (3), 74–88.

Bukow, Wolf-Dietrich (1996), *Feindbild Minderheit – Zur Funktion von Ethnisierung*, Opladen: Leske and Budrich.

Bundesagentur für Arbeit (2007), *Amtliche Nachrichten der Bundesagentur für Arbeit: Arbeitsmarkt Sondernummer*, **1** (55), Nürnberg.

Burzan, Nicole, Brigitta Lökenhoff, Uwe Schimank and Nadine Schöneck (2008), *Das Publikum der Gesellschaft. Inklusionsverhältnisse und Inklusionsprofile in Deutschland*, Wiesbaden: VS.

Busch, Anne and Elke Holst (2008), 'Verdienstdifferenzen zwischen Frauen und Männern nur teilweise durch Strukturmerkmale zu erklären', *DIW-Wochenbericht*, **75** (15), 184–90.

Butler, Judith (2004), *Undoing Gender*, New York: Routledge.
Commission of European Communities (2006), *Green Paper Confronting Demographic Change: A New Solidarity*, Brussels.
Council of Europe (1998), *Gender Mainstreaming: Conceptual Framework, Methodology and Presentation of Good Practices*, EG-S-MS (98) 2, Strasbourg: Council of Europe.
Cox, Taylor (1993), *Cultural Diversity in Organizations. Theory, Research, Practice*, San Francisco, CA: Berrett-Koehler.
Crenshaw, Kimberle W. (2000), 'The intersectionality of gender and race discrimination', www.womensplace.osu.edu/Archives/crenshaw.pdf, 20 May 2008.
Dippel, Alexander von (2007), 'Management aus der Sicht von Führungskräften in öffentlichen Verwaltungen', in Iris Koall, Verena Bruchhagen and Friederike Höher (eds), *Diversity Outlook – Managing Diversity zwischen Ethik, Profit und Antidiskriminierung*, Hamburg: LIT, pp. 68–81.
Domsch, Michel (2006), 'Quality management in gender and diversity – the role of social auditing', in European Commission, *Women in Science and Technology – The Business Perspective*, Brussels, pp. 37–48.
Domsch, Michel and Antje Hadler (1989), 'Marketing for women in management', *European Management Journal*, **7** (4), 510–15.
Domsch, Michel and Maria Krüger-Basner (1989), 'Laufbahnentwicklung von Dual Career Couples (DCC's). Ergebnisse einer empirischen Untersuchung', *Personalführung*, **22** (3), 285–9.
Domsch, Michel and Desirée Ladwig (1998), 'Dual Career Couples: Die unerkannte Zielgruppe', in Werner Gross (ed.), *Karriere 2000, Hoffnungen, Chancen, Perspektiven, Probleme, Risiken*, Bonn: Management International Review Edition, pp. 126–43.
Domsch, Michel and Desirée H. Ladwig (2003), 'Management Diversity: Das Hidden-Cost-Benefit-Phänomen', in Ursula Pasero (ed.), *Gender – from Costs to Benefits*, Wiesbaden: Westdeutscher Verlag, pp. 253–70.
Domsch, Michel and Erika Regnet (1990), 'Personalentwicklung für weibliche Fach- und Führungskräfte', in Michel Domsch and Erika Regnet (eds), *Weibliche Fach- und Führungskräfte. Wege zur Chancengleichheit*, Stuttgart: Schaeffer-Poeschel, pp. 101–23.
Domsch, Michel, Maria Krüger-Basner and Andrea Schneble (1988), 'Zeitliche Abstimmungsprobleme der Laufbahnentwicklung von "Dual Career Couples"', in Herbert Hax, Werner Kern und Hans-Horst Schröder (eds), *Zeitaspekte in betriebswirtschaftlicher Theorie und Praxis*, Stuttgart: Schaeffer-Poeschel, pp. 331–48.
Drumm, Hans J. (ed.) (1989a), *Individualisierung der Personalwirtschaft. Grundlagen, Lösungsansätze und Grenzen*, Bern and Stuttgart: Haupt.
Drumm, Hans J. (1989b), 'Vom Einheitskonzept zur Individualisierung: Neue Entwicklungen in der Personalwirtschaft', in Hans J. Drumm (ed.), *Individualisierung der Personalwirtschaft. Grundlagen, Lösungsansätze und Grenzen*, Bern and Stuttgart: Haupt, pp. 1–13.
Drumm, Hans J. (2000), *Personalwirtschaftslehre*, 4th edn, Berlin: Springer.
Einsiedler, Herbert E. (1993), 'Werte und Wertewandel aus der Sicht der Personalpolitik – Einige Gedanken zum Thema', in Lutz von Rosenstiel, Maryam Djarrahzadeh, Herbert E. Einsiedler and Richard K. Streich (eds), *Wertewandel*, Stuttgart: Schaeffer-Poeschel, pp. 115–38.
Elmerich, Kathrin (2007), *Personenbezogene Wahrnehmung des Diversity Managements*, Frankfurt/M.: Lang.
Frerichs, Frerich (1998), *Älterwerden im Betrieb. Beschäftigungschancen und -risiken im demographischen Wandel*, Opladen: Westdeutscher Verlag.
Frerichs, Frerich and Mirko Sporket (2007), *Employment and Labour Market Policies for an Aging Workforce and Initiatives at the Workplace*, National Overview Report: Germany. European Foundation for the Improvement of Living and Working Conditions, Dublin.
Friedrich-Ebert-Stiftung (ed.) (2006), *Kompetenzen stärken, Qualifikationen verbessern, Potenziale nutzen. Berufliche Bildung von Jugendlichen und Erwachsenen mit Migrationshintergrund*, Dokumentation einer Fachkonferenz, Bonn.
Fritsch, Stephan (1994), *Differentielle Personalpolitik: Einigung zielgruppenspezifischer Weiterbildung für ältere Arbeitnehmer*, Wiesbaden: DUV.
Frohnen, Anja (2005), 'Diversity in Action. Multinationalität in globalen Unternehmen am Beispiel Ford', Bielefeld: Transcript.
Gaugler, Eduard, Wolfgang Weber, Gerd Gille and Albert Martin (1985), *Ausländerintegration in deutschen Industriebetrieben. Eine empirische Untersuchung über individuelle und soziale Integration*, Königstein/Taunus: Athenäum.
Gebert, Diether (2004), 'Durch diversity zu mehr Teaminnovativität?', *Die Betriebswirtschaft*, **64** (4), 412–30.
Gergen, Kenneth J. (1999), *An Invitation to Social Construction*, London: Sage.
Grieger, Jürgen (2004), *Ökonomisierung in Personalwirtschaft und Personalwirtschaftslehre*, Wiesbaden: Gabler.
Habermas, Jürgen (1981), *Theorie des kommunikativen Handelns (Vol. 1: Handlungsrationalität und gesellschaftliche Rationalisierung, Vol. 2: Zur Kritik der funktionalistischen Vernunft)*, Frankfurt/M.: Suhrkamp.

Hansen, Katrin and Ursula Müller (2003), 'Diversity in Arbeits- und Bildungsorganisationen', in Eszter Belinsky, Katrin Hansen and Ursula Müller (eds), *Diversity Management Best Practices im internationalen Feld*, Hamburg: LIT, pp. 7–60.

Hardmeier, Sybille and Dagmar Vinz (2007), 'Diversity und Intersectionality – Eine kritische Würdigung der Ansätze für die Politikwissenschaft', *Femina Politica, Zeitschrift für Feministische Politikwissenschaft*, **16** (1), 23–33.

Harms, Martina and Patrick Müller (2004), 'Diversity Management', in Uwe G. Seebacher and Gaby Klaus (eds), *Handbuch Führungskräfteentwicklung: Theorie, Praxis, Fallstudien*, Oberhaching: USP Publishing, pp. 97–111.

Hermes, Gisela and Eckhard Rohrmann (eds) (2006), *'Nichts über uns – ohne uns!' Disability Studies als neuer Ansatz emanzipatorischer und interdisziplinärer Forschung über Behinderung*, Neu-Ulm: AG SPAK.

Herrmann-Pillath, Carsten (2007), 'Diversity: Management der offenen Unternehmung', in Iris Koall, Verena Bruchhagen and Friederike Höher (eds), *Diversity Outlooks – Managing Diversity zwischen Ethik, Profit und Antidiskriminierung*, Hamburg: LIT, pp. 202–23.

Holst, Elke (2007), 'Women in managerial positions in Europe: Focus on Germany', *Management Revue*, **17** (2), 122–42.

Inglehard, Ronald (1998), *Modernisierung und Postmodernisierung*, Frankfurt/M. and New York: Campus.

Jung, Dörthe and Junghild Küpper (eds) (2001), *Gender Mainstreaming und betriebliche Veränderungsprozesse*, Bielefeld: Kleine.

Jung, Rüdiger H., Helmut M. Schäfer and Friedrich W. Seibel (eds) (1994), *Vielfalt gestalten – Managing Diversity*, Frankfurt/M.: IKO.

Kappler, Ekkehard (1976), 'Zum Theorie-Praxis-Verhältnis einer noch zu entwickelnden kritischen Theorie der Betriebswirtschaftspolitik', in Hans Ulrich (ed.), *Zum Praxisbezug der Betriebswirtschaftslehre in wissensteoretischer Sicht*, Bern and Stuttgart: Haupt, pp. 107–33.

Kiechl, Rolf (1993), 'Managing Diversity: Postmoderne Kulturarbeit in der Unternehmung', *Die Unternehmung*, **47** (1), 67–72.

Klinger, Cornelia, Gudrun-Axeli Knapp and Birgit Sauer (eds) (2007), *Achsen der Ungleichheit. Zum Verhältnis von Klasse, Geschlecht und Ethnizität*, Frankfurt/M.: Campus.

Knapp, Gudrun-Axeli (2001), 'Dezentriert und viel riskiert. Anmerkungen zur These vom Bedeutungsverlust der Kategorie Geschlecht', in Gudrun Axeli Knapp and Angelika Wetterer (eds), *Soziale Verortung der Geschlechter. Gesellschaftstheorie und feministische Kritik*, Münster: Westfälisches Dampfboot, pp. 15–62.

Knapp, Gudrun-Axeli (2005), 'Intersectionality – ein neues Paradigma feministischer Theorie? Zur transatlantischen Reise von "Race, Class, Gender"', *Feministische Studien*, **23** (1), 68–81.

Knoth, André (2006), *Managing Diversity – Skizzen einer Kulturtheorie*, Tönning: Der andere Verlag.

Koall, Iris (2001), *Managing Gender and Diversity. Von der Homogenität zur Heterogenität der Organisation der Unternehmung*, Hamburg: LIT.

Koall, Iris (2007), 'Gegen Elite – eine Polemik zum funktional-äquivalenten Managing Gender and Diversity', in Iris Koall, Verena Bruchhagen and Friederike Höher (eds), *Diversity Outlooks – Managing Diversity zwischen Ethik, Profit und Antidiskriminierung*, Hamburg: LIT, pp. 305–19.

Koall, Iris and Verena Bruchhagen (2002), 'Lust und Risiko in der Arbeit mit Verschiedenheit! Wissenschaftliche Weiterbildung "Managing Gender and Diversity"', *Zeitschrift für Frauen- und Geschlechterforschung*, **3** (22), 111–28.

Koall, Iris and Verena Bruchhagen (2009), 'Managing diverse social systems: diversity meets social systems theory – deconstructing binary and unfolding paradoxes', in Mustafa Özbilgin (ed.), *Equality, Diversity and Inclusion at Work. A Research Companion*, Cheltenham, UK and Northampton, MA, USA: Edward Elgar, pp. 120–35.

Koall, Iris, Verena Bruchhagen and Friederike Höher (2002) (eds), *Vielfalt statt Lei(d)tkultur – Managing Gender and Diversity*, Hamburg: LIT.

Koall, Iris, Verena Bruchhagen and Friederike Höher (2007) (eds), *Diversity Outlooks – Managing Diversity zwischen Ethik, Profit und Antidiskriminierung*, Hamburg: LIT.

Köppel, Petra, Junchen Yan and Jörg Lüdicke (2007), 'Cultural Diversity Management in Deutschland hinkt hinterher', www.bertelsmann-stiftung.de/cps/rde/xbcr/SID-0A000F14-5385B43A/bst/xcms_bst_dms_21374__2.pdf, 1 June 2008.

Krell, Gertraude (1996), 'Mono- oder multikulturelle Organisationen. "Managing Diversity" auf dem Prüfstand', *Industrielle Beziehungen*, **3** (4), 334–50.

Krell, Gertraude (2003), 'Die Ordnung der "Humanressourcen" als Ordnung der Geschlechter', in Richard Weiskopf (ed.), *Menschenregierungskünste. Anwenundungen poststrukturalistischer Analyse auf Management und Organisation*, Wiesbaden: Westdeutscher Verlag, pp. 65–90.

Krell, Gertraude (2008a), 'Diversity Management – Chancengleichheit für alle und auch als Wettbewerbsfaktor', in Gertraude Krell (ed.), *Chancengleichheit durch Personalpolitik. Gleichstellung von Männern und Frauen in*

Unternehmen und Verwaltungen. Rechtliche Regelungen – Problemanalysen – Lösungen, 5th edn, Wiesbaden: Gabler, pp. 63–80.

Krell, Gertraude (ed.) (2008b), *Chancengleichheit durch Personalpolitik. Gleichstellung von Frauen und Männern in Unternehmen und Verwaltungen. Rechtliche Regelungen – Problemanalysen – Lösungen*, 5th edn, Wiesbaden: Gabler.

Krell, Gertraude and Renate Ortlieb (2004), *Chancengleichheit von Frauen und Männern in der Privatwirtschaft. Eine Befragung des Managements von 500 Unternehmen zur Umsetzung der Vereinbarung zur Förderung der Chancengleichheit*, DGB, Abteilung Gleichstellungs- und Frauenpolitik: Positionen + Hintergründe, No. 2. Berlin.

Krell, Gertraude and Margit Osterloh (eds) (1993), *Personalpolitik aus der Sicht von Frauen – Frauen aus der Sicht der Personalpolitk*, München: Hampp.

Krell, Gertraude and Barbara Sieben (2007), 'Diversity Management und Personalforschung', in Gertraude Krell, Barbara Riedmüller, Barbara Sieben and Dagmar Vinz (eds), *Diversity Studies – Grundlagen und disziplinäre Ansätze*, Frankfurt/M. and New York: Campus, pp. 235–54.

Krell, Gertraude, Ulrich Mückenberger and Karin Tondorf (2008), 'Gender Mainstreaming: Chancengleichheit (nicht nur) für Politik und Verwaltung', in Gertraude Krell (ed.), *Chancengleichheit durch Personalpolitik. Gleichstellung von Männern und Frauen in Unternehmen und Verwaltungen. Rechtliche Regelungen – Problemanalysen – Lösungen*, 5th edn, Wiesbaden: Gabler, pp. 97–114.

Krell, Gertraude, Heike Pantelmann and Hartmut Wächter (2006), 'Diversity(-Dimensionen) und deren Management als Gegenstände der Personalforschung in Deutschland, Österreich und der Schweiz', in Gertraude Krell and Hartmut Wächter (eds), *Diversity Management. Impulse aus der Personalforschung*, München Mering: Hampp, pp. 25–56.

Krell, Gertraude, Barbara Riedmüller, Barbara Sieben and Dagmar Vinz (eds) (2007), *Diversity Studies – Grundlagen und disziplinäre Ansätze*, Frankfurt/M. and New York: Campus.

Labucay, Inéz (2006), 'Diversity Management – eine Analyse aus Sicht der systemtheoretischen und postmodernen Organisationsforschung', in Manfred Becker and Alina Seidel (eds), *Diversity Management – Unternehmens- und Personalpolitik der Vielfalt*, Stuttgart: Schaeffer-Poeschel, pp. 75–103.

Lederle, Sabine (2007), 'Die Einführung von Diversity Management in deutschen Organisationen: Eine neoinstitutionalistische Perspektive', *Zeitschrift für Personalforschung*, **21** (1), 22–41.

Lewis, Marianne W. (2000), 'Exploring paradox: toward a more comprehensive guide', *Academy of Management Review*, **25** (4), 760–76.

Lindsay, Carol (1993), 'Paradoxes of organizational diversity', *Journal of Managerial Issues*, **5** (4), 547–66.

Lorber, Judith (2000), 'Using gender to undo gender. A feminist degendering movement', *Feminist Theory – An International Interdisciplinary Journal*, **1** (1), 79–95.

Luhmann, Niklas (1970), *Soziologische Aufklärung*, Vol. 1, Opladen: Westdeutscher Verlag.

Luhmann, Niklas (1984), *Soziale Systeme*, Frankfurt/M.: Suhrkamp.

Luhmann, Niklas (2002), *Organisation und Entscheidung*, Opladen: Westdeutscher Verlag.

Luhmann, Niklas (2005), 'Haltlose Komplexität', in Niklas Luhmann, *Soziologische Aufklärung 5*, 3rd edn, Opladen: Westdeutscher Verlag, pp. 58–74.

McCall, Leslie (2005), 'The complexity of intersectionality', *Signs – Journal of Women in Culture and Society*, **30** (3), 1771–800.

Mag, Wolfgang (1989), 'Besondere Mitarbeitergruppen in der betrieblichen Personalplanung', *Zeitschrift für Personalforschung*, **3** (4), 123–38.

Manske, Alexandra and Hanna Meißner (1999), '"Und wer wollt, wer möchte, wer will, hat seine Chance auch gehabt." Ehemaliger Ostberliner Zweigstellenleiterinnen im betrieblichen Umstrukturierungsprozess der Landesbank Berlin', in Hildegard M. Nickel, Susanne Völker and Hasko Hüning (eds), *Transformation, Unternehmensreorganisation, Geschlechterforschung*, Opladen: Leske & Budrich, pp. 155–73.

Marr, Rainer (1989), 'Überlegungen zu einem Konzept einer "Differentiellen Personalwirtschaft"', in Hans J. Drumm (ed.), *Individualisierung der Personalwirtschaft. Grundlagen, Lösungsansätze und Grenzen*, Bern and Stuttgart: Haupt, pp. 37–47.

Marsden, David (1999), *A Theory of Employment Systems. Micro-Foundations of Societal Diversity*, Oxford and New York: Oxford University Press.

Martin, Albert (1991), 'Statusabgrenzung gegenüber ausländischen Arbeitnehmern', *Die Betriebswirtschaft*, **51** (5), 629–47.

Merx, Andreas and Joana Vassilopoulou (2007), 'Das arbeitsrechtliche AGG und Diversity-Perspektiven', in Iris Koall, Verena Bruchhagen and Friederike Höher (eds), *Diversity Outlooks – Managing Diversity zwischen Ethik, Profit und Antidiskriminierung*, Hamburg: LIT, pp. 354–85.

Meuser, Michael (2004), 'Gender Mainstreaming: Festschreibung oder Auflösung der Geschlechterdifferenz? Zum Verhältnis von Geschlechterforschung und Geschlechterpolitik', in Michael Meuser and Claudia Neusüß (eds), *Gender Mainstreaming. Konzepte – Handlungsfelder – Instrumente*, Bonn: Bundeszentrale für politische Bildung, pp. 322–36.

Meuser, Michael (2005), '"Gender Matters" – Zur Entdeckung von Geschlecht als Organisationsressource', *Zeitschrift für Frauenforschung und Geschlechterstudien*, **23** (3), 61–73.

Meuser, Michael and Claudia Neusüß (eds) (2004), *Gender Mainstreaming. Konzepte – Handlungsfelder – Instrumente*, Bonn: Bundeszentrale für politische Bildung.

Morick, Holger (2002), *Differentielle Personalwirtschaft. Theoretisches Fundament und praktische Konsequenzen*, Neubiberg: Gfw.

Münst, A. Sengenata (2008), 'Intersektionalität als Perspektive der Migrationsforschung: Theoretische Überlegungen und empiriegeleitete Konkretisierungen', *Femina Politica, Zeitschrift für Feministische Politikwissenschaft*, **17** (1), 41–55.

Naegele, Gerhard (2004), 'Verrentungspolitik und Herausforderungen des demografischen Wandels in der Arbeitswelt. Das Beispiel Deutschland', in Martin von Cranach, Horst-Dieter Schneider, Eberhard Ulich and Ruedi Winkler (eds), *Ältere Menschen im Unternehmen. Chancen, Risiken, Modelle*, Bern: Haupt, pp. 189–219.

Naegele, Gerhard (2005), 'Nachhaltige Arbeits- und Erwerbsfähigkeit für ältere Arbeitnehmer', *WSI Mitteilungen*, **58** (4), 214–18.

Nassehi, Armin (2005), 'Social system', in Austin Harrington, Barbara L. Marshall and Hans-Peter Müller (eds), *Encyclopedia of Social Theory*, London: Routledge, pp. 570–72.

Ong, Aihwa (2005), *Flexible Staatsbürgerschaften. Die kulturelle Logik von Transnationalität*, Frankfurt/M.: Suhrkamp.

Ortlieb, Renate and Barbara Sieben (2008a), 'Diversity strategies focused on employees with a migration background. An empirical investigation based on resource dependence theory', *Management Revue*, **19** (1–2), 70–93.

Ortlieb, Renate and Barbara Sieben (2008b), 'Exclusion, hazard, adding value, or learning? Diversity strategies focused on employees with a migration background', in George T. Solomon (ed.), *Best Papers Proceedings of the Sixty-seventh Annual Meeting of the Academy of Management* (CD), ISSN 1543-8643.

Ortlieb, Renate and Barbara Sieben (2010), 'Migrant employees in Germany: personnel structures and practices', *Equality, Diversity and Inclusion*, **28**, forthcoming.

Özbilgin, Mustafa and Ahu Tatlı (2008), *Global Diversity Management: An Evidence Based Approach*, Basingstoke: Palgrave Macmillan.

Pfarr, Heide (ed.) (2001), *Ein Gesetz zur Gleichstellung der Geschlechter in der Privatwirtschaft*, Düsseldorf: Hans-Böckler-Stiftung.

Pfriem, Reinhard (ed.) (1983), *Betriebswirtschaftslehre in sozialer und ökologischer Dimension*, Frankfurt/M. and New York: Campus.

Pless, Nicola (1999), 'Von der Dominanz zur Partnerschaft – Erfolgreiches Diversitätsmanagement erfordert einen Paradigmenwechsel', *Die Unternehmung*, **3** (53), 159–75.

Podsiadlowski, Astrid (2002), 'Diversität in Organisationen', in Jutta Allmendinger and Thomas Hinz (eds), *Organisationssoziologie. Kölner Zeitschrift für Soziologie und Sozialpsychologie Special Issue No. 42*, Opladen and Wiesbaden: Westdeutscher Verlag, pp. 260–83.

Pongratz, Hans J. and Günter G. Voß (2003), 'From employee to "entreployee": towards a "self-entrepreneurial" work force?', *Concepts and Transformation*, **8** (3), 239–54.

Ridder, Hans-Gerd (1990), *Technologische Entwicklung und Kontinuität der Betriebswirtschaftslehre*, Bern and Stuttgart: Haupt.

Ridder, Hans-Gerd, Peter Conrad, Frank Schirmer and Hans-Joachim Bruns (2001), *Strategisches Personalmanagement. Mitarbeiterführung, Integration und Wandel aus ressourcenorientierter Perspektive*, Landsberg and Lech: Moderne Industrie.

Sackmann, Sonja, Sandra Bissels and Thomas Bissels (2002), 'Kulturelle Vielfalt in Organisationen: Ansätze zum Umgang mit einem vernachlässigten Thema der Organisationsforschung', *Die Betriebswirtschaft*, **62** (1), 43–58.

Schanz, Günther (1977a), 'Wege zur individualisierten Organisation – Teil 1: Ein theoretisches Modell', *Zeitschrift für Organisation*, **46** (4), 183–92.

Schanz, Günther (1977b), 'Wege zur individualisierten Organisation – Teil 2: Praktische Konsequenzen', *Zeitschrift für Organisation*, **46** (6), 345–51.

Schmidt, Verena (2005), *Gender Mainstreaming – an Innovation in Europe?*, Opladen: Budrich.

Schmidt, Werner (2007), 'Arbeitsbeziehungen und Sozialintegration in Industriebetrieben mit Beschäftigten deutscher und ausländischer Herkunft', *Industrielle Beziehungen*, **14** (4), 334–56.

Schramm, Florian (2004), 'Arbeitnehmergruppen', in Eduard Gaugler, Walter A. Oechsler and Wolfgang Weber (eds), *Handwörterbuch des Personalwesens*, 3rd edn, Stuttgart: Schäffer-Poeschel, cols 121–9.

Schramm, Florian (ed.) (2007), 'Varieties of employment', *Management Revue, Special Issue*, **32** (3).

Schuchert-Güler, Pakize and Martin Eisend (2007), 'Ethno-Marketing: eine kritische Betrachung', in Gertraude Krell, Barbara Riedmüller, Barbara Sieben and Dagmar Vinz (eds), *Diversity Studies*, Frankfurt/M. and New York: Campus, pp. 217–33.

Seidel, Alina (2006), 'Kundenorientierung und Mitarbeitervielfalt. Interdependenzen und

Begründungszusammenhänge', in Manfred Becker and Alina Seidel (eds), *Diversity Management – Unternehmens- und Personalpolitik der Vielfalt*, Stuttgart: Schäffer-Poeschel, pp. 239–56.

Sepehri, Paivand (2002), *Diversity und Managing Diversity in internationalen Organisationen – Wahrnehmungen zum Verständnis und ökonomischer Relevanz*, München and Mering: Hampp.

Sinus Sociovision (2007), 'Die Milieus der Menschen mit Migrationshintergrund in Deutschland. Zentrale Ergebnisse', www.sinus-sociovision.de, 17 June 2008.

Sporket, Mirko (2008), 'Age Management – Betriebliche Motive und Umsetzungsstrategien' in Jürgen Deller, Stefanie Kern, Esther Hausmann and Yvonne Diederichs (eds), *Personalmanagement im demographischen Wandel. Ein Handbuch für Veränderungsprozesse*, Berlin: Springer, pp. 20–23.

Statistisches Bundesamt (2006), *Wirtschaft und Statistik*, 12/2006, Wiesbaden.

Statistisches Bundesamt (2008), *Bevölkerung und Erwerbstätigkeit. Bevölkerung mit Migrationshintergrund. Ergebnisse des Mikrozensus 2006*, Wiesbaden.

Steinmann, Horst, Hans Böhm, Wolfram Braun, Elmar Gerum and Georg Schreyögg (1976), 'Betriebswirtschaftslehre und Praxis – Vorüberlegungen auf der Grundlage der Konstruktiven Philosophie und Wissenschaftstheorie', in Hans Ulrich (ed.), *Zum Praxisbezug der Betriebswirtschaftslehre in wissenstheoretischer Sicht*, Bern and Stuttgart: Haupt, pp. 51–92.

Stiegler, Barbara (2005), 'Gender Mainstreaming, Frauenförderung, Diversity oder Antidiskriminierungspolitik – was führt wie zur Chancengleichheit?', *Zeitschrift für Frauenforschung and Geschlechterstudien*, **23** (3), 9–21.

Stuber, Michael (2006), *Das Allgemeine Gleichbehandlungsgesetz in der betrieblichen Praxis*, unter Mitarbeit von Sonja Leyendecker, Freiburg et al.: Haufe.

Stuber, Michael (2007), 'Die wirtschaftliche Gestaltung von Diversity', in Iris Koall, Verena Bruchhagen and Friederike Höher (eds), *Diversity Outlooks – Managing Diversity zwischen Ethik, Profit und Antidiskriminierung*, Hamburg: LIT, pp. 428–49.

Süß, Stefan (2009), 'Die Institutionalisierung von Managementkonzepten. Eine strukturationstheoretisch-mikropolitische Perspektive', *Zeitschrift für Betriebswirtschaft*, **79** (2), 187–212.

Süß, Stefan and Markus Kleiner (2006a), 'Diversity Management. Verbreitung in der deutschen Unternehmenspraxis und Erklärungen aus Neo-Institutionalistischer Perspektive', in Gertraude Krell and Hartmut Wächter (eds), *Diversity Management. Impulse aus der Personalforschung*, München and Mering, pp. 57–79.

Süß, Stefan and Markus Kleiner (2006b), 'Diversity Management in Deutschland: Mehr als eine Mode?', *Die Betriebswirtschaft*, **66** (5), 521–41.

Thomas, Roosevelt R. (2000), *Management of Diversity – neue Personalstrategien für Unternehmen*, Wiesbaden: Gabler.

Tondorf, Karin (2001), 'Gender Mainstreaming – verbindliches Leitprinzip für Politik und Verwaltung', *WSI-Mitteilungen*, **54** (4), 271–7.

Ulich, Eberhard (1978), 'Über das Prinzip der differentiellen Arbeitsgestaltung', *Management Zeitschrift io*, **47** (12), 566–8.

Vedder, Günther (2006), 'Die historische Entwicklung von Managing Diversity in den USA und in Deutschland', in Gertraude Krell and Hartmut Wächter (eds), *Diversity Management. Impulse aus der Personalforschung*, München and Mering: Hampp, pp. 1–23.

Voigt, Bernd-Friedrich and Dieter Wagner (2006), 'Numerische und alternative Darstellungsformen von Heterogenität in der Diversity-Forschung', in Gertraude Krell and Hartmut Wächter (eds), *Diversity Management. Impulse aus der Personalforschung*, München and Mering: Hampp, pp. 109–33.

Weißbach, Barbara and Elena Vorontsova-Schnell (2003), 'Zugehörigkeit und Identität von Migranten der ersten Generation. Arbeitsmigranten als Wanderer zwischen den Welten: Diversity als Chance und Herausforderung', *Personalführung*, **12** (36), 48–55.

Weißbach, Barbara, Theo Schülken and Doreen Hüttig (2007), 'Je mehr kulturelle Vielfalt, desto besser? Zufriedenheit bei der Arbeit in multikulturellen Teams', *Personalführung*, **40** (3), 40–47.

Wetterer, Angelika (2002), 'Strategien rhetorischer Modernisierung. Gender Mainstreaming, Managing Diversity und die Professionalisierung der Gender-Expertinnen', *Zeitschrift für Frauenforschung und Geschlechterstudien*, **20** (3), 129–48.

Wiegran, Gabriele (1996), *Entwicklungsansatz einer differentiellen Personalwirtschaft*, Dissertation, Neubiberg: Universität der Bundeswehr.

Williams, Katherine Y. and Charles O'Reilly (1998), 'Demography and diversity in organisations. A review of 40 years of research', in Barry M. Staw and Larry L. Cummings (eds), *Research on Organisational Behaviour*, 20, Greenwich, CT: JAI Press, pp. 77–140.

Witt, Frank (1994), *Theorietraditionen betriebswirtschaftlicher Forschung*, Wiesbaden: Gabler.

Yildiz, Erol (1997), *Die halbierte Gesellschaft der Postmoderne – Probleme des Minderheitendiskurses unter Berücksichtigung alternativer Ansätze in den Niederlanden*, Opladen: Leske & Budrich.

7 Affirmative action in India: caste-based reservations

Rana Haq and Abhoy K. Ojha

1. Introduction

India is unique in its outcome-based focus on numerical reservations, or quotas, for three designated groups: the Scheduled Castes (SC), the Scheduled Tribes (ST) and the Other Backward Classes (OBC) as part of its affirmative action policies. India's reservation system is based on earmarking a certain percentage of positions for persons belonging to these three socially and economically marginalized and disadvantaged groups. The three main sectors federally regulated by the central government under these policies are public employment, public education and legislative organizations. However, despite protection for over 60 years, these groups continue to be significantly underrepresented in all three sectors (Deshpande, 2006; Hasan, 2009). There may be a variety of reasons for this underrepresentation, but discrimination against these sections of society is argued to be a major reason (Hasan, 2009; Jodhka and Newman, 2007; Madheswaran and Attewell, 2007; Thorat and Attewell, 2007).

Reservation had been used as a tool to implement affirmative action before India's independence in 1947. Independent India adopted the same policy framework. After the formal adoption of the Constitution in 1950, there have been no substantive changes in the basic affirmative action prescription. Reservation as a tool for affirmative action has been adopted by the central government as well as the state governments. States have implemented reservations in educational institutions and public organizations. Some have also incorporated reservation for women and certain sections of religious groups in different spheres of activities. Since each state has tailored these policies within the constraints of its own context, there are many variations between India's 28 States and 7 Union Territories. Therefore this chapter focuses only on the initiatives of the central government. Although the central government's affirmative action policies have gone a long way to reduce barriers for these groups (Chattopadhyay and Dufloi, 2004; Corbridge, 2000; Hasan, 2009; Pande, 2003; Weisskopf, 2004), much more needs to be done to make Indian society truly inclusive.

2. The designated groups

Although the Indian Constitution grants the right to equality for women, only three formally designated groups have traditionally been targeted for affirmative action policies: the SC, ST and OBC.

2.1 Scheduled Castes (SC)

According to Gupta (2005), India has one of the most stratified societies in the world. Caste, religion, gender and community-based differences have evolved over the past 5000 years and deeply influence almost every aspect of Indian citizens' public and private lives.

Various efforts have been made to address the issues that have emerged from the prevalence of this stratification, including religious and social reform movements. However, the initiatives of the government have primarily focused on a caste-based system of reservation.

The caste system of India, which is one of the major roots of socioeconomic stratification, can be traced back thousands of years. In the Hindu religion, every person was believed to be born into a *jati* or caste, which in turn belonged to a *varna*. Castes were traditionally based on occupations, and being born into a caste automatically meant that the person was to follow the profession of his forefathers. This complex system of networks, relationships and obligations between the castes was formally known as the *jajmani* system, which mimicked the monetary economy as a form of a barter system. Within each village, each caste had a role to play in providing services to the whole community in turn for services received from others in that community (Srinivas, 1962).

This social structure had a four-level hierarchy based on the four *varnas*: the *Brahmins* or priests, *Kshatriyas* or the warriors and aristocrats, *Vaisyas* or the merchants, and *Sudras* or the peasants, labourers and servants. The *dalits* or the untouchables, who are now referred to as SCs, were in fact the 'outcastes' who were excluded from this hierarchy as they did the most 'dirty' jobs or janitorial services. The religious and social beliefs and values based on the caste system have continued in the daily lives of most Indians, especially in the rural areas where the SCs are often prohibited by higher-caste members from entering holy temples, using the community watering-well, and participating in village festivals, because of their unclean profession. Over the years many *dalits* converted to other religions to escape this persecution, yet the social stigma of the SC label remained embedded in their treatment within other religions despite the conversion. Therefore, while the origins of the caste system can be traced to Hindu practices, today the caste system is an 'Indian' problem as it influences treatment across religions, including Islam, Sikhism, Buddhism and Christianity that formally do not recognize castes (Hasan, 2009; Kakar and Kakar, 2007).

The caste system has been sustained over centuries, but is quite a fluid and dynamic social institution challenging the colonial notion of caste as static, rigid and unchanging. Srinivas (1952) theorized the concept of 'sanskritization' as a process by which castes lower in the caste hierarchy could seek upward mobility by emulating the rituals and practices of the upper or dominant castes:

> The caste system is far from a rigid system in which the position of each component caste is fixed for all time. Movement has always been possible, and especially in the middle regions of the hierarchy. A caste was able, in a generation or two, to rise to a higher position in the hierarchy by adopting vegetarianism and teetotalism, and by *sanskritizing* its ritual and pantheon. (Srinivas, 1952, p. 32)

Recognizing the disadvantage to the SC communities based on centuries of exclusion, the Constitution of India provides for reservation of 15 per cent in central government jobs and central-government-supported educational institutions of higher learning. Also, a proportion of the seats in the legislative organizations in the states and at the central level have been reserved for members of this segment of society. Interestingly, while Sikhs and Buddhists who earlier belonged to the SCs benefit from reservation, there is no provision for reservation for those who practise Christianity and Islam. More recently, Muslims from 'lower' castes, primarily in the states of Bihar, Uttar Pradesh and Andhra

Pradesh, and Christians in the state of Tamil Nadu have been provided with reservation protection under state legislation but not yet under central legislation (Hasan, 2009).

2.2   *Scheduled Tribes (ST)*

The second category of people that the Constitution of India recognizes for affirmative action is the STs. About 50 million Indians who belong to tribal communities that traditionally lived in geographically remote areas – forests, hills and mountain areas – are referred to as STs. They follow a lifestyle and religions based on nature and have different languages (Kijima, 2006). Although their societies do not come under the influence of the caste system, they have not been able to participate in mainstream activities because of lack of adequate facilities in their communities. The Constitution of India provides reservation of 7.5 per cent for them in central government jobs and institutions of higher learning. Unlike the case for SCs, the disadvantage for this group is not seen as accruing from traditional religious practices, so the reservation is available to all STs irrespective of the religion they practise.

2.3   *Other Backward Classes (OBC)*

The Constitution also provides for identifying and establishing affirmative action for other backward classes, beyond the SCs and STs. In pursuance of the directive principles in the Constitution, the government established the Kalelkar Commission to identify the OBC. Although the commission defined OBC in terms of four dimensions, due to lack of information on other parameters it relied primarily on caste, identifying 2339 groups as OBC in 1959. Quite inadvertently, OBC and castes became quite closely associated and the central government decided not to implement reservations based on the report because of the strong caste focus. In fact, Kalelkar, in a letter included in the report, distanced himself from the report of the commission he had chaired. He was worried that the caste-based inquiry conducted by his commission had increased caste-based loyalties and aspirations that he thought were harmful (Hasan, 2009; Zwart, 2000).

The fluid nature of the caste system, and the importance of regional dimensions of caste and local traditions of Hinduism make the debate on reservation for OBC quite divisive. The OBC groups demand affirmative action equivalent to the protection provided for SC and ST, claiming that they too belong to the *varna* called *sudras*, which is the lowest level in the caste hierarchy. However, the relationship between caste and privilege or dis-privilege for OBC is complex. As Deshpande and Yadav (2006) argue, caste confers only privilege on the forward castes and only dis-privilege on the SC/ST; it can potentially confer both on the OBCs. While the OBC have been lower in the caste hierarchy, they have not experienced overt oppression, as have the SC, and neither have they been deprived because of geography, as have the ST (Ghosh, 2006). However, these groups are numerically dominant in several parts of the country, and have used their political clout in a democratic system to have reservation implemented in various states and more recently at the central level.

However, the central government permitted the states to proceed with affirmative actions based on that report. Since the central government had allowed states to pursue relevant affirmative action suitable for local needs, each state created its own list of OBC. By the time the Mandal Commission, appointed by the central government in 1979, reviewed the reservation policy for OBC in central government service and public sector enterprises, about 18 states had actively implemented reservation policies. Each state had also used differing definitions of 'backwardness', reflecting the population distribution in the state and also the political strength of the groups. The average percentage of reservations for both education and employment for SC/ST and OBC over all states was about 34 per cent, ranging from 5 per cent in Punjab to 50 per cent in Karnataka and Kerala (Lansing and Kuruvilla, 1986). However, there was no reservation for political office or legislative bodies for the OBC.

The Mandal Commission considered four social, three educational, and four economic indicators, and included 3743 castes, which, in their estimate, constituted 52 per cent of the Indian population as OBC. Despite the overt commitment to root out the evils of the caste system, the basic approach of the Mandal Commission towards the definition of OBC remained caste-based, regardless of the apparent use of multiple criteria. Further, the definition of OBC included non-Hindu populations (Tummala, 1999). Ramaiah (1992) identified several flaws in the criteria used by the Mandal Commission both in terms of identifying the number of OBC employees in government employment, which formed the basis for the argument of reservation, and in terms of identifying groups that would be included as OBC. He essentially argued that, according to the Constitution, there are provisions for groups that are socially and educationally backward but not included in the SC/ST category to obtain government help, including reservation. He suggested that many groups listed as OBC by the Mandal Commission do not meet the criteria of social and educationally backward. Due to some concerns with the methodology used and the recommendations of the Mandal Commission, the central government at the time did not table the report in parliament.

However, the report was tabled in parliament by a different government in 1990. The central government implemented 27 per cent reservation for jobs in the central government services in 1990 by issuing an Office Memorandum. This was strongly opposed, largely by the upper-caste groups. The move was also challenged in the Supreme Court, which put the implementation on hold. In 1992, the Supreme Court upheld the decision of the government but directed that the affluent sections from the OBC, referred to as the 'creamy layer', be excluded from the provisions.

The central government's introduction of reservations in higher education is known as Mandal II. In January 2006, the Indian parliament approved a bill as the 93rd amendment to the Constitution, enabling the government to introduce reservations for the OBC. Following this, the government passed a bill in May 2006 reserving 27 per cent quotas for the OBC in institutions of higher education. This 27 per cent was in addition to the 15 per cent and 7.5 per cent reservations for the SC and ST already in place, for a maximum of 50 per cent capped by the Supreme Court of India. There were widespread protests while the bill was discussed, but the bill was passed almost unanimously in both houses of parliament. This reflects the power of the OBC in the political system. The implementation of the bill was held up as the bill was challenged in the Supreme Court. The Supreme Court has since approved the implementation of the provisions of the bill, but has again asked the 'creamy layer' to be excluded from benefiting from reservations.

2.4 Women
Another basis of disadvantage acknowledged in Indian society is gender. Women have traditionally found fewer opportunities to participate fully in mainstream activity. With

changes in social attitudes, participation by women has increased. However, reservation in education and employment through central legislation has not been extended to women. Further, central legislation to implement 33 per cent reservation in legislative organizations has been stalled for several years. As discussed later, an excessive reliance on caste as an indicator of disadvantage has divided support for these moves. However, several states have provided for reservation for women in education and employment and also in local governments.

2.5 Disability

More recently, disability has been formally acknowledged as a source of disadvantage. To address this, the central government has legislated 3 per cent reservation for persons with disability in central government employment and also in educational institutions. However, the implementation of these policies is still quite patchy.

3. Constitutional and legislative provisions for affirmative action

The policy of reservations for disadvantaged segments of Indian society started before India's independence, although the terms used varied and the communities that benefited also varied. A bill in 1919 provided for representation for backward classes in public bodies. In the 1920s, some state governments reserved positions in government employment and educational institutions for the depressed classes. In 1935, another act provided for representation in central and state governments for different communities (Lansing and Kuruvilla, 1986). The same spirit and concern for the disadvantaged groups was displayed when the Constitution for independent India was drafted. The Indian Constitution stresses social, economic and political justice and equality of status and opportunity for all citizens. It seeks to promote the educational and economic interests of the weaker sections of the population, and in particular the SC and the ST, and to protect them from social injustice and all forms of exploitation (Jain and Ratnam, 1994).

When India gained independence from British rule in 1947 and established itself as a democracy, it carried over the burden of centuries'-old socioeconomic discrimination as a result of the caste system. The Constitution of India was adopted on its first Republic Day, 26 January 1950. The Preamble declares:

WE THE PEOPLE OF INDIA, having solemnly resolved to constitute India into a SOVEREIGN DEMOCRATIC REPUBLIC and to secure to all its citizens:

JUSTICE, social, economic and political;
LIBERTY of thought, expression, belief, faith and worship;
EQUALITY of status and of opportunity, and to promote among them all
FRATERNITY assuring the dignity of the individual and the unity of the nation;

IN OUR CONSTITUENT ASSEMBLY this twenty-sixth day of November, 1949, do HEREBY ADOPT, ENACT AND GIVE TO OURSELVES THIS CONSTITUTION.

The Indian Constitution elaborates on the Fundamental Rights of Indian citizens, specifically granting 'the right to equality' in Section 14; 'prohibition of discrimination on grounds of religion, race, caste, sex, or place of birth' in Section 15; equality of opportunity in public employment in Section 16; and the abolition of untouchability in Section 17. Further, Articles 29, 45 and 46 protect minorities, provide free and compulsory education up to the age of 14 years, and protect the economic and educational needs of the SC and ST.

The Constitution provides for 15 per cent reservation for those belonging to the SC communities and 7.5 per cent reservation for those belonging to ST communities in central government jobs and educational institutions. A proportion of seats is also reserved in legislative bodies at the central and state levels for these groups. Although the list of communities has changed over time, there is significant clarity in terms of criteria that qualify a community to belong to an SC or ST community, but not to the OBC. At the time of independence it was believed that caste-based reservations would be required only for a limited timeframe of ten years, to bring the SCs and STs into the mainstream. However, reservations are still in place, and have not been an issue in any significant political debate. Although there are minor debates on its efficacy, it is largely perceived as necessary.

In 1995, the central government adopted the Persons with Disabilities (Equal Opportunities, Protection of Rights and Full Participation) Act. This legislation provides for 3 per cent reservation in central government jobs and in education institutions supported by the central government. This is divided into 1 per cent each for those who have physical, visual, or hearing disabilities. Since this requires looking again at job specifications and selection criteria that may have to be relaxed or modified, the implementation of the provisions of this Act has been slow. Due to paucity of active political support, activists have relied on the courts to promote its implementation.

The proposal to table a bill providing for 33 per cent reservation for women in parliament and state legislature was made almost a decade ago. However, despite attempts to have it tabled in parliament several times, it has not been successful. The proposal views women as one homogeneous group, while those opposed to it want the quota further divided along caste and community lines. The proposal, if accepted, is also likely to affect some sitting parliamentarians. As a result of a variety of reasons, the Women's Reservation Bill has not obtained legislative sanction to become an Act. Narasimhan (2002) suggested that gender, class and caste-based alignments and divisions have negatively influenced initiatives, including reservations, focused on making India society more inclusive for women. Patil (2002) highlighted the role of caste and community alignment in the political process in preventing initiatives to empower women.

4. Reservation as affirmative action in India

According to Osborne (2001), the reservation policies for the SC were designed to assist groups who had been suppressed and discriminated against for centuries based on religious beliefs, whereas the reservations for the ST were primarily designed to assist groups who were traditionally isolated from the modern world and mainstream society because of their remote tribal, rural lifestyle.

Tummala (1999) outlined five broad arguments that have been given in favour of reservations in India. The first argument is based on compensatory justice (Borooah et al., 2007). It suggests that reserving certain opportunities for those disadvantaged by historical discrimination is an attempt to make redress for past mistakes. Thorat (2006) refers to the need to pay the social debt to the groups that have been historically excluded from education and employment. Second, distributive justice arguments support reservation with the need to distribute social goods and wealth by providing equal opportunity and access to all. Third, social utility theory justifies reservation based on the idea that everyone in society has something to contribute and that society is better off when everyone can participate. Fourth, the concept of responsiveness suggests that as an organization becomes more diverse it will become more responsive to the needs of all. Finally, an argument for reservation is based on the notion that merit is not based solely on test scores, but requires a wider definition. This is discussed further in Section 5.

Tummala (1999) also outlined some arguments against reservation. Some view reservation for lower classes as reverse discrimination, arguing that reservation perpetuates discrimination even though it is now being practised on a different group. Others, while accepting reservations, suggest that preference should be given only to those individuals who actually experience discrimination and not to all members of that group. The third argument is that any preference is against the political philosophy of individualism as it favours or disadvantages individuals because of their family or social background but not because of their individual traits and skills. The fourth argument against reservation stems from the implementation process that has been followed in India, where it is suggested that any preference tends to be treated as an entitlement and not a time-bound programme to address a problem. The fifth criticism is based on the idea that the efforts at better representation might result in poor services as less-qualified people may be appointed even when there are persons with more merit and capability who are left out. In other words, there is an under-utilization of available human assets. Finally, there are arguments that reservation would lead to self-denigration and defensive behaviour on the part of those who avail themselves of the benefits and actually work against the very people whom they are supposed to help.

Ghosh (2006) listed some additional arguments that have been used during the most recent discussion on reservation of seats in institutions of higher learning supported by the central government. Some have argued that reservation in higher education is a cosmetic political exercise and does not address the basic problem of inadequate primary and secondary education, which is the real reason for underrepresentation of certain segments in higher education (Lansing and Kuruvilla, 1986). Even the government committee appointed to develop the implementation programme for reservation in higher education acknowledges this limitation (Moily, 2006). Others suggest that, by allowing qualifications to be awarded to persons with lower aptitude and performance, reservation hurts the concept of merit (Lansing and Kuruvilla, 1986). This is similar to the individualism argument examined above. Reservation leads to stronger caste identities (Zwart, 2000) and creates a sense of victimization among those not covered by these polices. This is quite evident in the protests that followed the reservation in jobs for OBC and more recently the reservation of seats in higher education. The 'creamy layer' argument suggests that reservation benefits those who deserve it the least, depriving the rest of the community that could actually benefit. This point has even been made by the government committee (Moily, 2006). Further, others have indicated that the current form of reservation privileges caste-based discrimination and therefore ignores other and possibly more desirable forms of inclusion (Deshpande and Yadav, 2006; Hasan, 2009). This criticism is based on the belief that caste is not the only factor that limits access to education and jobs in India. Finally, some criticize this form of affirmative action as it compresses the notion of social justice into reservation alone (Mehta, 2006), instead of encompassing broader socioeconomic policies such as land reform and other asset redistribution strategies of income generation (Ramaiah, 2006).

At one level, reservation is driven by the need to be inclusive, but it is difficult to separate the evolution of the policies and their implementation from a country's political context. Affirmative actions, including reservations, are a manifestation of the will of a democratic society to address issues of inequality. It is inherently a product of a political process (Tummala, 1999). Osborne (2001) analysed the role of castes as rent-seeking pressure groups that have displaced class- or occupation-based groups in India. Pande (2003) described how certain politically powerful groups obtained greater benefits than others from existing reservation policies. Killian (1991) compared the reservations policies of India with the affirmative action programmes in the USA to suggest that there are parallels in the political processes in their implementation. Lansing and Kuruvilla (1986) also described the political pressure on the private sector to provide employment to persons from the backward community even when there was no formal requirement to reserve seats for them.

4.1   Reservation for SC and ST
The argument for discrimination of SC was based on traditional practices of untouchability that had clearly excluded significant sections of Indian society from the mainstream. Something had to be done to correct that, and reservation was seen as a useful tool. Similarly, it was clearly accepted that since most ST communities lived far from urban and semi-urban centres and their economic situation was obviously very bad, reservation was a good tool to bring them into the mainstream (Deshpande and Yadav, 2006; Jain and Ratnam, 1994).

4.1.1   Job reservation for SC/ST in government and public sector enterprises   The central government has reserved 15 per cent and 7.5 per cent of jobs in the government and in public sector enterprises for SC and ST respectively. Initially, reservation was limited to the hiring process, but as this did not increase representation in higher levels in the hierarchy in government jobs, reservation was also introduced for promotions so that persons from these groups could obtain jobs at a higher level in the hierarchy. Borooah et al. (2007) concluded that job reservation succeeded in raising the representation of persons from SC and ST in regular salaried and wage employment by about 5 percentage points. Corbridge (2000) found that the reservation system for schedule tribes in Jharkhand has improved their lot.

Jain and Ratnam (1994) studied the impact of the reservation policies on employment by studying the actual percentage of SC/ST persons in different levels of hierarchy in government services and public sector enterprises run by the central government. Table 7.1 shows the data from their study of employment in government and Table 7.2 shows data on employment in central public sector enterprises from the Jain and Ratnam (1994) study. Groups A and B represent professional and managerial jobs, while Groups C and D typically reflect clerical and non-managerial blue- and white-collar jobs. The data suggest that there were significant improvements in representation of persons from the SC communities. The most significant increases in representation had happened for A- and B-level roles, although the targets had not yet been achieved. The increases in C

Table 7.1   Percentage of SC and ST employees in central government service

Group	% of SC employees		% of ST employees	
	As on 1 Jan. 1977	As on 1 Jan. 1987	As on 1 Jan. 1977	As on 1 Jan. 1987
A	4.16	8.23	0.77	2.05
B	6.07	10.40	0.77	1.92
C	11.84	14.46	2.78	4.23
D	19.04	20.09	4.35	5.84
Total	11.31	16.18	3.36	4.69

Table 7.2   Percentage of SC and ST employees in central public sector enterprises

Category	As on 1 Jan. 1977	As on 1 Jan. 1980	As on 1 Jan. 1985	As on 1 Jan. 1990
SC				
A	0.52	2.9	4.12	5.95
B	1.54	5.12	5.50	8.73
C	5.49	18.08	18.34	19.20
D (excl. sweepers*)	7.42	22.36	18.10	31.39
D (sweepers only)	81.75	64.69	75.30	81.93
Total	7.42	17.44	18.10	19.57
ST				
A	0.17	0.66	0.89	1.43
B	0.16	1.36	1.57	2.50
C	1.29	7.71	8.62	8.95
D (excl. sweepers)	5.94	10.76	15.12	19.82
D (sweepers only)	1.39	4.14	3.31	2.87
Total	2.24	7.53	8.71	9.78

Note: *Sweeper refers to those providing janitorial services.

and D levels have been more modest, but the targets had been nearly met or exceeded. The data also suggest that while there had been an increase in representation of persons from the ST communities, the policy of reservation has not worked so well for them.

Jain and Ratnam (1994) attributed much of the inability to meet the targets, particularly in higher-level jobs, to lack of education. As per the 1981 Census, only 2 per cent of SC and ST passed matriculation, and 0.25 per cent were graduates. They suggested that providing access to education and training should precede or proceed in parallel with the policy of reservation in jobs. In a recent study, Madheswaran and Attewell (2007) showed that while a major share of the earnings differential between SC/ST and others is due to differences in human capital endowments, about 15 per cent is due also to discrimination in the marketplace. They suggested that occupational discrimination was more pronounced than wage discrimination. In other words, a person from an SC/ST group is more likely to be discriminated against at the time of employment but less likely to be discriminated against in terms of compensation once he/she is employed in a role. Deshpande and Newman (2007) suggested that SC/ST candidates differ in terms of family connections, financial security during their university years and obligations to support parental households, which influence the careers they can pursue. In other words, the social and cultural capital of SC/ST candidates negatively influences their job prospects. Further, scepticism related to reservations leads potential employers to question the legitimacy of their credentials.

In short, reservation for SC/ST communities in government and public sector jobs has helped individuals and communities in many ways. However, there is much to be done in terms of access to education and building social and cultural capital to make the opportunities accessible to a wider cross-section of deserving people.

4.1.2   Reservation of seats for SC/ST in higher education   The government has reserved 15 per cent and 7½ per cent for SC and ST respectively in centrally supported institutes of higher education. Weisskopf (2004) conducted a detailed study on the role of reservation in higher education in increasing representation of persons from SC/ST communities. According to him, student enrolment in higher educational institutions in India increased from fewer than 200 000 in 1950 to almost 7 million by the year 2000, and the representation of SC/ST students had gone up significantly. The proportion of SC students increased from 7 per cent to 7.8 per cent, and proportion of ST students increased from 1.6 to 2.7 per cent between the late 1970s and the late 1990s. In terms of absolute numbers, a very large number of people from the SC/ST community are getting college education now, compared to the 1950s. However, there are reasons for concern. As in the case of employment, the increase in representation of SC has been better than that for ST. Weisskopf found that even after the minimum qualifying scores are set well below the cut-off point for general-entry applicants, some seats earmarked for SC/ST students go unfilled, particularly in premier schools. He estimated that nearly 50 per cent of seats for SC and 66 per cent of those for ST are unfilled. He also estimated that about one-sixth of the students would have been admitted without the cut-off point being lowered, suggesting that five-sixths of the increase in representation in higher education is due to reservation. He further argued that due to reservation, SC/ST candidates have access to higher-quality education than they would have obtained without reservation, and the policy has also encouraged others who might not have pursued higher education to enrol for it. According to him, most SC and ST students enrolled in elite higher educational institutions in India enter careers they would not have been able to pursue in the absence of reservation policies. However, he argued that most of the benefits have been obtained by better-off castes and families within the SC/ST communities.

Most analysts believe that reservation for the SC/ST communities in jobs and higher education is meeting many of its objectives. However, several scholars would want the benefits to be more fairly distributed. Deshpande and Newman (2007) found that many beneficiaries of reservation join many of their non-reservation counterparts in arguing that reservation should be better targeted so that the benefits are obtained by the poor and rural *dalits*, rather than by second- or third-generation recipients of quota admissions, who are viewed as an internal 'creamy layer'. As they put it, the search for the 'truly disadvantaged' continues in India as it does in the USA, with complex political agendas in the mix (Deshpande and Newman, 2007). Similarly, Borooah et al. (2007) argued that governments need to do much more to prepare such persons with the skills and abilities that will allow them to seek those jobs on an equal footing. They suggest that in addition to reserving places in management, engineering and medical schools that largely benefit those in the urban areas, the government needs to ensure access to good primary and secondary schools for all.

4.2 Reservation for OBC

While there is broad consensus on the desirability of reservation for SC/ST communities in jobs and education, there is less of a consensus on reservation for OBC. Reservation for OBC has been vigorously contested from the very beginning and the anti-reservation 'movement' in centrally supported institutions of higher education is the most recent example of this contest (Deshpande and Yadav, 2006). Many argue that today economic inequality has a greater role in excluding people from higher education and high-paying jobs.

The OBC, however, are politically powerful because many of them are self-sustaining farmers and owner–cultivators. Reservation helps them to convert their political and economic assets, which are currently rural, to urban jobs and related skill assets (Gupta, 2005). The system of reservations rewards relatively better-off groups within the OBC while excluding those who are more genuinely in need of special concessions within the groups and also in the general category (Ghosh, 2006). Even the Moily Commission, set up by the government, recognized the role of income, stating that on average poverty among OBC was double that of others while average poverty among SC/ST was three times that of others. The commission also stated that health indicators for the OBC were closer to the general category and even better than the general category in some states. Land ownership among OBC is vastly higher than among SC, and not significantly different from the general category. Asset ownership (including land) per household of OBC is double that of SC and ST, and two-thirds of 'Others' in both rural and urban areas (Moily, 2006). There are yet others who argue that some 'OBC' are not really socially, politically or economically backward, and have been included in the list mainly because of political pressure. Further, others criticize the reservation policy as it allows OBC who suffer no discrimination to benefit at the expense of the more deserving within them (Ghosh, 2006). It also excludes deserving candidates from regions that are less developed, allowing the southern states to benefit more than others.

4.2.1 Job reservation for OBC in government service and public sector enterprises Job reservation for OBCs was implemented in 1992, but no long-term study has examined the changes in employment patterns. However, other studies can be used to infer the implications. Table 7.3 shows the distribution of males between the ages of 25 and 45 across the categories of economic status by religion and caste.

The data show that both Muslim and non-Muslim OBC men were more likely to be in self-employment than men from SC. Also, both Muslim and non-Muslim OBC men were less likely to work as casual labourers than men from SC. However, forward-caste Hindu men were more likely to be in regular salaried or wage employment than OBC men, and forward-caste Hindu men were even less likely to work as casual labourers than men

Table 7.3   Economic status and caste/religion of men between 25 and 45 years (1999–2000)*

	Self-employed	Employer	Unpaid family worker	Regular employee	Casual worker	Seeking work	Total
ST (non-Christian)	34.85	0.32	9.18	12.54	42.22	0.9	100
	6.65	1.76	6.16	4.12	12.44	3.11	7.33
ST (Christian)	44.48	0.30	10.15	14.93	28.36	1.79	100
	0.5	0.1	0.4	0.29	0.49	0.37	0.43
SC	27.72	0.33	5.01	18.07	47.18	1.69	100
	11.67	4.11	7.41	13.09	30.67	12.93	16.18
OBC (non-Muslim)	40.69	1.27	12.38	19.13	24.95	1.59	100
	33.25	30.11	35.54	26.89	31.47	23.55	31.39
OBC (Muslim)	44.98	2.21	9.02	15.31	26.79	1.69	100
	4.10	5.87	2.89	2.40	3.77	2.81	3.5
Hindu (non-ST/SC/OBC)	39.7	1.91	13.40	31.55	10.23	3.20	100
	31.39	44.09	37.25	42.91	12.49	46.00	30.38
Muslim (non-ST/SC/OBC)	46.27	1.22	7.67	19.82	22.92	2.12	100
	9.83	7.53	5.71	7.24	7.51	8.18	8.16
Christian (non-ST/SC/OBC)	25.32	5.82	4.68	37.47	22.28	4.43	100
	0.67	4.50	0.44	1.71	0.91	2.14	1.02
Sikh (non-ST/SC/OBC)	46.30	1.61	28.70	18.65	3.54	1.21	100
	1.93	1.96	4.21	1.34	0.23	0.92	1.60
Total	38.42	1.32	10.93	22.33	24.89	2.11	100
	100	100	100	100	100	100	100

Note: * Top and bottom numbers in each category are row and column percentages respectively.

Source: Borooah et al. (2007).

from OBC. In short, on average SC and non-Christian ST are at the bottom; forward-caste Hindus are at the top, and OBC are in the middle (Borooah et al., 2007). However, while the proportions vary, there are persons from all religious and caste categories in each economic stratum. It is quite natural that there would be resentment if reservation in jobs is based only on caste.

Based on their study, Borooah et al. (2007) concluded that jobs reservation for persons from OBC are misconceived. They found that only 11 per cent of the employment deficit that non-Muslim OBC males faced, relative to forward-caste Hindus, could be attributed to 'discrimination', while between 33 and 37 per cent of the employment deficit faced by Muslims could be so attributed. So, if the object of jobs reservation is to correct for discriminatory bias in the jobs market, and if reservation is to be extended beyond SC and ST, then Muslims have a more compelling case than persons from the non-Muslim OBC (Borooah et al., 2007).

4.2.2   Reservation of seats for OBC in higher education   The implementation of reservation for OBC in centrally funded institutions is still in the early stages, so a longitudinal study has not yet been done. However, its implications can be assessed based on the reservation for OBC in higher education institutions run by the states. In his study, Weisskopf (2004) estimated that about five-sixths of OBC students would have obtained admissions without reservation. This suggests that reservation for OBC is unlikely to have a significant impact, even assuming that the admission standards for the central elite institutions are higher. Even the Moily Commission acknowledged that the real problem appears to be at the high-school level, especially in rural areas. The proportion of 'high-school pass' among OBC, even in the top two income classes in rural areas, is only about 15 per cent as compared to around 20 per cent for so-called forward castes. In urban areas, matters are much better for OBC except in a few states – Madhya Pradesh, Maharashtra, Punjab, Tamil Nadu and Uttar Pradesh (Moily, 2006). The report indicates that there is no significant difference in the proportion of students who pass high school between SC and ST, and the OBC. However, the proportion of OBC who graduate from school is closer to forward castes in the southern states. The report clearly stated that 'The true benefit of reservations will be realized only when the high school enrolment of OBCs, especially in rural areas, increases significantly' (Moily, 2006, p. 54).

The Moily Commission acknowledged that socially and educationally, as well as economically advanced members of the OBCs should be excluded from the benefits of reservation in view of the fact that the basis for such reservation is class and not caste (Moily, 2006), but refused to make a recommendation as it was beyond the scope of the Commission. This suggests that unless the creamy layer is excluded, the reserved seats will largely benefit the OBC from the top two income deciles at the cost of the poorer income deciles of the OBC. Thus almost all rural OBC as well as urban OBC from the northern, central and eastern regions of India will be deprived of the intended benefit of reservation (Moily, 2006).

4.3 Affirmative action in the private sector

In conditions of rising unemployment due to population growth outstripping the growth of employment generation in India, there is now a 'politics of scarcity' that further exaggerates the role of politics in the debate on reservation. In this context, different castes and communities are competing with each other for the 'backward' label in order to obtain preferential access to education and employment (Jain and Ratnam, 1994). While in the census conducted in 1872 and 1931, groups that otherwise might have been categorized as backward tried to portray themselves as forward castes (Bhagat, 2007), in recent times, several forward castes, including some sub-castes from among the Brahmins, have begun to claim backward status on economic criteria to obtain the benefits of reservation. More recently, there were clashes between a group that was already categorized as ST and another group that was seeking the same status. The former group saw the latter taking away part of the privileges that would have come to their group. Since the liberalization of the economy, the importance of higher education in lucrative jobs has become more important, and government jobs have become scarce while most of the new jobs are created in the private sector. This has led to demands for reservation in the private sector.

The Confederation of Indian Industries (CII) and Associated Chambers of Commerce and Industry of India set up a committee, chaired by the CII past president J.J. Irani, to look at reservations issues as related to the private sector. This committee's report clearly opposed any kind of reservation in the private sector. The report was not meant as a response to the government's move for equity legislation but to reconcile the differences between industry organizations and the political leadership on what each considered to be social initiatives. While industry has been working with economically backward people for a large number of years, they found a disconnect with what the political leadership expected when they talked of the socially backward. The report proposed three major cornerstones:

> 1) given that organised labour is just two per cent of the total work force in the country, no matter what the private sector did, it was not going to be possible to solve the problem of segregation and discrimination in society. 2) industry recognised its role and would be a part of the solution rather than offer the complete solution; whatever is done has to further the competitiveness of Indian industry and not erode it; and 3) the entire effort has to be voluntary and cannot be forced by legislation, which would be counter-productive. Industry bodies too could not mandate a particular behaviour of their members but would use all persuasive skills possible to ensure that the members moved forward.

In their report, the industry bodies set out four areas in which they would take concrete steps: (1) at the workplace; (2) entrepreneurship development; (3) employability; and (4) education. They specified milestones for the first year, which include adopting a code of conduct, creating 100 entrepreneurs from SC and ST, establishing coaching centres in ten universities for 10 000 students, establishing ten centres for coaching for entrance examinations to professional and technical courses to cover 5000 students, creating 50 new scholarships in national institutes of excellence and disclosing progress on proposed concrete steps in annual reports.

5.   An alternative model for reservation

The issues related to reservations in India are very complex. Clearly there are many grey areas, such as which are the creamy layers within the lower castes and the OBC, whether they should be included or excluded from the reservations quotas and how that determination should be made. Ghosh (2006) proposes several methods of dealing with the creamy layer such as an economic cut-off above which there would be no eligibility for a reserved seat, allowing two or three generations of a family to benefit from the reservation and so on, which are easily administered and ensure the system is just, fair and time-limited. The Supreme Court of India has repeatedly excluded the creamy layer from the benefits of reservation. Simultaneously, several other political parties have started demanding reservation for economically backward people irrespective of caste. These recent developments indicate that such challenges will further erode the use of caste only as an indicator of backwardness.

Many have argued that it is also difficult to equate caste with class, and hence disadvantage for those lower in the hierarchy, particularly in the context of OBC. Gupta (2005) argues that caste identities cannot be straitjacketed within a hierarchical grid without running into empirical problems, as the caste order is characterized by contested notions of hierarchy and competitive assertions of caste identity. The actual hierarchy based on caste is strongly influenced by the local context. In some contexts, Brahmans were and are still dominant; in other cases it may be Jats, Rajputs, Marathas or Lingayats. He indicated that Jotiba Phule, the nineteenth-century leader of the non-

Brahman movement in Maharashtra, claimed that the lower castes or '*sudras*' were actually upper-caste Kshtriyas (or warriors) in pre-Aryan times. Phule portrayed them as 'kind and genial rulers of the land before the Brahmans and then the Muslim "robbers" from across the Himalayas took over by deceit and cruelty' (Gupta, 2005, p.412). In other words, it is difficult to sustain an argument for reservation based entirely on caste without acknowledging the variation in level of deprivation across the country that may be attributed to other factors.

On the other hand, Deshpande (2006) criticized the test-based notion of merit that has been used by opponents of the OBC reservations. According to Deshpande (2006), there are three broad kinds of resources necessary to ensure good performance in competitive exams and do well on indicators of merit that help candidates enter institutions of higher learning: (i) economic resources; (ii) social and cultural resources; and (iii) intrinsic ability and hard work. He argued that the position that merit is intrinsic to an individual is indefensible. Economic resources play a significant role in deciding the quality of schooling accessible to an individual. Social and cultural resources, including caste, influence the extent to which an individual can benefit from schooling, and also influence individuals' aspirations. Those from good economic and sociocultural backgrounds have an advantage over candidates from weaker contexts (Madheswaran and Attewell, 2007). There are several scholars who accept reservation as a useful tool to make a more inclusive society, but argue for a system of reservation based a wider range on parameters, rather than one based on caste alone. Deshpande and Yadav (2006) suggested a novel framework that extends the definition of merit so that a wider cross-section of disadvantaged groups obtains access to higher education.

Deshpande and Yadav (2006) presented an alternative proposal to reservations rooted in the recognition of both social justice and merit at an 80:20 ratio for 'a policy that is morally justified, intellectually sound, politically defensible, and administratively viable'. Their proposal involves combining the scores for academic merit and social disadvantage into the criteria for admission into institutions of higher education. While academic merit is non-controversial, social disadvantage would be measured on caste, community and gender, and region based on data from the National Sample Survey (NSS). The academic score would be converted into a standardized score on a scale of 0–80 and the social disadvantage score would range between 0–20.

Table 7.4 shows the percentage of persons aged 25 to 45 from different groups with graduate degrees. It is quite clear that as a percentage share of the urban population, Hindu upper castes and Christians have nearly twice the number of graduates, Sikhs and others have marginally higher levels of graduates, while all 'others' have fewer graduates. OBC have about half the percentage of graduates as a proportion of urban population, Muslims have less than half and SC have close to two-fifths. After one glance at the data, it is quite obvious that variation in proportion of graduates among the groups is not normal. However, as Deshpande (2006) argued, the data suggest the existence of inequality and discrimination but not necessarily the existence of injustice. They suggest that inequality and discrimination may be valid because entry into higher education requires some level of discrimination. Further, even if there is injustice, caste-based reservation for OBC may not be the most prudent option to correct the injustice. As shown in the table, and also highlighted by Borooah et al. (2007) based on the data, Muslims may have more of a claim to reservation than OBC. Further, Deshpande and Yadav (2006)

Table 7.4   Proportion of persons with graduate degrees, NSSO, 1999–2000

Castes and communities	% share of graduates in various castes and communities				% share of urban population
	Agriculture	Engineering	Medicine	Other	
Hindu ST	2.4	1.3	1.8	1.3	2.6
Hindu SC	3.8	2.2	1.8	3.6	12.9
All Muslim	9.4	5.0	10.0	5.7	17.0
Hindu OBC	10.0	14.9	10.4	13.7	24.2
Hindu – upper	62.1	66.8	65.3	65.9	36.9
All Christian	8.4	5.2	6.6	4.0	2.8
All Sikh	1.7	2.2	2.1	2.4	1.6
All others	2.4	2.4	1.9	3.3	2.0

Source: Deshpande (2006).

argue that while caste-based reservation may be easy to administer and monitor, and may be relatively resistant to appropriation by other groups, it is not necessarily the best solution to all affirmative action problems. According to Deshpande and Yadav, apart from attaining the social objectives, policies should also attempt to ensure efficiency by minimizing unavoidable costs and maximizing potential benefits. By unavoidable costs, they refer to the social disharmony, potential loss of life and property, and long-term caste solidarity; and by maximizing benefits they refer to the need to fine-tune the reservation programme to target the benefits to the really needy.

Table 7.5 illustrates the interaction effects among different types or sources of disadvantage, in this case those of caste and community, class and gender. The data suggest that caste and community disadvantage certain groups, economic class disadvantages the poorer sections, and women are also disadvantaged.

Deshpande and Yadav (2006) believe that there are other sources of disadvantage that prevent access to higher education and jobs. They also draw attention to the urban–rural divide in the country. Table 7.6 shows the percentage of graduates in the population aged 20 years or above in different castes and communities in rural and urban India. It is quite clear that access to higher education is much better for those in urban India relative to rural India. The proportion of SC with graduate degrees in urban India is comparable to those of upper castes in rural India. Hence any system of reservation that does not compensate for the rural–urban divide disadvantages people from the rural areas of every caste and community grouping.

Deshpande and Yadav (2007) suggest that there are regional variations. In some parts of the country, access to education and general economic conditions are better than in others. A reservation policy that does not compensate for regional variations disadvantages persons from parts of the country that are underdeveloped. Even the government commission argued that since OBC in the South are better off, they are more likely to take advantage of the scheme relative to those from other parts of the country (Moily, 2006).

Drawing on these conclusions, Deshpande and Yadav (2007) suggested a system that combines academic merit with social disadvantage as a basis for admission to higher

Table 7.5   Percentage of postgraduates and professional degree holders by caste/community, class and gender

Castes/communities	Gender	All classes	Rich	Middle	Lower middle	Poor	Very poor
All castes/comms	All	2.5	8.1	6.8	1.6	0.8	0.6
	Men	3.4	9.8	9.1	2.2	1.2	1.0
	Women	1.4	5.8	3.9	0.8	0.4	0.1
Hindu Dwija upper caste	All	5.6	13.6	8.8	2.7	1.7	0.5
	Men	7.4	17.8	10.3	3.9	2.7	1.0
	Women	3.5	8.3	7.3	1.4	0.3	0.0
Hindu and Sikh intermediate castes	All	2.8	6.2	4.6	0.7	1.2	0.8
	Men	3.5	7.3	5.8	1.2	0.9	1.7
	Women	2.0	4.8	3.4	0.0	2.2	0.0
OBC	All	1.8	5.8	6.6	1.1	0.7	0.7
	Men	2.7	6.2	10.1	1.6	1.3	1.3
	Women	0.8	5.2	1.9	0.4	0.1	0.1
SC (any religion)	All	1.4	4.2	8.0	1.6	0.5	0.4
	Men	2.1	2.3	11.7	2.8	0.7	0.8
	Women	0.6	5.0	2.6	0.2	0.2	0.1
ST (any religion)	All	0.9	1.9	6.1	1.4	0.6	0.4
	Men	1.3	3.3	10.0	1.6	0.3	0.7
	Women	0.5	0.0	1.8	1.1	0.5	0.2
Muslims	All	1.8	7.1	4.0	1.5	0.3	0.0
	Men	2.5	10.1	6.0	1.2	0.5	0.0
	Women	0.9	1.7	1.6	2.0	0.0	0.0
Christians	All	3.3	13.2	7.8	1.8	0.8	0.0
	Men	3.0	11.1	5.7	3.3	1.5	0.0
	Women	3.7	15.0	9.5	0.0	0.0	0.0

Source: Deshpande and Yadav (2006).

Table 7.6   Percentage of graduates in the population aged 20 years or above in different castes and communities in rural and urban India

Caste/community	Rural India	Urban India
ST	1.1	10.19
SC	1.2	4.7
Muslim	1.3	6.1
Hindu – OBC	2.1	8.6
Sikh	2.8	25.0
Christian	4.7	23.7
Hindu – upper caste	5.3	25.3
Other religions	5.4	31.5
All India average	2.6	15.5

Source: Deshpande and Yadav (2006).

education institutions. Their model for reservation is based on a system already in use at the Jawaharlal Nehru University (one of the universities that will be affected by the new law) wherein candidates from SC/ST/OBC communities, girls and students with disabilities obtain bonus points to compensate for social and economic disadvantage. The Moily Commission appreciated this system as a means of making higher education more inclusive (Moily, 2006).

Deshpande and Yadav's (2007) model is based on the notion that the social disadvantage score should be divided into group and individual components. The group component derives from disadvantages based on caste and community, gender, region, and whether the candidate is from a rural or an urban background. They suggest that these disadvantages should be calibrated on the basis of available statistics on representation in higher education of different castes/communities, regions, and urban–rural place of residence. Each of these should be considered separately for males and females. The individual component of social disadvantage includes education level in the family and economic condition of the family, as they both influence the child's learning environment. They suggested that parental occupation and the type of school where a person passed the high-school examination were two robust indicators to capture individual disadvantage. They believe that this model meets the criteria of effectiveness in terms of targeting the benefits to the more deserving, and also efficient as it is less disadvantageous to those left out only because of caste. Further, their model is based on a points system that is continuously updated and excludes from the purview of reservation those who are already doing as well as the rest of society. However, they do acknowledge that unlike the caste-based reservation that is relatively less amenable to cheating, there is some scope for cheating by individuals who can present credentials, which may not be easy to verify, to benefit from the reservation.

7. Conclusions

India's reservations policy is applicable to all public sector organizations, legislative representation and education. Variations in policy and implementation are apparent between the central and state governments. As in the experience of other countries, India too has faced considerable backlash towards it reservations policies, resulting in increased identity-based divisions. It has also taken a highly political, emotional and violent turn, which is expected to continue into the future. Private sector organizations are not governed by affirmative action policies and most have not shown any interest in implementing any voluntary programmes to address these issues. Many of the new firms in the emerging knowledge-based industry, particularly multinational corporations, however, have implemented affirmative action policies for women in the workplace.

Borooah et al. (2001) report that the reservations policy does nothing to improve the job-related attributes of those benefiting from these programmes and there remains a huge gulf between the educational standards achieved by the higher-caste Hindus. They recommend that rather than reserving places in management, engineering and medical schools in urban areas, the focus should be on the many dysfunctional primary and secondary schools in rural India, where learning and education for millions of children is stifled by an absence of learning materials, teachers and even classrooms. Compounding the problem of dysfunctional schools is the poverty of the SC, ST and Muslim parents who cannot afford to send their children to school. Hasan and Mehta's (2006) analysis

Summary table for India

Existence of anti-discrimination legislation	Yes, *Constitution of India* (1950)
Criteria covered by anti-discrimination legislation	• Section (15) prohibits discrimination based on grounds of religion, race, caste, sex, or place of birth • Section (17) abolished 'untouchability'
Criteria for which the reporting of quantitative data and their communication to a public administration are compulsory	• The Constitution provides for 15 per cent reservation for the SC and 7.5 per cent for the ST in central government jobs, educational institutions, and legislative organizations • It provides for states to establish a list of OBC for affirmative action purposes • The Supreme Court of India has established the total combined ceiling, on quotas for all designated groups, at 50 per cent
Criteria covered by 'affirmative' or 'positive' action legislation other than unemployment- or income-based	Scheduled Castes (SC) Scheduled Tribes (ST) Other Backward Classes (OBC) Women Disability
Existence of a discourse or debate about 'non-discrimination' or 'equality'	Yes, over 3000 years!
Existence of a discourse or debate about 'diversity'	Yes, but very recent
Year or period when the 'discrimination' concept started to disseminate in management literature in the country	1940s – before independence from the British Raj
Year or period when the diversity concept started to disseminate in management literature in the country	2000s
Who pushed the 'diversity' agenda?	• Management scholars and practitioners • Multinational corporations • Minorities not included in the existing protected groups
Existence of a professional association representing diversity professionals and year of creation	Yes, Indian Academy of Management (IAOM), 2009
Existence of a professional association representing diversity scholars and year of creation	Yes, Indian Academy of Management (IAOM), 2009

of the NSS data reveals that SC, ST, OBC and Muslims are seriously underrepresented in India's colleges relative to their population shares, and explain this phenomenon as a result of their lower high-school completion rates. They recommend attention to quality education at the lower rungs as the best economic response rather than reservations at the higher education levels.

Sowell (2003, p. 48) remarks that 'as the country with the longest history of preferences and quotas for the purpose of advancing poor and disadvantaged groups, India's experience is particularly relevant to the actual consequences of such programmes, as distinguished from their hopes and consequences'. In fact, India's 50-year experiment with reservations quotas has been emulated in other countries such as Nigeria, Malaysia and Sri Lanka (Borooah et al., 2007). It would be interesting for equity researchers and practitioners to further pursue comparative experiences of diversity policies in these countries to assess where positive gains have been made and where there remains more to be accomplished.

Managing diversity, for groups outside of the reservations policy framework, is a fairly recent phenomenon in India. It is promoted primarily by the multinational corporations, and follows more of a Western approach to accommodating diversity in the workplace for gaining a competitive business advantage, with their primary focus on women.

In conclusion, caste-based reservation as a tool of affirmative action in India is still a work-in-progress. It has worked well in many ways, but also created new challenges. A more elaborate model that recognizes a wider range of sources of disadvantage will be required to make Indian society really more inclusive in the future as India becomes a significant player in the global economy.

References

Bhagat, R.B. (2007), 'Caste census looking back, looking forward', *Economic and Political Weekly*, **42**, 1902–5.

Borooah, Vani K., Dubey, Amaresh and Iyer, Sriya (2007), 'The effectiveness of jobs reservation: caste, religion and economic status in India', *Development and Change*, **38** (3), 423–45.

Chattopadhyay, Raghabendra and Dufloi, Esther (2004), 'Women as policy makers: evidence from a randomised policy experiment in India', *Econometrica*, **72** (5), 1409–43.

The Constitution of India (1972), as modified up to 15 May 1972. Ministry of Law and Justice. New Delhi: Government of India Press.

Corbridge, Stuart (2000), 'Competing inequalities: the scheduled tribes and the reservations system in India's Jharkhand', *The Journal of Asian Studies*, **59** (1), 62–85.

Deshpande, Ashwini and Newman, Katherine (2007), 'Where the path leads: the role of caste in post-university employment expectations', *Economic and Political Weekly*, **42**, 4133–40.

Deshpande, Satish (2006), 'Exclusive inequalities: merit, caste and discrimination in Indian higher education today', *Economic and Political Weekly*, **41**, 2438–44.

Deshpande, Satish and Yadav, Yogendra (2006), 'Redesigning affirmative action castes and benefits in higher education', *Economic and Political Weekly*, **41**, 2419–24.

Ghosh, J. (2006), 'Case for caste-based quotas in higher education', *Economic and Political Weekly*, **41**, 2428–32.

Gupta, Dipankar (2005), 'Caste and politics: identity over system', *Annual Review of Anthropology*, **21**, 409–27.

Hasan, Rana and Mehta, Aashish (2006), 'Under-representation of disadvantaged classes in colleges: what do the data tell us?', *Economic and Political Weekly*, **41**, 3791–6.

Hasan, Zoya (2009), *Politics of Inclusion: Casts, Minorities, and Affirmative Action*, New Delhi: Oxford University Press.

Jain, Harish C. and Ratnam, C.S. Venkata (1994), 'Affirmative action in employment for the scheduled castes and the scheduled tribes in India', *International Journal of Manpower*, **15** (7), 6–25.

Jodhka, Surinder S. and Newman, Katherine (2007), 'In the name of globalisation meritocracy, productivity and the hidden language of caste', *Economic and Political Weekly*, **42**, 4125–32.

Kakar, S. and Kakar, K. (2007), *The Indians: Portrait of a People*, New Delhi: Penguin Books India.

Kijima, Yoko (2006), 'Caste and tribe inequality: evidence from India, 1983–1999', *Economic Development and Cultural Change*, **54** (2), 369–404.

Killian, L.M. (1991), 'Gandhi, Frederick Douglass and affirmative action', *International Journal of Politics, Culture, and Society*, **5** (2), 167–82.

Lansing, Paul and Kuruvilla, Sarosh (1986), 'Job reservation in India', *Labour Law Journal*, September, 653–9.

Madheswaran, S. and Attewell, Paul (2007), 'Caste discrimination in the Indian urban labour market: evidence from the National Sample Survey', *Economic and Political Weekly*, **42**, 4146–53.

Mehta, Pratap Bhanu (2006), 'Democracy, disagreement and merit', *Economic and Political Weekly*, **41**, 2425–7.

Moily, M. Veerappa (2006), 'Final Report of the Oversight Committee on the Implementation of the New Reservation Policy in Higher Educational Institutions', Government Document, available at http://over sightcommittee.gov.in/ocrep.pdf.

Narasimhan, Sakuntala (2002), 'Gender, class, and caste schisms in affirmative action policies: the curious case of India's Women's Reservation Bill', *Feminist Economics*, **8** (2), 183–90.

Osborne, Evan (2001), 'Culture, development and government; reservation in India', *Economic Development and Cultural Change*, **49** (3), 659–85.

Pande, Rohini (2003), 'Can mandated political representation increase policy influence for disadvantaged minorities? Theory and evidence from India', *The American Economic Review*, **93** (4), 1132–51.

Patil, Padmaja A. (2002), 'Socio-economic and political policies in the 1990s and the status of women in India', *Journal of Third World Studies*, **21** (1), 195–205.

Ramaiah, Avatthi (1992), 'Identifying other backward classes', *Economic and Political Weekly*, **37**, 1203–7.

Ramaiah, Avatthi (2006), 'Cultural diversity acclaimed but social and economic diversity ignored', *International Journal of Diversity*, **5** (5), 173–90.

Sowell, T. (2003), *Affirmative Action around the World: An Empirical Study*, New Haven, CT: Yale University Press.

Srinivas, M.N. (1952), *Religion and Society among the Coorgs of South India*, Oxford: Clarendon Press.

Srinivas, M.N. (1962), *Caste in Modern India and Other Essays*, Bombay: Asia Publishing House.

Thorat, Sukhadeo (2006), 'Paying the social debt', *Economic and Political Weekly*, **41**, 2432–5.

Thorat, Sukhadeo and Attewell, Paul (2007), 'The legacy of social exclusion. A correspondence study of job discrimination in India', *Economic and Political Weekly*, **42**, 4141–5.

Tummala, Krishna K. (1999), 'Policy of preference: lessons from India, the United States, and South Africa', *Public Administration Review*, **59** (6), 495–508.

Weisskopf, Thomas E. (2004), 'Impact of reservation on admissions to higher education in India', *Economic and Political Weekly*, **39**, 4339–49.

Zwart, Frank De (2000), 'Practical knowledge and institutional design in India's affirmative action programme', *Anthropology Today*, **16** (3), 4–7.

8 The development of diversity management in the Italian context: a slow process
Annalisa Murgia and Barbara Poggio[1]

1. Introduction

In recent years the concepts of diversity and diversity management have spread in the public debate and the managerial lexicon in Italy as well. Various public and private organizations have launched projects that use this label or adopt this orientation.

The main reasons for the diffusion of these concepts have been: (a) the growth of the multinationals and the spread of international cooperation agreements that imply inter-cultural management (Decastri, 1993; Ambrosini, 2001); (b) the progressive feminization of the labour market and the growing female presence in traditionally masculine sectors (Bombelli, 2000; Gherardi and Poggio, 2007); (c) the increasing importance of knowledge in organizations (Gherardi, 2006) and the diversification of organizational tasks; (d) the demands made by individuals of organizations regarding self-realization and a better balance between work and personal life (Piazza et al., 1999; Cuomo and Mapelli, 2007; Signorelli, 2007).

Nevertheless, in comparison with other Western countries, in Italy the concrete implementation of diversity management practices in firms and organizations is still rather limited. It tends to focus on gender differences and often consists in circumscribed actions with scant efficacy with regard to the cultural change that should be the basis of such an approach.

Our aim here is to conduct a reasoned analysis of diversity management in Italy, considering the situation of the Italian labour market, the legislative context, and the main schemes of organizational development undertaken in Italy by enterprises and consulting firms to enhance diversity. We shall try to show the strengths and weaknesses that characterize such developments. We shall focus in particular on gender diversity, because this is the dimension most widely considered in Italy.

2. Labour market changes and trends

Italy is characterized by a strong segmentation of its labour market due in particular to the differences between the South and the North of the country. However, within this framework of territorial segmentation, consideration should be given to at least two other dimensions of the national labour market that share features with employment trends in the rest of Europe: segmentation by gender and segmentation by age.

Moreover, of increasing importance, although to a much lesser extent than in the other countries of the European Union (EU), is the growth of employment among the non-EU population in Italy lawfully registered following regularization of immigrants without stay permits for work purposes (Istat, 2004).

Despite these ongoing changes, the dynamics of the labour market in recent years have not enabled Italy significantly to narrow its gap *vis-à-vis* the EU's objectives, even if it has gradually moved closer to the targets set by the European Strategy for Employment.

In order to comply with the Lisbon strategy, it would be necessary not only to increase employment opportunities but also to increase participation by persons currently out of the labour market, enhancing the employability of the weak segments of the labour supply.

In what follows we shall describe the segmentation and the quality of work in Italy, specifically focusing on differences in gender, age, ethnicity and sexual orientation, and with regard to differently abled workers. The weakness of the productive system produces not only barriers to entry into employment but also the under-utilization of the capacities of the employed, with harmful effects on the quality of employment. The aim of this chapter is to grasp aspects of participation or non-participation in the labour market that have been little analysed in recent years. More detailed investigation of these weak areas will highlight the situations of discrimination associated with such conditions, so that actions that acknowledge the specificities of each worker, and enhance social differences, can be designed and implemented.

2.1 Gender differences

In all the European countries the most important and evident trend in recent decades as regards employment dynamics has been the increased female participation in paid work. The activity rate for the total population aged between 15 and 64 rose in Italy from 52.1 per cent in 1996 to 58.9 per cent in 2006, a figure difficult to interpret without disaggregating the data by sex. Whilst for men the increase was five percentage points (from 66 per cent to 71 per cent), for women it was almost nine percentage points (from 38.2 per cent to 46.7 per cent). Nevertheless, the female employment rate in Italy still lags behind that of the 25-member EU (46.7 per cent against 58.5 per cent), whilst for men the differential with the European average is only two percentage points (71.1 per cent against 73.4 per cent) (Istat, 2007).

However, the rapid and high growth of female participation in the labour market, in education (particularly at university level, although not yet sufficiently in the scientific–technological faculties) and in cultural activities is not matched by adequate integration into the world of work, given that there are still evident imbalances between male and female careers in terms of both grade and pay (Saraceno, 1992). If it is true that the increase in female employment is the most striking phenomenon of recent years, nevertheless not only the quantity but also the quality of female participation in the Italian labour market should be emphasized.

Women often have access to jobs in which they find it difficult to stay in the market or re-enter after long periods of absence. Moreover, they are largely overrepresented in the majority of 'atypical' and precarious jobs (Semenza, 2004; Bertolini, 2006).

The question that thus arises is whether women's entry into ever broader areas of the labour market is indicative of decreased gender discrimination in workplaces, or whether different and new forms of inequality are emerging. Increased female participation and employment does not seem to have affected the vertical and horizontal segregation (Bianco, 1997) due to the gendered structure of work itself (Gherardi, 1995).

Women's increased entry into the labour market has come about almost exclusively in the services sector, which in Italy employs 79.3 per cent of women, as opposed to 55.9 per cent of men (CNEL, 2007). As regards vertical segregation, or women's underrepresenta-tion in managerial jobs, cultural factors still hinder the development of female careers. In dependent employment, women occupy only 26.4 per cent of medium-to-high positions; and in self-employment, they represent 20.4 per cent of all entrepreneurs and 28.2 per cent of free professionals (Istat, 2006).

The asymmetrical presence of men and women in the Italian labour market is due to two further factors: the persistence of traditional patterns in the division of roles within families; and the predominance of an organizational culture that often rewards physical strength and presence in the workplace and the willingness to work overtime, rather than the quality of work performance. This is highlighted by the variance in female employ-ment rates according to changes in the family role and the number of children – which have absolutely no influence on male careers. Examination of the 35–44 age group shows that unmarried women record the highest female employment rate (85.1 per cent), fol-lowed by women living in couples without children (75.4 per cent), and finally by those living in couples with children (56.9 per cent). Among the last group, the highest rates relate to women with just one child (66.8 per cent), and the lowest rates to women with three children or more (40.5 per cent).

The promotion of schemes that respond appropriately to the radical changes taking place in the socioeconomic circumstances of individuals, and especially of women, is therefore not only an ethical obligation but also a prerequisite for the country's develop-ment. Accordingly, policies that adopt a gender diversity management approach should not be understood as having purely (and exclusively) 'social' purposes, but rather as being development policies in the strict sense and, as such, able to affect economic and social growth.

2.2   Differences due to age
The Italian population, like those of the other Western European countries, is progres-sively ageing. As of 1 January 2006, the old-age index – the ratio between the population aged over 65 and that aged under 15 – recorded a further gradual increase, rising from the 137.8 per cent of the previous year to 140.4 per cent (Istat, 2006). Data issued by the National Institute of Statistics in 2006 showed that almost one Italian in every five is aged 65 or over, and that individuals aged over 80 exceed 5 per cent of the total population.

Italy is thus the country in the EU with the largest proportion of elderly citizens, with persons aged over 65 representing 19.8 per cent of the population, as opposed to the 13.9 per cent recorded in the Netherlands, or the 15.9 per cent in the UK (Carpenter, 2005).

The factors responsible for the ageing of the Italian population are, on the one hand, advances in medicine and an improved quality of life (average life expectancy rose from 65.4 years in 1951 to 78 in 1995), and, on the other, a decline in the birth rate. Since 1995, when the total fertility rate reached its historical minimum of 1.19 children per woman, it has slowly increased, standing in 2005 at 1.32 children per every woman of child-bearing age. Moreover, procreative choices are increasingly being postponed: the average age at birth of the first child has risen from the minimum of 24.7 years in 1975–76 to 28.7 years in 2001, to 30.4 years in 2004, and there are no signs of reversal in the trend (Istat, 2005).

The implementation of policies that set value on the differences in the Italian popula-tion must therefore necessarily take due account of the generational dimension, since the elderly constitute a significant part of society, not only in numerical terms but also from the point of view of their potential contribution to the country's economic and social growth.

On the other hand, young people also suffer hardships that cannot be neglected. The recent increase in fixed-term contracts has mainly concerned workers aged under 40 (Istat, 2006). This is closely connected with the difficulties encountered by young people in achieving independence in terms of economic self-sufficiency. Such difficulties also determine the scant propensity of young people to have children, with an obvious influence on the decrease in the birth rate. A survey by the National Institute of Statistics has shown that in 2000 single young people aged between 18 and 34 living with at least one parent numbered fully 8.06 million, a figure equal to 60.2 per cent of all young people in the same age class (Istat, 2000).

Ongoing demographic change therefore makes reorganization of the labour market essential, with removal of every structural and cultural factor that may cause exclusion or discrimination, both direct and indirect, due to the vulnerability of individuals due to their age.

2.3 Ethnic and religious differences

Italian society is becoming increasingly multicultural, with the presence of significant numbers of immigrants from around 200 different countries. Immigration has grown exponentially in recent years and has had a pronounced impact on the composition of the labour force.

According to data published in the *Statistical Dossier on Immigration* (Caritas/Migrantes, 2008), there are more than 3 million immigrants (EU and non-EU citizens) in Italy, a figure equivalent to 6.2 per cent of the Italian population. Immigrants are distributed throughout the country, although not uniformly: 59.6 per cent in the North, 26.6 per cent in the Centre and 13.8 per cent in the South and Islands.

The majority of stay permits are stable, so that more than nine in every ten immigrants are present in the country for work (56.5 per cent) and family (35.6 per cent) reasons. The increase of inflows is therefore also due to 'family reunifications', which increased from 29.3 per cent in 2005 to 35.6 per cent in 2006, and involved mainly women and minors.

The great diversity of countries of origin also produces the co-presence of numerous religions in Italy: whilst almost 90 per cent of Italian citizens profess themselves Catholic, among foreigners 49.1 per cent declare that they are Christian, 33.2 per cent Muslim, and almost 5 per cent Hindu and Buddhist.

The increase in the foreign population has offset the negative growth trend of the Italian population, which, as said, occupies one of the lowest positions among Western countries and is also growing older. In the space of ten years, after the 8000 births in foreign families recorded in 1994, the number rose to 49000 in 2004, with a positive (+45994 units) natural rate (difference between births and deaths) offsetting the negative rate (−30053) among the native Italian population. This has significantly changed the sociodemographic and cultural structure of Italian society, with the presence of second-generation immigrants, which has had major repercussions on both the education system and the world of work.

Foreign workers represent around 12 per cent of the labour force in Italy. They are mainly employed in construction, manufacturing, hotels and catering, agriculture, commerce, domestic work, and personal care services (Caritas and Migrantes, 2008). In regard to racial discrimination, employment and access to housing are the areas in which the greatest number of reports of discriminatory behaviour are made, with an incidence of respectively 28.4 per cent and 20.2 per cent (Unar, 2005).

The issue of ethnic and religious diversity is therefore of the utmost importance in business management, and in firms that do not have relationships with foreign countries but nevertheless need to value ethnic and cultural differences among their employees.

2.4   Disability

Despite great normative efforts for the social inclusion of the disabled, discrimination still persists in workplaces, in schools, on public transport, and in access to goods and services, and the handicapped suffer generally from social exclusion.

According to a report submitted to parliament on implementation of policies for the handicapped (Ministero del Lavoro e delle Politiche Sociali, 2005), in Italy people with disabilities number 2615 million, equal to circa 5 per cent of the population aged over 6 living with their families.

The number of disabled people of working age – that is, belonging to the 15–64 age group – amounts to 584 000, of which over 55 per cent are women. Work entry is the main problem in this area of intervention as well. Among people with disabilities, 26.5 per cent are in employment, and of these 32 per cent are afflicted by severe disability. Some 82.3 per cent of those in employment work on open-ended contracts, the majority of them in the private for-profit sector (56.1 per cent). Conversely, 13.5 per cent of disabled persons aged between 15 and 67 have never worked (Istat, 2005).

Whilst unemployment is much more frequent among the disabled than among other workers, multi-discrimination especially affects women with disabilities (only one in three disabled workers is a woman). Twice as many disabled women than men are in search of employment, and when they find jobs they are penalized in terms of both career and professional responsibility.

Entry into the labour market is closely conditioned by other needs, given that, without access to transport, the education system, or new technologies, work integration is difficult.

2.5   Differences due to sexual orientation

Still today, sexual orientation causes discrimination both from the normative point of view and that of prevention and awareness-raising campaigns designed to change cultural attitudes towards homosexuality.

According to a statistical survey conducted in 2005 by Arcigay and the National Institute of Health on the homosexual and bisexual population of Italy (Lelleri, 2006), still today homosexuality tends to be concealed. The setting in which it is most difficult to 'come out' is the workplace, where only 24.1 per cent of the interviewees did not conceal their homosexuality, against 37.3 per cent who had never mentioned it. Of the three broad areas of the country, and for both gays and lesbians, it appears easier to declare one's homosexuality in the North and the Centre than in the South.

In regard to discrimination, episodes of violence and aggression against homosexual women and men are frequently recorded. According to the above-mentioned survey by the National Institute of Health, 18.4 per cent of lesbians had been harassed in the 12 months before the interview because of their sexual orientation. Among men, around 20 per cent declared that they had been subject at least sometimes to insults or harassment, with a larger proportion (26 per cent) among homosexual males resident in the South of Italy.

The recent legislative decree no. 216 of 9 July 2003 has transposed into Italian law the provisions of Directive 2000/78/EC on equal treatment in occupation and employment, so that discrimination based on sexual orientation has been banned for the first time in Italy. Also significant is the recent amendment to article 15 of the Workers' Statute increasing the coverage of the prohibition on discrimination. Nevertheless, as in all the other issues discussed, despite the great importance of this legislation as regards the rights of workers, further and greater effort is required before it can be effectively implemented.

3. The legislative situation

In Italy, as in the rest of Europe, a legislative framework has been put in place to enhance diversity and to promote equal opportunities for all individuals in economic, social, political and cultural life.

The Italian Constitution enshrines the principle that all citizens have equal dignity and are equal before the law, without distinction of sex, race, language, religion, political opinions, or social and personal circumstances. The Italian state has enacted a series of legal provisions directed at the formation and promotion of instruments to counter discrimination. The specific purpose of this legislation is to combat discrimination in the labour market as regards gender, ethnicity and disability. Added to these provisions are broader ones concerning equality of treatment in employment and working conditions.

3.1 Gender discrimination

As regards gender balance in the labour market, Italy has shifted from protective regulations to parity of treatment, established by a law intended to increase employment among women (law no. 903 of 9 December on the equal treatment of men and women at work).

In the 1980s, however, it was realized that the law did not cover certain forms of indirect discrimination against women, and specifically situations of uniform treatment that in fact had differential effects on the two sexes. It was the advent of the concept of indirect discrimination that flanked the obligation to abstain from unlawful behaviour – a principle already laid down by law 903/77 – with recognition that positive actions should be undertaken to favour and achieve equal opportunities. However, it was not until 1991 that the concept of positive action was incorporated into law no. 125 of 10 April 1991 on positive actions for gender equality in the workplace.

3.1.1 Positive actions to achieve male/female equality at work (law 125/1991 and legislative decree no. 145/2005) The provisions of this law are intended to favour female employment and to achieve substantial equality between men and women in the workplace through the adoption of measures – called positive actions – aimed at removing the obstacles that prevent the achievement of equal opportunities. Specifically, the purpose of positive actions is to:

(a) eliminate the disparities to which women are subject in education and vocational training, access to employment, career advancement, working life and periods of mobility;
(b) diversify the occupational choices available to women, particularly through educational and professional guidance and training provision, and favouring access to self-employment and business training, and the professional development of female self-employed workers and entrepreneurs;
(c) eliminate working conditions, and the organization and distribution of work, that provoke gender-differentiated effects among employees, with prejudice to training, professional and career advancement, or pay;
(d) promote the inclusion of women in the activities, professional sectors and levels where they are underrepresented and particularly in technologically advanced sectors and with levels of responsibility;
(e) favour, also through the different organization of work, and of working conditions and schedules, the balance between work and family responsibilities and a better division of such responsibilities between the sexes.

Proposals for positive actions may be submitted by enterprises, and by cooperatives, consortia, public economic bodies, trade unions, and vocational training centres, which may apply to the Deputy Minister for Family Policies for total or partial reimbursement of the costs arising from implementing projects.

Besides 'positive actions', law no. 125 has made significant improvements to the anti-discrimination provisions already contained in law no. 903/1977. A worker is also protected against forms of indirect discrimination, by which is meant any prejudicial treatment consequent on the adoption of criteria that penalize workers of a particular sex.

A national committee has been created to implement principles of parity of treatment and equality of opportunity between male and female workers, and the figure of the 'equality adviser' at national, regional and provincial levels acting on behalf of the local authorities of promotion of equal opportunities and monitoring of gender discrimination. In all cases of discrimination against workers, and on their delegation, the equality adviser may take legal action before a labour tribunal or a competent administrative court.

Another important element of law is the obligation on public and private companies with more than 100 employees to furnish information on the situation of their male and female personnel by compiling and transmitting to the in-company trade union representatives and the regional equality adviser a report on the essential aspects of personnel policies (hirings, mobility, pay levels, dismissals), with separate information for male and female workers.

The legislative decree implementing EEC Directive 2002/73 on equal treatment between men and women (no. 145/2005) innovated the previous legal norms, which came into effect with law 125/1991, by making a series of amendments to them. Overall, the intervention changes the notion of direct and indirect discrimination (applicable to work performed 'in subordinate, autonomous or in any other form'), and for the first time introduces the definition of sexual harassment in workplaces into Italian labour law.

During the 1990s, intense legislative activity established the normative framework for gender policies and created the bodies tasked with their definition and implementation, for example, law no. 215 of 25 February 1992 – which introduced positive actions on female entrepreneurship – and the appointment in 1996 of a Minister for Equal Opportunities.

3.1.2   Provisions to support maternity and paternity, for the right to care and training and for coordinating times in cities (law 53/2000)   Law 53/2000 transposed the EC Directive on parental leave (Council Directive 96/34/EC of 3 June 1996 implementing the framework agreement on parental leave). The purpose of the law is to enhance the balance among work, care, training and relational time. It deals in particular with:

- parental leave and the extension of support to the parents of handicapped children;
- leave for continuing training and extended leave for vocational training;
- the coordination of city service schedules and promotion of the use of time for the purposes of social solidarity.

The contents of the law respond to EC recommendations on increasing employment levels among women and promoting new forms of reconciliation between paid and unpaid work. Specifically as regards parental leave, the law establishes that, upon conclusion of compulsory maternity leave, during the first eight years of the child's life the parents are entitled to take leave of absence from work – simultaneously and regardless of the other parent's working conditions – for a period that is either continuous or divided by six months for each parent, for up to ten months overall. Before enactment of this law, the father was entitled to take leave of absence only in the child's first year of life and only if the mother was a dependent employee and agreed to forego her right to leave of absence. The new norm therefore marks a shift from the protection of women to the promotion of carework by both parents.

This legislation has innovated social, economic and cultural models by furnishing the means with which to reconcile work and the private sphere through redistribution of care responsibilities between the couple, the reorganization of work and city service schedules, as well as the coordination of public-interest services.

A related item of legislation is article 9 of law 53/2000, which provides for the payment of grants – of which at least 50 per cent is allocated to firms with up to 50 employees – to firms that undertake positive actions for flexibility, and to self-employed workers or the owners of firms that intend to develop actions for family–work reconciliation.

The aim of this instrument is to facilitate reconciliation between family and work times by financing projects that introduce new ways to organize and manage working time or services that qualify the firm as family-friendly.

Also foreseen is payment by the Deputy Minister for Family Policies of grants for the implementation of the following positive actions for flexibility:

(a) projects so that working fathers or mothers can utilize particular forms of working time and work organization flexibility, with priority given to the parents of children aged up to 12, or up to 15 in the case of fostering or adoption;
(b) training courses for workers on their re-entry from more than 60 days of leave for reconciliation;

(c) projects to allow the substitution of the owners of firms or self-employed workers – for exigencies analogous to those covered by the rules on compulsory leave or parental leave – by other entrepreneurs or self-employed workers, with priority given to the parents with children of less than one year of age or with particular care responsibilities;

(d) initiatives and actions designed to enhance reconciliation measures already applied in the organization and/or to introduce new solutions for work–care reconciliation by workers with dependent disabled children or non-self-sufficient elderly members of the family.

Law 53/2000 has been amended and integrated by legislative decree no. 151 of 26 March 2001, which constitutes the consolidated text of the legislation on protection and support of maternity and paternity, subsequently amended by legislative decree no. 115 of 23 April 2003.

3.1.3   The code on equal opportunities between men and women   The legislative decree no. 198 of 11 April 2006 – 'Code on equal opportunities between men and women', in pursuance of article 6 of law no. 246 of 28 November 2005, consolidated text of provisions on parity between men and women.

The provisions of the decree concern measures to eliminate all sex-based distinctions, exclusions or limitations whose result, or purpose, is the obstruction or impediment of the recognition, enjoyment or exercise of human rights and fundamental freedoms in the political, economic, social, cultural and civil sphere. Specifically, the decree:

(a) prohibits discrimination between men and women in their access to work, rights to the same pay, and career advancement;

(b) annuls actions, pacts or provisions adopted in consequence of rejection or submission to harassment, including sexual harassment;

(c) creates an Equal Opportunities Commission at the Department for Equal Opportunities;

(d) creates the National Committee for Implementation of the Principles of Equality of Treatment and Opportunity between Male and Female Workers and tasks the committee with promotion and verification;

(e) institutes a Board of Investigation charged with identifying and removing discriminatory acts.

The issue of equal opportunities has received increasing legislative attention in recent years. The heterogeneity of these measures is due first to historical factors – because the legislation has stratified in time – and second to thematic ones, because numerous areas of civil, political and social life are subject to dispositions designed to promote equal opportunities.

This has required action to systematize the norms promoting equal opportunities by combining the legal texts and rationalizing the current legislation, which is often confused owing to overlaps or duplications among notions and instruments. To this end, a consolidated text has been enacted that gathers and reorganizes all extant provisions and the norms in the Italian legislation on equal opportunities.

3.2 Discrimination because of ethnicity

The first legal provision in regard to discrimination connected with immigrant status was contained in law no. 654 of 13 October 1975, which ratified and implemented the international convention on the elimination of all forms of racial discrimination. The second main intervention occurred in 1993 with the conversion into law of legislative decree no. 122 of 26 April 1993 on urgent measures in regard to racial, ethnic and religious discrimination. Finally, legislative decree no. 215 of 9 July 2003 and the subsequent Decree of the President of the Council of Ministers (DPCM) of 11 December 2003 transposed Directive 2000/43/EC promoting equal treatment and non-discrimination in regard to all foreigners resident in Italy.

The decree applies to both the public and private sectors in regard to the following areas:

(a) access to employment and work, on both a self-employed and dependent basis, including selection criteria and hiring conditions;
(b) employment conditions, including career advancement, pay and conditions for dismissal;
(c) access to all types and levels of vocational guidance and training, professional updating and retraining, including professional apprenticeships;
(d) membership of and activity within organizations representing workers and employers, or other professional organizations, and services provided by such organizations;
(e) social protection, including social security;
(f) healthcare;
(g) social services;
(h) education;
(i) access to goods and services, including housing.

Specifically, Article 7 of legislative decree no. 215/2003 implementing article 13 of the EC Directive creates the National Anti-Racial Discrimination Office (UNAR) at the Presidency of the Council of Ministers – Department for Rights and Equal Opportunities.

Since November 2004, the UNAR has performed the following functions: it furnishes assistance in judicial or administrative proceedings to persons who deem themselves injured by discriminatory behaviour; it conducts investigations to verify the existence of such behaviour; it promotes the adoption of specific measures, including positive action projects, to prevent situations of disadvantage due to race or ethnicity origin; it promotes the greatest knowledge possible of the protective measures in force by raising public awareness of the principle of equal treatment and mounting information and communication campaigns; it draws up recommendations and opinions on matters concerning discrimination on grounds of race and ethnicity, as well as proposing changes to the law; it compiles an annual report for parliament on concrete application of the principle of equal treatment and on the effectiveness of protective measures; it promotes studies, research, training courses and conferences with the other non-government organizations working in the sector and with statistical survey institutes, also with the purpose of drawing up guidelines for the repression of discrimination.

However, unlike the law on parity between men and women, the decree does not allocate specific grants to firms undertaking positive actions for the promotion of equal treatment and the elimination of discrimination on grounds of race or ethnicity.

3.3   Discrimination because of disability

At the end of the 1980s, the first measures taken to eliminate discrimination against the differently abled concerned the removal of architectural barriers in buildings open to the public. Enacted in 1992 was law no. 104 on the assistance, social integration and rights of handicapped people, and in 1999, law no. 68 setting out 'norms for the right to work of disabled persons'. This latter law introduced a new notion of job placement, the aim being to supersede the impositional approach of the previous rules with appraisal of the actual and potential capacities of disabled persons in view of their work integration.

Finally, law no. 67 of 1 March 2006, 'measures for the judicial protection of disabled victims of discrimination', was patterned – in terms of legal protection measures and definitions of discrimination and harassment – on legislative decree no. 216/2003 (implementing EC Directive 2000/78 on equal treatment in employment and occupation) and provided the same judicial protection against discriminatory acts and legitimation for associations advocating the rights of the disabled to take legal action on their behalf.

The law extends the special legal protection already afforded to disabled victims of discrimination in the workplace to all situations in which the disabled are subject to discriminatory treatment outside the employment relationship. On the one hand, this is an effective response to the demands of numerous categories of disabled persons; on the other, it meets the need to complete the system so that it guarantees the disabled full equality of treatment in every sphere of life.

In regard to indirect discrimination, it should be stressed that the aim of the legislator is above all to combat behaviour that, although apparently neutral, gives rise to discrimination against the disabled. Considered a case of indirect discrimination is, for instance, the impossibility for a citizen to access services – public or private – because of his or her disability.

3.4   Discrimination in the workplace

Law no. 300 of 1970 – known as 'the Workers' Statute' – forbids discrimination on the grounds of political opinion, religion, of race, language, sex, handicap, age, sexual orientation or personal circumstances, and in regard to economic treatment (articles 15 and 16).

As said above, legislative decree no. 216 of 9 July 2003 transposed Directive 2000/78/EC on equal treatment in regard to employment and working conditions. The decree applies to all discrimination based on religion, personal convictions, handicap, age and sexual orientation in the workplace, from job entry to working conditions to trade union membership. However, the entry into force of this decree was accompanied by a heated debate on certain incongruities apparent in it. Included in the Italian legislation is a provision envisaging exceptions to the extremely generic principle of equal treatment, so that the European Directive was rendered less effective, although some corrections were made by the subsequent legislative decree no. 256 of 2 August 2004 (Di Paola, 2003).

The legislative decree acknowledges the possibility of 'differences in treatment due to a person's religion, personal convictions, handicap, age or sexual orientation if these are characteristics which affect the performance of work or constitute decisive requisites for its carrying out'. Nor does the decree transpose the phrase 'regardless of the branch of activity and at all levels of the professional hierarchy, as well as promotion'. This means that the decree imposes limits on the range of application of equal treatment provisions, thus leaving the branch of activity, the hierarchy and professional advancement ambiguous in the case of non-application of the principle of equal treatment. It therefore seems that the Italian decree gives less importance to discrimination in regard to job and career advancement than to access to employment and working conditions.

The complex nature of the phenomenon, and the plurality of objectives pursued, highlight the inadequacy of reliance on legal measures alone in combating discrimination and promoting equal opportunities. As a consequence active policies are necessary, both in the public arena and within private organizations, to counter discrimination and to value differences.

4. Diversity management in Italy

In this last section we outline the current situation in regard to the application of diversity management policies in Italian organizations, describing the main types of intervention and presenting some projects and experiments for organizational change from a diversity management perspective.

The Italian situation of diversity management exhibits a number of differences with respect to other territorial contexts. In particular, Italy's substantial delay should be stressed compared with other countries, where diversity management policies have long been implemented. It is no coincidence that the most significant schemes in Italy have been those undertaken by multinational companies, which transfer initiatives designed in cultural contexts more sensitive to diversity issues, and experimental projects financed out of public funds, mainly the European Social Fund, which have not always been able to survive once the funding has been exhausted. A second difference is that the diversity management approach has been developed in Italy with particular reference to gender differences, which have become a sort of testing ground for corporate practices that may then be applied in other areas of diversity.

Analysis of current Italian legislation on discrimination and diversity enhancement in workplaces reveals a broad set of norms centred on gender equality but without equivalent attention being paid to other forms of occupational segregation. To be noted in particular is the lack of financing for firms wanting to pilot and implement innovative actions to increase labour market participation, in all sectors and at all professional levels, and able to promote diversity as beneficial to the individual and the organization.

Only in more recent years have experiments been conducted with regard to other types of difference, particularly those of ethnicity, age and disability. It should also be stressed that, in the majority of cases, the predominant approach has been to 'protect' a category considered to be weaker than, and 'different from', a hegemonic model, rather than recognize the 'diversity' of single individuals. The consequence has been the prevalence of initiatives designed to empower women (for instance through work–life balance policies), rather than to change prevailing roles and cultural orders by questioning predominant organizational practices and models.

4.1   Main types of intervention
The three main areas in which diversity policies have been developed in Italy are gender
and – but only recently – age and ethnicity.

4.1.1   Initiatives in regard to gender differences   In Italy, gender differences constitute
the area in which the widest range of diversity management initiatives have been developed. The majority of projects have been financed from funds allocated by specific laws
(e.g. law 125 and law 53) on promoting equal opportunities and work–family reconciliation, or by drawing on European Community structural funds (for example, through
EQUAL projects). The main types of actions are the following:

- schemes to empower women by means of training, counselling and accompaniment;
- policies to enhance the work–personal life balance of employees (particularly
  women) through services, facilities and leave entitlements;
- schemes for the reorganization of human resources management so as to redress
  gender balances (organization of work schedules, criteria for evaluating and hiring
  employees, incentives systems);
- awareness-raising initiatives to promote a culture of gender equality.

4.1.2   Initiatives in regard to age differences   In recent years, companies have begun to
pay specific attention to age differences and to acknowledge the need for policies and
actions designed to close the widening gap between generations. Most notable of these
initiatives are:

- schemes for labour market re-entry (especially by women) after early exit;
- update and refresher courses, both personal and professional;
- awareness and assessment meetings for employees aged over 45;
- training courses and team coaching sessions for specific target groups in order to
  enhance commitment, self-agency, skills and competitive value.

4.1.3   Initiatives in regard to ethnic differences   As far as ethnic differences are concerned, the most significant initiatives in diversity management in Italy have been undertaken by multinational companies, which have already addressed this issue in other
countries. The declared intent is often to create a heterogeneous workforce reflecting the
diversity of the customer base, thus facilitating forecasts of its preferences. Among the
most notable actions implemented are:

- training and support initiatives to favour hiring of persons of different ethnicities;
- specific training courses for personnel to improve their knowledge of other cultures
  and to develop the intercultural skills of human resources managers;
- opening of information desks on matters of interest to immigrant employees;
- organization of events.

4.2   Best practices of diversity management in Italy
In what follows we consider three examples of the application of diversity management
in Italy centred on gender, age and ethnicity differences.

The first case concerns a leading telephony company, which has implemented conciliation policies through the use of positive action programmes and the management of economic resources from a gender and development standpoint. The second deals with an accounting services company that has adopted diversity development policies targeted on age, and particularly on the difficulties, real or supposed, that firms encounter in managing older workers The last case is that of a multinational company operating in the large-scale furniture retail sector that has adopted a diversity management approach with particular regard to ethnic differences.

A critical factor that persists within companies undertaking diversity management projects is the difficult survival of good practice over the long term. The consequence has been the failure of organizational innovation, although not for the people directly involved. The goodness of a good practice, in fact, does not reside simply in the intrinsic value of the project, but in its capacity to act on the organizational culture and generate processes able to survive over time, even when the financial incentive no longer operates. Hence structural funds are essential for the launching of projects. But if these are to have significant results, it is necessary to go further and work on the culture, coordination and local development.

Therefore of greatest success are schemes targeted on change in personnel management strategies with a view to diversity, rather than those connected with individual and temporary planning processes.

4.2.1 The TIM case   TIM (Telecom Italia Mobile) is the brand with which Telecom Italia, the largest Italian telephony company, markets its mobile telephony services. It has around 10000 employees, of whom around half work in call centres. The average age of the workforce is rather low (30 years), and the company has a large proportion of female workers (42 per cent).

TIM has developed numerous initiatives in regard to work–life balance. These were initially positive actions aimed exclusively at women. The TIM 'Valore Donna' project, for example, was a positive action financed under law 125/1991 and aimed at facilitating the labour market re-entry of women aged over 40 through employment as TIM customer service workers on open-ended part-time contracts.

Positive gender projects were subsequently extended to men. For example, in 2004 the company launched a new brand, 'Timpeople', in order to create a direct link between employees and the company. The result of this philosophy was the 'I care' project, which comprises a variety of different initiatives:

- for flexibility: this concerns measures that affect working-time arrangements, for instance the 'hours bank' system whereby a worker can accumulate leave to be taken for personal reasons. The service is intended for mothers with children aged up to 8 years old;
- for unemployed women aged over 40: hirings on 50 per cent part-time open-ended contracts as operators in the company's customer assistance call centres;
- for families: introduction of time utility services designed to help employees save time by enabling them to perform routine tasks that tend to reduce non-work time (e.g. shopping, laundry, paperwork, ticketing) directly within the company;

- for employees' children: creation of a company crèche to encourage participation by parents;
- for staff: transport services, appointment of a 'mobility manager' to devise solutions to facilitate home/work travel, initiatives for psycho-physical well-being (company gyms, agreements with sports or wellness centres), newspaper kiosks and VHS and DVD rentals, creation of staff relaxation areas;
- for maternity: flexible arrangements for maternity leave, a vademecum on rights and duties between the company and pregnant employees, initiatives to favour contact between the company and women on leave.

Initiatives intended for mothers have recently been extended to include fathers, who are granted a day's leave on full pay for the birth of a child and hourly leave to attend prenatal courses.

4.2.2   The UniCredit Processes & Administration case   UniCredit Processes & Administration provides administrative and accounting services to the banks and companies belonging to the UniCredit Group – a banking group created by the merger of seven Italian banks. UPA's core business covers all aspects of back-office operations. It has 2197 employees located in nine cities. Around 56 per cent of employees are women, around 53 per cent are aged over 45, and the number of older workers is increasing. The company's human resources department recently implemented age management initiatives dealing with the redeployment of about 1000 workers after the merger of seven large banks into one group.

Here we discuss two schemes, for workers aged over 45 and over 50, and which involved various initiatives, among them:

- training courses to develop relearning skills and to build confidence in cognitive and memorization processes;
- English courses;
- celebration of the 25th or 35th year of service with the company, to reward the worker and to strengthen team spirit;
- voluntary initiatives to facilitate labour market exit upon retirement through the payment (at the same rate as work) of voluntary work at assistance facilities.

The UPA scheme has achieved excellent results. They reveal that the company's older employees identify strongly with their work, feel self-confident and believe that they can make a real contribution to the company. The results also show that older UPA workers have good relationships with their colleagues and are satisfied that the company appreciates their experience and professionalism.

4.2.3   The IKEA Italia case   IKEA is a Swedish multinational company furnishing sector. It has a commercial network of 186 stores in 31 countries with 154 sales outlets and 70000 workers. IKEA Italia has 5500 employees and 13 sales outlets. The company has consolidated experience in diversity management, which responds to its declared value of 'plurality' – meaning workforce diversity in terms of gender, culture, ethnicity and religion – and which is also pursued at its Italian stores. Two projects in particular should be mentioned: Work & Life Balance and Plurality (Cuomo and Mapelli, 2007).

The purpose of the Work & Life Balance Project is to identify strategies for a better balance between work and life needs of people, through the creation of an innovative work organization. In particular, the project focuses on the management of maternity and parental leave. Addressing this issue means planning the absence of an employee by reorganizing staff or using temporary replacements and then reintegrating the employee upon his/her return to work. The project moves through two stages: a first one in which absent employees are provided with data and information so that they can keep abreast of the company's business and that of their department; a second stage in which employees returning from leave are given training to facilitate their work re-entry. This project initially received ministerial funding but continued when the funding finished.

The Plurality project meets both the company's aim of valorizing workforce plurality and its need to address change in the context and the market. Three main indicators have been emphasized: customer diversification, workforce diversification, and recognition that diversity is a factor of innovation of crucial importance for the company (Mapelli and Scarpaleggia, 2004). The decision to develop a pilot project on ethnic differences in IKEA Italia was taken in 2002, the year in which the store in Florence was opened. The aims of the project were to enhance workforce diversity, seen as a source of creativity but also as a means to manage change; to create a staff representative of the local social context; and to foster intercultural integration between Italian and immigrant workers.

In the initial phase, the most representative ethnic communities in the local area were identified. After a first, unsuccessful attempt to involve the Chinese community, careful analysis was made of the ethnic groups resident in the Florence area. Some of these communities were involved in the project, while contacts were established with various organizations and institutions working with immigrants. Three hundred and fifty CVs were then collected, and after screening, 125 candidates were identified. Following evaluation by assessment groups, 25 people from non-EU countries and 12 from other EU countries were finally hired by IKEA. To foster the integration of these workers, specific training courses were organized, not only for the personnel concerned but also for the store's group leaders and department heads, the purpose being to improve knowledge of other cultures and to develop the intercultural skills of human resources managers. Moreover, in collaboration with the trade union, IKEA opened an information desk on matters of interest to immigrant employees. The company has also organized a film festival on the theme of integration.

5. Conclusions

Despite significant ongoing changes in the Italian labour market, which now seems to require closer attention to diversity issues, diversity management policies are still rarely applied in Italy. They are largely restricted to specific concerns, gender especially, and tend to privilege actions directed to protection rather than cultural change. The predominance in the Italian production system of small and medium-sized firms seemingly hampers the spread of human resources management practices centred on diversity. These practices are instead more frequent in large firms, and particularly in multinationals, where they respond to the parent companies' strategies and the cultures of their countries of origin. It is no coincidence that the three examples considered, among the few present in Italy, concern multinationals or large companies. In small and medium-sized firms, often family-run and based on patriarchal cultural models, there is less awareness of the need to implement diversity management policies.

Moreover, diversity management schemes seem unable to obtain the favour and support of trade union representatives concerned about the excessive individualization of bargaining practices, with the consequent risk that both the worker and the trade union will lose negotiating power.

A further weakness of the Italian system is its excessively burdensome bureaucratic–administrative apparatus, which tends to obstruct the introduction of alternative managerial solutions and impedes access to the existing incentives for the implementation of good practice.

The strategies that strike us as most effective in encouraging the spread of organizational practices for diversity management in Italy are the following:

Summary table for Italy

Existence of anti-discrimination legislation	Yes
Criteria covered by anti-discrimination legislation	Political opinion, religion, race, language, gender, pregnancy, handicap, age, sexual orientation, personal circumstances, economic treatment, union activity
Criteria for which the reporting of quantitative data and their communication to a public administration are compulsory	Gender (for organizations with more than 100 employees)
Criteria covered by 'affirmative' or 'positive' action legislation other than unemployment- or income-based	Gender
Existence of a discourse or debate about 'non-discrimination' or 'equality'	Yes
Existence of a discourse or debate about 'diversity'	Yes
Year or period when the 'discrimination' concept started to disseminate in management literature in the country	2000
Year or period when the diversity concept started to disseminate in management literature in the country	2000
Who pushed the 'diversity' agenda?	The European and Italian legislation for Gender. Influence of multinational companies in favour of positive action for age and ethnicity
Existence of a professional association representing diversity professionals and year of creation	Laboratorio Armonia (founded in 1971) www.sdabocconi.it/armonia
Existence of a professional association representing diversity scholars and year of creation	No

- promotional actions designed to highlight the convenience of such practices by publicizing both successes and the possible instruments and areas of intervention, and the advantages deriving from the adoption of such policies to foster organizational change and innovation (it is no coincidence that the three examples considered concern organizations with a particularly marked orientation to innovation);
- raising the awareness among trade unions that workers have diversified needs, and that stubborn defence of equality restricts attention to shared needs, without entering an 'ecological' dimension, where development is sustained in an equilibrium of differences (Callari Galli et al., 1998).
- the introduction of public economic incentives (e.g. the enhancement of diversity management policies by awarding points when adjudicating bids for tender);
- replacing protection with actions to change the dominant cultural models in organizations and proposing a broader definition of organizational practices;
- finally – and importantly – the implementation of diversity management practices that reflect the multiple differences within organizations but avoid essentialism (attempting to identify and exploit the specific suitability of people for particular jobs and positions, thus running the risk of reifying and reproducing inequalities), but instead emphasizing plurality and recognizing that success of the organization must also acknowledge the central importance of people and their needs.

Note

1. This chapter is a totally collaborative effort by the two authors, whose names appear in alphabetical order. If, however, for academic reasons individual responsibility is to be assigned, Annalisa Murgia wrote Sections 1, 2 and 3; Barbara Poggio wrote Sections 4 and 5.

References

Ambrosini, Maurizio (2001), *La fatica di integrarsi*, Bologna: Il Mulino.
Bertolini, Sonia (2006), 'La conciliazione per le lavoratrici atipiche', *Economia & Lavoro*, **40** (1), 57–71.
Bianco, Maria Luisa (1997), *Donne al lavoro. Cinque itinerari fra le diseguaglianze di genere*, Torino: Scriptorium.
Bombelli, Maria Cristina (2000), *Soffitto di vetro e dintorni: il management al femminile*, Milano: ETAS.
Callari Galli, Matilde, Mauro Ceruti and Telmo Pievani (1998), *Pensare la diversità. Per un'educazione alla complessità umana*, Roma: Meltemi.
Caritas/Migrantes (2008), *Dossier statistico Immigrazione 2007*, XVI Rapporto, Roma.
Carpenter, George Ian (2005), 'Aging in the UK and Europe – a snapshot of the future', *Journal of the American Geriatrics Society*, **53** (4), 310–13.
CNEL (2007), *Rapporto sul mercato del lavoro 2006*, Roma.
Cuomo, Simona and Adele Mapelli (2007), *Diversity management. Gestire e valorizzare le differenze individuali nell'organizzazione che cambia*, Milano: Guerini.
Decastri, Maurizio (1993), *Verso l'internazionalità*, Milano: Guerini.
Di Paola, Luigi (2003), 'Discriminazioni sul posto di lavoro: si amplia l'area dei divieti (d.lgs. 9 luglio 2003 n. 216)', *Le nuove leggi civili commentate*, fasc. 4–5, 855–90.
Gherardi, Silvia (1995), *Gender, Symbolism and Organizational Cultures*, London: Sage.
Gherardi, Silvia (2006), *Organizational Knowledge: The Texture of Workplace Learning*, Oxford: Blackwell.
Gherardi, Silvia and Barbara Poggio (2007), *Gendertelling in Organizations: Narratives from Male-dominated Environments*, Stockholm: Liber AB.
Istat (2000), *Rapporto annuale. La situazione del Paese nel 1999*, Roma: Istat.
Istat (2004), *Rapporto annuale. La situazione del Paese nel 2003*, Roma: Istat.
Istat (2005), *Rapporto annuale. La situazione del Paese nel 2004*, Roma: Istat.
Istat (2006), *Rapporto annuale. La situazione del Paese nel 2005*, Roma: Istat.
Istat (2007), *Rapporto annuale. La situazione del Paese nel 2006*, Roma: Istat.
Lelleri, Raffaele (2006), *Survey nazionale su stato di salute, comportamenti protettivi e percezione del rischio HIV nella popolazione omo-bisessuale*, Bologna: Arcigay.

Mapelli, Adele and Simona Scarpaleggia (2004), 'Il "progetto Plurality" di Ikea', in Luigi Mauri and Luca M. Visconti (eds), *Diversity management e società multiculturale. Teoria e prassi*, Milano: Angeli, pp. 161–72.

Ministero del Lavoro e delle Politiche Sociali (2005), *Relazione al Parlamento sui dati relativi allo stato di attuazione delle Politiche per l'Handicap in Italia per gli anni 2004–2005*, Roma.

Piazza, Marina, Anna M. Ponzellini, Elena Provengano and Anna Tempia (1999), *Riprogettare il tempo. Manuale per la progettazione degli orari di lavoro*, Roma: Edizioni Lavoro.

Saraceno, Chiara (1992), 'Donne e lavoro o strutture di genere del lavoro?', *Polis*, **6** (1), 5–22.

Semenza, Renata (2004), *Le trasformazioni del lavoro. Flessibilità, disuguaglianze, responsabilità dell'impresa*, Roma: Carocci.

Signorelli, Adriana (ed.) (2007), *Lavoro e politiche di genere. Strategie e strumenti per una nuova divisione del lavoro sociale*, Milano: Angeli.

Unar (2005), *Un anno di attività contro la discriminazione razziale*, Roma.

9 Laws, policies and practices of diversity management in the Netherlands

Inge Bleijenbergh, Marloes van Engen and Ashley Terlouw

Introduction

Workplace diversity is definitely a hot issue in current Dutch public debate. As a small country by the sea, the Netherlands has a long history of trade and immigration. Today, about 20 per cent of the population are immigrants, who come from both Western and non-Western countries. Workplace diversity, with regard to ethnical background, is the most pressing issue in the Dutch public diversity debate, and reference is often made to the freedom that immigrants should or should not have to act in the workplace according to their own cultural or religious beliefs. The issue of gender is another topic that is also intensively debated. In spite of the international image of the Netherlands as having a progressive and tolerant culture, the labour market position of women in the Netherlands is rather weak. Only a small minority of Dutch women are economically independent of their husbands, and there are very few women who fill top positions in for-profit and non-profit organizations in the Netherlands. Since the Dutch population is steadily ageing, Dutch organizations are increasingly feeling the need to develop the labour potential of immigrants and women. The ageing of the population has also created another diversity issue in the public debate, namely the public pension age. Many workers already retire from work before the age of 65, but the government has just decided, due to the economic crisis, to raise the retirement age to 67, in order to ensure that the public pension system can be afforded. Furthermore, the issue of sexual preference is discussed in regard to workplace diversity. Discrimination on the basis of sexual preference is prohibited, but religious organizations, such as schools, still claim the right to dismiss teachers who are openly homosexual.

In this chapter we shall first present the facts and figures that represent the current Dutch situation in regard to diversity at work. In the second section, we discuss Dutch equal treatment legislation. In the third section the public debate regarding diversity is explained. The fourth section discusses workplace practices on diversity. In the conclusion, we elaborate on the Dutch situation, and we discuss the most important problems and challenges related to workplace diversity.

Facts and figures

Migration

The Netherlands, as a trading nation, has a history of receiving immigrants. In previous centuries the immigrants were mainly of European descent. In the second half of the twentieth century, immigrants arrived from the former Dutch colonies in the Caribbean and South-East Asia, followed by migrant labourers from the Mediterranean countries, and subsequently refugees from all over the world. The current Dutch population consists of

16.41 million people, of whom 1.45 million are Western immigrants (Europe, the USA, Oceania, Indonesia and Japan),[1] and 1.77 million are non-Western immigrants (Africa, other parts of Asia, Latin America and Turkey). The largest groups of immigrants are of Turkish descent (373 000) followed by Surinamese immigrants (336 000), Moroccan immigrants (335 000) and immigrants from the Netherlands Antilles/Aruba (132 000). Of the non-Western immigrants, 1.02 million are first-generation immigrants and 750 000 are of the second generation, which means that they were born in the Netherlands and that they had at least one immigrant parent (Statistics Netherlands [CBS], 2008a.)

After the Second World War, the Dutch immigrants formed a heterogeneous group, which came to the Netherlands possessing a wide variety of backgrounds, during different periods and for different reasons. The first group of immigrants were repatriates of the Dutch East Indies. Immigrants from mixed Dutch–Indonesian descent returned or came to the Netherlands between 1949 and 1958 (Schaafsma, 2006). At the end of the war for independence in the Moluccas, the former soldiers of the Dutch colonial army and their relatives settled in the Netherlands. The second group of immigrants were from other Dutch colonies in the Caribbean, including Suriname and the Netherlands Antilles. These immigrants came mainly to receive further education or to escape the political and economic instability in their home countries (Schaafsma, 2006).

The third group of immigrants consisted of 'guest workers' in the 1960s and 1970s. Employers, confronted with a tight labour market, invited low-skilled labourers, mainly from Morocco and Turkey, to come to the Netherlands. Policy-makers assumed that the guest workers would return to their home countries after several years had passed. However, most of these immigrants decided to stay, and via the legal right to family reunion, they invited their families from their home countries to come and join them. Since the 1980s, the main immigration flow from Morocco and Turkey has consisted of marriage partners from their countries of origin. In the 1980s and 1990s, political refugees from a large number of countries composed the fourth group of immigrants. In the 1980s and 1990s, about half of the refugees were given a residence permit, but since the year 2000 immigration policies have become increasingly restrictive and now the Netherlands has one of Europe's most stringent immigration policies. A considerable number of refugees who were not granted a residence permit went into hiding in order to remain in the Netherlands, and they have become illegal immigrants.[2]

The labour market position of most migrants is problematic. The participation rate is the lowest among Moroccan–Dutch (50 per cent) and Turkish–Dutch (51 per cent) and the unemployment rates are the highest among Moroccan–Dutch (11 per cent) and Antillean–Dutch (10 per cent) (Statistics Netherlands, 2008a; see Table 9.1). There are several possible explanations for the lower labour market position of migrant groups.

Table 9.1   Labour participation of migrant groups in 2007

	Turkish–Dutch	Moroccan–Dutch	Surinamese–Dutch	Antillean–Dutch	Dutch
Unemployment rate	9	11	8	10	4
Participation rate	51	50	63	59	68

Source: Statistics Netherlands (2008a).

First of all, the educational level of most migrants groups is considerably lower. Almost 13 per cent of the migrants (and 17 per cent of the non-Western migrants) have only received primary education compared to 7.4 per cent of the native Dutch population (Statistics Netherlands, 2008b). The level of education of migrant groups is steadily increasing. On average, the lower education level explains part of the lower participation rates of migrant groups. If one looks at the participation rates that correspond to the level of education, the differences between migrants and native Dutch groups appear to be the lowest for the highly educated (Statistics Netherlands, 2008c). Nevertheless, discrimination by employers is also part of the explanation. Kruisbergen and Veld (2002) showed that 24 per cent of employers were reluctant to hire migrants. An experimental study showed that the Moroccan applicants for an apprenticeship, with the same personal résumé as native Dutch applicants, were 30 per cent less likely to be invited to a job interview (Groen Links, 2006). Moreover, certain groups of migrants earn less than the native Dutch do. This is true when the comparison is corrected for personal characteristics such as education. The Antillean–Dutch citizens and the Moroccan–Dutch earn on average 5 per cent less than the native Dutch, whereas the Surinamese–Dutch earn on average 10 per cent less (Van der Vliet, 2005).

Gender diversity

The labour market participation rate of women in the Netherlands was 57 per cent in 2007, whereas the participation rate of men was 75 per cent. It is worth noting that the Netherlands has the highest number of part-time workers in the EU: 69 per cent of Dutch women work part time versus 16 per cent of Dutch men. As a consequence, the percentage of economically independent women is relatively low at 43 per cent. Economic independence is defined as earning an income above the level of Dutch public assistance (Merens and Hermans, 2009). Most women depend on the income of a partner in addition to their own earnings.

The number of women placed in management positions in the Netherlands is relatively low. Although 26 per cent of managers in the for-profit sector are women, women comprise only 7 per cent of the top positions in business (Merens and Hermans, 2009). Nearly half of these women on boards, namely 49 per cent, are of foreign descent (of the executive board members 2 per cent are female, of whom 83 per cent are non-Dutch; Lückerath-Rovers, 2008). In the non-profit sector the figures are comparably low: in Dutch universities only 11 per cent of full professors are female (van den Brink, 2009).[3]

Not only are women underrepresented in higher and top positions, they earn considerably less than men. According to the European Foundation of Living and Working Conditions (2007, p. 26), with a gender wage gap of 20 per cent the Netherlands is among the group of countries with the highest gender wage gap in Europe. The labour market position of migrant women is on average worse than that of native Dutch women. In particular, Turkish and Moroccan women have a low participation rate of 27 per cent in comparison to the 59 per cent of native Dutch women. However, Caribbean women, of both Surinamese and Antillean/Aruban descent, have a participation rate of 61 per cent, which is higher than the participation rate of native Dutch women.

There are several explanations for the lower labour market position of women in the Netherlands in comparison with men. One can be found in the historically strong motherhood ideology in the Netherlands (van Engen et al., 2009). In the second half

Table 9.2   Labour participation of men and women with children (0–17) in 2007

	Primary school	Lower level	Middle level	Higher level	Total
Women	20	37	66	81	58
Men	41	60	88	96	87

Source: Merens and Hermans (2009).

of the twentieth century, married women were institutionally and culturally supported to stay at home. Until 1990, childcare facilities were nearly absent in the Netherlands (Bleijenbergh et al., 2006). Although the percentage of children (0–3 years) in day care increased from 13 per cent in 1996 to 25 per cent in 2006, still a majority of the Dutch population believe that mothers of young children should ideally not work more than three days a week (Merens and Hermans, 2009, pp. 132, 141). It is in particular women who possess a lower level of education who are more sensitive towards the motherhood ideology. As illustrated in Table 9.2, of all the women who have children aged between 0 and 17, 37 per cent of those with a low level of education are participating actively in the labour market, compared to 81 per cent of women who have a high level of education (ibid., p. 87).

Disability
The inability to perform paid employment is a problem for about 16 per cent of the labour force (those between 15 and 64 years old). This means that about 1.7 million people have reported that they have had difficulty trying to enter or to perform paid employment because of being chronically ill or disabled. Nearly 40 per cent of the chronically ill or disabled are in paid employment, which is far below the Dutch average of 65 per cent (Statistics Netherlands, 2007). The percentage of those ill or disabled who have an open-ended contract is similar to the average for the total Dutch population, but a considerably higher percentage of people with chronic illness or disabilities are self-employed. It appears that self-employment provides better opportunities for performing tasks that are more suited to the physical abilities of such people. Women are overrepresented among the disabled and chronically ill, since 54 per cent of the disabled are women. Furthermore, the low educated are overrepresented, since nearly half of the people with chronic illness or disabilities are low educated, compared to 33 per cent of the total population. The majority of people who have a chronic illness or a disability are older: 58 per cent of this group is over 45 years old compared to 40 per cent of the total labour force (Statistics Netherlands, 2007, pp. 12–15). The average income received by disabled people in employment is 9 per cent below the average income of people without a chronic illness or disability.

Equal treatment legislation
Equal treatment legislation will be discussed in two steps, the historical development and the current situation. The focus will be on equal treatment legislation with regard to labour, but in addition, attention will be paid to other provisions made in the labour legislation that are relevant for the position of groups that have a weak labour market position.

Equal treatment is a basic principle of Dutch law. Since 1983, under the influence of international treaties, the prohibition of discrimination has been clearly outlined in Article 1 of the Dutch Constitution. Art. 1 is formulated as follows: 'All persons in the Netherlands shall be treated equally in equal circumstances. Discrimination on the grounds of religion, belief, political opinion, race or sex or on any other grounds whatsoever shall not be permitted.' Discrimination on the grounds of nationality, sexual orientation, disability/chronic illness and age is not explicitly forbidden, but the prohibition of discrimination on these grounds is covered by: 'or on any other grounds whatsoever'. The prohibition is aimed at the vertical relation between government and citizens: to prevent discrimination by government. With regard to horizontal relations (to prevent discrimination between citizens), Art. 1 is implemented in the Equal Treatment Act (ETA) and other equal treatment legislation.

As the discussion of the Dutch figures makes clear, formal equality (equality before the law) does not necessarily result in procedural equality (equal bargaining/negotiation position in procedure) and material equality (equal outcomes, results). Legislation is nevertheless important for the recognition and confirmation of rights and obligations, and the possibility of starting a lawsuit. The Netherlands has many equal treatment provisions. However, observance is left mainly to individuals and it is dependent on the nature of their complaints. Since victims of discrimination are often not in the best position to complain, this is a noteworthy omission (Havinga, 2002). Dutch equal treatment legislation is highly influenced by European Directives, and the importance of these Directives has increased. Since the first evaluation was made of the ETA in 1999, the Dutch government has had the intention to integrate all Dutch equal treatment acts and provisions into one Integration Act (Equal Treatment Commission, 2005). At present, in 2009, this Act is still being developed.

The legislator has not yet regulated all of the situations in which equal treatment rights might conflict with each other. As will be made clear in the following sections, these are the type of situations that attract the most media attention nowadays. For example, the right of equal treatment with regard to religion can conflict with the right of equal treatment concerning sexual preference if a Christian school does not want to appoint a homosexual teacher. Likewise, the right of equal treatment on the basis of religion conflicts with the right of equal treatment on the basis of gender when a company does not want to hire a Muslim man who refuses to shake hands with women. Furthermore, the legislator has not regulated all of the situations in which constitutional rights might pose a conflict. This could lead to problems, for example if the constitutional right of equal treatment conflicts with the constitutional freedoms of education, religion or association.

Historical development
Dutch equal treatment legislation is still in its infancy. Until 1957, married women were even not able to undertake legally binding actions (concluding contracts) by themselves. The first Dutch equality legislation on race and gender followed international developments. The Dutch Criminal Code of 1971 contained the first legal instruments against discrimination, but only with regard to race, after having been inspired by the UN treaty against racial discrimination.[4] Subsequently, the implementation of EC Directives on the equal treatment of men and women resulted in the first Dutch Equal Treatment

Act, namely, The Equal Pay Act of 1975. Gradually, the scope of anti-discrimination legislation widened from equal payment for men and women to equal treatment of men and women in any area related to work: recruitment, terms and conditions of employment and dismissal, namely, the Act on Equal Treatment of Men and Women (Wet Gelijke Behandeling Mannen en Vrouwen).[5] In 1994 the Equal Treatment Act came into effect.[6] This extended the scope of equal treatment law from gender to other areas. From that moment on, discrimination on the grounds of race, religion, nationality, political opinion, hetero- and homosexual preference and marital status was also explicitly prohibited. Of course this did not mean that discrimination had ended; it is not even certain that discrimination has diminished, but it offered victims the possibility to start a legal procedure or to request an opinion from the Equal Treatment Commission (ETC). Powers, activity and outcomes of the ETC will be mentioned later in this chapter.

The Equal Treatment Act applies to all aspects of employment and profession, in the supply of goods and services. Since 1996, unequal treatment on grounds of part-time or full-time employment has been prohibited as well.[7] Since 2002, under the influence of European legislation, discrimination on the basis of a temporary labour contract has also been prohibited.[8] Further extension took place in 2003 with the Equal Treatment Act in regard to handicaps and chronic illness[9] and in 2004 with the Equal Treatment Act with regard to age, thus prohibiting age discrimination.[10] Apart from the equal treatment legislation as such, labour legislation contains provisions that aim at empowering those groups that are weakly represented on the labour market. These provisions refer mainly to women and ethnic minorities. Between 1994 and 2004, the legislator tried to encourage the participation of migrants in the Dutch labour market by creating special legislation. This special legislation, the first Employment Equity Act (Wet Bevordering Evenredige Arbeidsdeelname Allochtonen, WetBAA) dates from 1994, and included the obligation for employers who had more than 35 employees to register the ethnicity of employees (although the employees had to grant their permission for this).[11] The employees had to fill in a registration form (self-declaration) and, depending on their place of birth and the place of birth of their parents, they were registered as autochthonous (Dutch origin) or allochthonous (non-Dutch origin). In addition, employers had to issue a public report on the results, and a policy plan to increase the number of workers having a migrant background, including target figures.

Employers were highly resistant to this legislation, which in their opinion would mainly result in reams of administrative obligations. Since the legislators had not attached any sanctions to non-compliance with the legislation, in practice it produced very few results. The law had an extremely limited compliance rate; only 20 per cent of the employers who were obliged to register actually did so (Jonkers, 2003). Moreover, although the Employment Equity Act allowed preferential treatment on the basis of gender and race in specific situations, affirmative action as an instrument for promoting the labour participation of migrants in the labour market became controversial. On the one hand, this was caused by the increasingly strict conditions imposed by the EU Court of Justice in Luxembourg on cases concerning affirmative action that were aimed at gender equality. A backward position of the group, subject to the preferential treatment, had to be proved and to be related to the jobs available. Preferential treatment in application procedures is only allowed if the candidates are equally suited to the task. Preferential treatment should be in proportion to the goal, and serve as an adequate and effective means for ending or diminishing the backlash. Besides, it must be transparent for all potential candidates that a policy of preferential treatment has been chosen in regard to the jobs in question. These criteria were, according to the Dutch ETC, also applicable in cases concerning policy or preferential treatment in regard to ethnic minorities. On the other hand, a detrimental societal climate towards affirmative action lessens the political support for implementation (Rodrigues, 2007).

Following an evaluation of this legislation, the second Employment Equity Act (Wet SAMEN, which literally means the Act on Stimulating Labour Participation of Ethnic Minorities) was introduced in 1998. This time, the employers' organizations were closely involved in the evaluation of the former legislation and the drafting of this new law. In this second Equal Opportunity Act, the administrative burden for the employer was considerably reduced, but non-compliance had not yet been sanctioned. This law ceased to exist in 2004. The evaluation revealed that there was too much resistance from the employers' side; employers felt that the law produced too few results (Rodrigues, 2007).

It is hard to say if the situation of ethnic minorities has improved as a result of this legislation. The unemployment rates of ethnic minorities diminished in the period of the Wet BAA and especially in the period of the Wet SAMEN (Jonkers, 2003, p. 246). However, this might also have been caused by the economic progress that took place during this period. After 2004, government policy on migrants' labour market participation shifted from legislation to self-regulation. The employment position of non-Western migrants is supported by means of covenants, which are ambassador networks supported by facilitative organizations and collective labour agreements.

With regard to gender equality, there are also other laws than equal treatment legislation which are relevant, mainly in Book 7 of the Dutch Civil Code and in the Law on Civil Servants (Ambtenarenwet). This legislation refers to the rights of married women and of mothers in employment. The first step was the abolition in 1971 of the provision that obliged governmental organizations to dismiss female public servants when they became pregnant. Important later improvements gave the right to breastfeed at work in the Law on Working Hours, the right to 16 weeks' paid pregnancy leave in the Health Law and the right to 26 weeks' (unpaid) parental leave for half of the working time (since 1997). The right to parental leave is also a right for fathers and for foster parents. In 2001, legislation to support care for dependants became integrated in 'Act on Work and Care', which is called in Dutch the 'Wet Arbeid en Zorg'.[12]

Present-day legislation
At present, the main Dutch equal treatment legislation is the Equal Treatment Act of 1994. In this Act only discrimination on specific grounds is prohibited. For example, unequal treatment on the basis of wealth, titles, education and length thereof is not prohibited. The 1980 Act on Equal Treatment in regard to men and women is still relevant in situations of gender discrimination, because it prevails over the general Equal Treatment Act of 1999 as far as gender discrimination is concerned. Since the differences with the ETA provisions on gender are minimal, this has had few consequences.

The equal treatment legislation is not only restricted to specific grounds (as described above); it also only covers specific fields, mainly labour, goods and services. The most important field is labour. Dutch equal treatment legislation protects against discrimination in employment relations and this should be interpreted very broadly. Various kinds of labour relations fall within the scope of the protection, for instance, voluntary work, self-employed professionals (dentists, architects, doctors, lawyers, solicitors and tax advisers) and vocational education and training. Unequal treatment is forbidden in any area that is related to paid work, from job advertisement to the actual employment contract. This includes salary, holidays and promotion, training and professional education, dismissal, application and working conditions. The law does not only address employers; it also addresses all those involved in labour relations and in the framing of working conditions. Thus temporary agency work, such as trade unions and employers' confederations, also fall within the scope of equal treatment legislation. An exception is made for those organizations that have been founded on religious, ideological or political principles. For example, schools with a religious denomination are allowed to refuse teachers who openly express their homosexuality if this is not in accordance with their denomination.

The second important field in which equal treatment legislation applies is the offering or permitting of access to goods and services by professionals and public services. This might involve institutions working in the fields of housing, social services, healthcare, cultural affairs and education. Unequal treatment is also forbidden in concluding, implementing or terminating agreements or contracts with regard to goods and services, and in providing information on those matters and in giving career orientation and advice about educational or career opportunities.

With regard to the grounds of disability or chronic illness and age, up until March 2009 the prohibition of discrimination was restricted to employment, including vocational training. This legislation is meant to be extended to the other fields, especially the field of goods and services provision. As of 15 March 2009, the scope of coverage of the Act on Equal Treatment on the Grounds of Disability and Chronic Illness (WGBH/CZ) has been extended to the field of housing. Refusing to rent or sell housing to people with disabilities or chronic illnesses is prohibited. As of 1 August 2009, the law's coverage will be expanded to primary and secondary education (Staatsblad, 2009, p. 101).[13]

With regard to age, prohibition of discrimination is still restricted to employment and professional education. With regard to the grounds based on race, discrimination has also been forbidden – as a result of the European Directive against Race and Ethnic Discrimination[14] – in social protection, including social security and social advantages since 2004. This means that a branch of the public sector, besides the field of employment, now falls under the Equal Opportunity Commission's activities.[15]

Supervision on how closely these Acts are adhered to is a task for both the Dutch Courts and the Equal Treatment Commission (ETC). The ETC was established by the Dutch government in 1994. It is an independent, professional organization. People can ask the ETC questions about Dutch equal treatment law or ask the ETC to give an opinion in specific cases. Each time the ETC receives a request for an opinion, it investigates whether the equal treatment law has been violated. In some respects, the ETC is similar to a court. However, an important difference is that the opinions of the ETC are not binding. Moreover, the ETC searches for information independently, whereas the courts depend mainly on evidence that lawyers put forward. Other differences are that filing a complaint with the ETC is free of charge and that a lawyer is not required. The ETC does not have to wait for petitions to be filed either. It is also entitled to investigate on its own initiative in specific areas where systematic or persistent patterns of discrimination are suspected. The ETC cannot inflict fines on employers or impose settlements on either party.

Public debate and policy

In the present Dutch public debate on diversity at work, the most prominent themes are those of gender, ethnicity (related to religion) and homosexuality. Chronic illness and disabilities were debated in the 1980s, and this resulted in public cuts in disability insurances. The ageing population raises the question of whether the public pension system, which is under pressure because of the economic crisis, can continue to pay out. But the biggest public controversies surround the tension between constitutional rights regarding religion (equal treatment with regard to religion, freedom of religion and freedom of education) and the right to equal treatment on the basis of gender and sexual preference. For example, in the public debate Islamic immigrants are criticized for subordinating women and discriminating against homosexuals. A question frequently raised is whether public officials should be allowed to wear a headscarf and whether this is a symbol that represents a belief in an inferior position of women. The same question arises with regard to officials who refuse to shake hands with colleagues of the opposite sex on the basis of their religious conviction, as this can also be interpreted as a lack of respect or even as discrimination against women.

Public debate on migrants

Since the mid-1990s, Dutch policies have placed increasing emphasis on the duties of immigrants. For instance, new immigrants, whether guest workers, marriage partners, dependants or political refugees, have to pass a citizenship exam as a condition for being granted a residence permit. In the new millennium, migration has become a dominant theme in Dutch public debate. This has partly been caused by global developments such as 9/11 and its aftermath, and partly by national incidents such as two political murders and some controversial films. In May 2002 Dutch society was shocked by the murder of Pim Fortuyn, the party leader of a right-wing political party, by an environmental activist. Fortuyn's main political arguments had been directed against the threats that Islam poses to the liberal values of Dutch society. The murder resulted in a rise of hostilities towards left-wing political parties for their assumed tolerance towards immigrants (van Donselaar and Rodrigues, 2004, p. 18). Two years later, a second political murder further propelled the debate in the direction of intolerance. In November 2004 a Dutch Moroccan Muslim extremist murdered filmmaker Theo Van Gogh, who had been very outspoken in the media, describing Islamic culture as backward. At the time of his murder, Van Gogh was preparing a movie on the suppression of Muslim women by Muslim men, together with Ayaan Hirsi Ali, a female member of parliament for the liberal People's Party for Freedom and Democracy (VVD). The murder resulted in an intensification of public debate on the tension between freedom of religion and freedom of expression. Since the murder came at a moment when political support for the government was at a historic low, politicians rapidly adopted a firmer tone when speaking about immigrants (van Donselaar and Rodrigues, 2006, p. 139). Hirsi Ali had to go into hiding after doubts were expressed about whether she had been honest about her background when applying for asylum in the Netherlands. In 2006 she resigned from the Dutch parliament and left for the USA.

Geert Wilders, leader of the right-wing Party for Freedom, was one of the politicians who filled the political gap left by Fortuyn's murder. In 2008 Wilders released a political film, *Fitna*, which charges that Islam is a threat to Western society. In the period before its release, the film caused widespread media attention and protest among the international Muslim community. The Dutch Prime Minister Jan Peter Balkenende publicly distanced himself from the content of the film and Dutch Muslim organizations reacted calmly. Initially, the Dutch Public Prosecutor decided not to prosecute Wilders for discrimination and incitement to hatred, despite reports from diverse human rights organizations. However, in 2009 the Amsterdam Appellate Court prosecuted Wilders for discrimination. The focus was on the offensive nature of the assertions he had made in the media, in which he likened Islam to Nazism (Hof Amsterdam, 2009).

At the same time the political parties in the middle of the political spectrum, the Christian Democrats and the Social Democrats, have increasingly adopted a negative stance towards immigrants. In the media, representatives of immigrant groups complain about being treated as a homogeneous rather than a heterogeneous group. Muslim women who wear headscarves complain about being discriminated against in the labour market.

Public debate on gender relations
Dutch policies aimed at achieving gender equality were introduced in the 1980s. EU equality directives introduced gender equality legislation into the labour market and social security matters. The ratification of the UN Charter on the Elimination of All Forms of Discrimination against Women in 1991 has broadened the coverage of anti-discrimination legislation to include politics, schooling, healthcare and bodily integrity. The Dutch government must report to the United Nations on its progress in the field of gender equality every four years (Heringa et al., 1994).

The three main issues covered by Dutch gender policy are the participation of women in the labour market, the position of migrant women, and the elimination of violence against women (Ministerie van Onderwijs, Cultuur en Wetenschap, 2008). Because our focus here is on diversity in the labour market, we discuss the first two issues in more detail. Since the majority of Dutch women work part time, women receive encouragement for working longer hours, for example in the form of tax advantages. Initiatives to increase the number of women in leadership positions have included voluntary agreements between managers in the for-profit and non-profit sectors. The Dutch government has pledged to have 25 per cent of its leadership positions filled by women in 2011 (Ministerie van Onderwijs, Cultuur en Wetenschap, 2008, p. 34). In addition, childcare facilities have been extended to make it easier for women and men to combine work and family life. Migrant women in particular have been the target of support measures aimed at increasing their participation in society, such as integration courses (*inburgeringstrajecten*), which teach Dutch language and general knowledge of Dutch society, and provide orientation on labour market participation.

The Dutch public debate on gender equality is less extreme than the debate on migration. The general tenor of the debate is that gender inequality is more of a problem among migrant groups than among the indigenous Dutch population (Merens and Hermans, 2009, p. 16). As discussed earlier, the debate focuses on the wearing of headscarves by Muslim women and the weaker labour market position of women of Moroccan and Turkish descent. The general tendency is to allow the wearing of head-scarves at work, but not for public functions that require a uniform, such as police officers (although the ETC, 2008, advised differently). Another discussion refers to the freedom that religious groups have to ignore Dutch gender norms. A Dutch imam who refused to shake hands with a female secretary of state sparked off hostile debates. His refusal was inspired by his religious beliefs, but in the Dutch context refusing to shake hands is considered very impolite. The general feeling expressed in the media is that in professional situations migrants should behave as the native Dutch do; in this respect, equal treatment of women is considered more important than freedom of religion. The Dutch Equal Treatment Commission, however, expressed a different opinion, arguing that, in the cases concerned, the prohibition of discrimination on religious grounds had been violated (Equal Treatment Commission, see http://www.cgb.nl).

Another issue that is debated publicly is the use of quotas for women in leadership positions. Although Dutch public policy supports an increase in the number of women in leadership positions in both the for-profit and non-profit sector, the implementation of these policies is controversial. In the public arena affirmative action initiatives towards women are often interpreted as discrimination against men.

Public debate on homosexuality
Acceptance of homosexuality is seen by many as an achievement of Dutch culture. The Netherlands was the first country to introduce same-sex marriage (in 2001). Prominent politicians including the late Minister of the Interior Ien Dales (Dutch Labour Party, died in office in 1994), the late Pim Fortuyn (founder of the right-wing LPF Party, mur-dered in 2001) and Boris Dittrich (D66, Social–Liberal Party leader up to 2004) were all open about their homosexuality and championed equal rights for this group. As argued, in the recent public debates Islam is seen as the main threat to the tolerant attitude of the Dutch towards homosexuals, although orthodox Christians also openly disapprove of or even condemn homosexuals. Dutch public policy regarding homosexuality is directed at increasing public acceptance and tolerance by extending financial support to grass-roots organizations and at eliminating violence against homosexuals (Ministerie van Onderwijs, Cultuur en Wetenschap, 2007). There are no specific policies directed towards improving the position of homosexuals in the workplace.

In the public debate, however, homosexuality in the workplace is a topic for discus-sion. The tension between the right to equal treatment on the basis of religion and on the basis of sexual preference is very prominent at present, and presents a challenge to marriage officials and teachers in particular. Since the introduction of same-sex mar-riage, some Protestant marriage officials with conservative beliefs have claimed the right to refuse to officiate at such ceremonies. The initial advice of the Dutch Equal Treatment Commission was that municipalities should allow individual officials to refrain from officiating if they wished, since there are enough marriage officials available who are prepared to marry same-sex couples (ETC, 2002). Recently, however, refusal to conduct same-sex marriage ceremonies has become prohibited (ETC, 2008). Another example is that of the boards of a number of conservative Protestant schools that have claimed the right to refuse to employ or to dismiss schoolteachers who are openly homosexual. However, the Dutch Equal Treatment Commission argues that boards are not allowed to refuse to employ homosexual teachers on the grounds of their sexual preference (ETC, 1999).

In summary, the tone of the public debate in the Netherlands has become less tolerant towards immigrants. Gender equality has become an issue linked to migrant women rather than to native Dutch women. Migrants are increasingly being required to participate in integration courses where they learn the Dutch language and about the values promoted by Dutch society. Basic social rights such as the right to social assistance and public health insurance are provided only on condition that migrants perform these citizenship duties. Diversity policies to support the participation of migrants and women in the labour market combine legal anti-discrimination arrangements with voluntary agreements between employers and employees. Dutch policies aimed at making it easier to combine work and family life are an exception to this rule. They make use of social services such as childcare facilities and (paid) parental leave to support the participation of young parents in the labour market. Policies regarding homosexuality consist mainly of legal prohibition of discrimination.

Organizational practices
In this section we will discuss the extent to which equal treatment regulations and the public debate on diversity are reflected in the practices of organizations. We start with a general overview of human resources initiatives by organizations, and then go on to discuss some diversity practices in more detail. We shall argue that organizations steer a course between special treatment of groups with a specific identity (target groups) and 'valuing differences' practices that show appreciation of differences between individuals (without reference to specific identities).

Research performed in 2005 shows that most Dutch organizations do not have any kind of diversity policy. However, initiatives directed at individual differences (a focus on individual qualities, needs and work–family initiatives) are much more common than initiatives directed at target groups (e.g. women, migrants, the elderly, people with disabilities). De Vries et al. (2005) carried out a telephone survey among CEOs or HR directors of a representative sample of 500 Dutch organizations. Initiatives that address individual differences proved to be very common in the organizations. Nearly all organizations reported that they focused on individual qualities (94 per cent), while 81 per cent said they focused on individual needs, and work–family initiatives had been taken by 71 per cent. Of all target group initiatives, targeting older workers' employability was the one most often adopted by the organizations (33 per cent), followed by initiatives targeted at advancement of women (31 per cent), and actions to prevent turnover of people with disabilities. Initiatives for hiring people from ethnic minorities were mentioned by 15 per cent and initiatives for hiring people with disabilities by 13 per cent of the organizations surveyed. Thirteen per cent of the organizations had practices in place to enhance the advancement of migrants within the organization. With regard to diversity initiatives directed at migrants, similar findings were found in a study among 500 small and medium-sized businesses (Ait Moha et al., 2008). This study showed that 29 per cent of the companies had implemented diversity initiatives in their hiring practices. The initiatives ranged from active selection procedures for hiring migrants (18 per cent), equal treatment procedures (18 per cent), advertisements in which migrant groups are explicitly invited to apply for job openings (16 per cent), and searching for migrants through specific networks.

In general, non-profit organizations and larger organizations are much more active in carrying out diversity initiatives compared to for-profit organizations and smaller organizations (De Vries et al., 2005). De Vries et al. also studied whether the presence of initiatives was related to the representation of target groups in the organization (only cross-sectional data were available, so no causal inferences can be made). The correlation between initiatives and the representation of target groups in the organizations was highest for initiatives concerning migrants (0.42 for hiring, 0.40 for promotion) and for initiatives concerning the advancement of women (0.27). In contrast to the dominant perspective in both equality policies and in the public debate, initiatives that combined gender and ethnic background were rare. For example, in organizations that had initiated practices to promote the entry of migrant groups into the organization, only 7 per cent also had initiatives supporting the advancement of women within the organization. This suggests that organizational practices aimed at integrating the multiple dimensions of diversity are rare.

Although governmental institutions have the best record of implementing diversity practices (De Vries et al., 2005), there is still no coherent, integral perspective guiding diversity initiatives in governmental departments (Henderikse et al., 2007). Although most governmental departments have developed some initiatives on diversity, these are often short-term projects and seem to be characterized by amateurism and fragmentation (ibid.). Henderikse et al. (2007) conclude that while some efforts to improve the representation of target groups (women, migrants, elderly workers) have been partially successful, diversity practices are not anchored in the core HR practices and in public policies of these departments. The current Dutch government, however, has intensified its efforts to implement a diversity programme in all governmental departments. Target figures concerning the number of women, migrants and elderly workers have been set for each department. Moreover, the government has made the department heads responsible for delivering these targets (VNG and FORUM, 2009). Interestingly, the registration procedure for migrant groups, which was abandoned in 2004 (see above, Wet SAMEN), has been reinstated in government departments, enabling changes in the representation of different identity groups to be measured. In summary, both governmental and for-profit organizations have made efforts to deal with diversity. In the following sections we present some examples of common practices concerning migration and gender in Dutch organizations.

Practices directed at migrant groups

Scholars in diversity management have outlined three general reasons for organizations to implement diversity programmes: (1) ideological reasons (corporate responsibility for challenging discrimination, providing equal opportunities and having a workforce that is representative of the general population); (2) legal reasons (legal obligations and public sector procedures); and (3) 'business case' arguments (the need to recruit talent, open new markets, support creativity and innovation, and reduce conflict and misunderstandings; Kottke and Agars, 2003). As we shall show in our discussion of diversity initiatives on migration, all three reasons underlie the practices of Dutch organizations.

We start with the Dutch police organization, which has been actively involved in diversity programmes for many years. The diversity programmes that the police use are supported by ideological arguments, namely that equal representation of migrant groups within the police force would support the legitimacy of the police in Dutch society (LECD, 2009). In the past, however, practices that facilitated the hiring of officers with a migrant background by adapting standards for candidates of these groups have been devastating for the status of migrants within the police (Houdijk et al., 1997). These programmes have now been replaced by initiatives to fill possible skill gaps (e.g. in Dutch language skills) or to support adaptation (e.g. by implementing 'buddy projects' in which new police recruits are matched with an experienced police officer). Equal representation of migrant groups is still a strategic goal of the police, but no longer through affirmative discrimination means. Furthermore, the police force states that it aims to dissolve discrimination within the organization and to prevent unwanted turnover. Apart from these ideological arguments for supporting diversity initiatives, the police force uses legal arguments, explicitly aiming to set an example by observing the Equal Treatment Act. In 2007, the Minister of the Interior at the time, Guusje Ter Horst, who is responsible for the police force, decided that 50 per cent of the leadership vacancies in the regional police force and at least 30 per cent of the vacancies for top management positions within the national police corps should be filled by women or migrants (Ter Horst, 2007). In spring 2009, Ter Horst twice postponed the appointment of a white male to a high management position as thus far the police had failed to appoint more women and migrants to positions of leadership. This postponement is at odds with the current Dutch Equal Treatment Act and EC anti-discrimination directives, which do not allow preferential treatment, and consequently has met resistance within the police organization. Finally, the Dutch police organization also uses business-case arguments for supporting diversity initiatives. It argues that it needs expertise on migration issues, particularly since migrant groups are overrepresented in the crime statistics. Moreover, future labour shortages need to be prevented by attracting employees from new groups (LECD, 2009). Thus the practices of the Dutch police organization over the years show that diversity initiatives have been implemented on the basis of ideological, legal and business-case arguments.

Business-case arguments are perhaps even more salient in the justifications offered by for-profit organizations for implementing diversity initiatives. By attracting employees from migrant groups in the vicinity, organizations in the banking sector (e.g. Rabobank Group, 2007) and retail sector (Albert Heijn, 2009) hope to attract new customer markets. Research shows that initiatives supported by 'access and legitimacy' arguments (Luijters, 2008; Ely and Thomas, 2001) tend to result in feelings of alienation by minorities. In these inititiatives, migrants are valued for what they are (potential customers) rather than for who they are (groups with a specific identity). This perspective differs from a perspective of 'learning and integration' (Ely and Thomas, 2001), in which the organizations' main argument for diversity initiatives is to support rethinking the organization's core business and core processes with the aim of introducing innovations in the company. An example of this perspective can be seen in initiatives that have been taken by Philips, the Dutch multinational that produces consumer 'lifestyle' electronics, healthcare and lighting. In recent years Philips has restructured the company from an organization that consisted of separate divisions providing lifelong careers into an integrated organization in which people from different functional, national and continental backgrounds rotate regularly. Philips believes that this helps to create synergy, creativity and innovative ideas (van den Berg, 2009). Part of the multinational's strategy is also to actively search for and support female talent, as women are the major decision-makers for consumer product purchases. Moreover, Philips actively searches for talent among the upcoming economies, particularly Brazil, Russia, India and China. It should be noted that these diversity initiatives are tailored towards the higher-level employees.

It can be argued that large multinational corporations such as Shell, Philips and Unilever are at the forefront of implementing diversity initiatives just because of their status. Multinational organizations are, for instance, confronted with strong equal opportunity legislation in the USA. Moreover, public procurement in the USA is conditional on evidence of diversity initiatives in the organizations. The majority of for-profit organizations in the Netherlands, however, use mainly 'discrimination and fairness' arguments, striving for the prevention of unequal treatment of employees in their processes of hiring, reward and promotion. A strong belief that 'in our organization all employees are equal' is characteristic of this perspective. As the facts and figures presented earlier in this chapter show, material equality in labour participation, income and division of power between migrant groups and the native Dutch population, and between men and women, is still a long way off.

In addition to fulfilling legal obligations, diversity initiatives are also spread via informal networks. With regard to initiatives and the arguments used to support them, organizations show 'mimicking behaviour' (Paauwe and Boselie, 2003). Corporate diversity officers are part of formal and informal networks and frequently adapt the 'best practices' they have learned from each other. This is furthered by the presence of organizations for the enhancement of diversity such as the government-sponsored E-Quality, Dutch Network of Diversity Management, FORUM Institute for Multicultural Development, Opportunity in Bedrijf, 'Talent naar de Top' (literally 'Talent to the Top') and the Ambassador networks.

Practices directed at gender equality
In addition to the initiatives directed at migrant groups, a considerable number of Dutch organizations have taken initiatives aimed at improving the position of women in their organizations. These include mentoring programmes, women's development programmes and professional networks for women. There are (and have been) a number of ambassador networks active in the Netherlands, where prominent figures from profit and non-profit organizations have put a personal effort into increasing the number of women in top positions. According to a recent evaluation of Dutch Ambassador networks, these networks are effective in so far as they have succeeded in putting the issue on the agenda (Henderikse et al., 2006). Ambassadors are less positive about the actual rise in the number of women in the top layers of organizations. Since 2008, collaboration between governmental departments, labour unions, employers' organizations and companies has resulted in a taskforce that invites organizations to sign a 'Talent to the Top Charter'. In this charter, organizations make a unilateral commitment to increasing the number of women in their top management layers and to implementing the practices needed to reach this goal. The results of these initiatives will subsequently be monitored by the Minister of Education, Culture and Science (Talent naar de Top, 2009).

Conclusion and discussion
The previous sections have shown that the prominent issues in the Dutch public debate on workplace diversity concern clashes between the constitutional right to equal

treatment on the grounds of religion, and the right to equal treatment on the grounds of gender and sexual preference, and between the constitutional right to equal treatment on the one hand and constitutional rights such as freedom of expression and freedom of religion on the other. Public feeling is sometimes at odds with the constitutional rights that are protected under the Equal Treatment Act. Islam in particular is criticized for not respecting the principle of equal treatment regarding gender and sexual orientation, whereas violations of these rights by conservative Christian individuals or institutions are seen as less problematic. Conservative Protestantism has a long tradition in the Netherlands and is considered less of a threat to Dutch culture than Islam is. During the past few decades the polemic of Dutch public debate on diversity has seen a change from a pluralist perspective in the 1980s to more of an assimilation perspective in the twenty-first century (Maussen, 2006). Especially the tolerance of religious and cultural pluralism, which the Netherlands is known for historically, is declining. To some extent these changes in debates are reflected in national and local public policy, and in organizational programmes and practices. Some, especially small, organizations claim equal treatment of all their personnel, regardless of their (gender, ethnic, sexual preference) identity. However, in contrast to the emphasis in the public arena on assimilation, large organizations in particular have tended to introduce diversity practices aimed at creating opportunities for disadvantaged groups such as women and immigrants. Diversity initiatives vary from supporting the hiring and promotion of specific disadvantaged groups, to creating networks and mentoring systems and supporting the combination of work and care. Diversity practices are often legitimized by the business-side argument that organizations can derive a benefit from diversity because it supports growth, innovation and better adaptation to a society that is becoming increasingly globalized. Changes in legislation have had some effects on the development and implementation of diversity programmes, but to a more limited extent (e.g. the Wet SAMEN, which was withdrawn after six years).

The lack of effectiveness that Dutch organizations show in addressing diversity may stem from tensions between opposing legal, political and strategic demands. This has resulted in a number of paradoxical situations. The first paradox is that whereas there is political and strategic support for affirmative action policies, both Dutch and European laws place restrictions on initiatives that might result in benefits for one particular group. An example can be found in the introduction of quotas for increasing female and migrant representation in the top layers of organizations. Organizations that have introduced quotas have not only received negative press coverage, but they have often faced criticism from the ETC (see, e.g., the example of appointing women as police deputies discussed above). The second paradox can be found in the registration of ethnic identity, the aim of which is to monitor organizations' efforts to create a more diverse workforce, on the one hand, and the social resistance that this registration has met with.

The third paradox can be seen in organizational practices that are aimed at improving the position of target groups (e.g. the introduction of training, networks and mentoring systems for target groups) and the public debates surrounding these issues. Opponents of these policies have argued that they stigmatize the target groups. Public awareness that differential treatment of groups might be needed to create equal results, however, is generally low. Finally, organizational initiatives aimed at making it easier to combine

Summary table for the Netherlands

Existence of anti-discrimination legislation	Yes
Criteria covered by anti-discrimination legislation	Religious and political conviction, race, nationality, gender, marital status, sexual orientation, permanent or temporary labour contracts, working hours, handicap and chronic illness, age
Criteria for which the reporting of quantitative data and their communication to a public administration are compulsory	Abolished in 2004
Criteria covered by 'affirmative' or 'positive' action legislation other than unemployment- or income-based	Absent
Existence of a discourse or debate about 'non-discrimination' or 'equality'	Yes
Existence of a discourse or debate about 'diversity'	Yes
Year or period when the 'discrimination' concept started to disseminate in management literature in the country	About 1990
Year or period when the diversity concept started to disseminate in management literature in the country	About 2000
Who pushed the 'diversity' agenda?	Semi-governmental and non-governmental organizations such as FORUM and E-Quality
Existence of a professional association representing diversity professionals and year of creation	No, although there are a number of national platform and knowledge organizations (Div-Netwerk, 2004, Opportunity-in-Bedrijf, 2005, E-Quality, 1998)
Existence of a professional association representing diversity scholars and year of creation	Only single university-based associations, such as Babylon (Tilburg University, 2002)

work and care, although introduced for both men and women, may actually reinforce traditional gender relations. While it is argued that these policies support women's participation in the labour market, the emphasis on women's caring role may, on the one hand, consequently hamper their position. On the other hand, the Dutch emphasis on work–life balance policies also highlights the traditionally strong cultural value attached to being able to care for children and, to a lesser extent, the elderly. Indeed, in the Netherlands, more men and women work part time than employees in any other OECD country.

Notes

1. Interestingly, Japan and Indonesia are considered Western countries. Probably the welfare level is more important as a selection criterion than the geographical position.
2. No official statistics are available on the number of illegal immigrants.
3. In the Netherlands assistant professors or associate professors are not allowed to use the title 'professor'. This figure therefore refers to 'full professors'.

4. International Convention on the Elimination of All Forms of Racial Discrimination, 21 December 1965, entered into force on 4 January 1969.
5. Directive 76/207 of 9 February 1976· Equal treatment for men and women as regards access to employment, vocational training and promotion, and working conditions.
6. Equal Treatment Act of 2 March 1994.
7. Act of 3 July 1996, to adjust the Dutch Civil Code and the Dutch Code for Civil Servants with regard to the prohibition of discrimination of employees on the basis of working hours.
8. Act of 7 November 2002 to implement EC Directive 1999/70/EG of 28 June 1999.
9. Equal Treatment Act of 3 April 2003 with regard to the prohibition of discrimination on the basis of handicap or chronic illness.
10. Act of 17 December 2003 with regard to equal treatment at work, profession and professional education on the basis of age.
11. Act of 11 May 1994 with regard the promotion of equal participation of migrants on the labour market.
12. Act of 16 November 2001 to determine regulation on the achievement of a new equilibrium between work and care.
13. Change of the Equal Treatment Act with regard to the prohibition of discrimination on the basis of handicap or chronic illness in connection with extension to the field of education.
14. Council Directive 2000/43/EC of 29 June 2000, implementing the principle of equal treatment between persons irrespective of racial or ethnic origin.
15. This aspect of the Race Directive is implemented in Section 7a of the Dutch ETA.

References

Ait Moha, A., Verheggen, P.P. and Gijsbers, L. (2008), TrendMeter 2008: Werkgevers over nieuwe nederlanders als werknemers. Amsterdam: Motivations, Utrecht: Forum.
Albert Heijn (2009), 'Albert Heijn en medewerkers: diversiteit, de kracht van het verschil', retrieved from http://www.ah.nl/albertheijn/article.jsp?trg=albertheijn/article.omv.medewerkers, 30 March.
Bleijenbergh, I., M. Bussemaker and J. de Bruijn (2006), 'Trading well-being for economic efficiency: the 1990 shift in EU childcare policies', *Marriage & Family Review*, **39** (3/4), 315–36.
De Vries, S., van de Ven, C., Nuyens, M., Stark, K., van Schie, J. and van Sloten, G.C. (2005), Diversiteit op de werkvloer: hoe werkt dat? Voorbeelden van diversiteitsbeleid in de praktijk. Hoofddorp: TNO Kwaliteit van leven.
Ely, Robin J., and Thomas, David A. (2001), 'Cultural diversity at work: the effect of diversity perspectives on work group processes and outcomes', *Administrative Science Quarterly*, **46** (2), 229–73.
Equal Treatment Commission (1999–2008), For opinions of the Commission, see http://www.cgb.nl/.
European Foundation for the Improvement of Living and Working Conditions (2007), 'Pay developments 2007', http://www.eurofound.europa.eu/docs/eiro/tn0804019s/tn0804019s.pdf viewed 10 March 2009.
Groen Links (2006), 'Onderzoek GroenLinks toont ernstige discriminatie bij stages', http://tweedekamer.groenlinks.nl/nieuws/2006/11/09/onderzoek-groenlinks-toont-ernstige-discriminatie-bij-stages.
Havinga, T. (2002), 'The effects and limits of anti-discrimination law in the Netherlands', *International Journal of the Sociology of Law*, **30** (1), 75–90.
Henderikse, W., Hentenaar, F. and Schalkwijk, S. (2006), Ambassadeursnetwerk gevolgd. Een evaluatieonderzoek naar de effecten van het beleidsinstrument, Ambassadeursnetwerk Doorbreken Glazen Plafond. Utrecht: van Doorne-Huiskes en partners.
Henderikse, W., van Doorne-Huiskes, A. and Schippers, J. (2007), Diversiteit geïnventariseerd. Een onderzoek naar nieuwe bevindingen op het gebied van diversiteitsbeleid. Utrecht: van Doorne-Huiskes en partners.
Heringa, A.W., Hes, J. and Lijnzaad, L. (1994), Het vrouwenverdrag: een beeld van een verdrag. Maklu Uitgevers: Antwerpen Apeldoorn.
Hof Amsterdam (2009), Hof Amsterdam beveelt de strafvervolging van het Tweede Kamerlid Geert Wilders, LJN BH0496, http://www.rechtspraak.nl/Gerechten/Gerechtshoven/Amsterdam/Actualiteiten/Hof+Amsterdam+beveelt+de+strafvervolging+van+het+Tweede+Kamerlid+Geert+Wilders.htm viewed 1 March.
Houdijk, D., van Viersen, D. and de Vries, S. (1997), Acceptatie van allochtone agenten. Een onderzoek naar factoren die acceptatie bevorderen en bemoeijlijken. Leiden: Rijksuniversiteit Leiden.
Jonkers, P. (2003), Diskwalificatie van wetgeving. De totstandkoming en uitvoering van de Wet bevordering evenredige arbeidsdeelname allochtonen. Nijmegen: Aksant.
Kottke, J. and Agars, M. (2003), 'Models and practice of diversity management: a historical review and presentation of a new integration theory', in M.S. Stockdale and F.J. Crosby (eds), *The Psychology and Management of Workplace Diversity*, Oxford: Blackwell Press, pp. 55–77.
Kruisbergen, E. and Veld, T. (2002), *Een gekleurd beeld: Over beelden, beoordeling en selectie van jonge allochtone werknemers* [A coloured picture: About images, judgements and selection of young ethnic minority employees], Assen: Van Gorcum.

Landelijk Expertise Centrum Diversiteit (LECD) (2009), 'Waarom diversiteitsbeleid bij de politie?', http://www.lecd.nl/algemeen/waarom diversiteitsbeleid bij de politie?, accessed 24 September.

Lückerath-Rovers, M. (2008), 'The Dutch Female Board Index 2008: female executive and non-executive directors on corporate boards of Dutch listed companies', Erasmus Institute Monitoring & Compliance.

Luijters, K. (2008), 'Making diversity bloom: coping effectively with cultural differences at work', Dissertation, Groningen: University of Groningen.

Maussen, M. (2006), *Ruimte voor Islam? Stedelijk beleid, voorzieningen, organisaties*, Amsterdam: Het Spinhuis.

Merens, A. and Hermans, B. (2009), Emancipatiemonitor 2008, Sociaal en Cultureel Planbureau, Den Haag.

Ministerie van Onderwijs, Cultuur en Wetenschap (2007), Gewoon homo zijn. Lesbisch en homo-emancipatiebeleid 2008–2011, Den Haag.

Ministerie van Onderwijs, Cultuur en Wetenschap (2008), Meer kansen voor vrouwen; emancipatiebeleid 2008–2011, Den Haag.

Paauwe, J. and Boselie, P. (2003), 'Challenging "strategic HRM" and the relevance of the institutional setting', *Human Resource Management Journal*, **13**, 56–70.

Politieacademie (2008), Rapportage homofoob geweld; politiegegevens periode 1 januari – 1 juli 2008. Apeldoorn, September 2008.

Rabobank Groep (2007), 'Rabobank duurzaam in de markt: Biedt nieuw beleid kansen voor diversiteit?', retrieved from http://overons.rabobank.com/content/images/diversiteit_tcm64-75776.pdf, 30 March.

Rodrigues, P. (2007). 'The collection of data on ethnic or national origin for antidiscrimination policies: equality, privacy and diversity in a European perspective: the Dutch experience' (written version of a presentation at the Ethnic Data Conference, Brussels, 9 November 2007).

Schaafsma, J. (2006), *Ethnic Diversity at Work. Diversity attitudes and experiences in Dutch organisations*, Amsterdam: Aksant Academic Publishers.

Staatsblad (2009), Wet van 29 januari 2009, houdende wijziging van de Wet gelijke behandeling op grond van handicap of chronische ziekte in verband met de uitbreiding met onderwijs als bedoeld in de Wet op het primair onderwijs en de Wet op het voortgezet onderwijs en met wonen, Staatsblad van het Koninkrijk der Nederlanden, nr. 101, dinsdag 10 maart.

Statistics Netherlands (CBS) (2008a), *Jaarrapport Migratie 2008*, Den Haag: CBS.

Statistics Netherlands (CBS) (2008b), 'Beroepsbevolking; Behaalde onderwijs naar herkomst, geslacht en leeftijd, 25 november 2008', retrieved from http://statline.cbs.nl/StatWeb/publication, 30 March 2009.

Statistics Netherlands (CBS) (2008c), 'Bevolking; herkomstgroepering, generatie, geslacht en leeftijd, 1 januari', retrieved from: http://statline.cbs.nl/StatWeb/publication, 10 March 2009.

Statistics Netherlands (2007), *Arbeidsgehandicapten 2006; Arbeidssituatie van mensen met een langdurige aandoening*, Den Haag: CBS.

Talent naar de Top (2009), 'Het initiatief voor meer vrouwen naar de top', retrieved from http://www.talentnaardetop.nl/Charter/Commissie-Monitoring-Talent-naar-de-Top.htm, 30 March.

Ter Horst, Guusje (2007), 'Toespraak minister Ter Horst bij uitreiking diversiteitsprijs politie, 15 maart 2007', accessed 24 September 2009 (http://www.minbzk.nl/aspx/get.aspx?xdl=/views/corporate/xdl/page&VarIdt=109 &ItmIdt=102150&ActItmIdt=104777).

Van den Berg, B. (2009), 'Philips: diversity and inclusion', Guest Lecture Philips Global D&I, 10 November 2008.

Van den Brink, M. (2009), *Behind the Scenes of Science: Gender Practices in the Recruitment and Selection of Professors in the Netherlands*, Nijmegen: Ipskamp drukkers.

Van der Leun, J.P., G. Engbersen and P. van der Heijden (1998), Illegaliteit en criminaliteit: schattingen, aanhoudingen en uitzettingen. Rotterdam: Erasmus Universiteit Rotterdam.

Van der Vliet, R. (2005), *Krijgen allochtone werknemers minder betaald? Loonverschillen tussen autochtone en allochtone werknemers. Sociaal-Economische trends*, Den Haag: CBS.

Van Donselaar, J. and P. Rodrigues (2004), *Monitor Racisme and Extreem Rechts; zesde rapportage*, Amsterdam: Anne Frankstichting; Leiden: Departement Bestuurskunde Universiteit Leiden.

Van Donselaar, J. and P. Rodrigues (2006), *Monitor Racisme and Extremisme; zevende rapportage*, Amsterdam: Anne Frankstichting; Leiden: Departement Bestuurskunde Universiteit Leiden.

Van Engen, M.L., Dikkers, J.S.E., Vinkenburg, C.J., and de Rooy, P. (2009), 'Carrière succes van vaders en moeders: De rol van moederschapsideologie, werk-thuis cultuur en het gebruik van werk-thuis arrangementen', *Gedrag & Organisatie* (2).

VNG and FORUM (2009), 'Datgene wat ons bindt: Gemeenschappelijke integratieagenda van rijk en gemeenten (2e druk)', retrieved from http://www.vrom.nl/pagina.html?id=2706&sp=2&dn=w1090, 30 March.

Wikipedia (2009) Fitna (film), http://nl.wikipedia.org/wiki/Fitna_(film)#cite_note-51, viewed 29 January 2009.

10 Singapore: equality, harmony and fair employment
Audrey Chia and Angeline Lim

Introduction

> We, the citizens of Singapore
> Pledge ourselves as one united people
> Regardless of race, language or religion
> To build a democratic society
> Based on justice and equality
> So as to achieve happiness, prosperity and
> Progress for our nation.

(The Singapore Pledge, 1966)

Equality has been an important aspect of nation-building ever since Singapore gained independence in 1965. It was originally a small fishing village inhabited by Malays and *Orang Lauts*; however, British colonialism brought with it not only trade but an influx of immigrants from the Malay Archipelago, China, the Indian subcontinent and Sri Lanka. These immigrants often fought among themselves. The most prominent clash was the racial riots in 1964 between the Malays and the Chinese that left more than 30 people dead and more than 500 injured. Therefore, when Singapore gained independence, achieving harmony was considered an important goal by the founders of the Republic of Singapore.

Over the years, many efforts were made to maintain harmony among its citizens. This was done through legislation, the development of a national identity, housing policies and education. In the early years of Singapore's independence, legislation and national symbols were used to convey the message of equality. Article 12(2) of the Constitution of the Republic of Singapore (hereafter referred to as Article 12(2)) states that

> there shall be no discrimination against citizens of Singapore on the ground only of religion, race, descent or place of birth in any law or in the appointment to any office or employment under a public authority or in the administration of any law relating to the acquisition, holding or disposition of property or the establishing or carrying on of any trade, business, profession, vocation or employment.

A national identity was also created that incorporated equality as one of the five key values of Singapore. National symbols such as the National Flag, the National Pledge, the Lion Head Symbol and the National Anthem emphasize equality among its citizens.

In the last two decades, efforts at promoting equality and harmony went beyond legislation and national symbols. On 1 March 1989, the Ethnic Integration Policy (EIP) was introduced to promote racial integration and harmony, and prevent the formation of racial enclaves by ensuring that every public housing estate had a balanced ethnic mix. This is discussed further in the section on ethnicity.

National education (NE) was also introduced into schools on 17 May 1997 to develop national cohesion, as well as to cultivate survival instincts and instil confidence in the future. As part of the NE programme's efforts to promote harmony, schools celebrate Racial Harmony Day on 21 July every year in commemoration of the racial riots that occurred on the same day in 1964. Students are asked to reflect on the negative consequences of social division and the potential fault-lines created by racial and religious diversity in Singapore. Schools also celebrate the success Singapore has had with maintaining a harmonious multi-ethnic society.

Following decades of immigration, the CMIO (Chinese, Malay, Indian and Others) ethnic model that is the foundation of Singapore's multi-ethnic society remains more or less intact. As at June 2008, Singapore had a population of 4.84 million – 75.3 per cent of whom are residents (Singapore citizens and permanent residents) and 24.7 per cent are non-residents. The Singapore resident population comprises 74.7 per cent Chinese, 13.6 per cent Malays, 8.9 per cent Indians and 2.8 per cent other ethnic groups (MCYS, 2008). Of the resident population aged 15 years and over, 42.5 per cent are Buddhists, 14.6 per cent are Christians, 13.9 per cent Muslims, 8.5 per cent Taoists, 4.0 per cent Hindus, 14.8 per cent have no religion and 0.6 per cent practice other religions (MCYS, 2008; data from Singapore Census 2000).

Singapore's labour force totalled 2 939 900 as of June 2008 (Ministry of Manpower, 2008). Despite efforts at maintaining racial and religious harmony, and the emphasis on equality among Singapore citizens, the Singapore workplace is one built on meritocracy. Besides Article 12(2), which protects Singapore citizens based on race, religion, place of birth and descent in terms of gaining employment in public sector jobs, there is no legislation governing discrimination in the private sector or discrimination based on other demographic characteristics. Instead, a tripartite model has been used to promote fair employment practices in the workplace. This unique model is a collaborative effort between the unions, the employers and the Ministry of Manpower, and addresses matters relating to equality and fair employment differently from the legislative instruments used by most countries in the world.

The next section will elaborate on the tripartite model. In particular, we shall focus on the Tripartite Alliance for Fair Employment Practices (TAFEP) – the main vehicle in Singapore's promotion of non-discrimination and fairness in the workplace. The section that follows will then discuss the treatment of four types of diversity in Singapore – ethnicity, gender, sexual orientation and age – from a legislative and sociopolitical perspective. We shall also briefly address the academic discourse surrounding these. Finally, we shall end with a summary of the pertinent issues and the implications they have for both research and practice.

The tripartite model

The tripartite model was first employed in 1999, when the Ministry of Manpower (MOM), the Singapore National Employers' Federation/Singapore Business Federation (SNEF/SBF) and the National Trades Union Congress (NTUC) formed a tripartite body to investigate complaints about discriminating recruitment advertisements in the local newspapers. The newspapers had, for many years, allowed employers to state the demographic characteristics (e.g. race, gender, marital status, age) of the employee they wished to employ. To address this issue, the tripartite committee issued the Tripartite

Guidelines on Non-Discriminatory Job Advertisements. These guidelines promoted 'the use of objective criteria in the recruitment of job candidates' and gave examples of how recruitment advertisements can be crafted to highlight job-specific requirements without focusing on a particular demographic characteristic. For example, if the position requires someone who speaks Chinese, the advertisement should focus on the language skills needed rather than blatantly stating that they wish to hire a Chinese. The success of the implementation of these guidelines was noted from the significant drop in the number of job advertisements that would have been perceived to be discriminatory, from over 30 per cent in 1999 to less than 1 per cent in 2006 (Ng, 2007).

Riding on this success, other tripartite committees (involving the same representative groups) were formed. They include the Tripartite Committee on Employability of Older Workers, which introduced guidelines to the government for the re-employment of older workers and, more recently, the Tripartite Alliance for Fair Employment Practices.

The Tripartite Alliance for Fair Employment Practices (TAFEP)
Recognizing the importance of diversity and fair employment in the workplace, TAFEP was founded in 2006 to 'promote non-discriminatory employment practices and to shift mindsets among employers, employees and the general public toward fair employment practices for all workers'.

The alliance, representing the MOM, SNEF/SBF and NTUC, was formed in place of legislation after a team sent to survey countries that had anti-discrimination legislation deemed that such legislation would not be effective in Singapore. This decision was reported to stem from (a) the lack of success other countries had had with regard to equal treatment legislation, and (b) the previous success Singapore had had with a tripartite model. This model was thought to allow for more open negotiations and collaborations among the three parties.

TAFEP is a committee that is non-governmental and non-legislative. A promotional arm – Tripartite Centre for Fair Employment (TCFE) – was set up under this committee to organize and carry out various initiatives that promote fair employment. Examples of such initiatives are: providing guidelines on how to be fair employers; educating employers via workshops; and getting companies to pledge to build a fair workplace for their employees. As at May 2009, 1069 business organizations have signed the pledge.

As seen in Appendix 10.1, the pledge requires these organizations to be fair employers in terms of recruitment and selection, training, promotion opportunities and compensation. Business organizations pledge to recruit and select employees on the basis of merit and regardless of age, race, gender, religion, family status and disability.

The TCFE offers the following benefits to employers who pledge:[1]

- Free consultation on Fair Employment Practices will be provided on request
- Training on Fair Employment Practices such as recruitment and interview skills
- Resources such as guides and implementation tools
- Invitations to Learning events such as Workshops and Best Practice Seminars
- A Pledge Certificate (framed) will be issued to the Company and this can be displayed on the Company's premises
- The Company's name will be included on TCFE's website as well as in related publications and media advertorials.

At the moment, there is little public debate about TAFEP's efforts in promoting non-discrimination. This is probably a result of the non-legislative approach the government is taking towards encouraging diversity, and the sensitivity of some of the issues, particularly those relating to race and religion. However, it can be noted that despite TAFEP leaders' frequent mention of the success of the alliance, there are no explicit measures (besides the number of pledges and the decline in the number of perceived discriminatory job advertisements) or known research documenting the success of TAFEP. There also does not appear to be any monitoring of the progress of protected groups under TAFEP. While pledge figures may provide an indication of the number of businesses that publicly declare their support for fair employment practices, they do not reveal if these practices are actually in place. As such, one does question the adequacy of using pledge figures as an indicator of TAFEP's success. In addition, one cannot help but wonder if the 'business-case approach'[2] that TAFEP has adopted to encourage employers to pledge will be effective enough in bringing about the desired adoption of fair and non-discriminatory employment practices in Singaporean workplaces.

Key dimensions of diversity in Singapore
In this chapter, we focus on four types of diversity – ethnicity, gender, sexual orientation and age. We have chosen to focus on these dimensions because they cut across industries, functional areas and organizational levels. Age was included because it has become a growing concern not just for Singapore but for many other countries as well.

Another reason for choosing these four dimensions is the variation they provide in our discourse on diversity and equal treatment in Singapore. Of the four, ethnicity has been the most carefully and consciously managed by the state since Singapore's independence. While it is more recent, the movement to include older workers in the workforce was initiated by the government and has received explicit governmental support. The inclusion of women in the workforce began with subtle support from the government, but policies aimed at encouraging women to work have grown in prominence over the years. Sexual minorities (homosexuals, bisexuals and transsexuals), on the other hand, have received almost no governmental support, and men who have sex with men (MSM) may be prosecuted under Singaporean law despite an overt stand being taken by the government to hire openly gay men and lesbians for sensitive positions in government organizations. Through our discussion on the four dimensions of diversity, we hope to provide a better understanding of the ways in which diversity is managed in Singapore, and how equality, harmony and fair treatment are being discussed in this young and culturally pluralistic nation.

Ethnicity
The management of ethnic diversity in the Singaporean workplace should be understood in the context of Singapore's history of ethnic relations and public policies on ethnicity. Ethnic integration policies at work are a natural extension or subset of Singapore's highly managed social and public policy on ethnicity.

History   In the years under British rule, Singapore's ethnic groups were managed by a policy of segregation. The various ethnic groups were allocated to different geographical areas (Ooi, 2006). The Malays, many of whom made a living as fisher-folk, lived in the coastal regions. The Indians converged near the port, where many of them worked and the Chinese lived near the trading areas, where they worked as merchants or labourers.

Singapore attained self-government (under a British governor) in 1959. Then followed some turbulent years in which Singapore joined the Malayan Federation for mutually beneficial economic and political cooperation. From July to September 1964, there were sporadic inter-ethnic clashes between the Malays and Chinese in Singapore. These clashes left more than 30 dead and more than 500 injured.

Since then, the state has consciously sought to build inter-racial understanding and integration. These efforts permeate major social institutions such as the educational system and public housing. In addition, the state pays special attention to the progress of the Malays, the indigenous people of Singapore. Their progress has been regularly monitored in terms of indicators such as education, fertility and divorce rates, income, home ownership, occupation and possession of consumer durables.

Schools   School-going children, as young as age 6, learn in their social studies curriculum about the beliefs and practices of each ethnic group, and the benefits of racial harmony. There is a bilingual education policy: all school children learn two languages – English and their mother tongue (Chinese, Malay or Tamil). Textbooks, whether on mathematics, health education or even the mother tongue, contain stories, characters or illustrations about people of different races. For example, a Chinese textbook typically includes stories about Chinese children playing with their Malay, Eurasian and Indian schoolmates. Mathematics textbooks also illustrate mathematical concepts with pictures of children of different ethnic groups.

Racial Harmony Day (21 July) is observed in all schools as a chance for children to celebrate and share their ethnic heritage with one another. In addition, it is common for schools to celebrate festivals that are each identified with an ethnic group: Chinese New Year, Hari Raya Aidil-fitri (for Muslims who, in Singapore, are mostly Malay) and Deepavali (the Indian festival of the triumph of Good over Evil). During the observance of these festivals in schools, students are encouraged to dress in their own ethnic dress or the ethnic dress of other races, to build greater cultural appreciation.

Housing   Singapore has one of the world's most successful public housing programmes. Eighty-five per cent of the population reside in estates of high-rise blocks of flats built by the Housing and Development Board (HDB). Of these residents, 95 per cent own the flats that they occupy. Each housing estate is built with amenities and spaces for interaction. These spaces include playgrounds, basketball courts, gardens and coffee shops. In some blocks, there are empty spaces at ground level. These empty spaces, called 'void decks' can be used for social activities such as chess, conversations, an impromptu game of soccer, or more formal events such as weddings or funerals. All these interaction spaces provide opportunities for residents of different races to meet, mingle and socialize (Lai, 2009).

From the late 1960s into the 1980s, homebuyers had shown a preference for living with others of the same ethnic or religious group (Ooi, 2006). To prevent the formation of ethnic enclaves, the HDB introduced an Ethnic Integration Policy in 1989. Under this policy, each neighbourhood or block of flats is to be occupied by a representative proportion of each ethnic group – Malay, Chinese, Indian, Eurasian. A quota is assigned to each ethnic group. Once the quota has been reached, no other flats in that block or neighbourhood may be bought by members of that group. This policy ensures that people of different races become more familiar with one another, as well as with one another's way of life.

The movement away from ethnically defined to multi-ethnic housing estates also meant that residents could not rely on traditional social structures (such as village headmen) for support. To replace these, the state established residents' committees and grass-roots organizations with representation by members of different ethnic groups. However, these structures have had mixed results (Ooi, 2006). In some cases, the committees and grass-roots organizations have come to be dominated by Chinese members, with declining participation by other ethnic groups.

Since the 9/11 terrorist attacks in the USA, the Singapore government has been mindful of the need to strengthen inter-ethnic ties (National Library Board, Singapore, n.d.). Inter-racial confidence circles and harmony circles have been formed in housing estates, schools and workplaces to promote understanding. These circles work by organizing social and educational events (e.g. visits to places of worship) that increase understanding and allow for social relationships to develop. On the Internet, there is now a multi-lingual (English, Malay, Chinese, Tamil) portal for the Community Engagement Programme. The portal reports on activities that promote religious and ethnic harmony, and emphasize the need to maintain such harmony in the face of terrorist threats. In 2008, Singapore introduced the National Orange Ribbon celebrations to mark the peaceful coexistence of different ethnic and religious groups in Singapore. One indicator of increasing inter-racial acceptance is Singapore's rate of inter-ethnic marriages, which have risen steadily. The rate of inter-ethnic marriages registered under the Women's Charter (for non-Muslims) rose from 12 per cent in 2005 to 14 per cent in 2007. The rate of inter-ethnic marriages registered under the Muslim Law Act rose from 28 per cent to almost 30 per cent (Department of Statistics, 2008b).

Recently, Singapore acknowledged a new need to integrate an ever-growing number of migrants and new citizens (of different races and ex-nationalities) into its increasing population. This is being addressed by a National Integration Council, formed in April 2009. Members of the Council include professionals from academic, public and private organizations, and representatives from different ethnic groups and migrant groups.

Gender

In Singapore, education is mandatory and the national education system provides equal opportunities for boys and girls. Education has facilitated workforce participation, and allowed women to attain employment in higher-paying jobs in management and the professions. In 1999, Lee, Campbell and Chia (Lee et al., 1999) noted that employed Singaporean women faced three paradoxes. The first is at the national level, where policies encourage both high workforce participation and high reproductive rates. The second paradox, at the societal level, is that women were expected to contribute to their families financially while taking the primary responsibility for childcare, eldercare and domestic duties. The third paradox is that while women's workforce participation and educational levels have risen, their salaries and status still lag behind those of men. We shall examine each of these paradoxes in turn, to see what progress has been made in the last decade.

At the level of national policy, workplace legislation for women has improved steadily over the last decade. Provision for paid maternity leave has increased from two to three months, and, recently, to four months for full-time employees. Part-time employees are entitled to 12 weeks of paid maternity leave. Employers are prohibited from dismissing employees on maternity leave. This improved legislation clearly implies that women are encouraged to pursue motherhood along with economic work – the first paradox.

Some progress has been made towards reconciling the second paradox, that women are expected to earn a wage while taking care of the family and home. There have been recent changes in legislation, in the interest of promoting work–life harmony. These changes apply to both men and women. The provision of childcare leave for parents has been increased to 6 days per calendar year for each parent. Work–life programmes such as part-time and flex-time have also been made available to both men and women. The underlying message is that men should share family responsibilities with their wives.

To support legislation relating to work and life, the government also advises companies on the successful implementation of work–life strategies and gives out work–life excellence awards to companies.

Another piece of legislation does not directly address women's employment but is worth mentioning here because it contributes to women's participation in the workforce and lightens women's domestic burdens. Under Singaporean law, women from foreign countries can apply for work permits to do domestic work for a Singaporean employer on a contractual (usually two-year) basis. To obtain a work permit, these women have to pass an entry test, have a minimum level of education, pass a health check and also undergo training upon arrival in Singapore. Employers pay a government levy. They bear the responsibility of providing all the basic necessities and wages of the domestic worker, and also ensure that the worker goes for health checks every six months.

One in seven households in Singapore employ live-in, foreign domestic workers from neighbouring countries such as Indonesia, the Philippines, Sri Lanka and Myanmar. These domestic workers are an additional source of help for housework and care of family members, allowing women to seek work outside of the home. Currently, there are about 190 000 foreign domestic workers in Singapore. These domestic workers are also working women, but not covered by the Employment Act because of the domestic nature of their work. It may also be argued that because these domestic workers are all women, the gender-role beliefs that identify domestic work as women's work are reinforced rather than weakened. However, for Singaporean, employed women, the second paradox seems to have weakened. Women are expected to work outside the home, but there have been efforts to share family responsibilities with men and alleviate the burden of domestic work.

The workforce participation rate among women aged 25–64 has increased steadily over the last decade, rising from slightly over 50 per cent to slightly over 62.6 per cent in 2006. This is comparable with the workforce participation rate among women in other developed Asian countries[3] (Hong Kong, 60.7 per cent; Japan, 61.3 per cent; Taiwan, 57.4 per cent and South Korea, 56.6 per cent) but still 26 per cent lower than that of men in Singapore (89.1 per cent). More recent data from 2008 show a workforce participation rate by women of 55.6 per cent, but the slight dip can be explained by the inclusion of workers over the age of 64, and even those age 70 and over. The workforce participation of older workers is, as discussed in the section on older workers, lower than that of younger ones, but even among women, the rate of labour participation by those aged 64–69 has increased from 6.3 per cent in 1991 to 16.6 per cent in 2008, while participation by women aged 70 and above has risen from 2.9 per cent to 4.8 per cent in the same period (Ministry of Manpower, 2008).

Like many other countries, Singapore still faces the third paradox – that women lag men in earnings. Despite their increasing participation in the labour force, women still earn less than men in similar occupations. A 2007 Ministry of Manpower report on wages showed that, on average, women made less than men. Among managers, the difference was 5.4 per cent, among professionals 5 per cent, among semi-professionals and technicians 10.8 per cent, among clerical workers 9.2 per cent, among service workers 23.5 per cent, among machine operators 47.3 per cent and among labourers 30.8 per cent. The wage gap between men and women has persisted over the last few decades but there are signs that this might change. Among those aged 25 to 29, women actually earned more than men in professional, managerial and service work. However, the earning power of these women may diminish once they take on the demands of motherhood and family care, leading to interruptions in career paths, experience and social networks. Women may also consciously choose lower-paying jobs in an effort to balance work and family demands.

The provision of part-time, flextime and other work arrangements has benefited women (and men) in the Civil Service, but such schemes are still not available among the majority of employers. A survey of private sector employers showed that only one-fifth offered part-time arrangements. Fewer still offered staggered work hours (3.3 per cent) and flextime (3.5 per cent). Less than 2 per cent offered telework, working from home or job-sharing. That 80 per cent of employers have no work–life work arrangements makes it difficult for employees (and especially women) to attain work–life harmony, and may discourage women from staying employed or moving up at work.

Starting from January 2009, the government enhanced its existing schemes to help employed Singaporean mothers cope with the demands of parenthood. Singaporean working mothers can obtain a childcare subsidy of S$150 a month per child for half-day care and S$300 for full-day care. For infants (up to 18 months), the subsidy is higher at S$300 for half-day and S$600 for full-day care. In addition, women qualify for tax deductions such as the Working Mothers' Child Relief Tax of 15 per cent for the first child, 20 per cent for the next child and 25 per cent for subsequent children. Working mothers qualify for an additional relief of S$3000 if their child/children are cared for by their grandparents.

All the measures and incentives mentioned above are aimed at keeping women in the workforce while allowing them to better afford support services that will lighten their childcare and domestic loads. However, working mothers, and not all women, qualify for these schemes. The priority seems to be to address the steady decrease in labour force participation by women aged 30 and above, by reducing mothers' childcare challenges that might result in their leaving employment either temporarily or permanently.

What assumptions underlie these schemes for working women? Although the education of women, their participation in work and their positions attained at work have all risen in the last few decades, the underlying assumptions have not really changed. The first assumption is that women should have a family as well as work. Hence there are many more incentives and help schemes for married women with children than there are for single women or those married without children. The assumption seems to be that women should try to fulfil both work and family roles, and attain harmony between the two. The second assumption is that women, and not men, still bear more responsibility for the family. This is reflected in the breadth and depth of help schemes and benefits for married women compared with those for married men. Hence the approach to gender diversity is not so much one of equality but one that recognizes the different social roles assigned to men and women, and tries to relieve the conflicting or paradoxical roles that women must therefore assume.

Sexual orientation
Gay men and lesbians have been estimated to make up between 4 and 17 per cent of the workforce in the USA (Gonsiorek and Weinrich, 1991). However, it is not known what proportion of the Singaporean workforce they comprise. This is not surprising, for several reasons. First, homosexual behaviour is criminalized in Singapore. Second, attitudes toward gays and lesbians are generally negative. Third, there is a lack of research on gays and lesbians in Singapore, especially their presence in the workplace.

Under Section 377A of the Singapore Penal Code, 'any male person who, in public or private, commits, or abets the commission of, or procures or attempts to procure the commission by any male person of, any act of gross indecency with another male person, shall be punished with imprisonment for a term which may extend to 2 years'. Gross indecency here refers to non-penetrative sexual acts between men and includes mutual masturbation, genital contact and even lewd behaviour without any physical contact. Before the review of the Penal Code in October 2007, Section 377 of the Penal Code also criminalized 'carnal intercourse against the order of nature'. Under this section, anyone caught engaging in oral sex, anal sex, bestiality, or any form of unnatural sex could be arrested and punished. Oral and anal sex, if done in private between consenting adults aged 16 and above, has since been decriminalized.

Although not strictly enforced, these statutes may have led to general negativity towards gays and lesbians. A survey conducted by the Ministry of Community Development and Sports in 2001 found that 85 per cent of respondents felt that homosexual behaviour is unacceptable (MCDS, 2001). Lim (2002), in a study of tertiary students' attitudes towards homosexuals, also found that they generally harbour negative attitudes. However, these attitudes were reported to have improved in the last few years – a survey of 800 youths under the age of 30 conducted by Singapore Polytechnic found that half of the respondents find homosexuality acceptable (Channel NewsAsia, 2007).

The general negativity towards gays and lesbians can also be seen from the futile attempts made by People Like Us (PLU), Singapore's most prominent GLBT (gay, lesbian, bisexual and transsexual) advocacy group, to register itself as a society. It had tried twice (in 1997 and 2004) to register as an official society but was rejected by the Registrar of Societies, the main government board that approves the registration of societies in Singapore. As at May 2009, there are 2300 members in PLU's email discussion list. Other informal groups addressing GLBT issues also exist. These groups serve different functions for the GLBT community. For instance, some of these groups allow GLBT individuals who belong to the same faith to get together to pray, worship and support each other; some provide counselling and support services; some are activity groups and others do advocacy work. They have so far not attempted to register as official societies.

Given societal attitudes, it is not surprising that gay men and lesbians face discrimination in the workplace. Foo et al. (2005) found that if there are other potential candidates (with similar qualifications, skills and experience) available, hiring personnel are less likely to hire openly gay applicants. Their study also revealed that only 20.3 per cent of respondents indicated that their organization will hire openly gay individuals. The rest indicated that their organization will not hire gays and lesbians (20.7 per cent) or that they do not know if their organization will do so (41.5 per cent). A later study by Lim et al. (2006) further found that respondents are less likely to socialize with co-workers who appear to be gay or who are openly gay.

Contrary to the attitudes of the private sector, the Civil Service appears surprisingly positive towards hiring gays and lesbians. On 4 July 2003, then-Prime Minister Goh Chok Tong stated that the Civil Service is open to hiring gays and lesbians in sensitive positions if they openly declare their sexual orientation (*The Straits Times*, 2003). This was a change in attitude from the past, when 'if we know you're gay, we will not employ you'. While this was seen to be a move in a positive direction by some, there were strong protests by others and a debate ensued about the government's motives. Subsequently, a study by Tan (2009) presented field data from civil servants reporting that the relevant ministries and statutory boards had not acted upon the PM's statement. His data showed that while gay Singaporeans welcomed the move, they doubted the government's sincerity.

Academic research on gays and lesbians in Singapore is rather scarce. The few published journal articles mainly provide a sociopolitical commentary of the gay community or present findings of attitude surveys toward gays and lesbians. For example, Heng (2001) presented a historical perspective of the gay community in Singapore, Lim (2004) discussed the expression of homosexuality in Singapore, and Detenber et al. (2007) and Lim (2002) reported the attitudes of students and the general public towards gay men and lesbians. Books on GLBT issues also generally stay within the realm of personal biographies (Ng, 2006) and social issues (Lo and Huang, 2003). In terms of gay and lesbian issues in the workplace, two theses explored working experiences of gay men and lesbians (Goh, 2008; Low, 2002), while two conference papers investigated factors affecting the hiring of and socialization with gay men and lesbians at work (Foo et al., 2005; Lim et al., 2006).

Two issues emerge from the above discussion. First, the open-arm inclusion of gays and lesbians into society may not be as easy as with other minority groups because of (a) the remaining piece of legislation criminalizing their private bedroom activities, (b) the negative societal attitudes, and (c) the moral and religious admonishment of homosexual behaviour. Second, unlike the other three dimensions of diversity discussed in this chapter, it appears that the government does not have as much power to influence public opinion on issues related to gays and lesbians. Their attempts at doing so (acceptance of gays into the Civil Service, repeal of Section 377A of the Penal Code) have resulted in public backlash and heated debate. In conclusion, as Singapore strives to be a harmonious society where citizens are equal before the law, the move to integrate GLBT individuals into the fabric of mainstream society (be it inside or outside the workplace) will be easily one of the most challenging ones.

Age

In common with many of the economies around the world, Singapore has an ageing population, one of the fastest growing in the world (MCYS, 2008). The median age of the resident labour force has increased from 37 years in 1998 to 41 years in 2008. Currently, one-twelfth of the population is aged 65 and above. This proportion is expected to rise to one-fifth by 2030 (MCYS, 2009). The life expectancy of Singaporeans has also increased to 78 years for males and 82.9 years for females (Department of Statistics, 2008a).

There are two major work-related implications of Singapore's fast-ageing population. First, Singaporeans will need to extend their working lives to support themselves in their old age. Second, the country's economy may have to depend, among other things, on Singaporeans continuing to work in their later years. In 1993, the Retirement Age Act was introduced to mandate a minimum retirement age of 60 years. In 1999, the Act was amended to further extend the retirement age from 60 to 62 years. To encourage the continued employment of older workers, however, employers are allowed, under the Act, to reduce the wages paid to employees aged 60 and above. Although the Act covers the notice period and criteria/justification for wage reduction, and advises discretion on the part of employers, it also rather oddly allows wages to be cut more than once as long as each reduction is not more than 10 per cent. It also allows employers to retire employees at the age of 60 or after if they cannot reach agreement on their post-60 wages.

> To help ease the cost burden of retaining employees beyond the age of 60, employers are given the discretion under the Retirement Age Act to reduce the wages of such employees by up to 10 per cent when extending their employment beyond 60. . .
>
> If introduced, the wage reduction must be based on reasonable factors other than age, such as how entrenched is the seniority-based wage system in the company, any changes made to the scope of the (re-designed) job, the employee's productivity, duties and responsibilities.
>
> The Ministry of Manpower advises employers to be fair and judicious in implementing the wage cut. In deciding on the need and extent of the cut, employers should consider whether the older employee's salary reflects his/her job worth.
>
> The wage cut can be effected on or at any time after the employee turns 60. The wage cut (may) be effected more than once so long as the total magnitude of the cut does not exceed 10 per cent.
>
> The employee may disagree with the wage cut proposed by his employer . . . However, if an agreement cannot be reached after discussion, the employee may retire or his employer may retire him on or after he reaches the age of 60. (Ministry of Manpower, Retirement Age Act, updated 2008)

The Act is also silent on workers above the retirement age of 62, leaving it to employees and employers to work out the terms of employment.

To encourage workforce participation by older citizens, and also to encourage employers to continue employing older workers, the Tripartite Committee on Employability of Older Workers was formed to improve their employability. This Committee comprises representatives from unions, employers and the government. It recommended a four-pronged strategy: expanding employment opportunities for older workers; enhancing their cost competitiveness; improving their skills; and nurturing positive perceptions of older workers. Among the schemes that have been implemented is a retraining programme for professionals and an incentive programme for companies to redesign jobs for older workers. The Committee also highlighted positive examples of companies that had successfully integrated older workers into their workforce. In addition, the

Committee recognized that current legislation may be insufficient, hence 'a review of the retirement age is under way, with the purpose of enacting legislation by 2012 to enable more people to continue working beyond the current statutory retirement age of 62, up to 65 in the first instance and, later, up to 67'.

One of the positive outcomes of the Tripartite Committee's recommendations was the creation of the ADVANTAGE! scheme. This scheme was piloted by the Singapore Workforce Development Agency (WDA), NTUC and SNEF in 2005 and introduced in 2006 to promote the employment of mature workers (age 40 and above) and the re-employment of older workers (age 62 and above) by giving businesses incentives to hire and retain mature and older workers.

However, a survey of 2900 private establishments, each employing 25 or more employees, found that only 34 per cent of these establishments were aware of the ADVANTAGE! scheme. Establishments in the construction industry were very much less aware of the scheme (only one in five firms knew about it) compared to industries such as financial services (54 per cent), real estate and renting (45 per cent), and transport and storage (41 per cent). The survey also showed that larger firms were more aware of the scheme than smaller firms. Fifty-four per cent of establishments with more than 250 employees, as compared with 29 per cent of establishments employing 25 to 99 employees, knew about it.

In spite of efforts to retain an ageing workforce, it appears that there is a sharp drop in the employment rate for those 60 and above. The survey shows that while 97 per cent of the establishments surveyed hired mature Singapore citizens aged 40 to 49, the proportion employing workers in their 50s dropped to 89 per cent, and declined even further to 54 per cent for those who are older. A key reason for this appears to be related to the retirement age of 62. The survey went further to identify the reasons cited by these establishments for not hiring mature workers and retaining older ones. Their main reasons for not hiring mature workers were: high wage expectations (31.1 per cent); inability to meet the physical demands of the job (25.4 per cent); and lower receptivity to training and skills (13.4 per cent). The top three reasons given for not hiring older workers were: inability to meet the physical demands of the job (38.4 per cent); being less flexible and adaptable to change (18.9 per cent); and being less receptive to training and skills (16.9 per cent).

The survey also identified reasons why some workers were hired and re-employed despite their age. The three key reasons for workers aged 40 and above were: relevant skills and work experience; lower probability of job-hopping; and high competence. This suggests that, with increasing educational standards and retraining, mature and older workers can market themselves as skilled, stable and competent personnel with experience in order to be hired and retained (Ministry of Manpower, 2007).

Among older workers, there are differences by gender as well. The employment rate among older men is not only higher than that among women, but also above that of older men in developed countries other than Japan, South Korea and Sweden. However, the employment rate for older women in Singapore – which has increased in recent years – still lags behind that of many developed nations. It appears that female workers face twin barriers of age and gender to a far greater extent than men. However, the educational attainment and work experience of older female workers is also lower than that of male workers. This can be explained by the social roles assigned to men and women of their generation – women as homemakers and men as breadwinners. Education seems to be the key for women to find and continue employment. Among women aged 50 and above who had a university degree, nearly two-thirds were employed. However, among women aged 50 and above with below secondary education, only one-quarter were employed.

The increased emphasis in Singapore by government, employers and unions on enhancing skills and training among older workers is a step in the right direction. For women workers, these initiatives may make an even bigger difference. All these initiatives are even more urgent given the current economic crisis in which older workers may be more vulnerable to layoffs and find it harder to obtain work.

Moving forward

Issues and opportunities
Compared with many other developed nations, Singapore is at an early stage of the movement to manage workplace diversity. Besides the TAFEP, which tries to address discrimination issues at a non-legal level, no legislation has been enacted or is under way to protect individuals from being discriminated against. The public and academic discourse on workplace diversity in Singapore is also scarce. Public discourse on diversity at the societal level typically discusses diversity in terms of 'harmony' and 'equality'. However, such discourse usually refers to racial and religious diversity. At the workplace level, public discourse (influenced by TAFEP) revolves around the concept of 'fairness' and 'non-discrimination'. This differs from the typical terms (for example, 'diversity', 'discrimination') used in such discourse in the USA. Also, even though 'affirmative action' practices are being adopted in the area of housing, this cannot be observed when it comes to employment.

The above discussion presents merely a slice of the diversity issues that are of concern to Singapore, but we have selected four areas in which the treatment of diversity varies, in order to give the reader a better idea of the different ways in which diversity is managed here. Other groups that are gaining visibility in the public and academic discourse are foreign labour and ex-convicts. (A summary list of diversity types, relevant protective legislation and institutional support/NGOs can be found in Appendix 10.2.)

Foreign labour is divided into two main groups – foreign workers (low-skilled workers employed mainly in construction, manual work, cleaning and domestic work) and foreign talents (skilled labour employed mainly at the professional and managerial level; Yeoh, 2007). As at June 2008, only 65.6 per cent of the workforce were residents (Singapore citizens and permanent residents) while the rest were non-residents. There is no legal protection for these groups of employees either, but in 2001 the physical abuse that led to the death of an Indonesian domestic worker prompted the establishment of an *ad hoc* group – The Working Committee 2 (TWC2) – that sought to provide education, aid and support to foreign workers. This group was later formalized as an institution called Transient Workers Count Too (retaining the moniker of TWC2). Foreign talents generally possess more resources to relocate to Singapore and are generally respected. As such, there is no NGO that has been set up to advocate for their inclusion and their rights.

The reintegration of ex-convicts or ex-offenders into the workforce has been going on since 1945, when a work programme was introduced in Singaporean prisons. However, it was only in 1976 that a more active approach was taken by the government. Singapore Corporation Of Rehabilitative Enterprises (SCORE) was set up as a statutory board to oversee this. One of its initiatives, the Yellow Ribbon Project (which started in 2003), has seen great success nationwide. In a public perception survey conducted in 2007, 88 per cent of the respondents knew about the Yellow Ribbon Project. Fifty community partners had also offered to participate in the organizing of the Project for 2008.

Research implications

From what we have presented in this chapter, it is apparent that there is much room for workplace diversity and discrimination research. Lim et al. (2006) conducted a survey of businesses located in the Central Business District of Singapore in December 2005. They found that employees are not very aware of diversity management issues, with a mere 25.8 per cent of respondents indicating that their organization probably has diversity management policies. This could be a result of the lack of public or academic discourse on diversity management in Singapore at that time (note that TAFEP was only set up in 2006) or the different usage of diversity management terms in the American versus the Singaporean workplace. Further, since there is no non-discrimination legislation applied to the Singapore workplace, employers may not have enacted explicit policies addressing these issues, even though they may be carrying out fair employment practices.

Future research will do well to investigate the awareness and implementation of such practices in organizations, and perhaps include a follow-up study to see if awareness of diversity management policies has increased after the establishment of TAFEP. Studies should also be undertaken to measure the success of the diversity initiatives mentioned earlier in this chapter. Last but not least, it will be useful to monitor the perceptions of discrimination and the progress of the various 'protected' groups in the Singapore society at large and in the workplace.

With the different approaches Singapore is taking towards diversity management (e.g. government-led as with the reintegration of ex-offenders, government-initiated/tripartite model as with age, race, disability, religion, and public-initiated as with women, sexual minorities), it will be interesting to see which type of approach has the greatest positive impact on the inclusion of the various groups into the Singaporean workforce. Given the government's authority in Singapore, it would not be surprising if government-led initiatives were most successful. This will have implications for policy-makers as some groups might be left behind in this quest to manage diversity.

In general, the scarcity of diversity management research in Singapore provides an opportunity for scholars to contribute. As the country progresses and develops a comprehensive palette of workplace diversity initiatives, scholars should be encouraged to study these issues and to make recommendations for practice.

Overall, Singapore appears to be paying more attention in recent years to diversity issues in the workplace and broadening its scope to include different demographic characteristics. However, whether these measures are successful depends on how the various agencies and organizations monitor and measure success. While there are more types of diversity that need to be covered under the umbrella of initiatives that currently exist under TAFEP, such as ex-convicts, gays and lesbians, those with mental health issues and so on, it may be wise (as the government is doing) to take things one step at a time. Looking forward, it remains to be seen if the tripartite model will be a suitable one for

Summary table for Singapore

Existence of anti-discrimination legislation	Article 12(2) of the Singapore Constitution
Criteria covered by anti-discrimination legislation	Race, religion, descent, place of birth
Criteria for which the reporting of quantitative data and their communication to a public administration are compulsory	Foreign employees vs local employees
Criteria covered by 'affirmative' or 'positive' action legislation other than unemployment- or income-based	None. However, 'affirmative action' policies can be seen in terms of allocation of housing to people of different races
Existence of a discourse or debate about 'non-discrimination' or 'equality'	Yes
Existence of a discourse or debate about 'diversity'	Yes
Year or period when the 'discrimination' concept started to disseminate in management literature in the country	2003–2004
Year or period when the diversity concept started to disseminate in management literature in the country	2003–2004
Who promoted the 'diversity' agenda?	The government
Existence of a professional association representing diversity professionals and year of creation	No
Existence of a professional association representing diversity scholars and year of creation	No

managing diversity. If so, other countries may benefit from the implementation of a similar model.

Notes

1. This information is taken directly from the Tripartite Centre for Fair Employment website.
2. The 'business-case approach' is an approach in which parties campaigning for diversity and non-discrimination highlight the benefits of diversity management in terms of how it can be beneficial to the company. Employers have also been quoted on the TCFE website saying that adopting such practices will 'help small and medium sized enterprises attract good employees and remain competitive', and 'to attract and retain the best talents'.
3. 2005 data on these other countries.

References

AWARE, http://www.aware.org.sg, accessed 21 March 2009.
Channel NewsAsia (2007), 'Half of Singaporean youths think premarital sex is okay: survey', http://www.channelnewsasia.com/stories/singaporelocalnews/view/253054/1/.html, 17 January.
Community Engagement Programme Portal, http://www.singaporeunited.sg/cep/, accessed 5 May 2009.
Council for Third Age, http://www.c3a.org.sg/, accessed 21 March 2009.
Department of Statistics (2008a), 'Key indicators', http://www.singstat.gov.sg/stats/keyind.html, accessed 25 March 2009.
Department of Statistics (2008b), 'Statistics on marriages and divorces', http://www.singstat.gov.sg/pubn/catalogue.html#demo, accessed 30 April 2009.

Detenber, B.H., M. Cenite, M.K.Y. Ku, C.P.L. Ong, H.Y. Tong and L.H. Yeow (2007), 'Singaporeans' attitudes toward lesbians and gay men and their tolerance of media portrayals of homosexuality', *International Journal of Public Opinion Research*, **19** (3), 367–79.

Disabled People's Association (Singapore), http://www.dpa.org.sg/, accessed 21 March 2009.

Foo, M.D., A. Lim and Y.R. Choi (2005), 'Factors affecting the hirability of gay men and lesbians', paper presented at The Academy of Management Meetings, Honolulu, Hawaii.

Goh, E.Y.L. (2008), 'Performing queer femininities at (and after) work: queer women's workplace subjectivities in Singapore', unpublished honours thesis.

Gonsiorek, J.C. and Weinrich, J.D. (1991), 'The definition and scope of sexual orientation', in J.C. Gonsiorek and J.D. Weinrich (eds), *Homosexuality: Research Implications for Public Policy*, Newbury Park, CA: Sage, pp. 1–12.

Heng, R.H.K. (2001), 'Tiptoe out of the closet: the before and after of the increasingly visible gay community in Singapore', *Journal of Homosexuality*, **40** (3/4), 81–97.

H.O.M.E., http://www.home.org.sg/home/index.html, accessed 18 January 2010.

Housing Development Board (2009), 'Ethnic group eligibility of buyers', http://www.hdb.gov.sg/fi10/fi10201p.nsf/WPDis/Buying%20A%20Resale%20FlatEthnic%20Group%20Eligibility%20of%20Buyers?, updated 17 March.

Lai, A.E. (2009), 'A neighbourhood in Singapore: ordinary people's lives "downstairs"', Working Paper, Asia Research Institute, National University of Singapore, Singapore.

Lee, J., K. Campbell and A. Chia (1999), *The Three Paradoxes: Working Women in Singapore*, Singapore: AWARE.

Lim, A., M.D. Foo and Y.R. Choi (2006), 'Factors affecting coworkers' socialization with gay men and lesbians', paper presented at The Academy of Management Meetings, Atlanta, Georgia.

Lim, K.F. (2004), 'Where love dares (not) speak its name: the expression of homosexuality in Singapore', *Urban Studies*, **41** (9), 1759–88.

Lim, V.K.G. (2002), 'Gender differences and attitudes towards homosexuality', *Journal of Homosexuality*, **43** (1), 85–97.

Lo, J. and G. Huang (eds) (2003), *People Like Us: Sexual Minorities in Singapore*, Singapore: Select Publishing.

Low, W.P.L. (2002), 'Invisible diversity in the corporate world: the experiences of homosexuals in Singapore', unpublished honours thesis.

Ministry of Community Development and Sports (2001) 'Survey on social attitudes 2001', http://www.mcys.gov.sg/MCDSFiles/Resource/Materials/Attitudes_on_Family.pdf, accessed 29 April 2009.

Ministry of Community Development, Youth and Sports, http://www.mcys.gov.sg/.

Ministry of Education (2009), 'National education', http://www.ne.edu.sg/, updated 27 March.

Ministry of Information, Communication and the Arts, http://www.sg/explore/symbols.htm.

Ministry of Manpower, Singapore (2007), 'Paper No. 4/2007: firms' adoption of age-positive human resource practices', http://www.mom.gov.sg/publish/etc/medialib/mom-library/mrsd/ec.Par.33741.File.tmp/mrsd_AgePositiveHRPractices.pdf, accessed 24 March 2009.

National Heritage Board Education and Outreach Division (n.d.), 'National symbols', http://www.nhb.gov.sg/PE/resources/national_symbols/index.html, accessed 30 April 2009.

National Library Board, 'Singapore Infopaedia', http://infopedia.nl.sg/index.html, accessed 29 April 2009.

Ng, Eng Hen (2007), 'Speech by Dr Ng Eng Hen, Minister for Manpower and Second Minister for Defence at the launch of the Tripartite Centre for Fair Employment on 20 November 2007, 3:00pm', http://www.fairemployment.sg/index.aspx?id=58, accessed 20 April 2009.

National Trades Union Congress, 'Advantage! scheme', http://www.ntuc.org.sg/advantage/, accessed 25 March 2009.

Ng, Y.-S. (2006), *SQ21: Singapore Queers in the 21st Century*, Singapore: Oogachaga.

Ooi, G.L. (2006), 'The benefits of cultural tolerance: multi-ethnicity in Singapore', in J. Lidstone (ed.), *Cultural Issues of Our Time*, Cambridge: Cambridge University Press, pp. 168–77.

People Like Us, http://www.plu.sg, accessed 21 March 2009.

Singapore Business Federation (n.d.), 'Tripartite Advisory on the Re-employment of Older Workers', http://www.sbf.org.sg/download/docs/eventsvc/hrir/tripartite_advisoryolderworkers.pdf, accessed 25 March 2009.

Singapore Corporation Of Rehabilitative Enterprises, http://www.score.gov.sg/, accessed 21 March 2009.

Singapore Statutes Online, http://statutes.agc.gov.sg/, accessed 20 March 2009.

Tan, Chris K.K. (2009), 'Turning the Lion City pink: interrogating Singapore's gay Civil Servant statement', in E. Lewin and W.L. Leap (eds), *Out in Public: Reinventing Lesbian/Gay Anthropology in a Globalizing World*, Malden, MA: Blackwell, pp. 317–37.

The Straits Times (2003), 'Government more open to hiring gays now', 4 July.

Transient Workers Count Too, http://www.twc2.org.sg/site/, accessed 21 March 2009.

Tripartite Centre for Fair Employment, www.fairemployment.sg, accessed 17 September 2008.
Tripartite Centre for Fair Employment (2007), 'Speech by Dr Ng Eng Hen, Minister for Manpower and Second Minister for Defence at the launch of the Tripartite Centre for Fair Employment on 20 November 2007, 3:00pm', http://www.fairemployment.sg/index.aspx?id=58, accessed 29 April 2009.
Tripartism Singapore, www.tripartism.sg, accessed 30 April 2009.
Workforce Development Agency, 'Act now before the Re-employment Act starts in 2012 – be an early adopter with ADVANTAGE!', http://app2.wda.gov.sg/web/Contents/Contents.aspx?ContID=370, accessed 7 May 2009.
Yellow Ribbon Project, www.yellowribbon.org.sg, accessed 30 April 2009.
Yeoh, Brenda S.A. (2007), 'Migration and social diversity in Singapore', in T.H. Tan (ed.), *Singapore Perspectives 2007: A New Singapore*, Singapore: World Scientific Publishing.

Appendix 10.1   Employers' Pledge of Fair Employment Practices

Our shared vision is for Singapore to be one of the best places in the world to work; a place where every worker is given an equal opportunity for employment, rewarded according to his or her merit, treated fairly and with respect, and given the opportunity to optimize his or her unique talents; a place where businesses are able to attract, develop and retain valued employees, and create a harmonious and inclusive work environment, where employees are highly motivated and contribute to their fullest to their organizations and the economy.

With a view to achieving this vision, the Tripartite partners – the Singapore National Employers Federation/Singapore Business Federation, the National Trades Union Congress and the Ministry of Manpower – have unanimously endorsed the 5 key principles of fair employment practices for implementation:

- Recruit and select employees on the basis of merit (such as skills, experience or ability to perform the job), and regardless of age, race, gender, religion, family status or disability.
- Treat employees fairly and with respect and implement progressive human resource management systems.
- Provide employees with equal opportunity to be considered for training and development based on their strengths and needs, to help them achieve their full potential.
- Reward employees fairly based on their ability, performance, contribution and experience.
- Abide by labour laws and adopt Tripartite Guidelines which promote fair employment practices.

Shares the 5 key principles of fair employment practices and is committed to adopting these principles in the management of our human resources. We believe that the effective implementation of fair employment practices will bring about a more harmonious and progressive work environment within our organization, and contribute towards making Singapore a great place to work.

Source: Tripartite Centre for Fair Employment website.

Appendix 10.2

Table 10A.1   Summary of diversity type and legal/sociopolitical support

Diversity type	Key legislation/ code	TAFEP coverage	Key NGOs/political institutions
Race	Article 12(2) of the Singapore Constitution	Yes	National Steering Committee on Racial and Religious Harmony Mission: To be the national forum for apex ethnic and religious groups to dialogue and build trust across racial and religious groups in Singapore.
Religion	Article 12(2) of the Singapore Constitution; Declaration of Religious Harmony	Yes	
Language	–	–	–
Gender	–	Yes	Association of Women for Action and Research (AWARE) Mission: To identify areas for improvement in gender equality, encourage positive change, and support women in realizing their highest potential.
Sexual orientation /gender identity	–	–	People Like Us (PLU) Mission: We believe that everyone in Singapore should have a full and equal place in our society regardless of sexual orientation or gender identity, and to this end, we shall work for more informed understanding, the removal of barriers and a fuller integration of sexual minorities with the larger community.
Age	Retirement Age Act	Yes	Council for Third Age Mission: The Council helps people to form social networks through activities, so that the networks become the basis of mutual support towards achieving a better quality of life in all six dimensions of Wellness (social, intellectual, physical, vocational, emotional and spiritual).
Ex-offenders	–	Yes	Singapore Corporation Of Rehabilitative Enterprises (SCORE) Mission: To rehabilitate and reintegrate offenders to become responsible and contributing members of society.
Family status	–	Yes	–
Disability	–	Yes	Disabled People's Association Mission: To be the voice of people with disabilities, helping them achieve full participation and equal status in the society through independent living.

Table 10A.1   (continued)

Diversity type	Key legislation/ code	TAFEP coverage	Key NGOs/political institutions
Foreign workers	–	–	Transient Workers Count Too Mission: To promote respect for domestic workers through education, and secure better treatment of domestic workers through legislation and other means. Humanitarian Organization for Migration Economics (H.O.M.E) Mission: 1. To develop research and education on the socio-economics of migration on Singapore and the countries of origin. 2. To provide social integration services for emigrants and immigrants. 3. To provide humanitarian assistance for the effects of 'crisis' migration.
Foreign talent	–	–	–

Note: Mission statements are taken from the websites and published documents of the respective organizations.

11 Employment equity and diversity management in South Africa

Lize A.E. Booysen and Stella M. Nkomo

1. Introduction

In this chapter we begin with a brief overview of South African early history and cultures, the colonalization and the forming of a republic, the apartheid regime and the birth of its democracy. This is followed by a review of the legislation geared towards workplace equality and transformation in South Africa. The outcome of workplace equality legislative measures and the difference between employment equity (EE) and diversity management in the South African context will then be discussed, followed by the current debates surrounding cultural diversity in the workplace. This is followed by an overview of EE and diversity management research and practices in South African organizations, and the conclusion.

1.1 Early history of South Africa and its cultures

Booysen and van Wyk (2007, pp. 434–9) give a detailed overview of the early history of South Africa and its cultures, divided into the following three main eras.

1.1.1 Early history up to 1652
The Khoikhoi and San (Khoisan) inhabited the south and western areas of South Africa. Indigenous Bantu-speaking groups (Nguni and Sotho) were also present in most parts of Southern Africa. In 1488, Bartholomew Dias sailed around the southern tip of Africa, and named the Cape the 'Cape of Good Hope', other Portuguese explorers followed. Contact between the European seafarers and the Khoisan were mostly of a peaceful, commercial nature.

1.1.2 The period 1652–1948 – from colony to republic
The Dutch East India Company established a refreshment station at the Cape of Good Hope in 1652 under the command of Jan van Riebeeck, with strict instructions to preserve peace with the Khoisan. However, sporadic clashes occurred between the Khoisan and the Dutch. The Dutch were not permitted to enslave the local Khoisan; consequently slaves primarily came from present-day Java, Bali, Timor, Malaysia, Madagascar, China and parts of India to cultivate the land. In the early years of the colony, many white men married female slaves and the indigenous people. Such marriages were later regarded as socially undesirable.

From 1660 onwards, a new breed of Dutch settlers emerged, namely the 'Trekboers', who can be called the first white Africans. They caused the official area of the colony to expand, reaching the Great Fish River by 1778. In 1688, French Huguenot, poor, unemployed and landless refugees arrived in the Cape to further swell the ranks of the whites.

From 1771 onward, the Trekboers encountered the Xhosa. The first of eight 'frontier wars' between the colonialists and the Xhosa broke out in 1781. As a result of political events in Europe, the British colonized the Cape in 1795 until 1802; thereafter there was a brief return to Dutch rule, and then the British reoccupied the Cape in 1806. In 1854, representative government was granted to the Cape colony and in 1854, to the Boer Republic of the Orange Free State. In 1860, the Zuid Afrikaansche Republiek was established, and gold and diamonds were discovered. This mineral wealth caused the British government to invade the Republic. After failed negotiations, war was declared on 11 October 1899. Eventually, on 31 May 1902, a peace treaty was signed at Pretoria, bringing an end to the Anglo-Boer War.

On 31 May 1910, the Cape and Natal colonies united to form the Union of South Africa. The Act of Union excluded blacks, who then formed the forerunner of the ANC (African National Congress), the South African Native National Congress (SANNC), in 1912. In 1913, the notorious Natives' Land Act was passed by the Union government, which in time meant that blacks, the majority group, were entitled to a meager 13 per cent of the total land mass of South Africa.

1.1.3   The period 1948–94   The National Party (NP) won the election in 1948 on promises to preserve white power and particularly Afrikaner power. The NP instituted a battery of legislation to enforce segregation. In total an estimated 3.5 million black people were uprooted in the name of apartheid and resettled in 'homelands'. Oppressive laws and their brutal enforcement kept whites dominant over blacks. A racial hierarchy was entrenched, with whites at the apex followed by Asians, coloureds and blacks at the very bottom. Socioeconomic status and access to resources were commensurate with one's race. After having left the commonwealth, in 1961 South Africa became a republic, and the ANC adopted the strategy of the armed struggle. By the late 1980s, it became clear that although the overthrow of the government was not possible, neither was a decisive victory over the liberation forces. Booysen and van Wyk (2007, p. 439) identify two events that provided an opportunity to break this stalemate: first, the events in Eastern Europe removed the perceived threat that communism posed; and second, after having suffered a stroke, P.W. Botha, a staunch apartheid regime state president, was replaced by F.W. de Klerk as leader of the government in 1989.

De Klerk's announcement in parliament on 2 February 1990, lifting the ban on the ANC and the SACP, and of Nelson Mandela's release from prison, opened up the way for negotiating a new democratic constitutional dispensation in South Africa.

1.2   The birth of a new democracy
On 27 April 1994, after the first democratic elections in South Africa, formal political power moved from the National Party (NP), who had been in power for almost 50 years, towards the African National Congress (ANC), and Nelson Mandela became South Africa's first black state president.[1] He served a crucial and vibrant four years, then Thabo Mbeki became president for almost two terms. As a consequence of political and leadership struggles within the ANC, Mbeki was asked to resign in the last year of his second term. Kgalema Motlantle became the third black president in August 2008, and Jacob Zuma, a populist candidate, became the fourth black president of South Africa in April 2009.

South Africa has for the past 15 years been stable politically, with a steadily growing economy, and an example for peaceful transformation to the rest of the world. 'The

South African experience of regime change moved from being an archetypal illustration of conflict generation to the favourite case study of those involved in the emerging discipline of conflict resolution' (Stone and Rizova, 2007, p. 536).

Since this notable shift from a minority apartheid government to a democratically elected majority government, considerable and substantial changes have taken place in every sphere of South Africa's society at large, and especially in its workplaces.

2.   Cultural diversity in South Africa

From this brief introduction it can be seen that South Africa (SA) has a unique history of two powerful, antagonistic colonial rulers, the Dutch and the English, operating concurrently, followed by the apartheid governments of independent SA that systemically oppressed the native black population. The history of SA is in large part one of increasing racial divisiveness.

Apartheid was based on a system of legislated racial categorization and separation dividing the population into whites, which include Afrikaners and the English, and Africans, Asians, and coloureds (Littrell and Nkomo, 2005; Thomas and Bendixen, 2000). It furthermore maintained the system of inclusion and privileging whites as a group, and excluded not only the indigenous African people but also other groups who were classified as non-white, for example Asians.

Littrell and Nkomo (2005) show that this separation governed every sphere of life, from education to employment, and resulted in legislating discriminatory practices by minority whites towards the black majority. Non-white males were relegated to unskilled, menial jobs, while white males occupied skilled, professional and managerial positions. This historical racial division was accompanied by patriarchy, with women of all races subordinate to males. Women of all races were primarily expected to be homemakers and were legally classified as 'minors'. However, when they did work, black, coloured and Asian women worked primarily in domestic and unskilled factory jobs, while white women were employed in administrative and female occupations (e.g. nurses, teachers). The impact of this unique cultural history can be expected to produce unique behaviours and tensions in the workplace.

According to the latest 2008 census, the South African population is estimated at 48.7 million (Statistics South Africa, 2009). There are 52 per cent females and 48 per cent males, and South Africa has 31 different cultures. African blacks comprise about 79.2 per cent of the population and represent different ethnic groups, including Zulu, Xhosa, Ndebele, Pedi, Sotho and Swazi, as well as recent immigrants from other parts of Africa (particularly Zimbabwe and Nigeria). Whites comprise 9.2 per cent of the descendants of Dutch, French and British settlers who began arriving at the Cape from the late seventeenth century, immigrants from Europe who arrived in South Africa in the twentieth century, and Portuguese who left the former Portuguese colonies of southern Africa (Angola and Mozambique) after their independence in the mid-1970s. Coloureds, who represent 9 per cent, are 'mixed-race' people descended primarily from the earliest settlers, their slaves, and the indigenous peoples. The remaining 2.6 per cent are categorized as 'Indian/Asian', including the descendants of Indian indentured sugar-estate workers and traders who came to South Africa in the mid-nineteenth century (particularly around Natal), as well as a small Chinese population of approximately 100 000 people.

South Africa has relatively high rates of emigration (the majority of whom are white).

The estimated HIV prevalence rate is approximately 11 per cent; the HIV-positive population is estimated at approximately 5.35 million. South Africa ranked 183 out of 191 countries, with one of the lowest average life expectancy figures of 42 years (Swaub, 2008).

To cater for South Africa's diverse peoples, the Constitution (SA Constitution, 1996) provides for 11 official languages, which co-vary with the different ethnic groups in South Africa. According to the 2001 census, isiZulu is the mother tongue of 23.8 per cent of the population, followed by isiXhosa (17.6 per cent), Afrikaans (13.3 per cent), Sepedi (9.4 per cent), English and Setswana (8.2 per cent each), Sesotho (7.9 per cent), Xitsonga (4.4 per cent), siSwati (2.7 per cent) and Tshivenda (2.3 per cent). The least spoken official indigenous language in South Africa is isiNdebele, which is spoken by 1.6 per cent of the population. Recognizing the historically diminished use in formal settings and status of the indigenous languages (other than English and Afrikaans), the Constitution expects government to implement positive measures to elevate the status and advance the use of these languages. English is the unofficial official language of choice for business.

South Africa has eight religions and 25 denominations. Almost 80 per cent of South Africa's population follow the Christian faith. Other major religious groups are the Hindus, Muslims and Jews. Approximately 7 million of South Africa's population do not belong to any of the major religions, but regard themselves as traditionalists or of no specific religious affiliation. Freedom of worship is guaranteed by the South African Constitution (Act No. 108 of 1996) and the official policy is one of non-interference in religious practices. According to the Constitution, no discrimination is allowed based on difference; apart from the above this also include age, sexual orientation and disability.

As can be seen from the above, South Africa is a complex and diverse society, with many available different identities embedded in its societal fabric. Yet research shows that the most salient social identity groups in South Africa are race, gender, ethnicity and language (Booysen, 2007; Litrell and Nkomo, 2005; Booysen and Nkomo, 2007; Bornman, 1999; Cilliers and Smith, 2006; Cilliers and May, 2002; Ngambi, 2002). South African people are still classified by population group. However, now, unlike in the past, membership of a racial group is based on self-perception and self-classification, not on a legal definition.[2]

3. Review of the South African workplace equality legislative landscape

While statutorily based racial discrimination has systematically been abolished in South Africa since 1980, a number of significant law reform efforts have been initiated over the last 15 years (Horwitz et al., 2005).

After the democratic elections in April 1994, the new (ANC) Minister of Labour announced a five-year plan to revamp the industrial relations system in South Africa, and the following pieces of legislation were instituted:

- Labour Relations Act, 1995
- Constitution of South Africa (1996)
- Basic Conditions of Employment Act, 1997
- Employment Equity (EE) Act, 1998
- Skills Development Act, 1998
- Skills Development Levies Act, 1999

- Black Economic Empowerment (BEE) Act, 2003
  - – BEE Industry Charters, 2004
  - – BEE Draft Code of Practice, 2004
  - – BEE Codes, 2007

All this legislation is geared towards achieving greater social justice and equality, to redress past unfair discrimination, and to achieve proportional representation reflective of the national demographics.

3.1 Labour Relations Act (Act 66 of 1995)

On 11 November 1996 a new Labour Relations Act (Act 66 of 1995) came into force. This Act extended its ambit to cover almost all workers (including those employed in the public sector, farm and domestic workers). The goals of the Labour Relations Act (1995), are the following:

- to treat all people fairly as embodied in the South African Constitution;
- to regulate the organizational rights of trade unions;
- to promote and facilitate collective bargaining at the workplace and at sectoral level;
- to regulate the right to strike and the recourse to lockout in conformity with the SA Constitution;
- to promote employee participation in decision-making through the establishment of workplace forums;
- to provide simple procedures for the resolution of labour disputes through statutory conciliation, mediation and arbitration (for which purpose the Commission for Conciliation, Mediation and Arbitration (CCMA) is established), and through independent alternative dispute resolution services accredited for that purpose;
- to establish the Labour Court and Labour Appeal Court as superior courts, with exclusive jurisdiction to decide matters arising from the Act;
- to provide for a simplified procedure for the registration of trade unions and employers' organizations, and to provide for their regulation to ensure democratic practices and proper financial control;
- to give effect to the public international law obligations of the Republic relating to labour relations;
- to amend and repeal certain laws relating to labour relations; and
- to provide for incidental matters.

This Act has also led to the creation of the National Economic, Development and Labour Council ('NEDLAC'), in which the state, labour and capital negotiate national policies and jointly draft economic and labour legislative proposals for consideration by parliament. This act formally institutionalized social corporatism in the country.

3.2 Constitution of South Africa (1996)

South Africa's Constitution is one of the most progressive in the world, and enjoys high acclaim internationally. The Constitution is the cornerstone of democracy in South Africa. It enshrines the rights of all people in the country and affirms the democratic values of human dignity, equality and freedom. No discrimination is allowed on race, gender, ability, language, education, sexual orientation or any other difference. The Constitution is applicable to all SA citizens and all SA public and workplaces.

3.3   Basic Conditions of Employment Act (1997)

The goal of this Act is to give effect to the right to fair labour practices referred to in section 23(1) of the Constitution by establishing and making provision for the regulation of basic conditions of employment, such as employment contract (e.g. working hours and leave). The Basic Conditions of Employment Act is applicable to all SA workplaces, and an extension of the Labour Relations Act, 1995.

3.4   Employment Equity (EE) Act, 1998

The goal of the Employment Equity Act is to achieve employment equity by:

- promoting equal opportunity and fair treatment in employment through the elimination of unfair discrimination; and
- implementing affirmative action to redress the disadvantages in employment experienced by designated groups, in order to ensure their equitable representation in all occupational categories and levels in the workplace, through Employment equity policy (including psychometric testing, performance appraisal and affirmative action policies); Diversity management policy; Black empowerment policy.

The four designated groups are: African black, coloured, Indian, persons with disabilities and women.

The twofold purpose of the EEA 55 of 1998 is not only equitable representation or getting the numbers right, but also fair treatment in employment and the elimination of unfair discrimination. Therefore organizations should also focus on fairness perceptions and the principles of organizational justice, as highlighted in the following sections.

The main implications of complying with the legal requirements of the EEA 55 of 1998 for organizations, and specifically for designated employers, are to consult with employees, conduct a workplace analysis, prepare an employment equity plan (including affirmative action quotas), and report to the Department of Labour (DoL) and Commission for Employment Equity (CEE), through annual reports, on the progress made in implementing the employment equity plan. The EE plan needs to show how organizations intend to recruit people from the disadvantaged groups, through special measures, such as targeted searches, incentives and higher salaries for scarce skills and training and development.

The Commission for Employment Equity (CEE) is a statutory body established in terms of section 3 of the EE Act to advise the Minister of Labour, and to submit an annual report to the Minister on the implementation of EE. Reports should be given on the appointment, promotion, training and development and retention of all levels of employees in the organization per level, and per race and gender groups.

- Reports are publicly available on the DoL and the CEE websites;
- Reports are publicly available, and blaming and shaming is done with regard to non-compliance.

The EE Act is applicable to the following employer groups:

- All SA workplaces that employ 50 or more employees; but not members of the National Defence Force, National Intelligence Agency, and the SA secret service.
- Large employers with 150 or more employees must report on an annual basis to the Department of Labour (DoL).
- Small employers with fewer than 150 employees are required to report every two years to the DoL.
- Small employers with fewer than 50 employees, but with a turnover exceeding limits set for each major industry, are also required to report every two years to the DoL.

3.5   Skills Development Act (1998) and Skills Development Levies Act (1999)

Due to previous disadvantage, there is a lack of skilled people in the designated groups, and this Act is geared to developing, training and fast-tracking the designated groups. (See also the discussion on skills shortage in Section 6.2.)

The goals of the above Acts are, *inter alia*:

- To develop the skills of the South African workforce in order to improve productivity in the workplace and the competitiveness of employers.
- To increase the levels of investment in education and training in the labour market, and increase the return on investment.
- To use the workplace as an active learning environment to provide opportunities for new entrants to the labour market to gain work experience.
- To improve employment prospects of persons previously disadvantaged by unfair discrimination and to redress those disadvantages through training and education.

The Skills Development Act (1998) and Skills Development Levies Act (1999) are applicable to all SA workplaces that employ 50 and more employees.

Today South Africa has one of the most progressive labour law dispensations in the world, although there is concern that this is at the cost of an unacceptable level of unemployment and a worsening of the economy's inability to create new jobs, attract foreign investment and compete internationally.

In summary, then, the Labour Relations Act (Act 66 of 1995) covers almost all workers (including those employed in the public sector, farm and domestic workers). It provides job security for employees participating in a legal strike and awards organizational rights to trade unions. Through the structures of the CCMA, labour disputes are speedily resolved and the rights of workers under the new labour law are protected and ensured.

The Basic Conditions of Employment Act extends the basic floor of worker rights; and the Employment Equity Act provides for the prohibition of unfair discrimination and the compulsory introduction of affirmative action measures. The Skills Development Act of 1998 and the Skills Development Levies Act of 1999 shift the focus away from affirmative action alone to recruitment, succession and planning. It also addresses the skills gap in the disadvantaged groups through development and training (Helepi, 2000; Rautenbach, 2005; Swanepoel et al., 2003).

The above pieces of legislation were followed by the establishment of the Broad-Based Black Economic Empowerment (BBBEE) Commission in 1999, and the subsequent strategies and policies set by government and industry alike to increase black ownership of businesses and accelerate black representation in management.

3.6   Black Economic Empowerment Act (2003) (BEE), Broad Based Black Economic Empowerment (BBBEE), Industry Charters (2004), BBBEE Codes (2007)

The goal of BBBEE is to increase black ownership of businesses and accelerate black representation in management. It is applicable to all SA workplaces that employ 50 or more employees.

The Black Economic Empowerment Act was implemented in 2003 and the Black Economic Empowerment Industry Charters with proposed quotas by government for black ownership and management followed. In 2004, government sensed disparities and possible clashes between different industry charters (basic principles on BBBEE implementation in each industry) and published a draft Code of Practice aimed at providing specific guidelines to the various branches of industry on how to set up their BEE schemes (Bouche and Booysen, 2005; Mulholland, 2004; Rautenbach, 2005). During 2007 the draft BBBEE Codes of Good Practice became law, and now the BBBEE ratings (according to specific scorecard ratings) of organizations in SA are available in the public domain via the Department of Trade and Industry website (Wray et al., 2006).

South Africa's economic transformation or Reconstruction and Development Programme (RDP), and the Growth, Employment and Redistribution (GEAR) strategy, is part of the natural progression following the political transformation (Slabbert and De Villiers, 2003). RDP and GEAR are both aimed at systematic re-engineering of the South African political, social and economic landscape. A central objective of the RDP and GEAR is to de-racialize business ownership and control through focused policies of BBBEE. According to the BBBEE strategy document (Department of Trade and Industry, 2003a, p. 15), BBBEE is defined as 'an integrated and coherent socio-economic process, that directly contributes to the economic transformation of South Africa, and brings about significant increases in the number of black people that manage, own and control the country's economy, as well as significant decreases in income inequalities.' And naturally its also aimed to empower black people through mass creation of employment, and upward mobility in management and executive levels, through employment equity legislation.

Bouche and Booysen (2005) indicate that the first wave of BBBEE deals has for the most part come and gone. These deals could also not have been classified as BBBEE deals, but just BEE, since they did not empower a broad base of blacks on ownership, representation or stakeholder level across industries and organization size, but they focused very narrowly on ownership and big-corporation level. These deals have predominantly been completed by large corporations using speculative structures since legislation did not specify how these deals should be structured. Many of these initial BEE deals added no value to the market or organizations as a result of the Johannesburg Stock Exchange collapse of 1998 (Department of Trade and Industry, 2003a, p. 5). However, given the political, economic and social pressure placed on corporations by government, not to mention government's preferential procurement legislation and policies (Preferential Procurement Policy Framework Act, 2001), corporations have taken the lead in reviving BBBEE equity deals. Yet very few individuals from the designated groups are identified as viable partners in big corporate BBBEE deals. Deals also have predominantly involved only a privileged few black individuals with strong political influence, and at an ownership rather than a management or other stakeholder level, so that it has come to be seen as enrichment of a selected few as opposed to broad-based empowerment (Rautenbach, 2005; Terreblanche, 2003).

In spite of the general apathy regarding broad-based empowerment up to now, Bouche and Booysen (2005) and Wray (2004) point out that a new wave of broad-based empowerment deals has started. These deals are focused on empowering small and medium enterprises (SMEs), and on big corporate deals on management and other stakeholder representation. Since there is less capital and risk involved in deals at this level, and more pressure from clients, there is little doubt that the SME sector and other-than-ownership BBBEE deals alone will be the engine for future economic growth in South Africa (Kemp, 2003; Khanyile, 2004).

4. The outcome of workplace equality legislative measures

The aim of the above legislation is, *inter alia*, to redress the wrongs of apartheid, to transform the workplace and the economic landscape to be reflective of the demography of South Africa, and specifically to increase the numbers of previously disadvantaged individuals, namely blacks, women and the disabled, in the workplace and in business. This section will explore the effectiveness of the current battery of legislation in affecting these changes.

4.1 The economic landscape

A *Finance Week* study on the progress of BBBEE, published April 2005, showed that with regard to the direct and indirect shareholding and control on the Johannesburg Stock Exchange (JSE), SA whites effectively own and control a little more than 50 per cent of the JSE, compared to the 98 per cent they controlled in 1994 (Rautenbach, 2005). A 2008 study on ownership on the JSE indicates that JSE companies have transferred less than 25 per cent equity to BEE partners, that a majority of firms appear to support the social objectives of BEE, that external partners appear to best promote shareholder wealth, and that the primary source of funding for BEE equity transactions is third-party funding or the respondent companies themselves (Sartorius and Botha, 2008).

A survey carried out by Unisa's Bureau of Marketing Research (Rowen, 2000) showed a steep increase in the income level of African blacks and Indians, and a steady increase in the income of coloureds during the late 1990s. Yet, despite BBBEE and the government's declared intentions, inequality has increased since 1994. According to Rautenbach (2005) and Alexander (2006), inequality has also increased significantly within the black community, due to the development of a strong black middle class, as well as the so-called black elite. This economic shift is sadly, but perhaps realistically, class-related.

Although whites as a minority group have retained on a relative basis greater economic power (buying power and quantity) than other groups in South Africa, there are numerous corporate and government initiatives aimed at redressing the economic status of blacks. Blacks are gaining economic power with already visible positive movements towards parity as a result of legislation. With BBBEE gaining even more momentum in 2007 with the legislated Codes of Good Practice, the shift in economic power from whites to blacks will gain even further momentum. Booysen (2007, p.10) argues that 'even though the above indicates that blacks as a group have now much more economic power than historically, it is by no means an indication that blacks are approaching economic parity with whites yet, and the road towards economic equality is still a long and steep one'.

4.2   The workplace changes

Thomas (2002, 2004) and Horwitz et al (2005), Booysen and Nkomo (2007), and Selby and Sutherland (2006) all point out that only limited progress has been made in achieving employment equity since legislation was enacted in 1996. Booysen (2007) shows that, in 1994, management power resided almost exclusively with white males. White males held more than 80 per cent of management positions (Central Statistical Service, 1995a, 1995b). It seems as if now things are not much different. In its latest annual report the Commission for Employment Equity reports on the period April 2007–March 2008, and provides telling evidence on the (in)effectiveness of the workplace transformation legislation (Department of Labour, Annual Report – Commission for Employment Equity, 2008).

Table 11.1 provides a breakdown of the total number of employees in the categories top management, senior management, and professionals and middle management. Note that there are small percentages of foreigners in these occupation groups who are not reflected in this table and therefore the percentages do not add to 100.

From Table 11.1 it is evident that whites and males, and specifically white males, still dominate top management, senior management and professional and middle management positions. The top management level comprises in descending order 58.4 per cent white males, 12.9 per cent African black males, 9.8 per cent white females, 5.9 per cent African females, 5.0 per cent Indian males, 2.9 per cent coloured males, 1.1 per cent Indian females and 0.9 per cent coloured females.

The senior management level comprises in descending order 50.0 per cent white males, 15.2 per cent white females, 12.6 per cent African black males, 5.8 per cent Indian males, 5.5 per cent African black females, 4.3 per cent coloured males, 2.4 per cent Indian females and 1.8 per cent coloured females.

The professional and middle management level comprises in descending order 38.7 per

Table 11.1   Total number of employees in management level by race and gender

Occupational levels	Male				Female			
	African (%)	Coloured (%)	Indian (%)	White (%)	African (%)	Coloured (%)	Indian (%)	White (%)
Top management	12.9	2.9	5.0	58.4	5.9	1.0	1.1	9.8
Senior management	12.6	4.3	5.8	50.0	5.5	1.8	2.4	15.2
Professions and middle management	15.5	5.3	5.6	38.7	8.6	3.2	3.1	18.5

Source: Adapted from Department of Labour (2008, p.7).

cent white males, 18.5 per cent white females, 15.5 per cent African black males, 8.6 per cent African females, 5.6 per cent Indian males, 5.3 per cent coloured males, 3.2 per cent coloured females and 3.1 per cent Indian females.

From the above it is clear that the white group, particularly white males, still dominates management positions (54 per cent) proportionally (white males comprise approximately 4.5 per cent of the total population) and absolutely. White females (14.5 per cent, approximately 4.7 per cent of the total population) is the second-largest group, followed by African (13.7 per cent, approximately 39 per cent of total population), Indian (5.4 per cent, approximately 1.2 per cent of the total population) and coloured (4.1 per cent, approximately 4.3 per cent of the total population) males. Last in the row is coloured (2 per cent) females, and Indian (2.6 per cent). African black women (6.7 per cent, approximately 41 per cent of the total population) are the most underrepresented on all levels of management. There are 73.8 per cent males in management positions compared to 25.8 per cent females.

The 2008 Commission for EE Report (Department of Labour, 2008) tracks the progress in the implementation of the Employment Equity Act in top and senior management levels, from 2003 to 2007. It appears that momentum is building, as demonstrated by the 5 per cent increase of employment of blacks and a decrease of 7.8 per cent for whites in general as well as a 3.2 per cent increase for females in top and senior management positions, and a decrease of 5.9 per cent for males. As expected, the largest change was the 8.5 per cent decrease that has taken place for white males, since they are excluded from equal opportunity legislation. The previously disadvantaged group that showed the most progress is Africans, with a 3.9 per cent increase, with African males in second place with a 2 per cent increase followed by African females with a 1.9 per cent increase. The groups that showed the least increase are coloured males and females; both showed 0.1 per cent decrease. Both white females and Indian males showed an increase of 0.6 per cent, and Indian females 0.7 per cent.

What is disconcerting, though, is that at the professional and middle management level of employment, for the period from 2003 to 2007 there is a drop in the representation of blacks of 8.7 per cent, with Africans showing a decrease of 14.9 per cent, while there is a 7.7 per cent increase in white representation. There is also a decrease of females (3.0 per cent), with African females decreasing by 9.1 per cent and Indian females by 10.8 per cent, while white women increased by 3.6 per cent. African males decreased by 5.8 per cent, and white males showed the highest increase from all groups, by 4.4 per cent. This is worrisome in terms of employment equity progress, since the professional and middle management level is considered a 'feeder' to senior and top management positions. If this drop continues, it will not be possible to fill these positions with African males and females. Furthermore, the benefits have to a large extent not accrued to black females, who continue to be poorly represented in top management with a growth of only 2.2 per cent; and in senior management with a growth of only 1.5 per cent, coupled with the decrease of 9.1 per cent at the professional and middle management level of employment in 2003 to 2007 (Department of Labour, Annual Report – Commission for Employment Equity 2006, pp. 55–8; 2008, pp. 42–6).

4.3   Race and gender disparity in management
South Africa's unique political and social history raises the possibility of distinct differences in perceptions of managerial stereotypes across race *and* gender. As in most other

countries, there is an underrepresentation of women in management and a bias towards male management practices (Eagly and Carli, 2007; Marthur-Helm, 2004; Littrell and Nkomo, 2005; Booysen and Nkomo, 2006). In South Africa there is, however, also a bias towards western or Anglo-Saxon management practices and not Afro-centric practices (Booysen, 2001).

Historical racial hierarchies embedded in the system of apartheid created distinctive social locations, which structured gender and racial experiences in the workplace differently (Booysen, 2007; Erwee, 1994). The previous apartheid system simultaneously established a race and gender hierarchy. For example, while white women acquired some privileges due to their race, they were for the most part relegated to the home sphere or typically female jobs in the workplace (e.g. secretary, nurse etc.). African women, on the other hand, were largely confined to domestic work. The best and highest-paid jobs in the economy were designated for white men. Management positions were exclusively reserved for white men. Black men were primarily employed in unskilled jobs (Booysen, 2007). Despite a majority of the economically active population (74 per cent) being black South Africans, the current occupational representation of race and gender groups in the labour force largely reflects the pattern that existed during apartheid. Specifically, white males still dominate top, senior and middle management positions as well as professional jobs, followed by white females, black males and black females (Department of Labour, 2008). Black, Indian and coloured women are the most underrepresented groups on all levels of management. This pattern is consistent for senior management, middle-management and professional levels (Department of Labour, 2008). Generally, the position of women in the workplace does not reflect the government's commitment to gender equity as embodied in the South African Constitution. Women's representation in government has made steady progress since the ANC came into power and has increased in 2009, to 45 per cent, putting South Africa third in the international women in parliament rankings, behind Rwanda and Sweden. This puts the country firmly on course to achieve the Southern African Development Community (SADC) target of 50 per cent women in political decision-making by 2015 (Mbola, 2009).

4.4 The disabled and other marginalized groups

According to the Constitution of South Africa, workplaces are not allowed to discriminate against the disabled. In fact no discrimination is allowed based on any difference, and race, gender, religion, age, sexual orientation and disability are specifically listed. The employment equity legislation also included disability together with race and gender as specific categories on which organizations need to report. Yet little progress has been made in integrating disabled workers. Currently there are only 0.7 per cent disabled people in top management, 0.7 per cent in senior management and 9 per cent in middle management and professional levels. The is no significant difference in the race distribution of the disabled in the workforce.

The overall conclusion on the outcomes of workplace equality legislative measures in South Africa is thus that there are signs of progress. The progress is still at a snail's pace and far from the proportional representation expected for race. Women, and especially black women, are still largely underrepresented.

In the next section possible reasons for this slow progress of the workplace equality legislation will be discussed.

4.5   Possible reasons for the slow progress of workplace equality legislation
Most South African companies have all the necessary policies and formal procedures for good employee relations and practice, equity, equality, fairness, inclusion and non-discrimination in place. However, these policies have not yet been internalized, and are there mainly because of legislative compliance and not necessarily because of internal organization drivers. Therefore there is a hiatus or a lack of sufficient alignment between the formal policies and the implementation of the policies that affects the retention of blacks, and especially black women (Booysen, 2007; Department of Labour, Annual Report – Commission for EE, 2006; Horwitz et al., 2005; Ngambi, 2002; Selby and Sutherland, 2006; Thomas, 2004).

South African research (Bennet, 2001; Department of Labour, 2002, 2003, 2006, 2007, 2008; Sadler and Erasmus, 2003; Selby and Sutherland, 2006; Temkin, 2003; Thomas, 2002, 2004; Booysen, 2007) identify the following reasons for lack of progress in EE implementation and retention of previously disadvantaged groups:

- Slow EE progress at management level and inconsistent progress across departments in organizations
- Low commitment to EE from top management, with lip service by leadership about the need for EE
- Ineffective consultation and lack of shared understanding and communication about EE progress and implementation
- A lack of cultural sensitivity where new recruits are expected to assimilate into the current organizational culture
- A lack of cultural awareness programmes and of an organizational culture that values diversity
- A white male dominant organizational culture that continues to exclude black recruits (formally or informally through exclusionary network practices)
- Black people are perceived as tokens and not fully integrated into companies because of little delegation of real responsibility or decision-making authority, owing to persistent stereotypes
- Black staff are not systematically developed and trained – no effective talent management
- Lack of black mentors and role models or ineffective mentoring and coaching
- Lack of meaningful engagement of white males in the EE process in order to gain their commitment
- Failure to deal with white male fears and resistance to implementing EE legislation
- Insufficient focus, coordination and integration of existing implementation processes
- General lack of talent management, which includes training, development and growth opportunities, and career pathing and succession planning.

The above barriers all contribute to the gap between espoused EE policy and EE practices and progress. In conclusion it can be said that there is a general lack of progress and willingness on the part of corporate South Africa to embrace the transformation agenda. This leaves little room to introduce deregulation in the employment equity environment, and little or no sympathy for the outcry by organized business that the EE targets in the BBBEE Codes are too aggressive. South Africa still has a long way to go on its road to transformation and it seems that legislation alone is not enough; large-scale systemic change is needed.

5.   The relationship between workplace equality legislation and diversity management in the South African context

South African research (Booysen, 2007; Booysen and Nkomo, 2006; Horwitz et al., 2005; Selby and Sutherland, 2006; Thomas, 2002) and international research (Bartlett and Ghoshal, 2002; Kilian et al., 2005) show that while legislation is integral to address-ing unfair workplace discrimination, it is not enough. Organizational culture change also has to take place. Organizational transformation must be systemic; compliance with legislation is merely the beginning of the change process. EE implementation needs to be supported by coherent employment practice strategies focusing on human capital devel-opment, inclusive practices and organizational culture change.

In South Africa, as in the USA, much debate has taken place on the topics of diversity and related subjects such as affirmative action, understanding and valuing both differ-ences and diversity, as well as pluralism, multiculturalism and inclusion. Unfortunately, for several reasons, diversity is seen as akin to affirmative action and there is therefore a substantial amount of confusion (Van der Wal and Ramotsehoa, 2001; Booysen et al., 2002; Booysen, 2007).

5.1   Employment equity, affirmative action and diversity

Herholdt and Marx (1999) illustrate the evolution of affirmative action in South Africa very well in their affirmative action continuum. This framework suggests that organi-zations can implement a range of strategies along the affirmative action continuum to realize their employment equity objectives. Affirmative action varies from simple short-term reactive measures focusing on the removal of barriers to the creation of equal opportunities, to complex long-term proactive measures focusing on the development of disadvantaged groups and the harnessing of diversity.

Affirmative action and employment equity both refer to proactive policies that seek to redress work-related inequalities along racial, gender and disability lines. Diversity man-agement focuses on recognizing the uniqueness in everyone, valuing the contribution each can make, and creating an inclusive work environment where awareness of and respect for all cultures and genders are promoted. Jain et al. (2003, p. 2) maintain, however, that 'affirmative action and employment equity programmes are legislatively driven, whereas diversity management is strictly voluntary . . . and motivated by business objectives'.

The main purposes of affirmative action are to eradicate discriminatory practices, and to promote the skills and abilities of those who have suffered as a result of discriminatory practices, i.e. redress the imbalances of the past. This legislation is aimed at creating a diverse workforce that, at all levels, better reflects the society in which it operates. Once the diverse workforce is in place, organizations can start realizing the diverse interests of the workforce. Affirmative action is thus a process for creating diversity, and is the foundation on which diversity can build. Diversity management compels the organiza-tion and its culture to be renegotiated and reconceptualized from a perspective other than the dominant culture.

Table 11.2   The major differences between EE/AA and diversity

EE (employment equity)/AA (affirmative action)	Diversity
Government-initiated	Voluntary (company-driven)
Legally driven	Productivity- and business-case-driven
Quantitative – getting the numbers right	Qualitative – getting the organizational culture right
Problem-focused	Opportunity-focused
Assumes assimilation	Assumes integration
Internally focused	Internally and externally focused
Reactive – addressing historical discrimination	Proactive – addressing future inclusivity
Human-resources-focused	Human-capital and social-capital-focused
Can lead to stigmatism, tokenism and feelings of unfairness and polarization	Enhanced appreciation of cultural difference and inclusivity
Tools: EE plan, quotas and preferential treatment	Diversity vision and plan, training, development culture and systems change

Source: Adapted from Cascio (2003, p. 121).

The Employment Equity Act and the implementation of affirmative action are necessary steps and have their place in correcting the past imbalances and leading to diversification of the workforce in South Africa. There is need for diversity at all levels and in all categories of work before any useful efforts can be made to develop strategies for managing workforce diversity.

Even though there seem to be confusion in the minds of many, employment equity and affirmative action are distinctly different from valuing diversity, as shown in Table 11.2.

Both EE (Employment Equity Act in the case of South Africa) and AA are laws that are imposed on people and therefore have the potential to create an adversarial environment. Also, there is a belief that these two concepts mean that fewer qualified people should be given jobs, instead of more qualified, traditional employees. The insinuation is that we have to help the designated groups (protected classes of people) because they are not really qualified to succeed on their own merits. This only adds to the conflict and reinforces stereotypes, and disempowers the very same people it is meant to serve, especially if not accompanied by appropriate training and development to empower them to do the job. It thus leads to tokenism and perceptions of reverse discrimination.

Valuing diversity, on the other hand, says that people's differences are an asset rather than a burden to be tolerated. Similar to the USA experience, it is also found in SA organizations that affirmative action programmes and employment equity legislation have attempted to redress the imbalances of the past, but have not been successful on their own. Of more importance now is the management of diversity created by affirmative action and employment equity. Diversity is not simply a repackaging of equal employment opportunities and affirmative action. An organization that emphasizes quota filling as a major part of its diversity effort will undermine the true intent of valuing diversity. Instead, emphasis should be put on accelerated training and development of the previously disadvantaged groups to equip them with competences that will enable effective performance. There is a need to integrate EE and skills development planning to ensure that these support one another to facilitate workforce diversity management initiatives (Kossek et al., 2003; McCuiston et al., 2004).

Valuing diversity extends beyond EE and affirmative action; it builds the critical foundation laid by workplace equity initiatives, it creates an inclusive environment for all, and is viewed as a strategic imperative to the accomplishment of organizational goals – a business imperative. Changing laws is the easier part of moving towards valuing diversity in organizations; the hard part is changing the myriad everyday behaviours and assumptions that often unintentionally exclude, demean and limit the prospects of a culturally diverse workforce.

For diversity to succeed, it must form part of an institution's strategic management process, and must have the support of the highest-ranking official in an institution, and must be managed by highly qualified and skilled HR people or consultants (Thomas, 2002, 2004; Department of Labour, 2006, 2008; Selby and Sutherland, 2006; Booysen, 2007).

South African firms are on a daily basis busy with diversity management strategies, since they face the double challenge of recruiting and retaining competent previously disadvantaged employees and implementing training and development strategies while at the same time moving a step further forward by creating a uniquely South African working environment that truly values everyone's contribution, achieves business imperatives and is self-sustaining, through its achievement of organizational objectives (Horwitz et al., 2002; Horwitz et al., 2005; Sadler and Erasmus, 2003; Selby and Sutherland, 2006; Thomas, 2004).

6.   Diversity research and practices in South Africa

In contrast to the USA, which has seen over the past 30 years an evolution in the way organizations have managed diversity, in South Africa diversity management is a relatively new concept (Allard, 2002; Booysen, 2007). Before the democratic elections in 1994, diversity management and academic discourse on diversity were non-existent. However, that changed radically and in a matter of 15 years South Africa has seemingly successfully integrated its workforce and is seen as an example of best-practice diversity management. Diversity theory and practices in South Africa have, similar to those in the USA, moved away from the early discourses and practices of the melting-pot idea, where everyone becomes similar, automatically assimilated into the culture and part of the (dominant) homogeneous groups, to the acknowledgement of differences, with the institution of affirmative action and equal opportunity programmes, and an emphasis on differentiation. At present, the focus is on multiculturalism, which appreciates diversity while respecting the uniqueness of the individual, and is premised on integration. As in most other instances, diversity theory is way ahead of practice: while almost all organizations have EE and AA policies, few organizations have comprehensive diversity policies, and most initiatives seem to be limited to relatively simple hiring quotas or superficial training on peripheral diversity issues such as sexual harassment (Allard, 2002; Booysen and Ngambi, 2004).

Van der Wal and Ramotsehoa (2001) and Ocholla (2002) point out that even though best-practice diversity management is practised by some companies, most South African organizations are still stuck in the assimilation or differentiation modes, as described by Ely and Thomas (2001). These authors developed a theoretical paradigm of three

Table 11.3   Thomas and Ely's diversity paradigms as applied to South Africa

	Discrimination-fairness	Access-legitimacy	Learning-effectiveness
Focus	Creating equal opportunity, ensuring fair treatment, and compliance with state equal opportunity laws	Match internal employee demographics to customer and marketplace served	Incorporate diversity into the heart and fabric of the mission, work and culture of the organization
HR practices	Recruitment of women and Previously Disadvantaged Groups (PDGs). Mentoring and career development programmes for women and PDGs	Recruitment of diverse set of employee Key Selection Areas (KSAs) to match external demands. Rewards	Redesigned and transformed to enhance performance of all employees
Effectiveness measures	Recruitment numbers. Retention rates of women and PDGs	Niche markets captured. Degree of diversity among employees	All employees feel respected, valued and included. Committed employees
Weakness/ strengths	Does not capitalize on diversity of all employees. Emphasis on assimilation	Does not affect mainstream of company business; diversity confined to specific market segments	Inclusive organizations

Source: Adapted from Booysen and Ngambi (2004).

different perspectives on how organizations perceive the task of managing diversity. They classified the perspectives as discrimination and fairness, access and legitimacy, and learning and effectiveness. They assert that while most organizations in the USA have applied the first two perspectives, very few were using the third perspective. Ngambi's (2002) studies on diversity management in South Africa based on Thomas and Ely's (1996) paradigms found that it is the first paradigm, the discrimination–fairness perspective, that is prevalent in South African organizations. Table 11.3 shows the focus of diversity efforts, HR practices, effectiveness measures and strengths and weaknesses of each of the three paradigms as they relate to South Africa.

Both Ely and Thomas (2001) and Ngambi (2002) argue that it is only the third perspective (learning–effectiveness) that will enable organizations to benefit sufficiently from managing diversity. Ngambi's (2002) study clearly shows that in South Africa, with the legacy of apartheid still entrenched in the minds of leadership, management and the workers, most organizations are still 'trapped' in the discrimination-and-fairness perspective or what can be termed as 'righting the wrong', and still have a long way to go towards promoting the second paradigm of access–legitimacy, which centres on the 'business-case' argument, and the learning-effectiveness paradigm, which essentially promotes a valuing diversity paradigm and which would lead to organizations' adequately benefiting from workforce diversity. This finding is also corroborated by Selby and

Sutherland's (2006) and Kelly et al.'s (2007) studies on diversity management in South Africa. Selby and Sutherland (2006) maintain that while diversity management is seen as the ideal end-state of a transformed workplace, evidence suggests that most organizations are still focused on evolutionary strategies to create equal employment opportunities and, as such, maintain the *status quo*.

Booysen et al. (2007) concur with Ngambi's (2002) assessment of South African organizations' diversity management practices. These companies are far away from the 'learning and effectiveness' paradigm (Ely and Thomas, 2001), where transformation is measured by 'the degree to which new represented groups have the power to change the organisation and traditionally represented groups are willing to change'. Their study shows that diversity implementation is in some ways 'stuck' at the level of compliance, confirming other studies (Booysen and Ngambi, 2004) that find that very little seems to have changed in terms of diversity orientation.

In assessing the above differences and practices, it is important to bear in mind that South Africa is taking part in a concerted exercise to integrate the majority of people who were dispossessed during colonial rule and apartheid into the economic affluence of the minority. This is a very different scenario from that of the USA and Europe, where diversity has always been about integrating minorities into the majority cultures, and where a need has been experienced to 'justify' this integration.

It might be asked why South Africa needs to find a 'business case' for diversity when the moral one is so clearly evident. Booysen et al. (2007) suggested that the moral case is *not* clearly evident, as cultures of whiteness and power discourses of resistance actively continue to obscure enduring social and economic inequality, and legacies of apartheid (Steyn, 2005; Steyn and Foster, 2007), constructing EE intervention from government as 'political'. Government has identified organizations as important sites for social change.

> Thus SA's legislation straddles an uncomfortable divide between liberal capitalism and social interventionism, which often creates tensions in transformative exercises, the one pulling against the other. EE legislation is a powerful tool towards creating more equitable workplaces, if allowed to function as it should. It is evident from the case studies, however, that broader societal influences, such as discourses of whiteness which continue to pervade South Africa's discursive landscape, actively block this transformation. (Booysen et al., 2007, p. 8).

Even though South African research on diversity management is still in its infancy, there are a number of organizations such as SA Miller Breweries, Shell SA and First National Bank and others that do show progressive diversity management practices. The following best practices for achieving employment equity success are proposed by Booysen (2007), Selby and Sutherland (2006), Jain et al. (2003), Human et al. (1999) and Thomas (2002):

- active management commitment and accountability from senior, middle and line management, effective consultation and two-way communication between management and employees;
- effective employment practices that promote fair recruitment and selection procedures;
- continuous development through means such as parallel career-pathing and job rotation, and organizational culture that is inclusive of all;

- managing white male fears in order not to alienate or demotivate this valuable pool of talent;
- instituting a culture of valuing diversity that extends beyond just getting the numbers right.

In a review study of diversity management theory and practices in South Africa, Nkomo (2006) identified 16 best-practice strategies to create an organizational culture that values diversity:

- Create a superordinate social identity by establishing and evoking a compelling common organizational vision and set of values
- Adopt a human capital approach to human resources – where all employees are seen as valuable
- Link with and influence surrounding community
- Use strategy of cross-cutting categories and roles in work structures
- Develop programmes that promote appreciation of cultural differences and multiple realities
- Promote positive attitudes toward differences among ethnic groups
- Encourage cooperative intergroup contact
- Invest in training, development and succession planning that builds multifunctional, globally oriented employees
- Hold all managers accountable for valuing diversity
- Identify and address concerns and needs of previously disadvantage groups
- Involve representatives of all social identity groups in decision-making processes
- Challenge all stereotypes and assumptions about different groups
- Include 'everyone' in after-work engagements and company-sponsored events
- Recognize that differences in time consciousness may be due to real obstacles and not a sign of laziness
- Recognize that family and community responsibility may be a prime value of employees
- Be sensitive to religious holidays and use of religion in workplaces

Even though transformation in South Africa may present unique dynamics, its diversity industry has been heavily shaped by international trends (Nkomo and Stewart, 2006), and inextricably linked to EE and affirmative action. It was first argued by Roosevelt Thomas in the early 1990s that affirmative action should be reframed as affirming diversity. It was from this management focused idea that the 'business case' for diversity emerged – the idea that by affirming all our differences we bring out the best in each person, creating a more productive workforce (Nkomo and Stewart 2006; Kelly et al., 2007). Nkomo and Stewart (2006) argue that the business case emerged out of a need to make the politically overt practices of EE more palatable for white male management by stressing their 'economically viable' aspect, with only the fact of EE legislation drawing diversity in the direction of transformation. Clearly, it would be an error for South Africa to follow a similar pattern, since diversity management cannot be a substitute for employment equity given the continued large disparities in the access of blacks and other designated groups to the skilled, professional and managerial ranks in the workplace. The socioeconomic status of blacks in the broader society remains dire, with high levels of poverty, disease, illiteracy and lack of access to basic services such as water and electricity. It is important to recognize that the goal of employment equity and affirmative action in South Africa, unlike in the USA, is about empowering the majority black population after years of domination by a small white minority. Fundamentally, the transformation of South Africa is about social justice and normalizing an aberration where the majority black population was oppressed through a system of racial discrimination and force.

The next step for South Africa now is to move beyond just working towards the business case for diversity, towards the 'learning and effectiveness' paradigm of Ely and Thomas, where the learning that 'others' bring to the organization is internalized and changes the way the organization does business. Kelly et al. (2007) argue that this paradigm resonates with the principles of radical humanism, where people are motivated, *inter alia*, by a sense of self and community. Kelly et al. (2007, p. 18) conclude their argument by pointing out that questions diversity practitioners and management with a transformation portfolio in South Africa need to be asking themselves are:

> To what extent are 'transformation' activities driven by notions of transformation that are not transformational at all, and to what extent can this explain some of the difficulties organisations experience in relation to retaining black staff, continuing discrimination etc? Further to this, management must interrogate where the consultants they employ locate their definitions of diversity and the implications of that. For practitioners and management the challenge is finding a definition that embraces both 'the business case' and a social transformation agenda that is suitable for the South African context. This may mean redefining 'the business case', and 'the bottom line'.

6.   Current debates and issues surrounding cultural diversity

6.1   Faultlines on the effectiveness of AA

Currently there is much debate and tension around the actual effectiveness of affirmative action and employment equity in South Africa. Ironically, different groups seem to agree that it is not effective, but for very different reasons. The Black Management Forum, which is a non-government organization focusing on the transformation of South Africa, has called for more a punitive approach to addressing non-compliant organizations. They have also suggested that white women be excluded from the category of previously disadvantaged because they have made significant gains into management and professional positions relative to black men and black women. For blacks in general, progress seems rather slow 15 years after the end of apartheid. This is largely due to the high expectations of rapid access to better jobs, especially in corporate South Africa. In some cases, there is the perception that some designated appointments have been made at the expense of ensuring the right fit. Negative stereotyping of black appointees, tokenism and backlash against AA appointees are often commonplace. On the other hand, some whites and white advocacy organizations like Solidarity (a right-wing union) argue that AA and EE in South Africa have led to 'reverse discrimination' and loss of opportunities for whites. They see this as a contradiction to South Africa's goal to be a non-racial state. While there have been few studies to actually measure effectiveness, research shows there is a general focus on numbers versus true transformation. This is partly due to resistant organizational cultures, and management resistance, particularly white managers who often are the very ones with the responsibility to transform their organizations. As one white manager succinctly described the latter problem to one of the authors, 'It is like asking turkeys to vote for Christmas' (Booysen and Nkomo, 2006).

6.2   Skills shortage

On a national level, South Africa is experiencing a skills shortage, also referred to as skills gap, due to a limited pool of critical skills in designated groups, the historic exclusion of blacks from technical and professional jobs, inferior education of blacks, and 'brain drain' due to immigration from all demographic groups, predominantly whites. In 2005, an estimated 1.6 million white South Africans, was in Diaspora. This loss of scarce skills, e.g. those of engineers and medical doctors across all race groups due to better opportunities elsewhere, as well as to escape crime in South Africa, is a major challenge for organizations and the government (Mulholland and McKay, 2004; Theunissen, 2005; Statistics South Africa, 2009).

6.3   Xenophobia and integration of minorities

In their report on xenophobic violence, the Human Sciences Research Council (HSRC) indicated that South Africa's public culture had become increasingly xenophobic (Human Sciences Research Council, 2008, p. 18). The integration of foreigners, especially African migrants, into South African society and the workplace remains a challenge (Crush and Dodson, 2007). In 2008, South Africa experienced a horrific violent episode of xenophobia, in which 50 foreign African migrants were killed in urban informal settlements. Among the reasons found for this outbreak was the perceived threat these migrants posed to the livelihood of poor black South Africans, particularly competition for jobs and access to basic services (Human Sciences Research Council, 2008). At a different level, skilled professionals from other African countries often encounter problems in gaining work permits. Businesses in South Africa have voiced their unhappiness about this problem given the severe skills shortage in the country. Reporting on employment equity has been changed to clearly indicate the percentage of foreign blacks since there was a feeling that some companies were hiring them rather than black South Africans to fulfil employment equity goals.

6.4   Social identity changes in South Africa

Booysen (2007) maintains that as a result of radical societal power shifts in South Africa, primary identities and perceptions of inclusivity are shifting and new prototypes are evolving. These societal-level identity crises and conflicts are increasingly spilling over into the workplace (Booysen, 2007; Cilliers and May, 2002; Cilliers and Smit, 2006; Abram and Hogg, 2004; Haslam, 2001; Hogg and Terry, 2000; Tajfel and Turner, 1979). Booysen et al. (2007) argue that these social spillovers are most readily expressed through discourse which deeply informs organizational cultures that carry dominant ideologies, in particular masculinity and 'whiteness', articulated within social, historical and political contexts. Steyn and Foster (2007) explore how 'whiteness' continues to dominate public (and by extension organizational) discourse in South Africa. Their argument is that although there are a number of discursive positions open to white South Africans, including transformative positions, 'the central question for whiteness, as the orientation which takes its privilege as normal and appropriate, can be put simply: how to maintain its advantages in a situation in which black people have legally and legitimately achieved political power' (Steyn and Foster, 2007, p. 1).

According to Booysen et al. (2007), these ideological contestations are being articulated in the context of very particular and radical shifts in power and in-group/out-group dynamics. The most salient of these in South Africa today are the following:

- In terms of political power, the previously black subordinate group is becoming dominant and whites have lost their political dominance. However, blacks do not have the management power in the organizations due to the ineffectiveness of affirmative action and employment equity.
- For the group that had absolute power a little more than a decade ago, the white male, the perception is one of an increasing loss of future expectation and opportunity, resulting in a sense of disempowerment and great anxiety. The current reality, however, remains that most power is still held by the white male group. For instance, white males, who comprise approximately 4.3 per cent of the total South African population, held more than 80 per cent of management positions in 1994, and in 2007 they still held 51 per cent.
- White women do not gain the benefits of the push for gender equity in SA, but are still advantaged by race.
- The double disadvantage of black women in management, being black and women, should be turning into a double advantage due to employment equity legislation. Yet there is no real evidence that substantial changes towards equality for black women have taken place.
- Racial equity is tilted towards black males because the focus has been on closing racial divisions; gender equity in the workplace remains elusive.
- Coloured and Indian groups feel as if they are in the 'middle' and that there is a preoccupation with African blacks and whites.

Booysen (2007) argues that, at present, societal changes are still dictated by or bound within primarily racial categories, due to the polarization of South African society. The question remains as to how South Africans can un-think old categories of citizenship and redefine themselves as a nation, in order to move beyond racial categorization and their own political bondage. New social identities could conceivably be constructed, from categories coupled to professional identities, work identities, socioeconomic status or other new social identities rooted in some factor other than race.

7. Conclusion

Booysen et al. (2007) argue that South Africa's position with regard to transformation highlights the importance of bringing social identity into conversations about organizational transformation. South African societal transformation is a process of profound collective psychological work (Steyn, 2001) and requires reframing racial and gendered identities within a postcolonial context. It requires reflection on social processes of identification and on how organizations 'clone' (Essed, 2002) these identities. It appears that even 'good-practice' diversity interventions are not reaching the kind of depth and breadth needed to bring about this deep transformation, and that the task

Summary table for South Africa

Existence of anti-discrimination legislation	Yes
Criteria covered by anti-discrimination legislation	Race, gender, disability
Criteria for which the reporting of quantitative data and their communication to a public administration are compulsory	Report on race, gender and disability in terms of appointments, promotions, training and resignations, specified different employment levels, to the Commission for Employment Equity
Criteria covered by 'affirmative' or 'positive' action legislation other than unemployment- or income-based	Race, gender, disability
Existence of a discourse or debate about 'non-discrimination' or 'equality'	Yes, but really focuses on equity
Existence of a discourse or debate about 'diversity'	Yes
Year or period when the 'discrimination' concept started to disseminate in management literature in the country	Early 1980s
Year or period when the diversity concept started to disseminate in management literature in the country	Early 1990s
Who pushed the 'diversity' agenda?	Government
Existence of a professional association representing diversity professionals and year of creation	No
Existence of a professional association representing diversity scholars and year of creation	No

of finding 'what works' in such a context is far from concluded. Perhaps the positivist and instrumental approaches that dominate the literature on diversity management do not fit societies like South Africa, which need fundamentally to change their entire social and economic fabric to attain social justice for previously oppressed majorities while ensuring a new vision of inclusiveness for all. The summary table gives an overview of key issues of diversity management in South Africa.

Notes

1. According to the SA Constitution, people vote for a party during elections and then the head of the winning party normally becomes the president of the country.
2. It might be argued that the legal definition of the different race categories is still preserved by the employment equity legislation for purposes of positive and fair discrimination.

References

Abram, D. and Hogg, M.A. (2004), 'Metatheory: lessons from social identity research', *Personality and Social Psychology Review*, **8** (2), 98–106.
Alexander, M. (2006), 'Black economic empowerment', *South Africa.Info*, http://www.southafrica.info (accessed 16 May 2006).

Allard, M.J. (2002), 'Theoretical underpinnings of diversity', in C. Harvey and M.J. Allard (eds), *Understanding and Managing Diversity*, Englewood Cliffs, NJ: Prentice Hall, pp. 3–27.

Bartlett, C.A. and Ghoshal, S. (2002), 'Building competitive advantage through people', *MIT Sloan Management Review*, **43** (2), 34–41.

Bennet, J. (2001), 'Companies bleeding skilled blacks at a rapid rate', *Sunday Times*, 25 March.

Booysen, L. (2001), 'The duality in South African leadership: Afrocentric or Eurocentric?', *South African Journal of Labour Relations*, **25** (3 and 4), 36–64.

Booysen, L. (2007), 'Societal power shifts and changing social identities in South Africa: workplace implications', *Southern African Journal of Economic and Management Sciences*, **10** (1), 1–20.

Booysen, L. and Ngambi, H. (2004), 'Diversity management in South Africa', invited chapter for Catalyst Spectrum, Expert Contributions, http://www.catalystwomen.org.spectrum.

Booysen, L. and Nkomo, S.M. (2006), 'Think manager – think (fe)male: a South African perspective', *International Journal of Interdisciplinary Social Sciences*, **1** (2), 1833–82.

Booysen, L., Nkomo, S. and Beaty, D. (2002), 'Breaking through the numbers game: high impact diversity', *Management Today*, **18** (9), 22–4.

Booysen, Lize and Nkomo, Stella (2007), *Leadership Across Difference Report. The South African Scenario*, Centre for Creative Leadership in collaboration with the Graduate School for Business Leadership, Unisa, Midrand, January.

Booysen, Lize and Van Wyk, Marius (2007), 'Culture and leadership in South Africa', in J. Chhokar, F.C. Brodbeck and R. House (eds), *Global Leadership and Organizational Behavior Effectiveness (GLOBE Book 2)*, pp. 433–73, Culture and leadership across the world: The GLOBE Book of in-depth studies of 25 societies. Mahwah, NJ: Lawrence Erlbaum Associates.

Booysen, Lize, Kelly, Claire, Nkomo, Stella and Steyn, Melissa (2007), 'Rethinking the diversity paradigm: South African practices', *International Journal on Diversity in Organisations, Communities and Nations*, **7** (4), 1–10.

Bornman, E. (1999), 'Predictors of ethnic identification in a transitionary South Africa', *South African Journal of Psychology*, **29** (2), 62–72.

Bouche, J. and Booysen, L. (2005), 'Facing the unknown: introducing BEE into SMME's', *Management Today*, **21** (4), 46–7.

Cascio, W.F. (2003), *Managing Human Resources*, Boston, MA: Irwin.

Central Statistical Service (1995a), *October Household Survey 1994*, Pretoria: CSS.

Central Statistical Service (1995b), *Statistical Release PO317*, Pretoria: CSS.

Cilliers, F. and May, M. (2002), 'South African diversity dynamics: reporting on the 2000 Robben Island Diversity Experience, a group relations event', *South African Journal of Labour Relations*, **26** (3), 42–68.

Cilliers, F. and Smith, B. (2006), 'A systems psychodynamic interpretation to South African diversity dynamics: a comparative study', *South African Journal of Labour Relations*, **30** (2), 5–18.

Crush, J. and Dodson, B. (2007), 'Another lost decade: the failures of South Africa's post-apartheid migration policy', *Journal of Economic and Social Geography*, **98** (4), 436–54.

Department of Labour (2002), *Annual Report – Commission for Employment Equity 2001–2002*, Pretoria: Government Printer.

Department of Labour (2003), *Annual Report – Commission for Employment Equity 2002–2003*, Pretoria: Government Printer.

Department of Labour (2006), *Annual Report – Commission for Employment Equity 2005–2006*, Pretoria: Government Printer.

Department of Labour (2008), *Annual Report – Commission for Employment Equity 2007–2008*, Pretoria: Government Printer.

Department of Trade and Industry (2003a), *Broad-Based Black Economic Empowerment Act*, Pretoria: Government Printer.

Department of Trade and Industry (2003b), 'The Codes of Good Practice on Broad-Based Economic Empowerment', (draft), Pretoria: Government Printer.

Eagly, A.H. and Carli, L.L. (2007), *Through the Labyrinth: The Truth about how Women become Leaders*, Boston, MA: Harvard Business School Press.

Ely, R.J. and Thomas, D.A. (2001), 'Cultural diversity at work: the effects of diversity perspectives on work group processes and outcomes', *Administrative Science Quarterly*, **46**, 229–73.

Erwee, R. (1994), 'South African women: changing career patterns', in N.J. Adler and D.N. Izraeli (eds), *Competitive Frontiers*, Cambridge: Blackwell, pp. 325–42.

Essed, P. (2002), 'Cloning cultural homogeneity while talking diversity: old wine in new bottles in Dutch organizations', *Transforming Anthropology*, **11** (1), 2–12.

Haslam, S.A. (2001), *Psychology in Organisations: The Social Identity Approach*, London: Sage Publications.

Helepi, G. (2000), 'Moulding strategic affirmative training and development', *People Dynamics*, **18** (3), 34–6.

Herholdt, W. and Marx, M. (1999), *Employment Equity in South Africa: A Guide to Affirmative Action Success*, South Africa: Prentice Hall.

Hogg, M.A. and Terry, D.J. (2000), 'Social identity and self-categorization processes in organizational contexts', *Academy of Management Review*, **25** (1), 121–40.

Horwitz, F., Jain, H. and Mbabane, L. (2005), 'Trade union consultation by employers under Employment Equity legislation', *South African Journal of Labour Relations*, **29** (2–4), 4–32.

Horwitz, F.M., Browning, V. Jain, H. and Steenkamp, A.J. (2002), 'Human resource practices and discrimination in South Africa: overcoming the apartheid legacy', *International Journal of Human Resource Management*, **13** (7), 1105–18.

Human Sciences Research Council (2008), *Citizenship, Violence and Xenophia in South Africa: Perceptions from South African Communities*, Pretoria, June.

Human, L., Bluen, S. and Davies, R. (1999), *Baking a New Cake: How to Succeed at Employment Equity*, Randburg: Knowledge Resources.

Jain, H.C., Sloane, P.J. and Horwitz, F.M. (2003), *Employment Equity and Affirmative Action: An International Comparison*, New York: M.E. Sharpe.

Kelly, C., Wale, K., Soudien, C. and Steyn, M. (2007), 'Aligning the diversity "Rubik" cube: conceptualizing transformative practice', *Southern African Journal of Labour Relations*, **31** (2), 10–31.

Kemp, S. (2003), 'SME's needed: Mboweni', *Moneyweb*, retrieved 3 March 2004, from http://www.moneyweb.co.za.

Khanyile, T. (2004), 'Empowerment must bring clear value', *Business Day*, 16 September: 5.

Kilian, C.M., Hukai, D. and Mcarty, C.E. (2005), 'Building diversity in the pipleline to corporate leadership', *Journal of Management Development*, **24** (2), 155–68.

Kossek, E.E., Markel, K.S. and McHugh, P.P. (2003), 'Increasing diversity as an HRM change strategy', *Journal of Organizational Change Management*, **16** (3), 328–52.

Littrell, R.F. and Nkomo, S.M. (2005), 'Gender and race differences in leader behaviour preferences in South Africa', *Women in Management Review*, **20** (8), 562–80.

Mathur-Helm, B. (2004), 'Equal opportunity and affirmative action for South African women: a benefit or barrier?', *Women in Management Review*, **20** (1), 56–71.

Mbola, B. (2009), 'Women in Parliament on the rise, 6 May', www.southafrica.info (accessed 14 May 2009).

McCuiston, V.E., Wooldridge, B.R. and Pierce, C.K. (2004), 'Leading the diverse workforce: profit, prospects and progress', *The Leadership & Organization Development Journal*, **25** (1), 73–92.

Mulholland, S. (2004), 'Hijacking affirmative action – nothing sacred: openers', *Finance Week*, August, p. 17.

Mulholland, S. and McKay, D. (2004), 'Black mark, Mbeki: nothing sacred', *Finance Week*, May, p.15.

Ngambi, H.C. (2002), 'Exploring diversity perspective in South Africa and United States: different emphasis, different contexts', paper presented at a conference held at Göteborg, Sweden, 29–31 August.

Nkomo, S.M. (2006), 'Valuing diversity: best practices', unpublished MBA lecture 6, Graduate School of Business Leadership, University of South Africa, Johannesburg, August.

Nkomo, S.M. and Stewart, M. (2006), 'Diverse identities', in S. Clegg, W.R. Nord and S. Hardy (eds), *Handbook of Organization Studies*, 2nd edn, New York: Sage, pp. 520–40.

Ocholla, D.N. (2002), 'Diversity in the library and information workplace: a South African perspective', *Library Management*, **23** (1/2), 59–67.

Rautenbach, F. (2005), 'Indirect BEE Through the JSE. Is South Africa Making Progress?', *Finance Week Report*, April, pp. 1–37.

Rowen, P. (2000), 'Black income to out strip Whites', *Sunday Times*, 18 March.

Sadler, E. and Erasmus, B.T. (2003), 'Views of black trainee accountants in South Africa on matters related to a career as a chartered accountant', *Meditari Accountancy Research*, **11**, 129–49.

Sartorius, K. and Botha, G. (2008), 'Black economic empowerment ownership initiatives: a Johannesburg Stock Exchange perspective', *Development Southern Africa*, **25** (4), 437–53.

Selby, K and Sutherland, M. (2006), '"Space creation": a strategy for achieving employment equity at senior management level', *South African Journal of Labour Relations*, **30** (2), 36–64.

Slabbert, J.A. and De Villiers, A.S. (2003), 'The historical development of employee relations in South Africa', in J.A. Slabbert, B.J. Swanepoel, W. Backer and J.J. Prinsloo (eds), *Managing Employment Relations in South Africa*, Johannesburg: Juta, pp. 4-1–4-24.

South Africa (1995), *Labour Relations Act. No 66 of 1995*, Pretoria: Government Printer.

South Africa (1996), *Constitution of the Republic of South Africa*, Pretoria: Government Printer.

South Africa (1997), *Basic Conditions of Employment Act. No. 75 of 1997*, Pretoria: Government Printer.

South Africa (1998), *Employment Equity Act. No. 55 of 1998*, Pretoria: Government Printer.

South Africa (1998), *Skills Development Act. No. 97 of 1998*, Pretoria: Government Printer.

South Africa (1998), *Skills Development Levies Act. No. 9 of 1999*, Pretoria: Government Printer.

South Africa (2001), *Preferential Procurement Policy Framework Act*, Pretoria: Government Printer.

Statistics South Africa (2009), *Census 2008*, Pretoria: SSA.

Steyn, M. (2001), *Whiteness Just Isn't What It Used To Be: White Changing Identity in South Africa*, New York: State University of New York Press.

Steyn, M.E. (2005), 'White talk: the strategic management of diasporic whiteness', in A. Lopez (ed.), *Postcolonial Whiteness*, Albany, NY: State University of New York Press, pp. 119–36.

Steyn, M. and Foster, D. (2007), 'Repertoires for talking white: resistant whiteness in post apartheid South Africa', *Ethnic and Racial Studies*, **31** (1), 25–51.

Stone, J. and Rizova, P. (2007), 'Re-thinking racial conflict in an era of global terror', *Ethnic and Racial Studies*, **30** (4), 534–45.

Swanepoel, B., Erasmus, B., Van Wyk, M. and Schenck, H. (eds), (2003), *South African Human Resources Management: Theory And Practices*, 3rd rev. edn, Johannesburg: Juta.

Swaub, K. (2008), *The Global Competitiveness Report 2008–2010*, 2008 World Economic Forum, Lucern: Switzerland.

Tajfel, H. and Turner, J.C. (1979), 'An integrative theory of intergroup conflict', in W.G. Austin and S. Worchel (eds), *The Social Psychology of Intergroup Relations*, Monterey, CA: Brooks/Cole, pp. 33–47.

Temkin, S. (2003), 'Employment equity programmes taking root', *Business Times*, 14 July, p. 1.

Terreblanche, C. (2003), 'Elite empowerment must be stopped', *The Star*, 6 June, http://www.thestar.co.za (accessed 18 January 2005).

Theunissen, G. (2005), 'Exacerbating a shortfall – skills shortage: economic trends and analysis', *Finance Week*, March, pp. 48–9.

Thomas, A. (2002), 'Employment equity in South Africa: lessons from the global school', *International Journal of Manpower*, **23** (3), 237–55.

Thomas, A. (2004), 'Black economic empowerment: a study of South African companies', *Management Today*, May, pp. 35–8.

Thomas, A. and Bendixen, M. (2000), 'The management implications of ethnicity in South Africa', *Journal of International Business Studies*, **13** (3), 507–20.

Thomas, D.A. and Ely, R.J. (1996), 'Making differences matter: a new paradigm for managing diversity', *Harvard Business Review*, September–October, 79–90.

Van der Wal, R. and Ramotsehoa, M. (2001), 'A cultural diversity model for corporate South Africa', *Management Today*, **17** (6), 14–18.

Wray, Q. (2004), 'Empowerment apathy rules at SA Inc.', *Business Report*, March, p. 21.

Wray, Q., Sikhakane, J., Mokopanele, T. and Hamlyn, M. (2006), 'Cabinet approved BEE codes are already drawing criticism', *Business Report*, December, p. 2.

12 A possible brain drain: workplace diversity and equal treatment in Sweden

Viktorija Kalonaityte, Pushkala Prasad and Adiam Tedros

Introduction

Workplace diversity and equal treatment in the case of Sweden is an uneven and seemingly contradictory terrain. Sweden has been proclaimed to have the best migration integration framework within the European Union, based on data from 2006. The Migration Integration Policy Index, a research-based evaluation of the member countries' institutional and legal framework concerning migration integration, places Sweden as the exemplary case of best practice. Sweden is also the country with the best-educated taxi drivers. A recent report indicates that 44 per cent of taxi drivers in the third largest city in Sweden, Malmö, most of whom are foreign-born, have university education. Despite the high educational level, these taxi drivers have not yet been able to gain employment that reflects their academic vocation (Klapp et al., 2001). These two examples of Sweden's successes and failures in relation to the phenomenon of migration integration are very suggestive of the realities and particularities of workplace diversity in Sweden. In the most immediate sense, we would like to draw attention to the salience of the category of 'immigrant' and the term 'integration' as key concepts in the Swedish definition of diversity. We would also like to point to one major issue in relation to diversity in Sweden, namely the discrepancy between diversity policy and diversity in practice. Indeed, as for example Swedish researcher Birgitta Ornbrant (2007) pointed out, the Migration Integration Policy Index 2006 may give a fair description of Sweden's institutional framework, yet its actual results are less than flattering. Discrimination of the immigrant population does not seem to subside. Despite the fact that 30 per cent of the foreign citizens residing in Sweden have higher education, Sweden is particularly unsuccessful in employing foreign-born individuals with higher education – only 60 per cent of foreign-born residents of Sweden with higher education have job positions that reflect their educational level (Malmborg, 2006; OECD, 2008). In the light of these persistent employment problems for migrants with higher education, it is not surprising that the media repeatedly issues a 'brain drain' alert in the Swedish diversity debate (e.g. Malmborg, 2006).

With these broad characteristics of Sweden in mind, our aims with this chapter are to unravel the development and current state of equal treatment at work and workplace diversity in Sweden. Sweden, unlike many other countries, has appropriated the diversity management concept by merging it with the already existing immigrant integration framework, driven by the state. For an uninitiated reader it may seem strange that diversity management as a managerial concept receives so little attention in this chapter. The relative absence of diversity management is, however, a particularity of the Swedish context, where the diversity concept is very much a part of the state-driven public policies. Therefore the first section of this chapter is dedicated to discussion of the introduction and development of the term diversity, as a managerial discourse of diversity management and as an integrative term of migrant integration policy. We shall also discuss gender equality as one policy area where Sweden is considered to be successful, as well as the antidiscrimination and pro-equality initiatives that go beyond the category of gender. The purpose of the first section is to provide the reader with the Sweden-specific diversity terminology and the broader conceptual framework within which diversity needs to be viewed.

In the second section we move on to the review of the current research debates on the status and the challenges associated with workplace diversity and equality. The second section is therefore an overview of the existing research orientations concerning workplace diversity and equality in Sweden. In the third section we provide some empirically grounded examples from our own research on the current state of diversity management implementation in Sweden in order to illustrate the complexity of contextually grounded pro-diversity work.

Diversity and equal treatment in Sweden: legal and conceptual development
Sweden, not unlike many European countries, is in a process of building awareness and creating efforts to adequately transform its institutional framework in order to better represent its multicultural population. The development of pro-diversity and equal treatment practices in the Swedish context cannot be separated from the historical trajectory of increasing public and political awareness and efforts to create a pro-equality legislation. Furthermore, Sweden is characterized by a rather influential role of the public sector and public policy in relation to pro-equality work. Unlike many other countries, Sweden's political economy has a long history of state involvement and ownership, which has led to the development of an extensive social welfare and governmental subsidies system. Thus, although the past two decades of economic policies have led to increasing decentralization and privatization of state-owned monopolies and services, Sweden nevertheless remains quite distinct in terms of the state's responsibilities over its citizens' welfare.

Many diversity scholars, concerned with management research and organization studies, associate pro-diversity work with the introduction of the managerial business case for diversity in the 1980s in the North American context (e.g. Prasad and Mills, 1997). Since then, as Boxenbaum (2006) points out, diversity management has been appropriated in other national contexts, which have left their own contextual imprint of this management concept. Swedish appropriation of diversity management needs to be seen as a step and a development of the already ongoing national policy-making and institutionalized efforts to further equal treatment, migration management and gender equality.

The importation of diversity management into Sweden can be traced to a report, produced by a state–private sector intermediary organization, which described diversity management in the USA and made suggestions for how this framework could be used in the Swedish context (Fägerlind, 1999). The report focused on the profit and efficiency perspective of workplace diversity, and can be treated as relatively similar to diversity management philosophy in the USA. However, a significant factor in the Swedish case for diversity was changing migration management policy on the state level, a shift that has come to shape local understandings of diversity management. In the 1990s, the Swedish state reformulated its migration policies to shift the focus from migration policies to integration policies, explicitly stating that the migrant population of Sweden needed to be viewed and managed as diverse in terms of gender, educational level, time of stay in Sweden and age (Proposition 1997/98: 16). Interestingly, the state focus and involvement in pro-diversity work and the early insertion of the term diversity in the context of migration management have shaped diversity management initiatives in Sweden. State involvement and focus on ethnic diversity specifically remain two distinct characteristics of pro-diversity initiatives in Sweden.

Why then such a narrow focus on diversity as ethnic background and immigrant management? Sweden has a long history of gender equality work, and the arrival of the diversity concept in the mid-1990s could offer little to the already existing institutional framework of gender equality work. The successes of such work were, however, far greater than the attempts to establish equal treatment in the area of immigrant and refugee integration into the Swedish labour market. For example, Swedish anti-discrimination legislation in regard to ethnicity was passed in the 1990s, with consequent improvements, while gender equality legislation was already firmly in place. In consequence, gender equality and the diversity concept remain separate in the domain of public policy in Sweden.

Apart from the gender equality work in Sweden, which we review in detail in the section below, other social group identity categories such as sexual orientation have had their own trajectories of public policy and pro-equality lobby. Thus one could argue that Sweden has a history of focusing on separate groups and their rights rather than on civil rights or general non-discrimination. In consequence, immigrant background proved to be the greatest challenge for such a group-based public policy perspective, because immigrant population by definition consists of a variety of ethnic groups with different experiences of migration, different nationalities and different personal histories in Sweden. The difficulties of handling diversity within immigrant population are reflected in the lack of unanimous views on why immigrant integration has not succeeded despite the existing framework. Therefore, in the rest of this section we shall review the development of the gender equality framework, then continue with the development of the equality framework beyond gender and finally look at the specific implications of immigration policies and ethnicity in the Swedish context.

Gender equality
Sweden has come a long way in its efforts to achieve gender equality over the past 200 years. Early milestones in this process are the right to inheritance, given to women in Sweden in 1845 and the loss of men's right to strike their wives in 1864. These achievements were the beginning of a long list of rights that since then have been granted to women. The universal right to vote in national elections was introduced in 1919 in Sweden; however the first chance for women to exercise this right was in the national election of 1921; a total of five women were elected to parliament in that election. Since then a number of measures have been taken to ensure the equal rights of men and women, a number of these will be touched upon below.

The point of departure for the development of gender equality in the Swedish context was the limited rights for women, compared to men. Therefore the majority of such measures taken from that point onwards have sought to improve the situation for women. The efforts to grant opportunities for women continued with reforms such as access to all types of employment for women. In 1925 it was decided that women had equal access to employment as government officers as men, and in 1935 women were granted the same retirement benefits as men. Yet another advancement for women in the early part of the 1900s was that in 1939 women could no longer be discharged from employment due to marriage. The four first decades of the 1900s can thus be described as decades in which women sought to level the playing field, against heavy opposition, one should add, since the labour unions were at the same time fighting for higher wages for men so that they could afford a housewife. The women emerged victorious since a law from 1945 established that male and female government officials were entitled to equal pay. As the discussion above has shown, the women's movement played a big part in the reforms granting women equal rights. This was most visible in the 1960s and the 1970s, when a number of reforms were carried out to improve the situation for women. In 1965 Sweden became the first country in the world to have a law against rape in marriage. A slight difference compared with the reforms in the previous decades was that the aim of the latter reforms was not so much focused on achieving more rights for women but rather at alleviating some of the burdens on women. One example of this is the reform carried out in 1974 to allow shared parental leave, as opposed to the parental leave granted exclusively to women in 1931. Yet another measure in that direction was the establishment of a system of government-subsidized childcare for working parents. This was thought to serve the interests of children, as well as allowing parents to work or study. The reforms of the 1980s had to do with the labour market. A number of measures to stop the segregation on the labour market were taken and perhaps most important among these was the establishment of the Act on Equality between Men and Women at Work 1980. In January 2009 the Act was replaced by a new comprehensive law, the Discrimination Act; however, the law is of such magnitude in the discourse on equality in Sweden that a short background to the previous law is called for.

When the Act on Equality between Men and Women at Work was adopted in 1980, a government agency, the Office of the Equal Opportunities Act (Jämställdhetsombudsmannen) was established in order to ensure compliance with the Act. The Equal Opportunities Act from 1992 superseded the previous Act on Equality between Men and Women and while in existence it was amended a few times, the last time in 2001, but the main purpose of the Act was to promote equal rights for men and women, with a heavy focus on relations in the labour market. Besides prohibiting employers from discriminating against a person because of gender, the Act also required employers to take active steps to promote equality in the workplace. Another important aspect of the legal framework concerning gender equality is that transparency is built in as an important objective. The Official Statistics Act (2001:100), Article 14, states: 'Official statistics related to individuals should be disaggregated by sex, unless there are particular reasons for not doing so' (Statistics Sweden, 2006).

Despite the large gains when it comes to polices promoting equality, Sweden's reputation as a leading nation in this respect has been challenged on a number of issues. For instance, while the employment rate among women in Sweden is considerably higher than in most other European countries (80 per cent in 2005), the segregation within the labour market is still intact. Swedish women work in a more restricted sphere of the labour market than men do. Moreover, on average, women's monthly salaries are

92 per cent of men's monthly salaries when differences in the choice of profession and sector are taken into account (Statistics Sweden, 2006). Furthermore, due to the fact that women assume most of the responsibility for childcare, they work part time to a higher extent than men do. The representation of women in leading positions in the business sector is low in Sweden, as many as 95 per cent of all top executive positions in private firms are held by men (SOU 2007:108). While the business sector is marked by a low female presence, the opposite is true for the political arena, where Sweden distinguishes itself in the opposite direction. The representation of women in the Swedish parliament is highest in the world, next after Rwanda. As much as 47 per cent of the members of the Swedish parliament are women. Sweden, as opposed to Rwanda, does not practise an electoral quota system where women are guaranteed a number of seats in parliament. The high representation of women can in the Swedish case be explained by the fact that ever since 1994 the biggest party in the Sweden, the Social Democrats, started practising a system sometimes referred to as 'political party quotas'. This means that the parties adopt internal rules to include a certain percentage of women as candidates for office. This was later adopted by almost all the other parties, and in the last election, 2006, the two biggest parties (the Social Democrats and their counterparts, Sweden's conservative party Nya Moderaterna) had perfect representation. The left-wing Vänsterpartiet distinguished itself by having more women than men, 64 per cent of the parliament members are women. The representation of women is equally high in the executive branch. The current cabinet is equal: half of the appointed ministers are women.

The same trend can be observed on the local political scene, although the proportion of women is slightly lower than at the national level; because a number of local parties do not practise the system of political party quotas, the representation of women is still fairly high. Forty-two per cent of the councillors in the Swedish municipalities are women. The representation of women in the county councils and regions was even higher, at 48 per cent. The trend is thus that the national and regional/county councils demonstrate a far better degree of representativeness when it comes to gender than the municipalities. The almost equal representation of men and women in the local political arena as well as in the national arena is not, however, synonymous with equal power. Men still tend to hold higher positions and there is also a considerable amount of segregation concerning the specific political issues that women and men respectively work with. A study by Johanna Esseveld among politicians in the Swedish parliament confirmed that areas such as finance and defence are still male-dominated (Esseveld, 2005), while the female politicians are mostly assigned issues such as healthcare and other social issues. A recent study of the gender balance in the local councils revealed that the same kind of segregation was in place even there (Persson and Öhrwall, 2008). Table 12.1 demonstrates the number of men and women working with different policy areas at the local level.

To summarize, Sweden is a rather remarkable case of pro-gender equality efforts in an international comparison, both in terms of scope as well as in terms of progressive potential. For example, the Act Prohibiting the Purchase of Sexual Services from 1999, which makes the purchase of sexual services illegal only for the purchaser can be said to be an example of such progressive orientation. However, despite these gains, the goal that women and men should have the same opportunities, rights and responsibilities in all areas of life is far from accomplished.

Table 12.1   *Elected representatives in the local councils, 2007: distribution with regard to gender balance in different policy areas*

Policy area	Women (%)	Men (%)
Healthcare/social policies	58	42
Childcare/youth/education	50	50
Culture/leisure/tourism	45	55
Technology/environment/traffic	29	71
Miscellaneous	42	58

Source: Persson and Öhrwall (2008, p. 60).

Equal treatment beyond gender

A distinguishing feature of the measures in Sweden targeted towards achieving equality is that gender equality is separated from other kinds of equality. When referring to equality between men and women, the concept *Jämställdhet* is used, while *Jämlikhet* refers to equality on all other conceivable grounds. Both terms mean 'equality', yet have different connotations in the Swedish language. There is a slight difference in significance between the general concept of equality, meaning equal worth (*Jämlikhet*) and equality on the basis of gender (*Jämställdhet*), since the latter signifies 'to rank equally with' (Johansson, 1993: 18). The current laws on discrimination prohibit discrimination in four areas besides gender; these are ethnic origin, religion or other belief, sexual orientation or disability. While the use of a separate terminology for the various notions of equality might not *per se* be evidence of the privileged status of equality between men and women in Swedish politics (compared to equality on other grounds), it is however quite clear once the differences in the measures taken to promote the two different kinds of equality are taken into consideration. Gender equality, *Jämställdhet*, was given a far more privileged position in Swedish equality policies.

As previously mentioned, in January 2009 a new discrimination act was adopted in Sweden. The new Discrimination Act (Swedish Code of Statutes, 2008: 567) thus replaced the gender equity law and the other laws against various forms of discrimination with one single law, embracing all of these discrimination grounds. The laws that the new Discrimination Act replaced were: the Equal Opportunities Act, (Swedish Code of Statutes, 1991: 433); the Act on Measures against Discrimination in Working Life on Grounds of Ethnic Origin, Religion or Other Religious Faith (Swedish Code of Statutes, 1999: 130); the Prohibition of Discrimination in Working Life on Grounds of Disability Act (Swedish Code of Statutes, 1999: 132); the Prohibition of Discrimination in Working Life on Grounds of Sexual Orientation Act (Swedish Code of Statutes, 1999: 133); the Equal Treatment of Students at Universities Act (Swedish Code of Statutes, 2001: 1286); the Prohibition of Discrimination Act (Swedish Code of Statutes, 2003: 307); the Act Prohibiting Discriminatory and Other Degrading Treatment of Children and School Students (Swedish Code of Statutes, 2006: 67). Furthermore, the grounds for discrimination were extended to seven, adding age and transgender identity or expression to the previous five areas (gender, ethnic background, religion, disabilities and sexual orientation). The prohibition against discrimination in the new law applies to all areas of society, with the exception of age discrimination, which is covered only when it comes to education and employment.

At the same time that the new law came in force, a new agency, the Equality Ombudsman, was established to supervise compliance with the Act, which meant that the previous four ombudsmen agencies (the Equal Opportunities Ombudsman (gender), the Ombudsman against Ethnic Discrimination, the Disability Ombudsman and the Ombudsman against Discrimination because of Sexual Orientation) were replaced by one agency. The merging of the law and the introduction of one single agency, the Equality Ombudsman, was heavily resisted by the Ombudsman for Gender Equality. While the other four Ombudsman offices welcomed the merger, the Ombudsman for Gender Equality did not approve. This is not surprising given the vast differences among the different offices. Gender has had a privileged position in the discourse on equality in Sweden.

A first indication of the privileged position of gender-based equality was that an Ombudsman against Ethnic Discrimination (DO) was created in 1986, six years after the Ombudsman Against Gender Discrimination (established in 1980). The two other ombudsmen with the task of monitoring compliance with the existing laws against discrimination were established in the 1990s. Their area of responsibility, while in exist-ence, extended to: discrimination on the basis of disability (HO) and discrimination on the basis of sexual orientation (HomO). The ombudsman who used to be in charge of issues concerning discrimination on the grounds of disability (HO) came about through a UN charter and was established in 1994. HomO was the last ombudsman office that was introduced. It was established in 1999 and, despite its tardiness in comparison with the other Swedish ombudsman offices, it stands out in an international comparison since Sweden was the first country in the world to establish an office of that kind (DS, 2001: 01).

It should perhaps be mentioned that an ombudsman with the task of advocating the rights of children also exists (BO). The children's ombudsman (BO) was introduced in 1993; three years after the Swedish parliament ratified the UN Convention on the Rights of the Child, but it is not normally considered one of the ombudsmen against discrimina-tion, but rather an advocate for children's rights.

The common denominator of the previous anti-discrimination laws was that their primary function was to curb discrimination in the workforce, not least visible in the title of the previous laws, i.e. the Measures to Counteract Ethnic Discrimination *in Working Life* Act (1999:130), the Prohibition of Discrimination in *Working Life* of People with Disability Act (1999:132), and the Prohibition of Discrimination in *Working Life* because of Sexual Orientation Act (1999:133). The new law extends the scope by including more ground but also by extending the areas where the individual can claim legal discrimination. The heavy focus on the workforce has been extended to areas such as educational activities, labour market policy activities and employment, services not under public contract, starting or running a business, professional recognition, member-ship of certain organizations, goods, services and housing, meetings and public events, health and medical care, social services, social insurance, unemployment insurance, financial support for studies, national military service and civilian service and finally public employment.

The right to initiate legal proceedings by reference to the Discrimination Act is granted to individuals as well as to organizations that represent individual rights. For example, trade union organizations are entitled to institute proceedings in case of alleged discrimination in the Labour Court.

Yet another difference that has occurred with the establishment of the new Discrimination Act is that the concept of 'race', which was previously part of the definition of the 'ethnic origin' grounds of discrimination, has been removed. The issue has been debated for quite some time and the government finally decided on the exclusion of the term 'race'.

In summary, the Swedish development of the anti-discrimination legal framework beyond gender may be seen as relatively narrow, but the development suggests that Sweden is quite progressive when it comes to equality, e.g., on the basis of sexual orientation. Another development that is distinct in the case of Sweden is the integration of anti-discrimination laws and the anti-discrimination ombudsmen. One plausible explanation for this is the increasing awareness that discrimination grounds such as ethnicity and sexual orientation may be difficult to separate in the individual cases of discrimination. For that reason, the judicial praxis, driven by the Ombudsman, aims to be more integrative of the multifaceted identities of the discriminated individuals. Finally, it is important to keep in mind that the effects of the legal framework are highly dependent on the legal praxis, which makes it possible to try discrimination cases and implement equal treatment. In Sweden, the discrimination cases rarely reach the court due to the fact that the legal procedure must first be initiated and, it is hoped, resolved through the mediation of the Ombudsman. The central role of the state authority in the legal process has its advantages and disadvantages. The advantage is that the state authority such as the Ombudsman has the necessary resources to pursue all cases equally, thus relieving the individual of the possible legal costs. The disadvantage may be the fact that the mediation of the Ombudsman slows down the legal process and also cushions the offenders from high penalties, more likely to occur in case of civil trial.

The impact of integration policies on ethnic diversity
The laws regulating discrimination and the compliance with the Act can be said to be one set of rules that regulate diversity. Another way of managing diversity is by introducing laws that concern the rights and responsibilities of different groups in society; a common division is between the native population and the immigrant population. In Sweden a legal distinction is made between immigrants and Swedish ethnic minorities. In 1999 the Swedish ethnic minorities were officially recognized as national minorities and thus granted the right to speak their languages in official areas and receive services. The distinction is however only *de jure*, since Sweden has extensive service *de facto* even in the largest immigrant languages.

Sweden of today is a multicultural country of immigration. The modern era of immigration to Sweden can be divided into four phases, with each stage representing different types of immigrants and immigration. The first phase, late 1930s to late 1940s, consisted mainly of refugees from the war-torn neighbouring Nordic countries. The second phase was after the Second World War, and the immigrants were mainly labour migrations from Southern Europe and Finland, a period that lasted until the early 1970s, when the pattern of immigration altered somewhat and the large majority of those coming to Sweden were refugees from war-torn countries across the globe. Asylum seekers still

Table 12.2   Immigration flows by country of origin, 2007

Country	Number of immigrants
Swedish citizens (returning)	15 949
Iraq	15 200
Poland	7 525
Somalia	3 781
Germany	3 614
Romania	2 587
Thailand	2 548
China	2 386
Serbia	1 895

Source: Swedish Migration Board (2008).

make up a large percentage of those seeking refuge in Sweden. During 2007 a total of 99 485 persons migrated to Sweden, of whom approximately half (49 378) originated from non EU member states and/or Nordic countries. The ten largest immigrants groups in 2007 are accounted for in Table 12.2.

It is probably not far-fetched to argue that immigration policies in many ways have been before their time, in an international comparison, that is. The first legislation that regulated immigration was introduced in 1914. However, the first government agency set up to handle immigration, the Swedish Immigration Board, was set up in 1969, bringing together three separate fields of activity: (a) permit issues from what was then the Aliens Commission; (b) citizenship issues from the Ministry of Justice; and (c) assimilation issues from the Working Group for Immigrant Affairs at what was then the Ministry of the Interior. In other words, during the two first phases of immigration, up until the 1960s, Sweden had no official policy of incorporating migrants into mainstream society. A number of reasons can be given for that; however, the most probable one was that it was taken for granted that migrants from the neighbouring countries, who were deemed to be 'culturally similar', would assimilate. When the recruitment of foreign labour carried out by major industrial companies started increasing in the 1950s and onwards, the government cooperated closely with the Swedish trade union confederation. For instance, certain rules concerning the wage levels and access to unemployment benefits were laid down; foreign workers were to enjoy the same wage levels and rights as Swedes, including unemployment benefits. In accordance with many Western European countries, affected by the 1973 oil crisis, Sweden officially ended labour migration from non-Nordic countries in 1972 (Westin, 2000).

With the influx of migrants from other parts of the world, a unified policy was established in the mid-1970s. This was done after an Official Government Report (SOU 1974:69) recommended a new policy concerning the immigrants. A bill was presented to the parliament the following year, and this marked the initiation of a coherent Swedish policy concerning immigrants. The adopted policy had three overarching goals. The first goal was to achieve equality between Swedes and the migrant population. Secondly, the new policy wished to provide the immigrants with freedom of cultural choice, and thirdly, cooperation and solidarity between immigrants and Swedes was desired. The coherent immigrant and minorities' politics that has been conducted ever since the mid-1970s can be said to have a twofold purpose. On the one hand, facilitation for adjustment to the Swedish society has been sought, and on the other hand, efforts have been made to make it possible for the different groups to maintain and develop their native tongue and cultural heritage. The means to achieve this can be divided into two categories. The first category of measures has been of a general character. Through general measures, equality between native Swedes and immigrants has been sought. The general measures have included giving immigrants a legal position in society that differs as little as possible from that of the native population. Some of these measures are, for instance, that as early as 1974 foreign nationals who had resided in Sweden for more than three years were granted the right to vote in local elections. With Sweden's membership in the European Union in 1995, a division between migrants from EU countries, Iceland and Norway on the one hand and migrants from other countries has occurred since the former are granted voting rights in local elections without the waiting period of three years. Dual citizenship has been accepted only in recent years (from 1 July 2001).

The second type of means to achieve the goal has specifically targeted the immigrant groups (Lundh and Ohlsson, 1994: 125). One could label these measures of affirmative action, and the purpose has been to facilitate the integration of the immigrants in the new society and to assist them in preserving their native tongue. The mid-1970s was, besides the initiation of the coherent immigrant policies, also the point in time when the problem of ethnic segregation was identified (SOU 1975: 51). In 1985 an initiative was taken that aimed to distribute the responsibility for the refugees and asylum seekers to other municipalities than those already involved, which was mainly the metropolitan regions. One of the main reasons for this was that the metropolitan areas were becoming refugee-dense (Soininen, 1992). The immigrant density, together with a high number of highly deprived areas in the outskirts of the metropolitan region, brought about a number of initiatives targeted at the improvement of conditions in these areas. These measures culminated in a government bill in 1998, the Metropolitan Initiative, sometimes described as Sweden's first urban policy. The initiative, in accordance with other similar initiatives, could be described as one that focuses on the space-specific aspects of social inclusion since the government decided on special investments for 24 housing estates in Gothenburg, Stockholm and a further five municipalities in the metropolitan regions. In general, the focus in combating residential segregation has focused on combating socioeconomic segregation and class-related issues, and in Swedish policies to combat segregation this has had precedence over ethnicity (Tedros, 2008).

Concerning the Swedish integration policies, the most notable recent incident was the abolition in 2007 of two agencies dedicated to these issues: the Swedish Integration Board and the National Institute for Working Life. These bodies were very active in the funding and even production of data and research, and the closing down of the agencies has complicated data collection concerning these issues. Current Swedish integration policy states that special measures that focus on immigrants are only to take place for new immigrants who are in need of such measures, and that no other specific integration measures are necessary.

A study by OECD in 2008 pointed to a high degree of overqualification among immigrants compared to the native-born in countries in some of it member countries. There were two clusters of countries that stood out: countries with a high percentage of overqualified (Southern European countries, such as Italy, Greece and to a lesser extent Portugal and Spain, and two Northern countries, Norway and Sweden). The reasons for their divergence differed; while the situation for the immigrants in Southern Europe was attributed to the fact that immigration is a new phenomenon, the same could not be said for Sweden and Norway, with a long history of influx of relatively well-qualified refugees and a low degree of migrant workers (OECD, 2008).

In summary, as we stated in the opening section of the chapter, Sweden has a very advanced immigrant integration framework, and a considerable amount of social and economic resources are allocated to immigrant integration. However, the recent abolition of the two agencies dedicated to immigrant integration may be indicative of the changing policies in Sweden as a product of the current right-wing government. Also, the continuing problem in Sweden is the gap between the integration policies and the actual integration of immigrants. The labour market integration of immigrants as well as the residential integration suggests that immigrants continue to remain at a socio-economic disadvantage *vis-à-vis* the native Swedish population. More interestingly, the trajectory of the development of equal treatment policies in Sweden is quite different if we compare gender and ethnicity. The alleviation of gender inequality was early on focused on the increase of women's participation in various spheres in society, due to the recognition of the historical limitations of women's rights. There is no comparable recognition in relation to the immigrant population of Sweden, and it seems that the responsibilities of attaining socioeconomically viable positions in Swedish society remain up to the individuals with immigrant backgrounds. The political and public sectors have not attempted to create any type of quotas for immigrant integration in the public life of Sweden. The private sector is also interesting in this respect. The history of gender equality work in Sweden suggests that higher positions within private corporations are still male-dominated and very difficult to address despite the overall gender equality status in Sweden. In the light of such developments, immigrant integration in the Swedish labour market remains highly problematic for Swedish authorities and corporations, a topic that we address in the next section.

The researchers' response: the current debate on diversity, equality and integration in Sweden

Unlike the international trend, wherein diversity management and equal treatment in the workplace have become a prominent area for management research, Swedish research on equal treatment in the workplace remains concentrated in the areas outside management research. One plausible explanation for this development lies in the conflation of the diversity management concept, since its import into Sweden in the 1990s, with public integration policies. The Swedish translation of the diversity concept, the term *Mångfald*, is commonly associated with ethnic diversity and the public sector's attempts to work with ethnic diversity in various ways. Furthermore, the notion of diversity in the Swedish context is ambivalent in its connotation; it can mean the integration of immigrants through assimilatory practices, it can also mean work for increased ethnic diversity among the employees in a given organization (Kalonaityte, 2008). Thus, from the start, the notion of diversity in the Swedish context has been infused with associations to public policies, integration of immigrants and high degree of state involvement. This development was fuelled by the public sector's eager attempts to act as a good example in the late 1990s by introducing pro-diversity policies in most of Swedish municipal organizations (Integrationsverket, 2001). The vast majority of the policies targeted ethnicity specifically, as gender equality policies already existed. Furthermore, immigrant integration was perceived as the least developed and ethnic diversity as the least represented in the municipal organizations.

Another factor that contributed to the difficulties of implementing diversity in work organizations is the fact that in Sweden it is illegal to register or gather information about individuals' ethnic background. For that reason, it is practically impossible to measure ethnic diversity in organizations by other means than informal evaluations, based on personal knowledge of the employees. In consequence, the field of ethnic diversity suffers from lack of available data in regard to individual corporations, as it is also intertwined with notions of state policies and immigrant integrations. In the light of these specific conditions, it is rather difficult to generalize on what the corporate response to diversity management has been over the past decade in Sweden. Some corporate cases of managing diversity have received attention over the years, primarily in the media. The characteristic traits of these corporate attempts to manage diversity appear to be social integration projects, financed by the state funds, wherein immigrants would be hired for a limited period and paid salaries through government subsidies (e.g. Kalonaityte and Kawesa, 2002).

These context-specific conditions for pro-diversity work have influenced the research conducted in the area of diversity and equal treatment in Sweden. One prominent research area concerned with diversity is International Migration and Ethnic Relations (IMER) research. IMER research is an international research field, concerned with the topics of immigration and ethnic relations, studied from a sociological perspective, with all the variation that such a perspective entails. The IMER field examines issues that go beyond the area of equal treatment and diversity in the workplace; however, considering that this is the leading field in ethnic diversity research in Sweden, we shall review some of the major findings in this area in the first part of this section. The second part is dedicated to the relatively few and disparate findings within the field of management research concerned with workplace diversity. Finally, we end the section with an empirically grounded example from our own research on the current state of diversity management consultancy in Sweden, in order to provide an illustration of how the Swedish context shapes diversity management in a very particular fashion.

IMER research on diversity
The research conducted on issues concerning ethnic relations and international migration has a long history in Sweden. Since the early 1970s the field has steadily grown and presently there are close to 30 research centres in Sweden that identify themselves as centres for research on IMER. The IMER research centres are characterized by their interdisciplinary approach, with a slight predominance for the social sciences. Notwithstanding the research conducted within the centres, significant contributions to the field from researchers within the more traditional disciplines have been made. The many shifts that have occurred in Swedish integration policy have been well traced by researchers within the field (Södergran, 2000; Borevi, 2002; Dahlström, 2004). IMER research concerned with issues such as diversity and integration has been fuelled by

the growing concern for these issues in public policy. Often the picture presented in the policy discussion as well as in the media debate is depicted as if the current situation were a new one: implicitly one is to understand that the Sweden of yesterday was not diverse; the word sameness is used to describe the previous situation. A parallel can be drawn with Litvin's (2002, 2006) observations concerning the notion of diversity management in the USA; how a scenario of the sudden appearance of diversity is presented by the management literature, something that, according to Litvin is not an accurate description of the US population. Similarly, diversity and migration in Swedish society is not a new phenomenon.

It is difficult to summarize all the findings within the IMER research. However, several trends from the 1970s and onwards can be identified. The first trend is that the focus has been on how the immigrant population has integrated and adjusted to Swedish society. The opposite, or perhaps more correctly, complementary, perspective on how the Swedes have adjusted to multiculturalism in Sweden has not received much attention. The second trend of importance is the growing interest in issues such as racism/discrimination. Here, a number of recent research publications within the IMER field have dealt with the ethnic disadvantages in various areas of Swedish society. The latter trend can in part be explained by the increased presence of researchers with a foreign ethnic background at the Swedish universities. A number of studies in the last few years have clearly demonstrated ethnic inequalities in Swedish society (see, e.g., Andersson, 2002; Blomqvist, 2005; Kalonaityte et al., 2007; Molina, 1997; Neergaard, 2002). Furthermore, in 2003 and 2004 two government commissions were given the task of mapping the occurrence of ethnic discrimination in Sweden. The results were the reports: *Det blågula glashuset – strukturell diskriminering i Sverige* (SOU 2005:56) and *Integrationens svarta bok* (SOU 2006:79).

A rather gloomy image of Sweden emerges in these two government-commissioned research reports. Both emphasize that although earlier research has recognized the presence of ethnicized power structures in the Swedish society, the issue of discrimination has not yet been properly addressed. Both reports suggest that more research is required in order to map discrimination properly, and that there is a need to address the structural discrimination and ethnical inequalities in Sweden by broad-scale affirmative action efforts. Both reports opened up a rather fervent and polarized debate concerning discrimination. Several large trade unions and employers' associations opposed the call for affirmative action and mapping of discrimination. However, the reports contributed to one important step in the combating of discrimination – the proposal by SOU 2005:56 of the need to adopt a comprehensive anti-discrimination law, and supervision was realized in 2009 through the new Discrimination Act.

The two reports and their reception illustrate well the current situation concerning research and practice on ethnic diversity and equal treatment in Sweden. The state and corporate stakeholders generally support the notion of equal treatment. However, the diagnosis of the causes of poor immigrant integration, lower salary levels and lack of access to higher management positions among immigrants, despite their education levels, remains a controversial topic. The distribution of responsibility for integration problems remains a highly politicized debate, and many political stakeholders prefer not to focus on the research, which points to structural discrimination as one significant cause of immigrant disadvantage in the labour market in Sweden.

Diversity management research in Sweden

The above section on IMER research shows how research on ethnic diversity is intimately tied to the political debate on immigrant integration in Sweden. That is not very surprising, considering that the Swedish response to the notion of diversity was to integrate it into the existing framework of state policies. Therefore it is difficult to speak of any systematized researcher response to diversity management in Sweden, since it may be difficult to identify purely corporate diversity management practices in Sweden. Thus, in consequence, no systematized overview of diversity management practices in corporations in Sweden exists. Instead, what we have is a number of rather disparate studies of diversity management.

The existing studies on the corporate attempts to manage diversity in Sweden suggest that although corporations tend to attempt to include other aspects of diversity than ethnicity in their work, there is a tendency to focus on ethnicity, or conflate the terms diversity and ethnicity (Leijon and Omanovic, 2001; Leijon et al., 2002; Mlekov and Widell, 2002). Furthermore, a recent thesis on the implementation of diversity management in a Swedish organization suggests that the notion of diversity was infused with various interpretations of the notion of diversity, which were continuously reinvented by the different groups in the organization (Omanovic, 2006). A more overarching study of the way ethnicity, gender and physical disability are depicted in the diversity discourse in Sweden by de los Reyes (2001) suggests that the general tendency is to treat women, immigrants and the physically disabled as different and in consequence less than equal compared to the male, native Swedish, physically able workforce. These findings reflect the findings in international diversity research (e.g. Nkomo and Cox, 1996). Unfortunately, management research in Sweden has few responses to the international call to examine how organizations contribute to the maintenance of workplace inequalities.

One Swedish study that examines organizations' complicity in the production of workplace inequalities is Kalonaityte's (2008) thesis on the appropriation of diversity management philosophy by a Swedish municipal school for adults. The thesis suggests that despite the municipal ambition to implement diversity management in order to promote equal treatment and increase ethnic diversity among the municipal employees, this policy is understood in very specific ways by the organizations within the municipality. The studied municipal school for adults viewed itself as a leading stakeholder within the municipality in regard to diversity management. However, the school's understanding of diversity conflated the notion of diversity with the notion of immigrant integration, which, in turn, signified immigrant assimilation for the school. One explanation for such an appropriation of diversity management at this particular organization lies in the underlying cultural rationalities beyond the more recent and less well-established notions of diversity management. The cultural rationalities of the school were based on an underlying hierarchical view of gender and ethnicity, wherein immigrants were assumed to be either in possession of inferior cultural skills or lacking cultural skills and knowledge altogether. In consequence, the school's pro-diversity work was targeted to alleviate this supposed inferiority and lack by various assimilatory practices. It is worth pointing out that even if the immigrant students and employees did not live up to the images of lack and inferiority, the suspicion and expectations of inferiority lingered on and shaped the school's practices.

In summary, while IMER research in Sweden is at the forefront of the ethnic diversity debate, management research on equal treatment at work remains at the periphery of the contemporary Swedish debate on immigrant integration. It is clear that more research is needed when it comes to management practices in regard to the employment problems immigrants are facing in Swedish organizations. One plausible explanation for the lack of management research on the topic of diversity lies in that it is very difficult to identify corporate best practices and study the implementation of workplace diversity. The study of absence of diversity is always more difficult and ridden with other questions, such as the need for new personnel. The challenges of diversity implementation are also well illustrated in the section below on the work of diversity consultants in Sweden and the rather peculiar situation that their work conditions constitute.

The realities of workplace diversity in Sweden: the case of diversity management consultants

The diversity management philosophy is commonly associated with the establishment and expansion of the diversity management consultant industry. Such a development is, however, only partially true of Sweden. We have conducted interviews with two diversity management consultants' networks in Sweden and present here some of our findings. One striking fact concerning diversity management consultants in Sweden is that such consultancy services are quite limited. Our study, conducted in 2006, suggested that there were two major consultant networks specialized in diversity management specifically and working with independent consultancy. It appears that two types of diversity management services were in high demand. One type of service consisted of lectures and similar types of information spreading on issues such as gender equality and ethnic diversity. The second type of service was the actual diversity implementation. However, the interesting aspect of diversity implementation, as suggested by one of the consultant networks, consisted of helping the organization in question to apply for external, state or EU-based funding to finance the attempts to manage diversity. These findings suggest that there was a general unwillingness among the organizations to finance diversity management with their own funds. The consultants were expected to be quite skilled in applying for relevant funding because their services were financed with these funds as well. This is how a diversity consultant, Linda, explains the role of external funds:

> They used to finance a lot. Not only diversity, but immigrant integration projects. Projects for developing the business side of diversity aren't many within EU projects. That money is important, but it also makes you cynical, because organizations are willing to do something once someone else is paying – how much is that worth? But money also makes them do the analyses they otherwise wouldn't, since it is often a condition for receiving the money.

Another interesting aspect of the diversity management consultancy in Sweden was that our study revealed that state and public organizations were at least half of the total amount of clients the consultants had. The public organizations' interest in diversity management in part reflects the realities of the appropriation of the notion of diversity in Sweden, i.e. that the concept of diversity is closely linked to the notion of immigrant integration. Furthermore, state organizations are more likely to be in a position where they can apply for various project funds, provided by the state and the EU, as the diversity consultant Linda suggests. The type of diversity that is commonly asked for among the clients tends to be ethnic diversity. Linda describes the demand in the following fashion:

> I believe that organizations should work with a broad diversity concept, but often it becomes ethnic diversity only. It should be all discrimination factors, and many want a broader perspective, but in practice it becomes ethnicity. Perhaps because the lack of ethnic diversity is the greatest, and also the easiest to see, although it is not measured. It is visible, and many want to see results.

Considering that the diversity consultants have the best overview of the types of diversity demanded by the clients, it is clear that, as in the example given by Linda, the type of diversity that is practised and demanded in Swedish organizations revolves around ethnicity. Furthermore, the interviewed diversity consultants suggest that despite the attempts to secure external funds in order to finance pro-diversity work, many of the organizations they work for have not come very far in implementing diversity in the workplace. Diversity consultant Gunilla suggests that most clients hire them for short projects, which are mostly about spreading information about diversity:

> We have few clients that attempt implementation of diversity. There are few ideal situations. Normally there are short projects for the state, municipality and corporations. For example in the retail business we had a leadership for diversity programme where all the managers had a half-day about diversity.

The evaluation of the progress within workplace diversity that the consultants could provide us with indicates that many corporations and public organizations in Sweden are at very early stages of pro-diversity work, even if it means focusing on ethnic diversity specifically. This is how Linda describes the current situation in regard to the pro-diversity work she has encountered:

> I have seen some [organizations] take small steps, but those who are successful I have only heard of . . . Many need to recruit. I can imagine that I don't work with organizations that have come far. Those that are mainstream, on the other hand, don't know much [about diversity]. They are quite lost, the typical Swedish organizations, they recruit as usual, from universities, they mistrust university colleges, they define competencies in a very narrow fashion and also recruit the people that they like.

Thus it appears that Swedish organizations, even those that are more progressive and seek out consultant services in order to learn more about diversity, have not yet come far, according to the consultants. The organizations rely on external funding, prefer information before implementation and are generally keen on recruiting their workforce according to their traditional routines. It is, perhaps, not very surprising that diversity management research has not come very far in Sweden, as the empirical field of diversity management appears to be still in its cradle here.

Concluding reflections

We have argued in this chapter that Sweden has a history of focusing on separate groups and their rights rather than on civil rights or general non-discrimination. This may have changed now, at least at the policy level, through the introduction of the more comprehensive law in 2009. However, Sweden still faces severe challenges when it comes to actual immigrant integration in the labour market. This is evident in the very high levels of overqualification among the employees with immigrant backgrounds, as well as in the

Summary table for Sweden

Existence of anti-discrimination legislation	Yes
Criteria covered by anti-discrimination legislation	Gender, ethnicity, sexual orientation, religion, disability, age, transgender identity
Criteria for which the reporting of quantitative data and their communication to a public administration are compulsory	Organizations with ten or more employees are required to have a gender equality policy, which entails registration of gender distribution of the employees. Organizations with ten or more employees are also recommended to have a diversity policy. However, registration of employees' ethnical background is prohibited in Sweden
Criteria covered by 'affirmative' or 'positive' action legislation other than unemployment- or income-based	Under certain circumstances it is allowed to recruit the underrepresented gender, if all other merits are the same. Otherwise, there are many different locally driven projects, which support or in other ways attempt to improve different groups, such as youth, possibilities in the labour market without direct affirmative action measures
Existence of a discourse or debate about 'non-discrimination' or 'equality'	Yes
Existence of a discourse or debate about 'diversity'	Yes
Year or period when the 'discrimination' concept started to disseminate in management literature in the country	Discrimination as a general concept is seldom used in Swedish management literature, with the exception of gender
Year or period when the diversity concept started to disseminate in management literature in the country	1999–2001
Who pushed the 'diversity' agenda?	The Swedish government, also to some extent public–private intermediary organizations, the media, as well as the European Union and Swedish minority-driven NGOs. The involvement of the business sector is probably best characterized as responsive rather than driving in the questions of diversity
Existence of a professional association representing diversity professionals and year of creation	No
Existence of a professional association representing diversity scholars and year of creation	No. To some extent the International Migration and Ethnic Relations (IMER) Association founded in 1992 represents these questions

perpetuation of ethnic inequalities in various areas of Swedish society. Moreover, the labour market stakeholders' refusal to acknowledge and deal with the racism and discrimination in Swedish society, most recently manifested by the overtly hostile reception of the two government commissions, is indicative of the Swedish situation in regard to ethnic diversity. It appears that the Swedish progressive gender equality work has been driven by an explicit and collectively shared recognition of women's historical disadvantages and exclusion. The shared definition of the problem area has made it legitimate and broadly established to work for gender equality. Ethnic diversity and the integration of immigrants, it appears, is an area of high priority for both the Swedish state and for corporate Sweden. However, the historical and current disadvantages of immigrants remain to be acknowledged on a broad collective scale. In consequence, there remains a discrepancy between the desire to achieve ethnic diversity in the workplace and practices that contribute to the perpetuation of workplace inequalities. In the light of such development, it is perhaps not very surprising that concerned journalists and researchers regularly issue brain-drain alerts regarding Sweden's immigrant population. Our hope is that alerts issued by research such as the two government commissions are taken seriously by labour market stakeholders in Sweden before the unwanted consequences are too grave.

References

Andersson, Roger (2002), 'Boendesegregation och etniska hierarkier', in Ingemar Lindberg (ed.), *Det slutna folkhemmet. Om etniska klyftor och blågul självbild*, Stockholm: Agora.

Blomqvist Rodrigo, Paula (2005), *Närvarons politik och det mångetniska Sverige. Om att ta plats i demokratin*, Förvaltningshögskolan: University of Gothenburg.

Borevi, Karin (2002), *Välfärdsstaten i det mångkulturella samhället*, Uppsala: Uppsala University.

Boxenbaum, Eva (2006), 'Lost in translation: the making of Danish diversity management', *American Behavioral Scientist*, **49** (7), 939–48.

Dahlström, Carl (2004), *Nästan välkomna. Invandrarpolitikens retorik och praktik*, Göteborg: University of Gothenburg.

de los Reyes, Paulina (2001), *Mångfald och differentiering*, Stockholm: Arbetslivsinstitutet.

DS 2001: 10 Mänskliga rättigheter i Sverige- en kartläggning.

Esseveld, Johanna (2005), 'Toppolitiker i Sverige – politik, karriär, familj, omsorg', in Björn Fjæstad and Lars-Erik Wolvén (eds), *Arbetsliv och samhällsförändringar*, Lund: Studentlitteratur, pp. 19–34.

Fägerlind, G. (1999), *Managing Diversity – strategier för mångfald i USA*, Stockholm: Sveriges Tekniska Attachéer.

Fjaestad, B. and L.E. Wolvén (eds), *Arbetsliv och samhällsförändringar*, Lund: Studentlitteratur.

Integrationsverket (2001), *Kommunernas mångfaldsarbete*, Norrköping: Integrationsverkets rapportserie no. 10.

Johansson, Vicki (1996), *Vem gör vad när och var? Omsorgens organiseringsform i kommunerna och kvinnors och mäns omsorgsarbetsdelning*, Stockholm: Publica.

Kalonaityte, Viktorija (2008), *Off the Edge of the Map: A Study of Organizational Diversity as Identity Work*, Lund: Lund Institute of Economic Research.

Kalonaityte, Viktorija and Victoria Kawesa (2002), *Den tvåfaldiga mångfalden – en postkolonial dekonstruktion av mångfaldsdiskursen*, Master's thesis, Lund: Lund University, Department of Business Administration.

Kalonaityte, Viktorija, Victoria Kawesa and Adiam Tedros (2007), *Att färgas av Sverige: upplevelser av diskriminering och rasism bland ungdomar med afrikansk bakgrund*, Stockholm: Ombudsman mot etnisk diskriminering.

Klapp, E., G. Ivarsson, H. Bogomil and A. Eldenhed (2001), *Vem kör taxi? Broar Över Öresund*, Svenskt Näringsliv, Näringslivskontoret Malmö Stad.

Leijon, Svante and Vedran Omanovic (2001), *Mångfaldens mångfald – olika sätt att se på och leda olikheter*, Göteborg: Göteborgs Universitet, Handelshögskolan, FE-rapport no. 381.

Leijon, Svante, Ruth Lillhannus and Gill Widell (2002), *Reflecting Diversity – Viewpoints from Scandinavia*, Göteborg: BAS.

Litvin, D. (2002), 'The business case for diversity and the "iron cage"', in B. Czarniawska and H. Höpfl (eds), *Casting the Other: The Production and Maintenance of Inequalities in Work Organizations*, London: Routledge, pp. 160–85.

Litvin, D. (2006), 'Diversity: making space for a better case', in A. Konrad, P. Prasad and J. Pringle (eds), *Handbook of Workplace Diversity*, London Thousand Oaks, CA: Sage, pp. 75–94.

Lundh, Christer and Rolf Ohlsson (1994), *Från arbetskraftsimport till flyktinginvandring*, Stockholm: SNS Förlag.

Malmborg, Jonas (2006), 'Sveriges nya brain drain', *Ekonominyheterna*, 9 November.

Mlekov, Katarina and Gill Widell (2002), *Hur möter vi mångfalden på arbetsplatsen?*, Lund: Studentlitteratur.
Molina, Irene (1997), *Stadens rasifiering. Boendesegregation i folkhemmet*, Uppsala: Uppsala University.
Neergaard, Anders (2002), 'Arbetsmarknadens mönster – om rasifierad segmentering', in I. Lindberg and M. Dahlstedt (eds), *Det slutna folkhemmet: om etniska klyftor och blågul självbild*, Stockholm: Agora, pp. 116–34.
Nkomo, Stella and Taylor Cox (1996), 'Diverse identities in organizations', in S.R. Clegg, C. Hardy and W.R. Nord (eds), *Handbook of Organization Studies*, London Thousand Oaks, CA: Sage, pp. 338–56.
OECD (2008), *A Profile of Immigrant Populations in the 21st Century*, Paris: OECD.
Omanovic, Verdan (2006), *A Production of Diversity: Appearances, Ideas, Interests, Actions, Contradictions and Praxis*. Göteborg: BAS Publishing.
Ornbrant, Birgitta (2007), 'Att vara bäst är inte nog', in *Sydsvenskan*, 21 November.
Persson, Jessica and Richard Öhrwall (2008), *Förtroendevalda i kommuner och landsting 2007. En rapport om politikerantal och representativitet*, Statistics Sweden, Unit of Democracy Statistics.
Prasad, Pushkala and Albert J. Mills (1997), 'From showcase to shadow: understanding the dilemmas of managing workplace diversity', in P. Prasad, A.J. Mills, M. Elmes and A. Prasad (eds), *Managing the Organizational Melting Pot: Dilemmas of Workplace Diversity*, London: Sage, pp. 3–30.
Proposition 1997/98:16 Sverige, framtiden och mångfalden från invandrarpolitik till integrationspolitik, Government Bill.
Södergran, Lena (2000), *Svensk Invandrar- och Integrationspolitik. En fråga om jämlikhet, demokrati och mänskliga rättigheter*, Umeå: Umeå University.
Soininen, Maritta (1992), *Det kommunala flyktingmottagandet. Genomförande och organisation*, Stockholm: CEIFO, Centre for Research in International Migration and Ethnic Relations.
SOU 1974: 69 *Invandrarutredningen. Huvudbetänkandet; Invandrarna och minoriteterna*, Stockholm.
SOU 1975: 51 Bostadsförsörjning och bostadsbidrag, Stockholm.
SOU 2005: 56, *Det blågula glashuset – strukturell diskriminering i Sverige*, Stockholm.
SOU 2006: 79, *Integrationens svarta bok*, Stockholm.
SOU 2007: 108 Kön, makt och statistik, Stockholm.
Statistics Sweden (2006), *Women and Men in Sweden: Facts and Figures*, Stockholm: Statistics Sweden.
Swedish Code of Status (1996–2008).
Swedish Migration Board (2008), 'Migrationsverket, Kort om migration 2007', www.migrationsverket.se/ infomaterial/om_verket/statistik/kort_om_migration.pdf, accessed 21 April 2009.
Tedros, Adiam (2008), *Utanför storstaden. Konkurrerande framställningar av förorten i svensk storstadspolitik*, Förvaltningshögskolan: University of Gothenburg.
Westin, C. (2000), *Settlement and Integration Policies towards Immigrants and their Descendants in Sweden*, International Migration papers 34, Geneva: International Labour Office.

13 Diversity made in Switzerland: traditional and new plurality meets the business case[1]

Julia Nentwich, Chris Steyaert and Brigitte Liebig

Introduction

Switzerland is an amazingly diverse country. With only 7.2 million inhabitants, it has four official languages, two major religions and 26 cantons as sovereign legal and administrative entities. A federalist and democratic nation based on strong liberal values, Switzerland cherishes its myths about its rural origin as it also plays important global roles. The conception of the nation as 'unity in plurality' is at the heart of its national myth and forms an important discourse that establishes Switzerland as a special case[2] (Imhof, 2007, p. 36). It is in this sense – as a unitary and homogeneous national context – that Switzerland does not exist, but rather constantly has to be constructed.[3]

Despite Switzerland's long tradition of dealing with diversity, the public debate on diversity in the work context began only recently. The idea of managing diversity is very new to Swiss companies, even though workplaces are very strongly gender-segregated, both horizontally and vertically, and the Swiss economy depends heavily on immigration. A recent study showed that 68 per cent of Switzerland's top 500 companies do not measure aspects of diversity and that 80 per cent do not educate their managers on how to deal with diversity issues. Overall, the study concludes that diversity in Switzerland is undervalued as a business driver (Filler et al., 2006).

Generally speaking, two different approaches to diversity issues are used in Switzerland. First, the narration of the nation as 'unity in plurality' evokes concepts of difference, privileging cultural diversity as a traditional value within the national context of Switzerland. Second, Switzerland as a national context faces a range of modern challenges: it must deal with the diversity of globalized economies, along with issues like expatriation, immigration, emancipation and anti-discrimination.

This paradox[4] in the conception of diversity in Switzerland will guide us as we discuss the entry and establishment of diversity practices in Swiss corporate and organizational life. First, we sketch in general the recent entry of diversity management into Switzerland, and show how the historical and local context of a specific 'diverse' Switzerland is aligned with the global idea of diversity management as it travelled from the USA. In the second section, we outline the diversity of the Swiss labour market and work life in general with regard to those dimensions that are considered the most significant: gender and culture. Also here we note a tension between the historical, locally anchored variation and the new relationships that are being established as a consequence of globalization, immigration and (female) emancipation. In the third section, we sketch the legal dimensions of diversity management, again moving between the specifically Swiss legal context and the broader (mostly European) legislative changes. And finally, we review some recent research projects in order to shed some light on the extent to which Switzerland forms a special case.

Travelling concepts: diversity management as a growing field of practice

Only recently has the 'global idea' (Czarniawska and Sevón, 2005) of diversity management entered into Swiss discussions. The concept of diversity management travelled
to Switzerland from the USA via multinationals and Germany, where it became more
important in the 1990s (Aretz, 2006). In Switzerland, most companies started to introduce diversity management initiatives only between 2000 and 2006 (Benz, 2008; Filler et
al., 2006, p. 2).[5] In many cases, the more fashionable concept of diversity management
replaced locally grown equal opportunity initiatives, which have a longer tradition.
Thus, diversity management is seen as a 'timely and modern way of dealing with equal
opportunities' (Benz, 2008, p. 55). However, while initiatives with regard to gender
equality have a legal context in the federal act on gender equality, this is not directly
the case with diversity management. Yet the transition from equal opportunities to
diversity management also entails a shift from the logic of fairness and equal treatment
to economic rationales. Today, equal opportunities are associated with legal issues, anti-
discrimination and fairness, while diversity management is mainly associated with the
business case (Benz, 2008).

In November 2005, the *Neue Zürcher Zeitung*[6] published a special supplement on
diversity, featuring several articles on diversity management in Switzerland. This was the
first time the topic was prominently discussed in the Swiss print media, but it was neither
an important marketing argument nor a business topic. Companies tend to ignore issues
of diversity; being obliged to mention them in an annual report in order to testify good
governance practices would be considered 'bizarre from a Swiss point of view' (Gygi,
2005). One-third of the Swiss company websites investigated by Point and Singh (2003)
did not mention diversity or equal opportunity statements on their web pages; although
the researchers found enthusiasm for this practice in the UK, it was not reflected in the
communication strategies of Swiss companies. Nor did most Swiss companies specify the
meaning of diversity or specific dimensions on their web pages (Point and Singh 2003,
p. 755). Overall, diversity seems to be undervalued as a business topic and Swiss companies need to focus on it more strongly in the coming years (Filler et al., 2006).[7]

This rather late integration of diversity issues into Swiss workplaces can be explained
by several factors.[8] First, the 'management of diversity' is a US concept rooted in anti-
discrimination policies (Bendl, 2004, p. 56ff.) and therefore unfamiliar in the Swiss
legal context. Second, diversity as a management concept is often seen as a fashionable concept of the global economy, but is not judged important for everyday life in
Switzerland, which is strongly based on small- and medium-sized enterprises (SMEs).
Here, the main issues are family-friendliness or work–life balance (Ostendorp, 2007;
Ostendorp and Nentwich, 2005), and the topic of diversity attracts less attention. Third,
knowledge about the concept is quite limited: 'diversity' is primarily equated with race
and gender; the strong connection between 'diversity' and 'race', which is central in the
US context (Nkomo, 1992), is not seen as very salient in Switzerland. Similarly, people
often overlook the problems associated with the strong breadwinner culture in Swiss
working life, and the clear gender division that accompanies it.

Diversity management among Swiss employers

Filler et al. (2006) conducted the first study providing an overall picture of diversity management, and taking a closer look at Switzerland's top 500 companies.[9] They found that

only a small percentage of today's market leaders invest in the management of diversity. The majority of respondents said that what is being done with respect to diversity issues in their own organization is about right, and satisfies customer needs. But this optimistic opinion actually rests on a lack of facts: only 43 per cent of all companies systematically gathered and monitored basic data about the diversity of their workforce and diversity practices. Quite often, companies do not see the need to collect information on diversity-related practices such as hiring, promotion and development. Even more uncertainty exists around the returns on investment that might accrue from diversity management. Even today, many corporations neither know the basic preconditions for developing a 'multicultural organization' (Cox, 1993) nor measure the effects of investments in this area (Liebig, 2010b).

As of 2005, 30 per cent of the 'top 500' respondents had developed a clearly stated diversity policy – but the majority (71 per cent) of these firms are international companies, headquartered outside Switzerland. The investment in diversity clearly pays off: the percentage of foreigners and women at the CEO level is markedly higher in corporations that specifically invest in diversity practices (cf. Filler et al., 2006, p. 15). Overall, the key focus of their diversity management effort is on gender (81 per cent), followed by ethnicity (78 per cent) and age (70 per cent), and then by religion (43 per cent) and other dimensions (46 per cent) such as sexual orientation, educational background, race, professional experience, disabilities, regional language and leadership styles. On average, diversity employers in Switzerland are companies with headquarters outside Switzerland; they are either small (fewer than 250 employees) or large companies (more than 10 000 employees) and more often in the financial service or high-tech sectors. These companies provide good and comprehensive documentation and information on diversity, they seriously invest in diversity and implement human resource policies that are open, for example, to hire or promote diversity candidates (Filler et al., 2006, p. 19).

Although 31 per cent of the top 500 explicitly mention diversity in their business strategy, the authors of the survey evaluate the implementation of diversity policies as rather minimal (Filler et al., 2006, p. 19). Overall, they say, activities to support diversity are rather fragmented; that is, while many companies consider diversity as part of their hiring strategy, they do not incorporate it into their promotion procedures. Furthermore, these efforts seem to be segmented and focus mainly on women and culture; they do not focus on diversity or on other diversity categories as an overall philosophy. However, the strongest limitation on diversity management is illustrated by the fact that only 11 per cent of these companies employ a dedicated diversity manager; of those managers, few are doing that work full time or are members of the executive team (see Figure 13.1).

Establishing the position of a diversity manager counts as the most effective path to organizational change (Kalev et al., 2006). According to Filler et al., 20 per cent of the responding companies do invest in education on managing and dealing with diversity, but this is, as mentioned, not supported by appointing a diversity manager. The few diversity managers in place in Swiss companies are responsible for the development, rollout, evaluation and communication of all diversity-related initiatives, including strategy development, career development, recruiting and administration. The diversity managers of large (multi)national companies with more than 10 000 employees all participate in a network called 'roundtable diversity',[10] at which they discuss and exchange

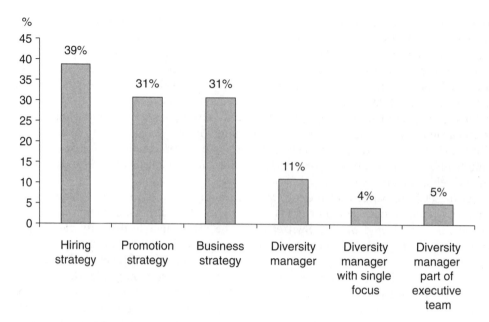

Source: Filler et al. (2006).

Figure 13.1 *Implementation of diversity policy (companies with diversity policy; more than one answer possible)*

best practices. Some of these are very visible in Switzerland's public discourse in the media and very well known for their commitment to diversity.

Obstacles to overcome
What are the obstacles that hinder the implementation of diversity in Swiss organizations? One is the lack of resources, which results in a low level of institutionalization: case studies on diversity management in Swiss SMEs and multinationals demonstrate how resource levels are related to the size of organizations (Liebig, 2010b). In SMEs, human resource managers are often delegated the task of institutionalizing and maintaining diversity efforts, which then depend heavily on their personal commitment; meanwhile, larger companies can more often invest in structural measurements and changes.

More important is the challenge of implementing diversity into the everyday practices of organizations. 'Synergy is not for free' (Brodbeck, 1999); as a case study on the cost-effectiveness of gender and diversity management in Swiss firms shows (Liebig, 2010a), cooperation in heterogeneous groups both enriches and challenges every member of a team. But this is only one of the reasons why structural measures are not sufficient to implement diversity in a sustainable way. SMEs and multinationals must develop institutional strategies to implement diversity cultures through everyday action and care (Liebig, 2010a). Proactive efforts to stimulate diversity involve a strong commitment on all levels of management; encouragement from the executive team and full support from the board of directors are only the start. Such efforts require the full understanding, confidence and participation of all employees. Quite often it is a lack of communication and understanding that keeps diversity policies from being accepted widely. In particular, measures set up to support selected groups of employees (e.g. women) suffer from being delegitimized and even ignored in the organization (see also Ostendorp, 2006). Liebig (2000) saw this happening with gender diversity measures; this dynamic then nourishes cultural reinterpretations and distortions of diversity practices, which can produce uncontrollable and counterproductive results.

Another important precondition for implementing diversity management is a functioning system to support gender equality. Stereotypical male concepts of leadership and professionalism in Swiss society and general anxieties related to cultural diversity and cultural change are at the core of traditional values, which have created obstacles to change (Filler et al., 2006). In addition to the lack of flexible working hours, especially in top management positions, day care and the Swiss schooling system are not supportive of working parents, especially working mothers. Public schooling still relies on traditional work arrangements between parents; more precisely, it is based on the idea of one parent being at home at midday preparing the meal (Bühler, 2004). This rigid situation has led to the development of private childcare services and day schools that are too expensive to be widely available. Two more disincentives for mothers to work are the high costs of childcare and the tax system that privileges breadwinners (cf. Bütler, 2007).

Filler et al. (2006) found that only 20 per cent of market leaders offer part-time work or the option of working from home at the senior executive level, and only a small number of top managers participate in programmes such as job-sharing (2 per cent) or work-based childcare programmes (8 per cent). On the whole, diversity measures in these companies primarily aim at individual change and development, but do not engage in cultural or structural change. 'Individual choice' is also the primary explanation given for the small numbers of women in leadership positions; respondents state plainly that women do not want to be in these positions and deliberately choose to engage in different activities (Filler et al., 2006; Osterloh and Littmann-Wernli, 2000).

Diversity dimensions
The literature on diversity indicates that gender, culture and more recently age (cf. Cranach et al., 2004; State Secretariat for Economic Affairs, 2005) are the most important diversity dimensions (Filler et al., 2006; Steyaert et al., 2011). This is true not only in Switzerland, but also in other European countries. Analysing the corporate web pages of the top 241 companies by market value in eight European countries, Point and Singh (2003) found that 48 per cent mentioned gender or sex, 45 per cent culture, 37 per cent race and ethnicity, 31 per cent age, 29 per cent nationality and country of origin, and 28 per cent disability. To sketch the situation in Switzerland, we shall discuss in greater detail the main dimensions of diversity, namely culture and gender.

Cultural diversity
As mentioned previously, the narrative of 'unity in plurality' plays a crucial role in the way Switzerland has invented itself as a nation. Switzerland is not built around a notion of ethnic nationalism, but instead sees itself as a volatile nation cherishing its plurality of languages and ethnicities and integrating them into a Swiss culture (Imhof, 2007). Its ethnic and cultural backgrounds are diverse and mostly related to language. Switzerland consists of four major cultural regions. The largest is the German-speaking part of

Switzerland with the major cities of Zürich, Basel, Lucerne and St Gallen making up 63.7 per cent of all Swiss inhabitants. Second largest is the francophone western region including Geneva, Lausanne and Neuchâtel (20.4 per cent). The cities of Fribourg and Berne are bilingual with both a French-speaking and a German-speaking population. Third, Ticino is an Italian-speaking region with Lugano and Locarno as its main cities (6.5 per cent). Finally, the Romansh spoken in the canton of Grisons is Switzerland's fourth official language at 0.5 per cent (Swiss Federal Statistical Office, 2009c).

Switzerland has also experienced immense migration during the past decades. In 2007, 26 per cent of the working population did not hold a Swiss passport, which is quite a high proportion compared to other European countries (Swiss Federal Statistical Office, 2009b). In 2004, 25 per cent of all migrants came from former Yugoslavian countries, followed by Italy, Portugal, Germany, Spain, Turkey, France and Austria (Bergmann and Mottier, 2004, p. 79). Compared to Swiss workers, foreign-born employees are on average younger, and more likely to be male and working full time. Migrants from Northern and Western Europe are more often in the health and educational sectors; they are working in academia or occupy top management positions. In contrast, migrants from Southern and Eastern European countries are more frequently found working in industry, the trades and construction (Swiss Federal Statistical Office, 2006). Overall, a higher proportion of the migrant population is affected by unemployment, mainly because of the more severe recession in the sectors of the labour market where they are usually active. In addition to the major wage gap between Swiss and non-Swiss workers, there is considerable variation among migrant workers depending on their work permits. Migrants with long-term permits earn significantly higher wages than those with short-term permits (Swiss Federal Statistical Office, 2006).

In terms of language plurality, this means that many more than the four official languages are spoken in Swiss workplaces. In addition to the official languages, 9 per cent of workers speak another language, including Serbian, Croatian, Albanian and Portuguese. As we shall see later, among the languages used in the work context, English also plays a major role (Jaworski and Piller, 2008; Steyaert et al., 2011). Furthermore, diglossia is an important aspect of the German-speaking region; most people use so-called Swiss-German in everyday speech contexts and high or standard German in written and more formal spoken contexts (Jaworski and Piller, 2008).

Although foreign workers and language diversity present important practical issues in everyday Swiss working life, they are not major issues in Swiss companies. While migration is an issue of law and order mainly in public places, neighbourhoods and immigration politics (cf. Ostendorp and Nentwich, 2009), language diversity is addressed under the label of early childhood education. Paradoxically, this enormous diversity of cultures and languages in Swiss working life is neither discussed nor managed in enterprises but is only addressed in two very small areas: expatriates and the cultural diversity of (top) management teams.

Looking at the comparably high numbers of non-Swiss on Switzerland's boards, the topic of non-Swiss expatriates emerges as an important one for diversity management in Switzerland. As Filler et al. (2006) show in the case of market leaders, 72 per cent of firms do employ non-Swiss nationals on their executive teams. Remarkably, the number of non-Swiss nationals increases with the size of the company (see Table 13.1), with the highest numbers in high-tech industry. Ruigrok and Greve (2008) looked at the diversity

Table 13.1 Ethnic and gender diversity of the executive board based on company size

Number of employees	Foreigners (%)	Women (%)	Total replies
Up to 250	34.0	16.6	7
251 to 500	18.4	5.0	17
500 to 1000	23.4	8.6	29
1001 to 5000	24.5	7.1	37
5001 to 10 000	29.8	6.9	17
More than 10 000	27.3	5.4	15

Source: Filler et al. (2006, p. 9).

of top management teams in large European non-financial firms in Denmark, Finland, the Netherlands, Norway, Sweden, Switzerland and the UK; they found similar percentages of foreigners in the top management teams (24 per cent in 2005, 21 per cent in 2000). Switzerland seems to be right in the middle of a group of Swiss, Dutch and Finnish firms that show a similar trend, gradually increasing their percentage of foreign executives.

However, the percentage of women in top management is consistently lower than that of non-Swiss nationals (see Table 13.1). In the next section we take a closer look at gender relations in Switzerland.

Gender diversity
In addition to language, cultural and regional diversity, gender is considered a crucial category of diversity in Switzerland. This is, of course, mainly due to the historical success of the women's movement (Lenzin, 2000; Schnegg and Stalder, 1984). The first women's movement focused on the issue of political participation: only in 1971 were women granted the right to vote (and also to run for office) on the level of the Swiss confederation. Following this milestone, the women's movement, still operating in the tradition of liberal feminism (cf. Nentwich, 2006a), turned its focus towards the practicalities of everyday gender relations in society, family and working life. This focus on the necessity of hands-on and everyday work to achieve change – based on a strong discourse of pragmatism – resulted in the development of a very rich variety of tools and guidelines. Many of them are published by the federal office of equality (www.topbox.ch), covering topics such as sexual harassment (Ducret, 2003), family friendliness (Fachstelle UND, 2000; State Secretariat for Economic Affairs, 2007), personnel selection and development (Baitsch and Steiner, 2004; Fried et al., 2000), assessment of key competences (Kadishi, 2001), job-sharing in leadership positions (Kuark, 2003), part-time work (Baillod et al., 2002), pay equity (Arioli et al., 2007) and gender equality controlling (Müller and Sander, 2005).

Although this list of guidelines may seem impressive, it is not sufficient to counteract overnight the large gender gap in Swiss working life. This prompted a writer for the *Neue Zürcher Zeitung* (Jacquemart, 2006) to comment upon a recent study of the International Labour Organization that 'it might really take another 962 years until gender equality is achieved'. While it might indeed take a considerable effort, as this headline suggests, gender relations are slowly beginning to change. For instance, while the rate of male participation in the labour force fell from 91.1 per cent in 1991 to 88 per cent in 2008, that of women increased constantly over the last decades from 68.2 per cent in 1991 to 76.6 per cent in 2008 (Swiss Federal Statistical Office, 2008b). Yet this increase must be put into perspective, when we consider how much of female employment is part time. As 57 per cent of women and only 12 per cent of men are working part time, part-time work is still considered to be for women and especially for mothers (Nentwich, 2004; Swiss Federal Statistical Office, 2008a, p. 12).

Furthermore, other major gender differences in Swiss working life seem hard to overcome (compare also Folini, 2007). First, differences in the educational levels of women and men are still considerable, although they have decreased over the last decades. Women have caught up on their level of university education and in 2007 they made up almost 50 per cent of all university graduates (Swiss Federal Statistical Office, 2008b, p. 7). On the other hand, occupational choice is still fundamentally segregated by gender and has resisted change over the last 20 years. While young men still prefer engineering, young women favour the humanities, social sciences and teaching (Swiss Federal Statistical Office, 2008b, p. 9). Second, an important wage gap persists (Flückiger and Ramirez, 2000; Sousa-Poza, 2002, 2003; Strub et al., 2008). The wages of men are 19.1 per cent higher than those of women, although the percentage has decreased slightly, from 23.8 per cent in 1994 (Swiss Federal Statistical Office, 2008a, p. 22).

Third, in Switzerland the roles of mother and father are perceived as fundamentally different (Nentwich, 2008). Even though the father's parental role and the mother's employment role have changed tremendously, the mother's primary responsibility is still the children's emotional well-being, while the father's is the family's financial well-being (Strub et al., 2005). The father's involvement is often limited to activities such as playing, bathing and soothing the child, rather than doing everyday tasks like meal preparation or housework (Strub, 2003; Willemsen, 2001).

This phenomenon also shows up in labour market statistics and career outcomes. For instance, the age of the youngest child is a strong predictor of the employment rate of mothers, and the labour force participation rate of women between ages 25 and 40 is significantly lower than that for men in the same age group and for younger and older women (Swiss Federal Statistical Office, 2008a, p. 11). Mothers with children under age seven are significantly less often engaged in employed work than mothers of older children (ibid., p. 14). Although family arrangements are changing slowly, the main changes can be found within the traditional bourgeois family: women are no longer working as housewives, but are taking part-time jobs (see Table 13.2).

To illustrate the persistence of gender inequality, we might turn to the situation of women in leadership positions. Although this figure has increased from 40000 in 1997 to 80000 in 2007 (Swiss Federal Statistical Office, 2008b), this is still an exception in corporate Switzerland, especially in the upper echelons. Davoine (2005) shows that out of 700 managers in the largest SPI companies,[11] only 3 per cent are female. While the 2008 WEF *Gender Gap Report* states that 30 per cent of legislators, senior officials and managers are women (Hausmann et al., 2008), in executive management there were only seven women compared to 230 men, and women made up only 12 per cent of the corporate boards of the 26 SMI companies (Actares, 2008).[12] And of these 26 companies, only one had a female CEO in 2006: Heliane Canepa of Nobel Biocare. And only one of the SMI companies, the Swatch Group, featured more than one woman on its executive management team and corporate board (Jacquemart, 2006).

Table 13.2   Changes in family arrangements: division of labour in families with children under 7 years

Arrangement	Woman	Man	In %, 1990	In %, 2000
Traditional–bourgeois	Not in paid employment	Full-time employment	59.8	37.3
Modern–bourgeois	Part-time employment	Full-time employment	23.2	36.5
Egalitarian–career oriented	Full-time employment	Full-time employment	10.7	12.1
Egalitarian–family oriented	Part-time employment	Part-time employment	1.5	3.5
Other combinations			4.8	10.7
			100%	100%

Source: Swiss Federal Statistical Office (2009a).

Ruigrok et al. (2007, p. 551) state that 'only 3 per cent of all directors on the boards of Swiss companies listed on the stock exchange in 2003 were women', compared to 11 per cent in the governing bodies of European companies in general (McKinsey and Company, 2007, p. 5). At the same time they report that non-Swiss nationals accounted for a total of 22.1 per cent of the board directors. Interestingly, 13 of the 50 female directors were also foreigners (Ruigrok et al. 2007, p. 555). Furthermore, 'women directors are more likely to have lower educational levels', and to come from outside the company and be affiliated with the founding family. As the authors point out, these findings differ significantly from findings in the USA, where women are more likely to be highly educated and to come from within the company.

Also, researchers have found that, as in other countries (Wajcman, 1998), the few women in leadership positions often do not have children (Folini, 2007). In 2008, only 24.8 per cent of the women in leadership positions had children, and only 41 per cent were married; in comparison, 80.2 per cent of the men were fathers and 90.3 per cent were married (Künzle, 2009). However, the female ratio in executive management did increase from 19 per cent in 1991 to 30.8 per cent in 2005 (Jacquemart, 2006). This is mainly due to women's progress in small and medium-sized businesses. While Swiss top 500 companies with fewer than 250 employees had 16.6 per cent women on their executive boards, companies with 500–1000 employees had only 8.6 per cent and companies with more than 10000 employees only 5.4 per cent (Filler et al., 2006).

Legal context(s)

While equal opportunity initiatives have been strongly supported by the Swiss Federal Act for Gender Equality, this is much less the case in regard to diversity management in general. Here, Switzerland's legal situation is not very clear or well defined; therefore it plays only a minor role in the implementation of diversity management in Swiss companies. Interviews with several diversity managers (Benz, 2008) confirmed the findings of Filler et al. (2006): anti-discrimination laws in other countries and the Swiss Federal Act for Gender Equality have served as major legal drivers towards diversity management. Otherwise, however, the rationales for diversity management are to be found primarily in business-related arguments: demography, innovation and customer orientation. However, there is also evidence that companies in the private sector are actually not aware of the legal requirements in place at an international level. For instance, in a New York court case, the Swiss pharmaceutical company Novartis was accused of systematic discrimination (Aiolfi, 2005).

In order to understand the legal situation it is important to acknowledge Switzerland's position as a special case within the European context (Epiney and Waldmann, 2004). Although it is located at the very heart of Europe, it might be the only European country that is not directly affected by the legislation of the European Union. Though it is not a member of the European Union, Switzerland closely follows the changes in European legislation, adopting some for domestic use and rejecting others. It adopts some laws through bilateral negotiations and others through plebiscite; many legislative changes are adopted by popular vote. For instance, the recently accepted EU directives for equal treatment on the basis of gender, race, sexual orientation, age and disability, which have resulted in anti-discrimination laws, are not effective in Switzerland. However, in bilateral agreements Switzerland agreed to the free movement of persons between member states; thus it is obliged to recognize professional qualifications, grant immigrants the right to buy property, and coordinate social security systems (cf. Amstutz and Müller, 2008, pp. 362–3).

Although Switzerland has not yet implemented a general anti-discrimination law and is not obliged to follow recent legislative developments in the European Union, Swiss federal legislation does provide some basis for the practice of diversity management in the public and, to a lesser extent, the private sector. An important passage in the Swiss Constitution guarantees the equality of all human beings before the law and outlaws discrimination. Also playing important roles are international human right conventions and several passages in the employment law.[13] And, to enforce this legislation in the private sector, an initiative was recently introduced in parliament supporting the idea of a 'diversity charter'.[14] This is a voluntary agreement by companies to ban any kind of discrimination in the workplace.

This strategy of voluntary agreements is quite typical of what could be called a 'Swiss way' of managing diversity. Drawing on liberal discourses of free will and choice, voluntary actions are generally preferred to normative, legal and mandatory consequences. In a similar vein, although the federal Constitution includes quotas to ensure that cultural regions and languages are appropriately represented in the Swiss Federal Council, they generate strong debate, for instance over gender diversity (Arioli, 1998). In the following paragraphs, we sketch out the various legal contexts of diversity management in Switzerland (see also Hausammann, 2008).

International and European conventions on human rights
Switzerland has signed several important international conventions, including the European Convention for the Protection of Human Rights and Fundamental Freedoms (ECHR); the United Nations Covenants I and II on Economic, Social and Cultural Rights (Covenant I) and Civil and Political rights (Covenant II); the International Convention on the Elimination of All Forms of Racial Discrimination (CERD); and

the UN Convention on the Elimination of All Forms of Discrimination against Women (CEDAW). All these require state parties to take suitable measures against all forms of discrimination. Also, they all have a programmatic character, which gives them a certain relevance in the economic sector, but they are not directly applicable to the situation of diversity management in companies except where those situations are governed by law.

The federal Constitution

Diversity is an important notion in the preamble of Switzerland's federal Constitution, which emphasizes the importance of Switzerland's historically developed cultural diversity, with its four languages and culturally specific regions. Specifically, the Swiss Constitution sets out the official languages,[15] guarantees cultural diversity[16] and defines the composition of the Swiss Federal Council (Bundesrat), and the appropriate representation of cultural regions and languages.[17] It takes diversity as a given and calls for tolerance, consideration and respect. However, these articles are not actionable and are mostly important as mission statements.

Article 8, Paragraph 1 of the Constitution tackles the general equality of all human beings before the law, and the paragraphs that follow lay out non-discrimination rules for several categories of diversity (Kälin 1999). Paragraph 2 states that 'No one may be discriminated against, in particular on grounds of origin, race, gender, age, language, social position, way of life, religious, ideological, or political convictions, or because of a physical, mental or psychological disability.' Gender equality is approached in Paragraph 3: 'Men and women shall have equal rights. The law shall ensure their equality, both in law and in practice, most particularly in the family, in education, and in the workplace. Men and women shall have the right to equal pay for work of equal value.' While the general non-discrimination rule requires activity from the legislature, the right to equal pay is directly applicable to the private sector (Epiney and Waldmann, 2004, p. 493).

Following the constitutional article on non-discrimination, several laws have been passed that apply to specific diversity categories (Hausammann, 2008). However, their level of detail and scope is very heterogeneous.

The Federal Act on Gender Equality (GEA)   This act constitutes the legal framework

for gender equality in work contexts (Freivogel, 1996; Kaufmann and Steiger-Sackmann, 2009). It prohibits any form of direct or indirect discrimination in the work context, which is applicable 'in particular to hiring, allocation of duties, setting of working conditions, pay, basic and advanced training, promotion and dismissal' (GEA, Art. 3.2). Also prohibited are sexual harassment and discrimination in the case of female employees, or on the basis of marital status, family situation or pregnancy.

The Federal Act on Gender Equality was established in 1996[18] and resulted in several structural measurements in Swiss companies. For instance, counselling services have been set up to respond to issues of sexual harassment and bullying, and human resource policies and practices have been analysed for potential discrimination and changed when necessary. Because the GEA reduces the burden of proof on a claimant,[19] companies are focusing more on non-discrimination and gender equality (Benz, 2008). Furthermore, this Act has both preventive and protective functions. In particular, Article 3.3 explicitly states that positive discrimination resulting from appropriate measures that aim at achieving true equality are not to be regarded as discriminatory. However, this has not been interpreted as a reasonable ground for the introduction of quotas. Furthermore, Articles 14 and 15 establish the basis for funding advice centres and for the Federal Office of Gender Equality to develop and implement specific measures in public or private institutions; this has resulted in a great variety of tools and measures becoming available free of charge (www.topbox.ch).

The Federal Act on Equal Rights for People with Disabilities (EPDA)   This Act, adopted in 2004, mandates improved conditions for the integration of people with disabilities. However, its primary focus is to ensure that those individuals have free access to public buildings, transport, services and education. As employment relations are only affected in the public sector on the federal level, this law has fairly marginal importance at the cantonal level and for the private sector.

Language diversity   Language diversity is, as already mentioned, at the heart of the federal Constitution (Art. 70). It stipulates that the federal confederation will operate in four official languages (German, French, Italian and Romansh), and all official documents are published in German, French and Italian. Although Romansh is an official language, its use is only compulsory when communicating with persons speaking Romansh. Again, this law is applicable for the public but not for the private sector.

Employment law: protection of the employee's personality and maternity leave
A third possible legal foundation for diversity management practices is the employment law. This law mandates the protection of personal integrity, particularly bodily, mental and sexual integrity, and protects the individual's social, personal and professional reputation.[20] The concept of protecting the integrity of the personality also covers discrimination on account of race, religion, ethnicity, sexuality and disabilities. However, the freedom of contract in employment relations is seen as having a higher claim than this law; therefore, under this law a case of arbitrary wage differences might not be a case of discrimination unless the employee's integrity of personality was severely disregarded or damaged. The protection of personal integrity obliges employers to proactively manage conflicts and to generally create a non-discriminatory work environment. It also protects employees against discriminatory dismissals.

While the employment law included maternity leave, which protects women during the first eight weeks after they give birth, it did not mandate that wages continue for that period.[21] Only since 2005 has the maternity leave benefit been in place, covering 80 per cent of the mother's salary for 14 weeks. There is no enforced parental leave for fathers, although the idea has been thoroughly debated and some companies have implemented it voluntarily.

Researching diversity management
In the sections above we have indicated that although Switzerland has a long tradition of dealing with diversity, the global concept of diversity management has been fairly slow to arrive in Switzerland's businesses and seems to be given more attention by multinational companies than by small and medium-sized enterprises (SMEs). In all domains of diversity, from culture to gender, and in both managerial and legal practices, a crucial tension exists: Switzerland is traditionally constructed around a discourse that it is a

'special case', but, like any other country, it is constantly influenced by global tendencies that could threaten and transform that uniqueness. By focusing on diversity management within Switzerland and writing a chapter to make this national case, we seem to have already done something that is typical of the research on diversity management: we have reified dimensions of diversity (in this case, nationality) and considered them as essential features of people, groups and even countries.

Instead of taking these reified categories for granted and assuming that there is something like a Swiss case of diversity, we have underlined that diversity studies have to enquire how diversity is 'made in Switzerland', which is itself an effect of a complex translation process between global and local conditions. Thus we must actually engage with reflexive and critical approaches for establishing studies of diversity management (with a national context). For instance, the paradox is that there is probably no country like Switzerland – notice our own narrative strategy here – that simultaneously draws upon its own invented myth of tradition and tries to recognize itself as a global player. In our view this paradox forms an intriguing starting point for studies in the field of diversity management; the aim of such studies is to understand how diversity management is practised by drawing upon global ideas, discourses of nation-making and more local narratives.

However, the research on diversity management has only recently gained momentum (in rhythm with the managerial practice of diversity) and seems to be following a line of development similar to that in other European countries where more normative and atheoretical research is complemented by more critical, conceptually based research (Lorbiecki and Jack, 2000). Rather than review this research and literature overall, we shall discuss a few theoretically grounded studies on how diversity management is practised; these can shed some light on how diversity management is translated into the Swiss work context.

With regard to the fashionable character of diversity management and the fact that many companies mostly engage in a kind of 'distant cheerleading' (Dick and Cassell, 2002), Prasad and Mills (1997, p. 8) clearly documented how diversity management is presented as a showcase; based on a discourse of 'success', workplace diversity is given 'enormously positive publicity . . . by highlighting its more striking accomplishments and attractive features'. Because of this emphasis on the success story, more critical studies have questioned whether diversity practices, by definition, bring differences along with them. These critical studies, based on discourse theory, look into more historical changes of discourses on diversity (Prasad, 2001; Runté and Mills, 2006) as well as the organizational contexts in which discourses are negotiated (Kirby and Harter, 2001; Tomlinson and Egan, 2002; Zanoni and Janssens, 2007). Such discursive and practice-based studies follow a similar line of critical and reflexive studies as currently observed in HRM studies in general (Janssens and Steyaert, 2009).

A first example of such a study in the Swiss context is that by Ostendorp (2006). The emphasis is on how *in vivo* diversity management is formed and practised through a complex negotiating process where several different discourses can be observed in action as people make sense of various diversity initiatives (Ostendorp and Steyaert, 2009). The study documents how the discourses of diversity management practised in Swiss companies are not simply mirroring the global concept, but are translated into local practices. From this perspective, diversity management is not as homogeneous as the simple categorization into either a 'business' or an 'equity' orientation might suggest. Rather, both normative-ethical and economic motives are treated as valid rationales for an investment in workforce diversity (Ryser, 2010).

For instance, Ostendorp (2006, 2009) and Ostendorp and Steyaert (2009) have conducted elaborate analyses of interviews with organizers of and participants in diversity management programmes in Swiss companies and have demonstrated that practices overlap and vary widely. For instance, when talking about diversity, a very broad range of initiatives and interventions has been subsumed under the label of diversity management and neighbouring fields. They range from issues such as different language groups, gender and disabilities to work–life balance, healthcare and corporate volunteering (Ostendorp and Steyaert, 2009). Analysing how these different initiatives and objectives are negotiated, Ostendorp and Steyaert differentiate four different interpretative repertoires of diversity management, all constructing a specific understanding of differences: differences as taboo, as need, as dispute and as *sine qua non*. In fact, the objectives of these initiatives also vary considerably (Nentwich, 2006a; Ostendorp and Nentwich, 2005). The authors conclude that the current use of such repertoires impedes the process of inscribing differences into the overall organization, rather than facilitating it. Furthermore, they suggest, the way diversity management travels as a global idea is strongly affected by the political negotiation through which the standard image of the ideal worker can be challenged and other images can be infused into a more hybrid organization.

A second study (Steyaert et al., 2008) considers how the multilingual situation is practised in Swiss organizations, especially as English gains influence as the global business language. This study forms part of a national research programme of the Swiss National Science Foundation, investigating how Switzerland should consider its linguistic policy for the future, based on research concerning the language education of youngsters and adults, and the legal, political, economic and social conditions in which language practices must be considered. As a multilingual country, Switzerland performs what can be called a linguistic peace-making, maintaining a balance, both legally and socially, between the linguistic rights of different groups.

While it is quite a balancing act to consider this multilingualism, globalization and immigration challenge the current solutions and practices in many ways. Illustrative of this tension is a manifesto for a lived, linguistic diversity in Switzerland, promoted by a group of for-profit and non-profit organizations as well as by prominent figures from politics, culture and business.[22] Although the group wanted to safeguard language diversity in general and promote linguistic competence in a wide range of languages, the media pointed out an underlying concern with the threat that emanates from 'the English wave' and the increasing weight of English as *lingua franca*.[23] There was talk of 'a lobby for language diversity'[24] that was erecting 'a barrier' and would 'enter the battlefield' (*'eine Kampfansage'*) against the English trend[25] and 'chase English' (*'chasse à l'Anglais'*).[26]

At the same time, the texts did not directly confront English, as the group sees that language diversity is a factor in Switzerland's economic success, which would hardly be imaginable without English competence, especially for the business lobby. The manifesto thus provoked a mixture of discourses on language diversity that contained instrumental referents ('competitive advantage', 'key to success'), as well as cultural ('it is about our identity') and 'political' ('confederal peace') argumentations (Janssens et al., 2004). In the analysis, Steyaert et al. (2008) suggest that multilingualism is performed as participants

Summary table for Switzerland

Existence of anti-discrimination legislation	Yes
Criteria covered by anti-discrimination legislation	Official languages, gender, disability
Criteria for which the reporting of quantitative data and their communication to a public administration are compulsory	n.a.
Criteria covered by 'affirmative' or 'positive' action legislation other than unemployment- or income-based	Official languages, gender
Existence of a discourse or debate about 'non-discrimination' or 'equality'	Yes
Existence of a discourse or debate about 'diversity'	Yes
Year or period when the 'discrimination' concept started to disseminate in management literature in the country	Mid-1980s for women in management and equal opportunity initiatives
Year or period when the diversity concept started to disseminate in management literature in the country	Around year 2000 in German-language journals and 2003/4 in the French literature
Who pushed the 'diversity' agenda?	Multinationals and US-based companies, NGOs and the women's movement, individual diversity managers, federal legislation on gender equality and anti-discrimination, gender and diversity scholars, Federal Office for Gender Equality
Existence of a professional association representing diversity professionals and year of creation	No
Existence of a professional association representing diversity scholars and year of creation	Network of researchers in Gender and Diversity Management Studies in Austria, Germany and Switzerland, 2006. Annual conference: www.genderportal.unisg.ch

negotiate over which languages can be spoken based on several sometimes incompatible rules of conduct. As a consequence, English cannot be seen as taking over the linguistic landscape of a company, but has to be situated within the whole range of alternatives a multilingual organization imagines it can draw upon to combine various languages.

Based on these examples of studies in the Swiss context, we suggest the following conclusion: the academic field seems to take a certain critical and reflexive approach to the global idea of diversity management and calls for more studies that contextualize their research process and that focus on the problems around the attempts to have diversity initiatives bring about change in everyday life. This orients research to questions of power, agency and participation, which are well summarized by Özbilgin and Tatlı (2008, p. 390): 'Can diversity managers engender the organizational change which they envision?' We think that research conducted with regard to these questions might make a considerable impact on the ways in which practitioners and professionals imagine that diversity issues can be managed. By understanding how diversity is made and negotiated in the Swiss context, both practitioners and researchers need to become sensitive to issues of change and change agency as they can be observed in tensions between the normal and the different, the local and the global, the known and the other. This would imply that researchers and practitioners alike consider diversity management to be a reflexive practice that can indeed transform organizations and the society in which they are embedded into more inclusive, social arenas.

Notes

1. We would like to thank Margot Benz for providing the solid background on the legal aspects discussed in this chapter and the interviews with diversity managers in her master's thesis; Professor Regula Kägi-Diener and Dr Kathrin Arioli for providing crucial feedback on the legal aspects; our colleagues Dr Anja Ostendorp and Claudine Gaibrois for several discussions on the chapter; and, last but not least, Dr Helen Snively for her language editing.
2. The term 'special case' translates as Sonderfall in German-speaking Switzerland, as insula elvetica in Ticino and as the Franco-German hybrid Le Sonderfall in the French-speaking part (Eberle, 2007, p. 7). The notion of Switzerland as a special case is based on the system of consociational democracy, the tradition that the Swiss confederation had a rural genesis, and the associated semantics of threat and resistance defied by a joint battle (Eberle, 2007, p. 7; Imhof, 2007).
3. The expression 'Switzerland doesn't exist' goes back to a piece of art by Ben Vautier, displayed at the world exhibition in Seville in 1992. Black hand-written letters on a white ground proclaim that 'la Suisse n'existe pas'. The expression plays with the notion of Switzerland as a volatile nation and a special case.
4. The Swiss novelist Thomas Hürlimann (2002) described this clash of logics, spaces and rhythms as Swiss schizophrenia.
5. Nentwich (2006b) investigated the importance of diversity management in Swiss universities. She points out that gender equality developed as an important topic in the 1990s and that other dimensions of diversity are yet to be discovered.
6. The *Neue Zürcher Zeitung* is a leading intellectual paper in the German-speaking part of Switzerland.
7. Similar results can be found in the Adecco study (2008) on the 'demographic fitness' of European companies. Switzerland, with 172 points, was situated near one end of a scale ranging from 100 to 400 points, but the variance of findings among countries is very small here. Nevertheless, the authors conclude that Swiss companies are rather badly prepared for the demographic change expected in the coming decades. At the same time, conditions in the Swiss labour market are very favourable for employees, so the Swiss will face the fewest difficulties in filling vacancies compared with other countries.
8. See also Nentwich (2006b, pp. 151–2).
9. The survey focused on companies listed as the 'Top 500' in Switzerland in the Swiss *Handelszeitung* (2004); 118 companies responded, yielding a response rate of 25 per cent. The questionnaire focused on the current mindset towards diversity within the executive levels in these organizations and the diversity practices in place. The study concentrated on two diversity dimensions: gender and nationality.
10. http://www.diversity-ch.ch/traegerschaft.html.
11. The Swiss Performance Index is Switzerland's most closely followed performance index.
12. This is the Swiss stock market index, the most important in Switzerland. According to the Ethos study, 8 per cent of board directors were females in these 26 SMI firms in 2005 (Biedermann et al., 2005).
13. See http://www.eda.admin.ch/eda/en/home.html, the homepage of the Swiss Federal Department of Foreign Affairs for details on the internationally relevant legal situation and the legal texts and http://www.humanrights.ch for details on the legal texts relevant to diversity management.
14. www.diversity-charta.ch.
15. Art. 4 and Art. 70, para. 3.
16. Art. 69, para. 3.
17. Art. 175, para. 4.
18. All legal cases conducted in German that lead to a sentence are published; commentary is available on the website www.gleichstellungsgesetz.ch.
19. Article 6 of the Gender Equality Act reads: 'In relation to the allocation of duties, setting of working conditions, pay, basic and advanced training, promotion and dismissal, discrimination is presumed if the person concerned can substantiate the same by prima facie evidence.'
20. Article 328, Swiss Code of Obligations (*Obligationenrecht*).
21. See Hauser (2004) for a historical perspective on the development of maternity leave insurance in both Switzerland and Germany.

22. These documents can be consulted on www.chstiftung.ch in three languages but not in English.
23. The term comes from Arabic 'lisan-al-farang', an intermediary language that speakers of Arabic use to communicate with travellers from Europe (House, 2003, p. 557).
24. Quote from the *Neue Zürcher Zeitung*, a leading intellectual paper in the German-speaking part of Switzerland, 5 May 2006.
25. Quotes from the general edition of a regional paper, *Sankt Galler Tagblatt*, 5 May 2006.
26. Quote from the *Journal du Jura*, a regional French-language paper, 5 May 2006.

References

Actares (2008), 'Auswertung zur Umfrage der Frauenvertretung im Verwaltungsrat und Top-Management', www.actares.ch/Downloads/ACTARES_Umfrage_2008_Frauenvertretung.pdf, 20 March 2009.

Adecco (2008), 'Press release: Swiss companies are hardly affected by demographic change – Switzerland's attraction compensates for the consequences'.

Aiolfi, S. (2005), 'Die Personalpolitik von Novartis am Pranger', *Neue Zürcher Zeitung*, 11 May, p. 63.

Amstutz, N. and C. Müller (2008), 'Diversity management', in W. Steiger and E. Lippmann (eds), *Handbuch Angewandte Psychologie für Führungskräfte*, Heidelberg: Springer, pp. 359–80.

Aretz, H.-J. (2006), 'Strukturwandel in der Weltgesellschaft und Diversity Management im Unternehmen', in M. Becker (ed.), *Diversity-Management Unternehmens- und Personalpolitik der Vielfalt*, Stuttgart: Schäffer-Poeschel, pp. 52–75.

Arioli, K. (1998), 'Die schweizerische Debatte um die Einführung von Frauenquoten in der Politik', *Schweizerische Zeitschrift für Politikwissenschaft*, **4** (2), 131–7.

Arioli, K., M. Hofer, S. Keller, R. Tobler and E. Violi (2007), *Der Lohngleichheitsreport. Ein Schulungsinstrument zur Förderung der Lohngleichheit*, Zürich: vdf Hochschulverlag.

Baillod, J., A. Blum et al. (eds) (2002), *Chance Teilzeitarbeit: Argumente und Materialien für Verantwortliche*, Zürich: vdf Hochschulverlag.

Baitsch, C. and E. Steiner (2004), *Zwei tun das Gleiche. Kommunikation zwischen Frauen und Männern im Berufsalltag*, Zürich: vdf Hochschulverlag.

Bendl, R. (2004), 'Gendermanagement und Gender- und Diversitätsmanagement – ein Vergleich der verschiedenen Ansätze', in R. Bendl, E. Hanappi-Egger and R. Hofmann (eds), *Interdisziplinäres Gender- und Diversitätsmanagement: Einführung in Theorie und Praxis*, Wien: Linde, pp. 43–72.

Benz, M. (2008), *Rechtliche Rahmenbedingungen des Diversity Management und ihre Bedeutung in der Praxis*, St Gallen: University of St Gallen.

Bergmann, M.M. and V. Mottier (2004), 'Kulturelle Vielfalt in der Schweiz', in C. Suter, I. Renschler and D. Joye (eds), *Sozialbericht 2004*, Zürich: Seismo, pp. 73–100.

Biedermann, Y., V. Kaufmann and V. Mathys (2005), *Corporate Governance der Schweizer Unternehmen*, Genf: Ethos.

Brodbeck, F.C. (1999), *Synergy is not for free. Theoretische Modelle und experimentelle Untersuchungen über Leistung und Leistungsveränderung in aufgabenorientierten Kleingruppen*, München: LMU.

Bühler, S. (ed.) (2004), *Kinder und Karriere – Vereinbarkeit von Beruf und Familie. Kurzfassung des OECD-Ländervergleichs zu Neuseeland, Portugal und der Schweiz mit besonderer Berücksichtigung der Teile zur Schweiz*, Bern: State Secretary for Economic Affairs (SECO).

Bütler, M. (2007), 'Arbeiten lohnt sich nicht – ein zweites Kind noch weniger. Zum Einfluss einkommensabhängiger Tarife in der Kinderbetreuung', *Perspektiven der Wirtschaftspolitik*, **8** (1), 1–19.

Cox, T.H. (1993), *Cultural Diversity in Organizations: Theory, Research and Practice*, San Francisco, CA: Berrett-Koehler Publishers.

Cranach, M. v., Netzwerk für sozial verantwortliche Wirtschaft, and Netzwerk für die Arbeitsgesellschaft (2004), *Ältere Menschen im Unternehmen Chancen, Risiken, Modelle*, Bern: Haupt.

Czarniawska, B. and G. Sevón (2005), *Global Ideas: How Ideas, Objects and Practices Travel in the Global Economy*, Malmö: Liber and Copenhagen Business School Press.

Davoine, E. (2005), 'Formation et parcours professionnel des dirigeants d'entreprise en Suisse', *Revue Economique et Sociale*, **64**, 93–103.

Dick, P. and C. Cassell (2002), 'Barriers to managing diversity in a UK constabulary: the role of discourse', *Journal of Management Studies*, **39** (7), 953–76.

Ducret, V. (2003), *Sexuelle Belästigung – was tun? Leitfaden für Betriebe*, Zürich: vdf-Verlag.

Eberle, T.S. (2007), 'Der Sonderfall Schweiz aus soziologischer Perspektive', in T.S. Eberle and K. Imhof (eds), *Sonderfall Schweiz*, Zürich: Seismo, pp. 7–22.

Epiney, A. and B. Waldmann (2004), *Gleichstellung von Frauen und Männern in der Schweiz und der EU*, Zürich: Schulthess.

Fachstelle UND (2000), 'Kriterien für Unternehmen und Verwaltungen', www.und-online.ch.

Filler, E., B. Liebig, M. Fengler-Veith and K. Varan (2006), *Diversity in Switzerland. A Study of the Top 500 Companies*, Chicago, IL: Heidrick and Struggles.

Flückiger, Y. and J. Ramirez (2000), 'Analyse comparative des salaires entre les hommes et les femmes sur la base de la LSE 1994 et 1996', *Observatoire Universitaire de l'Emploi*, Geneva: University of Geneva.

Folini, E. (2007), *Das Ende der gläsernen Decke. Die Entwicklung der Geschlechtergleichstellung am Beispiel eines Dienstleistungsunternehmens*, Bern: Haupt.

Freivogel, E. (1996), *Gleichstellung im Erwerbsleben. Informationen zum Bundesgesetz über die Gleichstellung von Frau und Mann*, Bern: EDMZ.

Fried, A., R. Wetzel and C. Baitsch (2000), *Wenn zwei das Gleiche tun . . . Diskriminierungsfreie Personalbeurteilung*, Zürich: vdf Hochschulverlag.

Gygi, B. (2005), 'Diversity wird in der Schweizer Wirtschaft eher beiläufig gepflegt', *Neue Zürcher Zeitung*, 29 November.

Hausammann, C. (2008), 'Instrumente gegen Diskriminierung im schweizerischen Recht – ein Überblick', Bern: Eidgenössisches Büro für die Gleichstellung von Menschen mit Behinderungen (EBGB) und Fachstelle für Rassismusbekämpfung (FRB).

Hauser, K. (2004), *Die Anfänge der Mutterschaftsversicherung. Deutschland und Schweiz im Vergleich*, Zürich: Chronos Verlag.

Hausmann, R., L.D. Tyson and S. Zahidi (eds) (2008), *The Global Gender Gap Report*, Geneva: World Economic Forum.

House, J. (2003), 'English as lingua franca: a threat to multilingualism?', *Journal of Sociolinguistics*, **7** (4), 556–78.

Hürlimann, T. (2002), 'Himmelshöhi, hilf! Mein Land in seiner grössten Krise', in T. Hürlimann (ed.), *Himmelshöhi, hilf! Über die Schweiz und andere Nester. Kleine Schriften vermischten Inhalts*, Zürich: Ammann.

Imhof, K. (2007), 'Sonderfalldiskurse und Pfadabhängigkeit: Der Fall Schweiz', in T.S. Eberle and K. Imhof (eds), *Sonderfall Schweiz*, Zürich: Seismo Verlag, pp. 25–55.

Jacquemart, C. (2006), 'Noch 962 Jahre bis zur Gleichstellung', *Neue Zürcher Zeitung*, 8 January, p. 23.

Janssens, M. and C. Steyaert (2009), 'HRM and performance: a plea for reflexivity in HRM-studies', *Journal of Management Studies*, **46** (1), 143–55.

Janssens, M., J. Lambert and C. Steyaert (2004), 'Developing language strategies for international companies: the contribution of translation studies', *Journal of World Business*, **39** (4), 414–30.

Jaworski, A. and I. Piller (2008), 'Linguascaping Switzerland: language ideologies in tourism', in M. Locher and J. Strässler (eds), *Standards and Norms in the English Language*, Berlin: Mouton de Gruyter, pp. 301–21.

Kadishi, B. (2001), *Schlüsselkompetenzen wirksam erfassen*, Altstätten: Tobler.

Kalev, A., F. Dobbin and E. Kelly (2006), 'Best practices or best guesses? Assessing the efficacy of corporate affirmative action and diversity policies', *American Sociological Review*, **71**, 589–617.

Kälin, W. (1999), *Das Verbot ethnisch-kultureller Diskriminierung verfassungs- und menschenrechtliche Aspekte*, Basel: Helbing u. Lichtenhahn.

Kaufmann, C. and S. Steiger-Sackmann (eds) (2009), *Kommentar zum Gleichstellungsgesetz* (2. Aufl. ed.), Basel: Helbing and Lichtenhahn.

Kirby, E.L. and L.M. Harter (2001), 'Discourses of diversity and the quality of work life', *Management Communication Quarterly*, **15** (1), 121–7.

Kuark, J.K. (2003), *Das Modell TopSharing. Gemeinsam an die Spitze*, Lenzburg: www.topsharing.ch.

Künzle, C. (2009), 'Intelligent, schön, erfolgreich – und Single. Der stille Schmerz von Frauen in Führungspositionen. Empirische Untersuchung zur Vereinbarkeit von Karriere und Familie bei weiblichen Führungskräften in der Schweiz in den Jahren 2004 und 2008', Zürich: Choice Executive and Business Coaching.

Lenzin, D. (2000), *Die Sache der Frauen: OFRA und die Frauenbewegung in der Schweiz*, Zürich: Rotpunktverlag.

Liebig, B. (2000), 'Organisationskultur und Geschlechtergleichstellung. Eine Typologie betrieblicher Geschlechterkulturen', *Zeitschrift für Frauenforschung & Geschlechterstudien*, **18** (3), 47–66.

Liebig, B. (ed.) (2010a), *Corporate Social Responsibility in der Schweiz. Massnahmen und Wirkungen*, Bern: Haupt.

Liebig, B. (ed.) (2010b), 'Gender and diversity: engagement im Bereich Gleichstellung und personelle Vielfalt', in B. Liebig (ed.), *Corporate Social Responsibility in der Schweiz. Massnahmen und Wirkungen*, Bern: Haupt, pp. 45–75.

Lorbiecki, A. and G. Jack (2000), 'Critical turns in the evolution of diversity management', *British Journal of Management*, **11**, 17–31.

McKinsey and Company (2007), 'Women matter. Gender diversity, a corporate performance driver', http://www.mckinsey.com/locations/swiss/news_publications/pdf/women_matter_english.pdf. Date accessed: 4 January 2010.

Müller, C. and G. Sander (2005), *Gleichstellungs-Controlling: das Handbuch für die Arbeitswelt*, Zürich: vdf Hochschulverlag.

Nentwich, J.C. (2004), *Die Gleichzeitigkeit von Differenz und Gleichheit. Neue Wege für die Gleichstellungsarbeit*, Königstein i.T.: Ulrike Helmer Verlag.

Nentwich, J.C. (2006a), 'Changing gender: the discursive construction of equal opportunities', *Gender, Work and Organization*, **13** (6), 499–521.

Nentwich, J.C. (2006b), 'Equity and diversity at universities in Switzerland', in G. Vedder (ed.), *Managing Equity and Diversity at Universities*, München/Mering: Rainer Hampp Verlag, pp. 149–64.

Nentwich, J.C. (2008), 'New fathers and mothers as gender trouble makers? Exploring discursive constructions of heterosexual parenthood and their subversive potential', *Feminism and Psychology*, **18** (2), 207–30.

Nkomo, S. (1992), 'The emperor has no clothes: rewriting race in organizations', *Academy of Management Review*, **17** (3), 487–513.

Ostendorp, A. (2006), 'Human resource and corporate social responsibility concepts between fashionable luxury, old conflicts of interests, and new lines of flight', doctoral thesis, Universität Zürich.

Ostendorp, A. (2007), 'Möglichkeiten für KMU und Grossunternehmen bei der Umsetzung eines Trends: Life Balance als Beitrag zu einer Kultur der Unterschiede?', in A. S. Esslinger and D. Schobert (eds), *Erfolgreiche Umsetzung von Work–Life Balance in Organisationen. Strategien, Konzepte, Massnahmen*, Wiesbaden: Deutscher Universitätsverlag, pp. 187–211.

Ostendorp, A. (2009), 'Consistency and variability in talk about "Diversity": An empirical analysis of discursive scope in Swiss large scale enterprises', *Forum Qualitative Sozialforschung/Forum: Qualitative Social Research*, North America, 10 February 2009, http://www.qualitative-research.net/index.php/fqs/article/view/451/2715.

Ostendorp, A. and J.C. Nentwich (2009), 'Weltoffenheit unter Gleichgesinnten: Widersprüchlicher Ein- und Ausschluss als diskursive Alltagspraxis', OPSY Working Paper, St Gallen: Research Institute for Organizational Psychology.

Ostendorp, A. and J.C. Nentwich (2005), 'Im Wettbewerb um "Familienfreundlichkeit". Konstruktionen familienfreundlicher Wirklichkeiten zwischen gleichstellerischen Idealen und pragmatischer Machbarkeit', *Zeitschrift für Familienforschung*, **17** (3), 333–56.

Ostendorp, A. and C. Steyaert (2009), 'How different can differences be(come)? Interpretative repertoires of diversity concepts in Swiss-based organizations', *Scandinavian Journal of Management*, **25** (4), 374–84.

Osterloh, M. and S. Littmann-Wernli (2000), 'Die "gläserne Decke": Realität und Widersprüche', in S. Peter and N. Bensel (eds), *Frauen ins Management. Diversity in Diskurs und Praxis*, Wiesbaden: Gabler Verlag, pp. 123–39.

Özbilgin, M.F. and A. Tatlı (2008), *Global Diversity Management. An Evidence-Based Approach*, New Hampshire, New York: Palgrave Macmillan.

Point, S. and V. Singh (2003), 'Defining and dimensionalising diversity: evidence from corporate websites across Europe', *European Management Journal*, **21** (6), 750–61.

Prasad, A. (2001), 'Understanding workplace empowerment as inclusion: a historical investigation of the discourse of difference in the United States', *The Journal of Applied Behavioral Science*, **37** (1), 51–69.

Prasad, P. and A.J. Mills (1997), 'From showcase to shadow. Understanding the dilemmas of managing workplace diversity', in P. Prasad, A.J. Mills, M. Elmes and A. Prasad (eds), *Managing the Organizational Melting Pot. Dilemmas of Workplace Diversity*, Thousand Oaks, CA: Sage, pp. 3–27.

Ruigrok, W. and P. Greve (2008), 'Does nationality still matter? (3) National identities still matter at top management teams', *European Business Forum*, **32**, 19–20.

Ruigrok, W., S. Peck and S. Tacheva (2007), 'Nationality and gender diversity on Swiss corporate boards', *An International Review*, **15**, 546–57.

Runté, M. and A.J. Mills (2006), 'Cold war, chilly climate: exploring the roots of gendered discourse in organization and management theory', *Human Relations*, **59** (5), 695–720.

Ryser, T. (2010), 'Der gesellschaftliche Beitrag von Schweizer Unternehmen – Leistungswirkungen einer strategisch motivierten Philanthropie', in B. Liebig (ed.), *Corporate Social Responsibility in der Schweiz. Massnahmen und Wirkungen*, Bern: Haupt, pp. 152–213.

Schnegg, B. and A.-M. Stalder (1984), 'Zur Geschichte der Schweizerischen Frauenbewegung', in The Federal Commission for Women's Issues (ed.), *Die Stellung der Frau in der Schweiz. Teil IV: Frauenpolitik*, Bern, pp. 5–27.

Schweizerische Handelszeitung (2004), 'Top 2003 – Die grössten Unternehmen in der Schweiz'.

Sousa-Poza, A. (2002), 'Labour market segmentation and the gender wage gap: an industry-level analysis for Switzerland', *Cahiers Economiques de Bruxelles*, **45** (2), 91–118.

Sousa-Poza, A. (2003), 'The gender wage gap and occupational segregation in Switzerland, 1991–2001', *Schweizerische Zeitschrift für Soziologie*, **29** (3), 399–416.

State Secretariat for Economic Affairs (2005), *Partizipation älterer Arbeitnehmerinnen und Arbeitnehmer:*

Massnahmenvorschläge: Bereich Sozialversicherungen, Gesundheit am Arbeitsplatz, Arbeitsmarktfähigkeit, Bern: SECO.

State Secretariat for Economic Affairs (ed.) (2007), *KMU-Handbuch Beruf und Familie*, Bern: SECO.

Steyaert, C., A. Ostendorp and C. Gaibrois (2011), 'Multilingual organizations as linguascapes: negotiating the position of English through discursive practices', *Journal of World Business*, **46**, 3.

Steyaert, C., A. Ostendorp, N.R. Soccodato and C. Gaibrois (2008), *Sprachenpolitik und Identität in Organisationen*, Schlussbericht 'Sprachenvielfalt und Sprachkompetenz in der Schweiz', Nationales Forschungsprogramm No. 56.

Strub, S. (2003), *Teilzeitarbeit in der Schweiz. Eine Untersuchung mit Fokus auf der Geschlechterverteilung und der familiären Situation der Erwerbstätigen*, Bern: Eidgenössisches Büro für die Gleichstellung von Mann und Frau.

Strub, S., M. Gerfin and A. Büttikofer (2008), 'Vergleichende Analyse der Löhne von Frauen und Männern anhand der Lohnstrukturerhebungen 1998–2006. Untersuchung im Rahmen der Evaluation der Wirksamkeit des Gleichstellungsgesetzes', Bern: Swiss Federal Statistical Office.

Strub, S., E. Hüttner and J. Guggisberg (2005), 'Arbeitsteilung in Paarhaushalten. Aufteilung von bezahlter und unbezahlter Arbeit in der Schweiz', Neuchâtel: Swiss Federal Statistical Office.

Swiss Federal Statistical Office (2006), 'Ausländerinnen und Ausländer in der Schweiz', Neuchâtel.

Swiss Federal Statistical Office (2008a), 'Auf dem Weg zur Gleichstellung von Mann und Frau. Stand und Entwicklung', Neuchâtel.

Swiss Federal Statistical Office (2008b), 'Schweizerische Arbeitskräfteerhebung (SAKE)', Neuchâtel.

Swiss Federal Statistical Office (2009a), 'Erwerbskombinatinen in Paarhaushalten mit Kindern unter 7 Jahren', Neuchâtel.

Swiss Federal Statistical Office (2009b), 'Panorama: Arbeit und Erwerb', Neuchâtel.

Swiss Federal Statistical Office (2009c), 'Wohnbevölkerung nach Hauptsprache', Neuchâtel.

Tomlinson, F. and S. Egan (2002), 'Organizational sensemaking in a culturally diverse setting: limits to the "valuing diversity" discourse', *Management Learning*, **33** (1), 79–97.

Wajcman, J. (1998), *Managing Like a Man: Women and Men in Corporate Management*, Oxford: Polity Press.

Willemsen, T. (2001), 'Patterns of work, childcare, and household tasks in Europe: results of a comparative study', *New Patterns of Work and Family in Europe: The Role of Policies*, Brussels, 11/12 October.

Zanoni, P. and M. Janssens (2007), 'Minority employees engaging with (diversity) management: an analysis of control, agency, and micro-emancipation', *Journal of Management Studies*, **44** (8), 1371–97.

14 Discourses and practices of diversity management in the UK

Ahu Tatlı

Introduction

Managing diversity has become a popular perspective in both the academic and practitioner circles in the last decades. The concept was originated in the USA with the publication of *Workforce 2000: Work and workers for the 21ˢᵗ century*, a report by the Hudson Institute in 1987 (Johnston and Packer, 1987). From the 1990s onwards, the concept has gained popularity as a new management approach in the UK. This chapter aims to provide a critical and evidence-based account of the discourses and practices of diversity management in the UK context. The chapter will present an analysis of qualitative and quantitative evidence from two field studies conducted with the diversity managers of public and private sector organizations.

The first section will provide a background to the development of the diversity management discourse and structures. To do that, the legislative and regulatory framework in the UK in relation to equality and diversity will be introduced. Then diverse scholarly perspectives developed in the UK context will be reviewed in order to account for the equal opportunities versus diversity management debate. More specifically, critical perspectives that are particularly related to two building blocks of the diversity management approach, i.e. the business-case arguments and individualized definition of difference and diversity, will be briefly sketched. In the second section, I shall explore the discourses and practices prevailing in the field of diversity management. The exploration will be informed by original empirical evidence, which includes the individual accounts of 12 diversity managers from large public and private sector organizations in the UK collected through semi-structured interviews and quantitative data from an online survey that produced 285 completed questionnaires from diversity managers. The complex and contested nature of diversity management processes will be uncovered by presenting compelling empirical evidence against simplistic, a-historical, a-contextual and a-political notions of diversity management in the mainstream literature. In the last section, conclusions will be drawn from the discussions introduced earlier in the chapter. In the light of empirical evidence, I shall discuss the impact of national anti-discrimination legislation on organizational diversity policies and practices and revisit the US-originated mainstream assumption that diversity management represents a break with equal opportunities.

The evolution of anti-discrimination law in the UK: a paradigm shift from equality to diversity?

Although it was originally presented as a replacement for equality of opportunity (Thomas, 1990), diversity management is also arguably built on the legacy of the equal opportunities (Liff, 1996). As such, legal compliance forms a major driver for employers to adopt diversity management policies and initiate diversity management programmes

(Tatlı et al., 2006a, 2008). Reviewing the EU's equal opportunities policies from 1950s to 2000s, Rees (1998) suggests that the EU has gone through three main periods: equal treatment (1970s); positive action (1980s); and gender mainstreaming (post-1990s). At the outset, the commitment of the EU to equal opportunities was limited to equal pay for equal work. In the 1970s, the EU issued several equal opportunities and equal treatment directives on pay, working conditions, social security, training, recruitment and promotion. The 1980s marked the beginning of the adoption of a more proactive policy stance by the EU, extending the scope of its approach to equal opportunities beyond legalistic commitment to pay equality. However, the EU's equal opportunity approach during the 1980s still had serious limitations due to its gender-neutral stance and treatment of equal opportunities policies just as an addendum to the general EU policies (Young, 2000). Rees (1998) identifies the 1990s as a period of gender mainstreaming. Coupled with raising concerns about the feminization of poverty in the EU since the Fourth UN World Conference on Women in Beijing in 1995, gender mainstreaming became a popular expression in the equal opportunities lexicon.

The 2000s witnessed another shift in the EU's equal opportunities approach towards inclusion of multiple equality strands within the legal framework. In terms of gender equality, the multiplicity of forms of discrimination has been identified as a major concern (EC, 2000a, 2000b). The scope of the anti-discrimination clause has been widened to cover different forms of discrimination (i.e. sex, racial or ethnic origin, religion and belief, disability, age or sexual orientation) through Article 13 of the Treaty of Amsterdam and council directives (EC, 2000a). It should be noted that the multiplication of the strands covered by the EU's equal opportunities framework can be interpreted as an indication of a move towards a diversity management approach at the EU level.

Despite the fact that the interpretation and implementation of the EU legislation vary across member states in line with their socioeconomic contexts (Hoskyns, 1996), the EU framework has an important influence on the national equality legislations of EU members. For instance, most recently, sexual orientation, religion and belief, and age have been introduced in employment equality legislation in the UK in order to implement the European Employment Directive of 2000 (EC, 2000a).

In terms of the historical evolution of the equality legislation, the UK has been one of the most progressive within the EU. The current anti-discrimation legislation in the country comprises separate pieces of legislation that have been introduced over the past four decades. The earliest equality legislation in the UK was related to race and gender. The current Race Relations Act (RRA) was introduced in 1976 and amended in 2000. The amended RRA included statutory duties[1] for the public authorities to promote racial equality. In relation to gender inequality, the Equal Pay Act was enacted in 1970, followed by the Sex Discrimination Act of 1975 (amended in 1999). The Gender Equality Duty for the public sector came into force in 2007. The third category that has been introduced within the scope of equality legislation is disability. The Disability Discrimination Act was enacted in 1995 (amended in 2005) and the Disability Equality Duty for public authorities came into force in 2006.

In order to ensure the implementation of the equality legislation, statutory bodies were established in each of these three areas: the Commission for Racial Equality (CRE), the Equal Opportunities Commission (EOC) and the Disability Rights Commission (DRC). These commissions issue statutory codes of practice[2] in order to provide public authorities with guidance to meet the obligations enforced by the statutory equality duties under the anti-discrimination legislation. In other words, the codes of practice offer practical guidance for the public sector on promoting equal opportunities and tackling discrimination in particular fields (EHRC, 2009). For example, in the past the EOC has issued codes of practice on sex discrimination, equal pay and Gender Equality Duty.

At present there are no statutory codes covering discrimination on the grounds of sexual orientation, religion and belief, or age. However, more recently, other equality strands have been introduced in the anti-discrimination law in the UK, partly as a result of the European Employment Directive of 2000. Within that framework, the following legislation has been passed:

- The Employment Equality (Religion or Belief) Regulations 2003
- The Employment Equality (Sexual Orientation) Regulations 2003
- The Employment Equality (Age) Regulations 2006
- The Equality Act (Sexual Orientation) Regulations 2007

Another important development in terms of the equality legislation has been the enactment of the Equality Act. In 2004, the Equality Bill was announced by Parliament, and then passed in 2006. As a result, the Equality Act came into force in 2007. The new Act established the new equality commission, the Equality and Human Rights Commission (EHRC), which brought together all six strands of equality covered by the law, i.e. race, gender, disability, religion and belief, age, and sexual orientation – under the roof of a single statutory body.

Most recently, another Equality Bill was developed by the Government Equalities Office and published in April 2009. The Bill introduces a single legal framework for tackling discimination by distilling seperate pieces of equality legislation into a single Equality Act. Accordingly, a single public sector Equality Duty is proposed to replace the three existing, separate duties, to cover age, sexual orientation, religion or belief, as well as race, disability and gender. Other significant aspects of the Bill are the proposals for provisions for a socioeconomic duty, tackling the gender pay gap, promoting equality through procurement, and clarifying aspects of discrimination law and positive action (Government Equalities Office, 2009).

Despite the legislative efforts of the last decades, both at the EU level and in the UK, discrimination on grounds of race, gender, disability, age, religion and belief, and sexual orientation still exists. For example, employment patterns in the EU countries, including the UK, are still gendered and women still suffer considerable disadvantages in the labour market in terms of employment rates, occupational segregation, both vertical and horizontal, and the gender pay gap (Women and Work Commission, 2006). This persistence of structural inequalities has been one of the reasons behind the critical appraisal of the frameworks and ideas of equality of opportunity in the UK. The key scholars of equality and discrimination research in the country, including Cockburn (1989), Jewson and Mason (1986), Liff and Wajcman (1996), criticized the equal opportunities approaches in terms of limitations of positive action measures and the legalistic stance to transform workplaces' practices and social structures that reproduce and sustain disadvantage, discrimination and inequality.

Simultaneously, in the USA the critique of equal opportunities approaches was associated with an advocacy of a new approach – diversity management (Ashkanasy et al., 2002; Thomas, 1990). In the mainstream diversity management literature, the importance of legal regulations is underplayed. Diversity management is claimed to be marked by a voluntary approach on the side of employers that emerges, reflected by the business realities of the era, rather than by legal enforcement, as in the case of equal opportunities practices (Gilbert and Ivancevich, 2000; Morrison, 1992; Thomas, 1990). However, it is important for scholars of diversity and equality to scrutinize the differences and similarities between the equal opportunities and diversity management approaches. Here, the discussion will focus on two basic philosophical building blocks of the managing diversity approach: sublimation of difference as an individually based phenomenon; and emphasis on the business case.

Definition of diversity: social groups or individuals
The idea of equal opportunities is based on the belief in principles of individualism and merit (Jaquette, 1990). There has been a lively debate in the UK on the pitfalls of the philosophy of equality of opportunity. The equal opportunities scholars in the country argued that one of the limitations of the approach is its ignorance of the hidden male bias in the merit-based criteria (Liff and Wajcman, 1996) and the underlying assumption that individuals can be easily unburdened of the historical disadvantages associated with their gender and ethnicity (Liff, 1996). It is noted that by focusing on the sameness of individuals, equal opportunities approaches implicitly posit male characteristics and behaviours as the universal norm (Liff and Wajcman, 1996). Rees (1998) argues that equal opportunities programmes have enhanced the position of professional, middle-class women without seriously threatening the *status quo* and challenging the discrimination experienced by less advantaged categories of women. Analysing the gendered employment patterns and changes to the gender pay gap in the context of labour market deregulation in the UK, Bruegel and Perrons (1998) point out the limitations of equal opportunities frameworks and policies that do not acknowledge and are not linked to wider economic policies.

In order to overcome the liberal bias in equal opportunities frameworks, Jewson and Mason (1986) propose a 'radical approach'. They distinguish between liberal and radical approaches to change, where the scope of the former is limited to equality of opportunity while the latter aims for equality and fairness in outcomes. On the other hand, Cockburn (1989) critiques the liberal and radical dichotomy posited by these authors and puts forward the terms 'short agenda' and 'long agenda', both of which are crucial for the equal opportunities initiatives and programmes. She states that short and long agendas should not be understood as contradictory but complementary within the equal opportunities framework, where the short agenda will focus on minimizing the bias in HRM procedures, whereas the long agenda will target the transformation of the field of employment and organizations to radically dissolve discrimination and inequality in the workplace (Cockburn, 1989, p. 218).

Within that context, Rees (1998) argues that mainstreaming is the way out of the deadlock position of the current state of the equal opportunities approach since it provides a solution both to the limited liberal scope of positive action measures and to the issue of multiple discrimination. Reviewing the EU-level equal opportunities policies, she argues that the mainstreaming approach has become more pronounced within the equal opportunities framework. On the other hand, Young (2000) points out the danger that, in the process of mainstreaming, equal opportunities measures may be diluted.

Simultaneous with these discussions, diversity management has been proposed in the USA as a way forward. It is alleged that the managing diversity perspective has an advantage over equal opportunities due to its emphasis on difference and inclusion as opposed to the latter's emphasis on sameness and focus on gender and ethnicity, which led to a backlash (Thomas, 1990). However, the ability of a diversity management approach to propose realistic policies and programmes to tackle inequality and discrimination in the workplace depends on the nature of the treatment of difference within that approach. The definition of diversity has varied widely in the literature, displaying a spectrum ranging from the narrow definition based on the traditional categories of race, ethnicity and gender to inclusion of a vast array of differences in age, sexual orientation, disability, employment status, tenure, function, educational background, lifestyle, religion, values and beliefs (Ashkanasy et al., 2002). Diversity management as a new saga has been introduced to the UK context by Kandola and Fullerton (1998), who produced the most influential definition of diversity management in the country. They include a wide range of differences in their definition:

> The basic concept of managing diversity accepts that the workforce consists of a diverse population of people. The diversity consists of visible and nonvisible differences which will include factors such as sex, age, background, race, disability, personality and workstyle. It is founded on the premise that harnessing these differences will create a productive environment in which everyone feels valued, where their talents are being fully utilised and in which organizational goals are met. (Ibid., p. 7)

This definition reveals two important aspects of the diversity management approach: reduction of workforce diversity into individually based differences and emphasis on organizational goals while avoiding any mention of discrimination on which equal opportunities discourses are focused. As a result, the literature on diversity management deals mostly with diagnoses of differences, instead of deeply rooted systemic inequality. This weakness in the literature is closely connected with its theoretical loyalty to social psychology, particularly to social identity, social categorization and attribution theories that result in a focus on ethnocentrism, prejudice and stereotyping rather than discrimination (DiTomaso and Hooijberg, 1996). Criticizing the mainstream literature on diversity management, Zanoni and Janssens (2003) point to the tendency to define diversity on individual terms and to ignore structures of power and inequality in the dominant discourses. However, difference and diversity are socially constructed phenomena that transcend the seemingly 'neutral' individual differences. Equating difference with individual preferences and choices, which supposedly reflect the uniqueness of each individual, entails the risk of blindness towards the wider historical and social dynamics that contribute to the construction of difference. As Bradley (1996), who is one of the most influential UK scholars in the field of discrimination and equality, states, differences based on race, ethnicity, gender, sexuality, disability or age are historically and socially constructed, and they draw the lines of inequality and discrimination in society. In turn, overcoming discrimination and inequality requires engagement with the effects of past discrimination and careful questioning of the commonsense assumptions that govern organizations and society (Lorbiecki and Jack, 2000).

Justification of diversity management: ethical case or business case

If one of the characteristics of the mainstream diversity management literature is its theoretical orientation to social psychology, the other is its emphasis on the business case. In the debates and policies on diversity management, discussions on business-related motivations and reasons for managing diversity replace the emphasis on ethics and justice that largely frames the equal opportunities efforts (Cox et al., 1991; Hambrick et al., 1996; McEnrue, 1993; Morrison, 1992). However, despite the growing body of literature on the effects of workforce diversity on business success, research in this field remains scant and unsystematic regarding what constitutes diversity in terms of unit of analysis and dependent variables under investigation (DiTomaso and Hooijberg, 1996). This situation in the literature on diversity renders it difficult to reach empirically substantiated conclusions on the impact of diversity on business performance. Still, workforce diversity is being treated by the proponents of diversity management as a magic formula that automatically provides employers with a competitive edge (Cox, 1991; Thomas, 1990). Ironically, as research in the UK context demonstrates, the most important business motive for UK companies to adopt diversity management policies continues to be legal compliance concerns (Tatlı et al., 2006a; Özbilgin and Tatlı, 2008).

The business-case rhetoric is one of the reasons for the cautious reception of the diversity management approach among scholars in the UK. For instance, Wrench (2005) and Noon (2007) considered the managing diversity approach as a challenge to moral, legal and social arguments for equality of opportunity. What appears striking in the business-case rhetoric for diversity management is the focus on employers' interest as opposed to the equal opportunities approach's focus on the interest of employees. Critics of diversity management argue that diversity management is a new right response to the 'political correctness' lobby of liberal policies and that it attempts to depoliticize the gender and racial conflicts in organizations (Lorbiecki, 2001; Lorbiecki and Jack, 2000; Prasad and Mills, 1997). Business-case rhetoric for diversity management is built upon the treatment of employees as assets and workforce diversity as an added value providing the organizations with a competitive edge (Liff, 1996). So it seems that, in the diversity management literature, employees' interests are an issue of consideration as long as they contribute to business outcomes. Liff (1996) argues that in contrast to the association of the equal opportunities approach with the traditional industrial relations framework, the diversity management approach fits well with the HRM perspective.

The industrial relations perspective of managing labour is based on the conception of the workforce as a collective and stresses the role of trade unions in representing workers' interests. Although trade unions are important actors in fighting inequality and discrimination, their one-sided approach based on the experience of white male employees as the 'norm' may prevent them from effectively tackling the issue of different forms of discrimination, experienced by different social groups other than white males (Kirton, 1999; Kirton and Greene, 2000). Nevertheless, it is important to note that recent years have witnessed increasing activity within trade unions in the UK in order to tackle discriminatory and exclusionary union practices and structures (Bradley, 1994; Bradley et al., 2002; Colgan and Ledwith, 1996; Healy et al., 2004a, b). Conversely, an HRM perspective treats employees as individuals rather than part of collectives, and emphasizes involvement, commitment and loyalty (Liff, 1996). In turn, the diversity management approach adopts a top-down orientation when dealing with equality and situates employees mainly as the receivers of the policies that are initiated, designed and approved by the senior management.

Perrons and Skyers (2003, p. 265), noting the rising popularity of concepts such as inclusion, participation and diversity in the academic circles of urban and regional studies, state that 'recognising and valuing diversity by genuinely giving people influence in their decisions affecting their future is a crucial prerequisite for finding solutions that reflect their needs and moving towards a fairer and more just society'. However, the authors are not convinced about the possibility of achieving such a democracy and inclusion in terms of discursive and material practices. Considering that managing diversity is hegemonically associated with a top-down approach, even some level of discursive inclusion seems unlikely, let alone the inclusion of employees in the making of decisions that affect their material conditions. Then, it is ambiguous how diversity management policies, which are based on the idea of individualistic career development strategies rather than collective action and bargaining, will provide all employees, not only a small number of individual members of minority groups from disadvantaged groups, with the means of empowerment.

Furthermore, the empirical research displays contrasting results on business benefits of diversity, which suggests that the business case for diversity is valid in some organizations and, more importantly, for only some categories of employees. In contrast to the cheerful welcoming and celebration of various differences between employees, diversity management literature keeps silent about social-class differences in the workplace (e.g. Cox and Blake, 1991; Gilbert and Ivancevich, 2000; Kandola and Fullerton, 1998; Thomas, 1990). In the UK, equality scholars such as Bradley and Hebson (1999) were cautious of disappearance, or, at best, marginalization of social class in equality and diversity research, as class is a key cross-cutting category intertwined with all other forms of difference.

A review of the discussions on definition of diversity and business-case arguments demonstrates the presence of a strong critical academic debate among UK scholars on diversity and equality. It also reveals that both advocates and critics of the managing diversity approach depict diversity management and equal opportunities at opposing poles. However, in practice, the two approaches display more similarities than are pictured in that ideal-typical framework, with differences being less clear cut. Referring to the UK context, Lawrence (2000) and Perrons (1995) point out that business-case arguments have been used in equal opportunities frameworks even before the development of the managing diversity approach. Despite the emphasis of individually based differences in the policies, diversity programmes designed to implement these policies are most of the time founded on group-based differences and have a high resemblance to equal opportunities initiatives and programmes. Liff (1996, p. 22), commenting on the review of the diversity policies of 300 organizations in the UK by Kandola and Fullerton, argues that 'of their list of the ten most frequently implemented diversity initiatives, the top three include the words of equal opportunities and four others are explicitly targeted at social groups'. Taking into account such similarities in practices of diversity management and equal opportunities, Liff (1996) and Kirton and Greene (2000) argue that integration of equal opportunities and diversity management approaches, rather than being presented as opposing philosophies, may be the way forward in combating discrimination in the field of employment.

Discourses and practices of diversity management in the UK
This section focuses on the analysis of discourse and practice prevailing in the diversity management field in the UK. By exploring and comparing the prevailing patterns, the section provides compelling empirical evidence against simplistic, a-historical, a-contextual and a-political notions of diversity management in the mainstream literature as it uncovers the complex and contested nature of the field.

The analysis here is based on qualitative and quantitative data on the state of diversity management in the UK. Semi-structured interviews were carried out in 2006 and 2007 with 12 diversity managers of large organizations with more than 10 000 employees. The interviews lasted between 45 minutes and one hour, were tape-recorded and transcribed *verbatim*. In addition, an online survey was carried out in 2006 on the website of the Chartered Instute of Personnel and Development (CIPD) through a self-completion online questionnaire. The survey, which is the first comprehensive diversity management survey administered nationally in the UK, generated 285 completed questionnaires from people with responsibility for diversity.

Discourses of diversity management
The analysis of dominant discourses in any field is crucial in order to understand the interrelationship between words and action, the ways in which words are translated into action, and actions transform the discursive space (Hamilton, 2001). Hence, in this section I provide an analysis of the main components of the diversity management discourse in the UK. During the interviews, I encountered a strong evidence of a blueprint terminology used by the diversity managers, particularly in the private sector, in terms of their definitions and narrations. The dominant discourse of diversity was built around business-case arguments, a top-down approach that regards senior management support as most prominent, and individual-based, a-political definitions of difference.

All respondents from private sector organizations claimed that there has been a shift from equal opportunities to diversity management in their organizations. A respondent from a large financial organization stated that this shift also brings out the shift from ethical and legal-case arguments to business-case arguments. The same respondent explained that using business-case arguments enabled them to implement and gain support for organizational diversity management programmes and policies. Similarly, the respondents from a large retail company emphasized that there is a strong business case for diversity management in terms of both employee and customer relations. They claimed that diversity management policies and programmes provided the company with a competitive edge for maintaining their market position, entering into new markets and designing new product ranges through reaching out 'to a broader group of customers and broader group of people in the talent pool'. The respondents also underlined the importance of gaining senior management support. The diversity manager of a private financial organization thought that convincing different organizational actors regarding the tangible benefits of diversity is one of the biggest challenges. In the same vein, the diversity manager of another large financial organization also reported that pitching diversity management through business-case arguments is the starting point for getting senior and line managers involved in the process.

Interestingly, all respondents from the public sector, except one, displayed a more reserved attitude in terms of engaging with the business-case rhetoric, unlike their counterparts in the private sector, whose narrations were dominated by business-case justifications. Still, it was evident that business-case arguments were gaining popularity in the public sector too. There was agreement between the respondents from the public sector on the necessity of making a business case in order to attract senior management support and financial resources for equality and diversity initiatives, as 'value for money' has increasingly become the most important criterion in scrutinizing performance in the public sector in the UK. For instance, the respondent from a local government organization explained the increased use of business-case arguments in recent years by the local authorities in the following words:

> Increasingly I think we use the business case. I wouldn't have said that a few years ago. I think, from a local authority point of view, we would have said we would go for the ethical, moral, the social responsibility. To some extent social responsibility as a local authority is still pretty high on our agenda. But I think the business case for doing a lot of things is becoming far higher on our agenda.

Nevertheless, diversity managers from the public sector put far more emphasis on the benefits of workforce diversity in terms of improving the social and relational fabric of their organization, compared with their colleagues in the private sector who capitalized on the direct and tangible impact of diversity on the bottom line. Still, gaining senior management support was mentioned by all respondents as crucial to the success of any diversity management initiative. However, respondents from public and private sectors followed different strategies to get the senior managers involved. Respondents from the public sector frequently emphasized the employment legislation and equality standards that have to be adopted by public sector organizations as important components of the business case. On the other hand, one of the research participants from the private sector said that the company's centralized diversity management programme had been initiated by the CEO, who would like to know 'how representative the company of the UK workforce and our customers' is. In a similar vein, the respondent from a large financial organization argued that it was only through a strong business case that they were able to gradually increase the resources devoted to diversity management.

In summary, the findings suggest that the discourse of diversity management in the UK is influenced by the US-originated neo-liberal managing diversity perspective, which treats workforce diversity as a commodity that will be subjected to cost and benefit calculations. The lexicon of the diversity management discourse, particularly in the case of the private sector, is shaped by business-case arguments, which prioritize needs of business, and is based on a top-down approach, which emphasizes the role of senior management within the process of managing diversity.

Interview evidence also found that an individually based definition of difference was another key component of the diversity management discourse. However, as in the case of adoption of business-case arguments, there is a difference between the public and the private sector in terms of the definition of diversity. When I asked them how they define diversity in their organizations, all respondents from the public sector, except one, confined their definitions to the categories of structural inequality covered by the anti-discrimination legislation in the UK:

> We've got sexual orientation, age, social class, race, religion, marital status, gender, disability.

> It is about the service users and employees, disability, gender, race and age, and obviously sexual orientation, religion, everything. As more legislation comes on line, we amend it.

On the other hand, the research participants from the private sector tend to define diversity on the basis of individual differences. In a nutshell, the respondent from a large global petrochemical company said that diversity is understood in her organization as 'all the ways in which we differ'. The respondent from a large retail company provided a more detailed definition of how diversity is understood in his organization:

> Instead of treating everybody the same it's more about celebrating the differences and to make sure that we are in business as a whole tuned in to those differences and how to use that to everybody's advantage from employees' point of view, customers' point of view.

Similarly, the research participant who works for a large financial organization defined diversity as follows:

> I think, in [this company], the diversity would be that we want to maximize the talents of all our employees irrespective of their personal characteristics and we want all our customers to benefit from high-level customer service and feel that the bank values them as customers. Initially it was about gender, race and disability. We focused on those three areas. But over time we moved a lot more to educating managers around non-visible differences. You know, diversity in its truest sense that everybody is different. Even a group of white men is different.

This definition of diversity clearly displays a break with the equal opportunities approach in terms of its focus on business benefits and lack of any reference to the issues of discrimination or the political nature of difference. Interestingly, the same respondent mentioned between the lines that although they have 'broken away from the traditional equal opportunities groups to recognise that everybody is different' and have moved to 'invisible differences', they 'still put a focus on gender differences or racial differences'. These examples from private sector companies show that the discourse of diversity management both in terms of business-case arguments and the individually based definition of difference does not always match the practice of diversity management. In the next section, I elaborate on what is actually done in the organizations in terms of diversity management.

The practice of diversity management
As discussed in the previous section, discourse of diversity management, particularly in the private sector, is to a large extent influenced by a neo-liberal discourse, which emphasizes the business case for diversity management and individualizes the notions of difference. In this discourse, diversity is treated as a marketable product and as a resource that contributes to the bottom line. Thus diversity concerns are deemed relevant as long as they relate to profit-and-cost considerations. Another pertinent feature in narrations of diversity managers from private sector organizations was related to what 'difference' means. Difference was reduced to the level of individuals, which rendered structural inequalities and group-based disadvantage invisible. So the curious question, with which this section deals, is to what extent the discourses of diversity management match the practices of managing diversity.

Why do organizations have diversity management programmes and policies? It is frequently claimed that diversity management is marked by a voluntary approach by employers and that it has emerged from business realities, rather than from a legal enforcement associated with equal opportunities practices (McDougall, 1996; Thomas, 1990). However, the evidence from the questionnaire survey revealed that business benefits of workforce diversity are not considered by UK organizations as key drivers for diversity management. One of the sections of the survey aimed to explore the key drivers for diversity management in organizations. Respondents were asked to rank a number of statements from 1 to 5 according to their importance in terms of being key drivers.

Although the literature claims that diversity management thrives on business-case arguments, the study findings suggest that diversity management is indeed predominantly driven by legal compliance in the UK. 'Legal pressures' were the most popular drivers for diversity management in both public and private sector organizations. However, the number of respondents who ranked legal pressures as key drivers for diversity was significantly higher in the public sector (47 per cent) compared to the private sector (22 per cent). The relatively greater importance attached to legal considerations by public sector organizations is not surprising given the presence of control and monitoring mechanisms designed to promote practices of equal opportunities in the public sector in the UK, including the Race Equality Duty of 2001, the Disability Equality Duty of 2006 and the Gender Equality Duty of 2007.

The second-most popular driver of diversity was 'because it makes business sense'. However, in total, only 17 per cent of the respondents ranked this statement as the most important driver for their organizations. In the light of the semi-structured interviews, one would expect the business case to be a more important driver for the private sector, but there was no statistically significant difference between sectors. In addition to the general statement of 'because it makes business sense', the survey specified different dimensions of business benefits of diversity management in line with the propositions put forward in the literature. This included the so-called business benefits of diversity, such as helping to meet the demands of diverse customers and increasing market share; enhancing labour relations and recruitment; responding to the needs of global markets and competition; improving the quality and performance of the internal workforce in terms of skills, creativity, innovation and decision-making (Chevrier, 2003; Cox and Blake, 1991; Fernandez, 1991; Hambrick et al., 1996; McEnrue, 1993; Morrison, 1992). The survey findings indicate that organizations do not consider most of these specific benefits of diversity as key drivers. For instance, 'desire to improve customer relations' was top-ranked by only 5.3 per cent of the respondents; 'desire to reach diverse markets' by 6 per cent; 'to respond to global markets' by 5.6 per cent; 'to respond to the competition in the market' by 5.6 per cent. Similarly, support for the statements regarding workforce productivity and efficiency was low, with 'to improve creativity and innovation' being ranked first by 5.6 per cent of the organizations; 'to improve products and services' by 9.5 per cent; and 'to enhance decision-making' by only 2.8 per cent. The highest-scoring top-ranking business-case driver was related to recruitment. A total of 13.3 per cent of the respondents ranked 'to recruit and retain best talent' as the top driver of diversity management in their organizations.

Thus the survey findings demonstrated that drivers of diversity management were to a large extent limited to legal compliance concerns for organizations in the UK. These results clearly conflict with the argument that diversity management policies are internally driven thanks to the business benefits, unlike the equal opportunities policies, which are externally driven by anti-discrimination legislation. Conversely, the most important motive for organizations to adopt diversity management policies and practices continues to be legislative pressures. Interestingly, despite the competence displayed by the semi-structured interview respondents from the private sector in terms of conveying business-case arguments, the survey results do not confirm a more significant presence of the business case as driving diversity management in the private sector. In fact, for the majority of statements related to the business-case drivers of diversity, there is no significant difference between the sectors. In cases where any significant differences exist, higher percentages of the organizations in the public sector are driven by business-case motives; e.g. larger numbers of respondents from the public sector, compared to those from the private sector, reported that 'desire to improve customer relations', 'to improve products and services', and 'to enhance decision making' are among the key drivers of diversity.

The importance of legislation as a key driver of diversity management programmes was also evident in the in-depth interviews with diversity managers. Although legislation was not rated high when respondents talked in general terms during the interviews, it proved to be a decisive factor for shaping the organizational diversity agenda in terms of actual programmes and activities. For example, the diversity manager of a global financial sector company compared the state of companies' diversity management practice in different countries as follows:

> I think different countries are making progress in different areas. Well, it's partly legislation as well, for example, in the UK about 95 per cent of our branches are fully compliant with the Disability Discrimination Act requirements, so that's an investment of 70 million, so you know, because we have legislation, but, whereas in other countries they may not have that legislation and their infrastructure may not be so developed and they may be doing very well in other areas.

So the legislation continues to be a key driving force behind the decisions regarding resources committed to and areas of target for diversity management. Business-case and legal-case arguments are often presented in dichotomous terms in the literature. However, there is also a historical dimension to the construction of the diversity management approach, and the equal opportunities perspective continues to influence the current practice of diversity management. In turn, organizations continue to use business- and legal-case arguments side by side. Survey results revealed that organizations that have legal-case arguments also have business-case arguments and vice versa. These findings sit uncomfortably with the discourse of diversity management, which is based mainly on the business-case rhetoric, and suggest that, arguably, the legal case is a key part of the business case.

The semi-structured interviews suggested that one of the most effective media through which diversity managers could communicate the business case for diversity across their organizations is to demonstrate the positive impacts of diversity management on the bottom line through 'hard data'. The survey also included a question on how the success of diversity management initiatives and their effect on the bottom line are monitored (Table 14.1). The question covered 15 measures through which organizations can evaluate the impact of diversity management on performance. These measures ranged from traditional HR measures such as employee attitude surveys, rates of labour turnover and absenteeism, to more contemporary measures, which link diversity management to the bottom line, such as monitoring customer satisfaction, employee commitment,

Table 14.1   *Which of the following measures do you use to monitor diversity in your organization?*

Measures	Number of respondents
Employee attitude surveys	206
Number of complaints and grievances	161
Labour turnover	159
Employee performance appraisals	132
Absenteeism	129
Ability to recruit	114
Number of tribunal cases	89
Impact assessment	77
Level of customer satisfaction	67
Employee commitment surveys	55
Business performance	53
Balanced scorecard	48
Diversification of customer base	37
Improvements to problem-solving and decision-making	19
Psychological contract issues	16

Note: Number of valid responses: 285.

problem-solving and decision-making, as well as balanced scorecard and impact assessment schemes.

As Table 14.1 illustrates, organizations overwhelmingly continue to use traditional measures, including employee attitude surveys, complaints and grievances, turnover rates, appraisal, recruitment and absenteeism figures. Strikingly, the number of public sector organizations that assess the impact of diversity management was significantly higher than their counterparts in private and voluntary sectors (see Table 14.2).

Only 10 per cent of private sector organizations and 11.1 per cent of the voluntary sector organizations reported that they conduct impact assessment in order to measure diversity, whereas the figure was as high as 51.7 for the public sector. This demonstrates that there is a more systematic effort in the public sector compared to the private sector in terms of diversity management, despite the fact that the managing diversity approach was more strongly advocated at the level of discourse by the latter. Furthermore, what seems to be missing from this picture are the measures that would assess the so-called business benefits of diversity management, such as employee commitment surveys, business performance, balanced scorecard, diversification of customer base; improvements to problem-solving and decision-making and psychological contract issues. Thus the survey findings suggest that organizations in the UK do not collect data on the business benefits of diversity. In the absence of evidence on the business case for diversity, it is unclear how diversity management activities could possibly have the necessary clout and be given the necessary resources to be effective, sustainable and far-reaching.

The focus of diversity management practice: groups or individuals?   Another area of discrepancy between discourse and practice was in terms of definition of diversity. The

Table 14.2   Cross-tabulation of measures for monitoring diversity: 'impact assessment' by sector

Sector		Impact assessment		Total
		No	Yes	
Private sector	No.	117	13	130
	%	90.0	10.0	100.0
Public sector	No.	56	60	116
	%	48.3	51.7	100.0
Voluntary sector	No.	32	4	36
	%	88.9	11.1	100.0
Total	No.	205	77	282
	%	72.7	27.3	100.0

Notes: Number of valid cases: 282. Pearson chi-square: 59.217; degrees of freedom: 2; asymptotic significance (two-sided): 0.000.

individual-based definition of diversity emerged as one of the major components of the diversity management discourse during the interviews. However, throughout the interviews, when diversity managers talked about the actual organizational diversity management practices, it was clear that nearly all diversity activity in both the public and the private sector was designed around group-based differences rather than individual-based differences. For example, in the financial sector company that claims to be one of the first organizations in the UK to break with the traditional equal opportunities approach and adopt a US-inspired managing diversity perspective, the focus of diversity management practice was still the traditional categories of disadvantage emphasized in equal opportunities frameworks; e.g. the company's positive action training programme mainly targeted ethnic minority, female and disabled employees.

When I asked the interview participants about the successful diversity management initiatives in their organizations, the examples they have given were mostly related to the improved representation of female and BME (black and minority ethnic) staff. Likewise, public sector organizations targeted their diversity and equality programmes and activities on the legally protected categories in the workforce. In the light of evidence from the semi-structured interviews, it was apparent that despite the rhetoric of 'welcoming all forms of difference', defining diversity in terms of 'all the ways in which we differ', the actual practice of diversity management targeted the strands of diversity that are protected under UK legislation and that have traditionally been the focus of equal opportunities initiatives.

In addition to monitoring recruitment of individuals from minority and disadvantaged backgrounds, another frequently cited diversity management initiative was diversity training programmes. Respondents from both the public and the private sector devoted extensive time to describing their training programmes. All the organizations had diversity training for managers and some had introduced a diversity and equality component into the induction training for all employees. The training initiatives were often limited to half-day programmes and aimed to raise awareness about organizations'

Table 14.3   *Which of the following categories does your diversity policy cover?*
              (Coverage of legally protected categories by sector, %)

Diversity strands	Private sector	Public sector	Voluntary sector
Disability	49.2	69.0	72.2
Ethnicity and race	45.4	70.7	69.4
Gender/sex	47.7	68.1	66.7
Religion	46.9	64.7	66.7
Sexual orientation	46.2	65.5	63.9
Nationality	38.5	55.2	66.7
Age	38.5	50.9	58.3

Note: Number of valid responses: 282.

anti-harassment and bullying policies, anti-discrimination legislation, and welcoming and respecting differences. Thus interviews suggest that the practice in the field of diversity management overwhelmingly focused on monitoring, recruitment and training activities, with substantial attention to legislation and group-based differences.

The questionnaire survey evidence also confirmed the findings that emerged from the interviews. The survey asked respondents which categories of diversity are covered by their organization's diversity policy. In terms of legally protected diversity and equality strands, 59.6 per cent of the participant organizations included disability in their diversity policies; 58.2 per cent race and ethnicity; 57.9 per cent gender; 56.1 per cent religion; 55.8 per cent sexual orientation; 48.4 per cent nationality; and 45.6 per cent age. Furthermore, the public and voluntary sector organizations were more likely to include these strands in their diversity policy compared to the organizations in the private sector (see Table 14.3).

As displayed in Table 14.3, diversity policies of fewer than half of the organizations in the private sector included seven legally protected diversity strands. In public and voluntary sectors, the figures were significantly higher, but they varied between 50 and 70 per cent, which can be considered low, particularly considering the fact that legislation as well as equal opportunities initiatives for some of these strands such as gender and race have existed for more than three decades in the UK. This picture clearly demonstrates that the organizational practices and awareness of equal opportunities and diversity management in the UK still require improvement.

Diversity management approaches emphasize the idea of inclusion, and valuing and respecting all forms of difference rather than limiting the diversity efforts to traditional equality categories. Strikingly, only 20 per cent of the survey respondents stated that the diversity policy covers 'all forms of difference' and there was no statistically significant difference between the public, private and voluntary sectors. This finding undermines the credibility of the diversity management paradigm in terms of promoting inclusive organizational practices and structures. Furthermore, non-traditional diversity categories were included in the diversity policy of very few organizations. Only 16.5 per cent of the participating organizations covered social and economic background; 10.9 per cent physical appearance; 3.2 per cent weight; 2.8 per cent postcode; 2.5 per cent accent; 13.7 per cent mental health; 9.5 per cent political ideology. Once again, the numbers of public and voluntary sector organizations that include different forms of diversity such as social and economic background, criminal conviction, marital and parental status, mental health, political ideology and trade union membership were significantly higher than the number of private sector organizations. Revealing the private sector's poor state in terms of inclusion of traditional and non-traditional categories of diversity and equality in their diversity policies, the survey findings raise several important questions; e.g. if many forms of diversity are not covered by diversity management policies of private sector organizations, then what do the managing diversity programmes involve and target? Or to what extent is diversity management used by private sector organizations as a decoy to avoid legislation and any serious effort to tackle workplace discrimination and inequality?

In summary, the survey findings demonstrated that the categories of diversity that are most frequently reported to be covered by the participant organizations' diversity management programmes and policies in all sectors were the legally protected categories. The focus on these categories reveals the gap between the rhetoric of managing diversity as an approach inclusive of all differences, and the practice of diversity management as a framework of activities around legal compliance.

The survey respondents were also asked which diversity activities their organizations have. The most popular diversity activities were awareness and diversity training for employees (65.6 per cent) and for managers (53.7 per cent), and employee attitude surveys (61.8 per cent). Unfortunately, neither employee attitude surveys nor training programmes are the most effective initiatives to promote diversity and equality in organizations. Employee attitude surveys will not serve to change discriminatory and exclusionary organizational structures and practices automatically unless they inform diversity management activities. Bradley et al. (2007), urging variation in the content and form of diversity training, argue that poor practice in diversity training may even be counterproductive, particularly in cases where such training activities are the result of compliance culture. Acker (2007) suggests that diversity and equality training programmes are among the least effective diversity initiatives in terms of achieving organizational change.

Within that framework, the question is to what extent diversity management approaches are capable of achieving progressive organizational outcomes that promote equality, diversity and inclusiveness. For instance, Kalev et al. (2006, p. 610), after assessing the efficacy of affirmative action and diversity management policies in the USA, conclude that the main reason for employers to adopt anti-discrimination and diversity measures is not to promote corporate equality, but they adopt these measures 'as window dressing, to inoculate themselves against liability, or to improve morale'. Thus one of the issues the survey results bring out is whether diversity initiatives and programmes aim to enhance organizational diversity and equality, or just pay lip service to the idea of equality and inclusion.

Interestingly, unlike employee attitude surveys and training programmes, which were present in the majority of the organizations that completed the survey, other types of diversity activities that would make diversity management a part of organizational mainstream, and enhance its legitimacy, importance and effectiveness were in place in only a small minority of organizations. A total of 69.8 per cent of the respondents stated that their organization does not set diversity objectives. It is hard to imagine how any diversity management policy or programme can be designed, implemented and sustained unless diversity objectives are set. However, it should be noted that the extremely low figures in terms of 'setting diversity objectives' were largely due to the low figures of the private sector in that respect. A total of 48.3 per cent of the public sector organizations set diversity objectives, whereas the figure for the private sector was only 14.6 per cent. Still, 48.3 per cent can be considered low for the public sector, since the organizations in the UK public sector are encouraged to set equality and diversity objectives, and monitor equality and diversity through mechanisms such as the Equality Standard for local government, Learning for All for schools, and Bridging the Gap and Measuring the Gap for community and health services (Özbilgin and Tatlı, 2006; Tatlı et al., 2006b).

Returning to the survey findings regarding organizational diversity activities, only 5 per cent of the organizations rewarded and recognized diversity achievements and just 30 per cent built diversity into their business goals. Similarly, only 20 per cent of the organizations that participated in the survey stated that they apply diversity standards. Furthermore, diversity was a performance criterion in only 18.6 per cent of the organizations and diversity-related goals were included in managers' performance assessment by only 15.8 per cent of the organizations. The survey results were even more revealing when data were dissected by sector. Responses demonstrated that the private sector consistently scored poorly for all types of diversity activities included in the question, with the exception of 'employee attitude surveys', which indeed proved a very popular activity in all sectors.

On the other hand, the public sector organizations were significantly ahead of their counterparts in the private sector with regard to the presence of different types of diversity activities. For instance, 87.1 per cent of the public sector organizations had awareness training and 72.4 per cent had diversity training for managers, whereas for the private sector the figures remained at as low as 44.6 per cent and 40.8 per cent respectively. More important for the organizational legitimacy accorded to diversity management, 41.4 per cent of the public sector organizations and 36.1 per cent of the voluntary sector organizations reported that they build diversity into business goals, as opposed to only 17.7 per cent in the private sector.

Although diversity was a performance criterion in only 26.7 per cent of the public sector organizations, the sector still achieved significantly better than the private sector, in which the figure was as low as 10.8 per cent. Similar results were evident also for 'inclusion of diversity in managers' performance assessments'. As Bradley et al. (2007) propose, integrating diversity targets into managers' performance appraisals is crucial in order to promote equality and diversity organization wide, and it is also an indication of structural support for diversity management policies and programmes. Ironically, the majority of organizations did not include diversity-related concerns in managers' performance assessments. Evidently, organizations in the UK are far from having a holistic and comprehensive approach to diversity management.

Conclusions

A number of common themes have emerged from the survey and interviews. These themes indicate the existence of a distinct diversity management field. The interview evidence suggests a discursive shift from ethical and legal arguments to business-case arguments, from group-based understanding of difference to individual-based definitions of difference, and from emphasis on the political and power-ridden nature of discrimination to prioritizing needs of employers and the role of senior management. However, there were differences between interviewees from the public and private sectors in terms of their use of diversity management discourse. These differences show that the discourse of diversity management is not completely homogeneous or uncontested.

Diversity managers from the private sector seemed to be more comfortable in using the mainstream diversity management discourse compared to their public sector counterparts, who appeared to be relatively reluctant in adopting that discourse, which is not surprising considering the fact that the dominant discourse of diversity management originates from the private sector and that the machinery of public relations in this sector has been churning out stories that draw attention to linkages between diversity and business performance. However, it should be noted that the aforementioned reluctance of public sector diversity managers in adopting the dominant discourse of diversity management does not suggest that they had contested or critiqued it. On the contrary, business-case arguments are gaining popularity in the public sector too, and diversity managers in this sector have adopted this dominant discourse unquestioningly throughout their narrations.

Surprisingly, at the level of actual practice the field of diversity management was more or less confined to the activities, initiatives and programmes previously associated with the equal opportunities framework. Having been historically more experienced in equal opportunities programmes and policies, public sector organizations led the agenda in terms of practice. Nevertheless, sectoral differences aside, the practice of diversity management with its overwhelming focus on HRM activities and procedures such as training, recruitment and promotion, as well as its exclusive targeting of legally protected categories, clearly conflicts with the discourse of diversity management, which pictures managing diversity as the new game in town and as an approach radically different from the equal opportunities perspective.

This study identified that there are both continuities and divergences between diversity management and equal opportunities approaches; thus we cannot talk about a clear break with equal opportunities, as suggested in the mainstream diversity literature. Although the practice in the field of diversity management presents a striking resemblance to that of equal opportunities, the discursive dimension of the field tells another story, a neo-liberal story that pushes the political nature of difference and discrimination under the carpet while bringing the profit concerns into the focus of debate. To summarize, the evidence from interview and survey data demonstrated that the field of diversity management is a curious hybrid of neo-liberal ideology and equal opportunities perspectives. The discourse prevailing in the field is largely informed by the neo-liberal ideology, whereas the practice of managing diversity is to a large extent confined to the activities traditionally part of equal opportunities frameworks. So, what is unique about managing diversity, or is it possible to talk about a separate field of diversity management? As the field research evidence uncovered, it is the very marriage of neo-liberal discourse and equal opportunities approaches itself that provides the field of diversity management with attributes of uniqueness and peculiarity. The unlikely combination of these two approaches into a single framework suggests that diversity management is a new phenomenon, distinguishable from the equal opportunities approach.

Summary table for the UK

Existence of anti-discrimination legislation	Yes
Criteria covered by anti-discrimination legislation	Race and ethnicity, gender, disability, sexual orientation, age, religion and belief
Criteria for which the reporting of quantitative data and their communication to a public administration are compulsory	Public authorities are legally bound by Equality Duties to produce equality schemes and monitor specific aspects of employment. Currently, the Public Duties cover race and ethnicity, gender, disability, but a new Equality Bill was published by the Government in April 2009. Should the Bill pass, a single public sector Equality Duty will replace the existing duties to cover age, sexual orientation, religion or belief, socioeconomic status as well as race, disability and gender
Criteria covered by 'affirmative' or 'positive' action legislation other than unemployment- or income-based	In line with public sector Equality Duties and statutory codes of practice, public sector organizations are expected to take action, including positive action measures to tackle disability, gender, and race discrimination. Positive action by the public sector on other strands of equality and by the private sector on all six strands of equality is voluntary, and varies locally and across organizations
Existence of a discourse or debate about 'non-discrimination' or 'equality'	Yes
Existence of a discourse or debate about 'diversity'	Yes
Year or period when the 'discrimination' concept started to disseminate in management literature in the country	The popular use of the concept of discrimination, particularly in relation to gender and race, dates back to the 1970s. The early 1980s were marked by more general debates on discrimination such as critique and assessment of equal opportunities frameworks
Year or period when the diversity concept started to disseminate in management literature in the country	1994, with the publication of *Diversity in Action: Managing the Mosaic*, by the Institute of Personnel and Development
Who pushed the 'diversity' agenda?	In the UK a shift from equal opportunities frameworks to a managing diversity approach was supported particularly by the large private sector organizations and the Chartered Institute of Personnel and Development. This trend has been further strengthened by the government and by EU legislation and discourse
Existence of a professional association representing diversity professionals and year of creation	No
Existence of a professional association representing diversity scholars and year of creation	No

Notes

1. Statutory duties, either general or specific, are the pieces of legislation that a public authority is legally bound to meet. The general duty applies to all public authorities, whilst specific duties have been placed on some public authorities that deliver important services. The duties include production of equality schemes and monitoring of specific aspects of employment.
2. The statutory Code of Practice is a document that is approved by Parliament and is admissible in evidence in court. It contains guidance on legislation and on implementation of specific and general duties. If a public body does not follow this guidance, it may need to demonstrate how it meets its legal obligations (EHRC, 2009). According to the Code of Practice for race equality, for instance, ethnic reporting is compulsory to monitor progress, but the setting of targets is not compulsory. This may vary according to local circumstances (Article 5.4, Statutory Code of Practice to Promote Race Equality, 2002).

References

Acker, J. (2007), 'Organising in search of equality and diversity: whose ends, what means?', unpublished paper presented at the First Annual Lecture of the Centre for Research in Diversity and Equality, Queen Mary, University of London, in 18 June.

Ashkanasy, N.M., Hartel, C.E.J. and Daus, C.S. (2002), 'Diversity and emotion: the new frontiers in organizational behaviour research', *Journal of Management*, **28** (3), 307–38.

Bradley, H. (1994), 'Divided we fall: unions and their members', *Employee Relations*, **16** (2), 41–52.

Bradley, H. (1996), *Fractured Identities: Changing Patterns of Inequality*, Cambridge: Polity Press.

Bradley, H. and Hebson, G. (1999), 'Breaking the silence: the need to re-articulate "class"', *International Journal of Sociology and Social Policy*, **19** (9), 178–203.

Bradley, H., Healy, G. and Mukherjee, N. (2002), *Inclusion, Exclusion and Separate Organization: Black Women in Trade Unions*, Working Paper No. 25, ESRC Future of Work Programme.

Bradley, H., Healy, G., Forson, C. and Kaul, P. (2007), *Workplace Cultures: What Does and Does Not Work*, EOC Working Paper Series, Manchester: EOC.

Bruegel, I. and Perrons, D. (1998), 'Deregulation and women's employment: the diverse experiences of women in Britain', *Feminist Economics*, **4** (1), 103–25.

Chevrier, S. (2003), 'Cross-cultural management in multinational project groups', *Journal of World Business*, **38**, 141–9.

Cockburn, C. (1989), 'Equal opportunities: the short and long agenda', *Industrial Relations Journal*, **20** (4), 213–25.

Colgan, F. and Ledwith, S. (1996), 'Sisters organising: women and their trade unions', in S. Ledwith and F. Colgan (eds), *Women and Organizations: Challenging Gender Politics*, London: Macmillan, pp. 152–87.

Cox, T.H. (1991), 'The multicultural organization', *Academy of Management Executive*, **5** (2), 34–47.

Cox, T.H. and Blake, B. (1991), 'Managing cultural diversity: implications for organizational competitiveness', *Academy of Management Executive*, **5** (3), 45–56.

Cox, T.H., Lobel, S. and McLeod, P. (1991), 'Effects of ethnic group cultural differences on competitive and cooperative behaviour on a group task', *Academy of Management Journal*, **34** (4), 827–47.

DiTomaso, N. and Hooijberg, R. (1996), 'Diversity and the demands of leadership', *Leadership Quarterly*, **7** (2), 163–87.

Equality and Human Rights Commission (2009), *Codes of Practice*, available at www.equalityhumanrights.com/advice-and-guidance/information-for-advisers/codes-of-practice/.

European Commission (2000a), 'Council Directive 2000/78/EC establishing a general framework for equal treatment in employment and occupation', *Official Journal of the European Communities*, L 303/16, 2 December.

European Commission (2000b), 'Council Decision 2000/750/EC establishing a Community Action Programme to Combat Discrimination (2001 to 2006)', *Official Journal of the European Communities*, L 303/16, 27 October.

Fernandez, J.P. (1991), *Managing a Diverse Work Force*, Lexington, MA: Lexington Books.

Gilbert, J.A. and Ivancevich, J.M. (2000), 'Valuing diversity: a tale of two organizations', *Academy of Management Executive*, **14** (1), 93–105.

Government Equalities Office (2009), *A Fairer Future: The Equality Bill and other Action to Make Equality a Reality*.

Hambrick, D.C., Cho, T. and Chen, M. (1996), 'The influence of top management team heterogeneity on firms' competitive moves', *Administrative Science Quarterly*, **41**, 659–84.

Hamilton, P. (2001), 'Rhetoric and employment relations', *British Journal of Industrial Relations*, **39** (3), 433–49.

Healy, G., Bradley, H. and Mukherjee, N. (2004a), 'Individualism and collectivism revisited: a study of black and minority ethnic women', *Industrial Relations Journal*, **35** (5), 451–66.

Healy, G., Bradley, H. and Mukherjee, N. (2004b), 'Inspiring activists: the experience of minority ethnic women in trade unions', in G. Healy, E. Heery and P. Taylor (eds), *The Future of Worker Representation*, Basingstoke: Palgrave Macmillan, pp. 103–26.

Hoskyns, C. (1996), *Integrating Gender: Women, Law and Politics in the European Union*, London: Verso.

Jaquette, J.S. (1990), 'Gender and justice in economic development', in I. Tinker (ed.), *Persistent Inequalities: Women and World Development*, Oxford: Oxford University Press, pp. 54–69.

Jewson, N. and Mason, D. (1986), 'The theory and practice of equal opportunity policies: liberal and radical approaches', *Sociological Review*, **34** (2), 307–29.

Johnston, W.B. and Packer, A.H. (1987), *Workforce 2000: Work and Workers for the 21st Century*, Washington, DC: Hudson Institute.

Kalev, A., Kelly, E. and Dobbin, F. (2006), 'Best practices or best guesses? Assessing the efficacy of corporate affirmative action and diversity policies', *American Sociological Review*, **71**, 589–617.

Kandola, R. and Fullerton, J. (1998), *Diversity in Action: Managing the Mosaic*, London: IPD.

Kirton, G. (1999), 'Sustaining and developing women's trade union activism: a gendered project?', *Gender Work and Organization*, **6**, 213–23.

Kirton, G. and Greene, A.M. (2000), *The Dynamics of Managing Diversity: A Critical Approach*, Oxford: Butterworth-Heinemann.

Lawrence, E. (2000), 'Equal opportunities officers and managing equality changes', *Personnel Review*, **29** (3), 381–401.

Liff, S. (1996), 'Two routes to managing diversity: individual differences or social group characteristics', *Employee Relations*, **19** (1), 11–26.

Liff, S. and Wajcman, J. (1996), '"Sameness" and "difference" revisited: which way forward for equal opportunity initiatives?', *Journal of Management Studies*, **33** (1), 79–94.

Lorbiecki, A. (2001), 'Changing views on diversity management: the rise of learning perspective and the need to recognise social and political contradictions', *Management Learning*, **32** (3), 345–61.

Lorbiecki, A. and Jack, G. (2000), 'Critical turns in the evolution of diversity management', *British Journal of Management*, **11**, 17–31.

McDougall, M. (1996), 'Equal opportunities versus managing diversity: another challenge for public sector management?', *International Journal of Public Sector Management*, **9** (5/6), 62–72.

McEnrue, M.P. (1993), 'Managing diversity: Los Angeles before and after the riots', *Organizational Dynamics*, **21** (3), 18–29.

Morrison, A.M. (1992), *The New Leader: Guidelines on Leadership Diversity in America*, San Francisco, CA: Jossey-Bass.

Noon, M. (2007), 'The fatal flaws of diversity and the business case for ethnic minorities', *Work, Employment and Society*, **21**, 773–84.

Özbilgin, M. and Tatlı, A. (2006), *Developing a Diagnostic Check for Equality*, Manchester: EOC.

Özbilgin, M. and Tatlı, A. (2008), *Global Diversity Management: An Evidence Based Approach*, London New York: Palgrave.

Perrons, D. (1995), 'Employment deregulation and equal opportunities: the case for monitoring gender work', in J. Shaw and D. Perrons (eds), *Making Gender Work: Managing Equal Opportunities*, Buckingham: Open University Press, pp. 72–88.

Perrons, D. and Skyers, S. (2003), 'Empowerment through participation? Conceptual explorations and a case study', *International Journal of Urban and Regional Research*, **27** (2), 265–85.

Prasad, P. and Mills, A.J. (1997), 'From showcase to shadow: understanding the dilemmas of managing workplace diversity', in P. Prasad, A.J. Mills, M. Elmes and A. Prasad (eds), *Managing the Organizational Melting Pot: Dilemmas of Workforce Diversity*, Thousand Oaks, CA: Sage, pp. 3–27.

Rees, T. (1998), *Mainstreaming Equality in the European Union: Education, Training and Labour Market Policies*, London: Routledge.

Tatlı, A., Özbilgin, M., Mulholland, G. and Worman, D. (2006a), *Survey Report 2006: Diversity in Business, How much Progress have Employers Made? First Findings*, London: CIPD.

Tatlı, A., Özbilgin, M., Mulholland, G. and Worman, D. (2006b), *Managing Diversity, Measuring Success*, London: CIPD.

Tatlı, A., Özbilgin, M., Worman, D. and Price, E. (2008), *State of the Nation, Diversity in Business: a Focus for Progress*, London: CIPD.

Thomas, R.R. (1990), 'From affirmative action to affirming diversity', *Harvard Business Review*, **68** (2), 107–17.

Women and Work Commission (2006), *Shaping a Fairer Future*, presented to the Prime Minister by Baroness Prosser of Battersea, Women and Work Commission, DTI, February.

Wrench, J. (2005), 'Diversity management can be bad for you', *Race and Class*, **46** (3), 73–84.

Young, B. (2000), 'Disciplinary neoliberalism in the European Union and gender politics', *New Political Economy*, **5** (1), 77–99.

Zanoni, P. and Janssens, M. (2003), 'Deconstructing difference: the rhetoric of human resource managers' diversity discourses', *Organization Studies*, **25** (1), 55–74.

15 Managing diversity in the USA: the evolution of inclusion in the workplace

Waheeda Lillevik, Gwendolyn M. Combs and Cheryl Wyrick

Introduction

Migration to the USA over the past century has created a diverse workforce, particularly in terms of race and ethnicity. Of particular importance to the development of equality and diversity discourse, are the employment rates of African Americans and of women. Even after nearly 50 years of affirmative action and equal employment opportunity policies, employment figures show persistent gaps between these two groups and the rest of the population. Although historically African Americans[1] constitute one of the largest groups of people in the US population, they comprise one of the smallest proportions of the workforce compared to other groups. The latest quarterly 2009 statistics for employment participation rates show considerable underrepresentation of minority subgroups in the labour force. The current overall unemployment rate in the USA is 9.2 per cent; this is much lower than the figures for African Americans (14.9 per cent), and for those of Hispanic origins (12 per cent) (Bureau of Labor Statistics, 2009). The unemployment rate for whites is 8.4 per cent (ibid.).

The employment ratios of Hispanics and Asians tend to be closer to those of whites than to those of African Americans; 53.6 per cent for the black population and 60.1 per cent for the Hispanic population, as compared with 60.6 per cent for the white population (Bureau of Labor Statistics, 2009) and 62.2 per cent for Asians (ibid.). However, the employment participation rates are rather different when the level/class of work is considered. In most reports that companies must submit to the Equal Employment Opportunity Commission (EEOC), underrepresentation of members of ethnic and gender minority subgroups appear to be rampant at the executive levels of organizations. For example, the minority workforce participation is 34.24 per cent, while minority participation at the executive and senior official levels is 12.58 per cent (US Census Bureau, 2007). Participation in executive positions by other subgroups is extremely low compared with the rates for whites, and in each case, women were represented at significantly lower levels than men in these high-level positions (see Appendix A for a further breakdown of employment participation rates in the executive ranks). The growth of females in the workforce has levelled out over the past 15 years, remaining around the 60 per cent participation rate, well under that of men, which is sustainably above 70 per cent. In addition, women are more likely to work in part-time rather than full-time employment than men (Bureau of Labor Statistics, 2006).

When discussing the employment of minorities in the USA, it is important to consider the concepts of equal opportunity employment, affirmative action and diversity management. These concepts are often (erroneously) used interchangeably (Jain et al., 2003) without truly understanding the drivers behind each concept, and their applicable usage.

304

In response to this discussion, there is often a backlash towards these policies, particularly with respect to claims of unequal treatment and reverse discrimination by managers and corporations.

After examining the early debates on gender and race equality in its first section, this chapter will discuss the relevant legislation and policies dealing with the treatment of minority groups in the workforce (second section). Enforcement issues, Supreme Court case law and critiques of affirmative action are dealt with in the third section. Next, research and public discourse about diversity management as a 'new' paradigm will be addressed (fourth section). This will include the definition of diversity, the rationales for the emergence of the concept of diversity, and a brief summary of US research and current debates on diversity, in particular as regards the relationship between equal opportunities, affirmative action and diversity management.

Early debates on race and gender equality
Discussion of the treatment of disadvantaged groups in the workforce began as early as the nineteenth century in the USA. Early writers took various viewpoints in their discourse on racial and gender differences. For example, W.E.B. Du Bois published *The Philadelphia Negro* in 1899, considered the first systematic and empirical study of the condition of blacks in America. In 1944 Gunnar Myrdal published *An American Dilemma*, which highlighted the dissonance resulting from the conflict between American democratic values and racism as experienced by whites. William Graham Sumner published *Folkways* in 1906, in which he introduced the term 'ethnocentrism' into the literature. In 1949 V.O. Key wrote *Southern Politics*, which postulated the 'harm thesis' of racial inequality. The harm thesis suggests that discriminatory actions by whites against blacks result in negative consequences for both blacks and whites (Key, 1949). Similarly, E. Franklin Frazier examined the integration of African Americans in such works as *The Free Negro Family: A Study of Family Origins Before the Civil War* in 1932 and *The Integration of the Negro into American Society* in 1951. Allport (1954) contributed the term 'contact hypothesis' of group interactions, which suggests that interactions between whites and blacks can be improved under conditions or contexts of equality. Specifically, discriminatory behaviours and negative stereotypes of diverse groups can be mitigated by frequency and quality of interracial contact. Such authors and others called the attention of social, political and educational constituencies to the need to analyse the disparities endured by particular segments of the American population.

The women's suffrage movement is considered by some as the beginning of systematic and organized discussions of gender equality in the USA. The concerns and pressures encountered in providing women the right to vote allowed women in the USA to sharpen their collective voices and political power. Early writings about sex discrimination or issues of gender diversity reflect similar issues as are represented in current literature. However, such writings were not as empirically based or systematic. For example, in 1861 Caroline Dall wrote three manuscripts ('Women's rights under the law') on the rights of women in the USA. Most writings such as those of Dall and her contemporaries dealt with the family and social roles of women, and social role differences between men and women. The establishment of the US Women's Bureau in 1920 propelled the debate and examination of issues and research related to women's equality in employment opportunities, wage disparities and other economic areas (Mastracci, 2004). In

1933, Carter and Strong published 'Sex differences in occupational interests of high school students'. This research, using Strong's 'Vocational Interest Blank', suggested different vocational preferences in men and women based on feminine and masculine traits, considered 'relatively stable traits which are intricately woven into the complex patterns of personality' (p. 170). High-school girls were found to have more cultural, linguistic and artistic interests while high-school boys had interests more related to mechanics, mathematics, and science. Gender research in the 1950s included topics such as pay equity between the sexes; the plight of career-oriented women; and the advancement of women into managerial and executive-level positions (e.g. Fisher, 1951; Wallin, 1950). For example, Fuller and Batchelder (1953) researched women in administrative and upper-level positions and the factors bearing on their advancement: the authors suggest economic conditions, prejudice regarding the ability of women to handle the work; and the notions of businessmen about the acceptance of women administrators by their generally male customers/clients. Additionally, women were thought to be more emotional than men, and had less earnest interest in the job. Fisher (1951) concludes that the differential in wages is based on 'custom and tradition' rather than on any real differences in productive output for men versus women.

The year 1963 witnessed the appearance of *The Feminine Mystique* by Betty Friedan, which openly discussed and labelled the identity crisis being experienced by women (Williams, 2001). Following the passage of the Civil Rights Act of 1964, research examining gender inequality increased. Also, there was research that centred on the need for sex as a protected class in the Act (Walters, 1967); and the responses of employers, men and women to its inclusion (Bowman et al., 1965). For example, Bowman et al. (1965) attempted to ascertain the perceptions of both executive-level men and women concerning the role of women in upper-level management. Both male and female respondents felt that women had to be 'exceptional, indeed overqualified to succeed in management' (p. 15). Additionally, both men and women respondents felt that access to opportunities for female managers could be found in the fields of education, social work and the arts; the retail trade industry; and the functions of office management and personnel.

Contemporary gender research continues to examine issues of pay inequity and wage gaps between men and women (Budig, 2002); differential access for women to developmental opportunities (Ragins, 1999; Smithey and Lewis, 1998); power, status and dominance in male–female work relationships (Fiske et al., 2002); women's roles as caregivers and issues of work–family balance (Greenhaus and Parasuraman, 1999); and sexual harassment, its antecedents, and the response of women as targets of harassing behaviours (Bowes-Sperry and Tata, 1999); and the intersection of race and gender and duality of discrimination/prejudice experienced by African American women (Bell and Nkomo, 2001).

The Civil Rights Movement in the USA
The Civil Rights Movement (CRM) of the 1940s, 1950s and 1960s was the catalyst for the resulting wave of change in the political, social and economic landscape of the USA relating to race relations and considerations of 'difference'. Diversity during this time was a dichotomy between black and white, and male and female. Although typical discussions of black protest centre on the activities of Rev. Dr Martin Luther King, Jr and his contemporaries, there is ample research evidencing the protest activities of blacks

before this time. For example, the National Association for the Advancement of Colored People (NAACP) was founded in 1909; in the 1920s the Marcus Garvey movement urged American blacks to return to Africa; and the literary protest of the Harlem Renaissance in the 1920s spoke clearly of the societal position of blacks and the need/demand for change (Lewis, 1998; Morris, 1999). Additionally, during slavery there were many protests and revolts by slaves. Figures such as Frederick Douglas and Harriett Tubman are examples of protest leaders during and immediately following slavery. Therefore the CRM might be perceived as developmental for the reason that a series of events and conditions precipitated it. Representative of these events and conditions are: the legal strategy of the NAACP, the writings of scholars (e.g. W.E.B. Du Bois, Carter G. Woodson, John Hope Franklin, Gunnar Myrdal, and Kenneth B. and Mamie Clark); economic opportunities produced for blacks by the Second World War; the growth in the number of civil rights organizations; the increase in educational opportunities for blacks; and the appointment of blacks to mid-level positions in the federal government and the coalition with the Roosevelt and Truman administrations (Franklin, 1989; Lewis, 1998).

The CRM was a response by blacks to laws and practices of whites following the end of slavery and particularly during the era of Jim Crow. Jim Crow represented a series of laws and widely used practices that subjugated and disenfranchised blacks (Morris, 1999). During Jim Crow, blacks were considered and treated as inferior to whites; were legally segregated in all facets of life (e.g. mandated separate housing, schools, medical facilities, eating establishments, entertainment facilities, public swimming pools, water fountains etc.); were barred from voting; and subject to extreme violence from whites for suspicion of wrongly looking at or speaking to a white person (Bennett-Alexander and Hartman, 2009; Graham, 2002). For example, Graham (2002) indicates that blacks recognized that their economic, social and political well-being required a systematic resistance to the debilitating conditions under which they lived. Blacks acquired the fortitude, courage, mindset of sacrifice and human agency to strategize and execute a political, social and economic movement.

The 1955 bus boycott in Montgomery, Alabama evidenced the ability of blacks to sustain a long-term protest. The actions of blacks, sympathetic whites, and the coalition of black religious institutions paved the way for more enduring and systematic actions to eradicate racial inequality (Lewis, 1998). It was in Montgomery that Rev. Dr Martin Luther King, Jr emerged as the prominent face and spirit of the CRM. Borrowing from the philosophy of Mahatmas Gandhi, King stipulated a non-violent direct action strategy that captivated blacks and solidified the support of whites (Morris, 1999). Non-violent sit-ins, boycotts, marches, protest rallies and voter registration drives were the activities of choice (Franklin, 1989; Lewis, 1998). From this platform black organizations worked together, including the Southern Christian Leadership Conference (SCLC), the Congress of Racial Equality (CORE), the Student Nonviolent Coordination Committee (SNCC), the NAACP and numerous other local grass-roots organizations. Other supporters were organizations such as the Anti-Defamation League, the American Jewish Congress, American Civil Liberties Union, and the American Federation of Labor–Congress of Industrial Organizations (AFL–CIO) (Franklin, 1989; Graham, 2002).

The confluence of these developments, activities and coalitions produced major pieces of civil rights legislation at the federal and state levels. At the federal level the centrepieces of legislation were the Civil Rights Acts of 1957, 1960 and 1964, the Voting Rights Act of 1965, and the Fair Housing Act of 1968. A major consequence of the CRM was an America that is a more racially diverse and open society. As a result of widespread social protest that rose to the national and international arenas, the US Congress and the Executive Branch joined the movement to ensure broad-based equality in America. In the next section we shall detail the Civil Rights Act of 1964 and other legislation important to employment equity and diversity in the USA.

Anti-discrimination laws in the USA

The laws in the USA that protect women and other disadvantaged groups in the workplace largely emanated from the turmoil and political unrest that occurred from the CRM described above. The following subsections outline the various laws that are still in practice today, as well as those that are currently in development.

Equal Pay Act of 1963

The Equal Pay Act ensures that men and women are paid equitably for the work that they perform. This Act outlaws disparity in pay on the basis of sex, for workers who work within the same firm and under similar working conditions. In determining jobs (and thus pay rates based on job grades, criteria etc.) that are considered similar for both males and females, effort, skill and responsibility are factored into the pay determination. Exceptions to this rule include differing pay based on piecerate compensation, merit or seniority compensation systems (US Equal Employment Opportunity Commission, 1997).

Civil Rights Act of 1964 (Title VII)

Legislation in the USA that prohibits discrimination on a variety of bases is encompassed in an assortment of different legal statutes. The first piece of legislation to emerge that widely outlawed discrimination in any manner was the Civil Rights Act of 1964, in particular Title VII. Title VII prohibits 'employment discrimination based on race, color, religion, sex and national origin' (US Equal Employment Opportunity Commission, 1964). The Civil Rights Act covers private employers who employ 15 or more employees (Jain et al., 2003). This Act also applies to labour unions, governments and governmental agencies, employment agencies and educational institutions. This particular document bars such employers from discriminating against individuals with respect to employment activities, including selection, training, termination, promotion and compensation (US Equal Employment Opportunity Commission, 1964).

Age Discrimination in Employment Act of 1967

The Age Discrimination in Employment Act of 1967 (ADEA) prohibits discrimination against current and potential workers who are 40 years of age or older from age-related prejudice in employment. The ADEA applies to employers with 20 or more employees, including government organizations, and public and private employees. As in much of the other legislation described, individuals who are 40 years and older may not be discriminated against regarding any condition or privilege of employment, and individuals are protected from retaliation if they oppose such discriminatory practices or if they file a discrimination complaint. In addition, job advertisements may not specify any preference or limitations of an applicant based on age, except in the extremely rare circumstance where age is shown to be a 'bona fide occupational qualification' (BFOQ) that is necessary to the essence of the business (US Equal Employment Opportunity Commission, 1967).

Rehabilitation Act for War Veterans of 1973
Certain veterans fall under affirmative action principles under this Act developed in the early 1970s (US Office of Personnel Management, 2009). This provision focuses primarily on veterans who are disabled. Under Section 4214 of Title 38 of this Act, employers are encouraged to consider and place veterans who are disabled, using appropriate merit-based hiring criteria and creation of affirmative action plans for recruitment, selection and advancement of disabled war veterans (US Office of Personnel Management, 2009). To be considered a disabled veteran, individuals must be have a disability according to the guidelines set forth in the Americans with Disabilities Act (see below) (US Equal Employment Opportunity Commission, 1990).

Pregnancy Discrimination Act of 1978
The Pregnancy Discrimination Act is an amendment to Title VII of the Civil Rights Act of 1964 (US Equal Employment Opportunity Commission, 2008a). Discrimination on the basis of pregnancy, childbirth or related medical conditions is forbidden. Women affected by pregnancy or related conditions must be treated in the same manner as other employees with similar abilities or limitations. Similarly to disability legislation (described below), employers cannot refuse to hire a person because of a pregnancy-related condition as long as she is able to perform the essential tasks of her job. If a worker cannot perform her job due to pregnancy, the employer must provide some type of accommodation, such as providing modified tasks, alternative assignments, disability leave or leave without pay (US Equal Employment Opportunity Commission, 2008a).

Americans with Disabilities Act (ADA) 1990
Title I of the Americans with Disabilities Act of 1990 forbids private employers with 15 or more employees, state and local governments, employment agencies and labour unions from discriminating against qualified individuals with disabilities in job application procedures, hiring, firing, advancement, compensation, job training, and other terms, conditions and privileges of employment (US Equal Employment Opportunity Commission, 1990). Those considered having a disability include individuals with major physical or mental impairments that limit or affect major life activities or events, or who have a history of this or are perceived to be disabled. As long as the individual can perform the core requirements of a job, he/she is considered to be a qualified employee with a disability, and it is expected that a firm should make what is termed a 'reasonable accommodation' where necessary to enable the individual to perform his/her job. Such accommodations may include modifying work facilities, the job itself, work schedules, equipment etc. so that the individual can perform to the best of his/her ability. Exceptions to this requirement can be made in the case where an employer feels that such modifications would impose 'undue hardship' on the operation of the employer's business. This can include incurring significant expenses or other difficulties in the consideration of a company's size, financial resources and organizational structure. In addition, workers who oppose employment practices that discriminate based on disability or who

file a discrimination grievance are protected against retaliation (US Equal Employment Opportunity Commission, 1990).

ADA Amendment Act of 2008
As of 1 January 2009, the first legislative amendment to the ADA legislation became effective. In late 2008, after activists and advocacy groups appealed for a review of the narrow definitions under which the Supreme Court interpreted the ADA, President Bush signed the Americans with Disabilities Act Amendments Act of 2008, which broadens the definition of disability (US Equal Employment Opportunity Commission, 2008b). This significant change in the ADA laws will, in short, broaden coverage to include more employees under the definition of 'disabled', and thus more employees will require reasonable accommodation to stay within the ADA guidelines (Bleau, 2008). This was meant to bridge the gap for those who were too disabled to obtain employment, but not disabled enough to be covered by ADA legislation (Hoyer, 2007). This coverage now includes instruction to the courts to consider broad interpretations of disability instead of the previously very narrow definition; substantially (i.e. life-altering) limiting impairments are to be considered under the ADA as a disability in a broader sense; treatment of an individual based on perception of his/her disability will be considered and focused on, rather than just focusing on the proof of the perception of a disability; job treatment (hiring, firing etc.) will also be considered beyond reasonable accommodation procedures; and in most cases, mitigating circumstances of the disability are not to be considered when determining the existence of a disability (Bleau, 2008). This coverage is extremely broad and the potential for a barrage of lawsuits is apparent (ibid.).

Genetic Information Nondiscrimination Act of 2008
The Genetic Information Nondiscrimination Act of 2008 is a reflection of modern science, prohibiting discrimination on the basis of genetic information provided to both employers and health insurers. This is a proactive and pre-emptive attempt to curb potential injustices that genetic testing may contribute to in the future. Under this Act, employers and health insurance companies are prohibited from requesting or requiring individuals to provide genetic tests or genetic information in most instances (it is recognized that this information may be required in very specific instances). As with many other acts and laws, any genetic information revealed must not be used to make employment decisions (Greaves and Smith, 2009). There are very specific exceptions to the use of genetic information, particularly where a company may inadvertently (which is still ambiguously defined) obtain the information for wellness programmes, compliance with the Family and Medical Leave Act (or state medical leave laws), genetic monitoring of toxic substances in the workplace, or for law enforcement purposes for identifying human remains (Government Publications Office, 2009; Greaves and Smith, 2009).

The enforcement of the US anti-discrimination laws
The Civil Rights Act of 1964 was an omnibus bill addressing discrimination in employment, voting, public accommodations and education (US Equal Employment Opportunity Commission, 2009a). Throughout the 1960s, however, issues of enforcement were crucial, particularly in the area of employment. It was found that during the years after the Civil Rights Act was enacted, compliance with the Act had been minimal

due to an ambiguous mandate that placed little pressure on employers (Edelman, 1992). As a response to this poor compliance, Congress passed the Equal Employment Opportunity Act of 1972 to provide the Equal Employment Opportunity Commission, founded in 1964, more authority to enforce civil rights laws. The Equal Employment Opportunity Act included giving the EEOC litigation authority to sue firms that continue to illegally discriminate, and Title VII coverage was extended to include the government bodies at all levels, as well as all levels of educational institutions, among other provisions (US Equal Employment Opportunity Commission, 2009b). It is at this time that the Equal Employment Opportunity Coordinating Council was established, composed of the EEOC, the Departments of Justice and Labor, the Civil Service Commission and the Civil Rights Commission in order to align the goals and create efficiency among the variety of federal discrimination programmes that existed.

The 1980s brought considerable turmoil and shake-up to the affirmative action (AA) and equal employment opportunity (EEO) momentum in the USA. President Reagan became very vocal in his opposition to AA during his presidential campaign, an attitude that carried forward subsequent actions in the form of dramatic reduction in administrative support for EEO and AA initiatives as well as appointments of federal judges who opposed AA and regulation as a whole. These steps, combined with proposed changes to reduce the number of companies filing AA plans and support for challengers of these plans, meant that it was only firms with considerable AA programmes that went beyond compliance that would be likely to keep such programmes in place (Kelly and Dobbin, 1998). In essence, the effectiveness of AA programmes was reduced (Leonard, 1984).

Momentum for diversity management, however, was picked up surprisingly by a report by Johnston and Packer (1987) entitled *Workforce 2000: Work and Workers for the 21st Century*, in which the authors identified dramatic future changes in the composition of the workforce, particularly on dimensions of race, national origin and ethnicity (this is further discussed below). It is the sense of urgency emanating from the publication of this report that seems to have spawned a renewed interest in diversity management (Edelman et al., 2001). However, another blow for EEO initiatives arose during the Clinton Administration, as he was the first Democrat leader to refrain from lending strong support to AA and EEO programmes. Combined with the crisis presented by the *Workforce 2000* study, EEO and AA specialists developed and reframed these efforts as business-oriented needs for creating and sustaining efforts to develop and nurture a diverse workforce (Kelly and Dobbin, 1998). During the early 1990s, the EEOC's authority and jurisdiction were increased once again by the enactment of important legislation, including the Americans with Disabilities Act of 1990, the Older Workers Benefit Protection Act of 1990, and the Civil Rights Act of 1991 (US Equal Employment Opportunity Commission, 2009c). The enforcement responsibilities of the ADA provided the EEOC with considerable authority and influence, as this is a significant piece of legislation that affected many employees. During the 1990s, the EEOC issued eight enforcement guidances that have provided explanations for a variety of key ADA concerns, including 'pre-employment inquiries and medical examinations, workers' compensation benefits, psychiatric conditions, the meaning of the term "qualified," and the requirement that employers provide reasonable accommodations' (US Equal Employment Opportunity Commission, 2009d). In addition, a definition of the term 'disability' was developed and explained in a comprehensive chapter of the EEOC's

Compliance Manual (US Equal Employment Opportunity Commission, 2009d), signalling another significant contribution to the EEOC's scope and importance.

Office of Federal Contract Compliance Programs (OFCCP)
The Employment Standards Administration's Office of Federal Contract Compliance Programs (OFCCP) enforces Executive Order 11246, Section 503 of the Rehabilitation Act of 1973, and the affirmative action provisions (Section 4212) of the Vietnam Era Veterans' Readjustment Assistance Act (US Department of Labor, 2002). These laws prohibit discrimination and require federal contractors and subcontractors to ensure that all individuals have an equal opportunity for employment, without regard to a variety of bases, including race, colour, religion, sex, national origin, disability or status as a Vietnam era or special disabled veteran (US Department of Labor, 2002). The OFCCP requires a federal contractor to conduct an organizational analysis in order to highlight and identify any barriers to equal employment opportunity. The outcome of this self-audit is a written affirmative action programme (AAP), which comprises result-oriented procedures that a contractor commits to enforcing in good faith. Where under-utilization of women and minorities arises, the contractor must develop goals to increase the pool of qualified minorities and females. It is important to note that contractors are not permitted to be penalized for failing to meet goals; the primary aim of these AAPs is to measure the effectiveness of affirmative action for the purpose of eliminating discrimination among federal contractors (US Department of Labor, 2002). However, if strictly meeting the goals is not an obligation, employers have to demonstrate effort and 'acceptable' progress: 'failure to develop and implement an acceptable AA programme within a specified time could result in cancellation or termination of existing contracts, withholding of payments by the government, and disbarment from competing for future contracts' (Jain et al., 2003, p. 19).

Civil Rights Act of 1991
The Civil Rights Act of 1991 was introduced to strengthen the original Act of 1964 by taking stock of Supreme Court cases on disparate impact. At least seven Supreme Court cases were addressed in the enactment of this Act, and as a result, this Act is seen as launching the reshaping of the legal landscape of immigration law through rebuffing current legal precedent (US Equal Employment Opportunity Commission, 2009e). Among the decisions that Congress addressed were *Price Waterhouse v. Hopkins* (1989) and *Wards Cove Packing Co. v. Antonio* (1989), where the ability to prove that a discriminatory practice would still have occurred even if done through business justification or lawful motives would have removed culpability for the employer with regard to discrimination. The main purposes of this Act were to introduce punitive damages to those employers who intentionally or maliciously discriminate, to formalize the concept of 'business necessity' (demonstrated by conducting validity testing between job requirements and predictors of job success), and to assert the Act's jurisdiction over claims of disparate impact (US Equal Employment Opportunity Commission, 2009e). The 1991 amendment essentially requires that employment procedures (particularly employment tests) be validated in order to demonstrate that they are non-biased – and in the event that such tests are biased against any covered subgroup, that such tests do demonstrate that they are job-related and necessary for the job in question (Biddle and Nooren,

2006). The Uniform Guidelines detailed below provide indications on how to prevent disparate impact.

Uniform Guidelines on Employee Selection Procedures
Disparate impact occurs when an objective selection procedure results in disproportionately low numbers of a protected subgroup being hired into an organization (Pybum et al., 2008), even though the employer may not intend to discriminate, or without him or her being aware of this disproportion. The difference in passing rates for a particular group can be either statistically or practically significant (Biddle and Nooren, 2006). The Uniform Guidelines formalize the procedures that employers should follow to prevent what is termed 'adverse impact'.

Adverse impact is measured through the four-fifths rule, described as occurring when the selection rate for any race, sex, or ethnic group is less than four-fifths (or 80 per cent) of the rate for the group with the highest selection rate (US Department of Labor, 1990). Validation is the establishment of a clear correlation between a selection procedure and successful job performance as a dependent variable. The Uniform Guidelines recognize three aspects of validity: criterion validity, content validity and construct validity. Criterion-related validity uses empirical data to demonstrate whether a selection procedure is predictive of or significantly correlated with aspects of work behaviour and job performance. A content-valid instrument is indicated by the comprehensive representation of the important aspects of performance on the job. Construct validity is established by data indicating that the instrument measures whether and to what degree job candidates have the necessary characteristics to achieve successful job performance.

US Supreme Court case law
Important to an understanding of past and current research agendas regarding diversity is the history of cases deliberated in the US Supreme Court that helped to frame the dialogue regarding race and gender differences in the USA. We shall refer here to a sampling of the cases that have set the stage for diversity research interest and operationalization in the USA. Early cases had given a base for a continuation of race segregation even after the Civil War and after the African Americans had been theoretically emancipated. Such cases include: The Dred Scott Decision [*Dred Scott v. Standford*, 60 U.S. 393, 396, (1857)] that classified blacks as non-legal persons, questioned the humanity of blacks (slaves or free), and placed them at the bottom of the nation's social and political stratification; and *Plessy v. Ferguson* [163 U.S. 537 (1896)] gave support for mandated segregation of the races through 'separate but equal' state laws and policies. The conclusion in *Plessy* was overturned by the Supreme Court decision in *Brown v. Topeka Board of Education* [347 U.S. 483 (1954)], which made segregation in public schools impermissible under the law.

From the late nineteenth century to the twentieth century, numerous court decisions gave rise to, and informed, social and political discourse regarding diversity. The cases discussed below are not intended to represent the entire body of judicial proceedings that affect diversity and equal employment issues in the USA. They are presented to show, although briefly, how the judicial system has addressed and clarified issues of discrimination involving race, sex, equity in pay, criteria for hiring and promotion, pregnancy and sexual harassment, age and other terms or conditions of employment. Precedent for employer actions and overall discussions of diversity and equal employment are instructed by these proceedings.

Title VII of the Civil Rights Act of 1964 provides the basis for most litigation claiming discrimination, harassment, and in some instances pay equity in the USA. Under Title VII, claims of discrimination fall into two main categories: disparate treatment or disparate/adverse impact. Disparate treatment is considered intentional discrimination and is defined as 'treating similarly situated employees differently because of prohibited Title VII factors' (Bennett-Alexander and Hartman, 2009, p.93). Disparate impact is considered unintentional discrimination that emanates from the employer's application of a 'facially neutral workplace policy that applies equally to all appropriate employees but has a disparate or adverse impact on a protected Title VII group' (ibid., p.97). Two seminal race cases involving black employees lay out the Court's interpretation of Title VII in relationship to these categories of discrimination. *McDonnell Douglas v. Green* [411 U.S. 792 (1973)] involves disparate treatment discrimination. It is critically important to all disparate treatment cases because it presents the Court's guidelines for establishing an inference of discrimination (*prima facie* case) related to enquiries regarding the person claiming discrimination and the employer's actions towards the individual. *Prima facie* is a four-pronged test. Once *prima facie* has been established, the burden of proof falls on the employer to show a legitimate, non-discriminatory reason for its action; or that the action is based on a reasonably necessary *bone fide* occupational qualification. If the employer is able to show a non-discriminatory reason, the employee then has opportunity to prove that the employer's stated reason is a pretext for discrimination. The process articulated in *McDonnell* continues to be the requirement and process for adjudication of disparate treatment cases involving individuals in all protected class groups.

Disparate impact discrimination is considered unintentional discrimination affecting protected class groups. The Court in *Griggs v. Duke Power Co.* [401 U.S. 424 (1971)] articulated the judicial precedent and thus organizational considerations in disparate or adverse impact complaints. *Griggs* involved black employees who, before the Civil Rights Act of 1964, were permitted employment only in the labour department of the company, without the ability to transfer to other departments. The wages of the highest-paid black were lower than the wages of the lowest-paid white. After the passage of the Civil Rights Act, Duke changed its policy such that new hires to all departments except the labour department must have a high-school diploma and pass two general intelligence tests. Also, employees desiring to transfer from the labour and coal-handling department must have a high-school diploma or pass two general intelligence tests. These requirements did not apply to whites already employed in other departments. In examining the complaint of discrimination brought by a group of black employees, the Court concluded that disparate impact did occur in that blacks as a group were adversely affected by hiring and promotion criteria. Important to the decision was that the criteria (high-school diploma and intelligence testing) were not shown to be job related, nor a reasonable measure of job performance. The message to employers was that seemingly neutral policies must be evaluated for the potential for disparate or adverse impact on Title VII protected groups, and that any and all components of selection procedures must demonstrate job relatedness (Barker et al., 1999; Bennett-Alexander and Hartman, 2009).

The ambiguity in the definition of what constitutes a disability under the 'substantially limits a major life activity' requirement of the Americans with Disabilities Act has been addressed in the Court. The Court has attempted to provide clarity on this question. In *School Board Nassau County, FL v. Arline* [480 U.S. 273 (1987)] the Court considered tuberculosis as a chronic contagious disease and therefore a protected disability under the Rehabilitation Act of 1963. And later, in *Bragdon v. Abbott* [118 S. Ct. 2196 (1998)], the Court further clarified what constitutes a disability in its decision that HIV infection was a disability under the Americans with Disabilities Act of 1990. The Supreme Court further set forth a stringent standard in establishing conditions that would fall under disability protection in *Toyota Motor Manufacturing, Kentucky, Inc. v. Williams* [534 U.S. 184 (2002)]. Here the Court associated 'substantially limiting' to impairments that prevent or severely restrict participation in activities fundamental in the daily lives of most individuals (Bennett-Alexander and Hartman, 2009).

An examination of Supreme Court cases dealing with sex and gender issues reveals several judicial decisions that maintained the inequality of men and women (see, e.g., *Muller v. Oregon* [200 U.S. 412 (1908)] and *Goesaert v. Cleary* [335 U.S. 464 (1948)]). However, beginning in the 1970s, following the 1964 Civil Rights Act, the Court began to recognize sex/gender discrimination (Barker et al., 1999). For example, in *Phillips v. Martin Marietta Corp.* [400 U.S. 542 (1971) the Court addressed sex/gender-based hiring discrimination. Martin Marietta had a policy of not hiring women with preschool-aged children. The policy was premised on the conclusion that women with such children would encounter conflicts and situations that would interfere with their ability to work. The company did not hold the same requirement for men. The Court saw this as a direct violation to Title VII. In *Dothard v. Rawlinson* [433 U.S. 321 (1977)] seemingly neutral height and weight requirements for employment as an Alabama prison guard were found to constitute gender discrimination. Sex was also the focus in the *Johnson v. Transportation Agency, Santa Clara County* [480 U.S. 616 (1987)] finding, which allows sex as a factor in promotion decisions when made in accordance with an organization's affirmative action plan.

Balancing the complexity surrounding work issues and reproduction has led to judicial deliberations. Resulting from the Supreme Court's decision in *General Electric v. Gilbert* [429 U.S. 125 (1976)] that sex discrimination under Title VII did not include pregnancy, the US Congress amended Title VII through passage of the Pregnancy Discrimination Act of 1978 (PDA). Since the PDA, pregnancy and foetal protection as issues of gender discrimination have been clarified by the Court's decisions in *Cleveland Board of Education v. LaFleur* [414 U.S. 632 (1974)] and *UAW v. Johnson Controls, Inc.* [499 U.S. 187 (1991)]. In *LaFleur* a group of teachers sued the County School Board for requiring specific and stringent requirements that public school teachers begin their maternity leave three months before childbirth, regardless of their ability or desire to continue working. Also, teachers must wait three months from childbirth to be reinstated. The Court found these rules arbitrary, irrational and, most importantly, unconstitutional. Similarly, in *Johnson Controls* the Court decided that neither a *bone fide* occupational qualification nor a safety defence could justify a policy prohibiting female employees of childbearing age from certain jobs without the same policy for childbearing-age male employees. Finally, the retroactivity of organizational maternity leave policies that adversely affect the pension of workers was deliberated in *AT&T v. Hulteen* [556 U.S. ___ (18 May 2009)]. Here the Court decided that the employer's seniority-based pension plan that operated before the passage of the PDA and resulted in less retirement credit for maternity leave than for other disability leaves was not discriminatory under the PDA. In essence the PDA could not be applied retroactively for affected women.

Other prominent cases associated with women's employment have been reviewed by the Court and have helped to delineate legal and social frameworks for examining barriers to women's employment (Barker et al., 1999). In the Court's decision in *Meritor Savings Bank v. Vinson* [477 U.S. 57 (1986)], hostile environment was determined to be a form of sex discrimination actionable under Title VII. It was also concluded that unlike *quid pro quo* sexual harassment, economic or tangible detriment does not have to exist to substantiate hostile environment sex discrimination. *Price Waterhouse v. Hopkins* [490 U.S. 228 (1989)] centres on sex stereotyping when characteristics or mannerisms associated with men versus women (e.g. aggressiveness, language, dress) are used in decision-making. The targeted employee was told that, in spite of her outstanding performance, she would not be promoted to partner and was advised to be more feminine and to take a charm-school class. The Court found sex discrimination and violation of Title VII. In the area of pay equity, *County of Washington, Oregon v. Gunther* [452 U.S. 161 (1981)] was said to hold long-range significance in that it determined that Title VII was not limited to the equal pay for equal work standard set forth in the Equal Pay Act, 1963. The statute of limitations for filing pay discrimination complaints under Title VII was reviewed in the recent *Ledbetter v. Goodyear Tire & Rubber Company* [550 U.S. 618 (2007)]. Although the 180-day filing period had passed regarding the initial pay decision, Lilly Ledbetter contended that each time discriminatory pay was issued (each pay cheque) constituted a decision on the part of the employer to discriminate regarding pay. Ledbetter discovered the discrepancy in pay as she planned for early retirement. The Supreme Court disagreed with her contention and ruled against her, upholding the 180-day statutory filing requirement. In direct response to this decision and public protest, the Congress passed the Lily Ledbetter Fair Pay Act of 2009, which in effect reversed the Court's decision. Under the Ledbetter Act, the statutory time for filing pay discrimination cases resets each time pay is dispensed.

Judicial precedent in age-related complaints requires the interpretation of the Age Discrimination in Employment Act of 1967 (ADEA), which was designed to protect the employment of workers age 40 and above. Cases such as *Western Air Lines, Inc. v. Criswell* [472 U.S. 400 (1985)]; *Hazen Paper Co. v. Biggins* [507 U.S. 604 (1993)]; and *O'Connor v. Consolidated Coin Caters, Inc.* [517 U.S. 308, 116 S. Ct. 1307 (1996)] are reflective of the major judicial precedents in this area. *Western* involved the establishment of a mandatory retirement age of 60 for flight engineers. Not only were flight engineers required to retire at 60, but pilots 60 years of age or older were not allowed to be reassigned to the flight engineer position. The company contended that the retirement age of 60 was necessary for safe operation of the business. The point of decision in this case was that age could be a *bona fide* occupational qualification only if (a), Western Air Lines could not determine a method to individually assess each flight engineer's ability to safely perform the job; and if (b), there was some credible evidence that some flight engineers 60 or above had traits that affected safe operation of the job for which age could legitimately be a proxy. The Supreme Court ruled that the lower court was correct in its instructions, thus establishing precedent for age-based mandatory retirement provisions (Bennett-Alexander and Hartman, 2009).

In *Hazen*, the Court examined whether the number of years to investing in a pension plan could be construed as an age-based motivation for termination, which would be in violation of the ADEA. The case states, 'Whatever the employer's decision making process, a disparate treatment claim cannot succeed unless the employee's protected trait [here age] actually played a role in that process and had a determinative influence on the outcome.' At Hazen, investing in pension occurred at 10 years of service. Mr Biggins claimed that the company terminated him to prevent his becoming invested in the pension programme. The Supreme Court ruled that age and years of service are distinct and, therefore, years of service do not construe age. There was not disparate treatment under the ADEA because the decision was based on years of service, not age. Finally, the *O'Connor* case set forth the precedent that the ADEA applies and provides protection within the protected group. O'Connor at age 56 was fired by Consolidated and replaced with a person 40 years old. Given that the ADEA protected those age 40 and above, the Court had to decide whether O'Connor met the requirements of establishing a *prima facie* inference of discrimination. The Court decided that the ADEA protected individuals based on their age and the fact that the age discrimination involved individuals within the protected class was irrelevant.

Judicial decisions related to the interface of social-group categories inform the way in which workplace diversity issues are framed, practised and researched. This is exemplified in the recent Supreme Court decision of *Ricci v. DeStefano* [557 U.S. ____ (2009)] that dealt with test validity and the diversity of firefighters in the City of New Haven. In *Ricci*, the Civil Service Board of New Haven, CT decided to not certify two exams that would have provided the list of firefighter candidates for promotion to captain and lieutenant. This decision to not certify was made because the test would result in promotion of a disproportionate number of white candidates and demonstrate disparate impact in violation of Title VII. White and Hispanic firefighters who would have been on the promotion list sued City officials, claiming disparate treatment or intentional discrimination under Title VII. The Supreme Court ruled in favour of the white and Hispanic firefighters. This particular situation has already created debate that will no doubt result in research into the implications for organizational practices regarding affirmative action and the integration of human resource management policy with Title VII requirements. A further example is the Supreme Court cases that have examined the permissibility of affirmative action programmes. The cases *Regents of the University of California v. Bakke* [438 U.S. 265,387 (1978)]; *United Steel Workers of America, AFL-CIO v. Webber* [443 U.S. 193 (1979)]; *Johnson v. Transportation Agency, Santa Clara County* [480 U.S. 616 (1987)]; *Grutter v. Bollinger* [123 S. Ct. 2325 (2003)]; and *Gratz v. Bollinger* [123 S. Ct. 2411 (2003)] reflect the ebb and flow of the debate on how organizations are to ensure equal employment opportunity and affirmative action. In *Bakke, Grutter* and *Gratz*, the Supreme Court attempted to provide clarity on the use of affirmative action and diversity plans that specified numerical objectives to satisfy inclusionary goals. In *Bakke* it was determined that race could be a factor in admission decisions, but not the only factor. The companion cases of *Grutter* and *Gratz* build upon the *Bakke* decision particularly given that *Grutter* (ambiguous non-numerical affirmative action policy) was determined constitutional and *Gratz* (straightforward numerical affirmative action policy) was determined unconstitutional. Taken together, the decisions of the cases suggest that race and other factors may be utilized in organizational decision-making (e.g. admissions and hiring/selection) only if the process does not intimate or potentially suggest the use of quotas. These decisions provide insights into the Supreme Court's perceptions and ideation of how organizational programmes to ensure inclusion should be developed and implemented.

Although *Bakke, Gratz* and *Grutter* involved admissions policies of educational institutions, the decisions interface, shape and instruct the affirmative action and diversity policies and practices of organizational entities across industries. For example, the 1979 *Webber* case, where affirmative action plans were deemed permissible in a manufacturing environment, extended the discourse on the applicability of race-based preferences in decision-making that was presented in *Bakke* in 1978. Additionally, the decision in *Johnson* that sex and race are appropriate criteria in employment-related decisions as part of an affirmative action policy when underrepresentation exists bridges affirmative action precedent across organization types. *Weber, Johnson* and *Ricci* are case examples that linked the application of affirmative action in the contexts of employment decisions and admissions criteria. The decisions in these cases show how similar issues occurring in different contexts can affect judicial decision-making, and subsequent understanding and interpretation of judicial precedent.

Critique of US affirmative action policy
Much of the discussion concerning rights and equality of treatment occurred during the civil rights period in the USA. Identification of the term 'minority' and the groups that would fall in this category began before the discussion of affirmative action, and a formalized attempt occurred in the early 1940s with President F. Roosevelt's ban on discrimination in the war industries and the establishment of the Fair Employment Practices Commission which operated from 1941 to 1945 (Skrentny, 2002). In 1948, then President Harry Truman issued Executive Order 9980, by which the Fair Employment Board was charged with improving federal government sector employment for minorities by means of 'constructive action' (Konrad and Linnehan, 1995). The constructive action approach was a precursor to the affirmative action concept. The term 'affirmative action' was first used in Executive Order 10925 issued by President John F. Kennedy in 1961. However, it was President Lyndon B. Johnson who, with Executive Order 11246 in 1965 and 11375 in 1967, is credited with instilling substantive enforcement for the Executive Orders by creating the Office of Federal Contract Compliance Programs (OFCCP). The OFCCP has the authority to investigate complaints, initiate compliance reviews, levy penalties and disbar contractors for non-compliance (Bennett-Alexander and Hartman, 2009; Konrad and Linnehan, 1995). While the outcomes of affirmative action programmes may be linked to Title VII remedies, affirmative action is not a legal requirement under Title VII. However, The Rehabilitation Act of 1973 and The Vietnam Veterans Readjustment Assistance Act of 1974 have a requirement for affirmative action for all persons qualified as disabled under the Acts.

A considerable amount of the debate in terms of who fits into the 'minority' category has continued into recent commentary. The reason for this debate is due particularly to a couple of reasons: (1) understanding who is considered to be truly 'disadvantaged' in American society (and based on which criteria); and (2) continual immigration into the USA (immigrants fall into the Hispanic and Asian categories and are eligible for the minority status) (Skrentny, 2002). Hispanic Americans pose an illustrative example of this predicament. Hispanic Americans are reported to be the fastest-growing population group, representing 15.1 per cent of the US population (Toussaint-Comeau and Rhine, 2004; US Census Bureau, 2009). One of the difficulties regarding identification of Hispanics is the definition of racial category. Similarly to the Asian American, in the Hispanic population group, there are several subgroups (e.g. Mexican American, Latino, Puerto Rican, Cuban etc.) who may identify based on geographic origin (Toussaint-Comeau, 2004). Subgroup identification may have implications for diversity research and the discourse on minority status because, across studies and investigations, the Hispanic categorization may be differently operationalized. This can lead to global group comparisons that are based on ill-defined populations (Hayes-Bautista, 1980). Unless subgroup reference is pertinent, most studies and facilitators of affirmative action plans use the 'Hispanic' designation applied to these groups by the federal government.

In spite of this difficulty in defining minority status, affirmative action plans normally target African Americans, Hispanic Americans, Asian Americans, Native Americans and women. While there is debate regarding the effectiveness of affirmative action programmes, there is support for the usefulness of such programmes in improving the social and economic position of women and racial/ethnic minorities (Bennett-Alexander and Hartman, 2009; Konrad and Linnehan, 1995; Leonard, 1984).

Debates continue around whether other sub-categories such as religion should be considered, or background, skin colour etc., because there seems to be relatively little in the way of a solid definition of what a diverse nation really entails. Additionally, immigration of individuals to the USA has resulted in an 'underground' debate of the numbers of immigrants who are benefiting from affirmative action programmes. Graham (2002) provides a blunt and intriguing account of the number and types of organizations that focus on hiring foreign nationals rather than hiring native US racial/ethnic minorities to positively affect their espoused affirmative action position. Graham reports accounts of illegal and legal immigrants receiving jobs under affirmative action programmes, and where large percentages of minority faculty at colleges and universities are not US-born. Policy concerning affirmative action has evolved and been influenced through political lobbying and actions of special-interests groups. Several states have had to contend with the push from outside interest groups for anti-affirmative action voter referendums. Led by an organization that calls itself the American Civil Rights Institute, voters in several states, including California, Washington and Nebraska, have approved bans on racial and gender preferences in employment. These initiatives have weakened the ability of public sector employers to execute affirmative action plans (Graham, 2002). The success of these voter initiatives is unfortunate in that research suggests that affirmative action programmes have resulted in improved human resource management practices (e.g. job posting, selection processes, access to training/developmental opportunities). Also, attention to identify conscious programmes and activities increases the representation of racial/ethnic minorities and women at all levels in the workforce (Konrad and Linnehan, 1995).

In spite of its achievements, affirmative action can have a negative stigma in the public domain (Mangum, 2008), often due to the misinterpretation that affirmative action policies promote the use of 'quotas' for minority groups. Affirmative action is sometimes confused with the term 'diversity', which has caused this term to be negatively construed (Young, 2007). This has resulted in a considerable amount of public backlash, so that affirmative action has become a highly contentious political issue. Critics of AA and

EEO initiatives have asserted that focus on minority groups has resulted in discrimination against 'majority' groups, resulting in what is termed 'reverse discrimination' (Menache and Kleiner, 1999). Although the EEOC asserts that the term reverse discrimination is a misnomer, the term continues to be used primarily by white males alleging discrimination due to employer affirmative action efforts. While white males may consider themselves to be the primary victims of affirmative action, scholars generally maintain that white women benefit the most from these initiatives (Mangum, 2008).

Affirmative action programmes have two fundamental goals in their implementation and purpose: increasing the level of diversity and inclusivity in a firm; and serving as a form of redress for past injustices in the workplace. While one of the key arguments in support of the claims of reverse discrimination is that all individuals, regardless of subgroup membership, should not be discriminated against in employment, voluntary affirmative action programmes falling under Title VII of the Civil Rights Act (1964) should be designed to reduce or eliminate 'traditionally segregated' job categories that were historically lacking minority representation (Gullett, 2000). Many authors have critically argued that preferential treatment of minorities is justified on the basis of 'making up' for past injustices, through the claim that applicants have rights to 'equal consideration' (Simon, 1974) and equal opportunity (Gross, 1978). In addition, many feel that affirmative action initiatives promote tokenism in the workplace, regardless of the consideration that these programmes have enabled those who are historically disadvantaged in the labour market to obtain positions they may not have been able to in the past (Hoffarth, 1996).

Research and public discourse on diversity in the USA
Social interest in population diversity in the USA has been a process of evolution, from an initial discourse primarily concerning black and white racial attitudes and women's rights to one that attempts to delineate interactions between multifaceted concepts of difference (Bond and Pyle, 1998). Research on diversity is intricately linked to the social history of the USA. In this regard the research perspectives and the approaches to research on diversity have also evolved. Diversity research has experienced contributions from multidisciplinary origins, including historical, anthropological, political and sociological perspectives (Bell, 2007; Konrad, 2003). Among others, the focus of diversity research in the USA includes examination of the organizational integration of demographic diversity (Dovidio and Gaertner, 2005a; Greenhaus et al., 1993; McLaughlin et al., 2004; Willis-Esqueda and Swanson, 1997); the relationship between American value systems and diversity (Konrad, 2003; Thomas and Proudford, 2000); the interfacing of American and organizational cultures and issues of diversity (Tsui and Gutek, 1999); the factors that influence minorities and women in their selection of referent groups and their engagement with the larger organization population (Combs and Sommer, 2004; Pettigrew, 1998), tensions between organization structures and diversity integration (Cox and Blake, 1991), issues of sexual harassment and gender equity (Ely and Meyerson, 2000; Benokraitis, 1997); religion in the workplace (Rao, 2005); diversity and firm performance (Richard, 2000); emotions and affect regulation (Ashkanasy et al., 2002; Combs and Griffith, 2007); the influence of age on individual and organizational decision-making (Rosen et al., 1981; Deal, 2007); diversity training and development (Combs and Luthans, 2007; Roberson et al., 2009); and group identity, social catego-

rization and stigma (Ibarra, 1999; Linnehan et al., 2006; Tajfel, 1978; Terry and Hogg, 2001); affirmative action programmes and effects (Combs and Nadkarni, 2005; Harrison et al., 2006; Kelly and Dobbin, 1998); mentoring relationships and race and gender issues that may impact the mentoring experience and outcomes (Murrell et al., 1999); and, the complexities of individual and organizational resistance to diversity initiatives (Thomas, 2008).

The advent of diversity as a research focus

Defining diversity   One of the first writers to promote and encourage diversity in the workplace as a competitive advantage is R. Roosevelt Thomas. Thomas defines diversity as the 'mixture of differences, similarities, and tensions that can exist among the elements of a pluralistic mixture' (Thomas, 2005, p. 93). Thomas is credited with coining the term 'diversity management' to signal the strategic movement from reliance on affirmative action programming and minority and gender group representation to organizational development and change process to effectively manage workplace diversity (Thomas, 1992). Before 1990, much of the discussion of inequality in the workforce revolved around affirmative action and equal employment opportunity (Pitts, 2009). Thomas sought to expand the definition of diversity beyond the traditional subcategories covered under existing legislation, with the goal of creating competitive advantage to improve job performance and other work-related outcomes (Thomas, 1990).

How diversity is defined in the USA is a function of a rich history of interdisciplinary research on individual- and group-level differences. The viewpoints from which diversity is defined and researched also differ. For example, Konrad (2003) suggests that dominance and power differentials are the bases of discrimination and should be the key elements in conceptualizing the outcomes of diversity in organizations. In this instance, definitions of diversity rest on the categories of groups who have been historically victimized by discrimination (African Americans, Hispanic Americans, women, etc.). The trait model of diversity posits that individual differences (inclusive of all differences in people) influence the attitudinal and behavioural outcomes resulting from a diverse work population. Here diversity is simply defined as all differences among people. (For a more complete discussion see Ashkanasy et al., 2002; Bell, 2007; Konrad, 2003.)

Another delineation of the concept of diversity is the distinction between surface- and deep-level diversity. Harrison et al. (1998) describe surface-level diversity as 'differences among group members in overt, biological characteristics that are typically reflected in physical features' (p. 97). This type of diversity is considered as visible, relatively unchangeable and often referred to as defining the primary dimensions of diversity. These dimensions include age, sex/gender, race/ethnicity, and physical disabilities. Deep-level diversity references characteristics that are not as easily observable, such as expectations, attitudes, preferences values and belief systems, religion and sexual orientation (Harrison et al., 1998; Jehn et al., 1999). Studies have demonstrated that individual similarity in surface-level diversity (e.g. race, gender) may not equate to similarity in deep-level diversity (e.g. values, task preference) (Jehn et al., 1999). Specifically, Phillips and Loyd (2006) examine the simultaneous existence of surface- and deep-level diversity and their influence on willingness to voice unique perspectives in similar and dissimilar groups. The study found that participants expected more agreement with their deep-level task perspective from surface-level similar others than from surface-level dissimilar others. Also, social majority members (those belonging to the dominant surface-level group) felt less acceptance in surface-level homogeneous groups when offering a unique/ dissenting opinion.

The rationale for diversity: the business case   The seminal research study in advocating the business case for diversity, *Workforce 2000: Work and Workers in the 21st Century,* published by the Hudson Institute (Johnston and Packer, 1987) projected huge and dramatic shifts in the composition of the US labour force that would demand changes in organizational perspectives on acquiring and deploying talent (Konrad, 2003). Competitive advantage would depend on the organization's ability to effectively manage and nurture a more diverse workforce. The study predicted that by the year 2000, women and racial/ethnic minorities would comprise 85 per cent of new entrants into the US workforce. Additionally, predictions of the increase of older workers choosing to remain in the workplace and the impact of immigration policies and globalization were high- lighted (Bell, 2007). These predictions, coupled with existing EEO and AA initiatives, greatly stimulated research on diversity and its correlate constructs.

Research at the governmental level also added to the influx of research on diversity (Goodman et al., 2003). In 1991, the US Department of Labor established the Glass Ceiling Commission, whose members were charged to identify the barriers to minorities and women to advancement in organizations; to examine the readiness of women and minorities for advancement to upper-level positions; and to conduct comparative inves- tigation into selection decision for upper-level positions (US Glass Ceiling Commission, 1995). The Commission's 1995 report, *Good for Business: Making Full Use of the Nations Human Capital,* found that the upper-level management of Fortune 100 and 500 corpo- rations was 97 per cent male and 95–7 per cent white. The 2008 report *Women in U.S. Management* shows that while women hold 50.8 per cent of managerial/professional/ related position in the US Labor Force, only 15.7 per cent hold corporate officer posi- tions in Fortune 500 companies (Catalyst Reports, 2009). The situation of these small numbers of minorities and women has been exacerbated by the pay disparities between high-ranking white males, and minorities and women. Salaries were found to be much lower for minorities and women than for white men. Corporate leaders and the govern- ment concur that this is not good for businesses in particular, and the US labour market in general (US Glass Ceiling Commission, 1995).

The predictions of workforce demographic changes and the attention given to the complexion of US corporations contributed to a renewed, yet different, interest in diversity. Studies proliferated that looked at the culture and structure of organizations and how they could effectively manage workforce diversity and the individual and col- lective differences of organizational members (Ivancevich and Gilbert, 2000). Research concentrated on providing rationales for the importance of effectively managing diversity, appropriately defining diversity, identifying and examining the components of diversity management, assessing outcomes of diversity, and examining individual and organizational variables that affect employee interactions and employer response (Ashkanasy et al., 2002). What follows is a discussion of each of these elements of diversity research.

Soon after the *Workforce 2000* study (Johnston and Packer, 1987), theoretical and empirical research attempted to offer support for organizational diversity efforts. Researchers also identified components of diversity programmes that contributed to positive organizational outcomes (Konrad, 2003). The justification for diversity basically falls into three categories. First, the evolutionary argument suggests that attention to diversity is inevitable due to the changes in labour force demographics. Second, the moral imperative explanation for attention to diversity speaks to the natural responsibility of organizations to incorporate policies that support and promote a good and just society. And, third, the business case for diversity rationalization concentrates on bottom-line results and improvement in overall competitive posture (Bucher, 2004). For example, Cox and Blake (1991) linked managing diversity to organizational competitiveness and advantage. Their model offers ways in which diversity contributes to organizational competitive advantage: cost of poor integration of diverse workers; enhanced employer reputation; improved creativity; better group decision-making and problem-solving; and organizational systems flexibility.

Diversity research obtained leverage with findings from Wright et al. (1995). The authors investigated the response of the financial markets to positive and negative announcements of discriminatory organizational practices. Basically they hypothesized that announcements of firms receiving awards for high-quality affirmative action programmes would correlate with significant and positive stock price changes. And, conversely, publication of firms guilty of discrimination (settlement awards, loss of court cases etc.) would correlate with significant negative stock returns. The study hypotheses were supported. Announcements of firms' participation in high-quality award-winning affirmative action programmes were associated with positive stock price changes. And announcements of discrimination settlements were associated with lowered stock price changes. Similarly, Richard (2000) found that firms with a growth orientation benefited more from diversity in terms of productivity and market position.

A brief summary of US research on diversity
In addition to the predictions of vast differences in the composition of the US population (Johnson and Packard, 1987), concern was voiced about the academic research community and its attention to race and its influence in organizations. Academic publications were found to rarely incorporate race as a primary variable for examination (Cox and Nkomo, 1990; Nkomo, 1992). Nkomo (1992) is considered a seminal work on the need for diversity within research studies. The above influences strengthened the focus on diversity in organizations and the importance of effective research focus. On the individual, group and organizational levels, there is a plethora of variables that have been studied as independent, dependent, mediating, moderating, and interaction variables in diversity research (Bond and Pyle, 1998; Konrad, 2003; Tosi and Einbender, 1985). While it is impossible to present the entire spectrum of variables studied in this chapter, some variables studied include: candidate desirability, employment decisions, sex and racio-ethnicity of subordinates and supervisors, salary recommendations, the model minority myth, subtle and aversive racism, race/ethnicity achievement, task perspectives, language differences, newcomers and social validation, race and gender effects on mentoring, behavioural and attitudinal attributions, work–life initiatives, performance management and evaluation, name effects on decisions, job embeddedness, similarity preferences, conflict generation and management, group processes, and career

interest and personal confidence (see, e.g., Ashkanasy et al., 2002; Bell, 2007; Konrad, 2003; Powell, 1999). A few examples of studies on the individual and group level are presented below.

The entrepreneurial pursuits of many early Asian immigrants led whites to promote their assimilation as an example for other racial/ethnic groups to follow. In spite of the social and employment segregation of Asians (i.e. Chinatowns in large metropolitan areas and labourer/service sector industries) the portrayal of Asians as the model minority was supported in the research (Cho, 1997; Woo, 2000). For example, Caudill and De Vos (1956) suggested that Japanese Americans' achievements reflected cultural and personality factors giving credence to the model minority myth. This false representation of Asian Americans persisted until later studies stressed the disaggregation of Asian populations and identified the within-group differences among different Asian population groups (e.g. Chinese, Vietnamese, Korean, Cambodian, Laotian etc.) (Chou and Feagin, 2008; Woo, 2000).

Cox et al. (2005) used a mixed methods approach to examine the differences between white women and Mexican American women on methods of coping following sexual harassment. They found that Mexican American women were less likely than white women to confront, but more likely than white women to assess, self-blame, and to ignore the harassment. Further, sexual harassment research had traditionally centred on the repercussions and reactions to sexual harassment from the perspective of the individual target. Raver and Gelfand (2005) extends the sexual harassment research to the group level of analysis linking the assessment of the outcomes of such behaviour to team process and team financial performance.

Stanley and Jarrell (1998) found that while wage discrepancies may exist between men and women, it is important to take into consideration experiences and account for selection bias in their analysis. In another study Mallol et al. (2007) assessed the differences in job embeddedness and voluntary turnover between Hispanics and whites. Job embeddedness refers to the 'links an employee has to other people or the community, how he or she fits in the organization or environment, and lastly, what the employee would sacrifice upon leaving the organization' (p. 36). They found that Hispanics tend to be more embedded in their communities than whites, and that job embeddedness in the organization predicts Hispanic voluntary turnover.

In the USA ageing is not always a process accompanied by honour and respect. Ageing can be associated with derogatory stereotypes regarding performance ability, decreased creativity, reduced decision-making flexibility, work adaptability and attitudes, and discrimination in employment decisions and career mobility. (For a detailed discussion, see Shultz and Adams, 2007.) The projected and experienced increase in older workers in the labour force, coupled with the generational differences exhibited between older and younger workers, is causing organizations to reassess how they manage age diversity (Ansoorian et al., 2003).

Just as important as individual and group variables in the study of diversity are considerations of task and organizational context (Jehn et al., 1999). Context for diversity includes the physical and social elements of the organizational environment, and work/task nature and composition. Bond and Pyle (1998) explore the complexity of environmental variables. The researchers propose that explanations of human behaviour in organizations based on individual characteristics are incomplete at best. What is required is recognition that arrangements of what they call the 'eco-logical conditions' of organizations affect individual behaviour. Consequently, human behaviour regarding diversity cannot be wholly understood without consideration of the environmental context. This perspective is congruent with other research that calls for strong top management support and adjustments of structural components (e.g. organizational norms, values, resource allocations, communication patterns and socializations systems) in ensuring effective diversity programming (Bond and Pyle, 1998; Cox, 2001).

Given the research result attempting to address the level and impact of varying dimensions of diversity, it has been suggested that organizations identify meaningful diversity emphasis through a process of self-assessment (Bucher, 2004). By far most organizations in the USA include social category characteristics as components of their diversity plans. The organization's strategic needs, workforce composition, compliance requirements and social consciousness tend to coalesce into significant diversity programming initiatives (Cox, 2001).

The debate: the relationship among diversity management, affirmative action and equal employment opportunity
The debate in the USA over the implementation and operationalization of diversity management in the workplace has often been narrowed in focus to affirmative action initiatives, which, as previously discussed, includes setting targets for companies that do not appear to be successfully including a diverse workforce.

While many firms are adopting voluntary diversity management programmes, the current debate on the benefits and drawbacks of affirmative action has often clouded diversity management initiatives as they are often seen as one and the same (see the section devoted to affirmative action above for critiques of affirmative action). The existence of a difference of approach between diversity management and its predecessors, equal employment opportunity and affirmative action, continues to be a key area of discussion among scholars, government, media and workers.

Thomas and Ely (1996) suggest that leaders often view diversity through a discrimination-and-fairness paradigm, where managers tend to focus on compliance with the laws and equal opportunity for all in the workplace. The goal is to have a workplace that is reflective of the demographics of the applicable labor force. The discrimination-and-fairness paradigm is presented as going beyond numerical analysis of demographic representation, with firms often undertaking more inclusive programmes such as mentoring and career development for women and minorities. However, the measurement of success often reverts to assessing recruitment and retention goals in terms of numerical representation, rather than on an understanding of how to disseminate the talents of diverse individuals so that they are well utilized and nurtured in the firm (Thomas and Ely, 1996). In this perspective, due process is highly valued, and people are often treated as 'equals' rather than highlighting and taking advantage of the unique talents and perspectives that individuals bring to the organization.

Kelly and Dobbin (1998), who have analysed 'how affirmative action became diversity management', link the advent of diversity management as a distinctive concept to the 'rise and decline of antidiscrimination enforcement': EEO or AA officers present in most major corporations reacted to the plans of the Reagan Administration to dismantle the anti-discrimination mandates that had been built over the two preceding decades, and fears that this legislation would totally disappear, by becoming 'the beachheads for diversity programmes', as the authors put it. R.R. Thomas (1990) was the most prominent among these advocates, candidly stating that the premises upon which affirmative action was developed are now outdated and possibly harmful to women and minorities, as they really only promote these disadvantaged groups upon organizational entry, but not further in the organization (Thomas, 1990). When they look at content rather than discourse, Kelly and Dobbin explain, diversity programmes differ from EEO and AA programmes mainly on their espoused rationales, not on their content, which is a continuation of existing EEO/AA initiatives. Kelly and Dobbin's comparative table is particularly explicit, and the authors themselves use the expression 'old wine in new wineskins' to suggest how, although the packaging and discourses have changed, the content indeed remains similar. For instance, goals and timetables are used in diversity programmes as they were used in EEO/AA programmes. EEO/AA offices were often renamed 'diversity' officers, but continued their activity with the same manpower and programmes as before, trying to utilize data (particularly developed through the *Workforce 2000* study) to bolster support for continuing EEO and AA initiatives, regardless of the attempts to politically dismantle them (Kelly and Dobbin, 1998).

Thomas and Ely (1996) suggest that in order for diversity to be truly embraced and utilized for the benefit not only of organizations, but for all workers, the attitude toward diversity within firms must evolve to foster individuals' perspectives and experience, which are often developed through their cultural and gender differences, into the work and organizational culture. The main contribution of diversity management, not in discourse but in terms of practice, is thus through the implementation of culture audits and use of proactive measures others than those found among the former EEO/AA practices (Kelly and Dobbin, 1998). However, Kelly and Dobbin suggest that these culture audits are rarely practised, in comparison to more traditional EEO/AA-related practices. This analysis helps understand why people perceive diversity management and EEO/AA to be one and the same, and therefore express the same criticism or backlash. Thomas and Ely (1996) identify eight preconditions for shifting the philosophical view of diversity in the workplace to embrace inclusiveness, most of which discuss key elements of organizational culture and a focus on continuous learning. Thomas (1990) sums it up aptly by stating that the 'wrong question' is 'how are we doing on race relations?', while the 'right question' is 'is this a workplace where *we* is everyone?' (ibid., p. 109).

Scholars have examined the intersection of definitions of diversity and the legal prescriptions of EEO and AA provisions of the law (Edelman, 1992; Edelman et al., 2001; Konrad, 2003). The push for the concept of diversity has emerged from organizational efforts to get away from the hard questions concerning racial and gender inequalities. Practitioners and scholars have seemingly shifted their attention and focus. Demographics encompassed in the law (e.g. race and gender) have been construed by organizations as components of a larger view of diversity rather than as focal points of inclusion. For example, Edelman (1992) speaks of organizations mediating EEO law to protect managerial prerogatives and to protect managerial interests. The basis for this mediation is attributed to ambiguities of the law (e.g. lack of definition of terms such as discrimination and compliance) and weak enforcement mechanisms. Similarly, Edelman et al. (2001) suggest that the rhetoric of diversity has had the effect of reframing the intent and ideals of civil rights law. They contend that 'diversity rhetoric expands the conception of diversity so that it includes a wide array of characteristics (e.g., education, thinking styles) not explicitly covered by any law' (Edelman et al., 2001, p. 1590). The authors further suggest that this expansion of definition of diversity has been influenced and institutionalized through the language of managerial consultants, management professionals and professional associations.

The more systematic movement of organizations into global markets and concerns regarding competitive advantage (Cox and Blake, 1991) also heightened the rhetoric of diversity as a solution to the problem of inclusion, the ability of organizations to effectively manage individual and group differences, and the need for all employees to flourish and apply creative forces to organizational productivity. The rationales for inclusion have moved from political to economic perspectives (Kelly and Dobbin, 1998). Konrad (2003) discusses the expansion of dimensions of diversity in terms of problems that may be associated with the dominance of the trait model of workplace diversity. The trait model couches diversity in terms of individual differences in 'values, knowledge, beliefs, attitudes and behaviors' (ibid., p. 6). A focus on these levels of difference ignores the power and dominance differential that exists among identity groups in societal and organizational settings. Therefore the expansion of the definition of diversity and associated dimensions may serve more to dilute the meaning of diversity and its associated power and dominance stakes. The effect of this dilution may result in attention to less conflictual issues.

Conclusion

Diversity management in the USA is a concept that, while quite new in its scope, has historical roots dating back to the nineteenth century, with particular importance placed on it during the renowned and revolutionary civil rights movement that blossomed during the 1960s. As the concepts of equal opportunity and diversity management have been deeply intertwined and embedded in the social and political construction of the USA over the past century, the result today includes legislation that continues to be active in the literature base, and somewhat controversial in practice. However, there are tangible benefits to having not only legislation but also voluntary diversity management programmes implemented; in fact, current research has shown that having a diverse workforce has led to increases in such job performance outcomes as sales revenue, customers, market share and profits (Herring, 2009). While there is debate over this value-in-diversity hypothesis (ibid.), which promotes a business case for inclusion and diversity in the workplace, business can and does benefit from diversity management and related programmes. However, with misidentification and often misuse of the terms affirmative action, equal employment opportunity and diversity management programmes, public opinion can often challenge and/or support their primary goals. Diversity management programmes still remain voluntary in the USA. It is hoped that the continued enforcement of and compliance with federal discrimination laws will continue to encourage firms to adopt diversity management programmes as a means to increase diversity and inclusiveness in the workforce and enhance organizational competitiveness.

Summary table for the USA

Existence of anti-discrimination legislation	Yes
Criteria covered by anti-discrimination legislation	Age, colour, disability, national origin, pregnancy, race, religion, sex, genetic characteristics, status of war veteran
Criteria for which the reporting of quantitative data and their communication to a public administration are compulsory	Age, disability, national origin, race, religion, sex
Criteria covered by 'affirmative' or 'positive' action legislation other than unemployment- or income-based	Any historically disadvantaged group as described above
Existence of a discourse or debate about 'non-discrimination' or 'equality'	Yes
Existence of a discourse or debate about 'diversity'	Yes
Year or period when the 'discrimination' concept started to disseminate in management literature in the country	1940s
Year or period when the diversity concept started to disseminate in management literature in the country	Late 1980s (1987/1988)
Who pushed the 'diversity' agenda?	EEO and AA specialists who reframed these efforts as diversity management programmes; federal government administration bodies during the 1990s and 2000s
Existence of a professional association representing diversity professionals and year of creation	Various associations, often discipline-specific or subgroup-specific. Primary groups include the American Institute for Managing Diversity (www.aimd.org), founded in 1984; and the American Association for Affirmative Action (www.affirmativeaction.org), founded in 1974
Existence of a professional association representing diversity scholars and year of creation	The Gender and Diversity in Organizations (GDO) group of the Academy of Management, created 10 December 1983 (originally called the Women in Management Interest Group)

Note

1. Throughout this chapter we use the terms African American and black interchangeably to preserve the integrity of the reports and research studies presented.

References

Allport, Gordon W. (1954), *The Nature of Prejudice*, Reading, MA: Addison-Wesley.
Ansoorian, A., P. Good and D. Samuelson (2003), 'Managing generational differences', *Leadership*, **32** (5), 34–6.
Ashkanasy, N.M., C. Härtel and C. Daus (2002), 'Diversity and emotion: the new frontiers in organizational behaviour research', *Journal of Management*, **28** (3), 307–38.
Barker, Lucius J., Twiley W. Barker, Michael W. Combs, Kevin L. Lyles and Huey Perry (1999), *Civil Liberties and the Constitution*, 8th edn, Englewood Cliffs, NJ: Prentice Hall.

Bell, Ella L.J. and Stella M. Nkomo (2001), *Our Separate Ways: Black and White Women and the Struggle for Professiona Identity*, Boston, MA: Harvard University Press.

Bell, Myrtle P. (2007), *Diversity in Organizations*, Mason, OH: Thomsen South-Western.

Bennett-Alexander, Dawn and Laura Hartman (2009), *Employment Law for Business*, 6th edn, Burr Ridge, IL: McGraw-Hill.

Benokraitis, Nijole V. (1997), *Subtle Sexism: Current Practice and Prospects for Change*, Thousand Oaks, CA: Sage Publications.

Biddle, D. and P. Nooren (2006), 'Validity generalization vs. Title VII: can employers successfully defend tests without conducting local validation studies?', *Labor Law Journal*, **57** (4), 216–37.

Bleau, D. (2008), 'The ADA amendments of act of 2008', *Labor Law Journal*, **59** (4), 277–96.

Bond, M. and J. Pyle (1998), 'The ecology of diversity in organizational settings: lessons from a case study', *Human Relations*, **51** (5), 589–623.

Bowes-Sperry, Lynne and Jasmine Tata (1999), 'A multiperspective framework of sexual harassment', in Gary N. Powell (ed.), *Handbook of Gender & Work*, Thousand Oaks, CA: Sage Publications, pp. 263–80.

Bowman, G.W., N.B. Worthy and S.A. Greyser (1965), 'Are women executives people?', *Harvard Business Review*, July–August, 14–28 and 164–78.

Bucher, Richard D. (2004), *Diversity Consciousness: Opening our Minds to People, Cultures, and Opportunities*, 2nd edn, Upper Saddle River, NJ: Pearson/Prentice Hall.

Budig, Michelle (2002), 'Male advantage and the gender composition of jobs: who rides the glass escalator?', *Social Problems*, **49** (2), 258–77.

Bureau of Labor Statistics (2006), 'Charting the US labour market in 2006', http://www.bls.gov/cps/labour2006/home.htm, 25 April 2008.

Bureau of Labor Statistics (2009), 'Employment status of the civilian population by race, sex, and age', accessed 24 August 2009.

Carter, H. and E. Strong (1933), 'Sex differences in occupational interests of high school students', *Personnel Journal*, **12**, 166–75.

Catalyst Reports (2009), *Women in U.S. Management*, New York.

Caudill, William and George A. De Vos (1956), 'Achievement, culture and personality: the case of the Japanese Americans', *American Anthropologist*, **58** (6), 1102–26.

Cho, S. (1997), 'Converging stereotypes in racialized sexual harassment: where the model minority meets Suzie Wong', *Journal of Gender, Race, & Justice*, **1** (1), 177–211.

Chou, Rosalind S. and Joe Feagin (2008), *The Myth of the Model Minority: Asian Americans and Racism*, Boulder, CO: Paradigm Press.

Combs, G. and F. Luthans (2007), 'Diversity training: analysis of the impact of self-efficacy', *Human Resource Development Quarterly*, **18** (1), 91–120.

Combs, G.M. and J. Griffith (2007), 'An examination of interracial contact: the influence of cross-race interpersonal efficacy and affect regulation', *Human Resource Development Review*, **6** (3), 222–44.

Combs, G.M. and S. Nadkarni (2005), 'A tale of two cultures: attitudes towards affirmative action in the United States and India', *The Journal of World Business*, **40** (2), 158–71.

Combs, G.M. and S. Sommer (2004), 'Social comparison theory and contact theory: implications for African American managers career development', paper presented at the Academy of Management Conference, New Orleans, LA.

Cox, R., P. Dorfman and W. Stephan (2005), 'Determinants of sexual harassment coping strategies in Mexican American and Anglo women', paper presented at the annual meeting of the Academy of Management Conference, Honolulu, HI.

Cox, Taylor H. Jr (2001), *Creating the Multicultural Organization: A Strategy for Capturing the Power of Diversity*, San Francisco, CA: Jossey-Bass.

Cox, T. and S. Blake (1991), 'Managing cultural diversity: implications for organizational competitiveness', *Academy of Management Executive*, **5** (3), 45–56.

Cox, T. and S. Nkomo (1990), 'Invisible men and women: a status report on race as a variable in organizations behaviour research', *Journal of Organizational Behaviour*, **11**, 419–31.

Dall, Caroline W.H. (1861), *Woman's Rights under the Law: In Three Lectures, Delivered in Boston, January, 1861*, Boston, MA: Walker, Wise and Company.

Deal, Jennifer J. (2007), *Retiring the Generation Gap: How Employees Young and Old can Find Common Ground*, San Francisco, CA: Jossey-Bass and CCL.

Dovidio, John F. and Sam L. Gaertner (2005a), 'Aversive racism', in Mark P. Zanna (ed.), *Advances in Experimental Social Psychology*, vol. 36, San Diego, CA: Academic Press, pp. 1–52.

Dovidio, J. and S. Gaertner (2005b), 'Understanding and addressing contemporary racism: from aversive racism to the common ingroup identity model', *Journal of Social Issues*, **61** (3), 615–39.

Du Bois, Burghardt W.E. (1899), *The Philadelphia Negro: A social study*, Philadelphia, PA: University of Philadelphia Press.

Edelman, L.B. (1992), 'Legal ambiguity and symbolic structures: organizational mediation of civil rights law', *American Journal of Sociology,* **97** (6), 1531–76.

Edelman, L.B., S.R. Fuller and I. Mara-Drita (2001), 'Diversity rhetoric and the managerialization of law', *American Journal of Sociology,* **106** (6), 1589–641.

Ely, R. and D. Meyerson (2000), 'Advancing gender equity in organizations: the challenge and importance of maintaining a gender narrative', *Organization,* **7** (4), 589–608.

Fisher, M.J. (1951), 'Equal-pay-for-equal-work legislation', *Labor Law Journal,* **2** (8), 578–87.

Fiske, Susan T., Amy J. Cuddy, Peter Glick and Jun Xu (2002), 'A model of (often mixed) stereotype content: competence and warmth respectively follow from perceived status and competition', *Journal of Personality and Social Psychology,* **82**, 878–902.

Franklin, John Hope (1989), *Race and History,* Baton Rouge, LA: Louisiana State University Press.

Frazier, E.F. (1932), *The Free Negro Family: A study of Family Origins Before the Civil War,* Nashville, TN: Fisk University Press.

Frazier, E. Franklin (1951), *The Integration of the Negro in American Society,* Washington, DC: Howard University Press.

Friedan, Betty (1963), *The Feminine Mystique,* New York: W.W. Norton and Co.

Fuller, F.M. and M.B. Batchelder (1953), 'Opportunities for women at the administrative level', *Harvard Business Review,* **31** (1), 111–28.

Goodman, J., D. Fields and T. Blum (2003), 'Cracks in the glass ceiling: in what kinds of organizations do women make it to the top?', *Group & Organization Management,* **28** (4), 475–501.

Government Publications Office (2009), *Regulations under the Genetic Information Nondiscrimination Act of 2008,* http://www.gpo.gov/fdsys/pkg/PLAW-110publ233/html/PLAW-110publ233.htm, 12 August 2009.

Graham, Hugh D. (2002), *Collision Course: The Strange Convergence of Affirmative Action and Immigration Policy in America,* New York: Oxford University Press.

Greaves, M.B. and A.E. Smith (2009), 'The new Genetic Information Non-Discrimination Act', *Defense Counsel Journal,* **76** (1), 137–40.

Greenhaus, Jeffery and Saroj Parasuraman (1999), 'Research on work, family, and gender: current status and future directions', in Gary N. Powell (ed.), *Handbook of Gender & Work,* Thousand Oaks, CA: Sage Publications, pp. 371–90.

Greenhaus, J., S. Parasuraman and W. Wormley (1990), 'Effects of race on organizational experience, job performance evaluations, and career outcomes', *Academy of Management Journal,* **33** (1), 64–86.

Gross, Barry R. (1978), *Discrimination in Reverse: Is Turnabout Fair Play?,* New York: New York University Press.

Gullett, C.R. (2000), 'Reverse discrimination and remedial affirmative action in employment: dealing with the paradox of nondiscrimination', *Public Personnel Management,* **29** (1), 107–18.

Harrison, D., K. Price and M. Bell (1998), 'Beyond relational demography: time and the effects of surface- and deep-level diversity on work group cohesion', *Academy of Management Journal,* **41** (1), 96–107.

Harrison, D., D. Kravitz, D. Mayer, L. Leslie and D. Lev-Arey (2006), 'Understanding attitudes toward affirmative action programmes in employment: summary and meta-analysis of 35 years of research', *Journal of Applied Psychology,* **91** (5), 1013–36.

Hayes-Bautista, D. (1980), 'Identifying "Hispanic" populations: the influence of research methodology upon public policy (editorial)', *American Journal of Public Health,* **70** (4), 353–6.

Herring, C. (2009), 'Does diversity pay?: Race, gender, and the business case for diversity', *American Sociological Review,* **74** (2), 208–24.

Hoffarth, V. (1996), 'Perspectives on career development of women in management', *Equal Opportunities International,* **15** (3), 21–53.

Hoyer, S.H. (2007), Testimony of House Majority Leader, *House Judiciary Committee, Subcommittee on Constitution, Civil Rights, and Civil Liberties,* Hearing on H.R. 3195, ADA Restoration Act of 2007.

Ibarra, H. (1999), 'Provisional selves: experimenting with image and identity in professional adaptation', *Administrative Science Quarterly,* **44** (4), 764–91.

Ivancevich, J. and J. Gilbert (2000), 'Diversity management', *Public Personnel Management,* **29** (1), 75–92.

Jain, Harish C., Peter Sloane and Frank Horwitz (2003), 'Introduction', *Employment Equity and Affirmative Action: An International Comparison,* New York, NY: M.E. Sharpe.

Jehn, K., G. Northcraft and M. Neale (1999), 'Why differences make a difference: a field study of diversity, conflict, and performance in workgroups', *Administrative Science Quarterly,* **44** (4), 741–63.

Johnston, William B. and Arnold E. Packer (1987), *Workforce 2000, Work and Workers for the 21st Century,* Indianapolis, IN: Hudson Institute.

Kelly, E. and F. Dobbin (1998), 'How affirmative action became diversity management', *American Behavioral Scientist,* **41** (7), 960.

Key, Valdimer O. Jr (1949), *Southern Politics in State and Nation,* New York: Random House.

Konrad, A. (2003), 'Special issue introduction: defining the domain of workplace diversity scholarship', *Group and Organization Management*, **28** (1), 4–17.

Konrad, A. and F. Linnehan (1995), 'Formalized HRM structures: coordinating equal employment opportunity or concealing organizational practices?', *Academy of Management Journal*, **38** (3), 787–820.

Leonard, J.S. (1984), 'The impact of affirmative action on employment', *The Journal of Labor Economics*, **2** (4), 439–63.

Lewis, John (1998), *Walking with the Wind: A Memoir of the Movement*, San Diego, CA: Harcourt Brace & Company.

Linnehan, F., D. Chrobot-Mason and A. Konrad (2006), 'Diversity attitudes and norms: the role of ethnic identity and relational demography', *Journal of Organizational Behaviour*, **27** (4), 419–42.

Mallol, C., B. Holtom and T. Lee (2007), 'Job embeddedness in a culturally diverse environment', *Journal of Business and Psychology*, **22** (1), 35–44.

Mangum, M. (2008), 'Testing competing explanations of black opinions on affirmative action', *Policy Studies Journal*, **36** (3), 347–66.

Mastracci, S. (2004), 'Backstage and spotlight activism: one survival strategy of the women's bureau and its price', *Labor History*, **45** (1), 85–99.

McLaughlin, M., M. Bell and D. Stringer (2004), 'Stigma and acceptance of persons with disabilities: understudied aspects of workforce diversity', *Group & Organization Management*, **29** (3), 302–33.

Menache, R. and B. Kleiner (1999), 'New developments in reverse discrimination', *Equal Opportunities International*, **18** (2–4), 41–2.

Morris, A. (1999), 'A retrospective on the civil rights movement: political and intellectual landmarks', *Annual Review of Sociology*, **25**, 517–39.

Murrell, Audrey J., Faye J. Crosby and Robin J. Ely (1999), *Mentoring Dilemmas: Developmental Relationships in Multicultural Organizations*, Princeton, NJ: Lawrence Erlbaum Associates.

Myrdal, Gunnar (1944), *An American Dilemma: The Negro Problem and American Democracy*, New York: Harper & Row.

Nkomo, S.M. (1992), 'The emperor has no clothes: rewriting race in organizations', *Academy of Management Review*, **17**, 487–513.

Pettigrew, T. (1998). 'Intergroup contact theory', *Annual Review of Psychology*, **49**, 65–85.

Phillips, K. and D. Loyd (2006), 'When surface and deep-level diversity collide: the effects on dissenting group members', *Organizational Behaviour & Human Decision Processes*, **99** (2), 143–60.

Pitts, D. (2009), 'Diversity management, job satisfaction and job performance: evidence from U.S. federal agencies', *Public Administration Review*, **69** (2), 314–27.

Powell, Gary N. (1999), *Handbook of Gender & Work*, Thousand Oaks, CA: Sage Publications.

Pybum, K., R. Ployhart and D. Kravitz (2008), 'The diversity–validity dilemma: overview and legal context', *Personnel Psychology*, **61** (1), 143–51.

Ragins, B.R. (1999), 'Gender and mentoring relationships: a review and research agenda for the next decade', in Gary N. Powell (ed.), *Handbook of Gender & Work*, Thousand Oaks, CA: Sage Publications, pp. 347–70.

Rao, Asha (2005), 'Religion, culture, and management in the new millennium', in Carol P. Harvey and June Allard (eds), *Understanding and Managing Diversity*, Upper Saddle River, NJ: Pearson/Prentice Hall, pp. 149–57.

Raver, J. and M. Gelfand (2005), 'Beyond the individual victim: linking sexual harassment, team processes, and team performance', *Academy of Management Journal*, **48** (3), 387–400.

Richard, O. (2000), 'Racial diversity, business strategy, and firm performance: a resource-based view', *Academy of Management Journal*, **43** (2), 164–77.

Roberson, L., C. Kulik and M. Pepper (2009), 'Individual and environmental factors influencing the use of transfer strategies after diversity training', *Group & Organization Management*, **34** (1), 67–89.

Rosen, B., T. Jerdee and R. Lunn (1981), 'Effects of performance appraisal format, age, and performance level on retirement decisions', *Journal of Applied Psychology*, **66** (4), 515–19.

Shultz, Kenneth S. and Gary Adams (2007), *Aging and Work in the 21st Century*, Florence, KE: Routledge.

Simon, R. (1978), 'Statistical justification of discrimination', *Analysis*, **38**, 37–42.

Skrentny, John D. (2002), *The Minority Rights Revolution*, Cambridge, MA: Harvard University Press.

Smithey, Philippa N. and Gregory B. Lewis (1998), 'Gender, race and training in the federal civil service', *Public Administration Quarterly*, **22**, 204–28.

Stanley, T. and S. Jarrell (1998), 'Gender wage discrimination bias? A meta-regression analysis', *Journal of Human Resources*, **33** (4), 947–73.

Sumner, William G. (1906), *Folkways: A Study of the Sociological Importance of Usages, Manners, Customs, Mores, and Morals*, Boston, MA: The Athenaeum Press.

Tajfel, H. (1978), *Differentiation between Social Groups: Studies in the Social Psychology of Intergroup Relations*, Oxford: Academic Press.

Terry, Deborah J. and Michael Hogg (2001), 'Attitudes, behaviour, and social context: the role of norms and group membership in social influence processes', in Joseph P. Forgas and Kipling D. Williams (eds), *Social Influence: Direct and Indirect Processes,* New York: Psychology Press, pp. 253–70.

Thomas, D. and R. Ely (1996), 'Making differences matter', *Harvard Business Review,* **74** (5), 79–90.

Thomas, David A. and Karen Proudfoid (2000), 'Making sense of race relations in organizations: theories for practice', in Robert T. Carter (ed.), *Addressing Cultural Issues in Organizations: Beyond the Corporate Context,* New York: Guilford Press, pp. 51–68.

Thomas, Kecia M. (2008), *Diversity Resistance in Organizations,* New York: Lawrence Earlbaum Associates.

Thomas, R. (1990), 'From affirmative action to affirming diversity', *Harvard Business Review,* **68**, 107–17.

Thomas, Roosevelt R. Jr (1992), *Beyond Race and Gender: Unleashing the Power of your Total Work Force by Managing Diversity,* New York: AMACOM Division of American Management Association.

Thomas, Roosevelt R. Jr (2005). *Building on the Promise of Diversity: How we can Move to the Next Level in our Workplace, our Communities, and our Society,* New York: AMACOM Division American Management Association.

Tosi, H. and S. Einbender (1985), 'The effects of the type and amount of information in sex discrimination research: a meta-analysis', *Academy of Management Journal,* **28** (3), 712–23.

Toussaint-Comeau, Maude and Sherrie Rhine (2004), 'Tenure choice with location selection: the case of Hispanic neighborhoods in Chicago', *Contemporary Economic Policy,* **22** (1), 95–110.

Tsui, Anne S. and Barbara A. Gutek (1999), *Demographic Differences in Organizations: Current Research and Future Directions,* New York: Lexington Books/Macmillan.

US Census Bureau (2007), 'The African American Community', http://www.census.gov/prod/2007pubs/acs-04.pdf, 25 April 2008.

US Census Bureau (2009), 'Hispanic Fact Sheet', www.hispanictips.com/2009/08/25/us-census-2009-hispanic-fact-sheet-hispanic-heritage-month-sept-15-%E2%80%93-oct-15/, January 2010.

US Department of Labor (1990). 'Federal Contract Compliance Manual (FCCM), Chapter 7 – Identification & Remedy of Employment Discrimination', http://www.dol.gov/esa/ofccp/regs/compliance/fccm/ofcpch7.htm, 31 August 2009.

US Department of Labor (2002), 'Facts on Executive Order 11246', http://www.dol.gov/esa/regs/compliance/ofccp/aa.htm, 16 April 2008.

US Department of Transportation (2008), 'Executive Orders', http://www.dotcr.ost.dot.gov/asp/execorders.asp, 21 April 2008.

US Equal Employment Opportunity Commission (1964), 'Civil Rights Act of 1964', http://www.eeoc.gov/policy/vii.html, 8 July 2009.

US Equal Employment Opportunity Commission (1967), 'Facts about Age Discrimination in Employment Act', http://www.eeoc.gov/facts/age.html, 21 April 2008.

US Equal Employment Opportunity Commission (1990), 'Americans with Disabilities Act', http://www.eeoc.gov/policy/ada.html, 14 April 2008.

US Equal Employment Opportunity Commission (1991), 'Civil Rights Act of 1991', http://www.eeoc.gov/policy/cra91.html, 8 July 2009.

US Equal Employment Opportunity Commission (1997), 'Equal Pay Act of 1963', http://www.eeoc.gov/policy/epa.html, 21 April 2008.

US Equal Employment Opportunity Commission (2002), 'Federal Laws Prohibiting Job Discrimination', http://www.eeoc.gov/facts/qanda.html, 21 April 2008.

US Equal Employment Opportunity Commission (2005), 'EEOC Litigation Settlements April 2005, EEOC v. Abercrombie & Fitch Stores, Inc. No. 04-4731 (N.D. Cal. April 14, 2005)', http://www.eeoc.gov/litigation/settlements/settlement04-05.html, 5 June 2009.

US Equal Employment Opportunity Commission (2008a), 'Facts about Pregnancy Discrimination Act of 1978', http://www.eeoc.gov/facts/fs-preg.html, 21 April 2008.

US Equal Employment Opportunity Commission (2008b), 'Information about Americans with Disabilities Act Amendments Act of 2008', http://www.eeoc.gov/laws/statutes/adaaa_info.cfm.

US Equal Employment Opportunity Commission (2009a), 'Pre-1965 – Events Leading to the Creation of the EEOC', http://www.eeoc.gov/abouteeoc/35th/pre1965/index.html, 8 July 2009.

US Equal Employment Opportunity Commission (2009b), 'The 1970's – The Toothless Tiger Gets Its Teeth – A New Era of Enforcement', http://www.eeoc.gov/abouteeoc/35th/1970s/index.html, 8 July 2009.

US Equal Employment Opportunity Commission (2009c), 'The 1990's – New Laws, New Strategies', http://www.eeoc.gov/abouteeoc/35th/1990s/index.html, 8 July 2009.

US Equal Employment Opportunity Commission (2009d), 'Combating New Forms of Age Discrimination', http://www.eeoc.gov/abouteeoc/35th/1990s/ada.html, 8 July 2009.

US Equal Employment Opportunity Commission (2009e), 'Combating New Forms of Age Discrimination', http://www.eeoc.gov/abouteeoc/35th/1990s/civilrights.html, 8 July 2009.

US Glass Ceiling Commission (1995), *Good for Business: Making Full Use of the Nation's Human Capital,*

Washington, DC: U.S. Government Printing Office, http://digitalcommons.ilr.cornell.edu/key_workplace/116, 8 July 2009.

US Office of Personnel Management (2009), *VetsInfo Guide: Affirmative Action For Certain Veterans Under Title 38*, http://www.opm.gov/veterans/html/vetsinfo.asp, 12 August 2009.

Wallin, P. (1950), 'Cultural contradictions and sex roles: a repeat study', *American Sociological Review*, **15** (2), 288–93.

Walters, G.E. (1967), 'Sex, state protective laws and the civil rights act of 1964', *Labor Law Journal*, **18** (6), 344–52.

Williams, J. (2001), 'Building a movement: Betty Friedan and the feminine mystique', *Radical History Review*, **80**, 149–54.

Willis-Esqueda, C. and K. Swanson (1997), 'The effects of stereotypical crime and alcohol use on criminal culpability attributions for Native Americans and European Americans', *American Indian Culture and Research Journal*, **21**, 229–54.

Woo, Deborah (2000), *Glass Ceiling and Asian Americans: The New Face of Workplace Barriers*, Walnut Creek, CA: Altamira Press.

Wright, P., S. Ferris, J. Hiller and M. Kroll (1995), 'Competitiveness through management of diversity: effects on stock price valuation', *Academy of Management Journal*, **38** (1), 272–87.

Young, C. (2007), 'Organization culture change: the bottom line of diversity', *The Diversity Factor*, **15** (1), 26–31.

Appendix

Table 15A.1   Selected managerial participation rates by gender, race and ethnicity by companies reporting to the EEOC, 2007 (all numbers listed in percentages)

Subgroup	Executive and senior-level officials	First/mid-level officials
All employees	100.00	100.00
Men	71.40	62.52
Women	28.60	37.48
White	87.42	80.54
Men	63.26	51.12
Women	24.17	29.42
Minority	12.58	19.47
Men	8.14	11.41
Women	4.43	8.06
Black	3.57	7.27
Men	1.89	3.74
Women	1.67	3.54
Hispanic	4.46	6.76
Men	3.03	4.32
Women	1.42	2.44
Asian American	3.70	4.50
Men	2.67	2.81
Women	1.03	1.69
American Indian	0.33	0.42
Men	0.22	0.26
Women	0.12	0.16

Source: 2007 EEO-1 National Aggregate Report, US Equal Employment Opportunity Commission, http://www.eeoc.gov/stats/jobpat/2007/us/national.html.

Index